CRUSADER WARFARE

Crusader Warfare

VOLUME II

Muslims, Mongols and the Struggle against the Crusades 1050–1300 AD

David Nicolle

hambledon
continuum

Hambledon Continuum is an imprint of Continuum Books
Continuum UK, The Tower Building, 11 York Road, London SE1 7NX
Continuum US, 80 Maiden Lane, Suite 704, New York, NY 10038

www.continuumbooks.com

First published 2007

British Library Cataloguing-in-Publication Data
A catalogue record for this book is available from the British Library.

ISBN 978 1 84725 146 6

Typeset by Egan Reid, Auckland, New Zealand
Printed and bound by Cromwell Press Ltd, Trowbridge, Wiltshire, Great Britain

Contents

Illustrations

For Dr Shihab al-Sarraf,
for opening further new windows on to what was really
happening during these centuries.

Introduction

To a large extent the current interest in the Crusades reflects the perceived danger of a so-called 'clash of civilizations'. While warnings of such a supposed clash in our own times are based upon a misunderstanding of the natures of both 'Western' and 'Islamic' civilizations, some commentators have looked to the medieval Crusades as an earlier example of such a confrontation. In reality they were no such thing. Instead the wars between Christian, Islamic and other forces during the Crusades resulted from a variety of political, economic and cultural as well as religious factors. The wars of the Crusades, even excluding the Baltic or so-called Northern Crusades, also involved an extraordinary array of states, dynasties, ethnic or linguistic groups and their fighting forces.

This book focuses on the Mediterranean Crusades plus associated military activities in the Balkans, the Black Sea, along the Atlantic coasts of the Iberian peninsula and north-west Africa. It does not look at the Baltic Crusades, but will deal with those non-Christian peoples along the southern stretches of Latin or Catholic Europe's 'eastern front'.

The fluid nature of politics and warfare within the Islamic World, not to mention culture and religion, makes it necessary to look closely at Islamic and other regional armies which campaigned outside the immediate sphere of Middle Eastern or Crusading warfare. Furthermore, research into the military affairs of the medieval Islamic World is still at a relatively early stage when compared with medieval European or even Byzantine military studies. Hence the Islamic net needs to be cast wider in order to get a better understanding of what forces were involved, how they were motivated, maintained and led, as well as the military traditions or expectations which spurred their commanders to victory or defeat.

The Mongols also have their own smaller section within the book. This is because the Mongols, though casting a giant shadow across the history of medieval Asia and eastern Europe, were latecomers and relatively minor players where Crusading warfare was concerned. Within this specific context the Mongols' greatest military impact was less their conquests than their impact upon subsequent developments within Islamic military history. This impact can be seen in organization and equipment, though to a lesser extent in tactics or combat skills. One of the most surprising aspects of warfare during this period was, in fact, the way in which the 'world conquering' Mongols who established states in Western Asia, adopted so much of the military heritage of the Islamic regions they had overrun.

Of course the phenomenon of the wars of the Crusades cannot be understood without looking at prior events. These were not only the conquest of most of the eastern and middle-eastern Islamic world by the Seljuk Turks and the Byzantine loss of Anatolia to these same Turks, but also the struggle between Sunni and Shi'a Islam for domination within Islamic civilization. Equally important was Islamic resistance to the rise of Italian naval power in the Mediterranean and the establishment of a warlike Norman state in previously Islamic-ruled Sicily. Similarly, Islamic resistance to the early phases of what became known as the Christian Reconquista in the Iberian peninsula, the spread of Islam south of the Sahara and the resulting emergence of a reforming Murabit (Almoravid) Islamic state, as well as the clash between these Murabitun and the expanding Christian states within what are now Spain and Portugal, all need to be looked at in detail.

There were major variations between the military forces and potentials of those regions which would be involved in Crusading warfare from the eleventh to the early fourteenth centuries, not to mention those peripherals which were drawn into these conflicts. Nothing could be more inaccurate or misleading than to see all 'Crusaders' or all 'Saracens, Turks and Moors' as alike. Similarly, what could be called the pre-existing military–political status quo in these widespread regions varied enormously, as did the socio-economic foundations, wealth and international connections of such regions.

The Islamic world (although in retreat in the Iberian Peninsula) expanded steadily elsewhere; to Sicily and, quite recently, even the Middle East. Islam was spreading into and beyond the Sahara, down and into East Africa, dramatically across northern India, more steadily and peacefully into Inner Asia, and even across the Indian Ocean towards south-east Asia. Muslims did not feel themselves to be under cultural threat or to be in political retreat, except in those few peripheral Mediterranean regions already mentioned. Meanwhile the faith of Islam was spreading within the vast political entity we call the medieval Islamic world. In many regions Muslims were still in a minority, although forming political, military and cultural élites. Elsewhere non-Muslims, most notably Christians of various churches regarded as heretical by Latin Western European churchmen, formed substantial and economically powerful minorities. In addition there were significant Jewish, Zoroastrian, Sabaean, Yazidi, Buddhist, Hindu and other communities in several areas. The fact that they continued to exist and indeed to flourish, says much for the tolerance or cultural self-confidence of the Islamic ruling communities. This confidence was further emphasized by clear evidence of military participation by many of these communities. This was despite an Islamic or *Sharia* Law excusing non-Muslims from direct military obligation in return for the taxation which provided the sinews of war, namely the money which enabled an Islamic state to defend all its citizens, Muslims and non-Muslims alike. This would, however, change during the course of the Crusades and associated Christian assaults upon the Islamic world.

All these factors formed the general background of the Crusades. Then came the event which served as the immediate catalyst. The Seljuk Turkish conquest of the Middle East during the second half of the eleventh century altered a long-established yet fluid status quo and caused a major disruption of international trade, most notably within the Arab regions. This was followed by a prolonged and widespread Western European assault upon the Islamic Mediterranean, justified and to some extent motivated by religion. Such an assault eventually led to a Western European, or more particularly Italian, domination of Mediterranean maritime trade. The relative importance of secular, economic and political motivation and that of religious enthusiasm remains a matter of debate. It probably always will, and to a large extent such an argument sheds more light on the values of its own time and place than it does upon the personal priorities of those who responded to the call of counter-Crusade or *Jihad*, and of those Christians who went on Crusade.

Another factor which is too often ignored is that of relative population sizes and densities. All sides tended to proclaim that their enemies greatly out-numbered themselves, not only on the battlefield but in general. The foe tended to be numberless as well as nameless, and as early Western historians have largely relied upon European sources they have too often assumed that Islamic armies were huge, and that the defeat or even annihilation of a Muslim fighting force was of little significance to an Islamic society whose manpower resources were so great that armies could easily be replaced.

Only in Iberia did Islam probably enjoy a significant numerical advantage because it held the urbanized and irrigated south of the peninsula. The diverse population of Egypt remained at around two million, as did that of Syria which, during this period, can be seen to include part of what is now south-central Turkey, the western half of modern Syria, plus Lebanon, Palestine-Israel, and Jordan. The Arabian Peninsula had a population of around a million, largely concentrated in Yemen and to a lesser extent other coastal areas. By far the most significant concentration of largely Islamic population was in the Jazira and Iraq, numbering an estimated eight million. These two highly developed regions, consisting of what are now eastern Syria, northern and north-central Iraq, and much of present-day south-eastern Turkey, had flourished since the golden age of early Islamic and 'Abbasid rule. They continued to do so until the Mongol invasions of the thirteenth century. Some four million people were under Islamic rule in Anatolia, consisting of some three-quarters of modern Turkey, but the great majority were still Christian so the situation was rather different in this newly acquired province of the medieval Islamic world.

The overall health of the populations of the Islamic world tended to be high, possibly higher than it would be again until the introduction of modern medicine, but why its numbers remained largely static is unknown. Furthermore, it was characterized by an imbalance of males and females with an estimated ratio of 12 men to ten women. Apart from rendering ridiculous the popular image of medieval Muslim men lording it over teeming 'harems', these figures suggest that some degree of hidden female infanticide persisted. A comparable disparity is believed to have existed in medieval Europe, beneath the same shadow of the killing of unwanted baby girls.[1]

Similarities between the religious motivations of the Christian Crusade and of the Islamic Jihad are astonishing, yet this was probably not a result of mutual influence. Instead it seems more likely that both emerged from common ancient roots which included both Old Testament Judaic, Romano-Byzantine and early Christian concepts of religiously justified warfare. It is also interesting to note that religious authorities, such as the Pope on one side and Muslim legal scholars on the other, tended to be more keen on major battles to 'settle' the rivalry between these two faiths than were most of the rulers, commanders or soldiers immediately involved.[2]

While the religious and political realities of the Crusades were more complex than is generally realized, the military realities of Crusading warfare have been even more obscured by myth and misconception. There is still a widespread tendency to see the history of warfare in terms of major battles and to regard campaigns of devastation or raiding as somehow second-rate, inferior or lacking in strategy. Where the medieval period is concerned, this approach is wholly wrong. Although medieval commanders tended to avoid full-scale battles for a variety of reasons, not merely the uncertainty of their outcome or fear of irreversible defeat, there were many occasions when a commander felt confident or desperate enough to risk everything. In fact set-piece battles were just one of several aspects of medieval warfare, as were sieges and campaigns of devastation, each to be employed when the circumstances seemed correct. Meanwhile the taking of fortified places remained central to medieval strategy, especially during the wars of the Crusades and related conflicts.

Where discipline, command and control are concerned, historians still too often tend to assume that these were virtually lacking in medieval warfare. However, the evidence shows that on all sides of Crusading warfare, there were armies, which shows considerable discipline, organization and training. There were also plenty of rabbles. At the same time the most successful commanders of this period tended to be those who understood the limitations, not only of their troops but of their own ability to control such armies. These limitations themselves reflected inadequate systems of communication and transport rather than skill, knowledge or experience on the part of both leaders and men. Even the sometimes seemingly irrational behaviour of those involved might only appear irrational from a modern standpoint.

Questions of transport and communications will be looked at in detail. However, the Mediterranean imposed certain basic parameters on all who used it. Almost all sailing was undertaken during those months from spring to autumn when the seas were 'open' – in other words not during the winter when the weather permitted only the most urgent of voyages. Furthermore, navigation in the Mediterranean and its connected inland seas was largely by using islands and peninsulas as stepping stones. The main sailing routes tended to follow the coasts while open water was normally only crossed when there was no alternative and where the distances involved were relatively small. These features were most obvious along the east–west sea-lanes, but were also true of those running north–south. Only when this is fully understood can the vital strategic significance of major eastern Mediterranean islands such as Crete, Rhodes and Cyprus be appreciated.

Other factors deforestation, or a simple lack of trees, in certain politically, economically and militarily important regions. This was almost certainly the root cause of a technological shift from hull-first to frame-first ship construction. Given these ecological considerations, this change is most likely to have begun in the eastern Mediterranean, perhaps even in the Islamic world which, by its control of both Mediterranean and Indian Ocean coastlines, had access to a much greater variety of shipbuilding or maritime traditions than did ancient Greece or Rome. Developments in ship construction and design then played a part in the changes which would characterize medieval Mediterranean naval warfare. Finally, there was the fact that the period of the Crusades saw piracy flourish, yet piracy was not necessarily seen as a dishonourable activity. In the conditions of the time, what today would be condemned as utterly disreputable was often regarded as an acceptable means of livelihood when state structures were rarely strong enough to impose control on their adjacent seas. If this naval aggression was directed against unbelievers, it might well be graced with the title of Jihad or Crusade.

The medieval Islamic world

THE MILITARY TECHNOLOGICAL BACKGROUND

In military terms the early Islamic world was heir to several very ancient tradi-tions. The most obvious were the Graeco-Roman and early Byzantine heritages of Syria, Egypt and North Africa, and the heritage of the Sassanian Empire in Iran and Iraq. Both of these great empires had, by the time of the rise of Islam in the seventh century AD, been under strong Turkish military influence from peoples of the steppes to the north. A third 'military culture' which tends to be overlooked in the context of what became medieval Islamic military traditions was that of the Arabs themselves. This stemmed not only from central Arabia where the Prophet Muhammad preached, but perhaps more significantly from the ancient urbanized civilizations of Southern Arabia, that is Yemen.

It is clear that warfare in immediately pre-Islamic Arabia was dominated by infantry, especially in Yemen. It is also clear that archers played a significant role, but this was infantry archery rather than the horse-archery which became so characteristic of the later Islamic Middle East. Furthermore the infantry archery techniques, tactics and indeed the bow involved, seem to have had more in common with those of Byzantine armies than Sassanian armies. The bows appear to have been larger, stronger, slower and more tiring to use but also greater in impact than the bows associated with Iran.

Things are less clear where the organizational traditions of pre- and very early Islamic Arab armies were concerned. For example the term *khamis* later came to mean the five main tactical elements of a battle array or a line-of-march: centre, vanguard, rearguard and two wings or flanks. However, the word was also used in pre-Islamic South Arabia where it seems to have referred to an almost entirely infantry force of perhaps professional or high status infantry, with no clear association with the number five.[1] Here it is also worth noting that the tiny cavalry forces available to pre-Islamic rulers in Southern Arabia were entirely separate, as, apparently, were some or most of the low-status communal levies. This neglected military heritage deserves more attention than it has received in the study of the astonishing initial waves of Arab-Islamic conquest during the first half of the seventh century. This was, of course, when tribes from Yemen and neighbouring areas provided much of the military manpower.

The subsequent century of the Umayyad Caliphate saw continued expansion, consolidation, the absorption of an astonishing variety of different military influences, and the emergence of what could be identified as a specifically Islamic military tradition.[2] This was followed by the golden age of the 'Abbasid Caliphate when all aspects of Islamic military culture, organization, tactics, strategy and technology reached a remarkable level of sophistication. Though again being far less well known and understood than it deserved, this 'Abbasid classical period continued to draw upon and to refine numerous traditions while also now influencing its neighbours.

The Islamic impact upon Byzantine military culture, upon the Iberian Peninsula and to a lesser extent upon parts of the rest of Western Europe, has already been mentioned (see *Crusader Warfare* vol. 1). This influence was similarly felt in India, Central Asia, even Russia and China. At the same time the regional variation which had characterized Islamic armies and equipment since the early days seems to have become more pronounced. In some areas these reflected climatic, ecological and economic factors. In others the strongest factors were probably cultural. In Iran and what is now Afghanistan, for example, the pre-Islamic, largely Iranian cultural heritage remained very strong and remained so under the Ghaznawid and Seljuk Turkish rulers of the eleventh and twelfth centuries. Visibly most obvious in terms of costume and ceremonial, this Iranian heritage also had an impact upon military organization, tactics and weaponry.

This was a period of profound political and military changes within the Islamic world, some of which also had a deep though localized cultural impact. For example, the declining importance and status of infantry within most though not all Islamic armies contributed to a decline in the enlistment of slave-recruited black African soldiers in Egypt.[3] Here the most dramatic change in such recruitment coincided with the fall of the Fatimid Caliphate and its replacement by the Ayyubid Sultanate founded by Saladin. Central Asia had been by far the most important source of such *mamluks*, *ghulams* or slave-recruits since the ninth century and would rapidly become the most significant source of external military influences.[4]

Although not all the men recruited in or via Central Asia were Turks, most were and as a result Turkish would become a virtual lingua franca amongst the military élites of the later medieval Islamic East and Middle East. For some centuries the evidence for this widespread use of Turkish was secondary, as any Muslim who claimed any degree of education, whether he was a soldier or otherwise, would write in Arabic or Persian. Nevertheless, the importance of Turkish amongst less educated soldiers was evidenced by little-known sources such as a fourteenth- or fifteenth-century Arabic-Kipchaq Turkish dictionary written in the Mamluk

Sultanate of Egypt and Syria. It seems to have been intended to help Arab clerks or bureaucrats in their dealing with the largely Turkish *mamluk* soldiery.[5] A little-known Turkish literature also emerged amongst the Mamluk ruling and military class in later medieval Egypt and Syria.[6] Yet the status of Turkish as a language remained extraordinarily low until the rise of Turkish nationalism in the late nineteenth and twentieth centuries.

The dramatic cultural, social and political changes reflected in, and to a substantial extent resulting from, military developments within the early and classical Islamic periods were associated with several significant technological advances. Some were already under way in the pre-Islamic period. One of the most important was the invention and spread of the superior north Arabian camel saddle. Unlike the old padded camel saddle currently associated with the peoples of southern Arabia, this northern type incorporated a wooden frame or tree.

It has even been suggested that, coming before the wood-framed horse-saddle, it was the predecessor of that historically even more significant development. Because the new type of saddle could be placed on the camel's hump, rather than having to be attached behind it, the camel became a more efficient riding and baggage animal. The camel also became, for the first time, a reasonably useful military mount though it could never compete with the horse,[7] all of which meant that the camel-raising peoples of the desert and its steppe-like fringes could themselves become potent military and political forces.[8]

While changes in the structure of camel saddles could be seen as a military-technological influence spreading from northern Arabia into Syria, horse-breeding and especially the raising of that most intelligent of riding animals, the Arabian horse, spread from Syria into Arabia. It eventually reached Yemen in the south not long before the rise of Islam itself.

The composite bow, made of wood, sinew, sometimes horn and other materials, had been known for many centuries but it was still in a state of evolution, improvement or alterations to its overall size to make it more suitable under varying circumstances. Hence the technological or stylistic changes in the composite bows used by Islamic as well as Byzantine, Central Asian, Far Eastern and latterly also Indian armies were part of a much longer story with many strands and variations in different parts of the world.[9]

The history of metallurgy within the medieval Islamic world, both for civilian and military purposes, was very different. This was true for iron, steel and non-ferrous metals. Here, to a much greater degree than in any other aspects of Islamic culture outside religion itself, there was an astonishing degree of cultural unity across the vast Islamic world. There were also regional variations, usually reflecting the availablity of raw materials and long distance trade links or more localized trading connections with non-Islamic neighbours. Nevertheless, to take one long-distance connection as an example, the similarities between the metal technologies of Egypt in the Middle East and al-Andalus on the furthest western frontier of the medieval Islamic world were quite remarkable.[10]

The conscious drawing upon different and sometimes geographically or chronologically distant technologies became a feature of Islamic technical treatises, especially those dealing with military matters. One of the few that are reasonably well-known is that by Murda al-Tarsusi who wrote a wide-ranging military text for Saladin which drew upon numerous and varied earlier sources. It may actually have been produced as early as 1169 and should perhaps be seen as containing the military wisdom of the preceding Fatimid and Seljuk periods rather than that of an Ayyubid era which had barely begun.

Another, material example of the way medieval Islamic military technology absorbed, refined and then disseminated earlier technologies can be seen in soft armour. Quilted fabrics are understood to have been a widespread technology within the pre-Islamic Sassanian Empire of Iraq, Iraq, much of present-day Afghanistan and parts of Central Asia, though it is less clear to what degree it was given military application. Quilted fabrics were then adopted with enthusiasm across the Islamic Middle East and beyond, becoming what might be regarded as a basic technology.[11] This was now given widespread military application, both as soft-armour and as horse-armour (see below), and was thus spread to the Byzantine Empire and eventually to Western Europe. Its popularity in India, however, may have long pre-dated the Islamic period. Indeed it is possible that quilting technology actually originated in the sub-continent.

On the other hand, the medieval period was clearly not one of continuous technological advance in the Islamic world, at least not in the sense that such advances necessarily went hand in hand with increasing power or effectiveness. Some quite dramatic technological improvements seem, in fact, to have been in response to military, political or naval decline, perhaps reflecting efforts to combat such a decline which, in the event, proved to be inexorable. The story of the decline of Islamic naval power in the Mediterranean from the tenth century onwards would seem to be a case in point. It was almost entirely caused by geographical factors and a worsening shortage of timber that were challenged, albeit unsuccessfully, by some remarkable technological innovations.

Another broad aspect of medieval Islamic culture that is widely misunderstood, and therefore needs clarification, was the role and status of women. Women in medieval Islamic society were certainly not 'oppressed', to use the popular modern jargon. They may, in fact, have had a higher and certainly more clearly defined legal and social status than in virtually all the other major civilizations of the Middle Ages. This was clearly the case within the social élites where, in most cultures, the role of women tended to be more confined than that of their sisters lower down the social scale. The major influence of women, including mothers, wives and concubines, in the aristocratic and military classes of medieval Islamic civilization was significant and occasionally surprising. Yet their power was almost always exercised from behind the scenes, or perhaps 'behind the screen' of the harem.[12]

This might have been expected in Turkish societies, but it was also characteristic of Arab regions of the Islamic world and sometimes, though to a lesser degree, of the Persian or Iranian. One notable example was the role of educated women in Fatimid court and society. This may, however, have also resulted from the distinctive character of the Isma'ili sect of Shi'a Islam. Although Muslim women rarely came to the forefront as rulers in their own right, one ruler of the Isma'ili Sulayhid dynasty in Yemen was a woman. She maintained close links with the Fatimid dynasty in Egypt for many years, from 1084 until 1138, actually recognizing Fatimid suzerainty during the early years of her reign. This relationship weakened after the First Crusade occupied Palestine and the Fatimid Caliphate lost suzerainty over the Hijaz and its Islamic holy cities in western Arabia.[13] In this context it is also worth noting that the Arab rulers of what is now southern Pakistan had also earlier recognized the distant supremacy of the Fatimid Caliph.

Back in the Middle East the Syrian Arab soldier, writer, politican and scholar Usama Ibn Munqidh described how some of the senior women of the Banu Munqidh family which held the castle of Shayzar in the later eleventh and early twelfth century, put on armour to help repel an attack by neighbouring Isma'ilis.[14] Further west in Granada, in what is now southern Spain, the wives of the soldiers exerted such influence in the eleventh century as to become something of a problem for the ruling Zirid *amir*.[15] There would be many such cases later, not least within the Mamluk Sultanate of Egypt and Syria.

THE CULTURAL, POLITICAL AND MILITARY CONTEXT

The First Crusade struck the Islamic Middle East at a time of exceptional political and cultural fragmentation. Meanwhile the initial successes of the Iberian Reconquista had already been in a context of political and military fragmentation on the Islamic side, as had the Byzantine reconquest of so much territory in what is now eastern Turkey and north-western Syria before that. Much the same had recently been true of the Norman conquest of Islamic-ruled Sicily, so the weakness of the Islamic Middle East during the final years of the eleventh century was neither a new nor unusual phenomenon. It may perhaps be more accurate to suggest that the First Crusade was just one in a series of events where a revived Christendom took advantage, consciously or otherwise, of sometimes passing weaknesses within various parts of the Islamic world.

What might have made the context of the First Crusade particularly dramatic, and particularly fleeting, was the fragmentation of a Great Seljuk Sultanate which had, little more than a generation earlier, inflicted a devastating blow upon the Byzantine Empire. This would be cruelly demonstrated in the way in which the Seljuk commander Kerbogha's allies deserted him in battle against the Crusaders outside Antioch in 1098. Kerbogha's resulting defeat paved the way for his subordinates' de facto independence while also leading to a virtual political and military vacuum within which the Crusader Kingdom of Jerusalem and the other Latin States could be established.[16]

This Seljuk weakness was not, as has sometimes been suggested, mirrored in the rival Fatimid Caliphate of Egypt. The latter, having effectively abandoned its ambitions of conquest, was nevertheless in a period of relative military revival. Even the major financial problems which had undermined Fatimid efforts to dominate eleventh century Syria[17] had been partially resolved. Nevertheless, the rivalry between Fatimids and Seljuks, Arabs and Turks, Shi'a and Sunni Muslims, added to the vulnerability of the Islamic Middle East at a moment when a huge army of religiously excited, indeed increasingly fanatical Crusaders burst upon the scene.

It is clear that the Islamic rulers and peoples of the Middle East did not understand the motivation of the First Crusade. Many regarded this assault as an extension of the old struggle between Muslims and Byzantines, believing that the Crusaders' aims were limited and that reasonable negotiation could resolve the question of political control over Jerusalem. In fact it took the Islamic political and military élites some time to grasp the seriousness of the threat posed by these newcomers from Western Europe.[18]

There was also a huge lack of knowledge about Europeans, based upon centuries of assumed cultural superiority when Western Europe was dismissed as a fringe area inhabited by virtual barbarians of no interest to the Islamic peoples of the Middle East. Indeed this ignorance often mirrored that of the Western Europeans where the Islamic world was concerned, resulting in some strange myths, prejudices and distorted beliefs.[19] For example, the European idea that the Saracens had less blood, and thus courage, in their veins because of the heat of their homelands, found parallels in al-Mas'udi's tenth century comments on the Europeans:

> As for the people of the northern region ... the Franks ... they have little warm temperament in them, their bodies have become enormous, their character dry, their morals crude, their intellect stupid and their tongues sluggish ... Their beliefs have no solidity, and this is because of the cold character and lack of warmth [of their homeland].[20]

Several of these prejudices persisted throughout the period of the Crusades, and were probably strengthened by them. The *Sirat Baybars* is that part of the traditional Arabic epic and poetic hero-cycle most concerned with the Crusades. It includes various strands of fantasy that were hardly concerned with the historical Mamluk Sultan Baybars and are closer in spirit to *Alf Layla wa Layla*, 'The Thousand and One Nights' stories better known in the West as the Arabian Nights, than to the medieval European *chansons de geste*.[21]

Nevertheless those parts of the epic which do refer to the Crusades portray them as a more significant threat than that posed by the Byzantines. Furthermore the *Franks* or Western Europeans in such stories tend to be savage, uncivilized and hugely strong. For example the character Bohemond, who is largely based upon Bohemond of Taranto, one of the most successful leaders of the First Crusade, is said to have once imprisoned his own father and was capable of punching right through a man with his fist, mail hauberk, backbone and all.[22] Generally speaking, Turkish epics from this period, and those written in Persian for a Turkish military aristocracy, were closer in spirit to the twelfth and thirteenth century European *chansons de geste* than were those written for Arab or Persian readers.[23] These Turkish tales tended to be relatively simple adventure stories, full of battles, heroism and clever stratagems. Persian tales tended to focus on the might and splendour of rulers, with sweeping descriptions of massive events with casts of thousands. Arab tales were characterized by more humour, more subtlety, frequently a very ambiguous attitude towards authority and much less uncritical admiration of military prowess.

Despite many and obvious cultural, political and military similarities across the medieval Islamic world, there were also significant differences, even between regions which were under pressure from Western European Christendom during this period. Al-Andalus, or that part of the Iberian Peninsula which was under Islamic rule, was very distinctive in several ways. Here Arabic was, of course, the language of culture, government and of the educated élite, while *romance, latinia* or *aljamia*, a Latin-based dialect which was one of the forerunners of Spanish and Portuguese, was the language of ordinary people. It is also likely to have been used by much of the indigenous Islamic élite in their homes.[24]

During the tenth century the once powerful Umayyad Caliphate in al-Andalus collapsed and the country fragmented into small, sometimes quite tiny independent realms commonly known as the *ta'ifa* or 'party' states. The strong tradition of local particularism within al-Andalus made such fragmentation easy,[25] but it was these new statelets that now bore the brunt of an upsurge in Christian aggression from northern Iberia in the eleventh century. It was also soon clear that the *ta'ifa* states and their fractious rulers were unprepared for the realities of a changed balance of power within the Iberian Peninsula.[26] Overconfident in their own traditions of political and military as well as cultural superiority over the Christian northerners, their fragmentation was just one example of a process which was seen in many parts of the Islamic world at that time.

What was different in al-Andalus was the seriousness of the threat that these Islamic states faced. Even in Syria, the Byzantine Empire seemed content to win control of a strategic frontier zone and then to halt. Elsewhere, on the other frontiers of the Islamic world, there were no neighbours capable of mounting a major threat. Paradoxically the fact that most of the *ta'ifa* rulers in al-Andalus had strong local support weakened them, at least initially, as they had not felt the need for large armies to maintain their authority.[27] Those that fell first, including the *ta'ifa* kingdom of Toledo, were in sparsely populated central regions. Elsewhere the density of Islamic population and the strength of the many, often fortified, cities enabled other *ta'ifa* states to resist the first dramatic advances of the Iberian Reconquista.

In strategic terms, the *ta'ifa* states' survival in the seemingly almost isolated Ebro valley in north-eastern Spain might look surprising, but this was one such densely populated, intensively cultivated and urbanized region. Furthermore, it had been a strongly fortified frontier zone for centuries, developing its own distinctive regional culture even in military terms.[28] Here the Banu Hud or Hudid dynasty ruled a *ta'ifa* state which had greater military potential than many of the others further south, several of which it actually absorbed. The Hudids also formed occasional alliances with the neighbouring Christian Kingdom of Aragon in order to preserve their independence, not only from the Christian states but from the North African Murabitun (Almoravid) empire which saved the remainder of al-Andalus by conquering it. The Murabitun finally took the Hudid capital of Saragossa in 1110, only to lose it to the Christians eight years later.[29]

A second, briefer and less well-known *ta'ifa* period followed the collapse of Murabitun in al-Andalus in the mid-twelfth century. There was also another advance by the Christian Reconquista. In *al-Gharb* or 'the west' of al-Andalus, including the southernmost Algarve region of present-day Portugal, a remarkable local leader named Ahmad Ibn Qasi emerged. He combined Sufi Islamic mysticism with an appeal to regional patriotism in an effort to build a local Islamic state, independent of both Christian and North African domination. Ibn Qasi failed, but he was not alone in such an attempt. Another local Islamic leader was Muhammad Ibn Mardanish who established himself in Murcia. Known as King Lobo by the Spaniards, he reportedly spoke Spanish, dressed in Spanish style and used Spanish military equipment. Furthermore, he employed such large numbers of Christian mercenaries that his army was eventually described as being largely Christian, while receiving naval help from Italy in his effort to fend off the Muwahhidun (Almohades) from Morocco. The latter again 'saved' what remained of Islamic al-Andalus by conquering it.[30]

Western European military influences, via the Christian kingdoms of northern Iberia, were clearly strong and getting stronger in Andalusian armies, particularly during the second *ta'ifa* period of the twelfth century. It was even more obvious in the third and final *ta'ifa* period which followed the collapse of the Muwahhidun in the mid-thirteenth century. This would not be followed by another wave of conquest from North Africa. Instead the fragmented states which emerged were largely left on their own and fell, one by one, to the Christian Reconquista; all except the remarkable *amirate* of Granada. Here the ruling dynasty established by Ibn al-Ahmar formed a strategic alliance with the most powerful of the Christian kingdoms, becoming a vassal of the ruler of Castile and agreeing to supply troops to his army when required.[31] Despite occasional clashes, this arrangement helped preserve Granada's independence until 1492. Early Granadan armies will be discussed in greater detail below, but it is worth noting that, as just one aspect of the significant degree of Spanish influence upon Granada's defensive systems, this last surviving Andalusian Islamic outpost often referred to its own frontier region as *al-farantira*, from the Spanish term *frontera*.[32]

Al-Maghrib or 'The West' of the medieval Islamic world was generally considered to include North Africa excluding Egypt, Malta, Sicily and al-Andalus. However, the cultural and military circumstances of North Africa were mostly very different to those of the Iberian Peninsula. The only exception was the northernmost part of Morocco which sometimes seems to have had more in common with al-Andalus than with regions further south and east. There were also similarities, of course. The Fatimid withdrawal from most of North Africa in the tenth century left powerful and initially vassal rulers in control of most of what is now Tunisia and Algeria but not across much of Morocco. Here the Fatimid withdrawal and the collapse of the Umayyad Caliphate in al-Andalus resulted in a *ta'ifa*-like situation.

One of the most extraordinary of these largely tribal *ta'ifa* states was that of the Berber Barghawata who are said to have been able to raise an army of 10,000 horsemen plus a further 12,000 from amongst the 16 tribes they dominated. Furthermore the Barghawata had adopted such an unusual version of Islam that they were themselves eventually condemned as *kafirs*, non-Muslims or pagans.[33] The Moroccan *ta'ifa* state which had most in common with those of al-Andalus was centred upon the port-city of Sabta (now Spanish-ruled Ceuta) and Tangier on the southern side of the Straits of Gibraltar. It may have had some association with the strange Barghawata in the 1060s but fell to the Murabitun in 1078–9.[34]

All these small states were taken over quite easily to the rising power of the Murabitun,[35] a reformist Islamic movement which had originated far to the south, on the other side of the Sahara desert in what are now Senegal and southern Mauritania. As already stated, these Murabitun next crossed the straits

and took over a large part of the Iberian Peninsula, thus extending an African
'empire' into Europe. Nevertheless, Sabta (Ceuta) continued to have close links to
al-Andalus, winning real or partial independence whenever central government
was weak in the rest of Morocco. This was what happened around 1250, after the
fall of the Muwahhidun, when Sabta (Ceuta) emerged as a significant naval power
in its own right, defended by an effective army, strong urban fortifications and
several outposts further inland. Even the Christian Spanish Kingdom of Castile,
an increasingly dominant power in the area, was obliged to treat tiny Sabta with
respect.[36] Elsewhere, from the mid-thirteenth century onwards, weaker Islamic
states often sought alliances with Christian powers against their stronger Islamic
neighbours. One such were the Zayyanid rulers of western Algeria who, as
rivals of the Marinids of Morocco, established political, economic and military
links with the Spanish Kingdom of Aragon.[37] This, perhaps above everything
else, illustrated a fundamental shift in the balance of power between Islam and
Christendom which characterized the later Middle Ages.

Sicily had only been conquered by the Muslims in the ninth century. Indeed
Taormina did not fall until 902. Islamic Sicily never produced its own strong
internal leadership, usually being dependent upon North Africa, though a
dynasty of governors known as the Kalbids were in place from the mid-tenth
to mid-eleventh centuries.[38] Under Islamic rule the island's closest cultural
connections were not with al-Andalus to the west, though there were some
military links, but with Egypt to the east. Nor did Islamic civilization have time
to strike deep local roots. On the other hand Islamic Sicily, and the Islamic culture
which survived on the island for over a century under Norman and even early
Angevin rule, did serve as a very important channel of cultural, scientific and
even military influences from the medieval Islamic world into Europe; most
obviously into mainland Italy itself.[39]

North Africa had been drawn into the Islamic World at a much earlier date, and
remained there ever since. The lack of a strongly embedded Romano-Byzantine
culture also meant that the indigenous Berber peoples, a large proportion of
whom still appear to have been pagans when the first Arab-Islamic conquerors
arrived in the seventh century, converted to Islam in large numbers in the early
centuries of Islamic rule. The only substantial indigenous community to retain
a separate religious identity were the Jewish tribes, the largest numbers of whom
lived in Morocco. Having been converted to Judaism some centuries earlier,
these Berber Jews were already a significant cultural, political and even military
force. They rapidly came to terms with the Islamic conquest, probably took part
in the Islamic conquest of the Iberian Peninsula in the early eighth century, and
remained an integral part of North African civilization until modern times.

It is important to note that the substantial Arabization of North Africa did
not occur during the centuries immediately following the Islamic conquest. Not

until a new wave of essentially bedouin and tribal rather than state-organized Arab 'conquests' during and after the eleventh century did Arabs become numerically or culturally dominant west of Egypt, or at least west of Libya. These eleventh century invasions or migrations by the Banu Hilal and Banu Sulaym tribes were of considerable political, military, cultural and eventually linguistic significance, but the devastation that they were said to have caused was almost certainly exaggerated. The golden age of the early Islamic centuries had passed and the central regions of North Africa had been suffering economic decline for some time. In fact the remarkable military success of the Banu Hilal in the mid-eleventh century was more a result than a cause of the weakness of established government like that of the Zirids.[40] Yet this bedouin Arab influx did undermine the power and prosperity of the inland cities, contributing if not causing settled governments to concentrate upon the coastal towns and upon the sea beyond. Eventually they became what unsympathetic Western European historians have characterized as 'pirate states', including, of course, the famous Barbary Corsairs of later centuries.

Zirid authority in Tunisia had already fragmented by the time the new Norman rulers of southern Italy extended their 'crusade' from Sicily to North Africa. Here a number of petty local rulers were exerting their independence from the Zirids, most notably on the island of Jerba which had almost become a safe haven for pirates who preyed upon Christian and Islamic shipping alike.[41] In these circumstances it has been suggested that the Norman king may have been trying to inherit the regional domination and 'imperial' role that the Fatimid Caliphate of Egypt once played.[42] Certainly, the wealthy Norman rulers adopted several aspects of Fatimid court and military ceremonial, as reflected in the extraordinary Islamic painted panels which form the ceiling of the Cappella Palatina in their capital of Palermo.

The work of resident Muslim craftsmen as well as Greeks, Italians, men from southern France and even from Fatimid Egypt, has also been suggested in the similarly remarkable carved capitals in the cloisters of Monreale Cathedral in Sicily. Here the best carving has been described as 'Islamic' and the poorest as 'non-Muslim'.[43] Close inspection of some of the arms, armour, horse-harness and costume shown in both the Cappella Palatina ceiling-panels and the Monreale capitals show that it is often very different from the equipment illustrated in other European or even Byzantine art of the period.

The islands of Malta and Gozo between Sicily and North Africa may have had a Semitic-speaking population since Phoenician and Carthaginian times, before the rise of the Roman Empire. Their Semitic culture was clearly reinforced or re-established during the early medieval centuries of Islamic rule and the Maltese language remains essentially an Arabic dialect to this day. The population of the islands was still largely Muslim until the thirteenth century, long after they had been conquered by a Norman fleet from Sicily, so that Malta and Gozo could be regarded as all that remains of the Siculo-Norman kings' attempts to carve out a North African empire in the centre of the Islamic Maghrib.

Egypt had become the economic powerhouse and military centre of the Fatimid state in the mid-tenth century when this Isma'ili Shi'a Caliphate and bitter rival of the Sunni 'Abbasid Caliphate in Baghdad first conquered the country and then transferred its capital to the new city of al-Qahira, Cairo. For many years the Fatimids clung to a dream of extending their conquests even further eastward and overthrowing the 'Abbasids by military means. However, their North African and Egyptian powerbase was never strong enough to achieve this ambition, while the majority of their own subjects remained Sunni rather than Shi'a Muslims or were still Christians. Indeed the Fatimids even found it difficult to maintain control over those parts of Syria which they did conquer.

A serious military decline then set in, most notably under the Caliph al-Hakim whose unorthodox religious claims resulted in many people regarding him as mad. His persecution of Christians and Jews, which ran counter to the normal policy of his predecessors and his successors, further alienated these communities. News of his actions, filtering back to Western Europe, added to a growing hostility and would be remembered a century later during the emotional build-up to the First Crusade. On the other hand many of those converted to Shi'a Islam by al-Duruzi, an Isma'ili missionary supported by the Caliph al-Hakim, came to revere al-Hakim as an incarnation of God. Known as the Druze, they were themselves eventually regarded by many Muslims as no longer forming part of the worldwide *umma* or Islamic community.

In many respects it is remarkable that the Fatimid Caliphate survived and recovered from the military decline, administrative chaos and general demoralization which characterized the reign of al-Hakim and some of his successors.[44] It did, though at a cost, and in 1074 an Armenian convert to Islam named Badr al-Jamali became *wazir*, vizier or chief minister of state. As an efficient administrator as well as an effective military commander, Badr al-Jamali gathered the reins of power into his own hands, reduced the Caliph to a dignified figurehead and turned the state into what could be described as a military dictatorship.[45] It was just in time, for the Seljuk Turks were overrunning Syria and Palestine and the seeds of the First Crusade had already been planted in Europe.

Most histories of the Crusades tend to be dismissive of the Fatimid army and its achievements. Badr al-Jamali was succeeded as *wazir* and effective if not official ruler by his son al-Afdal, a man with the same skills and determination as his father. He commanded a well equipped army which, though not as large as many chroniclers claimed, was more effective than most historians allow. Under al-Afdal and his sometimes successful, sometimes less so, successors the Fatimid Caliphate survived until 1171. The state had now virtually become the servant of the army,[46] existing to support the army which in turn either defended it or preyed upon it.

Al-Afdal's time as *wazir* before and during the early years of the Crusader threat was a period of fundamental reforms. Those affecting the military administration showed considerable eastern influence from the Seljuk Turkish Sultanate which was recognized as having the most powerful army in the Islamic Middle East. These new ideas seem to have reached the Fatimid state via those large numbers of Armenian soldiers and others in its service, most of whom probably came from regions now under Seljuk rule.[47] There were also continuing efforts to raise larger cavalry forces, especially of horse-archers, and to reduce the Fatimids' traditional reliance on infantry. This reflected military trends elsewhere in the Islamic Middle East.

Nevertheless the Fatimid army found it difficult to compete in such matters because Egypt had always been short of pasture to maintain large numbers of cavalry and was also unable to recruit many horse-archers, even as slaves. The great majority of the latter would have come from Central Asia, on the far side of the Fatimid Shi'a Caliphate's great rivals, the Sunni Muslim Seljuk Turks.[48] This must surely have been the main reason why the Fatimid army continued to rely on such large numbers of infantry, many still recruited from sub-Saharan Africa via Nubia.

The Fatimid Caliphate was eventually abolished by Saladin in 1171, two years after he, as a Sunni who owed his allegiance to Nur al-Din, the Zangid Turkish ruler of Syria, had become the Fatimid Caliph's *wazir*. Saladin used Egypt as his economic and military powerbase, but recruited the most important part of his army from further north and east. Nominally loyal to Nur al-Din until the latter's death ten years later, Saladin then seems to have put more effort into dominating Nur al-Din's successors and relatives in Syria and northern Iraq, than against the Crusader States. Inevitably this gradually undermined Saladin's claim to be in the forefront of the struggle to liberate Jerusalem.

Before his great victory over the Crusader Kingdom of Jerusalem at Hattin in 1187 and his retaking of Jerusalem that same year, Saladin is believed to have been campaigning far beyond his financial and military means. He needed a victory, not only for booty to pay his troops but to maintain their morale and to restore his somewhat tarnished reputation.[49] Hattin and Jerusalem gave him that victory, but it resulted in a Third Crusade which almost proved a disaster for the Islamic leader. In the event this epic campaign ended in stalemate with Saladin surviving an onslaught by the three most powerful rulers in Western Europe: Frederick of Germany, Philip Augustus of France and Richard of England. He even managed to retain his greatest prize, the liberated Holy City of Jerusalem, though a nominal or rump Kingdom of Jerusalem was recreated around the Crusader-held coastal city of Acre. Yet it had been a close-run thing and almost certainly accounted for the caution thereafter demonstrated by Saladin, and the Ayyubid dynasty which he founded, in their dealings with the Latin States.[50]

Saladin's Ayyubid dynasty came to an end in Egypt in 1250, though minor Ayyubid princes continued to rule in several parts of Syria and the Jazira for a few more decades. One part of the family retained at least nominal control of Hama and its surroundings until 1332 while another ruled Hisn Kayfa (Hasankayf) in what is now south-eastern Turkey until the later fifteenth century. In Egypt and subsquently in Syria the Ayyubids were, however, replaced by the Mamluk Sultanate. This remarkably successful and long-lasting state was dominated by, and for most of its history ruled by, *mamluk* soldiers of slave origin. It was another example of a military realm in which the state itself seems to have existed for the benefit of the army and its military élite. Yet at the same time this Mamluk Sultanate produced some of the finest architecture and craftsmanship in the long history of Islamic civilization.

Baybars al-Bunduqdari, 'Baybars the Pellet-Bow Man', was not the first Mamluk sultan but he came to power ten years after the overthrow of the Ayyubids and ruled until 1277. He is also seen as the real founder of the Mamluk military system which proved extraordinarily effective for such a long time. He seems to have regarded the organization of the invading Mongols as a sort of military ideal,[51] and although this could not be replicated in a settled, urbanized and Islamic state such as the Mamluk Sultanate, it did provide the Mamluks with new ideas which they successfully grafted on to existing and sometimes long-established Islamic military traditions.

Arabia tends to be virtually ignored when studying the history of the Crusades, especially their military aspects. Nevertheless the peoples of the Arabian Peninsula did have a part to play. Here the nomadic and semi-nomadic bedouin still lived much as their ancestors had done in the time of the Prophet Muhammad. In warfare they mostly fought on foot, usually as archers or with javelins, with a small number of cavalry drawn from tribal élites. The camel served, as it had always done, primarily as a source of food, as a beast of burden and a means of mobility in the desert.[52]

Surprisingly perhaps, the older, unframed and padded form of camel saddle continued to be widely used in southern Arabia, perhaps because it was adequate for all non-military purposes while the tribes of Yemen and other southern regions of Arabia did not adopt the long-range, camel-riding, raiding warfare characteric of central and northern Arabian tribes.[53] Furthermore, horse-riding cavalry were reportly numerous in Yemen by the thirteenth century, despite the horse having been a relative newcomer to this region.[54] Yemen itself flourished in a degree of political if not cultural and economic isolation from the Arab, Persian, Turkish and other Islamic lands north of Arabia. Even when Yemen's strategic location, dominating one side of the hugely important Bab al-Mandab Straits, resulted in it being occupied by armies from the north, these invaders found it almost impossible to control the Yemeni highlands. Saladin, for example, sent an army to conquer Yemen but then found that he had to send more and more men to keep order, until this new conquest became more of a problem than a benefit.[55]

Of all the Islamic lands involved in the history of Crusading warfare, none was more important than or as deeply impacted as Syria. This region also had a tradition of independence or autonomy, and of fractiousness. From the fall of the Umayyad Caliphate of Damascus in 750 AD, until the rise of Nur al-Din in the mid-twelfth century, the cities of what are now Syria, Lebanon, Palestine, Jordan and some parts of south-eastern Turkey frequently resisted distant central governments, whether they were based in Iraq like the 'Abbasid Caliphate or in Egypt like the Fatimid Caliphate. On the other hand, when facing revolts by the bedouin of nearby deserts or steppes, these cities tended to rally to whatever government held power at the time, clearly preferring order to disorder,[56] though preferring quiet autonomy above both.

The relationship between the bedouin and the settled peoples of the Fertile Crescent, including Syria, was usually one of economic symbiosis. Yet the nomads were always at an economic disadvantage because they relied upon settled peoples, peasants or townsmen, for cereals and manufactured items including most of their clothing and virtually all their military equipment. In return their own economic produce, largely consisting of sheepmeat, was not essential for either the cultivators or the urban population. The only real exception was the horses which the bedouin raised and which were in constantly high demand by rulers and their armies.[57] When these mutually dependent but also rival communities clashed, the nomads had to rely on their greater physical endurance, their knowledge of terrain and their tradition of very clever, indeed devious, tactics to balance the greater wealth, numbers and military equipment of their settled foes.

The only real advantage which the bedouin enjoyed was their strategic ability to conduct selected raids and then to retreat into the desert where their superior knowledge of water sources normally enabled them to escape.[58] The bedouin themselves were usually, though not always, unsympathetic to central governments. For their part, city-based governments had to balance the nuisance potential of the bedouin and the disruption they could cause with their own need for horses raised by these same nomadic tribes. As a result, the Syrian and neighbouring towns often found themselves caught between the competing interests of bedouin and central goverment.[59]

A great deal of unsubstantiated or oversimplified nonsense has been written about the impact that the initial Arab-Islamic conquest had upon settled life and cultivation in the seventh century. In reality the impact varied greatly between different parts of the Fertile Crescent; even between neighbouring provinces. Nor were localized changes in the balance between settled agricultural and nomadic pastoral ways of life permanent. There were, in fact, significant fluctuations throughout the early medieval period, even after the impact of the initial Arab-Islamic conquest was long past. The Ummayad period from the mid-seventh to mid-eighth centuries was, for example, one of huge wealth and splendour for most parts of Syria, even including the semi-desert steppes, but this golden age soon came to an end after the Umayyads were overthrown and the centre of the Caliphate moved east to Iraq.

There also appears to have been a significant decrease in the cultivated areas of northern Syria during the troubled tenth and eleventh centuries, before the arrival of the First Crusade further disrupted life, communications and trade. One symptom of this change was an increase in camel-raising amongst Arab tribes of the inland plains of Syria which lay between the deserts and the mountains. Here several Arab tribes had lived as settled agriculturalists for generations if not centuries.[60] Nevertheless these and other tribes remained rich and militarily powerful, reportedly capable of fielding 7,000 cavalrymen. Into this complex situation a new tribal nomadic people, the Turcomans, suddenly erupted during the second half of the eleventh century. In this context the term Turcomans is used to distinguish such tribes from the Turkish Seljuk states and armies.

Previously dominant Arab tribes, including the Banu Kilab, suffered a sudden and drastic political and military decline.[61] One of the main reasons for this collapse was the Arabs' shortage of archers, most particularly of the horse-archers who had never been a significant feature in Arab tribal forces, but also of infantry archers which is more surprising. During their unsuccessful resistance to the encroaching Turcomans, some local Arab armies even recruited archers from their erstwhile Byzantine enemies.[62]

Prior to the arrival of the Seljuk armies and Turcoman tribes in the later eleventh century, a reduction in Byzantine aggression earlier in that century had resulted in a noticeable economic revival in the hills and mountains of north-western Syria. This in turn led to a localized recolonization of agricultural land,[63] in apparent contrast to an abandonment of agriculture in some of the lowlands to the east. Much of this resettlement appears to have been grouped around the numerous fortifications which characterized this part of Syria, and which the Crusaders would subsequently often enlarge.

Another upland area further south, the Golan Heights and plateau between Damascus and Palestine, had, unlike the hills of north-western Syria, been virtually unfortified until the arrival of the Crusaders at the start of the twelfth century. In fact the local Islamic rulers had felt no threat in this region.[64] Nor was there any longer evidence of the coastal *ribats* or communities of local, religiously motivated volunteers who had defended the Syrian-Palestinian coasts against Byzantine naval raiding in earlier centuries.[65]

What the First Crusade found when it reached Syria at the end of the eleventh century were local political and military systems which had remained in place after the Fatimids had been forced out by the Seljuks. The land was fragmented, with petty local rulers or governors owing allegiance, real or nominal, to the distant Great Seljuk Sultan or, on the coast, to a similarly distant Fatimid Caliph. In a few places local rulers were truly independent, though only one or two seemed confident enough to state this publicly. Whether Turkish or Arab, they usually controlled a few fortified centres and had small, sometimes tiny, armies of a few hundred cavalry, some armoured some not, headed by élites which could be numbered in dozens rather than hundreds.[66]

The Seljuk Great Sultanate was already begining to decline when the First Crusade arrived, and in its aftermath this decline accelerated. As a result a number of Turcoman tribes or groups seized control in Syria, the Jazira and parts of northern Iraq. This fragmentation resulted in the emergence of new Turkish or Turcoman dynasties such as the Artuqids and Zangids which initially controlled quite small states with small armies, not dissimilar to the petty dynasties of Arab tribal origin which had characterized the period just before the Seljuk invasions.[67] Many are now referred to as *atabeg* states, having been founded or taken over by the 'elder guardians', or *atabegs* in Turkish, who had been put in place to supervise young princelings of the Seljuk ruling house.

The Byzantine Princess Anna Comnena, in a biography of her father the Emperor Alexius I, maintained that the Turks were more civilized than the Franks or Western Europeans.[68] Such a statement might sound surprising to those who think of the eleventh and twelfth century Turks as ferocious nomadic tribesmen recently erupted from Central Asia and still only superficially converted to Islam. When Anna was referring to the Turks, however, she was probably thinking of the Seljuk and other Turkish élites who now ruled most of the ancient cultural heartlands of the eastern and Middle Eastern Islamic world. More specifically she may have had in mind those who created new Turkish-Islamic states in Anatolia, in what had been one of the heartlands of Byzantine civilization.

These new states were under considerable Byzantine, Greek and Armenian cultural influence while the bulk of their populations would remain Orthodox Christian for many generations.[69] The most powerful was the Seljuk Sultanate of Rum, Rum or 'Rome' being the Arab, Persian and Turkish name for the Byzantine Empire. By the end of the twelfth century it had conquered its Turkish-Islamic rivals but would itself be defeated and made a vassal of the Mongols in the mid-thirteenth century. By the start of the fourteenth century the Seljuk Sultanate of Rum had effectively ceased to exist, its territories fragmented into an array of tiny Turkish statelets often known as *beyliks*. From amongst them one would emerge that not only absorbed the others but went on to obliterate the last traces of the Byzantine Empire, to conquer virtually the entire Middle East and most of North Africa, and whose armies would one day be knocking at the gates of Vienna. The *beylik* or *amirate* with such an astonishing military history before it was, of course, that of the Ottoman Turks.

Very little is known about the army or indeed the military organization of the Seljuk Sultanate of Rum in the twelfth century,[70] though it probably mirrored or attempted to mirror that of the Great Seljuk Sultanate of Iran and Iraq. Considerably more information becomes available in the thirteenth century, but even during that period the degree of Byzantine military influence remains a matter of scholarly debate.[71] One of the most interesting sources of information for this period of military transition, from the Turco-Iranian armies of twelfth century Islamic Anatolia to the distinctive armies of the Ottoman Empire, is a work of literature rather than a supposedly factual chronicle. It is the *Danishmandname* by 'Arif 'Ali of Toqat. The story itself was reportedly written for 'Izz al-Din Kay Kawus, the Seljuk Sultan of Rum immediately after the Seljuks had been defeated by the invading Mongols. The original text of this epic is unfortunately lost, but the story survives in a mid-fourteenth-century Ottoman version which is said to have been written in 'better Turkish' while leaving the text largely unchanged. As such the *Danishmandname* also stands as one of the earliest examples of Ottoman literature.[72]

At the start of the eleventh century the greater part of the Islamic world was in a remarkably fragmented state and largely under indigenous local rulers, with many Andalusian dynasties in al-Andalus, Berber dynasties in North Africa, Arab rulers from Egypt to Syria, Kurds and others in eastern Anatolia. The situation in Iraq was rather different and rather strange. In this largely Arab country the 'Abbasid, Sunni Muslim Caliphate was dominated and supposedly 'protected' by the Shi'a Islamic Buwayhids or Buyids, a dynasty of northern Iranian origin. The Buwayhid system of government was decentralized to the point of fragmentation with different sections of the family ruling different parts of Iraq and Iran until the mid-eleventh century.

Elsewhere in Iran there was further fragmentation with the country being divided between local dynasties. Apart from the Buwayhid realms, and before the rise of the Seljuks, the only other substantial states were those of the originally Turkish Ghaznawids in much of what is now Afghanistan and Pakistan, and the still tribal Turkish Qarakhanids whose realm spread from Transoxania across the Tien Shan Mountains to Kashgaria in what is now Chinese eastern Turkestan.

What distinguished the eastern frontier of the Islamic world from those of the Mediterranean and Iberian Peninsula was that here Islam was advancing rather than retreating. The Ghaznawids of Afghanistan would extend Islamic territory deep into northern India while Islam was spreading fast, and by more peaceful means, beyond its traditional frontiers in Central Asia. In the latter region the spread of the Islamic faith was, in fact, almost exactly in the opposite direction as the general flow of political and military conquest.

The Seljuk Turks originally formed a small part of the Oghuz or Ghuzz Turkish people who had dominated much of the Central Asian steppes for several centuries. Converted to Islam in the later tenth century they, like so many other nomadic groups, migrated into Islamic territory and found service as auxiliary troops. As the power of the existing, competing local powers declined, these Seljuks were able to carve out a territory for themselves in the prosperous and urbanized province of Khurasan. From there they expanded with remarkable success, forcing back the Ghaznawids and encouraging them to seek their fortune in India rather than Iran.

By declaring themselves as loyal Sunnis, the Seljuks won support from those who resented Shi'a rule, and here it is important to remember that Iran, which is today the only major Shi'a Islamic state in the world, was largely Sunni during the medieval period. Having defeated the Shi'a Buwayhids, the Seljuk leader Toghrïl entered Baghdad in 1055 and had his title of Sultan confirmed by the 'liberated' 'Abbasid Caliph.

The eleventh-century Turkish conquests by the Seljuks, Qarakhanids and Ghaznawids in Central Asian Transoxania, in Iraq, Iran, Afghanistan, what is now Pakistan and much of northern India, brought significant changes to these regions. While these were visible in their government and administrative structure, they were even more significant where military structures and subsequent traditions were concerned.

RECRUITMENT

Warfare, military élites and what might be termed military virtues were never as highly regarded in Islamic culture as they were, and to some extent still are, in Western Europe. In this repect the medieval Islamic world had more in common with Byzantine civilization. Warfare might be seen as a necessity, but it remained an unpleasant if not necessarily evil one. The greatest social, ethical and cultural prestige was offered to religious leaders or those who were considered to be living religious lives even if they did not hold positions of authority. People of cultural and above all literary achievement were also given generally higher status than 'mere soldiers'. Even political leaders were often regarded as a necessity to be respected and obeyed, but only if they themselves showed due respect to religion and culture. Military men had little prestige unless they were recognized as having other achievements or virtues as well.

Medieval Islamic civilization was also essentially urban and had, to a significant extent, always been so. The Prophet Muhammad was himself a townsman from Mecca, and the first Islamic community had been focused upon a town, Medina. The role of Arab bedouin tribes, so romanticized by Western historians, was secondary, even during the great age of Arab-Islamic expansion in the seventh and eighth centuries. They may have provided much of the military manpower and military skills, though even this has been exaggerated, but the leadership remained urban in outlook and to a large extent in aspiration. In these respects Islamic civilization was, or soon became, typically Middle Eastern. This was also true of almost the entire, and now vast, eleventh century Islamic world.

These fundamental characteristics had a profound impact upon military recruitment and organization, as well as upon the attitudes of governments and societies to the armies which either protected or occasionally preyed upon them. The still largely Iranian-speaking north-eastern frontier regions of Sughd and Transoxania had been strongly urbanized since the Islamic conquest. Here, for example, many of the existing urban élites turned to the newly arrived and still semi-barbarian Seljuk Turks to balance the power of their Qarakhanid rulers in the early or mid-eleventh century.[73] By the twelfth century, after Seljuk power had spread westward to include Iran and most of the Fertile Crescent, the 'Abbasid Caliphs of Baghdad frequently formed alliances with Seljuk *atabeg* provincial governors or rulers against the power of the Arab tribes in Iraq. In so doing they were able to free themselves from both, and to restore the Sunni 'Abbasid Caliphate to some of its previous glory.[74]

In neighbouring northern Syria at the end of the eleventh century the Seljuk princes or governors, perhaps recognizing that they themselves were a barely civilized warrior class only recently converted to Islam, largely left local administration to leading local urban families. Some of the latter were Muslim, some Christian, and they were often the same groups that had been running local affairs for generations.[75] The great northern Syrian city of Aleppo illustrates several of these points, undergoing huge changes from the eleventh to thirteenth centuries. What had been an Arab city, with a strong Shi'a element in its religiously mixed population, became an ethnically mixed centre of Sunni orthodoxy. This change was itself associated with a migration of Turks and Turcomans into the area and into the city. Aleppo did not, however, become a Turkish city, perhaps because so many Turks were attracted to the new and expanding Turkish states in Anatolia. Here a tribal people that had originated in Central Asia found the high plateau of central Anatolia much more suited to their semi-nomadic, sheep-raising way of life.

Aleppo subsequently became the vital northern bastion of the Ayyubid and Mamluk states, but by then there had been major changes in military recruitment patterns within northern Syria. The Arab Mirdasid, Turkish Zangid and Kurdish early Ayyubid rulers had largely relied on a traditional patron–client relationship between the ruling family and entire tribal groups. The latter then tended to become integrated into the fabric of the city of Aleppo. On the other hand, this centuries-old system was in decline as the *'iqta* or fief system grew (see below): the *'iqta* system favoured an individual relationship between a recruit-fief holder and a ruler. Another change was the sudden availability of large numbers of slaves as military recruits during the first half of the thirteenth century, reflecting major population upheavals, conflicts and migrations within Central Asia. These were in turn associated with the rise of Genghis Khan and the Mongol conquests. Rulers could now recruit larger numbers of previously expensive, rather scarce and traditionally élite *mamluk* or *ghulam* military slaves. Here again, however, the Aleppo region or more particularly its northern or eastern neighbours still differed in its continued reliance upon traditional patron–client relationships between local rulers and tribal groups such as those Turkish tribes which formed a military buffer between Aleppo and the Turkish Anatolian states.[76]

The situation was very different in Egypt. Here the nomadic, semi-settled and in some cases settled bedouin Arab tribes continued to form a state-within-a-state until they were largely crushed or expelled by the Mamluk Sultans in the late thirteenth and early fourteenth centuries; although the Coptic Christian population, which still probably formed a majority in some areas such as Upper Egypt, had been largely demilitarized during the early centuries of Islamic rule. This was not, however, yet the case with the Islamic population. Their effective demilitarization did not occur until well into the Mamluk Sultanate. Indeed the inhabitants of several Lower or northern Egyptian cities were described as quite warlike in the eleventh century, and were still fully capable of taking up arms in defence of their towns against Crusader invaders in the twelfth century. The most often mentioned in this respect were the capital Cairo and its older, sprawling southern suburb of Fustat, plus Bilbays and Tinnis which stood at the edge of the cultivated Nile Delta.[77]

Theoretically, the non-Muslim inhabitants of Islamic states were excused military service which, in the early Islamic period, had been seen as a form of *sajar* or 'humiliation' that was required of Muslims as a duty to protect the Islamic state. Instead *dhimmis*, or non-Muslims who had accepted Islamic protection, were obliged to pay a special tax which was intended to help pay the costs of the Muslim army.[78] This concept continued to be an essential part of Islamic law but by the eleventh century the armies of the Islamic states had become increasingly professionalized, and much of the Muslim population was also paying taxes instead of doing military service. The theory of universal Muslim military obligation remained but in reality the only non-professional or non-volunteer troops were urban militias; and even these were more characteristic of some regions than of others.

Such a legal framework did not mean that indigenous Christians and other non-Muslims had no part to play in the armies of the medieval Islamic states. They were almost certainly active, as well as having a supporting role, in defence of the Seljuk Sultanate of Rum though the degree of Byzantine military influence that they brought to new Turkish Anatolian states is a matter of debate.[79] A substantial migration by sections of the Armenian military classes to Syria and above all Egypt in the eleventh century has already been mentioned. Christian Armenian soldiers had served in these countries in earlier centuries but they now became perhaps the most important, though not the most numerous, element in the later Fatimid army. A number of *wazirs* or chief ministers were drawn from their ranks, usually though not invariably converts to Islam. The most significant were Badr al-Jamali and his son al-Afdal before and during the years of Crusader occupation in Palestine and parts of Syria.[80]

Indigenous Coptic and Syrian Christian scribes and bureaucrats may have dominated the military administration of the Fatimid Caliphate in Egypt and Syria.[81] Their role in support of the armies of the subsequent Ayyubid dynasty remained important and it was not until the time of Baybars I, ruler of the Mamluk Sultanate in the 1260s and 1270s, that many minor civilian offices were militarized and given to *mamluks*. This trend was itself part of the overall militarization and what might be called the '*mamlukization*' of the state during the later thirteenth century.[82] Even in North Africa where the Christian community, always in a minority, had been in decline since the seventh century, there were substantial Christian communities in Tunis and Tlemcen in the early twelfth century.[83] It is possible that they may still have supplied bureaucrats to the military administration of their relevant governments.

When one looks at patterns and systems of military recruitment across the medieval Islamic world it is clear that there were significant differences between regions. These not only reflected the availability of certain ethnic or cultural groups and their willingness to serve as soldiers, but also the wealth of local rulers. Wealth, or the lack of it, had a particular impact upon the dynasty's ability to recruit high-status troops from outside its own realm or sometimes from far distant lands. Changes in the ethnic origins, cultural and even religious affiliations of ruling groups resulted in changes in military recruitment. Furthermore, one notable characteristic of Islamic history during this period was the tendency of some major dynasties to rule several regions at once, or to migrate, willingly or otherwise, from one region to another. This is why it often makes more sense to study armies on a dynastic rather than geographical basis, and to look at regional variations within the armies of those dynasties which dominated particularly large parts of the medieval Islamic world.

Despite a widespread impression, resulting from the prominence and high status offered to troops from outside a particular realm, the great bulk of military recruitment was usually internal. This applied to the Islamic world as a whole and to the dynastic states of which it consisted. Nevertheless certain groups did tend to predominate. These were usually from the geographical as well as economic and social margins. Many such groups used the military power which resulted from their own recruitment to establish ruling dynasties, thus bringing themselves to the social and economic though more rarely the cultural centre of affairs. When such dynasties were overthrown and replaced, the ethnic or cultural groups from whom they had emerged, and which had provided their military muscle, tended to return to a marginal state. This phenomenon was not, of course, restricted to medieval Islamic civilization though it may have been more dramatic here than in most other parts of the world.

A fascinating account of the life of one otherwise unknown young man illustrates this marginalism as perceived and related by a writer who was himself part of a social élite which tended to look down upon soldiers. He told how, in tenth century southern Iraq, a young man of good family but bad character inherited a great deal of money which he then frittered away in bad company, drinking, singing and playing the tambourine. Now almost penniless, the young man decided to become a soldier. Having often associated with the northern Iranian Daylami infantrymen who formed the backbone of Buwayhid armies, he knew their language and their habits, so he used the last of his money to purchase the mules, horses, armour and weapons required of a soldier. He also changed his appearance, ate garlic to make his breath smell bad and pretended to be from Daylam. In the event the young man proved quite successful as a soldier and rose to be a confidant of the local commander.[84] There seem to be no reasons why almost identical but unrecorded careers were not just as common in the eleventh to thirteenth centuries, and probably later as well.

Much more attention was, however, focused on the more exotic and usually higher prestige soldiers recruited as slaves. This *ghulam* or *mamluk* system has continued to absorb the interest of modern historians. Consequently the real, and certainly the numerical, importance of such troops has probably been exaggerated, at least until the rise of a number of *mamluk*-based Mamluk Sultanates in the later medieval period, most notably in Egypt–Syria and Islamic India. The mostly highly esteemed and highly paid troops recruited as slaves were Turks and others mistakenly referred to as Turks who came from or via the Eurasian steppes.

Other sources of military slaves might occasionally have been numerous, but had a more localized impact. Africa, for example, remained a major source of slaves but it was really only in Egypt and to a lesser extent parts of North Africa that these men played a major military role. The main reason for this was that they came from sub-Saharan Africa which remained a militarily backward region with as yet little tradition of cavalry warfare.[85] The Turks, in contrast, came from a region with exceptionally advanced military traditions, technologies and skills, not only in cavalry warfare but in the horse-archery which was so highly prized in medieval Islamic armies. From the eleventh century onwards India was another significant source of prisoners-of-war who could be recruited as soldiers, but their military traditions were not highly regarded and their impact was almost entirely regional.[86]

Ghulam and *mamluk* slave-recruited soldiers had been a feature of wealthier Islamic armies for centuries, especially in the eastern provinces of what are now the ex-Soviet Central Asian republics, Afghanistan, Iran, the Fertile Crescent and Egypt. They would rise to greater prominence in the later twelfth and thirteenth centuries, eventually establishing their own Mamluk Sultanate in Egypt and Syria. Even in early eleventh century Fatimid Egypt, however, such troops were prominent, though few in number.

The origins and career of one such man, Anushtakin al-Dizbari, is known in some detail. A Turk, born in the Khuttal region north of the river Amu Darya (Oxus), he was captured by an enemy tribe as a young man and was taken to Kashgar to be sold. However Anushtakin escaped and made his way to Bukhara, heading further into the Islamic world rather than trying to return home. This fact alone sheds an interesting light on the attitudes of many of those who, supposedly as slaves, seemed eager to seek their fortunes in the wealthy and highly civilized Islamic world whose streets, to a poverty-stricken young tribesman from the steppes, may have been thought to be paved with gold. As it happened, Anushtakin was recaptured in Bukhara and was taken first to Baghdad and then to Cairo where he arrived in 1009.

Now probably aged over 20, he was purchased by a Fatimid army officer called Dizbar, from whom Anushtakin took his name of al-Dizbari. For three years the young man served in an administrative role before being given to the Fatimid Caliph. Only a slave who showed great promise would have been given to the ruler by an army officer. Two years' training in the palace followed, during which Anushtakin al-Dizbari showed such ability that he was freed and promoted to the rank of an army officer by the Caliph al-Hakim. In 1015 he was sent to Damascus on a tour of duty to learn about Syria, before returning to Cairo.

Anushtakin's next promotion saw him becoming governor of Ba'albak in Lebanon, where he started to buy his own *ghulam* slave-recruited soldiers. For a while he was governor of Qaysariya (Caesarea) before becoming governor of the entire province of Palestine in 1023. This involved Anushtakin in frequent military operations where he honed his skills as a commander.

Next he was sent to govern the strategically vital city of Aleppo. When this rose in rebellion it was retaken in the name of the Fatimid Caliph by part of Anushtakin al-Dizbari's own army under a *ghulam* named Toghan. Service in the upper echelons of the Fatimid Caliphate was notoriously uncertain and

Anushtakin al-Dizbari's career saw several ups and down before he died in 1042 at the age of around 55.[87] Al-Dizbari was, of course, a notably successful member of an élite and his career cannot be seen as typical, though it may have represented what many young soldiers hoped to achieve. Most did not; nor did most members of the slave-recruited class of *ghulams* or *mamluks*.

Bukhara, where Anushtakin's career as a *mamluk* could be said to have started, soldiers was one of the great commercial cities of Transoxania. This region lay at the centre of the so-called Silk Road network which had for centuries linked China, Iran and the Mediterranean world. During the immediate pre-Islamic period its wealthy merchant class seem to have had some sort of military command role, leading their own armed retinues and defending their fortified trading cities against Turkish nomad raiders. Some historians have even seen the possible origins of the *ghulam* or *mamluk* system of slave-recruited soldiers in these merchants' military retinues.

Another significant pool of military manpower in pre-Islamic Transoxania, eastern Iran and much of what became Afghanistan had been the prosperous *dihqan* lower aristocracy or 'landlord' class. Although their status declined after the Arab-Islamic conquest, these *dihqans* formed the political and military basis of several local Iranian-Islamic dynasties following the fragmentation of the 'Abbasid Caliphate. Military units described as *dihqans* were found in Ghaznawid armies, but thereafter disappeared as distinct formations. Under the Turkish and essentially tribal Qarakhanids, men refered to as *dihqans* still had important though non-military roles.[88] It seems likely that many Iranians from the *dihqan* class of society were numbered amongst the *muttawiya* volunteers who featured so prominently in eastern Islamic armies of the tenth and early eleventh centuries. They were, however, largely though not entirely replaced by professional troops and slave-recruited Turkish *ghulams* during the eleventh and twelfth centuries.[89] Many of the latter were maintained by an expanding system of state-allocated *'iqta* military fiefs rather than freehold properties as had been the case with the earlier *dihqans*. Despite this decline in influence and military role, the term *dihqan* was still applied to the lower level of Iranian landholders and village leaders in the eastern regions of the sprawling Turkish-ruled Seljuk Sultanate.[90]

During the early decades of the Seljuk Sultanate, particularly during its period of most dramatic expansion, the backbone of the Seljuk army consisted of free Turkish tribesmen who served out of loyalty to their leaders and in hope of booty or land. Even as early as 1091, however, the influential and highly educated Iranian *wazir* chief minister, Nizam al-Mulk, wrote a famous book on the art of government for the Great Seljuk Sultan Malik Shah I. How much actual influence this *Siyasat Nama* had at the time it was written is debatable, but it did become one of the most famous books on the subject in later years and contributed to the revival of several aspects of Iranian government under Turkish Seljuk rule.

Nizam al-Mulk had been educated within established Iranian-Islamic traditions of government, warfare and military recruitement which themselves owed a huge amount to pre-Islamic Iranian concepts of imperial government. Consequently his *Siyasat Nama* consisted of largely traditional ideas based upon the practice of previous Iranian dynasties. Where military matters were concerned, Nizam al-Mulk emphasized the need to have a reliable and well equipped but also splendid looking élite guard regiment in order to impress foreign ambassadors. This attitude was clearly shared by the Byzantine Empire. He also recommended that a standing army of professional infantry be recruited from a variety of different ethnic or cultural groups; 1,000 for the ruler's own retinue and 4,000 to be placed under the command of regional governors and army commanders.[91] Nizam al-Mulk considered that recruiting élite palace troops from a single ethnic group was dangerous, tending to make them 'disorderly', potentially disloyal or overmighty. Instead he suggested they consist of Daylamis from northern Iran and Khurasanis from eastern Iran, to create a mixed guard in battle and to foster rivalry between ethnic groups.[92] One group might also be played off against another in case such palace formations became a threat to the ruler.

To some extent this advice was followed by later Seljuk rulers who also continued the tradition of recruiting largely Turkish *mamluks* of slave origin. So did the smaller Turkish dynasties which emerged as the Great Seljuk Sultanate fragmented in the later twelfth and early thirteenth centuries, at least when they could afford to do so. The last such state, before the invading Mongols burst upon the eastern Islamic world, was that of the Khwarazmshahs. Their powerbase was initially in Transoxania and eastern Iran where their armies largely consisted of Turkish tribal troops and freely recruited professionals, though the Khwarazmshahs might also have had small numbers of *mamluks*.[93]

The rulers of the new Turkish states established in Anatolia in the later eleventh century faced different problems from those seen in Iran. This new territory was ex-Byzantine, with a still overwhelmingly Christian rather than Muslim population and with very different, indeed initially hostile, military traditions. The existing Christian population was itself mixed, largely consisting of Greeks and Armenians but also with other denominations or sects. This was particularly apparent in the east and south-east where there were many groups who were neither Christian nor Muslim, as well as substantial Islamic communities. The latter included the Kurds, Armenian converts, Arabs and Persians.

Of course the warlike *ghazis* who for many decades had been defending this Islamic frontier against Byzantine expansion included Turks as well as non-Turks well before the arrival of the Seljuks. Many took part in raids which eventually undermined Byzantine defences, but most such non-Turkish *ghazis* appear to have been absorbed within the Turkish community or to have been Turcified during the twelfth century.[94] The only major exceptions were the Kurds. Great numbers of more recent converts from Christianity to Islam were similarly Turcified, though this process sometimes took several generations.

It is clear that many Byzantine military leaders handed over their fortifications, including frontier castles, to the invading Seljuks during the collapse which followed the battle of Manzikert. In return many were given official positions, including military positions, or estates within the new Seljuk Sultanate of Rum. They were joined by refugees from what remained of the Byzantine Empire as it was torn apart by civil war,[95] though most would have converted to Islam before finding a place in Turkish military service. Some Armenian lords and castle-holding members of the military class in the old Armenian heartlands of eastern Anatolia similarly accepted Seljuk or other Turkish suzerainty, remaining in possession of their lands and fortifications into the 1090s. After that they mostly disappear, either dispossessed or Turcified.[96]

The Danishmandid *amirs* who established a separate Turkish state in north-eastern Turkey similarly absorbed much of the old Byzantine and Armenian military élites. As under Seljuk rule, a few families probably remained Christian though now serving an Islamic ruler for a generation or so, but then converted and disappeared as a distinct cultural or ethnic group.[97] One such aristocratic family were the Gabras who held lands and played a major role in defence of Byzantine Trebizond in the eleventh century. However, they clashed with the new Comnenid Imperial dynasty established by Alexius I and went over to the Turks. The Gabras family did not, however, lose its identity and in the late twelfth century a Muslim Gabras commanded a military following of 200 cavalry.[98]

Such distinct or separate groups were never a dominant or even particularly important part of the armies of early Turkish Anatolia. In the Seljuk Sultanate of Rum, for example, Turcoman horse-archers recruited on a tribal basis played the primary role in the initial conquest and continued to do so through the twelfth and into the early thirteenth century. Nor did they disappear even then.[99] Meanwhile some of the earliest hired troops, professionals or mercenaries were drawn from Turks who had settled as farmers or in the towns, plus local converts.[100]

The first half of the thirteenth century then saw significant changes in recruitment to the army of the Seljuk Sultanate of Rum. In fact the resulting army, consisting of Turcoman nomads, slave-recruited *ghulams* and freedmen, regional mercenaries known as *jira khvar*, 'Frankish' mercenaries of Latin, Western European or Crusader origin, and various allied contingents,[101] was now considered to consist of two separate 'armies'. That part known as the Ancient Army was, as its name suggests, essentially the same as the army which had served the Seljuks of Rum in the twelfth century. It consisted of the *havashi* or retainers of the main cavalry commanders, most such *havashis* probably being freely recruited Turcomans with a smaller number of slave-recruited *ghulams*.[102] Many slave recruits would have been Greek-speaking prisoners of war taken

in battle or captives seized during frontier raids. Their numbers apparently
increased in the second half of the twelfth century, large numbers coming from
the Kastamonou region of northern Anatolia. Such men appear to have been
particularly favoured as *jandars* or members of the guard units who were also
used to garrison fortified towns. They were converts to Islam and were known
for their loyalty and for the technical skills that they brought with them from
previous Byzantine service.[103]

The *igdish* or *ikdish* are a less clear military group within the Seljuk Sultanate of
Rum's 'Ancient Army'. They were not *ghulams* of slave origin but may have been,
or have included large numbers of, the descendants of such *ghulams*.[104] Another
possibility is that they were Muslims of mixed origins, and they clearly had high
standing in the towns of the Sultanate, serving as a local police or militia.[105]
Another new and apparently urban or militia force known as the *fityan* was first
mentioned in 1220, serving alongside the regular army and gradually increasing
in importance, particularly during the period of the Mongol invasion.[106]
Whether these *fityan* officially counted as part of the Ancient or the New Army
is unclear. It is similarly unclear whether the *jira khvar* local mercenaries counted
as Ancient or New. They clearly included large numbers of foot soldiers and were
drawn from all over the Sultanate of Rum.[107]

In general terms the 'New Army' of the thirteenth century Seljuk Sultanate
of Rum consisted of mercenaries, or at least properly paid, soldiers. They came
from a remarkable variety of sources, some as groups, some as individuals,
and included cavalry, infantry and perhaps technical specialists as well. The
result was an equally remarkably mixed army.[108] With perhaps few exceptions
amongst the ex-Byzantine and ex-Armenian aristocracies, the Seljuks of Rum
did not normally recruit local unconverted Christians into their army before
the period of Mongol conquest and occupation. This was for the simple reason
that their most likely foes would be fellow Greeks or Armenians. The only major
exception was in 1127 when Armenian troops were used against the rival Turkish
Danishmandids.[109]

The employment of Christian mercenaries from beyond the borders of the
state was a different matter. The Latin Catholic Church condemned European
mercenaries enlisted in Islamic armies if they were to fight against fellow-
Christians, though it was less of a problem if they were involved in wars between
Muslims. Consequently, Western mercenaries were very rare in places like Syria.
Anatolia was regarded in a different light, and European mercenaries became
common in the Seljuk Sultanate of Rum,[110] perhaps because ex-Byzantine Rum
or Anatolia was not seen as being so 'foreign' as the Arab lands. It is possible
that some of the Crusaders defeated by the Turks at Antalya in 1148 entered
Seljuk service, and in the early thirteenth century the Sultanate of Rum certainly
enlisted Crusader captives whom the Turks had liberated from Ayyubid hands

in northern Syria. Others soon arrived directly from Western Europe and during the first half of the thirteenth century such men included Gascons from France, Italians, Normands from south Italy, and probably many others.

Men also arrived from the declining Latin Crusader States and fought in Seljuk ranks against the invading Mongols. Furthermore, it seems likely that European mercenaries, including knightly cavalry and infantry crossbowmen, were numbered amongst the vassal or allied contingents from Cilician Armenia, Crusader Antioch, Byzantine Trebizond and Byzantine Nicaea.[111] Even before the Mongols appeared, the Seljuk army of Rum that fought against the Khwarazmshah in 1230 was a babel of tongues; including men described as Turks from Anatolia, Syria and the Caucasus mountains, plus unspecified *Ujis* 'frontiersmen', 'Franks', Georgians, Greeks, Russians and Arabs. An even greater mix fought the Ayyubids in 1233.[112]

A slow decline almost inevitably set in after the Mongol conquest and under Mongol suzerainty. From then on tribal Turcoman troops are rarely mentioned, expensive *ghulam* slaves became more difficult to recruit because of the Sultanate's economic decay, and *muqtas* holding *'iqta* military fiefs disappeared as the system gradually collapsed. In contrast *jira khvar* local mercenaries became more important, especially those from the Germiyan tribe, along with Western European mercenaries and those from other Islamic states. In this time of widespread confusion as a consequence of the Mongol assaults, such recruits included Khwarazmians from the defeated and dispersed army of the last Khwarazmshah, Kipchaq Turks from north of the Black Sea and the Balkans, Kurds, Arabs, probably Greeks and Europeans late of Nicaean Byzantine service, others from the remnant Crusader States in Syria and Palestine, and the Crusader States of Greece. However, the distinction between mercenaries and allies in some of these groups remained unclear.[113]

The army of the Sultanate of Rum disappeared with the last feeble Seljuk rulers in the last years of the thirteenth century and the first of the fourteenth. With them went the mercenaries. What remained were the autonomous Turcoman tribal forces and various largely urban militias, by then usually known as *ikhvan* or 'brotherhoods'. Many of the Turcoman forces were, however, numerous, well equipped and highly motivated, not only against the still largely pagan Mongols but against their Byzantine Christian neighbours. They and the *ikhvan* would form the highly effective if generally small armies of the small Turkish *beylik* states which now emerged from the breakup of the Seljuk Sultanate of Rum.[114]

South of Anatolia is the Fertile Crescent within which lies not only a large part of the history of mankind, but also the primary geographical, ecological and human factors which governed the history and outcome of the Crusades. It consists of three main regions. The eastern part consists of Iraq. In the north-centre of the crescent is the Jazira, which in Arabic means 'island' or what the ancient Greeks called Mesopotamia between the rivers Tigris and Euphrates. The western part of the crescent consists of greater Syria including what are now Syria west of the Euphrates, part of south-central Turkey, Lebanon, Jordan and Palestine-Israel.

North and east of the Fertile Crescent lay the mountains of Iran and Anatolia. West of it lies the Mediterranean Sea, while to the south and partially enclosed within the 'Crescent' are steppe, semi-desert and deep desert which are now divided between Iraq, Syria, Jordan and Saudi Arabia. The eastern tip of the Fertile Crescent touches the Persian or Arabian Gulf which leads to the Indian Ocean, India, South-east Asia and eventually to the Far East. The western tip of the Crescent almost touches the Red Sea which similarly leads to the Indian Ocean and to East Africa. This western tip also almost touches Egypt on the other side of the barren but relatively small Sinai desert.

In military terms the decline of the 'Abbasid Caliphate, based in Iraq in the eastern part of the Fertile Crescent, really began in the later ninth century, though political fragmentation had started earlier. Baghdad itself came under the control of the Shi'a Buwayhids in 945, reducing the 'Abbasid Caliphs to little more than puppets though their spiritual authority as heads of most, though not all, of Sunni Islam remained. The Umayyad rulers of far away al-Andalus also adopted the title of Caliph in the mid-tenth century while a third, this time Shi'a, Caliphate was proclaimed by the Fatimid in North Africa and then in Egypt.

The dignity of the 'Abbasid Caliph was to some extent restored when Baghdad and Iraq came under Seljuk rule in the mid-eleventh century, these new Turkish rulers being Sunni rather than Shi'a Muslims, but it was not until the Caliph al-Muqtafi threw off the domination of a secular 'protector' that the 'Abbasid Caliphate was re-established as a political and military rather than merely spiritual power. Under the Caliph al-Nasir, whose 45-year reign spanned the late twelfth- and early thirteenth century, the 'Abbasid Caliphate expanded to become one of the larger states in the Middle East, yet it remained little more than a local power whose major territorial and military preoccupations lay in western Iran and northern Iraq.

At the start of this revival, around 1133, most of the new 'Abbasid Caliphal troops seem to have been Turks or Turcomans,[115] as was another 'Abbasid army described in 1187. However, an 'Abbasid army campaigning in Iran in the mid-1190s largely consisted of Kurdish and bedouin Arab recruits.[116] In 1233–4 the 'Abbasid Caliph al-Mustansir enlisted many Khwarazmian soldiers who had fled into the area ahead of the Mongol invaders who had already destroyed the Khwarazmian state in eastern Iran.[117] Only a few decades earlier the Khwarazmian ruler or Shah had been the 'Abbasids' most serious opponent and when the Mongols approached Baghdad itself, the Caliph found himself unable to pay these new recruits. Most deserted and migrated westward again, to Syria, while Baghdad fell to the Mongols.[118]

During the medieval Islamic period, the Jazira region lying between Iraq and Syria was often regarded as including some of the mountainous terrain to the north, especially the broad and fertile valleys which contained several substantial cities and whose rivers formed part of the overall Tigris-Euphrates basin. The Taurus and other mountains which for centuries formed the real frontier with the Byzantine Empire and Armenian territory lay further north and west. Consequently the military as well as economic and cultural potential of the Jazira and its rulers included the Kurds of the hills as well as the Arabs of the valleys, plains and steppes, plus numerous other communities, some Muslim, some Christian and some neither.

Among those troops of essentially tribal origin, the Kurds were regarded as fine archers in the eleventh century, though it is not entirely clear whether their bowmen usually fought on foot or on horseback.[119] Certainly they did not normally use the harassment horse-archery tactics associated with the Turks. In the lower-lying regions of the Jazira, and in Syria to the west, most tenth- and eleventh century cavalry seem to have come from Arab bedouin tribes. This was clearly the case in what is now Jordan which, during the first half of the eleventh century, was dominated by powerful Arab tribes including the Banu Kilab. Their tribal army even included a force of heavily armoured cavalry riding caparisoned or armoured horses, a style of warfare that they probably learned in northern Syria rather than having inherited from the much earlier Umayyad or 'Abbasid centuries.[120]

In addition to local tribal forces and the small number of *ghulam* slave-recruited élite troops that local rulers could afford, the towns and cities of the eleventh century Jazira and Syria had their own often highly effective and warlike urban militias. They seem to have been particularly prominent in northern Syria which had been threatened by, or at least lay uncomfortably close to, the recently expanded frontiers of the Byzantine Empire. The Arab chronicler Ibn Abu Tayyi described urban society in the city of Aleppo as it was in the days of his grandfather, towards the end of the eleventh century and just as the First Crusade was preparing to march eastward: 'There was no person in Aleppo who did not have in his house a military costume and when war came, he went out at once, fully armed.' Much the same was true of the region around Shayzar, south of Aleppo, as related to Usama Ibn Munqidh by his father. To some extent this was a period of near anarchy, and so the role of urban militias in defence of their city walls should be no surprise.[121]

Statements that late eleventh century Syrian *ahdath* militias often consisted of local malcontents, may have reflected the attitudes of chroniclers rather than of the men actually involved.[122] The latter seem to have been surprisingly disciplined and were usually based in, or organized on the basis of, specific quarters of a town. As such the *ahdath* had a great deal in common with the slightly later urban militias of similarly urbanized and politically fragmented medieval Italy. Christian and Jewish citizens could also be summoned to defend cities like Aleppo during the eleventh century,[123] while the Jews of Jerusalem certainly helped defend that city against the First Crusade in 1099.

Aleppo had one such substantial Armenian community during the tenth and eleventh centuries which may have dominated the northern quarters of the city.[124] These would have been overwhelmingly Christian, but the Arevordik or Shamsiya al-Arman also provided soldiers to more than one Syrian ruler during the eleventh and twelfth centuries.[125] They were an Armenian-speaking community described as 'children the sun', perhaps as a form of religious shorthand to distinguish them from the Sabaean community of the Jazira region who were similarly simplistically and incorrectly described as 'moon worshippers'. Whether there was any real religious link between these Arevordik and the Paulicians of Anatolia who later reappeared as the Bogomils of the Balkans (see above) is unclear, though all were lumped together as wicked heretics by the Orthodox Christian church.[126] What is clear is that numerous religious minorities found refuge or flourished in these frontier regions of the early Islamic world, being tolerated by the Islamic authorities and occasionally assisting them against the much less tolerant Christian Byzantine Empire. Meanwhile there was even an isolated Daylami garrison from northern Iran in the Syrian town of Kafr Tab in 1012,[127] who seem to have been rather a long way from home.

The Seljuk Turkish conquest of most of Syria in the final third of the eleventh century was followed by a period of transition in the military systems of the region. While the steppes which bordered the desert remained a zone of competition between independent Arab bedouin tribes and Seljuk Turks who now dominated the cities, a few small Arab-ruled enclaves such as Shayzar retained their independence within the cultivated regions of Syria. These provided alternative sources of military employment. The remarkably detailed memoirs of Usama Ibn Munqidh shed a fascinating light on the ethnic composition of the army of Arab-ruled Shayzar and its immediate neighbours in the late eleventh and early twelfth century. Amongst governors, military leaders and senior officers over 18 per cent were Arabs, over 5 per cent Kurds, over 73 per cent freeborn Turks and over 2 per cent of slave origin. Amongst cavalry and junior officers over 44 per cent were Arabs, over 41 per cent Muslim Kurds, almost 3 per cent being Christian Kurds, over 5 per cent freeborn Turks and over 2 per cent of slave origin. Amongst infantry and unspecified soldiers 50 per cent were Arabs, over 21 per cent Kurds, none being Turks, over 14 per cent being of slave origin and over 14 per cent being Maghribis from North Africa.[128] Meanwhile much of the Syrian coast was also nominally under Fatimid rule or recognized Fatimid suzerainty, again providing alternative employment for non-Seljuk soldiers.

The Seljuks themselves employed some Arab or Kurdish troops and occasionally adopted autonomous leaders as their protegés. One such was a certain Ibn Khan who seized control of the large and important Syrian town of Ma'arat al-Nu'man in 1006. He did so with a force that reportedly consisted of 1,000 Turcomans, Kurds, Iranian Daylanis and Uj who may have been mixed peoples from the frontier regions.[129] Urban *ahdath* militias continued to play a role though they were not as important under the Seljuks as they had been earlier. Naturally they reflected the ethnic and religious character of the city in question, that of Ba'albek in eastern Lebanon probably being largely Shi'a during the twelfth century.[130] More surprisingly, Christian troops were similarly still present. The local Armenians are believed to have supported the Seljuk governor Yaghi Siyan in Antioch in the late eleventh century before turning against him on the arrival of the First Crusade.[131] Western European mercenaries were similarly recorded in late eleventh century northern Syria, probably having been in Byzantine service before the collapse of Imperial authority after the battle of Manzikert.[132]

Élite and expensive *ghulam* soldiers of slave-recruited origin soon reappeared in Damascus after the Seljuks took control, first being mentioned in the second half of the 1070s. These men were Turks and were commanded by a senior officer who was himself of slave origin, several rising to prominence later.[133] Distinguishing between free Turks from the Seljuk ruling class, tribal Turcomans and *ghulam-mamluks* of Turkish origin was not always easy. In fact the Turcoman tribes were now of considerable military and political importance. The Diyarbakr region of what is now south-eastern Turkey became a major zone of Turcoman settlement and nomadic way of life in the late eleventh and early twelfth centuries, the previous substantially Arab rural population almost disappearing or being Turcified or 'Kurdified'.

The main Turcoman tribe in Syria itself at the time the First Crusade arrived was the Nawakiya who had been invited in by the local Mirdasid Arab rulers and the independent Arab ruler of Tyre in 1063. The Nawakiya remained independent of the Seljuk Sultan for a while, but within a decade or so the greater part of Syria was under real or nominal Seljuk authority, including both the Arabs and the Turkish Nawakiya.[134]

A number of increasingly independent Turkish-ruled states, usually with the status of *amirates*, emerged within very few years of the Seljuk conquest of Syria and the Jazira. Their governors or rulers began recruiting armies on their own behalf with little reference to the Great Seljuk Sultan in Iran and this resulted in some interesting relationships developing between such states. One was the link between the Burids of Damascus and the Artuqids of the Diyarbakr region. The latter consisted of an almost enclosed, fertile plain amid the headwaters of the river Tigris. One of its main cities was Mayyafariqin, just north-east of the city of Amida which, somewhat confusingly, was itself coming to be known as the city of Diyarbakr as it still is. Mayyafariqin, meanwhile, emerged as a major centre of Turcoman military recruitment for the now Turkish-ruled *amirate* of Damascus far to the south.

Those enlisted as regulars tended to be known as Turks while temporary volunteers who often arrived in substantial groups were called Turcomans.[135] The former formed over three-quarters of the Damascene standing army and usually lived inside the city. The volunteers lived in surrounding districts,[136] probably either in villages or their own tented, almost nomad-like encampments. The resulting army of Damascus, which was to play such a significant role against the Crusaders during the first half of the twelfth century, consisted of six main elements. These were distinguished by the nature of their service as well as their origins.[137] They were the rulers, *askar*, small corps of full-time regular soldiers and the *ahdath* urban militia of Damascus, most of whom seem to have been drawn from the ranks of the poor.[138] Then there were the Turcoman volunteers, some Kurdish volunteers, the Arab bedouin who were more like regional allies than volunteers, and those volunteers from assorted backgrounds who joined up for specifically religious reasons as distinct from the tribal volunteers who might better be described as part-time warriors in search of payment, booty and adventure.

The largest numbers of tribal volunteers were the Turcomans. Kurdish troops had been mentioned in Damascus as early as 1076 and subsequently rose in importance by the mid-1140s. Yet their numbers remained relatively small and only one Kurdish *amir* or senior officer was mentioned.[139] Arabs were rarely mentioned in the regular army of Burid Damascus, though they did feature amongst volunteers fighting the Crusader invaders. Otherwise the Arab role was largely in logistical support.[140]

In some ways the local *mutatawiy'a* volunteers in the Burid army were more like a military reserve than the religiously motivated *jihadi* volunteers, and could be summoned when needed. Most of those recorded in the early twelfth century appear to have been refugees from territory lost to Crusader occupation, large numbers of whom had settled in and around Damascus. Examples included the garrisons of supposedly Fatimid Sidon and Tyre which moved to Damascus when these cities surrendered to the Crusaders. Many such groups were apparently under full government control and their military activities were authorized by the Burid ruler.[141]

Armenian soldiers were similarly present in central Syria, though in smaller numbers than in the north or in Egypt. For example Armenian *arevordik* so-called sun-worshippers served as light cavalry in Damascus in 1138.[142]

Another indication of how Muslim Armenians still played a significant role in mid-twelfth century Syria was the career of Altuntash, a Turkified Armenian convert to Islam and adventurer who established a short-lived autonomous fiefdom in the Hawran region of what is now southern Syria with Salkhad and

Bosra as his main centres. These lay between Turkish-ruled Damascus and the Crusader Kingdom of Jerusalem. Altuntash then rebelled against Damascus and tried to become a vassal of Jerusalem around 1147 but soon fell from power and disappeared.[143]

The Jazira region was not merely a source of troops for the armies of Syria. It was a thriving area whose autonomous rulers had considerable military strength and would eventually provide the foundations from which the initial Islamic counter-Crusades were launched during the twelfth century. One of the first rulers of this region to attempt to turn back the Crusader onslaught was Il-Ghazi I. In the early twelfth century he largely relied on the nomadic Turcoman tribes for troops, especially those living around his main city of Mardin, and was reportedly followed by no less than 10,000 Turcoman horsemen in 1105–6.[144] Such soldiers were fierce but also unruly, motivated by plunder and needed to be paid properly. In fact it is a tribute to Il-Ghazi's capacity as a leader than he was able to discipline and control such troops to the extent that he did.[145]

Another important military community in the Jazira region were the Armenians but they largely associated themselves with the invading Crusaders during the early twelfth century. Consequently, when Imad al-Din Zangi, the first really successful leader of the Islamic *jihad* or counter-crusade, retook Edessa (Urfa) in 1144 he expelled a large part of the pro-Crusader Armenian inhabitants and replaced them with Jews who were regarded as more sympathetic to Islam.[146] Elsewhere Armenians continued to serve in various Islamic armies. Some of these men were at least nominal converts to Islam but others remained Christian and managed to retain the trust of Islamic rulers. For example, after Jerusalem had been liberated by Saladin in 1187 an Armenian community either remained or was re-established within the city. During the thirteenth century it lived next to the Citadel which was at that time the only intact fortified structure in Jerusalem.[147]

Imad al-Din Zangi's son, Nur al-Din, continued his father's work and inflicted further significant defeats upon the Crusader States, laying the foundations for Saladin's even more dramatic successes. Nur al-Din had inherited his father's army and went on to improve and enlarge it. Turks and Turcomans remained the most numerous soldiers, the *tawashiya* being an élite force of free cavalry, each apparently assisted by a page. Auxiliary cavalry were drawn from the Arab bedouin tribes and there were increasing numbers of *ghazi* (pl. *ghuzat*) religiously motivated volunteers.[148] A perhaps new feature of Nur al-Din's army was the prominent role of Kurds, most of whom came from the Shahrazuriya tribe.[149] Nevertheless these Kurds remained secondary, both in importance and probably numerically, to the Turks. Saladin himself came from one of these Kurdish military families in Nur al-Din's service, yet it was certainly not one of the most powerful families in the state.[150]

Before looking at military recruitment in Egypt, which would eventually become the most important platform for the *jihad* or counter-crusade in the late twelfth and thirteenth centuries, it is worth looking at three areas or communities which sometimes tend to be overlooked, at least in military terms. The first was the tiny 'state' established by the so-called Assassins in the coastal mountains of north-western Syria around 1100. The name *Assassin* comes from the Arabic *hashishin* which reflected the myth that the volunteers who fought and gave their lives for the Nizari Isma'ili cause were doped up with *hashish*, cannabis.

This was a religiously based community which developed as a result of a split in the Isma'ili sect of Shi'a Islam on the death of the Fatimid Caliph al-Mustansir in 1094. His brother Nizar was pushed aside in a palace coup, but those who remained loyal to the belief that Nizar should have been Fatimid Caliph became known as Nizaris or Nizari Isma'ilis. While one group established a statelet in the mountains of northern Iran, another won control of several castles in the Syrian mountains. Since this was a community which sought converts in all sections of society, its *fidayin* or military arm probably included men of many different ethnic and cultural origins. Certainly their training emphasized an ability to blend into groups which surrounded and protected their intended targets. Otherwise almost nothing is known about the 'Assassin' fighting men who have been described as commandos, guerrillas or as terrorists depending upon who was describing them and when they were being described.

Sometimes regarded as enemies by all their neighbours, the Nizari Isma'ilis of the coastal mountains finally lost their independence with the fall of their last castle of Kahf to the Mamluk Sultanate in 1273. However, the Nizaris still held a few other castles under Mamluk suzerainty, being tolerated in Syria while the Nizaris of Iran were practically exterminated by the Mongols. It also seems possible that the Mamluks employed Nizari *fidayin* as assassins against their own enemies, including an attempt upon the life of the Crusading Prince Edward of England.[151] Presumably the Nizari leadership agreed to this in return for being left in peace in their remaining mountain strongholds.

Another mountain community with a ferocious military reputation were the Maronite Christians of Mount Lebanon. Their role as auxiliaries and allies of the Crusader States has already been discussed (see *Crusader Warfare* vol. 1) but their prowess continued after the fall of the final Crusader enclaves in the late thirteenth century. Early the following century Hayton of Armenia pointed out that there were still plenty of warlike Christian archers in the mountains near Tripoli in northern Lebanon, and that these men could be useful allies of any future Crusading expeditions to the Holy Land.[152]

The Arabian Peninsula largely fell out of the spotlight of Middle Eastern history after the 'Abbasid Caliphate lost control of the interior and much else besides in the tenth century. This was largely as a result of the rise of the Qarmatians, a radical Shi'a movement whose roots were in the revolutionary but less violent

Isma'ili branch of Shi'a Islam. The uprising started amongst the bedouin tribes of north-eastern Arabia in an area known as Bahrayn (the 'two seas') which included coastal regions on each side of the Qatar peninsula as well as the island now called Bahrayn. A formidable and initially almost communistic republic emerged which soon dominated most of Arabia including Oman while raiding deep inside Iraq, Syria and into Egypt.

The strongly egalitarian aspect of Qarmatian society faded, and even their raiding reduced in the eleventh century though the state remained warlike and strongly fortified until a joint Seljuk Turkish and 'Abbasid Caliphal expeditionary force helped a local Arab chieftain to overthrow the Qarmatians in 1078. Throughout this period and the subsequent centuries the bedouin Arab tribes, whether supporters or opponents of the Qarmatians, remained strong, warlike and in several cases rich and well equipped. Yet they now tended to avoid becoming too closely involved in the rivalries of the settled regions to their north and east. This included conflicts between the Crusader States and their Islamic neighbours. On a number of occasions Arab bedouin tribal forces defeated small or isolated Crusader units, but in general they avoided confrontation and seemed to prefer to be left alone to continue their traditional nomadic or semi-nomadic way of life.[153]

Egypt was conquered by the Fatimid Caliphate, operating from its original base in what is now Tunisia, in 969, overthrowing the previous Ikhshidid governing dynasty which had been loyal to the 'Abbasid Caliphs in Baghdad. The Fatimid army which seized Egypt was largely Berber, having been recruited amongst North African tribes which had supported the Fatimid Caliphate since its establishment 60 years earlier. For many decades after moving to their new capital of al-Qahira (Cairo) in Egypt, the Fatimid Caliphs continued to rely upon Berber troops.

Nevertheless, the limited success that these forces achieved in Syria, especially when they came up against numerically smaller forces of Turkish *ghulams*, convinced the Fatimids that they needed to modernize their army. Though their state was rich, there were almost unsurmountable problems in purchasing the largely Turkish slaves of Central Asian origin who filled the ranks of the *ghulam*, *mamluk* forces of 'Abbasid and other eastern Islamic armies. Not suprisingly, the 'Abbasids and their vassals were not keen on allowing such élite recruits to cross their territories and be enlisted by their enemies. The only other major source of slaves was sub-Saharan Africa, the Bilad al-Sudan or 'Land of the Blacks'. Consequently black African soldiers became the numerically dominant professional corps, though not the most prestigious élite, within the eleventh century Fatimid army, the overwhelming majority said to be sword-armed infantry. This was, of course, a time when cavalry had already become the dominant corps in virtually all other Islamic armies.

Such an employment of black African soldiers, some free volunteers or mercenaries and others of slave origin, had a long history in Egypt which went back long before the seventh century Islamic conquest. What changed under the Fatimids was the numbers involved which saw another significant rise in the mid-eleventh century. Some came down the Nile via Nubia, others across the Sahara desert via the oasis of Zawila in the Fezzan region of what is now southern Libya. Amongst the African mercenaries were a group known as the Masmuda who reportedly fought on foot with spears rather than swords and came from that ill-defined region 'south of the Nubians' known simply as 'the land of the Masmuda'.[154] This may actually have been a loose usage of the name Masmuda who were otherwise identified as a tribal group south of Morocco.

The Fatimids probably re-recruited some of the Turks, including *ghulams* of slave-origin, who had served the previous Ikhshidid governors of Egypt. Yet their numbers would have been small. Other Turkish slaves may have been purchased from Italian merchants who had bought these men in the Black Sea region. The fact that the sons of such élite soldiers, born in Egypt during the eleventh century, were themselves still seemingly listed as 'Turks' could be a sign of just how desperate the Fatimids were to recruit Turkish cavalry. In practically every other part of the early medieval Islamic world, including Egypt under the Fatimids' successors, the free-born sons of Turkish *ghulams* or *mamluks* were not allowed the same high military status as that accorded to their fathers.

Daylamis from northern Iran were clearly welcomed in the Fatimid army, not least because they were Shi'a rather than Sunni Muslims. Numerous such soldiers, largely serving on foot with their characteristic *zhupin* javelins and axes, were recorded in many Middle Eastern Islamic armies during the eleventh century. As higher status infantry than the black Africans, these Daylamis are also likely to have been found amongst the Fatimid army's *nafatin* 'Greek Fire throwers'. Because they had formed a military and political alliance with the Turkish *ghulams*, much as Daylami troops did in Iran and Iraq, these Daylamis were disbanded, along with the Turks, by Badr al-Jamali.[155]

Another distinctive feature of Fatimid armies, even in the tenth century, was the prominent role of Christians or men of Christian origin. In addition to Nubians from what is now Sudan (see vol. 1), Fatimids employed men described as *rumis* which suggests that they probably came from or via the Byzantine Empire, either as prisoners of war or slaves, or in a few cases perhaps as volunteers. However, these *rumis* seem to have disappeared from the ranks by the late eleventh century.[156] Then there were the even more obscure *saqaliba* whose name meant Slavs. They are believed to have been high status slaves of central, westerm or perhaps northern European origin who arrived via the Iberian Peninsula or northern Syria. Although always small in number, the *saqaliba* played a significant role in Fatimid state and military administration as well as in court.[157]

The Fatimid army which faced the First Crusade and the first campaigns by the newly established Latin Kingdom of Jerusalem was that recruited by Badr al-Jamali and maintained by his son al-Afdal. Changes in its patterns of recruitment usually reflected the international political situation outside the Fatimid state. Nevertheless, efforts to maintain a tradition of mixed recruitment continued, if with only limited success.[158] The army now consisted of three main elements; the *maghariba* 'westerners' which in the Islamic context meant men from North Africa, the *sudani* 'blacks' and the *mashariqa* 'easterners'. Each group was subdivided, often by a presumed ethnicity which included locally born descendants of recruits from the area in question. On the other hand a note of caution should be introduced because it is clear that regiments originally recruited on such an ethnic basis could change in composition over the years while retaining their original name or designation.[159]

By the twelfth century the *maghariba* had much reduced in number, the Fatimids having lost control of the regions beyond Barqa (Cyrenaica) in what is now eastern Libya. Nevertheless they still included regulars and irregulars from Barqa itself and from further west, recruited amongst the Berber tribes and sometimes the Arab tribes who had recently settled in these areas. Meanwhile the term Masri or Egyptian usually meant Fatimid forces actually based in Egypt. Whether there were any indigenous Coptic Egyptian Christians in the *ahdath* militias of Egyptian towns such as Tinnis during the Fatimid period is unclear, though the *ahdath* itself remained an active if limited local organization.[160]

The *sudani* were mostly of black African slave origin but also included freeborn mercenaries or volunteers from Nubia, Ethiopia and the Arabized nomadic tribes of southern Egypt and northern Sudan who are sometimes referred to as 'black bedouin'. The loyalty of the Fatimids' black African soldiers to the person of the Caliph became proverbial, perhaps because of a deep-seated tradition of divine kingship amongst many of the pagan peoples of sub-Saharan Africa (see below). It was probably for this reason, and because they were so rarely involved in palace coups which wracked the Fatimid Caliphate during the eleventh century, that the new Armenian *wazir* and virtual military dictator Badr al-Jamali did not disband them. In fact, while his own power was based firmly upon Armenian regiments, Badr al-Jamali also had his own black guard. With the death of Badr's son, the *wazir* al-Afdal, the Jamalid period ended, whereupon black African troops once again became the backbone of the Fatimid army.[161]

The most numerous and eventually the politically most potent Christian force in the armies of the Fatimid Caliphate were the Armenians. Most were archers and they had been increasing in Egyptian armies for several centuries, rising to particular prominence under the *wazir* Badr al-Jamali and his son al-Afdal. Even then, however, Armenian troops remained fewer in number than black Africans. It might seem strange that the Fatimid army, as one of the Crusaders' most important foes, should have relied to such an extent upon Christian Armenian soldiers. One reason was that the Armenians had a high military reputation and had served in Egyptian armies for generations though in small numbers. Meanwhile relations between Armenia and Egypt had been generally amicable since the early years of Islamic history. Both also had, for differing and changing reasons, tense relations with the other major power centres of the Middle East; namely the Byzantine Empire and the 'Abbasid Caliphate in Iraq. Furthermore there were plenty of such recruits available in the later eleventh century.

The result was a substantial migration, not just by Armenian soldiers but by entire families into Fatimid territory where there was no difficulty in their remaining Christian at a time when Coptic Christians may still have formed an overall majority in Egypt. Under the Jamalid *wazirs*, Armenians probably formed half of the regular military establishment in the capital, Cairo, and there was clearly also a large force of them in the Fatimid Caliphate's forward base of Ascalon facing the newly established Crusader Kingdom of Jerusalem in southern Palestine in 1110. Around this time there was a further substantial migration to Egypt from amongst the military class of the Kingdom of Lesser Armenia in Cilicia, largely as a result of Crusader attempts to take control of the Cilician kingdom.[162]

Four hundred Armenian troops were sent on a campaign to Yemen in the year that al-Afdal was assassinated, forming over one-third of this little-known expedition.[163] Thereafter Armenian troops declined in importance under the *wazirs* who succeeded al-Afdal, though they had a brief revival under the *wazir* Bahram al-Armani around 1134. By that time most Armenian soldiers in Egypt seem to have been based in the Nile Delta rather than Cairo.[164] Bahram himself was also unusual because he was the only one of the Fatimids' seven or perhaps eight Armenian *wazirs* to be a Christian rather than a convert to Islam.[165] The Armenian troops themselves were disbanded and in many cases slaughtered by Saladin after his take-over of the Egyptian government, but more because of their loyalty to the preceding Fatimids than any supposed sympathy with the Latin Crusader States.

The Fatimids' *mashariqa* now included Turks, Syrian Arabs, Arabs from the Arabian Peninsula and elsewhere, as well as the Armenians. Because the Turkish troops in the Fatimid army largely opposed Badr al-Jamali's seizure of the *wazirate*, he disbanded many of them. Those that remained seem to have served as individuals or as officers rather than forming distinct and politically unreliable units. His son and successor al-Afdal further reduced the numbers and influence of both the Turks and the remaining Berbers.[166] On the other hand it has been suggested that the Turkish, nominally Seljuk, garrison of Jerusalem enlisted under the Fatimids after the latter recaptured the city in 1098. Some may still have been in the now Fatimid garrison which defended the Holy City against the

Crusaders a year later. Others appear to have gone to Cairo or to have enlisted in Fatimid service as individual mercenaries.

Later Fatimid *wazirs* made largely unsuccessful attempts to recruit Turks to face the Crusaders during the twelfth century,[167] their numbers increasing slightly during the second quarter of the twelfth century, but they were never very numerous.[168] Furthermore, the Turkish and Syrian, perhaps largely Arabic-speaking, mercenaries whom the Fatimids recruited for single campaigns against the Crusader States were often indistinguishable from allied troops supplied by the Turkish *amirate* of Damascus.[169]

During the first century of Fatimid rule in Egypt, the new Shi'a government had copied their Sunni 'Abbasid rivals in creating a system of *hujra* barrack-schools to train and house military slave recruits. Naturally they claimed that such an organization was inspired by an earlier Caliph and not by the hated 'Abbasids. This *hujra* system seems to have slipped into disuse during the eleventh century because the Fatimids were unable to purchase sufficient recruits, but was subsequently revived by the *wazir* al-Afdal in the face of the Crusader threat.[170] Its recruits or *hujariya* were said to be the sons of soldiers and were not distinguished by ethnicity, perhaps in an attempt to avoid the factionalism which had previously caused so many problems.[171] Some are nevertheless known to have been of Armenian origin.[172]

Another military group which may have been of slave-recruited origin were the *farajiya, farahiya* or *faranjiya*. Occasionally mentioned from the time of the Caliph al-Hakim at the start of the eleventh century until the first years of Saladin's reign, they apparently consisted of infantry but were never numerous enough to become politically significant. Furthermore it remains possible that their name was simply a transcribing error for 'Frankish' *mamluks* or mercenaries.[173]

The Fatimid Caliphate's once numerous and largely tribal Berber cavalry, many of whom were recruited from the Kitama tribes, were disbanded in 1073, a year before the Armenian Badr al-Jamali came to power as *wazir*. Thereafter they seem to have been even less numerous than the Turks. The only real Berber tribal auxiliaries recorded in the early twelfth century were from the Lawata whose tribal territory stretched across the Western Desert from the edges of the Nile Delta to eastern Libya.[174] Other North African tribal cavalry from Barqa, the eastern province of Libya, were known as *barqiya* and probably included both Berbers and some Arabs. Their numbers increased under the mid-twelfth century *wazirs* Tal'ai and Dirgham.[175] Some such groups or communities of Berbers established small garrison-based dynasties along the coast between the Nile Delta and Tunisia.

In social, cultural and economic terms the Fatimid period could be described as a golden age for the Arab bedouin tribes of Egypt, despite the fact that they had initially resisted Fatimid conquest. Troops who could be clearly identified as

Arab then played a prominent role during the earlier part of Fatimid history in Egypt, though they were never particularly numerous and did not always support the current Caliph. The tendency of the Banu Hilal and Banu Sulaym tribes to volatile independent action, and their considerable military effectiveness, lay behind the Fatimid Caliph's decision to urge them to migrate westward in the 1050s and to seize land from the Caliph's disloyal vassals in Tunisia.[176]

Meanwhile a related Arab tribe, the Banu Qurra, remained in the north-western Nile Delta where their role was to provide auxiliary troops and act as a local garrison along the desert fringe. Other tribes lived elsewhere in the Fatimid Caliphate, on or near the fringes of the cultivated zone in Egypt proper, in the Sinai Peninsula and in southern Palestine. Others may have come from Arabia, particularly from the Hijaz on the western side of the peninsula. They provided substantial numbers of auxiliary cavalry,[177] and may also have guarded the main routes across the desert. But even under the Arab *wazirs* of the final decades of the Fatimid Caliphate they had little power or influence.[178]

In the far south of Egypt the Banu Kanz were a partially Arab, Arabized or Arabic-speaking tribal people who played a significant role in the history of Nubia (see vol. 1). Their own territory consisted of hills and desert mountains between the Red Sea and the river Nile, the southern part of which they had shared with the existing non-Arab Baja and Hadariba tribes since the early Islamic period. At various times the Banu Kanz also dominated neighbouring parts of the Nile Valley in southern Egypt, even occasionally the city of Aswan. It is similarly possible that Masmuda black African infantry mercenaries from the Sudan south of Nubia saw something of a revival in the twelfth century Fatimid armies.[179]

As the last *wazir* of the Fatimid Caliphate, Saladin commanded the existing Fatimid armies but also added troops who had been brought to Egypt by his uncle and himself. The result was, for a while, a mixed force, but within a short time of the death of the last Fatimid Caliph and the abolition of the Shi'a Caliphate, a large part of the old Fatimid army was disbanded. In some cases it was brutally destroyed, being regarded as loyal to the old regime rather than the new Sunni authority of Saladin and his suzerain in Syria, Nur al-Din. Nevertheless the two military traditions, essentially Fatimid and Seljuk, remained fundamental to the character of the new army which Saladin now built in Egypt. They would eventually fuse into something new, the military structure inherited by Saladin's Ayyubid successors and by the Mamluk Sultanate which took over from them in 1250.

Saladin himself was of Kurdish family origins, though entirely Arabized in culture and strongly influenced by the Turkish post-Seljuk court in which he had grown up and where both his father and uncles had served as military officers. The tradition of a senior commander or ruler relying on troops recruited from the same ethnic or cultural group as himself was deep rooted in medieval Islamic society. So it is not surprising to find that Kurds played a prominent part in Saladin's army and entourage, as they would continue to do under most of his successors. Nevertheless, there is considerable disagreement about quite how numerous and how important these Kurds were.[180] In general it seems that their significance had in the past been greatly exaggerated, even for the reign of Saladin himself.[181] Turks seem to have been more important from the start, and were almost always in a position to discriminate against their Kurdish rivals.[182] Meanwhile the true élite in all Ayyubid armies were *mamluks* recruited as slaves and usually of Central Asian Turkish origin.

Despite such reservations, there is no denying the Kurdish role. They were recruited in three different ways, as individuals, as tribal groups or units and, after the Mongol invasions of the Middle East, as larger regional groups such as the Qaymariya and Shahrazuriya. The latter period also saw social and tribal breakdowns with families on the move rather than merely Kurdish menfolk seeking military employment.

In the early days, Saladin's own army included Kurdish tribal units known by the name of the tribes from which they were drawn. The Hakkariya were the largest and most important, followed by the Humaydiya, Zarzariya and Mihraniya. They tended to be grouped together in a battle array and demonstrated great ethnic solidarity.[183] Under Saladin's successors, however, these large tribal battalions were usually broken up into smaller units and the importance of Kurdish soldiers steadily declined. This was often because they were seen as potentially disloyal, which seems surprising given the long tradition of ethnic solidarity in medieval Islamic armies.[184]

In addition to recruiting Turcoman, Kurdish and other soldiers directly into his army, Saladin was shown to be particularly keen on, and particularly adept at, winning over the troops of various defeated Islamic foes.[185] Some of the latter would have included *mamluks* comparable with those whom Saladin and his successors purchased and trained direct from the well-established slave trading network.

One of the last of the Ayyubid Sultans of Egypt was al-Salih. He greatly expanded his predecessors' purchase of *mamluks* and was able to do so because the Mongols' campaigns which were rampaging across the Eurasian steppes had uprooted so many peoples. Amongst the latter were the Kipchaq Turks who had previously dominated the steppes regions north of the Black and Caspian Seas. As a result true Turkish slaves, who had previously been relatively rare and expensive, suddenly came on to the market in droves.[186] Their number increased still further after the Mongol conquest of the Bulgar Khanate on the upper reaches of the Volga River in the east of what is now European Russia.

It was during this period that a new slave-trading route opened up from the Crimea, through what remained of the Byzantine Empire to Egypt, while the old route from Transoxania through Iran and Iraq effectively dried up.[187] The

Genoese soon dominated the maritime side of this trade while, by a poetic justice, it would be the army of uprooted and enslaved largely Kipchaq Turks who, as *mamluks* in the Egyptian army, would finally stop the Mongol flood in Syria.

With a state or array of associated states as widespread and as locally autonomous as the Ayyubid Sultanate it was inevitable that clear differences would develop between its regional and autonomous armies. The biggest and always most important was that of the Ayyubid Sultan of Egypt who was regarded as the senior member of the ruling family. Here most existing ex-Fatimid troops had been disbanded after a failed coup against Saladin in 1174, but not all. African military slaves, who had almost entirely served as infantry, similarly disappeared early in Saladin's reign.[188]

In the deep south of Egypt the Arab or Arabized Banu Kanz continued to play a major local role,[189] and are likely to have provided auxiliary troops to the main Egyptian army when required. Elsewhere the bedouin tribes of Egypt continued to prosper and although they lost their military prestige they were still called upon for auxiliaries.[190] Before being largely dispersed under Mamluk rule, the main areas inhabited by Arab bedouin in Egypt were the Sharqiya and Buhayra provinces, the Eastern Desert, the Jifar area or Sinai Peninsula, the Western Oases, along the northern part of the Western Desert and the coast as far as Barqa in Libya.[191] Despite their diminished military status, it remained important for the Sultan in Cairo to have at least the bedouin tribes' tacit support because their nuisance potential remained considerable.[192]

Another source of soldiers which has received less attention than might have been expected was Western European so-called renegades. It seems clear that many of the aristocracy of the Crusader States who lost their lands after Saladin's great victory at the battle of Hattin went on to find service in Islamic and subsequently also Mamluk ranks. Indeed in 1223 the Patriarch of Alexandria reported that 10,000 renegades were in Islamic service.[193] This was surely an exaggeration, though many sailors are known to have changed sides during the period of the Crusades, sometimes perhaps more than once. Occasionally individual 'renegades' are mentioned in the chronicles. For example De Joinville wrote about a French soldier who had been captured during a previous Crusade against Egypt, had converted to Islam and became a rich man though whether he still served as a soldier in the mid-thirteenth century is less clear.[194]

The armies of the autonomous Ayyubid rulers in Syria and the Jazira were relatively small and relied to a greater extent upon local recruits than did the Sultan of Egypt. In northern Syria, for example, Kurdish troops remained prominent and in the years following Saladin's death included *amirs* or senior officers who had fought for the great Sultan. Their descendants were still in place years later, especially men from the Hakkariya tribe who seem to have been particularly important in Aleppo.[195] Next in importance were men from the

Qaymariya tribe who were prominent in resisting the rising power of Turkish soldiers. Then came the Shahrazuriya from the area of that name between Irbil and Hamadan in western Iran. Most were refugees, fleeing ahead of the Mongol advance. Yet even here in northern Syria, Kurdish *amir* officers remained fewer than Turkish *amirs*.[196] After the Mamluk takeover in Egypt in 1250, the Kurdish soldiers tended to seek employment amongst the remaining Ayyubid sultans in Syria and the Jazira, particularly large numbers of Qaymariya serving al-Nasir Yusuf II of Aleppo and Damascus.[197]

Turks of free rather than *mamluk* status formed just over half the officers or *amir* rank in thirteenth-century Ayyubid armies in northern Syria, mostly drawn from the Turcoman tribes of the northern frontier regions and particularly from the Yaruqiya tribe. Such men had formed a dominant aristocracy in the smaller towns and castles since the mid-twelfth century, including Shayzar after the fall of the previous Banu Munqidh ruling family of Arab origin. Some of these Turkish aristocratic families were even powerful enough to undertake their own trading negotiations with the Venetians.[198]

Other officers and soldiers in Aleppo seem to have been independent Turkish adventurers or mercenaries with no apparent tribal connections, perhaps having arrived from the Seljuk Sultanate of Rum in Anatolia. While these free Turks were militarily important, the élite corps of Ayyubid Syrian armies still consisted of largely Turkish *mamluks*. Although fewer than in Egypt, they were nevertheless purchased, trained and freed in considerable numbers during the first half of the thirteenth century.[199] They tended to be exceptionally loyal, and as a result the Mamluk coup against the senior Ayyubid Sultan in Egypt caused them a crisis of conscience. Some deserted to serve the new Mamluk Sultan of Egypt but most apparently remained loyal to the Syrian Ayyubids.[200]

Another noticeable difference between Syrian and Egyptian Ayyubid armies was in their auxiliaries. In northern Syria and Jazira these were largely drawn from Turcoman tribes, especially the Yaruqiya (Yürük) in Aleppo where they also became a regular force. In Damascus most auxiliaries were again from Arab bedouin tribes and never achieved the status of semi-regular troops.[201] Muslim refugees from the Crusader States still featured in a number of Ayyubid forces, the commander of the citadel of Damietta in 1219 originally coming from Sidon in what is now southern Lebanon.[202] More remarkable, perhaps, were the so-called 'renegades' including prisoners-of-war who had changed their religion and taken service under the Ayyubids. In 1229, for example, the officer in command of Sultan al-Nasir II's troops stationed in the citadel of Damascus was reportedly a Spanish ex-Templar brother.[203]

The recruiting of slaves to be trained as high status professional soldiers was a phenomenon which went back to pre-Islamic times in some parts of what became the medieval Islamic world. The system was further developed and became an integral part of the military traditions of the Middle East during the first century or so of the 'Abbasid Caliphate. In fact some of the military treatises that deal with this subject, and which date from the later thirteenth to early sixteenth century Mamluk Sultanate were taken virtually word for word from classical 'Abbasid texts. One such was 'Lesson Eight' of the early Mamluk *Nihayat al-Su'l*, one of the best-known Mamluk works on *furusiya* or the military arts (see below) which deals with army recruitment and organization but is actually describing the 'Abbasid Diwan al-Jaysh or Ministry of War.[204]

The recruitment of suitable military slaves was so important for the Mamluk Sultanate that it had a major impact upon the state's foreign relations. For example, who controlled the Anatolian Black Sea ports of Sinop and Samsun, and the port of Kaffa on the northern side of the Black Sea, was a matter of serious concern. These received many of the slave recruits captured by the now Islamic Mongol Golden Horde to the north and exported via Italian colonial outposts in the Crimea.[205] The Mamluk Sultanate, itself to some extent dominated by men of Kipchaq Turkish origin from the western steppes, clearly preferred recruits from this area. Nor did the latter necessarily arrive unwillingly. Indeed these perhaps sometimes nominal slaves were soon followed by substantial numbers of Kipchaq women, both free and slaves.[206]

Other military slaves, or more accurately military captives, were neither of Kipchaq nor other Turkish origin. They were widely known as *cherkes* or Circassians and would subsequently come to dominate the Mamluk Sultanate. Most appear to have been ex-Christians, from Russia to the north of the steppes and Alans from the slopes of the Caucasus Mountains south of the steppes. Never as highly rated in military terms as the Turkish recruits, they had nevertheless been purchased in substantial numbers since at least the later Ayyubid period. Some were even allocated to the élite Bahriya regiment and the most famous of the early Mamluk Sultans, Baybars al-Bunduqdari, may actually have been a Circassian recruit. Their numbers continued to increase during the early Mamluk period and occasionally caused trouble for the dominant Turks, though the Circassian takeover of the Sultanate did not occur until 1382.[207]

Meanwhile the army of the Mamluk Sultanate remained open to freeborn Turkish and even Mongol recruits. The former included a small number of officers also arrived as remnants from the now defunct army of the last 'Abbasid Caliph of Baghdad.[208] The main source of freeborn recruits for Sultan Baybars I was, however, Turks and Mongols who were either fleeing ahead of, or had quarrelled with, the Mongol conquerors of Iran and Iraq. About 3,000 of them arrived in Syria during Baybars' reign. They were all described as horsemen and most were integrated with the status or designation of *amirs' mamluks* though they had not, of course, been recruited as slaves, nor were they allowed to keep a separate identity as a distinct unit.[209]

In 1296, a generation later, thousands of Mongol Oirat tribesmen, who had also fallen out with the Mongol Il-Khan ruler of Iran and Iraq, fled into Mamluk territory. Like their predecessors they almost certainly brought their own traditional arms and armour with them.[210] They were not, however, permitted into the prestigous slave-recruited *mamluk* regiments, though a few individuals did achieve quite high rank.[211] Instead these Oirats were allocated to the *Halqa* regiments which, consisting of freeborn rather than slave-recruits, now had lower and indeed declining military prestige.

Meanwhile the army of the Mamluk Sultanate increasingly consisted of, as well as being dominated by, Turks and to a lesser extent Circassians. Kurds continued to have a role, though a declining one, and tended to be allocated to units as individuals rather than on a tribal basis. Consequently, identifiable Kurdish units soon disappeared. The only exceptions were Kurdish auxiliary troops. This was probably the first time that Kurdish tribes had been summoned as auxiliaries, and they now served alongside bedouin Arab and Turcoman tribal auxiliaries.[212] Arab auxiliaries were, in fact, often found alongside *Halqa* troops garrisoning the coasts of the Mamluk Sultanate.[213]

Like the Ayyubid Sultanates before it, the Mamluk Sultanate had its largest army based in Egypt. Although there were differences between the Mamluk forces based here and elswhere, they were by no means as pronounced as had been the case in Ayyubid times. The most obvious difference was in the identity of tribal auxiliaries who were provided by the nomadic or semi-nomadic tribes of the region in question. In Egypt such auxiliaries were still drawn from Arab bedouin. In fact, the Sultan's government had the authority and power to oblige these tribes to remain in or close to the cultivated zone, to be ready if required, and not to return to their semi-desert pastures. Nevertheless relations between the Mamluk Sultanate and the bedouin tribes of Egypt rapidly worsened. In 1253 the Mamluks defeated the Arab tribes of Upper and Lower Egypt in two battles which were followed by large-scale massacres. Finally, in the early fourteenth century, the remaining Arab bedouin of Egypt were expelled into the surrounding deserts;[214] many migrating south into what is now Sudan.

The Mamluk government also had the authority to demand a horseman and a certain amount of military supplies from every settled village.[215] Otherwise the role of the *falahin* or peasantry had virtually disappeared, though there seems to have been less of a decline in Egypt's towns and cities. For example, in the time of Baybars I the *ra'is* commanders of the ports in Dumyat (Damietta), Rashid (Rosetta) and Alexandria was in each case a local man rather than a *mamluk*.[216]

Since the Mongol invasions of the second half of the thirteenth century the Jazira region north and east of the river Euphrates had been under Mongol Il-Khan rule or suzerainty (see below). Syria proper had also suffered massive damage as a result of a series of Mongol invasions and raids. However, as Islamic rule was re-established the area was largely brought under the direct rule of the Mamluk Sultanate, with a few remaining Ayyubid enclaves recognizing Mamluk suzerainty.

On the coast the shrinking outposts of the Latin Crusader States survived until 1291 with the tiny off-shore island of Ruad remaining under Western European occupation for a further decade. In Syria aristocratic military families continued to exist in some numbers, providing high status soldiers and leadership to the Mamluk army though not, of course, enjoying the same military prestige as men of slave-recruited *mamluk* origin. Their role was generally in the lower ranks of the officer corps or in the Halqa freeborn regiments.[217] As a result the Mamluk army in Syria, which formed the first line of defence against the ever threatening Mongols, was more mixed than that based in Egypt. In addition to *mamluk* regiments stationed in the main cities, there were locally recruited free troops, Arab, Kurdish and Turcoman auxiliaries, plus a remarkable variety of individual soldiers who had somehow found their way to Syria. These included Turks from neighbouring Anatolia, who were known as Rum; a term that might also have embraced men of Greek origin. Others were referred to as Russians, whose origins are even more obscure.[218] Given the massive dislocation and migrations caused by the Mongol conquests in the thirteenth century, the presence of people from practically any ethnic groups would not be surprising.

From the fall of the Fatimid Caliphate in the second half of the twelfth century until the Ottoman Turkish conquest of Egypt and most of North Africa in the sixteenth century, the military histories of Egypt and North Africa diverged. While Egypt returned to its traditional status as a major part of the Middle East, Islamic North Africa became something of a backwater in military as well as some other respects. This naturally had an impact upon military recruitment which was already changing. Given the massive purchases of sub-Saharan Africans as soldiers by the Fatimids after they conquered Egypt, it seems surprising that such troops had fallen out of favour when the Fatimids took over the Maghrib half a century earlier.[219] Black or *sudani* soldiers of both slave and free origin had been highly regarded by the previous Aghlabid rulers of the central Maghrib, showing the same dedicated loyalty to the Aghlabid *amirs* as the Fatimids' élite African regiments would offer the Caliph two centuries later.

Throughout its North African period and for many decades after the capital was transferred to Egypt, Berber troops, largely recruited and organized on a tribal basis, formed the bulk of Fatimid armies from the establishment of the Caliphate in 909. Berbers also provided the bulk of the army of the Zirid *amirs* who initially ruled most of the Maghrib as governors on behalf of the Fatimid Caliphs, but proclaimed their independence in the mid-eleventh century. By then the Zirid dynasty, itself of Sanhaja Berber origin, had divided with one line retaining the dynastic name of Zirids ruling what is now Tunisia and a second branch known as the Hammadids ruling eastern Algeria. While the rise of Zirid independence choked off much of the flow of Berber recruits to the Fatimids in Egypt, the Zirid *amirs* of Tunisia had already revived the policy of sub-Saharan recruitment. Their *'Abid* are believed to have been the Zirids' black élite palace regiments during the eleventh century and they proved particularly steadfast during the battle of Haydaran against invading Banu Hilal in 1057.[220]

Though weakened, the Zirid state survived an onslaught by the Banu Hilal and Banu Sulaym. They would also beat off a number of Norman attacks from Sicily in the mid-twelfth century. Yet this did not stop the Zirid rulers recruiting Christians and recent converts from Christianity in their armies, some of them possibly from the remaining indigenous Christian community in Tunisia.[221] This policy seems to have ended around 1140 and within little more than a decade both the Zirids and the Hammadids had been swept aside by Muwahhidun from Morocco.

The Muwahhidun in turn ceded authority to another dynasty, that of the Hafsids who, initially as Muwahhid governors and subsequently as independent rulers, would dominate Tunisia and part of eastern Algeria for three and a half centuries. These Hafsids developed close relations with some of their Christian neighbours on the other side of the Mediterranean, even recruiting a bodyguard unit of Catalan mercenaries from Spain in the thirteenth century. The presence of these men in Tunis would, in fact, give Aragonese rulers like King James considerable influence in this part of central North Africa.[222] To the east of Hafsid territory lay that of the similarly long-lasting Zayyanid dynasty of Tlemsen in what is now western Algeria. Though the Zayyanid army was largely recruited from local Berber tribesmen, the ruler of Tlemsen similarly recruited a guard of Catalan mercenaries in the late thirteenth and fourteenth centuries.[223]

The great island of Sicily had been conquered, in the face of bitter and prolonged Byzantine resistance, by an army launched, supplied and reinforced from North Africa. It was initially sent by the Aghlabid rulers of the central Maghrib as part of a series of naval campaigns which saw Islamic forces campaigning on various parts of the Italian mainland and even establishing a short-lived *amirate* in Apulia, in the heel of Italy. The army which conquered Sicily was mixed and consisted of a larger proportion of professional soldiers than that which conquered virtually all of the Iberian peninsula and part of southern France in the eighth century. Those troops involved included Arabs who provided most of the command leadership, Berbers who formed the bulk of the soldiers, plus black Africans, some Iranians and others. Numerous local Sicilians also converted to Islam and were incorporated into what became the *jund* or regional forces of Islamic Sicily.[224]

The evidence of surviving place-names and other historical sources show that, following this conquest, Islamic Arab and Berber colonization of Sicily was largely focused on the western end of the island, being particularly dense south-west of a line between Cefalu and Catania. The settlers themselves were initially a military occupation but soon settled down as farmers.[225] There is strong evidence of Arab Christians from Egypt and al-Andalus also settling in Sicily during this period of Islamic rule.[226]

Following the Norman Conquest in the later eleventh century, Islamic communities were concentrated in the western highlands of Sicily,[227] south-east of the capital Palermo, where they may have formed a majority. It is also worth noting that the North-African and indeed Semitic heritage of western Sicily went back many centuries, before the Roman Empire to the time of the Phoenicians and Carthaginians. Perhaps not surprisingly, it was into the mountainous centre of Sicily that Islamic 'rebels and runaway slaves' fled following a massacre of Muslims in Palermo in 1190. Here they achieved virtual independence for a few years until the Emperor Frederick II launched a serious campaign against them in 1222. A bitter but ultimately doomed guerrilla struggle ensued, with the Sicilian Muslims' main base being at Girgenti from which they may well have been in communication with the Islamic states of North Africa.[228]

Even in the initial stages of the Islamic conquest of Maghrib al-Aqsa, the 'Furthest West' or what is today Morocco, Arabs had been present in very limited numbers. Their role was to provide a military, cultural and of course religious leadership. Thereafter there is even less mention of specifically Arab troops. All armies were overwhelmingly recruited from the indigenous Western Berber peoples, largely from nomadic and semi-nomadic tribes such as the Sanhaja who inhabited the foothills and steppes south of the Atlas Mountains. Urban communities and the mountain tribes also played a part although less is usually heard about them.

Major change came with the rise of the Murabitun (Almoravids). Emerging as an Islamic reformist movement in the furthest western region of the Sahel semi-desert or steppe region south of the Sahara, the Murabitun expanded their power in several directions, most dramatically to the north along the Atlantic coast until they reached and conquered Morocco before crossing the Straits of Gibraltar to take over Islamic al-Andalus in the Iberian Peninsula.

The first Murabit army that we know much about consisted largely of Berber-speaking Lamtuna African tribesmen from the western Sahara. It seems as if, at an early stage, the names Murabitun and Lamtuna became virtually synonymous. After the establishment of a huge empire in north-west Africa and south-west Europe, the Murabitun army became more complex in organization and recruitment. The terms Rum and Nasara were probably both given to the same corps of European Christian mercenaries. Such troops, largely consisting of armoured cavalry, were certainly recruited by 'Ali Ibn Yusuf in the first half of the twelfth century and their role seems to have been to establish a firm position or base at the centre of the Murabit battle array. Some of these European troops may have been recruited as slaves or prisoners-of-war but by the later years of the Murabit state the Rum were important enough to warrant their own clergy and even a bishop in Morocco.[229]

The Hasham remained a separate and distinct group, more frequently mentioned during the later decades of the Murabit Empire than they had been earlier. They were also known earlier in al-Andalus at the time of the Umayyad Caliphate of Cordoba when they were probably mercenaries from outside the frontier of the state. However, the Hasham disappeared after the fall of the Murabitun but reappeared under the Marinids (see below). Within the Murabit army the term Hasham seems to have applied to various military groups or units who were not themselves regarded as proper Murabitun. These included some Sanhaja Berber tribesmen from the Sahara, related to but separate from the Lamtuna tribal federation which formed the bedrock of the Murabit state, but excluded black Africans from south of the Sahara, Christian mercenaries and European renegades.[230]

The name Zanata may have been given to Berber tribal troops in the Murabitun army, perhaps inherited from the pre-Murabit Zanata tribal states. Another group known as the Masmuda had meanwhile disappeared, having been crushed during the Murabit conquest of Morocco. Quite how these Masmuda of the Sus valley south of Marrakesh were related to the Masmuda whom the Fatimids and others recruited from the eastern Sudan is unknown. Arab troops are apparently only mentioned once in Murabit service and were clearly of minor importance, perhaps having been enlisted from the urban populations of Fez, Tangier and Sabta (Ceuta).[231]

The Muwahhidun (Almohades) who overthrew the Murabit state in the mid-twelfth century were Moroccan rather than Saharan but, like their predecessors, were emphatically Berber. The Muwahhidun army was largely recruited from the indigenous tribes of the Moroccan highlands, valleys and coasts. Nevertheless, it also included a remarkable variety of other units drawn from many sources. Even in the early days of the Muwahhid state there were references to ‘abid al-makhzan who consisted of black African slaves who may or may not have been freed, plus tribesmen of Saharan desert origin. The first such troops had previously fought for the Murabitun but were constantly renewed so that there were still ‘abid al-makhzan in the last Muwahhid armies.[232] Though of low status, they were not regarded as slaves or even as serfs. The Tabbala who played the great war-drums characteristic of Muwahhid armies were again of black African origin,[233] but little is otherwise known about the sub-Saharan, Sudani or black troops in Muwahhidun service.

Several elements or units within the Muwahhid army were apparently recruited because they possessed special skills, and were included in the *murtaziqa* of freely enlisted and perhaps full-time professionals as distinct from the *hushud* conscripts who were summoned for one specific campaign. The *mutatawwiya* were religiously motivated *jihad* volunteers, again probably joining up for one campaign and largely relying on booty to cover their expenses. Those recorded in al-Andalus probably included men from Morocco who crossed into Europe for a summer campaign then returned home in winter.[234]

Although Arabs were mentioned more frequently under Muwahhid rulers than in the preceding Murabit period, large-scale Arab settlement in Morocco did not take place until after the fall of the Muwahhidun. Nevertheless some Banu Hilal bedouin, having been defeated in the central Maghrib by the first Muwahhid Caliph 'Abd al-Mu'min in 1153, were incorporated into his army. Their descendants are believed to have been sent to al-Andalus 28 years later.[235]

There were also some Turks in the armies of the Muwahhidun. Known as *Ghuzz* (pl. *Aghzaz*) they fulfilled an important function as horse-archers, using their traditional skills in an area where Central Asian-style harassment horse-archery skills had been virtually unknown. An earlier reference to *ghuzzat* in 1062 probably meant simply archers rather than men claiming Ghuzz or Oghuz Turkish tribal origins. The largest group arrived from Egypt around 1172 and there seem to be no reasons why these troops should be regarded as Kurds, as has sometimes been suggested.[236] Small groups of Kurds, fleeing the Mongols and apparently unable or unwilling to find service under the new Mamluk Sultanate in Egypt, reached the Maghrib after 1258 but thereafter scattered or disappeared. Perhaps they were absorbed by the descendants of the previously arrived Turkish Ghuzz.[237] A unit of Ghuzz archers had, in fact, been inherited by the Ziyyanid rulers of western Algeria around 1235 following the fragmentation of the Muwahhid state.[238]

This phenomenon of a victorious dynasty inheriting military units from its defeated predecessor had been seen at the start of the Muwahhid period. One example was the ex-Murabit Rum, European mercenaries, who featured in the early Muwahhidun army, then disappeared before reappearing in the final decades of the Muwahhid state. This was after the latter had suffered a massive defeat at the hands of just such Spanish European troops at the battle of Las Navas de Tolosa in 1212. Around 1220 a guard unit of Western European mercenaries was recorded in the southern Moroccan city of Marrakesh, while further Castilian or Leonese were reported in the central Moroccan city of Meknes. Other sources refer to a small Christian Spanish or Portuguese élite fighting for the last Muwahhidun against the rising Marinids in the mid-thirteenth century.[239]

Large numbers of such Iberian Christian mercenaries were, however, killed during an anti-Christian reaction which followed the collapse of the Muwahhidun in 1269.[240] Nevertheless the new ruling dynasty from the Banu Marin, itself stemming from the nomadic Zanata Berber tribe of the north-western fringes of the Sahara, soon recruited a largely cavalry bodyguard of Christian mercenaries.

More surprisingly, the champion of one Marinid invading army within Spain was himself a Christian.[241] Otherwise the Marinid army was overwhelmingly tribal, largely being drawn from tribes favoured by the ruling dynasty; essentially their own and their closest allies.[242]

Al-Andalus was profoundly different to North Africa in a number of respects, not least in military matters. This reflected the fact that Islamic civilization was built upon Visigothic foundations which were themselves rooted in Late Roman and Germanic European traditions. Furthermore, al-Andalus to some extent separated from the Middle Eastern Islamic cultural mainstream at the time of the overthrow of the Umayyad Caliphate in Syria by the 'Abbasid Caliphate. An Umayyad state and subsquently Caliphate was re-established in al-Andalus, and its Syrian-Arab heritage was probably more important than is generally realized. This would in turn be reinforced by the ecological and cultural similarities between the Iberian Peninsula and Syria, lying at the opposite ends of the Mediterranean but at essentially the same latitudes.

Umayyad al-Andalus was not entirely divorced from the mainstreams of early medieval Islamic civilization but it went in its own way in several fields while also having strong military, economic and even cultural connections with Christian states to its north. These included not only the small Christian kingdoms within the Iberian Peninsula, but also France on the far side of the Pyrenean mountains and Italy on the other side of the western Mediterranean basin. What became known as the Umayyad Caliphate of Cordoba developed into a significant military power in the Iberian Peninsula and in the western regions of North Africa. In the early ninth century Caliph al-Hakam I reformed the army which had previously been recruited and organized along traditional early Islamic lines, enlisting much larger numbers of professional mercenaries known in al-Andalus as *hasham*, and purchasing largely European slaves to form an élite guards regiment of *mamluks*.

Military information can be found in the most unlikely sources, and one such is the so-called *Calendar of Cordoba* which was a guide to agricultural activities throughout the year. Written in al-Andalus in the mid-tenth century it stated that enlistment of troops for summer campaigns began on 28 February, this fact perhaps having relevance for those who also needed to know who would be available for agricultural work.

A generation or so later, during the late tenth century the enfeebled Caliphate fell under the control of the powerful *hajib* or first minister al-Mansur who became, in effect, the military dictator of al-Andalus. He introduced further military reforms which resulted in the Cordoban army consisting almost entirely of mercenaries, large numbers were Berbers from North Africa,[243] plus slave recruited *mamluks*. Many of the latter were referred to as Saqaliba or Slavs, having supposedly originated in north-eastern or eastern Europe. Al-Mansur was succeeded as *hajib* by his son al-Muzaffar, thus establishing a 'dynasty' of chief ministers known as the Amirids. However, the unity they maintained by force came crashing down following a sequence of military revolts in and around Cordoba which began in 1009.

The two main groups within the army of the Amirid *hajibs* were both of foreign origin; Berbers from North Africa and Saqaliba, supposed 'Slav' *mamluks*. Both lacked local roots,[244] and neither was able to take control of the entire country which rapidly fragmented in the *ta'ifa* or 'party' statelets which characterized eleventh-century al-Andalus. During this first *ta'ifa* period some Islamic Andalusian states were ruled by members of the Amirid family, others by the descendants of previously powerful frontier or *thughur* governors, while Cordoba even attempted to establish a republican government. Some were dominated by Berbers, some by so-called Slavs, some by indigenous Andalusians.

Their small-scale military recruitment usually reflected the origins of the ruling dynasty though there was a general decline in the employment of mercenaries. Berbers in particular fell from favour, perhaps because they were feared as potential coup-makers rather than being too expensive to employ.[245] Nevertheless, there were exceptions. The Zirid dynasty of Granada, for example, was Berber and Berber Sanhaja troops formed a large proportion of its *jund* local or militia armies. Even so these Berbers were a small minority within the overall population. In addition the Zirids of Granada maintained *'abid* who, in this context, are believed to have been European slave-recruited troops, while the *wusfana* appear to have been African slave-recruited troops, plus a small number of mercenaries. There were no references to local or specifically Andalusian troops who were generally hostile to the Zirid regime.[246] By the later eleventh century the mainstay of Granada's defence against the Murabitun saviour-invaders from North Africa are said to have been the *raqqusa*, a corps of supposed 'couriers' perhaps of African origin, but they deserted.[247]

Seville differed not only in apparently recruiting Christians from the north but by being more aggressive than its neighbours. Christian troops may have been present in the small army of Almeria but were probably recruited from prisoners rather than mercenaries. Initially neither of these *ta'ifa* states had frontiers with the Christian north; but Saragossa and Toledo did, which was probably why neither of them recruited Christian mercenaries.[248]

It has been calculated that Muslims finally became a majority in Islamic-ruled al-Andalus by the end of the tenth century. Nevertheless almost half the population could still have been Christian or from the smaller but still extremely significant Jewish population. Both these non-Islamic communities had limited and localized military obligation. The Christians were usually referred to as Mozarabs or those who were 'like Arabs' because of their adoption of virtually every aspect of Arab-Islamic culture except for Islam itself.

In some frontier regions of eleventh-century al-Andalus there was a locally powerful Mozarab aristocracy. One such was Count Sisnando of Tentugal, west of Coimbra in what is now central Portugal. He managed to maintain friendly relations with both al-Mutadid, the Islamic ruler of Seville, and King Ferdinand I of Leon.[249] Another powerful Mozarab Christian family dominated a small region towards the eastern end of the frontier between al-Andalus and the Christian states of northern Iberia during the second *ta'ifa* period, following the fall of the Murabitun. They were the Azagra clan who, having been vassals of the Islamic ruler of Valencia, declared their independence as rulers of Abin Rasin (Albarracin) on the mountains between Saragossa and Valencia around 1167. Fernando Ruiz de Azagra then became feudal lord of Daroca, a short distance to the north, under Aragonese suzerainty in 1182. In fact the Azagra family remained powerful until it died out just under a century later.[250]

The twelfth century Andalusian writer al-Turtushi is believed to have been working in Egypt when he produced his book of advice for rulers, the *Siraj al-Muluk* or *Lamp of Kings*. In it he specifically referred to what was customary in 'our country', namely al-Andalus, when writing about military matters. Here al-Turtushi advocated a return to early Islamic traditions with a reliance on a general military levy instead of a standing army of professional soldiers paid by treasury, implying that it was the latter who had failed in al-Andalus. He further explained Andalusian defeats by maintaining that state treasuries had focused on raising money rather than manpower. Nevertheless, while urging recruitment on the basis of all free men owing military service, al-Turtushi approved the existing Andalusian practice of assigning territorial fiefs to soldiers. Here it should be pointed out that the supposed early Islamic traditional methods of recruitment idealized by al-Turtushi, had never actually existed in al-Andalus which was conquered by Islamic forces after those primitive systems had almost fallen into disuse.[251]

The third and final *ta'ifa* period, following the collapse of the Muwahhid Empire, was so brief that no particular systems of military recruitment appeared. Most such states, including that of Granada, were at least in part a local revolt against the Muwahhidun. The armies that did emerge during this period seem to have been recruited in essentially the same ways as those of the second, and indeed the first, *ta'ifa* periods. Only one Islamic state now survived; that of the Nasrid rulers of Granada, and it did evolve its own highly distinctive military systems.

The Nasrid dynasty sprang from an important family of frontier soldiers and initially had to rely on its own tribe or clan, the Banu Nasr and their 'clients' or allied clans who formed the ruler's regular guard of cavalry and infantry archers. Thereafter the dynasty won support from most sections of Andalusian society. The ranks of its *jund* army were certainly swelled by Islamic refugees from other *ta'ifa* states as they fell to Christian conquest, these men joining distinct squadrons of cavalry or infantry.[252] Those of specifically Andalusian origin were known as *jundi mutadawwan* or territorial militias whose members were recorded on government registers, received salaries and were led by their own *ra'is* or commander.[253] Mercenaries and religiously motivated volunteers were called *muttawiya*,[254] the mercenaries being recruited for a specific campaign. Small numbers of Christian mercenaries were also enlisted, perhaps being political exiles from the north, and probably formed the ruler's closest bodyguard.[255]

The role of Berbers in the Granadan army changed over the years but they may at times have been the most numerous group. They included Berbers already resident in al-Andalus as well as exiles or defeated troops expelled from North Africa.[256] Relations between Granada and North Africa were not always good. Nevertheless Ibn al-Ahmar, the first Nasrid ruler of Granada, employed Zanata Berber mercenaries from Marinid Morocco quite early in his reign. These troops had initially crossed the straits into the Iberian Peninsula to take part in *jihad* against Christian invaders.[257] Many then stayed to become a regular part of the Nasrid army. This, however, led to political problems between the Nasrid ruling family and the powerful Banu Ashqilula clan of the Granadan frontier region, as a result of which a large part of the Banu Ashqilula migrated to Morocco in the late thirteenth century.[258] Tensions persisted and during the fourteenth century the rulers of Granada tried to reduce their dependence upon Berber mercenaries, though North African Berbers never disappeared from Granadan ranks, even if only as religious volunteers.[259]

ORGANIZATION

In general the systems of military organization seen in Islamic armies of this period were based upon those of the preceding 'Abbasid era, and in some cases remained virtually identical. Nevertheless the eleventh to fourteenth centuries also saw a number of significant new influences at work. One feature that remained constant, at least in theory, was the *'ard* or *isti'rad* military muster.[260] This served not only as a method of gathering troops at a designated location but also to review and inspect them. The methods involved dated back to the 'Abbasid and perhaps even the Umayyad periods which were widely regarded as a 'golden age' to be imitated as well as admired.

The *'ard* usually took place in an open area outside or near a city and was a very structured affair. The soldiers themselves, or at least those who could be described as professionals, were trained for such events, being reviewed in order of precedence or status. Cavalry paraded first, followed by infantry in what could be a very tough array, sometimes in full kit in the full sun. Men occasionally died from exhaustion in what was more than just a ceremony.[261]

Although the *'ard* might have been almost universal, the organization of military forces and the territorial divisions which sometimes underpinned such an organization did vary. Such variations tended to reflect the military or cultural heritage of the region in question, and that of the current ruling or dominant ethnic group. From the mid-eleventh century onwards the dominant group throughout most of the eastern Islamic territories was Turkish. Here the Great Seljuk Sultanate was divided into 24 military provinces by the highly influential Iranian *wazir* and writer on government, Nizam al-Mulk.

How far his plan was carried out in reality is not entirely clear, but these provinces were supposedly under military governors or commanders whose titles reflected the cultural traditions of the province in question. Thus, in Turkish areas the regional governor was a *Chad* or *Khan*, in Persian a *Shah*. Every such chief was expected to raise a certain number of troops each year, also being responsible for training and equipping them.[262] It has been estimated that the resulting armies of the later Seljuq period could number between 10,000 and 15,000 men.[263]

This Seljuq system of military administration owed as much, if not more, to Iranian traditions as it did to Turkish. Iranian traditions may have been even more fundamental to Ghaznawid armies further east, in what are now Afghanistan and Pakistan, as well as amongst the remaining smaller Iranian or non-Turkish Islamic states of the Caucasus region. The Shi'a Isma'ili enclave or statelet established in the mountains of northern Iran by Hasan al-Sabah in the 1090s, and which survived until its destruction by the Mongols in 1256, was in a different situation. Here the Isma'ili strongholds were surrounded by enemies, amongst the most antagonistic of whom were the strictly Sunni Muslim Seljuks. Consequently the Isma'ili *da'i* leader in Iran, like the Isma'ili leader in the mountains of north-western Syria, had to be a military as well as a spiritual commander and chief administrator.

In both enclaves, each member of the *da'wa* or community was employed according to his or her talents.[264] In Syria, Sinan Ibn Salman proved so effective and so feared by the Isma'ilis' enemies that he earned the nickname of 'The Old Man of the Mountain'. Beneath these leaders were the *rafiqs* or comrades who owed absolute obedience to their *da'i*. Next came the *fida'is* that was the active military arm of the Isma'ili community but had supposedly not been initiated into its 'higher mysteries'. Those in the main Isma'ili castle of Alamut in northern Iran were trained in foreign languages and in the practices of other religions so that they could move freely amid the ranks of their enemies. They were the feared soldiers who, operating in very small groups, or even as individuals, became known to their enemies, Muslim or Christian alike, as the Assassins. Lowest in rank were the *lasiqs* or beginners and the rest of the community.[265]

The Seljuk Sultanate of Rum, established amid the ruins of Byzantine rule in central Anatolia, clearly attempted to follow the principles of military organization used by the Great Seljuk Sultanate to the east. Here again military titles of Turkish, Persian and Arabic origin were used while the *Amir Akhur* or 'master of horse' was sometimes called the *kundestabl* which clearly came from French, perhaps via Armenian use.[266] The annual *'ard* muster was held in spring, usually near Kayseri in Cappadocia which, it is interesting to note, had also been a major mustering point during the Byzantine period. Here both veterans and new recruits assembled for what sometimes seemed more like a military festival with various forms of entertainment, juggling, recitations of poetry, displays of horsemanship and feasting.[267] There then followed a summer's campaigning in time of war or training in time of peace. This was normally done under the Sultan's own command before the men dispersed for winter when the weather was not suitable for campaigning except in cases of emergency.

In the early decades of the Sultanate of Rum the army was largely tribal and was organized as such. Cavalrymen were supported by *havashi* retainers, the most senior or wealthy men having as many as ten followers. Most of these tribal troops were horse-archers and were mainly concentrated in frontier zones, especially facing what remained of the Byzantine Empire. As already stated, the military forces of the Seljuk Sultanate of Rum consisted of two elements during the thirteenth century, the Qasim Ancient and Hadith New armies.[268] Elements of these could be based in different regions, in addition to the Turcoman tribal troops of frontier zones. For example, after the Seljuks took the eastern fortress city of Ahlat around 1231, the Sultan sent 1,000 of his top-rated slave-recruited 'royal' *ghulams* not merely to garrison the place but to settle there, perhaps accompanied by 500 *serhenk* (Persian *sarhang*),[269] who in this context may have been foot soldiers. Normally, however, such court *ghulams* formed a household corps with the best serving as the ruler's personal bodyguards.[270]

The *igdish* or *ikdish*, whose precise origin remains unclear (see above), were often used to maintain law and order in towns and cities under the command of their *igdishbaşis*.[271] The new and far from élite *fityan*, who first appeared fighting alongside regular soldiers in 1220 armed with *gurz* mace and *najakh* axe, were probably much the same as the subsequent *ikhvans* or *javans* who defended several cities when the Seljuk Sultanate of Rum collapsed. As such they seem to have been more like a religiously based urban militia than regular soldiers.[272] Western European and Latin mercenaries from the Crusader States had a separate status and organization amongst the other *jira khvars* or hired troops in Seljuk Rumi service, apparently being commanded or led by their own *za'im* leader in the late 1220s. How they were organized in other periods is unknown.[273]

Before the arrival of the Seljuk Turks, Syria and the Jazira were largely dominated by powerful Arab tribes and their armies were, of course, organized on a tribal basis. On the other hand, some of the leading men and commanders of the Banu Kilab tribe of north-western Syria were supported by *'iqta* fiefs along the fertile banks of the river Orontes.[274] It is also clear that local or regional *jund* militia armies still existed in both Syria and the Jazira, their organization probably dating from the 'Abbasid if not the even earlier Umayyad period. Furthermore, these militias were strong enough to cause occasional problems for unpopular rulers, including the Fatimid Caliphate of Egypt.[275]

Quite how, if at all, provincial *junds* fitted into the armies of the petty rulers who dominated so much of this part of the Islamic world in the eleventh and early twelfth centuries is again unclear. What is known is that a professional and perhaps largely full-time *askar* or household corps formed the centre of such rulers' military power and were the basis of his authority.[276] During the near anarchy of the early eleventh century, not only rulers and governor but even some of the leading men of cities like Aleppo had their own retinues of sword-armed, slave-recruited *ghulam* soldiers.[277]

Then there were the *ahdath* urban militias which sometimes seem to have answered to nobody other than their own *ra'is* or commander. At other times this post could be given by a local ruler to one of his own supporters. This appears to have happened in Aleppo in the early eleventh century when Salih Ibn Mirdas, the first of the Mirdasid dynasty, may have created the official post of *ra'is* of the *ahdath* for a certain *qa'id* officer named Salim Ibn Mustafah, himself the son of a *ghulam* of the famous Hamdanid ruler of northern Syria and patron of poets, Sayf al-Dawla. This position was powerful enough for Salim Ibn Mustafah to attempt an unsuccessful rebellion against the next Mirdasid ruler.[278]

In 1085, following the fall of the Mirdasids and the occupation of Aleppo by the rival 'Uqaylids, some 600 *ahdath* militiamen marched with the last Arab army of Aleppo against the invading Turks; but were defeated.[279] In addition to defending their city, these Syrian *ahdath* urban militias otherwise acted as a local fire-brigade and police force. Paid from local taxes, their loyalties were also entirely local and although they were the sources of a few minor local dynasties, the chroniclers all too often record them as gangs of troublemakers.[280]

Within a few years of the Seljuk conquest of the Jazira and Syria, the region again fragmented as it had tended to do throughout recorded history. At first, during the late eleventh and very early twelfth centuries, many of its provinces and cities were ruled by Seljuk *maliks* or sub-kings as deputies of the Great Seljuk Sultan in Iran and Iraq. They had authority to appoint and dismiss military commanders and other government officials while also normally taking personal command of the local army.[281] However, the role of the *maliks* was gradually taken over during the first half of the twelfth century by *atabegs*, a title which itself became virtually synonymous with that of *isfahsalah* or army commander.[282] This *atabeg-isfahsalah* was normally supported by several other powerful but secondary officials such as a *shihna* chief of police,[283] a governor of the citadel,[284] and the *ra'is* of the *ahdath*.[285]

The ruler's *askar* continued to form the centre or kernel of the often quite small armies of this fragmented period. They again largely consisted of highly trained, well paid and high prestige slave-recruited *ghulams* who, in addition to being responsible for protecting their ruler, supervised his siege machines and guarded the state's military arsenals. Freeborn troops consisted of mercenaries from outside the state and locals whose military obligations were in return for pensions or being included in state registers for regular payment. Virtually all these professional soldiers were cavalrymen, though they clearly also had other skills. Foot soldiers were normally mustered as and when needed, along with tribal auxiliaries.[286] The term *shihna* could be used for relatively small garrisons or military units as well as their commanders, including the cavalry escorts allocated to merchant caravans in troubled times. The fact that one such early twelfth century *shihna* escort was described as consisting of 'only ten horsemen' might suggest that they were usually more numerous.[287]

The army of the Seljuk and post-Seljuk or Burid *amirate* of Damascus has been studied in greater detail than most. It was clearly a major element in the state from the late eleventh- to mid-twelfth century,[288] and was commanded by several clearly distinct officer ranks. The most senior were the *isfahsalar* commander and leader in battle who often was ruler himself. Perhaps rather surprisingly, the *ra'is* of the *ahdath* militia was next in seniority, probably indicating how important the *ahdath* was in Damascus. Immediately beneath him was the *shihna* head of police who was in charge of internal law and security.[289]

The armies of the Zangid state of Mosul and Aleppo was in many ways a typical *atabeg* force. It has been suggested that under Nur al-Din, the son of the founder of the dynasty Imad al-Din Zangi, the Zangid army never lived in barracks because they had so many other active duties.[290] However, this might be a poetic exaggeration rather than a realistic description. The sources do, nevertheless, state that at the start of his reign in Damascus in 1147, Nur al-Din had an *askar* of 1,000 or so men which subsequently increased to 3,000. Each soldier formed part of a *tulb*, a Turkish word meaning something like a platoon, of 70 to 200 men, and his weapons were stored in the state *zardkhana* or arsenal to be distributed at the start of a campaign.[291]

As might be expected, the structure and organization of the forces of the tiny and almost constantly threatened Isma'ili enclave in the coastal mountains of north-western Syria differed from those of the city-based Seljuk and post-Seljuk states. It was much more like that of the other Isma'ili mountain enclave in northern Iran. Although the castle and small town of Masyaf is regarded as the centre of this remarkable statelet, the nearby castle of Kahf probably served as a training centre.[292] Otherwise, the military subordinates of the Syrian *da'i*, spiritual leader and effective ruler, had the ranks of *naqib* officer, *jamah* 'wing' or perhaps flank officer, and *nazir* keeper or inspector. After the death of Sinan

Ibn Salman, 'The Old Man of the Mountain' in 1192 or 1193, the *da'i* in charge of a Syrian Isma'ili castle was also called a *wali* or governor.[293]

The military organization of the Fatimid state was based upon that of the Sunni Muslim 'Abbasid Caliphate, although the Fatimid Caliphs, as leaders of a substantial section of Shi'a Islam, did not care to acknowledge this fact. Fatimid military organization, in its final form, then served as the foundation of subsequent Ayyubid and Mamluk military structures. Like the 'Abbasid officer corps, that of the early Fatimid army consisted of various grades of *amir* and *qa'id*, the highest of whom was the *Amir al-Umara* 'Amir of Amirs' or *Amir al-Juyush* 'Amir of soldiers' who was normally commander-in-chief of the Syrian garrisons. On the other hand the actual ranks do not seem to have been as significant as they had been under the 'Abbasid Caliphs.[294]

In its early form in North Africa and during the decades immediately following the conquest of Egypt, the Fatimid army largely consisted of tribal formations, the most organized of which were divided into traditional and smaller *'irafa* units. But as Fatimid recruitment changed, becoming more complex and more specialized, the army was increasingly based upon function, ethnic origins or sources of recruitment including the *ghulams* of freed slave-origin.[295] In many cases the latter formed regiments that were known by the names of the senior military officers or generals who had purchased and organized them. Very often the individual *ghulams*, and perhaps occasionally other soldiers as well, adopted their commander's or unit's name as an addition to their own name.

Here it needs to be understood that, in almost all sections of medieval Islamic society, individual names were built up from several elements. These included a personal name, a father's name sometimes followed by a string of real or claimed ancestors, plus a tribal, clan or family identification, often a place of geographical origin, and an indication of career or, in the case of many *mamluks*, of an early job or responsibility. Where clan, family or tribal origins were missing or deemed unimportant, as was the case with many men of slave origin, the name or title of the individual's first owner, patron or commander could be added.

The Fatimid Hujariya, soldiers normally recruited and trained since youth in *hujra* barrack rooms, were themselves divided according to their ages or date of recruitment rather like a modern school, then in units based upon multiples of ten. Another cavalry or partially mounted unit briefly mentioned in early eleventh-century Cairo were the Qaysariya whose name suggests that they might have been raised in or around Caesarea in Palestine, or have been drawn from that city's garrison.[296]

Following a number of defeats by considerably smaller forces of Turkish *ghulam* cavalry in Syria, the Fatimid Caliphate's attempts to raise comparable forces of its own resulted in virtually separate armies. The older, traditional and larger Berber forces remained on strength for many decades. The newer force seems to have included a sort of 'middleweight' professional cavalry, more heavily armoured than the bulk of Berber tribal horsemen but rarely including the very heavily armoured cavalry riding armoured horses who were numbered amongst 'Abbasid and ex-'Abbasid *ghulam* élite forces. The other part of this new army consisted of black African infantry. Meanwhile those bedouin tribal Arab auxiliaries who supported the Fatimids in both Syria and Egypt were almost like a third army, responsible for policing the frontiers and controlling, in so far as possible, the steppe regions of eastern Syria.[297]

Despite the fact that the most senior officer in the early Fatimid army, the *Amir al-Umara*, commanded the garrisons and field forces stationed in Syria, the bulk of Fatimid was concentrated in and around Cairo. The leading *amirs* had their own houses within the city, probably in the older southern suburb of Fustat rather than the fortified 'Caliphal city' of al-Qahira (Cairo) itself. These houses sometimes became competing centres of power at times when the authority of the Caliph was weak and may have served as barracks for an *amir*'s own loyal retainers.

Most of the black African infantry also lived in the Mansuriya quarter on the southern side of the Caliphal palace-city, this having been established as a barracks for them: it would subsequently be destroyed by Saladin and replaced by gardens.[298] At other times such *sudani* Africans were billeted in surrounding agricultural villages.[299] During the late tenth century those in Cairo are known to have been summoned when needed by public criers in the *suqs* or markets of the city. The men then presented themselves and were issued with weapons. Something similar is likely to have been done elsewhere in the country and in the later period as well.[300]

European and Crusader sources, followed by later historians, almost invariably exaggerated the size of those Fatimid armies which faced the Crusaders and Latin States. A widely accepted estimate that, at the time of Saladin's take-over of Egypt, there were still between 30,000 and 50,000 Armenians and Sudanese in the Fatimid Caliphal palace regiments seems improbable.[301] The twelfth-century Fatimid military establishment is unlikely to have numbered more than 25,000 men. Of these some 10,000 to 15,000 were based in or around Cairo of whom only 4,000 or 5,000 were cavalry, excluding youngsters under training. A similar number were scattered in garrisons elsewhere in Egypt.[302]

The largest field armies were those mustered in Egypt when Egypt itself was threatened. Otherwise, Fatimid field armies were relatively small. In the early days, Fatimid armies campaigning in Syria numbered from 5,000 to 10,000, plus local militias, and this figure also seems to have applied during early twelfth-century expeditions against the Latin Kingdom of Jerusalem. In such forces the proportion of cavalry to foot soldiers varied considerably because of the presence of largely infantry militias and often mounted tribal auxiliaries. In general, however, it seems that in these later expeditionary forces from one- to two-thirds were horsemen,[303] though some of the latter might have been mounted infantry rather than true cavalry.

More detailed information from the early Crusader period shows that the ranks of the Fatimid officer corps now included that of the 'Umara al-Mutawwaqun' 'Amirs of the necklace' who were comparable to the later Amirs of One Hundred or Amirs of One Thousand in the Mamluk Sultanate. Below them were the Arbab al-Qundub 'lords of maces' comparable to the fourteenth century Tablakhana. The lowest rank of officers was Amirs without maces comparable to the Mamluk Amirs of Ten or Amirs of Five. On the other hand the most common term for any form of officer was Ziman rather than Amir. The very senior ranks of Isfahsalar or Ziman of Zimans were now more of a governmental administrative role than a military command.[304] In fact the later Fatimid Isfahsalar seems to have been in charge of military ceremonial, not of a campaign.[305]

The structure of the Fatimid regular army had also changed, following the reforms of the wazir Badr al-Jamali and his son. It now consisted of two distinct parts, the Caliphal or palace regiments known as the Khawass al-Khilafa and the ordinary regiments or Tawa'if al-Ajnad.[306] The former included the Hujariya who, unlike the other units, seems to have been a constantly trained élite, permanently under arms and rising from 3,000 to 5,000 men at its largest.[307] They formed several units stationed around the Caliphal palace but not inside it, and were also available for military campaign outside Egypt itself.[308]

Other smaller Caliphal formations had a variety of sometimes specialized functions. For example the Ustadhs, both black and white, were a source of officers for other units, the most senior being known as Muhannak or experts. They also served as guards and administrators but were not eunuchs, as the corrupted term ustadh came to mean in Mamluk times. The Sibyan al-Rikab al-Khass or Rikabiya were a proper Caliphal bodyguard of attendants and companions who also had political duties as well as being a source of guards and officers. Otherwise it is unclear whether the 2,000 or so Sibyan al-Khass were cavalry or infantry.[309] A description of disturbances in Cairo in 1131–2 which led to the slaughter of around 300 Sibyan al-Khass by a new wazir does, however, seem to indicate that they were mounted.[310]

The ordinary regular regiments were now mostly named after their founders, their ethnic origin or the equipment which denoted their primary function. One such were the sibyan al-zarad or 'young men with mail armour' who numbered approximately 500 in 1134. Such regiments were semi-permanent in the sense that as old ones died out new ones were created, though some lasted a remarkably long time. Nor were their personnel necessarily permanent, as there were examples of soldiers being transferred from one regiment to another.[311] Some regiments also included both horse and foot. One such was the mid-twelfth century Juyushi regiment which included both black *Sudani* soldiers and others, being assembled from the best men available but excluding Armenians. Meanwhile the Rayhaniya regiment was described as being specifically *Sudani*.[312]

During the last years of Fatimid rule in Egypt the power of the Caliphs had declined to such an extent that the *wazirs* virtually had their own private armies, but even then the Caliph retained his loyal guard regiments of Armenian archers and black *Sudani* infantry.[313] The latter, in fact, remained a source of trouble for the wazirs to the very end,[314] including Saladin before he finally abolished the Fatimid Caliphate and shortly after he turned savagely upon the remaining largely slave-recruited black African soldiers.

Fatimid professional units were subdivided for tactical purposes, the smallest element apparently consisting of 100 men under a *ziman* officer. Perhaps these subdivisions were used as a means of rotating troops, so that only one went into battle at a time. It is also possible that several could be formed into something resembling a battalion under a more senior officer.[315] Meanwhile the *ahdath* urban militias declined in importance during the twelfth century. Nevertheless, this was more characteristic of Egypt than of the Fatimid Caliphate's remaining coastal possessions in Palestine and Lebanon where in some cases they may also have drawn upon the towns' Jewish populations. Here the local militias remained vital to the defence of their city fortifications and occasionally fought in the open, outside the walls. Nevertheless their equipment was poor, their pay low and unreliable, and their morale sinking.[316]

Within Egypt the Arab bedouin tribes were, as already mentioned, almost a state within a state, but as a community rather than as a geographical entity.[317] The only real exception was in the far south where the leaders of the Arabized Banu Kanz tribe were sometimes so powerful that the Fatimid government recognized them as hereditory governors and defenders of the frontier region of Aswan.[318]

Even before Saladin's abolition of the Fatimid Caliphate in 1171 he had, as *wazir* since 1169, started major changes to the organization of the Egyptian army.[319] Precise numbers also survive following more than one assessment or review of available troops. For example, in 1169 Saladin commanded 8,640 regular soldiers, excluding naval troops and sailors. These included the 500 Asadiya or followers of his late uncle Asad al-Din Shirkuh who had been sent to Egypt by Nur al-Din of Syria to prevent the now feeble Fatimid Caliphate falling under Crusader control. Saladin had then taken over with the nominal status of Fatimid *wazir* when Shirkuh died. In addition around 3,000 Ghuzz Turcoman tribal troops had also been sent from Syria.

In 1181 another review undertaken to impress visiting Byzantine and Crusader envoys showed that Saladin now had 174 *tulb* cavalry units with a further 20 absent, probably on garrison duties elsewhere. Each *tulb* consisted of from 70 to

200 horsemen, producing a total 14,000 regular cavalry immediately available, of whom 6,000 were *tawashiya* highly rated *mamluks* and 1,500 were *qaraghulamiya* who are usually interpreted as lower-rated *mamluks*. In addition there were 7,000 auxiliaries from the Arab Judham tribe, but these were regarded as being of dubiously loyalty to the new and not really Fatimid *wazir*, and were therefore soon reduced with a mere 1,300 being allowed on the military registers.[320]

Saladin's destruction of the old Fatimid army was not total, and there were a number of exceptions. One of the most interesting may shed light on the special situation in southern Egypt. Here Saladin chose an ex-Fatimid *amir* as deputy governor of the provinces of Qus, Aswan on the frontier with Nubia, and Aydhab on the Red Sea coast.[321] This must surely have been an attempt to soothe local sensibilities in a vulnerable and volatile region at a time when Saladin's main military priorities lay in Palestine and Syria.

The sometimes brutal military reforms after 1181 saw the disappearance of virtually all of what remained of the Fatimid army. Instead a new Ayyubid army emerged whose organization nevertheless owed much to the Fatimid past. Even after Saladin won control of Syria and much of the Jazira, the largest section of his army was still based in Egypt. This included up to 9,000 cavalry plus a further 1,000 under Sultan Saladin's immediate command. The cavalry forces of Egypt probably increased to 12,000 under Sultan al-Kamil during the first half of the thirteenth century. The supposedly subordinate Ayyubid rulers in Damascus probably had a further 3,000 cavalry though these also had to garrison what are now southern Syria, Jordan and most of Palestine. During the time of Nur al-Din in the third quarter of the twelfth century, the garrison of Damascus had probably numbered only 1,000 or so. Ayyubid Aleppo probably had a further 3,000 cavalry, but here there was a greater reliance of tribal auxiliaries than in the Sultanate of Damascus. The smaller Ayyubid sultanates of Hims and Hama in central Syria probably had no more than 1,000 cavalry apiece, with evidence from 1239 suggesting that these numbers were now no more than 400 or 500. Other Ayyubid sultanates or governorates in Syria could field even smaller armies, though those in the Jazira and Mosul in northern Iraq were much larger; perhaps 4,000 and 2,000 respectively.

All told, the Ayyubid family confederation of sultanates could probably draw upon a little over 22,000 regular cavalrymen,[322] but getting them all together into one army would have been a very different matter. Like the Fatimid Caliphs before them, Saladin and his successors could not send their entire military strength against the Latin States in the Holy Land and Syria. At least half normally remained in Egypt on garrison duties because of the constant threat of invasion or naval attack, while some of the eastern Ayyubid principalities were even more vulnerable to attack. In 1176, for example, Saladin mustered 6,000 regulars and over twice as many volunteers to field an army of around 20,000.[323] For his great

victory over the Latin Kingdom of Jerusalem at Hattin in 1187, Saladin managed
to assemble rather more; perhaps 12,000 professional cavalry plus retainers and
servants to make a total of 30,000 soldiers, plus numerous volunteers of dubious
training and reliability. They faced some 12,000 Latin or Crusader knights plus
15,000 to 18,000 *turcopoles* and infantry, probably not including camp-followers.
In other words the Muslim and Christian armies were not very different in size
when the crunch came.

Although the terminology of officer ranks changed during the Ayyubid period,
the basic system remained similar to what it had been under the Fatimids. There
were now only four senior officer ranks; *Ustadh al-Dar* of whom there was only
one, *hajib, amir hajib, amir jandar* and *khazindar*, the latter being the governor
of a major citadel. All could, however, rise from very lowly origins.[324] Otherwise
the ranks amongst the *amirs* seem to have been rather informal with the term
amir simply an officer, *amir kabir* being an unspecific senior officer and an
amir al-isfahsalar being higher still. Even so, the result was basically a three-tier
system amongst what might be called field officers, similar to that of the previous
Fatimid armies and of the subsequent Mamluk ones.[325]

Several studies have been made of the internal unit structure of Ayyubid
armies, especially those of Saladin himself. However, the very abundance of
sometimes conflicting and all too often obscure information resulted in varying
interpretations.[326] First there is the matter of terminology for varying units or
formations, some of which were probably permanent while others were ad hoc
responses to a particular military situation. The *tulb*, which has already been
mentioned, is generally accepted to have been a small unit 70 to 200 men, each
tulb being identified by its own *sanjaq* banner. The *katiba* was an old but now
rare term that seems to have meant much the same as *tulb*. A *jarida* was again a
small unit of perhaps 70 or so men, the term having been used in previous Zangid
forces, while a *jama'a* or 'assembly' normally seems to have consisted of three
jaridas, perhaps as an ad hoc field formation. A *sariya* was the smallest unit in
the army, clearly smaller than a *jarida*, possibly averaging around 20 cavalrymen
and often being used for ambushes. The name *saqah* was given to a separated unit
which went ahead or behind the main army, but further details are confusing.

The term *yazaq* seems to be applied to a specialist or élite unit forming part
of an advance guard and consisting of the best available cavalry. It was almost
certainly an ad hoc formation, organized as and when required. The *yazaq al-
da'im* almost appears to be an example of Special Forces used for reconnaissance,
poisoning the enemy's water supplies and such tasks. Another specialist unit was
the *jalish* who seem to have been associated with a Turkish-style banner having
tufts of animal hair upon it. The *jalish* may, in fact, have been a unit protecting
the standard-bearers who went ahead of the main army, though they could
also apparently be employed as shock cavalry to attack an enemy encampment.

Numbering an estimated 500 men, their other duties included encircling the foe and protecting military engineers or technicians. Their weapons show the *jalish* to have included a substantial proportion of horse-archers, and they may indeed all have been horse-archers, but their very exposed role surely precludes them from being light or unarmoured cavalry. Instead it seems more likely that they, and perhaps their horses, had more armour than usual.

Another term, *qufl*, which literally meant a fortress or strongpoint, was often applied to Arab auxiliaries who were employed to block the enemy's communications routes. The term *harafisha*, which literally meant a rabble, seems to have been given to infantry guerrillas while the *lisus* seem to have been cavalry raiders, again usually Arabs, whose task was to damage enemy supplies, attack supply caravans and so on. The *qufl*, *harafisha* and *lisus* were all, meanwhile, of low status but considerable military importance.

The soldiers with the highest prestige in Ayyubid armies were those of slave-recruited origins; namely the *ghulams* or *mamluks*. Their training and organization was based upon both Seljuk-Zangid and Fatimid systems which were, of couse, similar and owed their origins to the preceding 'Abbasid period. The resulting troops, once trained and freed, formed a fiercely disciplined and loyal force with a proud sense of its own identity and worth. They usually protected the ruler, formed the centre of field armies or battle arrays and lived in barracks or garrisoned some of the most important fortifications.

The men of the high status Tawashi regiments were, for example, *ghulams*. The word *tawashis* had earlier meant eunuch, and it appears that the men of slave-origin who had trained young *sibyan* and *ghulam* recruits during the Fatimid, Zangid and perhaps early Ayyubid periods had been eunuchs. The same may also have been true of some of the senior officers in command of *tawashiya* regiments, at least in the early days. Tawashi soldiers were normally supported by *'iqta* fiefs and they were often entrusted with administrative roles, which was probably evidence of their standard of education as well as military training. Meanwhile the *tawashi* regiments remained proper fighting units, usually placed at the centre of a line of battle but also being entrusted with particular strategic garrison duties.[327]

The status and origins of the Qaraghulams or 'black *ghulams*' is less clear. Some have suggested that they were initially African soldiers of slave origin who had previously served in Fatimid armies,[328] but this seem unlikely. Other evidence shows them to be lower status or lighter equipped cavalry, sometimes employed to secure an army's route. Some Tawashi troops were also *qaraghulams*, so it seems more likely that the term was being used in the way it had been in the eastern provinces of the Islamic world, to indicate inferior or second-rate *ghulams*. The Turkish word *qara*, meaning black, had of course long been used by the Turks themselves to indicate a lower or secondary status.

Under Saladin and his Ayyubid successors, the word Halqa was used to designate the prestigious units which assembled around the ruler both in peace and in battle, but which were more numerous than his immediate bodyguard.[329] They would be expected to stay with him during a retreat and would supply the men for a *yazaq* advance-guard. An Ayyubid Halqa could fight as an independent military formation, but its officers also provided the Sultan with political support in peace and acted as a sort of military staff in war. [330] Presumably this was why the Halqa often, or perhaps even normally, included 'men of the pen', who were the civilian bureaucrats as distinct from the military 'men of the sword'. The officers, and perhaps the bureaucrats, of the Halqa were normally supported by *'iqta* fiefs; the officers being expected to bring a specified number of soldiers with them, depending upon the size or value of their *'iqta*.[331]

The Jandariya were a smaller group within the Ayyubid Halqa, their role being to protect the person of the sultan. Headed by an officer known as a *naqib*, the trusted Jandariya also served as messengers, guards and supervisors of arsenals. They always remained close to a ruler in battle but could also fight in the centre of the line if necessary. Some were also sent to garrison vital locations in times of danger. In later Ayyubid times these Jandariya were exclusively Turkish *mamluks*, and in the Mamluk Sultanate they were given responsibility for inflicting serious punishments,[332] especially on high ranking people who had fallen into disgrace.

After the death of Saladin in 1193 the Ayyubid realm, which had always been something of a family affair, fragmented further with the emergence of more distinctly regional armies. One further effect was that some *amirs* developed strong family ties in the area in which they served, resulting in a sort of local landed aristocracy. Although this phenomenon should not be overstated, it did become characteristic in and around the northern Syrian city of Aleppo.[333]

The fragmentation characteristic of these later Ayyubid decades resulted in smaller localized forces with simplified internal structures, though the terminology remained much the same. An *askar* was still like a prince's or a leading *amir's* personal regiment, though the term could now be applied to the unit defending one city or one small principality. Furthermore, the *askar* was still clearly a real unit in terms of its pay, equipment and training. The term *tulb* was now rarely used and had become rather vague, sometimes referring to a parade unit and sometimes to a field unit. It is unclear whether the *tulb* was now permanent or drawn from a field army when required, and whether it would normally be divided into smaller *jama'a*, *jarida* or *sariya* units. Some evidence does, however, suggest that its size had stabilized at around 80 men.[334]

Al-Kamil, as Sultan of Egypt and thus the senior ruler in the Ayyubid family confederation, reportedly considered reviving the 'Abbasid and Fatimid Hujariyyah system of training the sons of soldiers as élite troops, but never did so.[335] The possibility itself points to the difficulty faced by even such a powerful and wealthy ruler as al-Kamil in recruiting sufficient numbers of suitable slaves to be trained and released as *mamluks*. Only a few years later in the 1240s the international situation, and above all that in Central Asia, had changed so such much that Sultan al-Salih of Egypt was able to purchase massive numbers of men. They would form his élite Bahriya and Jamdariya regiments. With this army of loyal and professional soldiers, al-Salih tried to reimpose the central authority which Saladin, the founder of the Ayyubid dynasty, had enjoyed in the late twelfth century. But by relying on his formidable military entourage rather than on family solidarity, al-Salih stirred up considerable resentment and although he achieved some success in southern Syria, his efforts failed in northern Syria and the Jazira.[336]

Al-Salih's policies also contained the seeds of other problems. Segregating his Bahriya and Jamdariya regiments from the rest of society in Cairo, providing them with barracks on the fortified island of Roda (now virtually in the centre of the Egyptian capital) was itself a new idea. Furthermore, the Sultan encouraged them to take more than usual pride in their largely Turkish origins as well as their *mamluk* status. Similar efforts had been made by the Ayyubid sultans of Aleppo since the early thirteenth century. Nevertheless, the increasingly proud *mamluk* regiments remained only a small part of the overall Ayyubid military structure. The Bahriya numbered from 800 to 1,000 men while the Jamdariya were only 200 or so, perhaps drawn from the ranks of the Bahriya; this within a military establishment of over 10,000.[337] Al-Salih's Bahriya regiment remained the model for the subsequent Mamluk Sultanate, but in the meantime the effect was to steadily undermine the prestige of traditional forces.[338]

This later Ayyubid period saw the decline of other, even earlier military groups. In the deep south of Egypt the power of the Banu Kanz ebbed away and this Arabized but largely Nubian tribe gradually migrated southwards into northern and north-western Sudan where it usually cooperated with the rulers of the similarly declining Christian Nubian kingdoms. In fact the leader of the Banu Kanz was often designated by the King of Makkuria as the *eparch* or senior military commander of his own northernmost province facing Egypt. Elsewhere the urban *ahdath* militias declined still further, though Aleppo apparently still had a *Shihnat al-Shurta* or chief of police in 1240.[339]

The Ayyubid Sultanate of Egypt was overthrown by its own *mamluk* troops, specifically those of the élite Bahriya Regiment which, after a brief interregnum, went on to establish their own government in what is now known as the Mamluk Sultanate. Initially limited to Egypt, this Mamluk Sultanate subsequently took control of what remained of Ayyubid territory in Syria south and west of the Euphrates while Ayyubid territory beyond that river, in the Jazira, was largely incorporated into the Mongol Il-Khanate.

Like Ayyubid and Fatimid forces before them, the armies of the Mamluk Sultanate were almost always assumed by the Crusader and other European foes to be much bigger than they really were. On the other hand the purchase of slaves to be trained and freed as *mamluk* soldiers did increase after the Mamluk coup. This was clearly the case with *mamlaka sultaniya* or 'royal' *mamluks*. Under Sultan Baybars I (1260–77) they rose to some 4,000 with the rest of the army consisting of another 12,000 ordinary *mamluks* and an estimated 24,000 *Halqa* free or non-*mamluk* troops.[340] Under Sultan Qalawun (1279–90) the *mamlaka sultaniya* numbered 6,000 to 7,000, forming the élite of the army which retook Acre in 1291 and brought the Latin or Crusader Kingdom of Jerusalem to an end.

A fascinating document to survive from this period is the *Devise des Chemins de Babiloine*, a Hospitaller intelligence report drawn up for a proposed crusade against the Mamluk Sultanate and written around the time of the fall of Acre. It was clearly the work of someone with accurate information and military understanding, perhaps being based upon a translation of a Mamluk administrative source. Nevertheless, the information in the *Devise des Chemins de Babiloine* reflects an earlier moment of relative Mamluk weakness.[341] One section of the report stated:

> First, the Sultan provides from his own household 1,000 cavalry, heavy and light. Then there are twenty-four great emirs, 'chieftains of the host' each of whom can field one hundred cavalry. Then there are eighty emirs of which some bring with them sixty cavalry, some fifty, some forty, and the sum total of this category amounts to 4,000 cavalry. Then there are thirty emirs, each of whom is followed by ten horsemen. Then there are seventy *elmecceden* [Arabic *al-muqaddimun*] and each *elmecceden* brings with him forty horsemen and they are called '*la Bahrye*' [the Bahriya regiment] who are always around the tent of the sultan. Then there are the other *elmeccedens* to the number of eighty, each of whom brings with him forty horsemen. And you should know that all the emirs can certainly produce from their *mesnies* [a French term meaning retinues] approximately a further 1,000 cavalry and more. The total sum for Babylon [Cairo or Egypt in general] is 14,700. And all the men-at-arms who are listed above are divided among the twenty-four chieftains also listed above. And that is the strength of Babylon ... The power of Syria; firstly in Gaza is 700 cavalry, then at Safed 900 cavalry, at Damascus 4,000 cavalry, at Hims 300 cavalry, at Hama 1,000 cavalry, at Aleppo 2,000 cavalry at Tripoli 1,000 cavalry. The sum for Syria is 9,900. The sum total of the power of the Sultan in Babylon and Syria is 24,600 men, of which at least 15,000 are so poor that they can hardly maintain their horses.[342]

Despite the fact that the Mongol threat remained, the numbers of *mamluk* soldiers in the Mamluk Sultanate appears to have dropped during the fourteenth century.[343] Nevertheless a rich and powerful Mamluk *amir* of the late thirteenth and early fourteenth century could himself have a retinue of 300 to 800 slave-recruited *mamluks*.[344] The organization of the first armies of the Mamluk Sultanate was the same as that of the late Ayyubid Sultanate that had been overthrown, and no significant structural changes were introduced until after the Mamluks' great victory over the Mongols at 'Ayn Jalut in 1260.[345] Baybars I became Sultan shortly after that battle; and it was he who created a new Mamluk army.

For the rest of the thirteenth century and throughout most of the fourteenth, the central or main armies of this remarkable military force consisted of three elements; the *mamlaka sultaniya* or *mamalik sultaniya*, the *umara'* or *amir*'s troops and the *halqa* recruited as free men. There had been comparable divisions within the Ayyubid armies, with each being of theoretically equal status. In the Mamluk Sultanate this was no longer the case, having been replaced by a clear hierarchy with the *mamalik sultaniya* at the top and the *halqa* at the bottom. The *mamalik sultaniya* themselves consisted of several elements; the *mushtarawat ajlab* or *julban mamluks* of the ruling Sultan, the *mustakhdamun* who were *mamluks* acquired by the current Sultan but not purchased by him, including the *qaranis* who had been raised by a former ruler and the *sayfiya* whose amir had died or been dismissed. These *mustakhdamun* had, of course, already been freed as fully trained soldiers by the time they were transferred to their new leader. Though the *mushtarawat* were the *mamluks* of the ruling Sultan, the *qaranis* were older and more experienced, so there was often antagonism between these two groups.[346]

The first and second major groups were, rather confusingly, also grouped together as the Mamalik al-Sultan.[347] The Khassakiya were the ruling Sultan's personal bodyguard of trained and freed *mamluks* and as such formed the élite of the *mamlaka sultaniya*. Based in the Citadel of Cairo they acted as pages to the Sultan and as junior military secretaries while also continuing their military training and making useful political contacts for their own future careers. In fact very few *mamluk* soldiers rose to become senior *amirs* unless they had been *khassakis*.[348] Nevertheless, the Khassakiya included in its ranks a few non-*mamluks* such as the chief military engineer.

The bulk of full-time troops in the Mamluk Sultanate were stationed in Lower (northern) Egypt, Upper (southern) Egypt and Syria. However, the relatively small size of the Mamluk military élite probably accounted for the elite largely being concentrated in Cairo. Those who were stationed in Syria served as followers of the *Kafils* and *Nayibs* or senior governors. These latter terms could themselves also overlap, the *Nayib al-Sultana* or Sultan's Deputy in Syria often also being called the *Kafil al-Mamlaka* or Defender of the Mamluk State.[349]

The terminology of smaller unit formations and officer ranks remained largely unchanged, though the precise meanings did alter over the decades. For example a *tulb* could now be a large military unit of around 1,000 men under a senior *amir*, or a personal entourage of *mamluk* soldiers.[350] The names given to several officer ranks have also caused confusion. During the Mamluk period the minimum number of soldiers led by an officer was based upon the value or revenues of his '*iqta* fief. So an *amir mi'a* (*amir* of 100) commanding 1,000 *halqa* troops on campaign might also be called a *muqaddam alf* (*muqaddam* of 1,000) or an *amir kabir* ('big' officer). An *amir arba'in* (*amir* of 40) or *amir tablkhana* could lead 100 soldiers while an *amir 'ashara* (*amir* of ten) actually led ten. Even so, these figures were probably an ideal rather than the reality by and during the fourteenth century.[351]

There were also other perhaps temporary ranks for officers commanding field units such as the 40 troopers led by a *muqaddamu al-halqa*.[352] Similarly an officer with the rank of *amir tablkhana* was on the same level as an *amir isfahsalar*, or might indeed be the same man; this rank normally being given to the leaders of Haj pilgrim caravans to and from Mecca and Medina. It was also given to the engineer in charge of the construction of large stone-throwing mangonels in Damascus for use against the Crusader fortress of Marqab, and this is unlikely to have been the only example of such ranking.[353] What is clear is that the Mamluk Sultanate's ranking system of 'Men of the Sword' allocated precise roles to senior officers in both Egypt and Syria. Furthermore, these men were supported by a highly developed and efficient bureaucracy and civilian administration.[354]

When Baybars I became Sultan in 1260, there were already large numbers of military refugees within Mamluk territory, including many ex-Ayyubid troops from Syria and the Jazira. The proportion that were sent back to those parts of Syria which came under the direct rule of the Mamluk Sultans after the battle of 'Ayn Jalut is unknown, but Baybars did not purge these Ayyubid remnants. Instead he incorporated them into his new army, many of these already trained soldiers entering the Halqa.[355] They included Kurdish troops, some of whose *amirs* rose to quite senior roles.[356]

Although a serious decline in the status of the Halqa really only started in the late thirteenth century,[357] the Halqa of the Mamluk Sultanate was very soon different from that of the Ayyubid period. Only about one-third of the army based in and around Cairo were Halqa whereas they now formed the bulk of troops in Syria. In both regions they received lower pay than both the Sultan's and the *amirs' mamluks*.[358] Of course Syria already differed from Egypt in having numerous indigenous soldiers and a centuries-old warlike tradition of self-defence. This, and the persistent threat from aggressive neighbours, led to the Mamluk Sultanate establishing a different system of local control and garrisons from that in largely peaceful Egypt. Whereas in the latter region the army was concentrated in Cairo with fewer garrisons in Alexandria and other places, Syria had numerous garrisons scattered across the country.

Furthermore, locally born or at least locally recruited free rather than *mamluk* soldiers played a much more important role in Syria than in Egypt. They included a much larger number of infantry, mainly from the cities but also from the peasants and semi-nomads, who proved useful in the mountain, hill and siege warfare which characterized most Syrian campaigns. As a result, these foot soldiers enjoyed greater prestige than elsewhere. Although it was still far lower than that of the cavalry, it contributed to a narrowing of the social gulf between local Syrians and foreign-born *mamluks*.

Within Mamluk Syria, troops fell into two main groups. The first and of higher prestige were those of the resident Mamluk governors and senior *amirs* in the main cities. Some were *mamluks* but many others were free recruits. The second and larger military group consisted of local *halqa* and the retinues of locally based junior *amirs*. The *'iqtas* allocated to the latter did not maintain more than 40 soldiers each. Nevertheless these local *amirs* formed a separate and formidable hierarchy within Syria. The Syrian Halqa similarly formed a proper standing army known as the *ajnad al-halqa* rather than a part-time militia.[359] These Halqa troops had a variety of important roles, including the garrisoning of seaports which was always an unpopular task amongst *mamluk* soldiers.[360] Nevertheless, the defence of the Syrian-Palestinian coast was considered so important that the Mamluk government settled a substantial number of military refugees from the Mongol conquests in this region. It was hoped they would remain a distinct fighting force but in the event they were soon assimilated by local communities.[361]

The role of tribal auxiliaries and *ahdath* urban militias remained important and those men involved were still organized in much the same way as earlier. This was particularly apparent in Syria, but in southern Egypt there was a significant change. Here tensions between the bedouin Arab tribes and the Mamluk government erupted into warfare, resulting in most of the tribes fleeing southward out of Mamluk territory. The Arabized Nubian Banu Kanz also tended to be more anti-Mamluk than otherwise, though there were occasional tense alliances between them.[362]

Much less is known about the organization of North African armies than those of Egypt or indeed of al-Andalus. Yet it is clear that their structures were simpler than both. It is also important to point out that cities played a vital military role here, as they did in virtually every corner of the medieval Islamic world. There has been much disagreement about the degree to which such Islamic cities, including the relatively small ones in North Africa, had a sense of corporate identity. Local patriotism would play an absolutely central role in the development of medieval Italian cities, including their military systems, and would be almost as significant elsewhere in medieval Europe. Yet most scholars have denied that Islamic cities developed anything similar.

This view has recently been disputed in a detailed study of the small but regionally important Libyan city and port of Tripoli. Known in Arabic as Trabalus al-Gharb or Western Tripoli to distinguish it from Trabalus al-Sham in what is now northern Lebanon, Libyan Tripoli was one of the first North African cities to become effectively independent in the eleventh century at a time of political fragmentation across the entire region. Such independence or autonomy would be maintained for centuries. Outside rulers including the Norman kings of Sicily would occasionally install small garrisons, as the Ottoman Turkish Sultans would do many centuries later, but the administration of the city was almost entirely left to the local authorities.[363] Even in the early fourteenth century, the citizens of Libyan Tripoli themselves saw to the defence and maintenance of the city's fortifications. They apparently willingly allocated a portion of their own taxes to repair the masonry and would do so as a matter of urgency when required.[364] How far Tripoli can be seen as typical of other Islamic cities, even within North Africa, is less clear. Yet the evidence suggests that it was not unique and that at least some localized urban defensive systems of this Libyan city could be found elsewhere within the medieval Islamic world.[365]

Further west, in what are now Tunisia and eastern Algeria, the armies of the Zirid and Hammadid *amirates* were organized along Fatimid lines, though being smaller and presumably simpler. They also had similarities with the forces of the earlier Aghlabid realm and of the Sanhaja Berber tribal confederation (see below) from which the Zirids had sprung. The Hafsid state which emerged in this same area as the huge Muwahhid state fragmented in the thirteenth century, maintained military structures which it had inherited from the Muwahhidun.[366] On the other hand the rising power of the Arab bedouin tribes who had been settling in this part of North Africa since the eleventh century considerably weakened the professional or 'official' army of the Hafsid state.[367] What impact this had on their organizational structure is less clear, and the Muwahhid heritage survived for several centuries.

While the Hafsid army may have increasingly relied upon tribal elements and tribal structures from the thirteenth and more particularly the fourteenth century onwards, the army of the Zayyanids to the west seems to have been largely tribal from the establishment of this state in the mid-thirteenth century. Based in Tlemsen in western Algeria, the Zayyanids proved to be a powerful rival of the Moroccan Marinids whose forces were again largely tribal.[368] The Zayyanids also drew strength from their close links with the Christian Kingdom of Aragon but this relationship does not seem to have had any impact on their military administration.

The Islamic conquest of Sicily had been almost entirely carried out by the *jund* armies of the North African Aghlabid state. As a consequence the *jund* system and its professional military personnel continued to dominate the island. Similarly, the splits between the higher status Arabs and the as yet lower status Berbers which had been a feature of the Aghlabid *jund* forces and the auxiliaries who accompanied them persisted within Sicily, as they did in North Africa.[369] This did not stop the island being divided into *iqlim* districts, each of which had its own *jund* provincial army.[370] This was still much the case when Sicily was conquered by the Normans in the later eleventh century and may have survived as the basis upon which local Sicilian Muslim troops were raised and organized by their new Norman rulers. It is even possible that the castle of Entella which, ruled by the daughter of the Islamic resistance hero Ibn 'Abbad and forming a base for several hundred infantry and cavalry, had itself been the military centre of one such *iqlim* military district.[371]

In the 'Further Maghrib' or Morocco, Berber military systems continued to dominate throughout the medieval period. Being essentially tribal, they were based upon the principle that every tribesman had some sort of military obligation. Consequently the states of this region were capable of fielding remarkably large armies. For example the Barghawata, who are sometimes regarded as a sub-group of the ill-defined Masmuda Berber tribal confederation from the eighth to eleventh century, were said to be able to summon 12,000 horsemen and played a significant military role in coastal regions of western Morocco until they were crushed by the Murabitun.[372]

The Sanhaja were another Berber tribal federation whose identity is clearer and whose territory lay in the western Sahara. Their forces, though still tribally organized, included two élites, one of cavalry and another of infantry. Meanwhile the bulk of tribesmen either served as ordinary, unarmoured light cavalry or as low status foot soldiers.[373] Before the rise of the Murabitun in the eleventh century, the Sanhaja appear to have been divided into rival 'drum-groups' or sub-tribes of which the Gudala and Lamtuna were two. In fact the Sanhaja tribal federation only seems to have remained united for a short time.[374] The Murabitun also used the tribal 'drum-group' as a method of military organization, these proving to be very effective fighting units in the early days of their empire.[375] It is also interesting to note that the *ettebel* or 'drum-group', from the Arabic word *tabl* meaning a large form of drum, still existed in Saharan Tuareg society in the nineteenth century.[376]

Yusuf Ibn Tashufin, who became the leader of the Murabitun movement in 1061 after the death of its preacher and founder 'Abd Allah Ibn Yasin, introduced a number of important changes to the army. Command had previously been based upon tribal or ethnic groups within what was in effect a religiously motivated confederation. Instead Yusuf Ibn Tashufin created a *hasham* permanent military formation recruited from African slaves and those regarded as 'foreigners'. The black African horsemen eventually numbered around 2,000. Within a few years he was also able to enlist a bodyguard of 50 non-Berber cavalry from elsewhere in North Africa, from Europe and from the Middle East.[377]

Despite being bitterly hostile to the preceding Murabitun, the Muwahhidun who overthrew them in the twelfth century still relied on tribal forces, this time largely recruited from Morocco. The bulk of the Muwahhid army was tribally structured and organized though its rulers, like the Murabitun rulers, soon had professional guard regiments structured along classic Islamic military lines. These included the élite *huffaz*[378] and, by the early thirteenth century, Christian mercenaries from the Iberian Peninsula. In 1220 a Portuguese 'prince' was in command of a 'Frankish' European guard unit based in Marrakesh while a Castilian or Leonese knight was in command of those at Meknes.[379]

Tribal forces played a part in Islamic al-Andalus but here military organization was more complex, more structured and in no real sense tribal. During the early eleventh century, at the end of the Umayyad Caliphate when al-Andalus was still united, the numbers of soldiers raised in the Cordoba region were said to number around 20,000 men while unspecified numbers came from outlying provinces. Towards the end of the eleventh century the neighbouring region of Sidonia was known to have raised 6,790 troops, representing one-third of the army of Cordoba which was by then merely one of the fragmented *ta'ifa* kingdoms of al-Andalus.[380]

A so-called 'Collection of Traditions' from this first *ta'ifa* period recalls the high point of Umayyad Caliphal power in Cordoba over a century earlier and in which the highest status local Andalusian cavalry seem to have been evolving into an almost European-style feudal landed aristocracy. How true this was in reality is less clear.[381] If such an indigenous Andalusian military aristocracy did exist, it would surely have included the resident *qa'id* commanders or leaders of the *thughur* frontier zones.[382] Several dynasties which ruled subsequent *ta'ifa* statelets in what had been the Andalusian *thughur* were from such *qa'id* families.

The eleventh and twelfth centuries were the period when *ribats* played their most important role in the defence of a now beleaguered al-Andalus. Manned by religiously motivated volunteers, their organization was remarkably similar to that of the earliest days of the Christian Crusading Military Orders.[383] Indeed the term *ribat*, which is generally taken to mean the fortification in which such volunteers served, may equally have applied to the unit of volunteers itself. Though probably declining in importance, this aspect of the defence of al-Andalus continued down to the time of the final Islamic state of Granada. Meanwhile the Military Orders and Almogávares on the Christian side of the border (see vol. 1) were, to a considerable extent, still mirrored by *thagri* frontiersmen and *murabit* volunteers along the frontiers of Granada in the late thirteenth and early fourteenth centuries.[384]

As already stated, most though not all of the Andalusian *ta'ifa* states were unmilitary and had tiny armies, some of only a few hundred men. During the first *ta'ifa* period their military organizations probably mirrored that of the Andalusian Umayyad Caliphate or that of the final period when the Caliphate had been dominated by Amirid *wazirs* or military dictators, though on a small scale. In eleventh-century Zirid Granada local *qa'ids* were responsible for organizing local military service while the defence and garrisoning of castles was organized by central government. All provincial governors also had to look to the defence of the *qasba* citadels in their main towns.[385]

The military organizations of the second *ta'ifa* period seem to have harked back to the first *ta'ifa* period rather than copying those of the collapsing Murabitun. In contrast, those of the third and final *ta'ifa* period had clearly been influenced by the now collapsing Muwahhid state. In southern Portugal, during each of these periods, major military estates sometimes clearly passed from father to son, rather like the fiefs of Western European aristocracy. They may indeed normally have done so, but not enough information survives to be certain.

Under the Muwahhidun the vulnerable and almost isolated Algarve region of southern Portugal probably formed a distinct military zone under its own *wali* or governor. It clearly seems to have become increasingly militarized; this being reflected in the fact that most surviving castles in the Algarve are largely of Islamic construction.[386] Here, during the final decades of Islamic rule, the main towns and cities each had a *qa'id* military governor in charge of garrisons which seem to have averaged about 100 men, but there is no evidence that the role of *qa'id* normally passed from one generation to the next.[387]

The Islamic military élite, perhaps now more correctly referred to as a resident military aristocracy, had similarly increased in number in the Valencia region at the eastern end of the Islamic–Christian frontier across the Iberian peninsula. Before the final collapse of Islamic rule they were holding numerous small castles dotted across the countryside. Many remained in place after the Christian conquest, to become Mudejar (Muslims under Christian rule) lords within the southern reaches of the Kingdom of Aragon and short-lived Kingdom of Murcia.[388] Here the Arabic term *qa'id* continued to be used, usually referring to an Islamic minor rural chieftain, castle *castellan* or governor. The Aragonese Christian conquerors themselves initially only took direct control of the most important or strategic castles.[389]

The Islamic military aristocracy of Valencia did not flee, nor was it expelled until after a series of failed uprisings against Aragonese rule. Nevertheless, it proved impossible to integrate the two military systems, Islamic and Christian. Despite some superficial similarities in the military field, Andalusian Islamic society was not really feudal. Instead it was built upon extended family networks and its social stratification or divisions were much less clearcut. Rather than depending upon a landed and largely rural military aristocracy, which only existed in al-Andalus to a limited degree and was only characteristic of a few periods, Islamic rulers looked to the cities for their military strength. Even the rural fortifications were of secondary significance.[390]

This would still be true of the last surviving *amirate* of Granada in its final centuries of existence. Here the army of the Nasrid ruling dynasty was organized through a Diwan al-Jaysh or Ministry of the Army which supervised and recorded territorial conscription as well as other military matters. Berber *ghuzat* volunteers from Morocco and Algeria were similarly under the general authority of this Diwan though a North African Berber militia, largely of Zanata tribal origin, had its own separate leadership based in Granada.[391] During the later thirteenth century, and probably other periods as well, the commander of the Andalusian part of Granada's army had the title or rank of *Wali*, while the commander of the North African ghuzat was known as the Shaykh al-Ghuzat.[392]

It is hardly surprising that military payment was of fundamental importance in Islamic armies as so many of the men involved were professional soldiers. Furthermore there was rarely anything truly comparable to the Western European feudal system within the medieval Islamic world. In those places where land was used as a means of rewarding military service or maintaining those who were expected to provide military service, its allocation had much more in common with the Byzantine *pronoia* than the western *fief*. Of course the *pronoia* itself probably owed a great deal to Islamic influence, though not necessarily to the Islamic system of *'iqta* fiefs in their fully developed form.

The *'iqta* should really be seen as a source of income rather than a piece of land and although the income in question could be the revenues of a designated territorial estate, it could equally be revenue from another source. Yet, territorial *'iqtas* seem to have become the norm as the years passed. This probably reflected changes, or indeed a decline, in the economy of the Islamic Middle East following the collapse of 'Abbasid Caliphal power in the tenth century. This, in turn, had reduced trade and perhaps more importantly the volume, value or trustworthiness of coinage. However, the most significant difference between an Islamic *'iqta* and a Western European fief was that the *'iqta* still belonged to the government in a much more real sense than the *fief* 'belonged' to a European ruler as the head of a feudal pyramid. The *'iqta* could be, and frequently was, taken back by the government, usually to be reallocated to someone else. Similarly, *muqta'* or holders of *'iqtas* often found their allocations being changed; sometimes as a result of promotion, or increasing political favour, or the reverse. Such changes might be for simple administrative convenience, as a result of a government overhaul of the *'iqtas* or changes in their value, or because a man had been permanently transferred to another part of the state. The Islamic *'iqta* system was, in fact, a remarkably flexible and efficient way of rewarding loyal supporters, whether they were military men or not.

In his *Siyasat Nama*, written for the Great Seljuk Sultan in 1091, Nizam al-Mulk pointed out that in 'olden times' there were no *'iqtas* and that troops were paid four times a year with cash and various supplies or necessities. In fact he was referring to the classic age of the 'Abbasid Caliphate. The Buyid dynasty which ruled most of Iran after the 'Abbasids but before the Seljuks used the *'iqta* system, though only in a limited manner. Nizam al-Mulk also claimed that the Seljuks' great rivals, the Ghaznawids, still paid their army in the old way. He may, however, have been overstating the case.

In fact Nizam al-Mulk regarded the use of *'iqta* fiefs as an inferior, though sometimes necessary, system of reward. He stated that, although the Seljuks made considerable use of *'iqtas*, some of their élite troops still received cash payments. He also warned that if men awarded *'iqtas* were absent from their posts this must be reported at once, implying that possession of such a fief could divert a soldier's attention away from his primary military duties.[393] Where Turcoman tribal warriors were concerned, rewards usually came in the form of booty from offensive raiding, though they were also expected to defend the states' border against enemy attacks.

This was very clearly the case in the Seljuk Sultanate of Rum where frontier defence against Byzantine or other raids initially, and perhaps largely, fell to the Turcoman tribes. In some cases such warriors may have received payment from their own chiefs, but not normally from the central government. For all these reasons the Turcoman tribal warriors were difficult for a Sultan to control.[394] In contrast some of their senior men were allocated *'iqta* fiefs which were not normally available to paid mercenaries, at least not in the Sultanate of Rum. The overall importance of the *'iqta* system in Turkish Anatolia remains a matter of debate because they may have been allocated to senior *ghulams*. In fact it has been suggested that *muqta'* or holders of *'iqtas* might actually have formed the core of the Seljuk Sultanate of Rum's 'Ancient Army' by the 1230s.[395] The relationship between the Anatolian Seljuk *'iqta* and the, very important, Ottoman Turkish *timar* system of fiefs is also unclear. Some degree of influence or even continuity might be assumed, but it is just as likely that the Byzantine *pronoia* lay behind the Ottoman later *timar* and may have been a more important predecessor.

The *'iqta* system was in use in northern Syria by the late eleventh century and the arrival of the Seljuk Turks merely increased its importance.[396] Here the leaders of the small *askar* permanent forces of local eleventh- and twelfth century rulers were usually supported by such fiefs,[397] though the *'iqtas* themselves were not expected to produce specific revenue.[398] Indeed they varied considerably in value and physical size but were still expected to allow the *'iqta* holder to carry out his expected duties and to maintain a suitable retinue.

The same was probably the case in the Jazira and perhaps southern Syria. In Damascus there were, however, several different methods of payment or reward during the first half of the twelfth century. The *jamakiya* was regular payment but only to regular *askar* troops and probably on a monthly basis. The *'iqta* appears to have been used for provincial *jund* forces, not in the city of Damascus or even in the surrounding irrigated and fertile Ghuta area but further afield. Thus *'iqtas* are recorded in Hims in central Syria, in the Hawran of what are now southern

Syria and northern Jordan, as well as in southern Jordan at Ma'ab and al-Jibal east of the Dead Sea, Wadi Musa near Petra and south of the Dead Sea.[399]

More details are known about payment in the Syrian army of Nur al-Din a generation or so later. Here a slave-recruited *ghulam* of the prestigious household troops got a *barak* or annual salary of 700 to 1,200 *dinars* for his equipment plus ten animals, horses, mules and camels. This would supposedly enable him to campaign for a certain number of months every year.[400] Much less is known about the payment of lower prestige *ahdath* urban militias, but those of eleventh-century Aleppo sometimes received an annual payment and, in troubled times, occasionally demanded more.[401]

The sometimes astonishing amount of detailed information about the larger, and perhaps more bureaucratic, Fatimid armies of Egypt show that if a soldier died, his name would be removed from the state's military registers. However, a man could also be moved from the cavalry to the infantry registers and vice-versa. His changed status would be noted and his pay altered accordingly. Many aspects of this system were continued throughout the Ayyubid period and into that of the Mamluk Sultanate.[402] On the other hand the Fatimid Caliphate's system of pensions for old or wounded soldiers seems to have disappeared under Saladin.[403] Under the Fatimids these state pensions for soldiers and their families proved very expesnive but had a major beneficial impact upon Egyptian society.[404]

In other respects the payment of Fatimid troops was done through the Diwan al-Jaysh or Army Ministry which was itself staffed by civilians.[405] Nasir-i Khusrau, who visited Egypt in 1047, wrote that each Fatimid soldier in Cairo was paid 20 *dinars*,[406] perhaps each month. This was notably less than the élite *ghulams* of Nur al-Din's army in the twelfth century but was a reasonable salary. Not that cash payment was always on time or adequate; failings or delay occasionally leading to unrest in the ranks.[407] Increasing financial problems probably lay behind an increasing use of *'iqtas* for officers from the mid-eleventh century onwards.[408]

In fact there appear to have been four systems of payment in Fatimid forces for four different categories of troops. Those assigned to fortified places and assimilated into the local area were paid directly by the treasury. Those stationed in one area but liable to be moved around by the government were paid in a variety of ways and seemingly included men who could alternate between the categories of cavalry and infantry, including the high status Hujariyyah. The payment of professional soldiers categorized as *'iqta jayshi* changed as a result of Fatimid military reforms, largely in the eleventh century. In the earlier system these men included Berbers, Turks, sub-Saharan Africans, Armenians and non-bedouin Arabs. In this case an *'iqta* was allocated to each individual soldier. Following the reforms, however, a new system called the *'iqta i'tidad* allocated a presumably larger *'iqta* to a named officer who was then expected to support a specified number of soldiers. This was the *'iqta* system inherited and continued by the Ayyubid Sultans.[409]

Although the Fatimid heritage was clear in the Ayyubid armies, most troops were now paid in kind or supplies and with an *'iqta*. Both forms of reward came through the Diwan al-Jaysh Army Ministry.[410] Saladin himself had gradually transferred the *'iqtas* allocated to Fatimid troops to his own men and also created more as land became available. Later in his reign he also established a system of *'iqtas* specifically to support the Egyptian navy and its personel.[411] Under the Ayyubid Sultan a son could inherit the military status of his father, which may indeed have been the case for many years. There were even occasions when the son of a *mamluk* did so, though this was not normal practice. Even so, sons did not have the right to inherit their fathers' *'iqta* fiefs; any such inheritance remaining a privilege rather than a right.[412]

In a few cases we know the size or value of such Ayyubid *'iqtas*. For example, in 1229 an *'iqta* consisting of the Muwaar area in the eastern provinces was expected to support 100 cavalrymen. The man who held this *'iqta* also had another in Egypt which supported 250 cavalrymen.[413] Further snippets of information concerning the thirteenth-century Ayyubid dynasties in Syria indicate that the commander of the army of the small sultanate of Salkhad in southern Syria had an *'iqta* worth 22,000 *dirhams* a year or 36 *dinars* a month, which was a substantial sum.[414] Surviving Ayyubid *tawqi* or documents allocating an *'iqta* instruct the *muqta'* or holder to 'be prepared', and to keep only brave men and horses under his command, the men in question being referred to as *ajnad*. Some *tawqi* even give instructions concerning clothing and appearance.[415]

Those unfortunate enough to lose their *'iqtas*, sometimes for poor service, were known as *battal* during the Ayyubid period. They could nevertheless be re-employed with a money salary rather than a fief. Some *battal* were included in the expedition to Yemen in 1182 and large numbers were also present at Saladin's siege of Acre in 1190.[416] Further detailed information about payment in Saladin's army during the early years of his reign is found in a text by al-Mammati. This stated that Turkish, Kurdish and Turcoman regular troops were paid what was called the full rate, while the ex-Fatimid *amirs* and *'iqta* holders of the Arab Banu Kinana tribe who had came from southern Palestine after the fall of Ascalon in 1153 received 'half rate'. So did the 'Asaqila former garrison troops of Ascalon and other soldiers who had been on the Fatimid military registers. Naval troops received a 'quarter rate' though another contradictoray source in al-Maqrizi reported that naval pay was increased from 'five-eighths' to 'three-quarters' of the full rate under Saladin.[417]

Yet other sources indicate that, in Saladin's army, élite armoured *tawashi* cavalry received from 120 to 1,000 *dinars* a year according to rank, while cavalry of lower status received 10 *dinars* a month, that is 120 *dinars* a year. The average annual pay in 1181 was 429 *dinars*, but there were such huge differentials between troops of different status, and between varying ranks, that such a figure is almost meaningless. On the other hand it is clear that military wages increased under the Ayyubids, as they did under the other successor states of the Great Seljuk Sultanate.[418] One thing that can be said with reasonable certainty, is that military pay generally compared favourably with that of other sections of society outside the ruling class.

Pay in the armies of the Mamluk Sultanate was similarly based upon existing Islamic systems though there does seem to have been an attempt to regularize and simplify it. As a result professional, full-time *mamluk* troops could receive *jamakiya* or monthly pay, an annual or half-yearly *kiswa* allowance to cover clothing expenses, and the *lahm* which was a daily meat ration, plus a *nafaqa* additional payment from the Sultan on the eve of a campaign.[419] Furthermore they received an *'aliq* for their horses consisting of fodder twice weekly, normally in the form of barley but sometimes as cash for horsefeed.[420]

The unification of Egypt and most of Syria by the Mamluk Sultan Baybars and his successors led to a rationalization of the *'iqta* system which now became more coherent. This was reflected in Mamluk officer ranks with such men being expected, at least in theory, to maintain military retinues of 10, 40 or 100 soldiers, with the *'iqtas* of very senior officers supposedly supporting 250 fighting men. This was, in fact, the first time that a formal link had been made between the size of an *'iqta* and the military rank of its holder.[421] It is also interesting to note that the smallest Mamluk allocation of pasture in Egypt was half a *feddan*, approximately half an acre which was probably just enough to feed one horse.[422]

The *'iqta* system had been used in Tunisia and the central Maghrib since at least the Aghlabid dynasty in the ninth century, though only to the same limited extent seen in the eastern Islamic world during this early period. It was also introduced to Sicily by the Aghlabids when they initiated the conquest of that island.[423] Thereafter it remained a fundamental aspect of military payment and is believed to have been incorporated into, or have formed the foundation of, the Norman system of military fiefs in twelfth-century Sicily.

In Morocco and other western regions of North Africa, it appears to have been the Murabitun who first introduced the idea of rewarding military service with allocations of land. This was later than the same process in the Middle East or further east, but developed into much the same sort of *'iqta* system.[424] As such it was continued by the Muwahhidun and their successors.

The *'iqta* appears to have been similarly late in reaching al-Andalus, or it may have been very early and then have either died out or been considerably modified. For instance, in the early ninth century the Umayyad ruler of Cordoba, al-Hakam I, reformed the traditional 'Syrian Umayyad' army which existed in al-Andalus when the new 'Spanish Umayyad' dynasty took power in the mid-eighth century.

As a result the descendants of *jundi* soldiers in the still territorially organized *jund* armies mostly lost their *'iqta* benefices. Instead the majority were thenceforth paid salaries in cash.[425] However, this earlier allocation of land does not seem to have been quite the same as the later *'iqta*. It may have been more permanent and seems initially to have been used a means of encouraging the recolonization of 'dead land'.[426]

In eleventh-century Zirid Granada the *jund* army received regular pay,[427] and this continued to be the case throughout the remaining years of Islamic civilization in al-Andalus, despite some seemingly limited introduction of the *'iqta* system and the emergence of permanent, heritable family estates which had much in common with later medieval Western European systems of land-holding.

FLAGS, INSIGNIA AND MUSIC

Flags, banners, other forms of military insignia and above all military music, were all highly developed in medieval Islamic civilization. In each respect the Muslims drew upon a variety of earlier traditions, not least the Arabs' own distinctive tribal banners.[428] The Romano-Byzantine heritage of various parts of the Mediterranean world may have played a lesser role, whereas those of the pre-Islamic Sassanian Empire in Iran and the pre-Islamic Turks of Central Asia were far more important.[429] Visual emblems such as flags, and to some extent clothing, similarly drew upon an Islamic tradition of colour coding. In this black was associated with the Mahdi, a religious figure who would one day bring justice to the world, and also with the 'Abbasids. White became the colour of the Fatimids having earlier been associated with the Umayyads. Red was the colour of martyrdom and of the Imam Husayn, one of the most important figures in Shi'a history, but was also used in public performances to identify a villain or prostitute. In earlier years red had been used by the fundamentalist and reformist Khariji movement while in India it later came to identify Sunni Muslims. Only later did green become particularly associated with the Shi'a 'Alids. Meanwhile, blue or purple, never very popular colours in Islamic society, represented mourning.[430]

One feature above all others which distinguished Islamic banners was the dominant role of written inscriptions. These were usually, though not invariably, of a religious nature and were far more important than abstract or representational motifs. Nor were banners normally used on their own as indications of political or religious affiliation. It seems to have been more common for a ruler or a spiritual leader to indicate or recognize the status of an individual by giving him a variety of symbolic objects. This was the case in literary fiction as well as historical reality. Hence, when the Caliph gave the Turkish tribal leader Melik Danishment 'permission to conquer Rum' or Byzantium in the *Danishmandname* poetic epic, the associated ceremony involved a donation of horses, robes of honour and assorted banners. The latter included a 'Caliphal *sancaq* and '*alam*', the '*sancaq* of Battal Gazi' and the ''*alam* of Abu'l-Muslim'. In addition Melik Danishment was given large *kus* kettledrums and smaller *naqar* side-drums.[431]

In the far west of the Islamic world, in al-Andalus, the keeping of banners in mosques and the fixing of them to their poles in a solemn ceremony at the start of a military expedition were normal practice at the time of the Umayyad Caliphate of Cordoba. Both continued until at least the Muwahhid period, being described in 1190, and are likely to have remained common practice until the fall of Granada in 1492.[432]

Medieval Islamic illustrations show that such flags came in a variety of shapes and sizes while written sources indicate that the most usual were the *liwa* and the *raya*. Furthermore, the medieval Islamic world's willingness to adopt styles of banner from other cultures was indicated in a number of ways, some of them rather surprising. One of the most remarkable must surely be the windsock military banners used by the Fatimid Caliphate. This dramatic device is normally associated with Late Roman armies, having been copied by them from their steppes neighbours and foes. Like these pre-Islamic versions, the Fatimid windsocks included an almost sculptural element that might be thought to run counter to the iconoclasm of Islamic civilization. In reality the Muslims' abhorrence of three-dimensional lifelike representation was much less apparent in medieval Islamic art than it would be in later centuries.

Even so the Fatimid windsock banners remain remarkable. One was described in detail as being made of red or yellow brocade, and others having 'lions with round discs in their mouths to catch the air'.[433] In the absence of information to the contrary it seems possible, even likely, that the banners resembling trousers used by Saladin's army during the period of the Third Crusade would have been constructed along similar lines. If, as seems to have been the case, such a form of banner had fallen out of use in western if not central Europe by this time, might not a French or English observer have likened a windsock to a man's hose?

A rigid emblem, usually called an '*alam*, was often attached to the tops of poles with or without flags, this first clearly appearing in Islamic art during the tenth century.[434] By the twelfth century *amir* officers in Nur al-Din's Syrian army were using such '*alams* to rally their men in battle.[435] Various shapes were known, ranging from a rectangle which, in later surviving examples, almost certainly represents the page of a book. Pages from the Koran had, in fact, been attached to the heads of lances as early as the battle of Siffin in 657, though on that occasion it was a call to negotiate by the side that felt it was losing in a conflict between two competing Islamic armies.

Another popular shape was what has become known as the 'Hand of Fatima'. Some historians have even suggested that this may have been used in pre-Islamic Arabia in much the same way that military eagles were used in earlier Roman armies. In medieval Islam, however, the 'Hand of Fatima' eventually became associated with the Shi'a martyrs Husayn and Hassan.[436]

The history of the *hilal* or crescent as an Islamic motif is more complicated; and in many ways is more misleading. Its earliest appearance in the Islamic world was with pre-Islamic or non-Islamic connotations. Later the *hilal* was adopted as a ruling rather than religious symbol both in 'Abbasid Baghdad and by some Seljuk rulers. It may also have been used slightly earlier by the Fatimids, but again as a mark of secular rather than religious authority. The crescent was certainly used as a heraldic blazon in the late thirteenth and early fourteenth century Mamluk Sultanate, but again in a secular context. Meanwhile *hilal* crescents had also been mounted on the tops of some mosques since the eleventh century. This was, of course, in a religious context.

The *hilal* remained just one of several Islamic religious symbols well into the Ottoman period and seems to have been first adopted as the most important abstract Islamic religious symbol by Christian artists, especially when trying to identify people, places or structures as Ottoman. Indeed it was not until the nineteenth century that the Islamic world fully accepted the crescent as 'their' symbol, and even then it continued to be associated with the Ottoman Turks in particular and Sunni Muslims in general; not really with Shi'a at all.[437]

Another device was the *tuq* horse or yak tail which was introduced to the Islamic Middle East from the steppes by Turks and Mongols. Though used by various armies in several parts of the medieval Islamic world, this *tuq* or *tug* remained an essentially Turkish insignia, often added to other forms of *'alam* and banner.

Heraldry is normally assumed to have been a Western European concept that was not even fully adopted by the similarly Christian Byzantines. In fact there is compelling evidence to suggest that simple proto-heraldic patterns as well as colours were used in the Islamic world at an early date, though they never evolved into a fully developed heraldic system.[438] The latter, in the way that it was understood in Europe from the later Middle Ages onwards, had a recognized system of authorities who could not only identify heraldic symbols and their users, but regulate the adoption of these symbols and arbitrate when quarrels arose. No such system of heraldic authority seems to have existed within the Islamic world. For example, senior *amirs* and officers in the Ayyubid and Mamluk Sultanates could adopt whatever armorial symbols they wanted. There was no controlling body of heralds as in Western Europe, not even, apparently, within a single state.[439]

Similarly the range of symbols used in the Mamluk Sultanate was very limited while the symbols themselves were assembled in a very specific, and again very limited, manner. Compared with previous centuries when Arab, Seljuk Turkish and Ayyubid rulers or governors had used birds of prey, animals such as lions and even hunting dogs as carved motifs on fortified gates,[440] the Mamluks rarely used animals in this symbolic manner. Plant motifs such as the rose and fleur-de-lys, however, do appear. The latter had occasionally been used as a perhaps symbolic piece of architectural decoration since the Umayyad early eighth century.

The most notable exception was Sultan Baybars I whose distinctive lion crops up across Egypt and Syria.[441] In addition to pieces of decorated metalwork, the 'Lion of Baybars' has recently been found painted on helmets, a military saddle and various other items of warlike equipment from a castle overlooking the Euphrates and a tower in the Citadel of Damascus.[442] Other senior Mamluk *amirs* used such objects as bows, horns or trumpets, polo-sticks, swords and napkins, each believed to reflect their role when they were junior *mamluks*. After the death of Baybars I, subsequent Mamluk Sultans increasingly limited themselves to inscribed cartouches as symbols of their status, domination or ownership.

Nothing comparable seems to have been used in North Africa, and the situation was also different in al-Andalus. Here early Islamic proto-heraldic designs including the *shatrang* or chessboard pattern had been used since at least the tenth century, long before 'checky' was adopted as one of the earliest Western European heraldic motifs. Subsequently other simple geometric patterns were used on military banners in a way that was rarely if ever seen in Islamic countries further east.

It seems highly likely that such Andalusian flags influenced the first stirrings of European heraldry, but it is equally likely that Western European heraldry subsequently turned the tables by influencing later medieval Islamic Andalusian military flags. The fourteenth-century Nasrid rulers of Granada were even 'given' a coat-of-arms by their nominal suzerain, the King of Castile. Though Islamicized with an Arabic inscription across the middle, this coat-of-arms was never worn or carried in the way that a Spanish nobleman or knight would display his emblem. Instead it seems to have been confined to walls and ceramics as a small and discreet element swamped by more typical 'Moorish' patterns.[443]

While there were no strictly defined uniforms within medieval Islamic armies, there was a well-established code of dress which supposedly governed what individual people wore. This was clearly more important among the élites than ordinary people and was accepted or imposed to varying degrees according to geographical location, period and culture. The 'Abbasid Caliphate had been characterized by particularly strong dress codes for both military and civilians, at least during its period of greatest splendour. Even so, this had probably been a phenomenon of the central regions, especially Iraq and Baghdad itself, rather than the outlying provinces. Rules or fashions also broke down in the later tenth and eleventh centuries with observers noting that even the prestigious descendants of the Ansar 'Companions of the Prophet Muhammad' no longer wore their distinctive yellow turbans.[444] It is unlikely to have been the only such sartorial change.

A more consistent aspect of the dress of senior civilians and military individuals was the *tiraz*. This band of fabric around the upper sleeves of various sorts of outer garment indicated affiliation or loyalty to a particular Caliph and, by this means, to the state or ruler who recognized the spiritual authority of that Caliph. It traditionally carried an inscription, usually in the form of a supplication to God followed by the name of the Caliph, his personal title or *laqab* and various benedictory phrases. Later and more elaborate types could be made of tapestry or be embroidered, painted or printed.[445] While the distinctively Islamic *tiraz* remained in use in much of the Middle East, Egypt and the western Islamic lands throughout most of the medieval period, it seemingly fell out of use in Iran during the Mongol period.[446]

Whereas there is no evidence of uniform military dress in particular armies, there is some reason to believe that particular colours were adopted by, or associated with certain high prestige units, regiments or the retinues of particular rulers. In other respects it was the style and cut of a soldier's or officer's garments that indicated his ethnic origin or current employment. Thus the largely Arab armies of early eleventh-century Syria would not be dressed in the same manner as the largely Turkish armies of the same area a century later. Equally, there were highly visible differences between military costume in the late thirteenth-century Mamluk Sultanate of Egypt and Syria, and those of the armies of Marinid Morocco or al-Andalus.

By the thirteenth century there was clearly considerable Christian influence from northern Iberia upon the military costume as well as the military equipment of early Nasrid Granada. The chronicler Ibn Sa'id described these armies as being 'the same as the Christians', even to the extent of their officers wearing red capes. Ibn Sa'id was further shocked to have personally seen Ibn Hud, the early thirteenth-century Islamic ruler of Murcia, going bareheaded in public.[447] Judging by surviving art from the period of the later Umayyad Caliphate of Cordoba, this otherwise unislamic lack of headcovering had also been common in the tenth century. In the early fourteenth century, another chronicler and commentator, Ibn al-Khatib wrote of Granada's army that:

> They wear long hauberks, hang their shields [on *guiges*], have ungilded helmets, have large iron [bladed] lances, saddles with ugly horsetail coverings [the rear part of caparisons] which make them one with the horse. These are the distinctive signs of their equipment and a mark by which they are known.[448]

The latter remark may also indicate that the horses' caparisons served a heraldic purpose, just as they did amongst the Christian knights of Spain during the same period.

Iran probably had the strongest or longest tradition of military music in the Middle East, although military music also had ancient roots among the Central Asian Turks. Both would have a profound impact upon the development of such music within the Islamic world during the medieval period and later. Musicians, including military or court bands, were a popular subject in medieval Islamic art which, though usually highly stylized, does give some indication of the sort of instruments used.

The late eleventh-century Syrian Arab *ahdath* urban militias often 'identified themselves' with fifes and drums,[449] perhaps indicating that they used such musical instruments to maintain cohesion in battle. The Turkish *Danishmandname*, originally written in mid-thirteenth century Seljuk Anatolia, mentioned *naqar* drums, *nefir* trumpets and *zurna* large clarinets being used to summon men to battle when referring to both Turks and Greeks.[450] The scholar al-Harawi, in a military treatise written for one of Saladin's immediate successors highlighted the importance of music and display in warfare, but also noted that they were not very effective against a determined foe.[451]

Although the term *tablkhana*, meaning an arsenal of drums and other musical instruments, was occasionally used during the Ayyubid period it seems to have become rarer in the Mamluk Sultanate. Nevertheless military music continued to play a major role, as noted by Fidenzio of Padua whose book on how to regain the Holy Land was written for the Pope in 1291. Fidenzio was clearly something of an expert on the Mamluks, noting that the 'Saracens', as he called the Mamluk army, used trumpets to reassemble military formations that had become dispersed in battle.[452]

Most performances by Islamic military bands consisted, naturally enough, of battle-songs and marches. In fact some of the music played today by the recreated Ottoman Mehter is ancient or traditional, being based on the music of Sufi Islamic mystics or dervishes.[453] One legend maintains that the famous Ottoman Turkish Tabl-i Ali-i Osman 'Great Ottoman Band', or as it is better known today the Mehterhane, began when the Seljuk Sultan of Rum recognized Osman Gazi, the eponymous founder of the Ottoman state, as an autonomous *amir* late in the thirteenth century. Part of this recognition ceremony entailed sending Osman various insignia of authority, including a large *kös* war-drum, *nekkare* small double kettle-drums and a *çevgen* set of bells mounted on a staff. The Seljuk Sultan also sent musicians to play them, their first concert traditionally being held at Eskişehir where, to show his respect for the Seljuk Sultan, Osman Gazi remained standing while the musicians played. All subsequent Ottoman rulers stood when the Mehter played until Sultan Mehmet II, the Conqueror of the Byzantine capital of Constantinople, declared that, 'one should not stand in respect to a ruler who has been dead two hundred years. This sort of respect does not suit the magnificence of the great Ottoman Empire,' and so abolished the custom.

Earlier bands would probably have been in many respects similar to the Ottoman Mehter, which remains the traditional Islamic military band about which most is known. Its wind instruments consisted of two kinds of seven-hole clarinet made from plum or apricot wood; the low pitched *kaba zurna* and the higher pitched *cura*. The *kurenay* or *boru* Turkish trumpet was a relatively simple brass instrument only used for keeping rhythm. Mehter *düdüğü* or Mehter 'whistles' sometimes completed the wind section. *Nekkare* doubled kettle-drums or 'tom-toms', *zil* cymbals, *davul* ordinary two-sided drums and the massive *kös* 'bass drum' formed the percussion section.

Traditionally the *kös* players were a separate musical organization only employed by the Sultan himself. There were, in fact, several sizes of *kös*; those carried on horseback, a middle sized for a camel and the largest mounted on an elephant, though all could be placed on the ground to form the final piece in a full Mehterhane. The Çevkâni singers who are now such a striking feature of the revived Turkish Mehter were only added in the late eighteenth century.

Drums seem to have played an even more prominent role in the military music of the western regions of the Islamic world, in North Africa and al-Andalus. Whereas 'Abd Allah Ibn Yasin, the religious reformer and founder of the Murabitun in what are now Mauritania and Senegal, disapproved of the traditional drums used in this region, his successor as leader of the Murabitun reintroduced them. In fact the massive and numerous war drums of the Murabitun became a vital aspect of the psychological tactics they used against their Christian foes within the Iberian Peninsula.[454] So much so that even the French, north of the Pyrenean mountains, knew about the Moors' *tabor* drums which then featured in the late eleventh century *Song of Roland*.[455] The subsequent Moroccan Muwahhid dynasty made even greater use of massed war drums, the largest and most important such instrument being kept in the Burj Tidaf or 'Watchman's Tower' of Tin Mal, the spiritual birthplace of the Muwahhidun movement high in the Atlas Mountains.[456]

MOTIVATION AND MORALE

Religion was a primary motivation for military action in the medieval Islamic world, just as it was in Christian Western Europe and the Byzantine Empire. It was not, of course, the only such driving force, yet it is clear that governments often tried to describe their wars as *jihads* in order to get their armies and peoples motivated. Similarly, having a war sanctioned as a *jihad* by sufficiently senior religious figures was rather like the clerical blessing of weapons in Christian Europe.[457] During this period the waging of *jihad*, which was always defensive in theory if not always in practice, was an important source of legitimacy for Islamic rulers, especially as so many of the latter achieved power through debatable means. This having been said, warlike or active *jihad* always remained secondary in terms of religious merit to spiritual *jihad* which was the individual struggle to lead a moral life.[458] The former was often called 'lesser *jihad*' and the latter 'greater *jihad*', as had been the case since the days of the Prophet Muhammad himself.

The Turks and their rulers were sometimes also motivated by another very different and initially pagan view of their place in the world. They, unlike the Arabs and the Persians, brought with them from pre-Islamic Inner Asia what might be described as a folk myth in which Turks were destined to one day dominate the world. This world view, inherited by or shared with the Mongols, probably dated back far beyond recorded history but it first appeared in written form in the earliest surviving version of the *Oghuz Epic*, in thirteenth century Uighur script. In this the Oghuz *Qaghan* or supreme ruler conquers the four corners of the world. Many of the symbols and emblems in this ancient Central Asian Turkish epic and its associated traditions were brought into the Islamic world by the Seljuk Turks in the eleventh century. Thereafter they continued to have an impact upon Turkish Islamic culture for many centuries, especially in military and secular fields though also upon Turkish forms of *sufi* Islamic mysticism. It is also interesting to note that these symbols and emblems can often be traced back to Indian iconographic influence via the Buddhism adopted by many Turks before their conversion to Islam.[459]

The ancient pagan Turkish belief that they would one day rule the world was Islamized into a belief that the Turks were a chosen people, selected by God to defend Islam. This came to be reflected in a supposed *hadith* or Saying of the Prophet Muhammad in which God said: 'I have an army in the east which I call Turk. I set them upon any people who kindle my wrath.' Many medieval Muslim scholars of the Seljuk and later periods accepted the view that the Turks did indeed 'save Islam', not only from Byzantine reconquest and Crusader invasion in the eleventh and twelfth centuries, but from the Mongol onslaught in the thirteenth century.[460]

This was, however, only one of several widespread myths about the Turks and their God-given military prowess that achieved popularity in the medieval and post-medieval Islamic world. There would also be a limited revival of the cult of world domination amongst the Ottoman Turks after the Mongol threat had faded.[461] The Kizil-Elma or Red Apple as the ultimate goal of Turkish conquests is normally associated with Constantinople. In earlier centuries it seems to have been an undefined place in Daghistan beyond the Demir-Kapu Pass on the northern slopes of the Caucasus Mountains. This early Kizil-Elma may date from the pre-Islamic period when the Khazars were the 'target'. Later, after the fall of Constantinople to the Ottoman Turks, the Kizil-Elma became Budapest, Vienna or Rome.[462]

Religious motivation was stronger in some regions than others and its significance also varied over time, usually in response to political events. When local Muslims felt that Islam was under threat, Islam became a more important motivating factor in warfare. It is therefore interesting to note that religious motivation and the urge to military or 'lesser' *jihad* was not particularly evident in the Islamic heartlands of the Middle East during the tenth and eleventh centuries. This was despite the Byzantine Empire's seizure of several frontier provinces which had been under Islamic rule for hundreds of years. Apparently the revival of Byzantine military strength and the Orthodox Christian Byzantine Empire itself were not viewed as significant threats to the Islamic religion or to Islamic culture. Perhaps this relaxed view of Byzantine expansionism resulted from centuries of more or less stable relations between the Islamic world and the Byzantine Empire as well as a view that recent events were just another stage in the ebb and flow of frontier warfare.

Classical or early medieval Islamic civilization seemingly felt no real threat to its eastern provinces either. Here the Muslims had been militarily dominant since the eighth century and Turkish incomers had embraced Islam, usually before crossing the frontiers of recognized Islamic states. The main conflicts in this region had, in fact, been between Islamic rulers or Islamic sects. Some of the states had been more doctrinal than others, but there was also a widespread attitude of toleration, both to non-Muslims and to Muslims of other persuasions. The vast Samanid state had, for example, been the major power in the eastern provinces of the Islamic world throughout most of the ninth and tenth centuries. Being Sunni but essentially non-sectarian, its rulers seemingly had no problem when some of their senior military commanders adopted 'heretical' religious views.[463] This is not to say that religion played no part in military motivation, as the Samanid *amirs* are known to have led public prayers for deceased soldiers.[464]

When the Seljuk Turks took control of most of eastern Islam, even their rulers seem to have been only superficially, though sometimes also enthusiastically, Muslim, while the tribal rank and file could hardly be regarded as Muslim at all. The Seljuk Sultans' adoption of the Sunni cause is also likely to have been political, though sincere. By the time Seljuk and other Turks overran most of Byzantine Anatolia in the late eleventh century their rulers and leadership in general would have been better educated in their adopted faith, though still occasionally unislamic in their behaviour. Nevertheless, the bulk of their tribal followers and warriors were still only superficially Muslim, this being particularly apparent in the publicly active and not infrequently warlike behaviour of their womenfolk.[465] To be fair it should also be pointed out that Muslim women had always played a significant role in all aspects of life, including the lesser or warlike *jihad*. But they had traditionally done so as supporters or financiers behind the scenes; this phenomenon having been noted amongst Syrian Arabs by the Byzantine Emperor Leo VI two centuries before the arrival of the Seljuk Turks.

The arrival of the latter in the Fertile Crescent and Syria resulted in significant conversion to Islam amongst certain groups that had previously not converted. For example, during the years immediately preceding the arrival of the First Crusade at the close of the eleventh century the newly dominant Armenian élite in Edessa (Urfa) had clung tenaciously to its Christian identity. In contrast in Antioch many Greek and Armenian 'young men', probably meaning those with military potential, were said to have been 'turkified', often through intermarriage with the new Seljuk conquerors.[466] This clearly did not lead to any demilitarization of the local population and may indeed have increased militarization. The name of the man who betrayed a tower in the fortified wall of Antioch to the besieging Crusaders in 1098 strongly suggests that he was a recent convert to Islam. Indeed it seems possible that unreliable crypto-Christians played a significant role in the defence of the Seljuk-ruled city, and in its fall.[467]

Following the fall of Jerusalem to the First Crusade in 1099 and the establishment of the Latin States in Syria, there was a gradual change in Islamic attitudes and reactions to the Crusades.[468] This nevertheless took time and was more obvious close to the Crusader frontier than it was further away. Here it is worth noting that the Artuqid Turkish ruler Il-Ghazi did not start employing *jihad* propaganda as a method of motivating his followers until 1119. He then found that the best response came from the cities rather than the Turcoman tribes, though the *jihad* did help Il-Ghazi revive his flagging authority over tribal troops.[469] Even this may have been a passing phase, as subsequent Artuqid rulers developed sometimes close relations with their Christian neighbours, both the Latin Crusader States and the Kingdom of Georgia, and it was not until the late twelfth century that *jihad* enthusiasm really took hold within the Artuqid state.[470]

Imad al-Din Zangi, who retook Edessa from the Crusaders in 1144 and is generally regarded as the Muslim ruler who started to roll back the Crusader conquests, was probably motivated by traditional political and secular ambitions rather than religious zeal. His son and successor, Nur al-Din was more obviously inspired by ideas of *jihad* and made very effective use of it to bolster his own position. Saladin, who was in reality Nur al-Din's successor as the most powerful Islamic ruler facing the Crusaders, made huge efforts to have himself portrayed as an almost archetypal *jihadi* commander. In this he largely succeeded and although some commentators at the time, as well as some modern historians, have cast doubt on his motivation, it is likely to have been genuine though also politically calculating.[471]

Where ordinary people, soldiers and religious leaders were concerned, the sanctity of the Holy City of Jerusalem seems to have increased for both Muslims and Christians after they lost control of it.[472] Certainly Jerusalem and its holy places played a major role in the motivation of the Islamic Counter-Crusade or *jihad* against the Latin States.[473] Eventually this revival of sacredness also applied to the Holy Land as a whole, with numerous pre-Islamic Patriarchal, Jewish, Christian and early Islamic holy sites being rediscovered, and in some cases probably newly invented, during the course of the history of the Crusades and Counter-Crusades. It has even been suggested that the fact that the site of Bayt al-Ahzan, the 'House of Lamentations' (now Vadum Iacob in Israel) overlooking the upper river Jordan, was sacred to Muslims as a place of minor pilgrimage added urgency to Saladin's decision to destroy the castle that the Crusaders were building there in 1179.[474]

In Damascus, during the first half of the twelfth century, the *mutatawiy'a* volunteers included some individuals who continued to serve until they were very old. One such was the scholar-soldier Abu'l-Hajjaj Yusuf al-Findalawi who was one of those who preached resistance to the Second Crusade in Damascus in 1148 and was eventually killed fighting the Crusaders.[475] It was also a tribute to Saladin's success in motivating his heterogeneous forces that there was rarely much friction between the Turkish and Kurdish troops within the Ayyubid armies, all of whom primarily saw themselves as Sunni Soldiers of Islam.[476]

Another characteristic of *jihad* preaching in Syria and the Jazira during this period was that it was essentially a Sunni phenomenon, directed not only against the Crusaders but against Shi'a Muslims and in particular the Isma'ilis.[477] There were major efforts to ensure that it was firmly rooted in a correct interpretation of Islamic law. For the lesser or military *jihad* to be effective it had to be both just and legal. This is clear in the work of the anonymous author of the *Bahr al-Fawa'id* who is believed to have been a Sunni scholar working in Syria at the time of the Crusades. He, for example, insisted that a ruler must not be secluded from his subjects and complained that current rulers: 'have deprived the Muslims of two things; their share from the public treasury and participation in raids for the Faith.'[478]

The author of the *Bahr al-Fawa'id* still made the usual distinction between the great or spiritual *jihad* and the inferior physical *jihad* against unbelievers, but pointed out that the latter was now necessary for the people of Damascus because there was a real threat on their doorstep. He argued that believers, meaning the Muslims, should make *ghazw* raids against unbelievers (the Latins and perhaps the Mongols, as the exact date of this text is unknown) at least once a year so that the enemy would not be able to prepare his plans against Islam. Furthermore, this was obligatory duty for both freemen and slaves, but not of the poor who lacked adequate military equipment. Clearly when the author was referring to 'slaves' he was meaning *mamluks* or *ghulams* and perhaps high status domestic servants. Muslims, he maintained, should not be employed as mercenaries in *jihad* as this undermined the aspect of duty or obligation implicit in the *jihad*. On the other hand a ruler could hire groups of *dhimmis*, that is local non-Muslims, and pay them from the public treasury. Finally, he proclaimed that the leaders of towns near the enemy frontier had a particular duty to undertake small raids against the nearest infidels.[479]

Rulers and members of the ruling or cultural élites made use of other factors to promote enthusiasm for the warlike lesser *jihad*, while in so doing they also strengthened their own positions and prestige. The role of buildings or highly visible inscriptions was very important and Nur al-Din was among the first to use, or to revive the use of, architecture in this respect. Saladin, his Ayyubid successors and the Mamluk Sultanate which followed, all did the same. As a result cities like Aleppo, Damascus and Cairo are full of magnificent buildings from the twelfth to fourteenth centuries which had more than their obvious initial functions. They, their prominent inscriptions, as well as the city gates, towers, fortresses, bridges and other structures often also proclaim their patrons' dedication to the defence of Islam.[480]

Victory monuments were not a particularly prominent feature in Islamic culture and architecture, but they did exist. One of the biggest and perhaps most unusual was ordered by the 'Abbasid Caliph Harun al-Rashid near Raqqa in north-eastern Syria following a campaign across Byzantine territory to the Black Sea coast in 802.[481] Saladin erected another and more modest monument on the Horns of Hattin following his great victory over the Latin Kingdom of Jerusalem in 1187. It was in the form of a small domed *musallah* prayer hall, and may have been built in response to the church the Crusaders built after defeating Saladin at Montgisard ten years earlier.[482]

Other modest battlefield victory monuments followed but remained rare. It was more common to mark a victory by changing the purpose of existing buildings, often in a very visible and symbolic manner. Saladin himself, after liberating Jerusalem in 1187, handed the Palace of the Christian Patriarchs over to a *sufi* Islamic brotherhood.[483] Militarized *sufi* movements had, in fact, been a notable development during Saladin's reign.[484] After the fall of Acre, the last major Crusader-held city, to the Muslims in 1291 the victorious Mamluk Sultan al-Ashraf Khalil had a finely carved Gothic portal transported stone by stone from Acre to be incorporated into the mausoleum-mosque of his father, the Sultan Qalawun, who had really done the groundwork for this final Islamic victory.

After the death of Saladin there was a general decline in enthusiasm for warlike *jihad* in the Middle East.[485] This only revived under the Mamluk Sultanate in the second half of the thirteenth century when Islam faced a truly mortal threat in the invading Mongols. Once the *jihadi* spirit did revive amongst Sunni

Muslims it was not merely preached by religious enthusiasts. Such individuals, including *sufi* mystics and *faqih* Islamic religious scholars, also volunteered in substantial numbers despite their almost complete lack of military training and equipment. Furthermore, this religious aggression was now directed against pagan Mongols, Christian Crusaders, Shi'a Muslims and, to a lesser extent, indigenous non-Muslim minorities within the Islamic Middle East. The Shi'a in Iraq and elsewhere had, all too often, made their satisfaction with the destruction of the Sunni 'Abbasid Caliphate in Baghdad very public. This was despite the fact that the Mongols had targeted the Shi'a Isma'ili or so-called Assassin community in Iran with particularly ferocity.[486]

The Sunni reaction really gathered pace after the Mamluks' remarkable victory over an invading Mongol army at the battle of 'Ayn Jalut in Palestine in 1260. It was the first time the Mongols had suffered a significant reverse, certainly in the Islamic Middle East, and this Mamluk victory had a huge moral impact throughout the Sunni Islamic world.[487] Enthusiasm for military *jihad* surged and had what was, from the Mamluk point of view, the beneficial side-effect of strengthening support for the Mamluk regime in both Egypt and Syria.[488]

Like Saladin after the battle of Hattin, Baybars al-Bunduqdari reportedly built a small victory moment on the battlefield when he became Mamluk Sultan shortly afterwards.[489] Sadly both Saladin's and Baybars' monuments have disappeared. Sultan Baybars clearly understood the power of architectural symbols to motivate his followers and subjects, erecting many shrines associated with Biblical Prophets and Companions of the Prophet Muhammad in territory retaken from the Latin States. These were generally supported by *waqfs* or Islamic charitable trusts.

Baybars also used ex-church land and reconquered knights' fiefs to support *sufis* and *faqihs*.[490] In 1261 Sultan Baybars authorized an official revival of the *futuwwa* system in Egypt. There has been a great deal of disagreement about what the *futuwwa* really was, with some suggesting that it was almost like an Islamic version of Christian knighthood. It included a number of quite elaborate ceremonies and was, in reality, more like a religious association with shared values and to some extent pooled resources which served as a method of motivating people to good behaviour, occasionally being associated with defending Islam by military means but not primarily being a military organization. The system that was revived amongst the ruling élites in Mamluk Egypt was based upon that seen in Iraq during the last decades of 'Abbasid Caliphal rule and was extended to a limited number of people in Syria in 1290.[491]

Another form of ceremonial that drew in a far greater number of people was the *Mahmal* procession. This celebrated the return of the annual Haj pilgrimage from Mecca to Cairo and although it had existed before, it was developed into a large scale military spectacle under Sultan Baybars I.[492]

A more identifiably Islamic rather than traditionally tribal or Turkish form of motivation began to appear amongst the armies of the Seljuk Sultanate of Rum in Anatolia in the later twelfth and thirteenth centuries. Here what was found in secular literature might have been a truer reflection of the attitudes of the secular élite than were the writings of religious leaders or scholars who had always been under stronger Arab and Persian cultural influence. One such source was the *Seljuknama*, a poetic and epic account of the Seljuk conquest written for an unknown urban patron in Anatolia late in the thirteenth century. This clearly illustrates the strong military and *ghazi* or religiously motivated warrior attitudes of the period, not only amongst the Turkish military aristocracy but also in the urban population.[493] Nevertheless the later *Danishmandname* epic still describes a Turkish hero arming and dressing himself for battle, and being careful to wear essentially pagan amulets to protect himself against the 'evil eye' of his foe.[494]

The defeat of the Seljuk Sultanate of Rum by the Mongols and its subsequent decline led to a gradual defection by the religiously motivated *ghazi* groups which had previously defended and expanded its frontiers. This process mirrored the defection of the Byzantine *akritoi* almost two centuries beforehand.[495] This time, however, the *ghazis* were accompanied by the Turcoman tribes which had similarly been urged into the frontier provinces by Seljuk rulers. These Turcoman tribes now established their own small states or *beyliks*, often seemingly in alliance with the *ghazis*, but whereas the latter were Islamic volunteers whose beliefs and attitudes were more or less orthodox, many of the Turcoman tribal groups still appear to have been only superficially Islamic. This is unlikely to have been a reversion to earlier behaviour. Instead it probably indicated that strong elements of pre-Islamic Turkish culture and shamanistic folk beliefs had survived years of merely nominal conversion to Islam.

Non- or pre-Islamic beliefs similarly survived in North Africa for centuries after the Muslim Arabs conquered the region. In most cases they manifested themselves in minor aspects of social behaviour or slightly unorthodox religious rites. In other cases they resulted in entire peoples going so far 'astray' that they were no longer accepted as part of the Islamic *Umma* or community. The Barghawata of Morocco's Atlantic coast fell into the latter category during the tenth and eleventh centuries, despite the fact that most aspects of their little-known beliefs were rooted in various branches of Islam.[496] More typical was the Berber love of saints who were widely revered, almost to the point of worship where, of course, such behaviour tipped beyond the limits of acceptability for orthodox Muslims. Perhaps as a counterweight to such a tendency, the Berber peoples of North Africa and the Sahara produced a number of very strict, almost fundamentalist Islamic reformist movements. Not all became militant, but one that did was the Murabitun. Another was that of the Muwahhidun a century later.

Al-Andalus did not produce comparable fundamentalist movements. Here

Islam tended to be both orthodox and extremely tolerant. Al-Andalus also produced a number of remarkable *sufi* or mystical teachers whose influence was felt beyond the borders of Islamic Andalus, in the Christian kingdoms of northern Iberia and beyond. Few can, for example, seriously dispute the *sufi* element in the ecstasies of St Teresa of Avila. In contrast there was a notable lack of *futuwwa*, *akhi* or *ahdath* organizations in early Islamic al-Andalus when compared to the Middle East, at least until a number of such religiously based and essentially urban associations appeared as a belated response to the Christian Reconquista.[497]

What might be termed the spirit of *jihad* was also largely lacking until the eleventh century when it was used almost as an excuse to invite the Murabitun to come and save Andalusian Islam.[498] Eventually an enthusiasm for *jihad* did then take hold in the western provinces of the Islamic world in response to Christian assaults in al-Andalus, Sicily and Tunisia. Once this happened, the position of Christian minorities in the Islamic west deteriorated rapidly. The last remnants of indigenous Christianity in Tunisia disappeared after the Muwahhidun took control of the area with the community in Tunis itself reportedly being faced with conversion or expulsion in 1159.[499] Thereafter the only Christians in Tunisia are believed to have been foreigners or slaves. The ancient Christian communities in al-Andalus gradually migrated northwards, seeking sanctuary in the Christian kingdoms where they were known as Mozarabs.

At the same time the indigenous Andalusian Islamic military élites, as distinct from the largely Berber occupying armies of the Murabitun and Muwahhidun, had evolved their own almost aristocratic code of military behaviour. This had remarkable similarities with that of Christian knights on the other side of the frontier.[500] Both included a strong religious commitment but both also highlighted a sense of personal honour plus a duty to protect the weak, poor, young or female. On the Islamic side this was rooted in earlier and indeed pre-Islamic Arab warrior values but there is also likely to have been two-way influence across the religious divide.

Another feature of the Islamic frontier in al-Andalus that was similar to what could be seen in Syria and Turkey was the significant role of religious mystics. Such individuals lived on the frontier and helped to defend it, living amongst and helping inspire the enthusiasm of more secular frontiersmen. These 'warrior mystics' were known at least as early as the tenth century and would still be present during the final struggle to preserve Granada in the late fifteenth century.

Historical chronicles tended to pay less attention to individual and secular motivation that they did to the broader sweep of religious inspiration. In contrast some literary sources such as epic poetry and satire were interested in this often less noble motivation. Family origins and heritage had always been important in Islamic culture but were rarely dominant. This was because there was also a deep-seated respect for what, in modern terminology, might be called the self-made man. The first generation to achieve power or to found a prestigious dynasty was treated with great respect both at the time and by subsequent chroniclers. This attitude was summed up in a popular account of a poor Arab who was taunted for his lowly origins, but who countered, 'My *nasab* [family line] begins with me, yours ends with you!'[501]

A sense of group identity, especially amongst soldiers, was called *sinf*. It could be based upon economic class, cultural or ethnic background.[502] It was similarly seen amongst leaders who had served in the same armies and who rose to power together like a military brotherhood.[503] Unity of purposes and fellow feeling were not necessarily the dominant motivation, however. They seem to have been notably lacking in many of the Buwayhid armies which dominated Iran and Iraq before the coming of the Seljuk Turks. Here elaborate public ceremonies were used in an attempt to cement the oaths of loyalty and mutual support which should have given cohesion to Buwayhid forces. Unfortunately these do not seem to have been very effective. Nor, necessarily, were the private and secret agreements confirmed by oaths within certain sections of these armies.[504] Factionalism was almost as great a problem in the armies of the similarly Shi'a Fatimid Caliphate of Egypt during the period of the early Crusades.[505]

A stronger variation on this sense of mutual *sinf* was that between slave-recruited soldiers who had been purchased, trained and freed by the same purchaser-patron at approximately the same time. The sense of loyalty and obligation which bound *ghulam* soldiers who had been purchased as slaves, then trained and freed as members of a military élite, to their patrons or purchasers was called *istina*.[506] This was also the name given to the loyalty felt by a 'client' or man from a humble family or tribal origin to the individual or tribe which had accepted him and sometimes his family as members of the 'superior' group. *Istina* often joined with the *asabiya* or feeling of family or tribal loyalty to form a wider group solidarity.[507]

Bonds of loyalty between soldiers and their patrons or commanders were naturally considered very important. So much so that military *istina* or patronage almost led the patron-commanders to be seen as foster-parents by their soldiers; the latter almost invariably being younger than themselves. The *istina* of a *mamluk* or *ghulam* to his master-patron after being freed could not, however, be passed on to the next generation or even to the son of a patron. Nevertheless it could be purchased by a new patron or indeed captor. This was why Islamic military regiments could sometimes last two or even three generations,[508] though one must assume that their *istina* was diluting all the time.

Since it was usual for a patron to die before his *ghulams*, the consequent transfer of allegiance was an important if sensitive matter and was usually done by a new patron treating a dead man's followers with respect, so earning their *istina*. A perceived lack of such honourable treatment could lead to problems. It was also normal for *ghulams* to gather around one of the senior and older men within their own unit and sometimes to adopt his name.[509] This was always a delicate matter with its own accepted code of proper conduct. Here it was, for example, considered bad form for *ghulams* to deal with a ruler directly rather than going through their patron.[510] All these factors contributed to a structure of power and influence in which a ruler's real strength depended upon his own *ghulams* whose loyalty to him was, of course, stronger and more direct than that of all other troops.[511]

Mamluk bonds of loyalty were referred to as *khushdash* and were clearly neither absolute nor fanatical. Instead it would be more correct to see the bonds which tied a *mamluk* soldier to his patron and to his fellow *mamluks* as being based on mutual self-interest. There was similarly little that could be described as a code of blood feud, as seen in so much of Europe during this period.[512] Mutual self-interest also underpinned a system of promotion which tended to be slow, steady and rather predictable within the Mamluk army, at least until the end of the largely Turkish Bahri Sultans in the late fourteenth century. It then speeded up under the Burji or Circassian Sultans along with a general decline in military standards, training and morale.[513]

Meanwhile there could be bitter rivalry between different military groups as each struggled to dominate the civilian staffs of the *diwans* or offices which controlled military registration, pay and postings. When the system failed, as it occasionally did, the result could be rioting and pillaging in the cities.[514] On the other hand medieval Islamic soldiers often demonstrated a sort of class solidarity. In Fatimid armies, for example, poor treatment of old, retired or infirm troops was known to harm the morale of existing or younger soldiers. A strong sense of shared identity and of a common fate between soldiers, even in opposing armies, often led to the merciful treatment of captives and tended to reduce unnecessary slaughter. This was most obvious in periods of political confusion when soldiers could not be sure whose side they would be on in a few years' time, or who would be their enemies or friends.[515]

Within the heartlands of Islamic civilization the ancient focus on city life remained central to Islamic culture. Aristocracies and military élites normally preferred to live in or very close to major cities and rural living, even in splendid castles, was rarely attractive to the upper classes of the medieval Islamic world. This was probably even truer of the later medieval Mamluk Sultanate in Egypt and Syria than elsewhere. Here high ranking or wealthy mamluks normally only went to live on their country estates if they had fallen from political favour.[516] Even those elderly and pious mamluks who did leave Cairo or Damascus tended to settle in other cities with strong religious associations such as Jerusalem in preference to disappearing into the countryside. If an entire military unit or group fell from favour, it might find itself effectively in exile, at least for a while. This happened to some members of the mamluk Bahriya regiment between 1254 and 1260. They had to leave Egypt and find service as mercenaries in Syria,[517] until political circumstances changed and they were allowed to return.

While Islamic soldiers often demonstrated a remarkable degree of corporate identity, the profession of arms did not necessarily carry much prestige. This was more apparent in Arab and to some extent Persian-speaking regions than amongst the traditionally warlike Turks, and of course was expressed by civilians rather than by the soldiers themselves. It may also have been more characteristic of the peaceful golden age of the 'Abbasid Caliphate than of the later struggle against Western European Crusaders and Mongols. Such a traditional interpretation of military psychology was nowhere better expressed than by the tenth century scholar and chronicler al-Jahiz:

> To confront an enemy at sword point is a difficult and meritorious act, but less so than the ignorant suppose ... Were there not something of equal weight on the other side [of the scales] to counterbalance the unpleasantness of going into battle, the soul would choose inaction rather than action ... Courage can be inspired by anger, alcohol, stupidity, inexperience or youth. It may be due to bloodthirstiness, jealousy, chauvinism or ambition, or to [opposing] qualities such as hardheartedness or clemency, generosity or meanness, dislike of punishment or resignation, but a man impelled solely by religious feelings will not go into battle. He needs to be actuated also by one of the motives mentioned above.[518]

Such a remarkably modern attitude towards warlike conduct is paralleled in al-Jahiz's comments on the qualities required of a military leader. He maintained that killing the greatest number of enemies and fighting hardest in battle were not the most important criteria for a fitness to command. Some of the greatest champions in personal combat and battle, he pointed out, were unable to wield authority. What a successful commander really required was an ability to take responsibility, to endure anxiety, worry and not be overwhelmed by problems. Failure or weakness in a commander, al-Jahiz stated, was worse than it would be in any other soldier. Furthermore, the commander must be able to face up to the possibility of blame and humiliation in case of defeat.[519]

The career of the Sultan Kilij Arslan I shows that success in battle was not essential for a successful and respected ruler even in late eleventh- and early twelfth-century Anatolia. Having been defeated by the First Crusade, he clashed with virtually all his Islamic neighbours but still came to be regarded as one of the great of the Seljuk Sultans of Rum.[520] By the late eleventh century, however, such sophisticated attitudes were largely limited to the educated bourgeoisie of the cities. In many regions power had returned to tribal peoples, many of whom took great pride in their military traditions and reputations.

This was clearly true of the Arab bedouin who controlled not only the Arabian Peninsula but substantial parts of the Fertile Crescent. They had frequently shown their military superiority over the largely Berber and more numerous armies that the Fatimid Caliphs of Egypt sent to Syria in the second half of the tenth century.[521] During the eleventh century tribes such as the Banu Kilab in northern Syria similarly demonstrated an independent minded volatility that characterized the bedouin since pre-Islamic times,[522] changing their allegiances suddenly and for what sometimes seemed very slight cause. The bedouin Arab tribes of Sinai, southern Palestine and what is now southern Jordan had a similar reputation for military unpredictability in the late twelfth century, especially during the period of Saladin's rule. Occasionally accused of being sympathetic to the Crusaders, it was probably more a case that these tribes were latently hostile to Saladin because they had previously been loyal to the Fatimids.[523]

The high military reputation of the Turks has already been mentioned, and it would continue down to modern times. This, together with a heritage of victory over most of their neighbours and capabilities as horse-archers above that of all rivals except perhaps the Mongols, gave Turkish or Turcoman tribal armies huge confidence. On the other hand the only Turkish Islamic states which were firmly based upon Central Asian tribal and nomadic traditions were those newly formed on or beyond the boundaries of what had been the early medieval Umayyad and 'Abbasid Caliphates. The most significant of these was the Qarakhanid state which straddled the Tien Shan Mountains on the furthest north-eastern frontier of the Islamic world. Here a new form of Islamic state appeared in the late tenth century, built upon pre-Islamic Turco-Altaic political and military traditions. Though the power of the pious Qarakhanid *khans* depended almost entirely upon nomadic Turkish tribesmen, these newly converted rulers tapped into earlier Islamic forms of military motivation, building many *ribats* which seem to have served as centres where religiously motivated volunteers could spend their time in prayer and in defence of Islam.[524] The degree to which these Islamic *ribats* owed anything to similarly militarized Buddhist monasteries which had in many cases preceded them remains a matter of controversy.

Even less is known about the motivation of urban militias, or the degree to which local patriotism played a part. During the tenth and eleventh centuries the young *hamalat al-silah* or arms bearers of Damascus and the surrounding irrigated Ghuta were described as the protectors of their communities.[525] Historical evidence shows that their morale and their effectiveness were often very high. The same was almost certainly true of the *ahdath* militia of Aleppo which had a reputation of being deeply hostile to the Turcoman tribes, briefly driving them out of the area in 1065, capturing their arms and horses.[526] During the first half of the twelfth century the *ahdath* took a leading role in defending Damascus, operating far beyond their city walls against Crusader raiding forces in the Hawran region to the south and resisting take-over by Nur al-Din of Aleppo. In the end Nur al-Din managed to win their grudging aquiescence and entered Damascus in 1154.[527]

Resistance by the local Muslim inhabitants of those regions occupied by the Latins in the wake of the First Crusade died down after the Crusader States were established. Nevertheless, local revolts broke out on several occasions, including that by the Shi'a Nusayris (now generally known as the Alawis) of the mountainous southern part of the Principality of Antioch in the 1130s and again in the early 1180s. Otherwise the local Islamic peasantry only tended to rise up against their Latin overlords if a Muslim army was also operating in the area.[528] Here it should also be noted that stories about the Isma'ili *fidayin* or 'Assassins' taking drugs such as *hashish* before setting out on their almost invariably suicidal missions are a myth.

A deepseated sense of personal honour and concern for reputation was characteristic of the professional military classes and officer corps of the Islamic world during this period. Usama Ibn Munqidh recalled in his collection of autobiographical stories how, in 1123, a soldier with a reputation as a 'champion' felt the need to redeem his own honour after being struck by a warrior of inferior reputation. This he did by charging right into the midst of an enemy force merely to 'touch' the man in question.[529]

The chonicler Ibn al-Athir similarly made it clear that senior *amirs* in Saladin's army were in the thick of the fighting and suffered notable casualties in the battle of Hattin and during the subsequent campaign to retake Jerusalem.[530] Detailed accounts of Mamluk losses in the final victorious siege of Acre in 1291 indicate that the proportion of officer losses in comparison to those of lower ranking soldiers was significantly higher among the more prestigious regiments; 1 to 4.3 amongst the *amir*'s troops but only 1 to 8.8 in the *halqa*.[531] To be fair it should be remembered that in the Mamluk Sultanate, despite its very public adherence to orthodox Sunni Islam, some distinctly unislamic habits seem to have been brought by *mamluk* slave recruits from Central Asia. These included collecting the heads of enemy dead after a battle,[532] and hanging them from the saddles of captured enemy horses.[533]

If the taking of the heads of dead enemies was a distasteful aspect of *mamluk* warfare in the later thirteenth-century Middle East, the Murabitun are said to have brought the habit of head-hunting from south of the Sahara to North Africa and the Iberian peninsula in the late eleventh century. This was then adopted by their Christian foes for many years, though it seems to have been normal to return the rest of the body to a victim's family for proper burial.[534]

LAWS OF WAR

Laws concerning proper conduct in war were more highly developed in the medieval Islamic world than they were in Latin Christian Western Europe or even the Orthodox Christian Byzantine Empire. Nevertheless, these were not 'Laws of war' in the modern sense. They only concerned the correct behaviour of Muslims under such circumstances. Nor were they the result of international attempts to minimize the horrors of war. Any such Islamic 'military laws' sprang from Islamic *Shari'a* or religious law, while other non-legal customs relating to conduct in time of conflict were reflections of deep-seated regional, cultural, ethnic or tribal attitudes.

Jihad of the lesser or military kind was the only form of war legitimized by *Shari'a* Islamic Law. Its function was not to enforce conversion but to defend and where appropriate to extend the Islamic state. Unbelievers incorporated into the Islamic state then had the choice of conversion with equal rights to those of existing Muslims, or payment of special tax which represented an alternative to the military obligations imposed upon Muslims. This was, in effect, regarded as the non-Muslims' contribution to the defence of the state. To translate *jihad* as Holy War is inaccurate as well as inadequate. Furthermore *jihad* or 'struggle' included both actions by the state and actions by those individuals taking part, with Paradise as the reward for those who fell.[535]

Not surprisingly, there was always a big contrast between this legal and religious theory and the reality of war within the medieval Islamic world.[536] Scholars discussed its finer points and the legal justifications of each conflict. They also discussed the true meaning and detailed application of *Hudna*, meaning armistice or peace.[537] Medieval Islamic civilization was, in fact, a very legalistic one and the first known formulation of Islamic Law by Imam Malik Ibn Anas, dating from the second half of the eighth century, included a substantial section on the rules governing warfare.[538]

The *Kitab al-Ahkam al-Sultaniya* by al-Mawardi (974–1058 AD) offered an even more detailed if academic survey of the theoretical legal basis. His six principles of *Jihad* warfare were organized as:[539]

One, on Mobilisation: 1 – The routemarch, bearing in mind the physical endurance of the troops so as to conserve their energy; 2 – Inspection of horses and special provision for them; 3 – Constitution of troops, a – Regulars as official servants of the state drawing stipends from the treasury, b – Volunteers comprising tribesmen, bedouin and peasantry, to be classified as young or old, poor or rich, infantry or cavalry, married or unmarried; 4 – Officers commanding each military unit receive commissions indicating the bond between them and the state; 5 – A war-cry (*shi'ar*) to be assigned to each army unit; 6 – Men regarded as an impediment to morale should be discharged; 7 – In order to ensure the solidarity of the ranks, the commander of an army shall abstain from partisanship.

Two, Polytheists in the Abode of War (Dar al-Harb) *being of two kinds:* 1 – Those who have rejected a call to Islam; 2 – Those unacquainted with Islam, who shall therefore not be subjected to a military attack unless they then reject the new faith.

Three: In presiding over an army a commander shall abide by the following regulations: 1 – As protection against a sudden thrust an intelligence service shall trace the movements of the enemy, and watchmen shall maintain a constant guard duty; 2 – Suitable military camps shall be established in strategic positions within reach of water and pasture; 3 – Maintainance of adequate food supply for the troops and of fodder for the animals; 4 – Troop units shall be dispatched to military positions according to a previously projected manoeuvring plan; 5 – Propaganda shall serve to stiffen the fibre of the troops and to whip up their will to win, also to be used as a means of undermining the strength of the enemy; 6 – Perseverance and patience shall be inspired by stressing God's reward for those who fall in battle and the abundance of earthly compensation for those surviving the conflict; 7 – A commander shall confer with his military aides and seek, by heeding the council of experts, to avoid blunders; 8 – Strict discipline in the fighting units shall be implemented by a severe penal code.

Four: Muslim warriors owe allegiance to God and to their commander: 1 – Allegiance to God implies, a – Outstripping the enemy in patience so as to prolong the fight until victory is won; though outnumbered by a ratio of two to one a Muslim warrior shall not flee the battle, b – The ever-to-be-remembered war aim is victory for the Faith of God, c – Spoils shall be assembled and later distributed among the fighters, d – Any form of friendship between a Muslim and a Polytheist dating back no matter how long a time shall, in time of war, be forgotten because allegiance to God overrules all other bonds; 2 – Allegiance to the commander implies, a – Complete submission to orders, b – By common consent among the fighters authority shall be vested in the commander, c – His orders become effective automatically, his disposal of spoils is not to be held in question.

Five: The commander is committed to the continuance of the war, regardless of duration, until the enemy yields.

Six: The commander is free to use means of destruction; siege artillery including 'arradas and manjaniqs, night raids, fire and devastation of the enemy's crops are all legitimate war measures.

Other scholars wrote comparable treatises on the legal basis of war and *jihad* in later centuries; the best known being that by Ibn Rushd (known in Europe as Averroes) in 1167. His work naturally deals with legality but also with who can or should take part, who can or should be considered an enemy and who was excluded according to different schools of *Shari'a* law, what damage was permissible, how and when safe conduct was given, who could and could not be killed, the fate of captives, the degree to which surprise attacks were allowed, and conditions for a truce.[540]

These laws and customs focused almost as much on ensuring a fair distribution of booty, including captives, as they did on the process of combat itself. By at least the early ninth century such rules and regulations were being incorporated in military manuals. One such was that by al-Harthami which, originally written for the 'Abbasid Caliph al-Ma'mun, survives in an edited version from the early fifteenth century Mamluk Sultanate. It stated that cavalry should get twice, or three times, as much booty as infantry because they had the additional expense of maintaining horses, the variation reflecting which school of Islamic law was being adopted.[541]

Conquered or reconquered land was another form of booty, sometimes being used as *fay'* or collective booty for the benefit of the Islamic community. Consequently a ruler could distribute such territory as if it belonged to the state rather than to the existing inhabitants, even if the latter were Muslim peasants, and use it as a source of *'iqta* fiefs or *'iqta tamlik* private property.[542] This concept probably lay behind attempts by the Mamluk Sultans to continue the preceding Crusader feudal-vassal system along parts of the reconquered coast, even adopting the terms *fasl* and *mafsula* from the French original word *vassal*.[543]

Attitudes towards captives changed according to circumstances and may have become harsher during the period of the Crusades. In tenth- and eleventh-century Syria, before the arrival of the Turks, we read of military pursuits during which only those who looked worth taking for ransom were taken captive, the remainder apparently being allowed to escape.[544] Where Christian and other non-Muslim prisoners-of-war were concerned, it has been suggested that Islamic armies and states were milder in times of military success but harsher in times of defeat or setback. Military captives were more likely to be killed than civilians, the old more likely than the young, while those seized during naval raids had a good chance of survival if they reached port in one piece. Higher ranks were, of course, more likely to be ransomed than lower ranks, who could face temporary or permanent enslavement. On the other hand captured members of the enemy élite were often sent to major cities or religious centres such as Cairo or Baghdad to be publicly paraded in victory celebrations.[545] For example, those taken by Saladin at the battle of Hattin were sent to Damascus.[546]

Such parades may have been humiliating for captured nobility but on other occasions Saladin's treatment of prisoners earned him a reputation for great humanity which was not always deserved. After liberating Jerusalem, for example, Saladin retook Ascalon in September 1187, large numbers of prisoners then being sent to Egypt. There they were released but remained throughout the winter, subsequently reporting that they had been particularly kindly treated in Alexandria.[547] A recent study of Saladin's behaviour towards prisoners taken in war concludes that he did not apply a specific code but reacted differently under various circumstances, and that his reputation for mercy was not always deserved.[548] In fact it seems that Saladin was, as in so many other aspects of his career, behaving in a thoughtful and even calculating manner, using prisoners as political, military and propaganda pawns. His successors tended to do the same;

for example the very large numbers of Crusaders captured during St Louis's invasion of Egypt in 1250 became political and military bargaining chips but were mostly released in the end.[549]

The actual experience of being a prisoner-of-war in the medieval Islamic world could be very hard. A captive might be kept in irons, not fed adequately and be used as virtual slave-labour carrying stones for the building of fortifications.[550] There was often pressure to convert to Islam, though conversion by force was rare and was, of course, illegal under Islamic law. Most who survived captivity were eventually ransomed and returned to Europe, though some converted and became Muslim soldiers.[551] The 'Franks' who helped defend the Ayyubid city of Harran in the Jazira against the Seljuks of Rum may actually have been prisoners-of-war. Clearly they were disliked and mistrusted by the local inhabitants who therefore opened their gates to the Seljuks.[552]

For reasons which are not very clear, the chances of members of the Christian Military Orders eventually being freed were better in the Iberian Peninsula than in the Middle East. Nevertheless the massacring of captured brethren from these Military Orders was not normal practice in either area, and only happened in special circumstances. There were numerous examples of Military Order garrisons negotiating safe conduct to friendly territory in return for surrendering their castles. Nevertheless, those who were captured could remain prisoners for a very long time and escapes were extremely rare. Islamic rulers seemed, in fact, reluctant to release such men even for ransoms during the twelfth century, preferring to use them as diplomatic pawns, though the acceptance of ransoms did increase in the thirteenth century.[553] In contrast, many of the Hospitallers, Templars and Teutonic Knights taken prisoner during the final collapse of the Latin States in the late thirteenth century were held for many years, some never being released. Other evidence suggests that numerous Templars captured during the fall of Acre in 1291 eventually converted to Islam, one brother knight named Pierre being recorded as an interpreter in the Mamluk Sultan's service in 1323.[554]

Most Muslims who fell into the hands of the First Crusade seem to have been slaughtered, though some survived, converted to Christianity and entered service in the newly established Latin States. They almost certainly included the earliest Turcopoles (see vol. 1). Many of the Jews who helped defend Jerusalem against the First Crusade were also slaughtered, though large numbers of this community were captured and sent to Italy as slaves. Most were, however, killed along the way. Many others found sanctuary as refugees in Fatimid-held Ascalon,[555] before moving into Egypt proper. They and the existing Egyptian Jewish community then made great efforts to ransom not only their captured co-religionists but also the many sacred books taken as booty by the Crusaders.[556]

Many Jewish women were reportedly raped by the Crusaders after the fall of Jerusalem. In traditional Arab warfare during the pre-Islamic and Islamic periods a clear distinction had been drawn between real rape of female captives and a symbolic rape which was a form of humiliation for those who had been supposed to protect the women in question.[557] This symbolic rape may at times have consisted of little more than the removal of veils or headcoverings. North African troops in Fatimid service also had a reputation for raping women but it is unclear whether this was real or symbolic.[558] In contrast, the Crusader raping of women after their conquest of Jerusalem appears to have been real.

Islamic military texts often emphasize the importance of not leaving men to be killed or captured on the battlefield because of the damage this did to military morale.[559] The release of Muslim prisoners from the Crusaders was, of course, a cause for joy, and the Mamluk Sultanate clearly orchestrated such events to maximize Mamluk prestige. An Islamic charitable *waqf* or trust was also established in Damascus for just this purpose and it being thought more pious to purchase their release in this way rather than by diplomatic treaty.[560] Rich individuals also ransomed prisoners and in 1266 a merchant from Damascus was recorded ransoming prisoners held by the Knights Hospitaller in Crac des Chevaliers.[561]

There was not always the opportunity of surrender and eventual ransom. In Sicily the leader of the Islamic resistance, Ibn Abbad, tried to surrender to the Emperor Frederick II but was hanged. This simply resulted in a further, more prolonged and bitter struggle which resulted in an estimated 16,000 Sicilian Muslim prisoners being forcibly transported to Lucera on the Italian mainland. There most of them were employed as agricultural slaves, though some had continuing military obligation to the Emperor and his successors in return for being allowed to remain Muslim.[562]

STRATEGY

Ecological factors probably had a more direct impact upon warfare in the Middle East than in many other regions of the world. The most important such factors were climate or weather, the limited availability of water or fodder, and the major barriers formed by mountains and deserts, above all the deep or true deserts in which substantial armies virtually never operated. For these reasons a map of the medieval Islamic world which illustrated the military realities and limitations of the time might well look more like an ocean dotted with relatively small land-masses and numerous islands than the huge land-mass lapped by peripheral seas that appears on an ordinary map of physical terrain. These imaginary 'oceans' would consist of deserts as well as the seas which exist in reality. The imaginary 'land-masses' would be the settled, irrigated, agricultural and more favoured pasturelands, whilst the imaginary 'islands' would be isolated oases, large or small, which dotted the deserts and semi-deserts of the Middle East.

Medieval armies had to 'navigate' these imaginary seas if they wished to campaign over long distances, sometimes 'island-hopping' the oases which marked the main lines of communication and trade. They would replenish their supplies and munitions in the fertile 'land-masses', each of which tended to be dominated by one or more cities.

The Islamic world inherited a number of highly literate military traditions and although only a few fragments of pre-Islamic military texts survive, they highlight the degree to which the sophisticated strategic and tactical theories of the medieval Islamic world owed a debt to the past. Furthermore, the varied traditions which the Islamic world inherited were not only rapidly absorbed but were soon fused into something new. They were updated and improved, in light of the Muslims' own military experience against very varied foes.

It is not known whether the rich pre-Islamic Arab civilization of Yemen or southern Arabia produced written manuals to be used by military and political leaders. Such texts did, however, form part of Sassanian Iranian culture and as a result Persian books of practical advice for rulers were soon translated into Arabic for the new ruling Caliphs. There was also some Greek influence from the Romano-Byzantine world, though this seems to have been of secondary importance. Within a few centuries books of advice for Islamic rulers were again being written in Persian. For reasons which presumably reflect the character of the two major strands within early Islamic civilization, books in Persian tended to be more practical whereas those in Arabic tended to be more literary.[563]

Two strands or forms of *furusiya* similarly appeared for the Islamic upper classes to follow; *al-furusiya al-nabila* which was a code of noble courtly behaviour based upon Sassanian traditions, and *al-furusiya al-harbiya* or military *furusiya* which primarily focused on cavalry training. The latter itself consisted of four main elements concerning the use of hand-held weapons, archery, polo and hunting.[564] As yet there was little concern with infantry skills. The term *furusiya* has itself been widely misunderstood or mistranslated. In essence it meant skill whereas *shuja'a* meant courage, though sometimes the terms blurred to the extent that *furusiya* took on some aspects of what in Western Europe would be regarded as 'chivalry' or chivalrous behaviour and its associated value systems.

Before looking at the strategies, tactics and individual skills described in medieval Islamic works on military command, leadership and *furusiya*, it should be pointed out that they described things which existed in reality, not merely in theoretical literature. This is not only clear in numerous Arabic, Persian and subsequently Turkish descriptions of warfare, battle and individual combat, but also in observations by the Muslims' enemies or neighbours. The Byzantine Emperor Leo VI made it clear in his *Taktica* that early tenth century Islamic armies fought in almost exactly the manner described in such texts.[565] The same proved to be the case when comparing the actions of Saladin's armies, as well as those of the Mamluks and other dynasties, with at least some of the theories proposed at the time. While such parallels are not exact, they are close enough to show that the writers of military works were not armchair generals or enthusiasts without experience of the reality of warfare. Indeed we know that many, perhaps most, of the writters in question were, or had been, officers, serving military specialists and in some cases senior commanders.

Among the earliest surviving texts, the *Mukhtasar Siyasat al-Hurub* by Abu Sa'id al-Sha'rani al-Harthami was written for the 'Abbasid Caliph al-Ma'mum in the early ninth century. This was, however, a work of military theory, strategy, tactics and army administration rather than *furusiya* as such. Unlike so many of the earliest texts which we know only by their titles and the occasional quotation,[566] al-Harthami's book survives in an abridged version, probably dating from the Fatimid period. Substantial pieces of text are also embedded within later Mamluk works such as that attributed to al-Ansari at the start of the fifteenth century.

Although this later book includes information on Mongol warfare, perhaps dating from the late thirteenth and fourteenth centuries, the bulk of the text is believed to be considerably earlier. Some historians have thus assumed that the essential features of 'Abbasid military theory still applied during the period of the Mamluk Sultanate, while others have tended to dismiss these Mamluk texts as archaic irrelevances which merely demonstrate a reader's erudition. If viewed as evidence of 'Abbasid, probably Fatimid and perhaps early Ayyubid tactical concepts, these quasi-Mamluk sources show infantry to have been used in a defensive and largely static manner while the cavalry was expected to launch repeated counter-attacks and withdrawals before a final, battle-winning charge.[567]

The identified surviving sections of al-Harthami's *Mukhtasar Siyasat al-Hurub* are deeply concerned with the qualities needed of a commander and how to impose effective leadership. These were primarily personnel management skills, including those of a political and diplomatic nature. However the text also focuses on the need for good sources of information and the importance of maintaining one's own secrecy, as well as how to ensure that commands were carried out speedily. Other sections of the book describe 30 different ways of arraying an army, what its constituent parts were called and what equipment was needed.[568]

Most of the text is, however, strategic though there are specific tactical chapters on the role of cavalry and infantry in battle.[569] These make it clear that infantry archers are arrayed in the front ranks to protect their own cavalry.[570] More specialized sections of the text deal with the making of night attacks and how to defend against the same, again with a major defensive role being given to infantry archers.[571] The sections on both offensive and defensive siege warfare include the same weaponry, personnel and tactics as would be found in later works.[572]

The traditional founder of true Islamic *furusiya* literature is considered to have been Ibn Akhi Hizam Muhammad Ibn Ya'qub, a late ninth and early tenth century 'Abbasid military commander and horse expert who was himself the nephew of a famous *Khurasani* or eastern Iranian military commander and stable master in 'Abbasid service. Ibn Akhi Hizam's work also highlights the importance of all aspects of military archery during this period: on horseback, on foot and in siege warfare.[573]

The next half century saw a remarkable flowering of *furusiya* literature, but there was then something of a decline until the mid-twelfth to mid-fourteenth century saw a sudden revival within the Ayyubid and Mamluk Sultanates of Egypt and Syria.[574] Writing from the intervening period tended to be derivative, but did preserve earlier knowledge which might otherwise have been lost. This is why the specialists who wrote for Saladin remain so important. In other respects the Mamluk period is generally considered to have seen the full development of classical *furusiya*. This now consisted of the following distinct branches: lance-play or skills with the spear on horseback, polo, horse-archery 'shooting at the gourd' which meant aiming upwards at a target in the form of a hollow gourd, horse-archery shooting downwards while passing a target at close range, archery shooting horizontally at an ordinary target usually on foot, 'skill in use of the bow' which involved techniques of draw, loose and so on, swordplay, use of the mace which seems to have been a rare addition to the list of required skills, crossbow shooting, wrestling, horse-racing, hunting, and 'games' associated with religious processions and other public displays.[575]

Although there was a widely accepted tradition or school of Islamic strategy, tactics and general military skills, it is clear that there were, in practice, a number of regional variations. These tended to reflect local conditions and the availability of different types of troops as well as deep-seated local military traditions. The Persian *Qabus Nama* was written by Qabus Ibn Washmagir, ruler of a minor northern Iranian state in the late tenth and early eleventh century. It was intended for his successors and is an example of a style of work known as a 'Mirror for Princes' which reflected a pre-Islamic Sassanian tradition of training manuals for government.

Unlike earlier Arabic works, the *Qabus Nama* based its precepts upon expediency and pragmatism. It accepted the need for coercive force to govern a state and reflected the fact that there was now a much deeper divide between the military and the ordinary population than there had been in the early Islamic period. Furthermore, the ruler and his government stood in the middle, needing to keep both the military and the people content if they hoped to retain power.[576]

Like Nizam al-Mulk in his *Siyasat Nama* written a century later, Sultan Qabus was also painfully aware that his troops might be unreliable and could pose a threat to his regime.[577] In fact his own reign was divided into two, with a period of Buwayhid occupation in between.

Another remarkable and more specifically military Persian text was the *Adab al-Harb* 'Science of War', by a Persian scholar named Muhammad Ibn Mansur Fakh al-Din Mubarakshah, also known as Fakhr-i Mudabbir. He worked for the last Ghurid and first Delhi Sultan rulers of the Punjab region of northern India and what is now Pakistan. The *Adab al-Harb* was itself written around 1230 and was dedicated to Sultan Shams al-Din Iltutmish of Delhi.[578] A remarkably wide-ranging book, it included information based upon current warfare against the Hindu rulers of India as well as a great deal of traditional material, including descriptions of the differing military arrays of pre- or non-Islamic peoples.[579] The section of this valuable work dealing with military archery appears to include fewer words of Arabic origin than was the case in most other Persian texts, and may therefore be closer to the original, pre-Islamic and pre-Turkish Persian archery tradition.[580]

Within the Arab Middle East at the start of the Crusader period, the strategy and tactics adopted by the armies of the Fatimids were theoretically based upon the Traditions of the Prophet Muhammad and of the revered Caliph 'Ali. In reality they were a direct continuation of those of the earlier and rival 'Abbasid Caliphate.[581] The threat posed by the Crusades and the establishment of the Latin States in the heart of the Islamic world sparked off another period of military writing. Some of this was intended for the ruling classes and senior commanders but other works were clearly aimed at middle or lower ranking military officers, especially those involved with training.

Most of these seemingly new works were again based firmly upon earlier 'Abbasid traditions and texts, quoting directly from them with or without acknowledgement of the first author. On the other hand the great majority also attempted to update this information and to make it relevant to the present day. How far they succeeded is, of course, still a matter of debate. The anonymous *Bahr al-fawa'id* was more original. Written in twelfth-century Syria, probably Aleppo, for an *atabeg* or autonomous governor of Adharbayjan, it strongly reflects an atmosphere of *jihad* resistance against the Crusaders.[582]

Three other very significant works were written a short time later for Saladin and his immediate successors. Al-Shayzari's *Al-Manhaj al-Masluk* focused on the administrative aspects of warfare and was in the 'Mirror for Princes' style. Al-Tarsusi's book focused largely on the technical but also the tactical, while al-Harawi's *Al-Tadhkirat al-Harawiyya* was primarily concerned with theoretical and strategic matters.[583] Little is known about al-Tarsusi, except that he may have had links with Cilician Armenia and might even have been of Armenian origin.

His book, generally known as the *Tabsira Arbab al-Lubab*,[584] was an example of the general or broad ranging *furusiya* type and may have been written as early as 1169 when Saladin took effective control of Egypt. Clearly it was based upon experience of the preceding Fatimid period.[585]

In contrast Abi Bakr al-Harawi was a famous scholar and traveller who is believed to have operated almost as a secret agent on behalf of Saladin, being present in Palestine, Syria and Egypt at the time of the Third Crusade. Written after 1192, his book was mainly concerned with military tricks and stratagems. Partly reflecting Saladin's victories and partly based on earlier traditional works, it includes a number of interesting case-studies in which al-Harawi endeavours to modernize long-accepted military practice.[586] Whether the theory reflected the practice or the practice reflected the theory is less easy to judge. Yet Saladin's siege of the Crusader-held castle at Bourzey almost exactly mirrored what al-Harawi wrote, with Muslim troops advancing in steady waves or lines to erect a shield-wall using large *januwiya* mantlets.[587]

A considerably larger number of works were written in the Mamluk Sultanate, some of them dating from its earliest decades and clearly reflecting the military practice of the late Ayyubid period. It was the Mamluk state which divided specifically military *furusiya* into cavalry and infantry skills, respectively known as upper and lower *furusiya*. There was also a third group which consisted of popularized and less scholarly texts which have, unfortunately, confused several modern scholars.[588] Another feature of several later *furusiya* books from the Mamluk Sultanate was that some of them included archaic non-Islamic texts which had little current application. For example the prolific fourteenth-century *furusiya* writer Muhammad Ibn Mangli al-Qahiri translated the *Taktica* of the late ninth/early tenth century Byzantine Emperor Leo. The late thirteenth-century al-Aqsara'i translated Sassanian Iranian sources as well as the Greek Polybius and the *Tactica* of Aelian as well as an abridged version of the 'Abbasid military scholar al-Harthami whose text was subsequently included in a fuller though incomplete form in al-Ansari's writings of the fifteenth century.[589]

The problems of interpretation posed by the *Nihayat al-Su'l* attributed to al-Aqsara'i are typical of this Mamluk period.[590] Some of the text clearly, and in some instances very specifically, dealt with current warfare against the Mongols along the Euphrates frontier. Other parts dealt with, or recalled recent conflicts with, the Crusaders and their Latin descendants in the Middle East. But then Chapter 9 of the *Nihayat al-Su'l* includes plans of battle formations which have very little relevance for the Mamluk Sultanate, mainly being copied from pre-Islamic, early Islamic and 'Abbasid sources.[591] This having been said, when the author of the *Nihayat al-Su'l* incorporates whole passages from the Greek *Tactica* of the second–third century Aelian whom he knew as Aylanus,[592] from his Latin Roman name Claudius Aelianus, al-Aqsara'i does more than merely copy and translate. He endeavours to use them critically and to put them into an Islamic military context, though also occasionally misunderstanding the original text.

The Mamluk Sultanate did produce some very important new treatises on archery, but these had to await the second half of the fourteenth century, previous Mamluk archery experts still largely relying on earlier Islamic sources.[593] The first of these truly original writers was the Syrian *ustadh* or archery instructor, Taybugha al-Baklamishi al-Yunani. He composed his *Ghunat al-Murami* in verse and dedicated it to Sultan Sha'ban, yet even he borrowed heavily from earlier Mamluk texts on military archery.[594]

Military treatises, both theoretical and practical, were similarly produced in the western regions of the medieval Islamic world. These were not fundamentally different from those written in the Middle East though they sometimes differed in emphasis. They also tended to be rather old fashioned. For example the *Siraj al-Muluk* of al-Turtushi reflected the military traditions and situation of al-Andalus under Murabit domination. It was nevertheless written around 1122 in Fatimid Egypt, where it was dedicated to the *amir* Abu Abdullah Ibn al-Bata'ihi who was briefly *wazir* after the murder of al-Afdal.[595] This period of the Fatimid Caliphate saw a ferocious attempt to return to the customs that had existed before the days of the Armenian wazirs Badr al-Jamali and al-Afdal. So it is possible that al-Turtushi's references to how military matters were conducted in 'his country', namely the Murabit state in general or al-Andalus in particular, were offered as examples of how such seemingly old fashioned systems could still achieve victory.

Old fashioned as the Islamic west might seem in hindsight, it clearly preserved a strong tradition of archery, especially on foot. So much so that Ibn Mangli, writing on military archery during the mid-fourteenth century in a Mamluk Sultanate which historians generally regard as the apogee of Islamic archery skills, largely relied upon a monumental work by the Moroccan, Abu Muhammad Jamal al-Din 'Abd Allah Ibn Maymun.[596] Part of Ibn Maymun's central thesis was an argument in favour of the traditional hand-held composite bow and against an increasing adoption of the crossbow. In this effort Ibn Maymun largely failed and one of the most interesting, indeed most original, sections of a work of general *furusiya* by the fourteenth-century Andalusian Ibn Hudayl was on the crossbows which now dominated archery in the last remaining Islamic state of Granada.[597]

Theory and reality were not, of course, necessarily synonymous when it came to strategy in any period of history, and this was as true of the medieval Islamic world as of any other. The military manuals rarely distinguished between the impact major natural obstacles had upon different peoples or types of army. For example, the largely Arab armies of the early Caliphates had been unable to permanently conquer the high plateau of central Anatolia though they seemed capable of invading or raiding it with relative impunity. On the other hand the Arab armies had taken control of a good part of the very rugged and mountainous eastern regions of Anatolia. They had also managed to break through the mountains which encircled the bleaker and hotter central plateau of Iran which they did conquer. Furthermore these early Islamic armies then went on to overrun the Central Asian regions of Transoxania with relative ease, plus the mountains of Afghanistan with greater difficulty.

Huge distances, shortage of suitable manpower and political problems at the centre were largely responsible for bringing these initial Arab-Islamic conquests to a halt, after which enthusiasm for further expansion seems to have been replaced by enthusiasm for developing a new, culturally brilliant and, for several centuries, hugely rich civilization; that of the 'Abbasid golden age. The next wave of enthusiastic conquerors was not Arab, nor indeed Persian, but Turkish. It was they who pushed Islam's political frontiers deeper into India, who conquered the central plateau of Byzantine Anatolia as the Arabs had never done, and who in later centuries would expand across south-eastern Europe to the gates of Vienna.

These Turkish or tribal Turcoman armies differed from those of the early Arab-Islamic period as, to a considerable degree, did their societies. Consequently they found some strategic barriers less of a problem, and some more so. Turkish nomads reputedly disliked forests because they could be ambushed; furthermore retreat was difficult and their herds were liable to be attacked by wild animals. This seems to have been less of a problem for the Mongols, many of whose tribes originated in densely wooded regions of Inner Asia. The Byzantine defenders of the Empires of Nicaea and Trebizond clearly used such forested zones as barriers during the thirteenth century and possibly even later. Mountains were less of a barrier to the Turks and Mongols, both of whom relied on Bactrian camels rather than dromedaries as did the Arabs.[598] The most obvious difference between bactrians and dromedaries, apart from their double or single humps, was the bactrians' ability to cope with extreme cold. Less well known is their different feet which, in the case of the bactrians, were less vulnerable to sharp rocky surfaces. Meanwhile major rivers were more a means of communication than a barrier to all these tribal and nomadic peoples.

Until modern times the term Desert Warfare has been something of a misnomer, as it was exceptionally rare for major fighting to take place in the deep deserts. These were, of course, a significant obstacle to all armies, though some could cope with them better than others. Arab forces were the most adept in crossing deserts and could also use them as a form of refuge, but their success in these respects was due to greater knowledge of the limited available water sources, of the routes between such sources, and of the restricted, seasonal and temporary fodder for animals. Arab and Middle Eastern Islamic states also developed more effective support systems to enable their armies to cross deserts, semi-deserts and all sorts of parched terrain.

According to one contemporary chronicler a Khwarazmian army from Iran, fleeing ahead of the Mongols in the early thirteenth century, tried to occupy the steppes of Syria but were unable to do so because there was not enough fodder to support their huge numbers of horses.[599] In fact there were many reasons for the Khwarazmian failure, but ecological factors undoubtedly played their part. The Mongols faced precisely the same problem only a few years later. The armies of Islamic dynasties and rulers based in Egypt may have developed the most effective desert-crossing capabilities amongst the major powers of the Middle East, yet even they were constrained by what was and was not possible. The Sinai Peninsula remained a major barrier to substantial forces and to their logistical support or 'tail'. In fact it normally took 40 days to move a large army from Cairo, across Sinai, through Palestine and Syria to Aleppo. Since Aleppo served as the Mamluk Sultanate's main military base facing the mountain frontier to the north and the Euphrates frontier to the east, there was clearly a need for the best and fastest system of communications from here to Cairo, to minimize delays in responding to an invasion.[600]

Back in the early eleventh century the Fatimid rulers of Cairo needed to respond speedily to crush a Syrian revolt. This they did by sending an army across Sinai in high summer, spearheaded by cavalry in which each man was given two horses, ten *dinars* in cash and accompanied by water carriers.[601] This was, incidentally, at a time when the Fatimid army was short of good cavalry. According to Crusader accounts the men of the Fatimid army defeated by the First Crusade outside Ascalon in 1099 similarly entered battle with waterbottles around their necks. Eighty-three years later, control of the limited sources of water near Husban in central Jordan was vital to the outcome of a local struggle between Saladin and the Latin Kingdom of Jerusalem, which the Muslims eventually won.[602]

The seasons could also affect the outcome in another way, if one side had demobilized its cavalry and sent their horses to recuperate in good pasture. This happened to Nur al-Din in 1163, and was the subject of a poem of consolation by 'Ubayd Allah al-Mawsili who described how, despite Nur al-Din's swift reaction to the crisis:

> Your lances were put aside and the bows unstrung,
> The horses were in the remotest pastures grazing with the young rams …
> You seized the swift horse, naked and unbridled,
> While the tawny lances were hung up,
> And the swords were in their scabbards.[603]

The availability of suitable or good quality troops in sufficient numbers was another constraint upon generally accepted strategy. The Fatimid Caliphate's shortage of cavalry was largely due to Egypt's shortage of pasture. This meant that, unlike the 'Abbasid forces which had dominated Syria for several centuries, Fatimid armies could rarely pursue dissident Syrian bedouin tribes into the desert fringes nor attack their semi-permanent *hilla* camps.[604] In complete contrast, eastern Iran and Transoxania could support huge numbers of horses while also straddling the trade routes which made a state rich. So it is no surprise to read that, according to Mawlana Minhaj al-Din in his *Tabakat-i Nasiri*, the early thirteenth century Khwarazmshah 'Ala' al-Din Muhammad defeated the Buddhist Qara Khitai or Western Liao from China with a massive cavalry army in which both men and animals were armoured.[605]

The Jazira region of northern Iraq and eastern Syria, like Syria itself, could sustain substantial cavalry forces, though not on the same level as Central Asia. According to the Crusader chronicler William of Tyre, Nur al-Din sent Shirkuh and his nephew Saladin to take control of Egypt with 9,000 armoured cavalry but only 300 archers.[606] The numbers are suspect, but the Syrians' advantage in cavalry was probably real enough. Having suitable troops readily available also enabled Saladin to support his allies at short notice, as happened in 1186 when the Sultan sent infantry, archers who may have been horse-archers, and supplies of weapons to Count Raymond of Tripoli during the latter's quarrel with the Latin King of Jerusalem.[607]

The professional nature of the core units of Islamic armies had become painfully apparent to many Western Europeans by the late thirteenth century, especially where the Mamluk Sultanate of Egypt and Syria was concerned. Even a powerful ruler such as the Angevin King Charles II of southern Italy, writing in the year that Crusader-held Acre finally fell in 1291, maintained that the 'Muslims' (meaning the Mamluks) were clever and more adroit in waging war than the Christians.[608] At around the same time Fidenzio of Padua, in his book on how to regain the Holy Land, warned that the Mamluks were especially good at using scouts and were therefore very difficult to surprise.[609] Beyond such a simple use of large numbers of scouts, the evidence shows that later medieval Islamic armies maintained their long established superiority in wars of movement. This applied not only when they were facing Western European forces, but in their internal struggles as well. Even the far from wealthy or well-equipped Hafsid army of the late thirteenth- and fourteenth-century Tunisia continued the Muwahhid tradition of rapid movements, sudden sieges, raids and, where necessary, guerrilla warfare, not only when combating local enemies but against Crusader invasions of North Africa.[610]

The offensive strategies adopted by Islamic armies during this period illustrated most of these advantages and constraints. Until recently explanations for the failure of most of the Fatimid counter-attacks against the newly established

Crusader Kingdom of Jerusalem in the early twelfth century have shed more light on the patronizing and racist attitudes of Western historians than on the military events themselves. They also tended to assume that the wealth of the Fatimid Caliphate could be translated into vast military resources and huge numbers of troops. The reality was rather different, with Fatimid armies based in Egypt being quite limited in both respects.[611]

Having been forced back upon their remaining Palestinian enclave of Ascalon (sometimes described as the Gaza Strip of the twelfth century),[612] the Fatimids always had to bring armies from the Nile valley and Delta across Sinai before reassembling at Ascalon. They could therefore never achieve real surprise. They also suffered from major problems of logistical support because the area around Ascalon, while capable of supporting the garrison of that fortified city, was inadequate for a full-scale field army.[613] In fact, after 1105 the Fatimids only used Ascalon as a forward defensive position and base from which to raid Latin territory, with no further major attempts at invasion. As such, the fortified city proved highly effective; its garrison remaining active and its raiders sometimes reaching as far as Jerusalem.[614]

The Islamic rulers of the Jazira and Syria also had to keep in mind the limits of their own logistical bases. On other occasions, however, even cautious early twelfth-century commanders like Il-Ghazi found themselves swept along by their followers' eagerness for a quick battle, sometimes with catastrophic results.[615] Saladin achieved greater control over his armies, though this was certainly never complete.

Like Il-Ghazi and virtually all the more successful Islamic commanders facing the Crusades, Saladin was normally very cautious when undertaking offensive operations. The main objective of almost all major attacks, as distinct from raids, was to besiege and capture a fortified place. This also involved protecting the besiegers' supply lines and communications as well as the siege positions themselves. Because the large Islamic armies employed in such offensives included substantial numbers of part-timers and volunteers, they could not normally remain in the field for long. One of Saladin's remarkable successes was, in fact, his ability to keep an army on campaign for much longer than was normal. Islamic commanders also knew that their Crusader enemies generally avoided major confrontations because Crusader field armies drew men from vital garrisons and defeat could leave cities and castles seriously undermanned.[616] Yet they were also aware that failure to defeat Islamic raids or to support places under siege could undermine a Latin ruler's authority.[617] Therefore fine judgement was required on both sides.

The conquest of certain regions was, of course, politically more significant than others. Such a conquest might result in obvious strategic advantages but might also have a cultural or religious impact. When Saladin retook Aqaba in

1171 he opened up the vital strategic overland link between Egypt and Syria. He also 'freed the Haj road', thus enabling Muslim pilgrims to travel overland in relative safety from Egypt to the Islamic Holy Cities of Mecca and Medina in Arabia. The former effect strengthened Saladin militarily while the latter impact earned him huge prestige. Furthermore, this seemingly localized success also forced the Latin Kingdom of Jerusalem to strengthen its own defences in southern Palestine and Oultrejordain.[618]

Other campaigns by Saladin highlighted different aspects of a strategy that was rooted in the Islamic military traditions of the time. When he launched a major cavalry raid against the Sidon area in the north of the Kingdom of Jerusalem in 1179, Saladin left his infantry at Banyas in the foothills of the Golan Heights. A Crusader force of cavalry and infantry tried to take advantage of this division of Islamic forces by attacking the foot soldiers defending Banyas, but were themselves then caught between Saladin's infantry and cavalry as the latter returned.[619] The resulting Crusader defeat was just one example of the superior speed and manoeuvrability of Islamic forces. Three years later Saladin attempted a more ambitious series of raids, sending troops against the Kingdom of Jerusalem from four separate directions, striking the Jordan Valley, Galilee, Beirut and northwards from Egypt.[620]

This achieved only limited results and Saladin was diverted by more pressing business elsewhere, but then came the climactic campaign of 1187, culminating in an overwhelming battlefield victory at the Horns of Hattin, the liberation of Jerusalem and the retaking of huge areas of the Latin States. This offensive is worth looking at in some detail because much of it reflected the theories seen in Arabic books of military advice from this period.

Saladin had assembled and reviewed his army at Tal 'Ashtara where there was abundant water and where he could await the arrival of further contingents from Aleppo. He may not have expected to fight a major battle but the campaign was necessary to justify Saladin's position as ruler and self-proclaimed champion against the European occupiers. He was also under criticism for seemingly directing more energy against his Islamic rivals than against the Latin States. In the event Saladin was challenged in the field by the main Latin army, then won a resounding victory at Hattin and liberated Jerusalem. What he did next was a clear demonstration of his strategic ideas, as mirrored in the writings of al-Harawi. Instead of aiming for the strongly fortified coastal city of Tyre, Saladin mopped up the enemy's weaker positions, thus maintaining the momentum of his campaign, the morale of his troops and his reputation as a winner.[621]

Although Saladin's failure to take Tyre, thus leaving a bridgehead for a future Crusade, has been strongly criticized by subsequent military historians, his cautious strategy seems to be vindicated by the final results of the Third Crusade. This massive and hugely expensive assault, launched in response to the loss of

Jerusalem, was headed by the three most powerful monarchs in Western Europe, yet its achievements were modest. In the event the Third Crusade was unable to destroy Saladin's field army or to retake Jerusalem. Instead it took a year and a half's campaigning to regain five of the cities which had fallen to Saladin in less than a month.[622]

Elsewhere Saladin had maintained the tradition of raiding or *razzia* which had been another characteristic of Islamic warfare for centuries. These included expeditions along the North African coast, down the Nile into Nubia, against the too-often pro-Crusader Arab bedouin tribes of southern Jordan and northern Hijaz, and down the Red Sea coast of Arabia to Yemen. Many if not all of these raids had a clear strategic purpose which was to expand the frontiers and influence of the Egyptian state which formed the foundation of Saladin's realm.[623] The Mamluk Sultanate continued most of this cautious strategic policy against the Latin Crusader States, and launched raids to weaken or dominate minor states on other frontiers.

The greatest of the early Mamluk Sultans, Baybars al-Bunduqdari, earned a reputation for putting even greater efforts than normal into maintaining military and strategic secrecy. This often entailed keeping both his enemies and his own subordinates in ignorance of his intentions. Baybars is even credited with using large-scale hunting expeditions as a cover for sudden military movements.[624] The result was to force his enemies, including the Crusader States, to spread their defences wide. This maintained a pattern of controlled and still rather cautious offensive warfare in which Baybars and his Mamluk successors kept a wary eye on the greater threat posed by the Mongols on the Euphrates frontier; meanwhile sending their armies to nibble away what remained of Crusader territory. Castle by castle, town by town, Latin territory on the Middle Eastern mainland was reduced until only Acre and a handful of other coastal enclaves remained. These were then crushed by an all-out offensive in 1291.

Medieval Islamic defensive warfare made use of many of those ecological factors which constrained offensive warfare. The problems faced in Syria by the 'refugee' army of the last Khwarazmian Shah, Jalal al-Din, where they could not find enough natural fodder for their horses, have already been mentioned. In Iraq the 'Abbasid Caliph of Baghdad went a step further by reportedly ordering all the agricultural land ahead of Jalal al-Din's line of march to be ploughed up, again to deny the Khwarazmians food for their horses.[625]

The limited number of routes across the Sinai Peninsula that an army could use also enabled Saladin to have a massive fortress built at Qal'at al-Jindi, overlooking a pass through the mountains of western Sinai. This was probably in response to an attack on al-Arish in north-east Sinai in 1182, raising fears of an invasion of the Egyptian heartland.[626] Qal'at al-Jindi's strategic location would be highlighted several times in later centuries, not least when Israel invaded

Egypt in 1956 and again in 1967. Instead of building fortifications to defend an area, Saladin, his Ayyubid successors and the Mamluk Sultans sometimes destroyed those that already existed in order to deny them to an enemy. In fact Saladin initiated the policy of demolishing coastal fortifications from al-Arish to Sidon immediately after regaining the territory in 1187. This low-lying coast was regarded as being particularly vulnerable to naval assault.[627] In contrast the steeper coasts north of Acre as far as Iskenderum were not so suitable for beach landings. Hence the destruction of its captured fortifications was not so thorough, though the Mamluks did demolish some ports.[628]

The strategic situation was again different closer to Cairo. Here, along the coast of the Nile Delta and part of northern Sinai most of the defences were strengthened because they were close to the main Ayyubid and Mamluk garrison centres and so could be quickly reinforced. During the later Mamluk period the defences of the ports of Dumyat (Damietta) and Alexandria were given particular attention because they were vital outlets for Egyptian trade. The port of Tinnis, however, stood on an island which, despite being in the Manzala coastal lake rather than on the coast, was still regarded as unduly vulnerable at a time when European naval domination could hardly be disputed. The town was therefore completely abandoned.[629]

The Mamluk Sultanate gave even greater attention to organizing the defence of their northern frontier. This faced the Mongol Il-Khanid Empire across the river Euphrates and in a vulnerable but mountainous gap between the great Euphrates bend and the Mediterranean coast.[630] The resulting defences consisted of a chain of fortresses quite as impressive as the better-known Crusader castles to the west. They were also linked by a very efficient communications system so that warnings of Mongol invasion could be sent to Aleppo, Damascus and Cairo within a few days if not hours (see below). Furthermore, the entire frontier zone was defended by frontline garrisons with reserves further back. In terms of sophistication and effectiveness the Mamluk Sultanate's Syrian frontier zone remained one of the most remarkable in military history, well able to stand alongside that of the Byzantine Empire's eastern frontier zone or the northern *thughur* of Islamic al-Andalus.

The Iberian Peninsula is divided by a series of Sierras or mountain ranges which mostly run east–west. With a few exceptions they are not particularly high, but for many centuries they formed the basis of frontier defence in al-Andalus. Unlike most other regions of the Islamic world, al-Andalus had been defended by fortifications from the start because it was isolated and faced a significant threat to its northern frontier. During the time of the Umayyad Caliphate of Cordoba these fortifications formed chains in the mountains across the country. They were also linked by an efficient communications system.[631] During the tenth century the Andalusians responded to the first Christian advances by building a small number of stronger fortifications with substantial garrisons such as those at Gormaz and Medinaceli.

However, Christian pressure continued and control of the crests of the Sierras was lost soon after the Caliphate of Cordoba fragmented in the first *ta'ifa* period during the early eleventh century.[632] This was followed by Christian colonization of the central mountains which would in turn provide a springboard for the next push southwards. Elsewhere the nature of the frontier differed. In north-east Iberia, for example, there was no line of Sierras to provide a reasonably clearly defined border. North of the river Ebro there was instead a broad no-man's-land between the main Islamic fortified city of Saragossa and the Christian citadel of Huesca. The intervening land, while far from empty, was subject to domination or raiding depending on whichever side was the stronger at any particular moment.[633]

Not much changed under the Murabitun, but the Muwahhidun greatly strengthened the Andalusian frontier which had, by then, been pushed further south. Cities like Caceres, Badajoz, Reina and Montemolin, some of which had been fortified by the Romans and then by the Umayyad Caliphs of Cordoba, were now provided with far stronger, more modern walls, towers and citadels. Apart from protecting the border itself, they also formed a defensive ring around the fertile region and great city of Seville which was the basis of Muwahhid rule in al-Andalus.[634]

The geography of the eastern and south-eastern parts of the Iberian Peninsula was yet again different. Here there were no clearcut ranges of sierras, but rather a tangled knot of mountains forming an extensive region which was rarely suitable for heavy cavalry warfare. Instead, infantry and fast moving light cavalry dominated. This region also had a substantial population of Muslim peasants as well as numerous small hilltop castles and several substantial towns. Not surprisingly, the Aragonese who eventually conquered the eastern part of Islamic al-Andalus found the going somewhat harder than their Castilian, Leónese and even Portuguese cousins did further west. This was easily defensive terrain and eventually the Christians only succeeded by taking major castles, installing substantial garrisons and controlling the richer coastal lowlands while leaving a largely autonomous Islamic population in place in the mountains. Even here it took many years for the Aragonese to consolidate their hold. Only after they had done so could they look to the hills, gradually grinding down a series of prolonged and savage revolts.[635]

The similarity between the resistance shown by the Islamic population inland from Valencia in the later thirteenth century and that put up by the Muslims of Sicily only a few decades earlier is remarkable. The terrain, probably the military organization and perhaps even the sense of isolation in both areas also had parallels. In fact the rebellion by Islamic communities in western Sicily against the Emperor Frederick II has been described as 'a war of attrition and desperation'.

The Emperor's eventual decision to deport the entire Islamic community was intended to ensure that they never again enjoyed autonomy within his kingdom while at the same time they remained a potent military force against Frederick I's enemies in the north of his Italian realm.[636]

TACTICS

Tactics were less influenced by ecological factors than strategy because they concerned more limited territorial space, such as a battlefield or a siege. Although ecology did play a part, cultural traditions and the availability of certain types of troops were more significant. In military terms these traditions were firmly rooted in the past while also being constantly updated in response to new problems or threats.[637]

The Arabs' own pre-Islamic tactical heritage has not received the attention that it might deserve. It was clearly taken seriously during the medieval period, even being described in detail by the Persian military scholar Fakhr al-Din Mubarakshah in a book written for an early thirteenth-century Turkish ruler of northern India. How much relevance the traditional battle array of the pre-Islamic rulers of Himyar and Yemen had for Sultan Shams al-Din Iltutmish of Delhi is debatable, but it might shed light on one of the origins of what became early Islamic, Umayyad and 'Abbasid tactical theory. From them the Fatimids, Ayyubids and eventually the Mamluk Sultans also drew inspiration.

This little-known 'Battle Array of the Kings of Himyar' clearly reflected a shortage of cavalry, a problem which some Middle Eastern Islamic states would also face, not least the Fatimids. The battle array itself is rather complex but could be interpreted as consisting of five parts; left and right wings, centre, left and right flanks which are further back. The number five needs to be remembered, but this interpretation of the plan in Fakhr al-Din Mubarakshah's book excludes other substantial formations which are, however, largely in a supporting rather than combat role. It also excludes a rear guard which seems to be so far back that it is effectively separate from the main fighting formations.[638] The term *khamis*, which can be interpreted as based upon the concept of 'five', was often used in association with the earliest Islamic armies and their arrays. Although it does not have to be translated in that way, it is generally assumed to have referred to a vanguard, a centre, a rearguard and two wings,[639] which is not quite what appears in Fakhr al-Din Mubarakshah's book.

The early 'Abbasid military manual by al-Harthami adds a great many details and variations when considering those factors to be borne in mind by an Islamic commander. This work continued to have a profound influence throughout the medieval period, so al-Harthami's work should not be dismissed as archaic. For example, he stated that it was preferable to draw up an army with hills to the rear as a guard against surprise attack from that direction. Otherwise the rear should be protected by a series of 'ambush positions'. The commander should attempt to have his centre on raised ground, free of dust, so that he could see the whole battlefield clearly. If that was not possible, he should delegate a reliable subordinate to command the centre while he himself went to a hill on the right, or failing that on the left. If there were no hills at all, he should have some sort of tall, rigid structure erected from which to observe events.[640]

Here it is worth noting that a camel was sometimes used as a command post, not only by early Islamic Arab armies but also in tenth-century Iran,[641] while an elephant fulfilled the same function in both Hindu and Islamic India. Camels with large *howdahs* or litters on their backs, perhaps including the highly visible flags as shown in some Islamic art from this period, were also used to signal an advance or counter-attack in tenth-century northern Syria.[642]

When considering the timing of an attack, al-Harthami recommended a moment when the sun and wind were from the rear, and thus in the enemy's eyes. Wind from the right was a second-best, but if the wind was disadvantageous the commander should order his cavalry to dismount because wind and therefore dust blowing into the faces of men and horses was a major disadvantage.[643]

Al-Harthami recommended that an army be drawn up in five lines if it was facing a numerically superior foe, in three divisions consisting of a centre and two wings each of which were subdivided into three, making nine battalions. Each battalion was to be commanded by a *muqaddam*, and a clear passage must be allowed between each section. The first two ranks consisted of 'fighters', meaning men who were to engage the enemy in front of them. The third rank was to protect that unit's baggage from the front, the fourth to protect the baggage from the rear, and the fifth to serve as rearguards.[644] The army's overall formation could be in straight lines or variations of a *hilali* crescent formation in which the centre was thicker and stronger than the wings. It is interesting to note that Hannibal is said to have employed a form of crescent formation in his great victory over the Romans at the battle of Cannae in 216 BC, which might indicate that it had a very ancient heritage amongst Semitic peoples.

Having suggested the overall layout and plan of a battle, al-Harthami referred to the role of *mubariz* or individual champions who fought between the opposing ranks of armies before a main clash occurred. This habit was certainly ancient and could on occasions settle the outcome without the need of further bloodshed. Al-Harthami did, however, warn that a successful *mubariz* should not pursue a fleeing foe more than two-thirds of the way towards the enemy's main line or he risked capture.[645]

When the army did advance against its enemy, al-Harthami advised that the infantry should go ahead of the cavalry to protect them from the enemy's foot soldiers. If these advancing ranks then had to retreat, they should fall back only to their starting position. If their advance was a success they still should not pursue the enemy more than one-third of the way to his main position, which rather asumes that the enemy had similarly moved forwards unless al-Harthami is referring to the enemy's camp rather than initial battle position. If the enemy appeared to be defeated, the commander's standard bearer should advance a short way to indicate this success, but again should not go too far.[646] The overall impression given by al-Harthami's work is very much one of caution and of concern about the enemy employing ruses and tricks such as feigned flight.

Al-Harthami and the military tradition which he represented were not too cautious to avoid night fighting. When launching a night attack, he advised that this should best be done on a dark, windy or rainy night to conceal the army's approach. If, however, the enemy was strong it was best to attack just before dawn when his troops would still be sleepy and confused.[647] The Byzantine Emperor and military writer, Leo VI the Wise, confirms that, in the late ninth and early tenth centuries, the 'Saracen' battle array followed at least some of these precepts, consisting of a long rectangle with strict order being maintained both in battle and on the march. He pointed out that the Muslims were indeed generally cautious, preferring to await an enemy attack to which they responded with archery and javelins before closing their shields together and counter-attacking in ranks. He also noted how they sometimes also made field fortifications from their baggage train.[648]

Military tricks and stratagems were as highly regarded in the Islamic Middle East as they were in the Byzantine Empire. The chronicles mention many, but that of fooling the enemy into thinking that you are stronger than you really are was amongst the favourites. As just one example, in 987/8 a force of Kurds was facing the largely Arab army of the Uqaylid governor of Mosul in northern Iraq. Feeling outnumbered, the Kurdish commander had cattle driven on to the mountaintops with some infantry amongst them. The latter then flashed their swords in the sun so that, from a distance, they looked like a substantial cavalry force.[649]

Such tactical traditions were continued throughout the history of the Fatimid Caliphate, well into the Crusader period, but were always constrained by Egypt's lack of pasture to support cavalry horses. Furthermore, the natural pasture which did exist was almost entirely limited to winter grazing. As a result armies based in Egypt, whether Fatimid or later, had to rely upon small numbers of very well equipped, well trained élite cavalry riding quite large, stall-fed horses.[650]

Some of the surviving information that supposedly related to Fatimid armies may in reality have been based upon theory rather than reality. Nevertheless, this would have a battle starting with close-combat foot soldiers and infantry archers advancing while cavalry protected their flanks. Men were supposedly trained never to break ranks and always to return to their original position. Pursuit of the enemy was done by archers, presumably on foot, and cavalry who should always check thickets and other such cover for possible ambushes. If the enemy charged, they should be met with archery and javelins while close-combat infantry thrust the bases of their shields into the ground to form a shield wall, with armoured men being placed in the front ranks. The slightest wavering in an enemy's attack must result in a counterattack but only by the minimum necessary number of men while the rest remained in position. An army must also leave the battlefield in the same formations in which it arrived, though whether this applied to both victory and retreat is less clear.[651]

Again according to theory, the positioning of the units of a Fatimid battle array was to be arranged and agreed before the battle, with the resulting formations and lines being checked by the commander. Normally these would be based upon a centre and two wings or flanks, while officers should be selected beforehand to liaise between such formations and presumably with the commander. As in earlier tactical traditions, single combat was an accepted feature before the main battle was joined.[652]

The many descriptions of the Fatimid army in battle show that theory and practice were closer than might have been expected. In tenth and eleventh century northern Syria, where the Fatimids were usually facing Arab forces often of at least a partially tribal nature, set-piece battle usually involved two armies facing each other. Each side would then try to break the opposition's line then turn and attack it from the rear. Such forces used false flight or otherwise attempted to lure their enemy into an ambush. Those in the front ranks were almost invariably infantry and were in danger of massacre if defeated, which also accounted for their tendency to panic. The main role of cavalry was, in real warfare as in theory, to protect the infantry's flanks against attempts by enemy cavalry to turn them.

In one battle against a Byzantine force near Afamiya in central Syria in 998 the centre of the Fatimid line specifically consisted of Daylami infantry recruited from Iran, these men being Shi'a Muslims like the Fatimid Caliphate itself. Although the centre stood firm, the outnumbered cavalry wings were driven back and the Byzantines would almost certainly have won had their commander not been killed.[653] Under such circumstances it is not surprising to find that the Fatimids made great efforts to ensure that their small numbers of élite horsemen were well armoured with mail and padded garments while many of their horses were also armoured.[654] Different troops were involved in the remarkable but little-known Fatimid defeat of an invading Turkish army outside Cairo in the later eleventh century. Here the Fatimid battle array was described by a Jewish poet writing in Hebrew. His sympathy, like that of his community, was strongly with the Fatimid Caliphate, as his verses made clear:

And there came forth the camp of the saved ones,
And among them was the chief of the wise,
And placed flags like columns for the sons of Kush [Sudanese],
The sons of Ham [possibly the Berbers],
And the chief came with great anger and with great terror,
And Arabians and Hagrites [Bedouin] to the left and to the right.[655]

These traditional tactics were still used by Fatimid armies that did battle with the Crusaders at the close of the eleventh and into the early twelfth century.[656] On such occasions the Armenian troops included both cavalry and foot soldiers, mounted and infantry archers, while the Sudanis were largely close-combat infantry,[657] the Turks and Arabs largely being cavalry, and all operated in a manner remarkably close to that outlined in written theory. During the First Battle of Ramla in 1101 the Fatimid army adopted just such a defensive array. The armoured cavalry of the Latin Kingdom of Jerusalem attacked but the first two waves were beaten off by Fatimid infantry and were seemingly pursued by some of the Fatimid horse. Then the rest of the Crusader army attacked and the centre of the Fatimid line was broken, resulting in complete defeat.[658] On other occasions, as in 1099 and 1123, Fatimid defeats clearly resulted from their cavalry deserting or being separated from the infantry.[659] However, at the Second Battle of Ramla the horse and foot worked together as they should, absorbing and defeating a ferocious and overconfident Crusader charge, then practically exterminating the enemy army.

It is clear that the Turks' horse-archery tactics gave them a huge advantage over the largely Arab armies of Syria during the second half of the eleventh century.[660] When the First Crusade arrived only a few years later, the only major technological difference between the invading Christians and the defending Muslims was the latter's composite bows. These the Turks used primarily on horseback and the Arabs largely on foot. The few crossbows used by the Crusaders as yet had little tactical impact.

With what the Christians described as its 'astonishing' range,[661] estimated pull of 27 to 36 kg and high rate of shooting the composite bow was, in the hands of fully trained soldiers, a potentially battle-winning weapon. Nevertheless its powers of penetration have tended to be exaggerated. The Islamic composite bow normally shot lighter arrows than the Western European simple or self-bow later called the longbow, and weight was required to punch through armour.

Even so, the success of the First Crusade seemed miraculous at the time and still divides military historians today. Some have pointed to a rise of light cavalry and a corresponding decline in heavily armoured cavalry in the Islamic Middle East as a result of the arrival of the Seljuk Turks during this period, along with a supposed decline in the Middle Eastern tactical tradition of close cooperation between horse and foot.[662] Others have highlighted the limitations of Turkish,

Central Asian style horse-archery tactics against disciplined and determined foes. A subsequent revival in or reversion to the use of horse-armour might indicate that, on the contrary, archery both on horse-back and on foot formed the major threat to cavalry during this period. Unfortunately even a poet as skilled at describing battle as 'Arif 'Ali of Toqat does not indicate which weapons predominated, but instead provided a snapshot of the din of Turkish battle: 'The neighing of horses, the rattle of *cevşen* armour [lamellar cuirasses], the clatter of swords, the crash of *gürz* [maces], the whistling of arrows, the shouts of warriors.'[663]

A clearer idea of how existing, largely Arab-Persian, Islamic tactical ideas were adopted and modified by the new Turkish ruling dynasties and their armies can be seen in later twelfth- and thirteenth-century Iran. Here it is clear that the tradition of single combat that had probably been shared by Arabs, Persians and Turks for centuries was still accepted. A remarkable example was recorded when the Khwarazmian Shah Jalal al-Din of Iran was besieging Ahlat in eastern Anatolia in 1230. The local Ayyubid prince, Mujir al-Din, emerged from the fortress to challenge the Shah to single combat and settle the issue without further bloodshed. However, Jalal al-Din's *wazir* claimed that it would be wrong for a mightly ruler like Jalal to fight a man who was regarded even by his own Ayyubid relatives as a dependant or follower. Jalal responded by stating that he had to accept, otherwise what would his own followers think of him?[664]

Such isolated anecdotes might illuminate the military attitudes of the time and of the Persianized Turks involved. They also fit remarkably well with the highly detailed and seemingly theoretical advice given by the Persian scholar Fakhr al-Din Mubarakshah writing around much the same time for another Turkish ruler, Sultan Iltutmish of Delhi. Some of his advice was identical to that found in earlier Arabic military manuals. For example the need to have a hill behind the army's battle position to avoid attack from the rear.[665] Fakhr al-Din's description of the cavalry as a 'castle' and the infantry ahead of them as a 'moat' also illuminates the basic concept within the traditional medieval Islamic battle array.[666] The account of how to 'array an army and deploy it for battle' in Chapter 17 of the Persian scholar's text is, in fact, detailed enough to warrant being quoted in full:

> Know that for this purpose it is necessary to have the first rank consisting of armed infantrymen with broad shields [*siparha-i farkh*] and spears [*harba* which are sometimes translated as heavy javelins or as an early form of pole-arm] and archers [*tir andazan*]. This is because their role is defensive. The second rank should be of infantry wearing a lamellar cuirass [*jawshan*] and tunic [*khaftan*, sometimes padded], and be armed with a sword [*shamshir*], shield [*sipar*] and spear [*niza*]. The third should be of infantry armed with a sword [*shamshir*], quiver [*tarkash*; note no mention of bows], iron-bound staves [*chubha-i ahan basta*, perhaps an early form of long-hafted infantry mace] and large daggers [*kardha-i buzurg*]. The fourth rank should consist of junior officers ['*arifan*],

with infantrymen armed with leather shields [*daraqa*], swords [*shamshir*] and maces [*'amud*].

Between such ranks there should be a wide space so that each rank of soldiers is able to see what is happening, so that there may be a way through for the cavalry, and so that the warriors in the forefront [assault troops] can go forward and get through.

The warriors are in four groups. The first are the daredevil warriors in the foremost or champions [*mubarizan*], who seek fame in the battle. These should be placed in the right wing. The second group are the outstandingly firm and steadfast troops in battle; these should be placed in the rearguard. The third group are the archers who may be necessary as a supporting force, and who bear a shield as protection for themselves and who get down on their knees to loose their arrows. These troops should be placed on the left wing. The fourth group comprise the non-combatants [*arayish*, literally 'ornamental' or 'auxiliary'] element of the army, such as standard-bearers, those holding partizans [*mitrad*, probably with an insignia on their tips], warriors with kettledrums of the *duhul* and *tabira* kinds, frames of bells [*zangiyana* or 'jingling johnny'], trumpets, wardrums and suchlike. There should also be a unit of valiant and hardy men who can inspire the troops with bravery, make them keen to throw themselves into battle and give heart to the army so that it becomes intrepid and fearless. The baggage and impedimenta, the treasury, the army bazaar and the artisans should be kept in the rear but near the centre and the two wings [of the main body of the army].

When the Caliph [the use of this term shows that the author is almost certainly recalling 'Abbasid military practice] is established in his place with his leading commanders, the arrangement should be that each group should be deployed in its allotted place with its field officers [*sarhangan*] and with its complete array of weapons. In particular, the cavalry troop commanders, and then grooms and attendants [*chakiran*], all fully armed, should be in their designated places. The generals [*hajiban*] and royal guards [*khassagan*] must stay very close to the ruler and the army's commander-in-chief [*sipahsalar*]. The guides who police and keep the routes open, with their aides, should be at the right side of the centre. The archers, the troops operating various mechanical weapons [*hilatgaran*] and fire-throwers [*naft andazan*] should be at the left side of the centre. Those who lead the baggage train, the men who lead the strings of remounts and the experts with lassoes [*kamand andazan*, perhaps throwers of scaling ropes] should be close at hand. The guard pickets [*harasbanan*], the men bearing calthrops [*hasakdaran*], the crews operating *manjaniq* and *'arradat* [both being forms of mangonel], the men with scaling ladders and ropes [*kamand halqa andazan*] and the outstandingly bold troops [*jigar-andazan*, lit. 'those who hazard their livers/the seats of their lives'], are held on the right [of the centre]. The animals, herds of horses, sheep and oxen, should be held away from the army. The riding camels dispersed [at pasture], the beasts carrying fodder and other loads and baggage, should be placed farthest back of all, with trusty, strong and full-armed men looking after them.

The great generals and senior field officers, the long-experienced veterans of the army, the religious scholars, the physicians, the ruler's boon-companions and the astrologers should remain near to the monarch and the supreme commander of the army. Servitors [*khadiman*, eunuchs] and slaves, both those of the ruler's personal retinue and those in general, should be placed at the right hand [of the preceding group], together with the *wazir* and two knowledgeable, sharp-witted and experienced men from amongst the ruler's trusted confidants [*aminan*]. A second [group] of the ruler's personal guards and protectors should be stationed on the army's right. The ruler's womenfolk [*harim*], treasury and armoury [*silah*] should invariably be near the centre, together with the ruler's personal kitchen. The rearguard remains stationed behind the ranks of the [front line] troops with its back to the main body of the army and its front placed so as to protect and watch over the army and the baggage train.

If the opposing army appears before the left wing, the following deployment should be made, in the manner which they [i.e. experienced commanders] usually make for the battlefield and for war and for drawing up the ranks of troops. A field officer or general moves from the centre to the right and left flanks in order to arrange and deploy the troops for battle and goes round the scouts [*talaya*] and the four fronts of the army [i.e. the centre, the two wings and the rearguard].

If the danger of attack [by the enemy] is coming from the front, one should throw forward half of the left wing towards [the opposing] line of troops, and another half, from the right wing, so that the centre is just behind them. In this way, the right and left wings and the centre remain compact and close together and maintaining their battle order. If battle has then to be engaged, then first of all the right wing gives battle in that place and then the rest [of the army joins in]. If the danger of attack comes from behind the army's centre, it is necessary to adopt the same procedure as has been described above. If it is unclear where the threat is going to come from or from which direction, the army should remain silent and calm, and scouts should be sent out. In any case, the ruler and the supreme commander who deploys the army should remain in the centre, with the treasury before him, and experienced cavalrymen and infantrymen drawn up behind him, so that the ruler may have a view over all his troops.

On the actual day of battle, an issue of two days' rations of fodder, hay, bread and meat should be given out. Every cavalryman intending to give battle should carefully check his saddle, bridle and weapons, for if some failure of these should occur in the midst of the fray, he will be thrown into a distressed state and pay for it with his life. He should ensure that five things are firm and strong: the leather straps of the bridle [*duwal-i 'inan*], the stirrup straps [*duwal-i rikab*], the girth [*tang*], the *pushtak* [an unknown strap or series of straps going over the horse's back or over the saddle] and surcingle [*hayasa*], for a cavalryman's effectiveness depends on these things. If a crupper strap (or crupper armour) [*par dum*] or collar (or neck armour) [*bar band*] is faulty, this is not usually a grave problem. A cavalryman should never be without a cobbler's awl [*dirafsh*], a large pack-needle [*juwalduz*], a sewing needle [*suzan*] and thread [*risman*], plus a leather strap and an [extra] piece of thread, so that if any damage occurs to any of these pieces of equipment, he can speedily put it right and sew it up. Also, if the leather strap is not long enough, he can take some hair from the horse's tail, twist it together and sew with that.[667]

Nothing as detailed as this is known to survive from the period of *atabeg* and Zangid rule in the Middle East, though other sources make it clear that Nur al-Din's army relied upon three main tactics; harassment, sieges and set-piece battle arrayed in lines; probably in a simplified version of that described by Fakhr al-Din Mubarakshah. One interesting variation of such an array was seen at the battle of Babayn in Egypt when the army sent by Nur al-Din and commanded by Saladin's uncle Shirkuh anchored its flanks on two hills and had its centre in the valley between. Shirkuh hoped to lure his enemies, an alliance of Crusader and Fatimid forces, into attacking the centre and thus being ambushed by his wings. In the event the Crusaders tried to charge the hills, but these were too steep and sandy for the Latin cavalry to achieve sufficient momentum and the battle ended as a draw.[668]

The first of the military manuals written for Saladin was the *Tabsira Arbab al-Lubab* by Murda al-Tarsusi. Since it was written in Egypt very early in Saladin's reign, it may be more relevant to late Fatimid forces than to Saladin's army, though other evidence concerning Saladin's actual campaigns suggests that there had been little tactical change other than an increased use of horse-archery. Once again al-Tarsusi's suggested battle array is worth quoting in full:

> Everyone agrees on principles but not on the details of their application ... Place infantry ahead of cavalry to make a firm fortress. In front of every infantryman place a *januwiya* or *tariqa* shield [both of these being tall or elongated shields or mantlets] or a parapet as a protection against those who attack with sword, spear or arrow. Behind each pair of men place an archer with a *jarkh* [crossbow] or with *nabala* [arrows to be shot from an ordinary handbow]. Their role is to drive back attackers. Thus the cavalry and *abtal* [champions] to the rear are separated from danger by these archers, and the *shuj'an* ('attack cavalry') wait to make a charge. Troops [of cavalry] are grouped into units with a prearranged gap ahead of them through which they charge, after which the infantry close up again. It is necessary on the field of battle to arrange the battle array by *karadis* [squadrons] and the horsemen by *'alam* [flag] and *khamis* by *khamis* [corps by corps] when it is the foes' habit to charge in a mass and rely for shock [on] their detachment of their army, this is the case with the Franks [Crusaders] and those neighbours who resemble them. This array is very effective because when one group of enemy attacks, it can be taken in the flank and surrounded.[669]

Al-Harawi's military manual was completed shortly after Saladin's death and clearly reflects what might be described as updated versions of long-accepted tactical and other traditions. Where the battle array was concerned, he advised putting the best men in the centre where the enemy was most likely to attack, but also to keep some of these best troops in reserve for use in stratagems. The infantry was still to be arrayed ahead of the cavalry, these foot soldiers to include archers with both ordinary and heavy arrows (note that the published translation by Sourdel-Thomine is wrong at this particular point) and two different types of javelins. The commander should always draw up his troops to match those of the foe, best for best and type for type. When the enemy attacked, then that section of his line from which the attack came should itself be immediately counter-attacked with cavalry and infantry because it could be assumed to have been depleted. Once again the men were strongly advised not to pursue an enemy too far as this could weaken their own position and make it vulnerable. A further interesting piece of advice by al-Harawi was that the prince or commander should keep those cavalry mounted on the best Arabian horses close to him.[670]

The practical application of such tactical traditions by Saladin often seems to have been more active and less passive than the theories indicate. Descriptions of earlier battles show that this had also been the case elsewhere in the Islamic world for many years. For example, when Saladin defeated a rival, lzz al-Din, near Hama in 1174, he did so by managing to separate the enemy's cavalry from their infantry and baggage.[671]

Breaking the enemy's force into more vulnerable sections might have been easier to do when the foe were on the march, and this seems to have been what Saladin attempted at the battle of Arsuf in 1191 during the Third Crusade.[672] Here Saladin launched his attack as the front of the Crusader column was approaching its designated campsite for the following night. This moment, often known as *nuzul* in Arabic, could be expected to result in some eager pressing ahead by those at the front, and perhaps some breakdown in cohesion and discipline which an attack might then seize upon (see below for such *nuzul* tactics in North Africa).

Saladin did not succeed at the battle of Arsuf, though the outcome was more of a draw than the great victory proclaimed by Crusader chroniclers. Four years earlier at the battle of Hattin the outcome had been far more clearcut. Before and during the early stages of this battle, volunteers in Saladin's army had been tasked with lighting brush fires to make conditions even worse for the tired and thirsty army of the Latin Kingdom of Jerusalem.[673] The latter had already been harassed while on the march but this time the battle culminated in the two armies facing each other in relatively static positions.

The predictability of events meant that, on the night before the main battle, Saladin was able to have 70 baggage camels loaded with additional arrows and stationed amongst his units.[674] The following day saw Saladin's units manoeuvring across the battlefield, showing much greater tactical flexibility than their Latin opponents whose only significant moves were a retreat to a final stand on the twin hilltops of the Horns of Hattin. The resulting rather confused battle nevertheless saw a combination of heavy cavalry charges supported by infantry in what was essentially a version of traditional Islamic tactics supplemented by horse-archery harassment.[675]

If the Ayyubid period can justly be described as a period of change, it is important to recognize that the subsequent Mamluk Sultanate saw a significant reversion to cavalry shock tactics, though not to the exclusion of horse-archery harassment. What changed was the role of infantry which certainly did not disappear but which did decline in importance and flexibility. Perhaps the Mamluks' greatest or most significant victory was their defeat of an invading Mongol force at 'Ayn Jalut in 1260. This battle clearly demonstrated the different tactical traditions of the two sides and the sophistication of those available to the Mamluk army.

Both sides are estimated to have been roughly equal in number, though the Mongols included large numbers of Georgian and Armenian auxiliaries or allies.[676] Given the political circumstances of the time it would almost certainly be wrong to see these Middle Eastern Christian troops as unwilling participants. One of the more convincing interpretations of the battle of 'Ayn Jalut describes it as a classic example of the Mamluks drawing their enemy into a trap. This was not really an ambush but meant that the Mongols found themselves in an unfavourable tactical position. The resulting battle is also interesting because of the vital role played by infantry in the Mamluk army, particularly on the left wing. The foot soldiers themselves were not members of the slave-recruited Mamluk élite. Nevertheless they were highly motivated and proved highly effective.

Part of the Mongol left wing was commanded by an Ayyubid prince whose men were probably unwilling allies of the pagan Mongols, and as a consequence many deserted to the Mamluks. Part of the Mongol centre then tried to fight its way into the hills to escape but, now outflanked on both sides, they were pursued and destroyed by infantry from the Mamluk army of Egypt, showing once again that cavalry could be at a serious disadvantage in steep, rough ground where nimble foot soldiers could operate more easily.[677]

In more classic or controlled manoeuvres in open or flat ground, the disciplined formations of Mamluk cavalry were sufficiently impressive for Fidenzio of Padua, in his book on how to regain the Holy Land written in 1291, to urge the Crusaders to imitate them.[678] In such open array the Mamluk Sultans continued the Ayyubid tradition of placing their Turcoman auxiliaries on one wing and their Arab bedouin auxiliaries on the other but whether this was primarily to avoid tension between competing groups or to make better use of their differing military skills is unknown.

The predominance of Berber tribal troops, and above all Berber cavalry in the armies of medieval North Africa inevitably had a major impact upon their tactics. Even when classic Islamic battlefield tactics were attempted, these were also always in a simplified form. Archery had taken root during the early Islamic period, but it was of the Arab infantry style. There were hardly any horse-archers and those that existed seem, until the later Middle Ages, to have been incomers from the Middle East.

This is not to suggest that some of the wealthier Islamic states of the Maghrib did not employ large numbers of professional and élite soldiers. It is just that their tactics and skills seemed remarkably old fashioned when compared with those of the Islamic Middle East. The Zirid Sultanate in Tunisia and eastern Algeria was, until the later eleventh century, wealthy enough to recruit well-trained and well-equipped infantry. Those in the ruler's household or escort may have been mounted infantry, accompanying the small élite of armoured true cavalry which also formed part of these guard units.[679] Unfortunately little is known about the arms and armour of the Zirid period, but it is likely to have been similar to that of the thirteenth- and fourteenth-century Hafsid state in almost exactly the same region. The latter made notable use of leather armour with iron armour limited to a few. Their cavalry now included plenty of archers but javelins remained the main missile weapon of the cavalry, plus some horse-archers whom the Zirids almost entirely lacked.[680]

The supposed greater abundance of armour worn by the best of Zirid forces was such that traditional Arabic accounts of the battle of Haydaran in 1057 have the leader of invading Banu Hilal ordering his men to aim for their enemies' eyes, since this was the only part of their body that remained unprotected.[681] Such legends probably contain more than a germ of truth. Accounts of the battle of Haydaran are difficult to interpret, but it does seem that the battle array of the Zirid army differed from that seen in the pre-Turkish Middle East by placing cavalry not only on the wings but also ahead of and behind the infantry who formed the centre.[682]

On the other hand this distribution of troops might have been used by an army on the march rather than fully arrayed. In fact the battle of Haydaran might better be intepreted as an attack by the Banu Hilal on the Zirid army as the latter were at the point of *nuzul*, completing their march but not yet either encamped or arrayed for battle. Their preparation clearly took time and they were attacked before they were fully prepared. The best translation of the term *nuzul* may actually be the process of congregating an army which had been strung out along its line of march.[683]

Surprisingly, more detail is known about the tactics employed by the originally Saharan and sub-Saharan Murabitun in the furthest west of the medieval Islamic world. This is probably because they were credited with introducing major changes to the traditional tactics of these regions. The Murabitun's 'new' tactics were supposedly based upon those of the first Islamic armies back in the seventh century and, having been introduced or taught by a religious reformer from the Middle East, they formed part of the Murabitun's religious and cultural identity. For example, the first Murabit armies astonished their local enemies by refusing to retreat when facing difficulties, and instead preferring to accept substantial casualties. This went against nomad Berber tribal traditions which had been rooted in an avoidance of manpower losses in a part of the world where life was precarious enough in the first place.[684]

The early Murabit armies largely consisted of infantry, some camel-riding mounted infantry, and a very small number of horsemen. According to the chronicler Ibn 'Idhari, the Murabit army which defeated the related but rival Masmuda tribes consisted of 400 cavalry, 800 camel riders and 2,000 men on foot. The latter reportedly fought in ordered ranks, the first of which carried long spears or pikes while those behind were armed with javelins of which each man had an adequate supply.[685]

Another account of this first victory by the first Murabit preacher 'Abd Allah Ibn Yasin in 1048/9, written by al-Bakri, has Ibn Yasin fighting on horseback or on a racing camel, while most of the Lamtuna Berbers who supported him were infantry lined up in ranks. Al-Bakri continued: 'In all their expeditions they put in the front rank a man with a flag. As long as the flag remained upright they remain unshakeable. If it falls, then they all sit on the ground where they remain as immobile as mountains.'[686] Apparently such early Murabit armies did not even pursue a defeated foe, all of which seems to be a conscious inversion of what had been traditional amongst the tribal Berbers.

Facing the Spanish Castillians at the battle Zallaqa less than 40 years later, the Murabitun army's best *sudani* black African *hasham* troops were again infantry equipped with *lamt* very large leather shields and *mizraq* javelins. However, they were not passive in battle but attacked and defeated the Christian Spanish cavalry.[687] Even so, swords were mentioned only occasionally and the overall impression is that of a largely infantry army armed with javelins and now also with bows. Their archers may, however, have largely been Andalusians and Moroccans rather that Saharan Berbers.

Muwahhid tactics were much the same as those of the later Murabitun, using a solid defensive phalanx supported by cavalry. According to an anonymous Muwahhid poem:

> We formed a square in the plain. On all four sides we stationed a row of men who held long spears in their hands. Behind them stood men holding shields and javelins in a second line, and at the back of them were men armed with 'nose bags' filled with stones [presumably slingers]. At the far back were the archers. The cavalry were in the middle of the square. Whenever the cavalry of the Murabitun [at that time the Muwahhidun's main enemy] charged towards them, they only met the long-pointed spears, the javelins, the stones and the loosed arrows. When they died in the charge or turned to flee, the cavalry of the Muwahhidun went out from lanes [in the ranks of foot soldiers] from which they had withdrawn their men, and through openings which they had prepared, and fell upon the enemy wounded and other casualties. If the Murabitun charged them again, they [the Muwahhid cavalry] entered within their forest of spears.[688]

The close-packed infantry formation or phalanx was probably common to both Morocco and al-Andalus during this period, with the cavalry being allocated the final and 'aristocratic' role of delivering a battle-winning charge.[689] In essence this was merely a variation on the earlier Islamic battlefield tactics seen in the Middle East. At Zallaqa in the Iberian peninsula in 1086, one version of the battle has the local Andalusians forming a first division or vanguard with the Murabitun formed up behind them. Furthermore there was said to have been a ditch excavated between them. The Andalusians clearly stood to receive the Christian charge, but were broken by it and fell back. The Murabit line then held, checking the Castillian assault while the Murabitun sent their reserves or troops on their flanks to go around the Christian formation and attack its camp in the rear. One thing is clear, and that is the remarkable steadiness and discipline shown by the Murabitun infantry.[690]

Writing in Egypt in the mid-twelfth century, al-Turtushi described the battle array used in 'his country', namely al-Andalus. Although it is not clear whether he is referring to Andalusian or Murabit tactics, there is unlikely to have been a great deal of difference between the two.[691] Only the emphasis on infantry archers tends to point to al-Andalus rather than the Sahara. The array that had been found 'most suitable against our enemies' was, according to al-Turtushi, as follows:

> The infantry, with their *daraqa kamil* [tall shields], their long *rumh* [spears] and their *mizraq* [javelins] of sharp and penetrating iron, are placed in many ranks, their *rumh* [spears] resting obliquely on their chests, the butt touching the ground, the point in the direction of the enemy. Every one is on his left knee, placed on the ground and the *qaim* [handles] of their *turs* [shields] between their hands. Behind the infantry are the archers, the best of whom can pierce a *dir'* [coat of mail] with their *saham* [arrows]. Behind the archers are the cavalry. When the Christians charge the Muslims, the infantry remain in their position, knees to the ground, the enemy reaches a short distance away, the archers discharge at them a hail of *nishab* [arrows] while the infantry throw their *mizraq* [javelins] and receive the enemy on the points of their *rumh* [spears]. After that the infantry and the archers open their ranks in an oblique movement to the left and right, and through the open space the Muslim cavalry fall on the enemy and put them to rout, if God will it to be so.[692]

Here it is worth noting that the Islamic cavalry élite of thirteenth century Valencia had an aristocratic code of behaviour which their Christian opposite numbers in Aragon regarded as comparable to their own. Both sides also indulged in single combat of champions before a battle, perhaps reflecting the deep-seated degree of traditional Islamic military influence in Christian northern Iberia as well as in the Andalusian south.[693]

The vulnerability of an army on the march, and more particularly when it is tired at the end of a march or eager to establish camp for the night, has already been mentioned in the context of the *nuzul*. So it is not surprising that Islamic military thinkers, theoreticians and generals put a lot of thought into minimizing such risks. Once again al-Harthami, in his military manual originally written for the 'Abbasid Caliph al-Ma'mun in the early ninth century, had interesting observations to make. Some of them deal with seemingly minor details, such as it being a commander's responsibility to tell his men when to put on their armour. Others are more obvious, such as the need to send scouting parties ahead of the line of march, followed by a group of pioneers consisting of the best men to repair roads, cut down trees, build bridges and dam rivers to make the passage of the army easier. Some of the tasks assigned to these supposed pioneers sound more like engineering. Behind them comes the *Muqaddama* which was a cavalry vanguard, perhaps close enough to ensure the safety of the pioneers. In narrow places or bottlenecks the commander must also supervise matters closely so as to avoid confusion or jealousy over precedence.[694]

According to al-Harthami, the actual order of march varied according to the threat posed by any nearby enemy. If the foe was near, the army should move in what was almost a battle formation with a *Muqaddama* vanguard, a *Maysara* right flank, a *Maymana* left flank, and a *Saqah* rearguard plus the main force in the centre. All should march with unsheathed weapons, banners flying and each man under the correct flag.[695] If the march was threatened from one side, then this should be reinforced with troops from the other sides. If the commander was not sure in which direction enemy lay, he should have scouting parties all around while the army marched in battle order with the commander in the centre.[696]

This was also the theory, and perhaps often the reality, in Fatimid armies of the Crusader period, such forces often defending even their temporary encampments with ditches.[697] The chronicles supply further detailed information from specific instances, as when the freelance Turkish *ghulam* commander Alp Takin led his men from Iraq to Syria, across the steppes of the Jazira. Greatly outnumbered by the local Arab bedouin tribes, the *ghulams* were ordered to wear their armour and put caparisons or horse-armour upon their horses. The bedouin were reportedly so impressed that they did not attack the little army, though it should be added that the Turkish *ghulams* were also noted for their remarkable standards of order and discipline which would have given tribal warriors reason to be cautious.[698]

Two centuries later Nur al-Din's army, marching through much the same region, was preceded by scouts who not only looked out for the enemy but reported back on the availability of drinking water. Behind Nur al-Din's scouts his advance guard looked for suitable camp sites. The main body and cavalry came next but there does not normally appear to have been a rearguard. The baggage train was supposedly placed ahead of this main body while the herds and flocks followed. What might seem even more remarkable was the 30 km a day which such an army could usually cover.[699]

The *Nihayat al-Su'l* attributed to al-Aqsara'i and dating from the late thirteenth century was largely based upon earlier sources but it does add a few interesting details. Here the march was in four mounted groups consisting of a vanguard which prepared and marked out the route and arranged camping places, a rearguard to pick up stragglers and so on, plus left and right wings to guard the flanks. Apparently the centre consisted of the 'soldiers' market' (see below), the infantry followed by the stores plus siege train, the staff organization and the commander.[700]

On the whole question of scouting and intelligence gathering, it is clear that medieval Islamic governments and armies took these issues very seriously. Frontier observation systems and networks of spies inside enemy territory were highly developed while serious efforts were also made to win enemy spies over to one's own side.[701] According to al-Harthami, a *tali'a* scouting party must always be selected from the best available men provided with the fastest and most easily controlled horses. The scouts themselves should each have a mail hauberk, a shield and archery equipment with a quiver of 20 arrows, but be otherwise unencumbered. They should avoid raising dust, never go more than two-thirds of the distance from their own main force to that of the enemy, never follow up an enemy retreat nor fall into ambush. Furthermore their commander should never send his whole party back with news, but should always keep some men available in case they were needed.[702] During the Ayyubid period, the *tala'i al-'askar* not only consisted of special reconnaissance troops and scouts to be sent ahead of the main army before hostilities broke out, but also included spies and informers. All such information seems to have come in to the commander via the *yazaq*.[703] Meanwhile considerable attention was paid to information gained from prisoners.[704]

At the end of a march an army made camp, and here again the Islamic armies of the medieval period had well established systems to draw upon, such as those described by al-Harthami in the early ninth century. When an army made camp, it should choose a spot where a hill or river protected one side from surprise attack. If this was not possible, then scouts should be placed all around the site. When there was a specific threat of attack, the camp should be surrounded by trenches with two or more entrances guarded by archers and cavalry. In 'Abbasid times the area immediately outside these camps would be protected by *zaqaziq* calthrops against horses' hooves and infantry's feet, but this habit seems to have been abandoned by the time al-Harthami's surviving text was copied and edited in the Mamluk Sultanate. According to al-Harthami, some military specialists considered it advisable to have a mounted guard unit called a *darraja* riding around the exterior of the camp all night, to watch out for any ambushes that an enemy might try to set up.[705]

It is clear that the Fatimids continued to construct such military camps surrounded by ditches in late tenth-century Syria. In such cases they placed their own troops inside but apparently insisted that local Arab tribal allies make camp outside.[706] A variation on this process was seen in a confrontation between Fatimid and Hamdanid armies in northern Syria in 991. On this occasion there appear to have been no natural obstacles, features or anchorpoints in the area, so both armies formed 'large circles', probably meaning encampments from which they sent their cavalry to attacks certain parts of the enemy's defences.[707]

The Banu Qurra were an Arab tribe closely related to the Banu Hilal, but which remained in Egypt as auxiliaries in Fatimid service after the Banu Hilal had migrated to Tunisia. Their traditional tactics seem to have been based upon a laager of tents containing their flocks and families, this also serving as a defensive position from which to launch cavalry charges and into which to retreat. Perhaps the largely tribal Arab armies of the Syrian Hamdanids did something similar when fighting the Fatimids. There does, in fact, seem to have been a notable increase in the military capabilities of nomadic and semi-nomadic Arab tribes around this time, including those such as the Banu Qurra in Fatimid service, though their tactics remained very traditional.[708]

The evidence indicates that much the same sort of tented encampments were still used in Syria, even under Turkish post-Seljuk rule. In the mid-twelfth century Nur al-Din's army usually erected its encampments as a circle with the commander's tent in the middle, then surrounding the camp with a ditch and the calthrops which may have been regarded as old-fashioned by Mamluk times. Once again an advance position called a *yazaq* was established in the direction of the enemy although, if the foe were too close, *karariya* 'shock troops' were also made ready in that direction.[709] Writing for Saladin or his immediate successor a few decades later, al-Harawi maintained that it was best to make the camp in two concentric circles, though again with sentinels and an advance guard in the direction of the enemy.[710] After an assassination attempt by Isma'ilis during his siege of Azaz in 1175, Saladin surrounded the tent, or perhaps the entire camp, with a guarded stockade.[711]

According to Fidenzio of Padua, in his book of 1291 on how to regain the Holy Land, the armies of the Mamluk Sultanate surrounded their military camps with a small ditch plus other unspecified obstacles.[712] At the battle of Köse Dağ in 1243, the Seljuk Sultan of Rum constructed field fortifications but was still defeated by the Mongols, while the 3,000 Greeks and Franks in his army are said to have retreated up a mountain or large hill in the hope of making a defensive position but were still showered by the Mongols' arrows.[713] Contemporary descriptions of field fortification and fortified camps are often difficult to interpret and have sometimes been overlaid with myth. One of the most notorious examples concerns the chained palisade almost certainly constructed by the Muwahhidun before their disastrous defeat at the battle of Las Navas de Tolosa in 1212. This eventually entered the mythology of the Christian Reconquista as a legend that the fanatical Muwahhidun chained themselves together so that no man would be tempted to flee, and were as a result slaughtered.

The dividing line between cavalry tactics and individual cavalry skills was a fine one. However, the general skills required of cavalry in open battle were listed as an ability to attack, to maintain an attack, to feign retreat, wheel around in formation, to evade the enemy and to renew an attack.[714] In has been suggested that the lightly armoured, close-combat cavalry which dominated Fatimid armies during the tenth and eleventh centuries may have been armed with swords rather than spears,[715] but this does not seem to be supported by evidence from comparable Arab and non-Turkish regions such as Syria and North Africa. Nor it is supported by the admittedly limited pictorial evidence from the Fatimid Caliphate itself.

It has been suggested that what is described as 'medium cavalry' were more important than 'heavy cavalry' during the early medieval Islamic period from the seventh to eleventh centuries. Furthermore, that there was not really a revival in 'heavy cavalry' until the Mamluk Sultanate in the second half of the thirteenth century.[716] This interpretation does, however, seem to oversimplify the situation and imply an unrealistic degree of uniformity in the cavalry of these periods. In fact, all forms of cavalry were in service, ranging from the entirely unarmoured to the heavily armoured riding armoured horses, and the proportion of one type to another reflected economic and cultural rather than strictly military factors.

Al-Andalus provided a particularly dramatic example of this sort of regional variation. Here, according to Ibn Hauqal, Andalusian horsemen still did not use stirrups even in the late tenth century.[717] Instead they rode and fought in the early Islamic Arab manner which had probably been superseded in practically all other regions of the Islamic world, with the exceptions of some bedouin Arab tribes as well as nomadic tribal peoples of the Sahara and Red Sea coasts of Africa. Nevertheless Andalusian Islamic cavalry had a major role in Iberian warfare, above all as light and fast moving raiding forces or in protecting the rear of an army on the march.[718]

Horse-archery had such a major impact upon warfare in the Middle East that it has inevitably received a great deal of scholarly attention. Its history goes far back into ancient times but it was always divided into two major forms. On one hand there was the harassment style of horse-archery normally associated with largely nomadic peoples of the Central Asian steppes or of recent Central Asian origin. This was usually done at a distance and on the move. It may also have become even more effective with the adoption of stirrups which, known on the borders of China for several centuries, reached Iran and the Middle East shortly before the emergence of Islam in the seventh century.

A second form of horse-archery is more closely associated with settled peoples, not only in Iran and the Middle East but also in China and some other regions bordering the great steppes of Central Asia. In essence this 'settled' style of horse-archery was based upon disciplined and highly trained cavalrymen acting in distinct units, either 'shower shooting' while their horses were standing still or delivering controlled charges which culminated in arrows being shot from close range before the cavalry units in question wheeled around and retired. This latter tactic would almost certainly have been made more effective by an adoption of stirrups. Of course there were many variations on these two basic styles of 'settled' mode of horse-archery, and aspects of them were also employed by nomadic steppe warriors. It is also important to realize that the stirrup itself was probably not developed to improve horse-archery, or indeed cavalry warfare of any sort, but emerged as a device to make long distance riding and long hours in the saddle more bearable.

Occasionally a description of a minor skirmish or small battle of no great historical significance can shed more light on the reality of current tactics than do several accounts of a larger engagement. One such was a clash between the Daylamite northern Iranian foot soldiers of a rebel named Ruzbahan at the Bridge of Arbaq near Baghdad in the year 957. The opposition was led by Ahmad Ibn Buya Mu'i al-Dawla, the Buwayhid *amir* or ruler of Iraq. The latter mistrusted his own Daylami troops, despite the fact that the Buwayhid dynasty had itself sprung from the mountainous region of Daylam. Instead he relied solely on his Turkish household cavalry who were almost all *ghulams* of slave-recruited origin. Thus traditional infantry in a static position were pitted against fully trained professional horse soldiers using the 'settled' rather than 'steppe nomadic' tradition of horse-archery. The following account was by Ibn Miskawaihi, a Persian chronicler writing in the early eleventh century: 'Mu'zz al-Dawlah then crossed [the river] and drew up his men in bodies which relieved each other in the charge till sunset. The Turks then flagged, their tactics being exhausted and their arrows spent.' The *ghulams* wanted to halt for the night and resume their assaults in the morning but Mu'zz al-Dawlah feared a Daylami counterattack. So he begged them to fight on, informing them that the *ghilman al-asaghir*, lesser or perhaps younger retainers, had arrows to spare. 'These *ghilman al-asaghir* were mounted on blood [fine bred] horses and were clothed with *jubbas* [quilted and sometimes mail-lined armour] and *tijfaf* [quilted armour, perhaps for the men or for their horses].'

They had wanted to fight but had not been allowed to do so, and when a junior officer was sent to collect their arrows they thought it was their turn to enter the battle. 'They, being fresh, charged, and their horses also were fresh. They dashed against the ranks of the Daylamis, broke them, hurling one against another, and got through to the rear. Mu'zz al-Dawla then charged and belaboured them with maces.'[719] The result was a victory for Mu'zz al-Dawla and demonstrated how *ghulam* horse-archery tactics were supposed to work.

It would appear that the skills involved had become rarer by the time the First Crusade reached Turkish Islamic territory in 1097. Or it may have been that the tactical limitations of horse-archery became brutally obvious when it was not adequately supported by other sorts of troops.[720] Various sources similarly made clear the vulnerability of the composite bow to variations in weather, especially if the weapon got wet,[721] and it is possible that its normal killing range and even its accuracy have been exaggerated except when in the hands of those recognized as 'archery masters'.[722] Such limitations would surely have been even more pronounced in non-élite, non-professional, part-time and tribal warriors who formed the bulk of Islamic armies at the time of the Crusades.

Recently a number of virtually complete composite bows have been found in the Middle East, and tests strongly suggest that they are of late twelfth- to early fourteenth century origin. They are also much less formidable and powerful than might have been expected.[723] While it is possible that this particular archaeological find is of weak practice bows, as described in the archery training manuals of the period, this cannot necessarily be assumed.

Various modern archery specialists have come up with different assessments of what the normal medieval Islamic composite war bow could achieve. One has suggested that the smooth recurved Turkish style had a killing range of over 150 m and could therefore be used out of range of the normal European hand-held crossbows used during the Crusader period.[724] However, this estimate must surely only be true against unarmoured targets. The archer would almost certainly have had to come closer when attacking men in any form of armour. This was, of course, the purpose behind the charge–shoot–retire tactic used at the Bridge of Arbaq as described above. Another scholar has maintained that, at a range of over 100 m, even ordinary mail was unlikely to have been penetrated by the light arrows normally used in the Islamic world. Furthermore, he notes that the form and weight of arrowheads and arrows, and their high-drag fletching, seem to be designed for them to be shot at close range. The resulting maximum armour-piercing range, against the sort of armour used before the introduction of European plate armour, was likely to have been from 35 to 55 m, which also happens to be the usual spacing of towers along fortified walls.[725] The latter feature was, incidentally, before those architectural changes resulting from the adoption of counterweight stone-throwing *trebuchets* (see below).

Certain practical considerations would similarly have influenced the way in which repeated waves of horse-archers charged to shoot and wheel. Hence the suggestion that there was probably at least ten seconds between each such wave, to allow the preceding wave to get out of the way. Each wave may have

approached in line abreast then shot before turning a right-angle and riding
nose-to-tail out of the way to the rear of the hindmost attacking wave or unit,
ready to charge when their turn came again. This also assumes that an archer's
horse or pony charged at about 30 kph.[726]

Having turned after shooting, however, it seems unlikely that the line of horse-
archers would simply have ridden along the face of an enemy unit, thus exposing
themselves to his defensive archery. Perhaps they formed their nose-to-tail
formation then curved away as soon as they were clear of the men behind. The
minimum safe distance for horse-archers to retire before turning to shoot once
more may be indicated by the final third of a *qabaq* 'training course' which was
described as 40 m. Practical experience has shown this to be about twice what a
horseman needed to recover his reins and turn his horse.[727] However, this would
only have taken the man out of the 'armour-piercing' range of enemy archers,
not beyond their harassment range.

The sum total of evidence from the later medieval period strongly suggests
that the armies of the Mamluk Sultanate relied upon the accuracy and volume
of their archery to balance the Mongols' mobility,[728] and indeed their numbers.
It has therefore been suggested that, when facing a Mongol 'arrow charge', a
properly trained Mamluk force stood its horses in four staggered lines in open
order with the front two ranks shooting rapidly as soon as the enemy came into
a designated killing zone. The third and fourth ranks are unlikely to have shot
over the heads of the men in front as this would have been too inaccurate, but
may have come forward as the first two ranks retired and while the Mongols
themselves reloaded.

Because of their superior training and their use of 'shower shooting' tactics
at rest, Mamluk soldiers would have been able to loose many more arrows than
the Mongols, especially if the latter shot on the move. In response the Mongols
would have needed a greatly superior number of men,[729] which usually seems
to have been the case. If the Mamluks began shooting at a range of 75 m, which
would have been the maximum for reasonable accuracy even at a designated zone
rather than individual targets, they would have been able to loose several arrows
before the Mongols reached their own maximum 'shooting on the move' range
of 50 m. This could have had a devastating impact upon the largely unarmoured
Mongols and their usually unarmoured horses.[730] The role of heavily armoured
Mongol cavalry on armoured horses will be discussed later. To follow up their
shower-shooting response to a Mongol horse-archery charge, the Mamluks often
counterattacked with spears, swords and other close-combat weapons where
their perhaps superior training and almost certainly heavier equipment gave
them an advantage.

Mamluk cavalry tactics were, as already stated, a culmination of several
existing traditions. The repeated charge had been central to Arab cavalry tactics

since pre-Islamic times, but not with archery. In 1030, for example, the Byzantine Emperor Romanus III was defeated near Antioch by small groups of Arab cavalry which attacked repeatedly. Furthermore, according to the Byzantine chronicler Psellus, the bedouin horsemen still did not use stirrups.[731] This was the *karr wa farr* tactic, almost identical to Romano-Byzantine *cursores defensores* and the *torna fuya* of medieval Spain.

Essentially the same tactic had been used by North Africa Berber cavalry since ancient times, though with javelins rather than other weapons. This was clearly still central to the battlefield practice of the Murabitun's Berber tribal allies in the eleventh century and perhaps later.[732] In his *Muqaddima*, the fourteenth-century Arab historian Ibn Khaldun, stated that both Arab and Berber nomads had made a sort of *majbudu* or field fortification with their pack animals and then employed *karr wa farr* tactics before retreating within this 'fortress'. While pointing out that such a form of defence required very large numbers of animals, Ibn Khaldun also noted that camels were notably passive in such a situation.[733]

In contrast the late thirteenth century *Nihayat al-Su'l* training manual from the Mamluk Sultanate dedicates only one small section to *karr wa farr*, and even this is believed to be taken from a much earlier work. Perhaps *karr wa farr* was by then regarded as an outdated cavalry tactic or one better suited to tribal auxiliaries rather than highly trained and professional *mamluks*. They, in contrast, relied on the shower-shooting described above, plus various forms of shock cavalry charges.

Shock and close-combat cavalry have sometimes been regarded as more typical of Western European and Crusader 'knightly' tactics. Nevertheless, the evidence clearly shows that they formed part of the skills expected of Islamic warriors, especially of the armoured élite. This was certainly true of fully trained *ghulams* and *mamluks* from an early date. A detailed description of armoured *ghulams* on armoured horses in late tenth-century northern Syria specifically stated that they charged their enemy in close-packed formations.[734] In this respect they were identical to Byzantine heavy cavalry and the vaunted cavalry *conrois* of medieval Western Europe, though the latter would not adopt horse-armour for another 200 years. Indeed the evidence rather suggests that the Western *conrois* was not merely inspired by Byzantine military practice, but might actually have owed its origins to the Islamic Middle East, via Byzantium.

Other detailed and personalized accounts of Islamic cavalry charges add further details. In Ibn al-Athir's description of the culmination of the battle of Manzikert against the Byzantines in 1071, the Seljuk Sultan cast aside his archery equipment, dressed in funeral white and sprinkled himself with the perfume used for corpses at funerals, took his sword and his mace and tied his hand to his horse's mane.[735] The latter action might have been to help him remain in his saddle if wounded or in danger of falling. Here it should also be remembered that the medieval Islamic military saddle did not provide the degree of support that a fully developed medieval Western European saddle did. On the other hand it permitted greater freedom of movement.

An account of the defeat of a Mongol invasion of Syria in 1303, written by the Ayyubid Sultan Abu'l Fida of Hama, describes how the defeated Mongols were surrounded. Refusing to surrender, they dismounted and used their horses' saddles as a field fortification from behind which they continued to shoot. The combined Mamluk and Ayyubid cavalry had no choice but to attack, so they launched a cavalry charge which overran the Mongol position.[736] This recalls the defeat of Attila's supposedly also nomadic Huns by Aetius in the fifth century when Attila is said to have retreated within a field fortification and prepared to burn himself upon a heap of saddles. Might the latter have, in reality, formed part of a field fortification?[737]

There was a general tendency for the wings to crumble before the centre in most medieval battles. This was also traditionally where the bulk of cavalry were stationed, so cavalry skills also entailed restraint, caution and how to watch out for traps or ambushes. Although al-Harthami, writing in the early ninth century, stated that only the wings should press hard against an apparently beaten foe while the commander in the centre should follow up more slowly. All those pursuing an enemy must, however, take precaution against ambushes.

If cavalry were pursuing cavalry, then their own infantry should attack the enemy infantry in order to stop the latter going to the defence of their horsemen or hindering the pursuit. Such advice indicates that cavalry could rarely be regarded as autonomous, and that they needed infantry support. How far this was still true by the twelfth and thirteenth centuries, especially in flat or open terrain, is open to doubt. Aspects of training in such caution and observation appear to be reflected at the battle of Mansura in 1250, when Islamic cavalry fell back some distance as soon as they saw Crusader infantry put their feet into the stirrups of their crossbows, preparatory to loading and shooting.[738]

Al-Harthami's further advice that the victors should not attempt the total destruction of a defeated foe because this merely provoked fiercer resistance[739] would seem to stand for all time. On the other hand it ran directly counter to the Mongols' tradition of annihilation which, perhaps reflecting competition for extremely limited means of life in parts of Inner Asia, came as a massive psychological shock to their European and Islamic enemies.

Skill at laying ambushes was just as important as not falling into them. Here again al-Harthami had some interesting advice. The same high quality horses should be used for ambushes as for scouting parties. Furthermore, they must be either all mares or all stallions; otherwise the animals might snort at each other. When a cavalry ambush was launched, it should be done in separate *kardus* formations or squadrons. A source from the mid-fourteenth century maintained that 128 men was the ideal number for such a *kardus*, and this may well have been repeating a long-established tradition.[740] With sufficient troops, large enemy supply columns could be attacked in open country. In 1077 the Banu Kilab of Syria summoned their tribal allies and assembled a force of about 1,000 cavalry and around 500 foot soldiers. These were able to defeat a column of 1,000 Turks who were bringing a siege train to support the siege of Aleppo by the Seljuk Turkish commander, Tutush.[741]

The highly detailed and specific section on ambushes in the early Mamluk *Nihayat al-Su'l* is mainly drawn from al-Harthami,[742] and shows no evidence of pre-Islamic derivation. As such it can be assumed to reflect current practice, certainly in the period prior to the Crusades and probably throughout the Crusader period as well. The main aims of such an ambush were to lure the enemy into a suitable position for a surprise attack, then to prevent the enemy getting reinforcement, and finally to stop members of one's own side deserting to or warning the enemy. It would seem that normal practice was to use between one- and two-thirds of available troops for the ambush itself, with the rest forming a reserve. It is also clear that these ambush units were expected to act independently and to be self-supporting in terms of water, food and other supplies. Although ambush troops were autonomous, they must also be close enough to the main army to remain in communication. A more elaborate tactic was the preparation of two such ambushes, one on each side of the enemy's anticipated route, but to launch only one at first.[743]

Inevitably, perhaps, these ambush tactics were sometimes overambitious. On one such occasion Saladin himself tried to ambush Crusader foragers in the Tibnin area of what is now southern Lebanon. Twenty men were selected from each of eight squadrons to act as bait, but the operation proved to be too complex and thus failed.[744] Greater success was achieved during the course of the Third Crusade when, on 17 June 1192, Muslim troops ambushed a Crusader column near Ramla in Palestine. This minor clash is of particular interest because it was described in some detail by chroniclers of both sides. According to the anonymous *Itinerarium Peregrinorum*, the 'Turkish cavalry burst from ambush, rushing upon the latter [the rear of the Crusader line] and endeavouring to get before them, passed right though the rear of the caravan [supply train]'.[745] This resulted in some extraordinary heroics by the chronicler's Christian heroes including Baldwin de Carron who was unhorsed three times and 'the valiant Earl of Leicester' who eventually rescued him.

Saladin often employed bedouin Arabs as ambush troops because they were lightly equipped and famously swift in movement,[746] and according to the chronicler Baha al-Din, that was done on this occasion. Writing from the Islamic side, he was rather more prosaic, stating that:

When the Muslims learnt that there were caravans uninterruptedly on the move, a detachment laid an ambush for them, taking along many bedouin. A caravan with a large number of men came by and the bedouin attacked. The cavalry escort chased them, as they gave way, retreating toward the Muslim troops. The Turks then appeared from the ambush, took some prisoners and killed others. Several of the Turks were wounded.[747]

The skills needed in an ambush were similar to those required of troops raiding enemy territory or harassing an invader's supply lines. Above all, such forces had to act autonomously and often needed to be self-sufficient. Al-Harthami's military manual also highlighted the difficulties of raiding at night. He insisted that the rest of the army must be ready to cover or protect such raiders. If the enemy attempted to surround them, the troops of the main force must ensure that the wings of the enemy army could not sweep round to surround the raiding force. Meanwhile the main function of night raiders themselves was said to be wounding, hamstringing or freeing the foe's tethered horses.[748]

This did not, of course, mean that they were necessarily acting far from their own bases. In fact those who conducted a form of guerrilla resistance campaign were usually in home territory where local knowledge was a great advantage. For example, the irrigated Ghuta area extending eastwards from Damascus was like a huge oasis. It was, and to a large degree still is, dotted with villages surrounded by market-gardens and orchards with stone or mudbrick walls, being criss-crossed with irrigation ditches spanned by flimsy wooden bridges. The medieval houses often had tall wooden platforms or balconies. The result offered abundant cover for those trying to intercept supply convoys or to cut off small groups of enemy foragers.

In fact the terrain of the Ghuta could prove a nightmare for an invader or would-be occupier as the Fatimids found in the tenth and eleventh centuries,[749] just as the Second Crusade found in the mid-twelfth century. Furthermore, the inhabitants of Damascus and its surroundings had a high military reputation, even though they were not professional soldiers. During the first half of the twelfth century the city's *mutatawiyya* volunteers included a group known as *al-haramiya*, 'The Robbers', who specialized in cutting enemy supply routes.[750] In North Africa the Berber warriors of the Zanata tribe earned a similar reputation in raiding and ambush, as well as for ferocity.[751]

Before looking at the tactical skills expected of foot soldiers, it is interesting to note that war-elephants were used by Islamic armies within India where the Ghaznawids and the Sultans of Delhi copied this tactic from their Hindu foes. The Ghaznawids also seem to have used these massive beasts elsewhere in their huge realm, in Afghanistan and in eastern Iran. More surprisingly, the Buwayhid rulers of western Iran and Iraq had a few war-elephants. A handful were also reported in the Fatimid Caliphate of Egypt and Syria, though here they were almost certainly restricted to parade purposes, probably only in Cairo.

It has been suggested that the Murabitun had some elephants and may even have taken one or two across the Straits of Gibraltar into the Iberian Peninsula,[752] though again only for parade purposes or as symbols of their power. Perhaps the animals in question were the last of the relatively small North African or Saharan breed used by Hannibal in ancient times, but which are generally thought to have been extinct by the Middle Ages. Perhaps they came from south of the Sahara, although the African elephant is normally thought to be quite unsuitable for such 'domestication'. Maybe they had somehow come from India, perhaps via Fatimid Egypt. Unfortunately, practically nothing else is known about them.

During the medieval period it is not always easy to differentiate between low status cavalry and mounted infantry. This can be particularly difficult in the Islamic world where there was not only a greater willingness by cavalry to fight on foot than was apparent amongst the knightly classes of Western Europe, but a seemingly greater use of fast-moving mounted infantry. Furthermore, the latter sometimes seemed quite willing, and indeed capable, of fighting on horseback. This is not to deny the existence of real mounted infantry. The latter were clearly noted in the Byzantine *De Administrando Imperio* governmental and military treatise attributed to the Emperor Constantine VII Porphyrogenitus during the first half of the tenth century. Referring to the Fatimid army, he wrote:

> They ride not horses but camels and in time of war they do not put on corslets [cuirasses] or coats of mail but pink-coloured jerkins [almost certainly quilted soft-armour] and have long spears and shields as tall as a man and enormous wooden [simple, not composite] bows which few can bend and that with difficulty.[753]

This tradition was continued by Saladin in the twelfth century, when the *janib* of his army sometimes seemed more like mounted infantry than cavalry, especially as they could ride mules rather than horses.[754] Military changes to the early Murabitun army, introduced by Yusuf Ibn Tashufin, which gave pride of place to the horse rather than the camel almost certainly reflected a shift from camel-riding mounted infantry to cavalry and perhaps mounted infantry now provided with horses.[755] The second Murabit ruler, 'Ali Ibn Yusuf, was credited with mounting his *sudani* black African troops on horses then employing them in the Iberian Peninsula.[756] Since these Africans had been élite infantry, it seems likely that they had been upgraded to mounted infantry rather than to cavalry.

The basic skills or qualities required of traditional Islamic infantry on the march and in open battle were listed by al-Harthami in the early ninth century as an ability to march long distances, to recognize dangerous or threatening enemy formations, to take cover, to chase cavalry, to check cavalry, and to scatter and startle their horses.[757] He then described what they should be trained to do in case of a sudden enemy attack. This is essentially the same as the battlefield tactic repeated by later Islamic authors, but with additional points. The foot soldiers must:

> Kneel on one knee and hold a spear and defend themselves with *daraqa* [leather shields] and *tawariqa* [long shields] in a single rank until the enemy retires or their own cavalry arrives in support. This can be very difficult for the inexperienced. If the attack comes after the battle array has been drawn up, the infantry should hold their spears against the upper parts of their chests, engaging the enemy but remaining in their places assisted by archers who shoot at the foe at close range. If the infantry cannot hold, then the cavalry intervenes. If the enemy reaches right to the trenches, then he must be driven back in a sortie, and be engaged in the sortie with *al-dababis al-muharrafa* or *muharraqa* [spiked or flanged maces], or *atbaru* [war-axes].[758]

The reference to the enemy reaching 'right to the trenches' suggests that the defending infantry initially met the enemy ahead of their field fortifications, to which they could find themslves forced back. This recalls the battle of Zallaqa when the Andalusians and Murabitun were separated by a ditch. Perhaps the Andalusians formed the battlefront with the Murabitun in reserve behind a trench.

The close cooperation between infantry and cavalry implied in this section of al-Harthami's work was clearly reflected in historical accounts. Sometimes it was successful, sometimes not. One of the happier military cooperations was that between ex-'Abbasid, now freelance, Turkish *ghulam* professional cavalry and part-time Syrian militias in the tenth and eleventh centuries. Apart from largely shared political objectives, this relationship was probably strengthened by the effectiveness of the local Syrian militias, itself largely resulting from the need by peasantry and urban populations to be able to defend themselves against bedouin Arab raiding or harassment. This seems to have been very characteristic of the villages of the exposed eastern part of the Ghuta of Damascus.[759]

In a part of the world where archery had long been a very major and even dominant aspect of warfare, it was obvious that properly trained foot soldiers had to develop skills as well as equipment to protect themselves. This would apply whether they were facing enemy archers on foot or on horseback. One of the more obscure devices was the *karwa* of Afghanistan and some neighbouring regions. It might have been a lightweight moveable hoarding or multiple mantlet that foot soldiers could push or carry ahead of them as a defence against arrows. As such it is said to have remained in use until the introduction of firearms.[760] One account of the use of a cotton-padded *karwa* concerned a battle between Ghurid infantry and the Ghaznawid ruler, Bahram Shah, in the mid-twelfth century. When the battle began, Bahram Shah's cavalry and elephants charged the Ghurid infantry line but the latter 'opened the ranks of *karwa*', and then closed the *karwa*, trapping their foes who were then slaughtered.[761] This is, however, a rather garbled account and the *karwa* can just as easily be interpreted as a form of padded soft armour (see below).

Various forms of mace are often mentioned as suitable weapons for foot soldiers to use against cavalry or their horses. These are likely to have been long-hafted weapons and imply infantry tactics which had much in common with those of later medieval Western Europe, not least with the specialized *goedendag* 'spiked mace' used so savagely by Flemish infantry militias against French knightly cavalry in the early fourteenth century.[762] Fatimid armoured infantry with flanged *lutut* maces proved particularly effective against armoured Crusader horsemen.[763] They often worked in coordination with the Fatimid army's *sudani* light infantry armed with a pair of *harba* javelins and small leather *daraqa* shields, and with the *zanj* who traditionally fought with swords.[764]

One thing is entirely clear where these Islamic infantry forces were concerned. They were not a disorganized horde in which men with different styles of weapon were jumbled up together. They were differentiated into groups which then operated in mutual support, all of which presupposes a perhaps considerable degree of training. However, it is equally clear that, although certain ethnic groups were traditionally associated with specific weapons, this sort of distinction must not be exaggerated. The Daylami infantry from northern Iran were, for example, famous for their supposedly double-ended *zhupin* javelins. However, the Daylami garrison of Kafr Tab in northern Syria in 1012 also included archers.[765]

Infantry archers included men with hand-held bows, usually though not invariably of composite construction, as well as crossbowmen at a considerably earlier date than such men are widely reported in Western Europe. One of the earliest Persian references to a crossbow was in Firdawsi's huge epic, the *Shahname* written around the year 1000 in eastern Iran. In this poem the *kaman charkh*, which was probably a substantial form of crossbow spanned by a winch, was used by the infantry of Baghdad in open battle. Normally, and perhaps always in reality, these large crossbows were weapons of siege warfare (see below). However, during the tenth and eleventh centuries apparently hand-held crossbows came into common use in the Middle East, especially in Fatimid forces and those of northern Syria and Cilicia. Even so archers and crossbowmen are still estimated to have only represented 10 to 15 per cent of Fatimid infantry in the early twelfth century.[766]

Al-Tarsusi, writing for Saladin but basing his work on late Fatimid practice, included a substantial section on infantry archery. He described how such troops operated in groups, were protected by a shield wall, how they were trained to defend themselves if attacked 'on a road' or while on the march, how they operated in difficult broken terrain where they enjoyed several advantages, and how they tried to trap an enemy against a natural obstacle such as a river. They were, furthermore, trained to make night attacks and to avoid drawing attention to themselves while encamped for the night, this being done by digging holes in which to light their campfires so that they were less visible.[767]

Other sources such as chronicles describe how Islamic archers could operate as light infantry skirmishers. During the Third Crusade, for example, the Crusader accounts noted that the bedouin, 'who fight on foot and carry a bow, quiver and round shield, and are a light and active people'.[768] Recalling the battle of Arsuf, Baha al-Din stated that marksmen were selected from each battalion in Saladin's army and were sent forward to harass the enemy preparations.[769] These men were Turkish cavalry rather than bedouin infantry. Nevertheless, as an anonymous Crusader chronicler recalled, many Turks 'had purposely dismounted from their horses in order to take better aim at our men with their darts and arrows'. Many were consequently caught by a sudden Crusader charge before they could remount.[770]

De Joinville who, like Baha al-Din, was recounting what he himself had seen, described the fighting outside Dumyat in Egypt two generations later. Here some of the best Islamic cavalry, probably meaning *mamluks*, dismounted and, still wearing their full armour, erected a *hourdeis de pierres taillié* or stone bulwark. From here they shot at the advancing Crusaders until they were forced to retreat by a Crusader warrior whose armour was proof against their arrows.[771]

This habit of even élite Islamic cavalrymen dismounting to use their bows on foot is mentioned in the *Book of Dede Korkut*, a Turkish epic probably written down in the second half of the thirteenth century but based upon a much more ancient story. Here, on one occasion, the main character dismounted, kept his bows with him but took the arrows from his quiver and thrust them into his belt. He then tucked up the hems of his tunic to make walking easier.[772] Another time the Turkish heroes dismount, tighten the straps of their shields and draw their swords to attack the foe.[773]

Yet by the fourteenth century most of the infantry archers of the Islamic Middle East were clearly not élite troops. Those of the Mamluk Sultanate were, in fact, dismissed in the writings of King Henry II of Cyprus as an unarmoured rabble lacking other weapons.[774] The one exception to this decline may have been in the far west of the medieval Islamic world, in Morocco and al-Andalus. Here a traditional or pre-Turkish school or style of infantry archery had flourished up to the twelfth century, and even then its decline was in favour of the crossbow rather than horse-archery.[775]

COMBAT SKILLS AND TRAINING

It is abundantly clear that standards of training and individual combat skills varied considerably across the medieval Islamic world. There were several reasons for this, not merely the availability of suitable troops but the ability of a state to pay its men. Furthermore, there was a tendency for even professional soldiers to seek additional forms of income if their military salaries or fiefs proved unreliable or inadequate. Morale and loyalty, or the lack of it, also played their part. Nevertheless, there was almost always an élite corps of professional soldiers at the centre of every political, territorial or dynastic entity. Sometimes these military élites were tiny. Sometimes military élites survived the collapse of the state which had raised them or most recently employed them. Thus we have the admittedly rare phenomenon of 'freelance' forces or armies moving around, usually in search of suitable employment, occasionally in the hope of establishing their own realms. These unemployed armies do, however, seem to have been rarer in the medieval Islamic world than in medieval Western Europe.

What tended to distinguish such freelancers was their above average military skills. Without these they could not really hope to find well-paid employment, and probably would not have survived long enough to be noted by the chroniclers. One feature that remained largely constant in such circumstances was the military superiority, unit for unit and perhaps man for man, of dedicated *ghulam* or *mamluk* soldiers of slave-recruited origin. They could be described as the true 'professionals' of this period of medieval Islamic history. Only when they had lost their initial employer, for whatever reason, could they justifiably be termed mercenaries. Even then this term tends to be misleading as such troops were almost always on the lookout for a permanent military home. Only rarely did they chop and change employers on the basis of who paid most. This simply did not seem to be characteristic of the great majority of medieval Islamic professional soldiers; occasionally rootless, perhaps, but hardly ever faithless.

The archetypal *ghulam* was of Central Asian Turkish origin, though there were plenty of variations on this theme. All sources confirm that, in general, such Turkish *ghulams* had superior military capabilities to those of Fatimid troops,[776] and this superiority was usually just as marked in relation to other non-*ghulam* soldiers. It was equally clearly a result of training at an individual and unit level, as well as the possession of generally superior or more advanced equipment. The latter factor must, however, be regarded with caution because there was no obvious reason why the best equipped minority of troops in, for example, the Fatimid army of the pre-Crusader period should not have had access to precisely the arms, armour, horse-harness and horses as the best-equipped *ghulams* and *mamluks*.

Nor did the military superiority shown by small numbers of Turkish *ghulams* in tenth- and eleventh-century Syria necessarily mean that their Fatimid opponents were no good. It merely means that, in the circumstances of the time, the *ghulams* were better. Hence the somewhat shambolic Fatimid force commanded by the Turkish ex-*mamluk* Anushtakin al-Dizbiri in early eleventh-century Syria were still able to hold their own against various bedouin Arab revolts.[777] Similarly, the exceptionally large force of Turcoman warriors, bedouin and Kurds sent into Egypt by the Turkish governor of Damascus in 1076 was totally defeated by a Fatimid army outside Cairo.[778] To be fair, this was three years after the Armenian Badr al-Jamali had been made *wazir*, and had instigated a series of ruthless military reforms.

Colourful poetic descriptions of battles rarely provide detailed information about specific military skills, but they can indicate the variety of such skills employed. Some of the most illuminating from the period of the Crusades either concern the Turks or are themselves in Turkish. One such is the *Warqah wa Gulshah* epic poem. Though written in Persian, it was probably intended for a mid- to late eleventh-century Seljuk Turkish-Islamic military aristocracy in what are now western Iran, the southern Caucasus and eastern Turkey who are assumed, like their Norman counterparts in Western Europe, to have had a professional interest in battle.

Such illuminating quotations include: 'The whistling of arrows, the smack of the bows; The blows of maces and the tearing [or breaking?] of lances',[779] and 'He turned a lance in his hand like a serpent'.[780] Elsewhere it indicates that horsemen slackened their reins as they entered combat,[781] fought first with spears until these broke then drew their swords.[782] A cavalryman targeted his enemy's thigh with a spear during combat on horseback and men could be pinned through their thigh to their saddle.[783] When a horseman threw a javelin at his foe, the latter took it on his shield.[784] The fourteenth-century Turkish *Danishmandname* stated that the noise of battle consisted of: 'The neighing of horses, the rattle of *cevşen* armour [lamellar cuirasses], the clatter of swords, the crash of *gürz* [maces], the whistling of arrows, the shouts of warriors.'[785]

Lesson Seven, Chapter Two of the Mamluk *Nihayat al-Su'l* military training manual consists of a fascinating and detailed description of the use of the bow, spear, sword, javelin, mace and dagger in different combat situations.[786] These are approached on the basis of a simple series of questions and answers, indicating what weapon a horseman should use when attacked by another horseman using one of the weapons in question. In this section all the weapons have a part to play, except that when a horseman is attacked by a man on foot there is no role for his dagger. Another sequence of questions dealt with the weapons a foot soldier should use when attacked by a mounted man using specific weapons. This time all weapons are applicable in one case or another.

To take just one example from each of the four situations:

Whom should a horseman armed with *nashib* [arrows] watch out for? If he comes up against a horseman armed with a dagger, drawn sword or mace, he must not hesitate to close and to go up against him, unless he does so as part of a cunning plan.[787] What infantryman may be overcome by a horseman with a mace? A horseman with a mace may prevail over an infantryman with a dagger or a sword in those places where the horseman may move freely around.[788] What type of infantry surpasses the cavalry? The infantry with the drawn sword surpasses the cavalry with the *khanjar* [dagger] and the drawn sword and the *'amud* (mace).[789]

It has been suggested that this part of the *Nihayat al-Su'l* was quoted verbatim from another but as yet unidentified source.[790] Nevertheless until that original can be identified, this text should perhaps be regarded as vital evidence for weapons training for both cavalry and infantry within the Mamluk Sultanate, or at least from the preceding Ayyubid era.

The skills or combat styles of various forms of cavalry can often be deduced from their equipment, even when other more specific information is lacking. One can, for example, state with certainty that a particular 400 strong élite cavalry regiment of the Fatimid army of the early Crusader period was intended for close combat, probably employing shock tactics, because it was issued with *kazaghand* (mail-lined and padded body armour), *tijfaf* (quilted soft armour for man or horse), sword and *latt* mace.[791] Being among the heaviest cavalry in Fatimid ranks, these may have been comparable in their expected skills to the *agulani* who attracted the attention of the anonymous Crusader author of the *Gesta Francorum* after the defeat of a Seljuk army outside the walls of Antioch. The writer, who probably came from southern Italy, stated that: 'The Agulani numbered three thousand; they feared neither spears nor arrows nor any other weapon for they and their horses are covered all over with plates of iron. They will not use any weapons except swords when they are fighting.'[792] The cavalrymen in question were, in reality, élite and notably heavily armoured *ghulams* and their armour was almost certainly lamellar. Here it is worth noting that the willingness of those opposing the First Crusade to fight at close quarters surely indicates confidence in their armour.[793]

In complete contrast the attention of the anonymous late twelfth-century author of the *Itinerarium Peregrinorum* was drawn to his enemies' relative lack of armour during the Third Crusade. He wrote that: 'The Turks were not loaded with armour like our men ... for the most part they were lightly armed, carrying only a bow, or a mace bristling with sharp teeth, a sword, a light spear with an iron head, and a dagger suspended lightly.'[794] The danger with such sources is that too many modern historians have assumed that what was described by one chronicler in one place was likely to have been typical of that period. In reality the evidence shows that medieval Islamic armies were distinguished above all by the variety of their military equipment. In the eleventh-century Persian *Warqa wa Gulshah* epic poem, for example, the military equipment is Persian, including lance, sword, bow, mace, *kamand* lasso, full iron armour and lots of javelins. The tactics and style of combat are also Turco-Persian although the story purports to be about the rivalry between Arab tribes.[795] The comment by the French Crusader, De Joinville, in the mid-thirteenth century that the bedouin Arabs despise armour and instead fight only with sword and spear was of course exaggerated. Nevertheless it did reflect their cavalry's traditional preference for light equipment and close-combat weapons.[796]

Nothing as detailed as the *Nihayat al-Su'l* survives from North Africa or al-Andalus, though other sources of evidence make it clear that various forms of javelin were traditional among the cavalry of both areas, along with the spear, sword and shield.[797] Horse-archery was, as already stated, rare, but western Islamic cavalry could still be very effective. At the battle of Las Navas de Tolosa the Murabit horsemen defeated the Spanish horse but were then held by the Spanish infantry.[798] The sources, whether documentary or illustrative, also show that Andalusian cavalry tended to be better or more heavily armoured than those from North Africa. One late thirteenth century Andalusian Islamic source specifically stated that while indigenous Andalusian cavalry had two horses, the Berber volunteers had only one. The Andalusians had mail hauberks and mail *mighfar* coifs, holding a heavy *rumh* lance in one hand and a large *turs* shield in the other, both of which they used in the same manner as their Christian Iberian opponents. In other words the indigenous cavalry of al-Andalus at the time of its collapse in the second half of the thirteenth century fought with the *couched* lance in Western European style. Meanwhile the Berbers had only swords and light spears but were regarded as 'more nimble' on horseback.[799]

This is not to say that Islamic Andalusian and Christian Spanish cavalry were therefore indistinguishable. A very detailed mid-thirteenth century description of an armoured Muslim cavalryman from the island of Majorca stated that he had *perpunt* soft armour, a long European style belted sword and shield, a helmet made in Saragossa or possibly Syracuse in Sicily.[800] This account in the *Libre dels feyts* of King James of Aragon also noted that in a combat against four Christian knights, the Moor killed the horse of one of his foes. Aiming for the horse, often in preference to aiming for the rider, had been a feature of Islamic military training for centuries and reflected a more realistic if less chivalrous attitude towards battle.[801]

Closer investigation of sources to discover how specific types of weapon were used is easier for medieval Islamic civilization than for most others because *furusiya* military training manuals provide a great deal of this sort of information. However, they also need to be studied in conjunction with other sources, literary and pictorial, to ensure that they were reflecting reality rather than some impractical or unpractised theory.

The spear or lance is given more attention in the traditional *furusiya* texts than any other weapon. The 'Abbasid system of training, which underpinned that of subsequent centuries, divided lance techniques into four main parts. The first concerned different types of charge and thrust, plus techniques of using the lance under difficult circumstances. The second part consisted of sets of movements or exercises as if the individual horseman was in a mêlée, including parrying in four different directions. These exercises were done by individuals on their own. The third concerned fencing combat between two lance- or spear-armed horsemen. The fourth consisted of collective or group exercises between two teams of horsemen to be undertaken in the *maydan* or training ground.

Once again Ibn Akhi Hizam's writings are the main source for the first group of exercises in subsequent texts dating from the Mamluk Sultanate. Other early sources form the basis for the third group of duelling techniques. None of the surviving early sources deal with the second group, though the names of the 'experts' mentioned are from the 'Abbasid period. It is now believed that the Mamluk Sultanate itself produced most of the team exercises in the fourth group. This would certainly find support in the prominent role of the training *maydan* during this later period. It is also interesting to note that the teachings of the great thirteenth-century Syrian 'lancemaster' Najm al-Din al-Rammah in this field of team exercises are likely to have been dictated as lessons to pupils, one of whom later put them down on paper as there is no evidence that Najm al-Din wrote them down himself.[802]

The methods of using a spear on horseback recorded in the *Nihayat al-Su'l* are each given names which, though traditional, might genuinely reflect the origins of the technique in question. Some do indeed seem to be reflected in the earlier history or arts of the regions or peoples in question. These were the Khurasani (eastern Iranian) style which involved 'rotating' the weapon in one hand; in other words passing the target and then extracting the weapon.[803] This was essentially the same exercise known as tent pegging which the British Army learned in India. It is also important to note that Khurasani methods were highly rated in various other aspects of lance exercises.[804] Next came the *Muwallad* method which usually, and perhaps always, used both hands and had been the standard technique in the Mediterranean world throughout Graeco-Roman and early Byzantine times.[805] The term *Muwallad* was, incidentally, often used for indigenous people in what became the Islamic Middle East who had converted and entered the Caliphal armies during the first centuries of Islam. Presumably they brought their traditions of lanceplay with them. Finally there was the Shami or 'Syrian' attack which was also called the Rumi (Byzantine) style, and which was clearly the *couched* lance by another name.[806]

Usama Ibn Munqidh's *Kitab al-I'tibar* book of personal recollections was not a work intended for military training purposes, but it does include detailed stories of combat and occasional advice on the best way to use weapons as well as avoiding errors. The author, as a member of the Arab military aristocracy of twelfth-century Syria, had plenty of first-hand knowledge of such matters. In one instance he recalled how, as an inexperienced youngster, he had used a *couched* lance overenthusiastically, lost his balance and almost fell from his horse.[807] Usama's descriptions of cavalry combat give greater priority to the lance than to any other weapon, even in the mêlée, making it clear that horsemen had a great fear of turning their backs on a lance-armed foe while also fearing to attack a lance-armed horseman if they themselves were not similarly armed.[808] Usama's stranger recollections include the time a man was thrown from his horse by trying to take the lance from an opponent who had just missed him,[809] and the man who tripped his own horse with his own lance, both then falling but being unhurt.[810]

Other snippets of information come from different sources, as when Baha al-Din described the death of a Muslim cavalryman during the Crusade, because he 'had dismounted to pick up his lance, and was trying to remount his horse which was very restive when the Franks [Crusaders] swooped down on him and killed him'.[811] In his *Adab al-Harb*, Fakhr al-Din Mubarakshah maintained that the heavy *nizah* lance was the best weapon for the man on an armoured horse.[812] The cavalry tactics illustrated on what is known as the Pila, an eleventh-century carved Andalusian Islamic basin in Jativa, shows a man thrusting his spear into his opponent's thigh, using two arms and carrying no shield.[813] Precisely the same technique is described in the text of the eleventh-century *Warqa wa Gulshah* poem, and is illustrated in the accompanying texts. It also appears in other illustrated sources from the Middle East and eastern provinces of the medieval Islamic world.

Back in the westernmost regions of the Islamic world there is an account of how, during the Muwahhidun siege of Murabit-held Marrakesh in 1147, an Andalusian frontier warrior fighting for the Murabitun observed how the enemy fought and came back to recommend that the Murabitun shorten their lances.[814]

There are very few details about the use of the javelin, though this was clearly an important weapon, especially amongst North African Berbers,[815] bedouin Arabs and as an alternative missile weapon for Mamluk cavalry. Given the preeminence of horse-archery amongst the Turks it might also be surprising to note the survival of *cirit*, a mounted combat game with blunted javelins based upon medieval cavalry training, in eastern Turkey itself.[816] The name comes from the Arabic word *jirid* meaning a light javelin and eastern Turkey was, of course, the heartland of the early medieval Armenian kingdoms whose cavalry almost certainly made considerable use of javelins, as shown in the rather later Armenian national epic, *David of Sassoun*.[817]

Greater attention is given to the sword, though less than might have been expected. One of the few specific instructions is found in al-Tarsusi's mid-twelfth-century *Tabsira*, but even this limits itself to close combat between horsemen when an individual was again advised to strike at his enemy's horse and to try to keep the enemy on his left side because this made it easier to defend oneself with a shield.[818] This lack of detailed instruction on fencing techniques with various types of sword in the *furusiya* manuals must surely indicate that the ability to use such a weapon was virtually assumed. It may have been regarded as almost a private or individual matter, and as part of a young man's education rather than a matter of military training.

In this respect it is worth noting that one of the few references to the correct method for a cavalryman to use his sword actually relates to his 'two swords'; the second being attached to his saddle. The earliest passing reference in an Islamic source to such a saddle-sword comes from the first quarter of the tenth century. In *furusiya* texts dating from the Mamluk Sultanate but, as so often, based upon considerably earlier works, the cavalryman is advised to use his saddle-sword after using or losing his mace, but before using the sword that he carried at his waist. The latter was regarded as the weapon of last resort, to be used if a man was unhorsed in battle and threatened by enemies.[819] In many respects the man's personal sword almost seems to have been more a symbol of status and manliness rather than a real weapon of war. It is also important to note that in medieval Islamic civilization, like that of the Byzantine Empire but unlike that of medieval Western Europe, the wearing of weapons in public was not the norm even, apparently, among off-duty soldiers and members of the military aristocracy.

The fact that the mace is given greater attention in military texts than the sword surely cannot mean that skill in its use was considered more important. It is more likely to have reflected the fact that any soldier was expected to be able to use a sword properly, whereas the mace was specifically military rather than personal and thus needed special training. Nevertheless, there seem to be no texts on 'The Arts of the *Dabbus*', a form of mace, in earlier works of *furusiya*, the only surviving chapter being found in a book from the Mamluk Sultanate.[820] Other historical sources nevertheless indicate that various forms of mace were important, perhaps from almost the earliest centuries of Islamic history.[821] They were essentially armour, helmet and shield breaking weapons, intended to stun and perhaps to break bones rather than to pierce and slay. The mace was also used highly effectively against the more massive muscle and bone of a foeman's horse, both in the hands of foot soldiers and cavalry.

The effectiveness of such weapons was described in gruesome detail by an anonymous French chonicler at the time of the Third Crusade: 'Manassier was unhorsed and when he was on the ground they beat him cruelly with iron maces, rough with teeth, and standing around so mangled him that they broke off his leg, bone and all, from his body.'[822] In 1250 the élite *mamluk* troops of the last Ayyubid Sultan of Egypt fought with the invading Crusaders in the narrow streets of Mansura, using their maces and their swords because there was not enough room to use lances.[823] In such close-quarter combat Islamic cavalry wielded their weapons against both enemy riders and horses. Writing about much the same event, the Crusader and chronicler De Joinville noted that these Ayyubid cavalry were still able to hit an unhorsed Crusader with their maces, suggesting that these weapons had quite long handles.[824]

Fakhr al-Din Mubarakshah, writing in Persian in early thirteenth-century Islamic northern India, listed various maces as being especially suitable against heavy armour and 'wooden helmets'.[825] Until recently the latter reference has been a mystery, but a substantial number of just such wood-lined medieval helmets have recently been found in Syria (see below) and would clearly have been vulnerable to smashing blows from a mace though perhaps more effective against glancing blows with a sword. The hero of the Turkish *Danishmandname* epic by 'Arif 'Ali of Toqat is armed with two *gurz* maces, one on his left and one on his right side, in addition to the other usual weapons.[826] However, this may have been merely a poetic device to show his exceptional prowess.

The *Danishmandname* also makes several references to a lasso being used to capture an enemy.[827] This was not a piece of poetic imagination. Lassoes had been used for hunting in Syria since at least the tenth century,[828] and the later thirteenth-century Mamluk *Nihayat al-Su'l* included detailed advice on how to avoid being caught by a lasso. The way this advice is expressed does, however, indicate that the lasso was more common in the hands of Mongols and perhaps Turks than in the armies of the Mamluk Sultanate.[829] The similarity and the differences between the advice which this text does provide on the use of the lasso and that of the archetypal American cowboy is fascinating:

> Question: How is the lasso thrown and what length should it be?
>
> Answer: Its length should be twenty cubits [about 10 m]. Thread the end of the rope through a ring [or knot] in the lasso until one third of it is through [to form the loop]. Now hold a further third in the hand, letting the final third hang free. Take the loop in the right hand, with the gathered-together third, holding the rest of the lasso in the left hand. Now spin it around your head, and this is the same for horsemen, infantry, or anyone else.
>
> Question: Where is it best for a horseman or infantryman to carry his lasso?
>
> Answer: Those who have experience consider it best for the horseman to hang it from his saddlebow [*qarnus* or the raised pommel at the front of a medieval Islamic military saddle] but not to tie it firmly there. Rather it should be fixed to the righthand side of the rear of the saddle by its end. As for the infantryman, it is considered best for him simply to carry it dangling from his left hand.[830]

Developments in the design of the Islamic composite bow during the period under consideration are believed to have focused on improving speed of shooting and range rather then power and penetration.[831] The early thirteenth-century Persian author, Fakhr al-Din Mubarakshah, listed a variety of bows, but this was mainly by place of origin. All were of composite construction and differed in minor details of overall shape, proportions and size. The only bow that Fakhr al-Din described as being wholly different was the traditional Indian bow which was made of reed or bamboo.[832] This is clearly illustrated in pre- and non-Islamic art from India and the Indies. The most famous, and perhaps only, Islamic example of such a reed bow is the weapon traditionally stated to have belonged to the Prophet Muhammad, now in the Reliquary of the Topkapi Palace Museum in Istanbul.

It is also widely believed that there had been an overall decline in archery skills, particularly those of horse-archery, during the Buwayhid and Fatimid periods of the tenth and eleventh centuries.[833] On the other hand any such decline is likely to have been a result of a reduction in the numbers and availability of the best Central Asian Turkish slave-recruits, as well as limited time and money for their training or for maintaining their highly specialized career-long skills. The best Islamic horse-archers were probably as good as ever, but such men would have been rarer than they had been during the golden age of the 'Abbasid Caliphate.

A revival probably began with the arrival of the Seljuk Turks, though the bulk of their troops would still have been tribal archers rather then fully trained *mamluk* or *ghulam*-style horse-archers. Nevertheless the Crusader chroniclers expressed their surprise at the range achieved by such men at the battle of Dorylaeum.[834] The steady revival of traditional Islamic horse-archery skills during the twelfth and thirteenth centuries undoubtedly play a significant part in the eventual defeat of the Crusaders, and in halting the Mongol onslaught. Even so, it has been suggested that a decline set in once again in the Mamluk Sultanate from the early fourteenth century onwards.[835] Fear of this decline may, indeed, have been what stimulated a subsequent upsurge in the writing of Mamluk training manuals.

Islamic archery inherited a variety of traditions from those regions conquered by the Muslim Arabs in the seventh and eighth centuries. These were added to, and to a large extent superseded, the Arabs' own effective if quite simple tradition of infantry archery. It is clear that the finger-draw and the thumb-draw were known and used by peoples of the Eastern Mediterranean before the rise of Islam. Both are also likely to have been known further west, at least in those Mediterranean regions which had formed parts of the Roman and early Byzantine Empire.

By the 'Abbasid period two main forms of draw were in use, the three-finger draw or *daniyyat* and thumb-draw or *bazm*, both probably being used on foot and on horseback. An unclear reference to a device called the *kustuban* in al-Tarsusi's twelfth-century military text was probably not a thumb-ring, as was known in the eastern and some central regions of the Islamic world, but may have been a form of archer's partial gauntlet to protect the fingers. This is understood to have come in two-, three- and four-fingered varieties but was not a full gauntlet. This *kustuban* is also assumed to be the same as the *dastaban* which had already been mentioned in tenth-century Arabic poetry from northern Syria; the term itself being of Persian rather than Arabic origin.[836] Such a device was used with versions of the finger rather than the thumb-draw. The latter is generally accepted to have been more powerful, but was also more tiring and demanded great skill or practice.

Despite the fact that many thumb-rings have been found in the Middle East, at least one dating from pre-Islamic times,[837] and many later examples bearing quite elaborate decoration, it has been suggested that they were not widely used in warfare. The texts make it clear that it was considered better to shoot with a bare thumb or to use a leather thumb guard as second best. The experience of specialist historians of archery also suggests that while a thumb-ring might be useful for long distance flight-shooting it tended to cause inaccurate shooting at short range.[838]

Islamic archery was not unique in recognizing that the stronger the bow, the heavier the arrow which it could shoot effectively.[839] Where Islamic archery was more sophisticated than that of Western Europe was in its variety of techniques which permitted a variety of missiles. In this respect medieval Islamic archery was probably a little more advanced than that of the Byzantine world and may even have exceeded that of Turco-Mongol Central Asia, despite the fact that so many of the ideas, techniques and equipment involved owed their origin to influence from that part of the world.

One of the most highly skilled techniques was that of flight-shooting, or shooting at very long range. It had a military application but is likely to have been of secondary importance as a military skill when compared with shower-shooting and close-range archery. The arrows used in flight-shooting were lighter and more fragile than usual. Consequently it required skill to loose the arrow cleanly and avoid it breaking as it bent around the bow. Strength was also needed to make an arrow fly far.[840] Fakhr al-Din Mubarakshah, in his *Adab al-Harb*, stated that ordinary arrows were normally of poplar and willow, while an arrow of reed was used for long range shooting. However, it was difficult to make such reed arrows really straight and thus accurate.[841] The large number of arrows dating from the late thirteenth to early sixteenth century recently uncovered in Syria have yet to be analysed, and it will be interesting to find what wood they are actually made of, though clearly none are of reed.

Another method of achieving great range was to use a *majra* or *siper* arrow-guide. These came in a variety of forms, but all required considerable skill to use effectively, and indeed without danger to the archer himself. The arrows shot with the aid of such guides could be considerably shorter than an ordinary arrow, but are assumed to have been correspondingly lighter and thus had less impact or penetration. On the other hand there seems little reason why a short dart-like missile should not be thicker than the ordinary arrow, and thus combine impact weight with greater aerodynamic efficiency. Though unproven, it may be that the 'darts' so often mentioned by Crusader chroniclers on the receiving end of Islamic archery were such short arrows shot from a *majra* or *siper* arrow-guide.

The astonishing variety of arrowheads used even with ordinary arrows by medieval Islamic archers is confirmed not only by the written texts and a small number of illustrated sources that are detailed enough to show such things. It has also been confirmed by abundant archaeological finds. Until recently these have tended to be scattered, difficult to date and sometimes unrelated to a specific army, political or ethnic group. More recently, however, a huge number and variety of arrowheads have been found in some specifically Mamluk contexts in Syria, mostly still attached to fragments of arrows. When these are eventually catalogued and published, they will hopefully clarify some of the basic forms as well as minor varieties within such forms.[842]

Documentary sources will nevertheless remain vitally important. At one end of the spectrum there are highly personal accounts of single events, as when Usama Ibn Munqidh recalled how a man was killed in battle by a particularly broad-headed arrow of the type normally used for hunting but which may, in war, have been aimed at horses rather than men.[843] At the other extreme there is Fakhr al-Din's extensive list of named forms of arrowhead and what forms of armour, shield and other targets they were most effective against.[844]

As already stated, very little that was new was written about horse-archery techniques after those of the 'Abbasid ninth and tenth centuries, until the later fourteenth century. In the absense of other evidence one may have to assume that the skills described in 'Abbasid sources remained those expected of properly trained Islamic horse-archers for the following four or five hundred years. They were clearly the basis of al-Tarsusi's chapters of archery skills, written for Saladin in the mid-to-late twelfth century. Here the Egyptian-based military scholar stated that the way a mounted archer reacted to an enemy cavalryman largely depended upon how the latter was armed and whether there was more than one opponent. A priority was to dismount the foe by shooting at his horse. If he was armed with a sword he should be allowed to come close so that there was no danger of missing. But if he was armed with a lance or a bow with an arrow-guide, the horse-archer should shoot from a distance and then be ready to defend himself with his sword and shield.[845] The text also suggested how to shoot if the archer himself also had a drawn sword, in which case he should suspend the weapon by its wrist loop, and what to do with his lance if he wanted to shoot, or indeed both weapons, which sounded remarkably complicated.[846]

Speed of shooting was one of the most valued skills, both on the move and at rest. In the latter case the horse-archer apparently held a bunch of up to five arrows in his hand,[847] nocking and loosing them at such a rate that it was possible to have several in the air at one time. On the other hand the often quoted claim that a fully trained *ghulam* could shoot three arrows in a second and a half was while he was on foot, not in the saddle.[848]

The little that is known about the limited use of horse-archery in al-Andalus shows it to have remained within the early Islamic, essentially Persian and Arab tradition, and not to have used Turco-Mongol harassment techniques.[849] Written and pictorial sources from the later medieval Iberian Peninsula confirm that the crossbow was used on horseback to an increasing extent, especially in the last surviving Islamic state of Granada. According to Taybugha al-Baklamishi writing in mid-fourteenth-century Mamluk Egypt, a crossbow with a stirrup could be used on horseback. It was spanned by the rider rising in his saddle, one foot in the weapon's stirrup while the spanning hook was attached to a shoulder strap rather than the usual waist or hip belt. In most surviving versions of this manuscript the crossbow itself is called a *qaws al-rijl* or footbow, though in what might be the earliest text it is called a *jarkh*.[850]

The weapons skills expected of infantry tended to be implied rather than specifically described in contemporary texts. Sometimes they can only be assumed by the sorts of weapons carried by specific units on parade. For example a big Fatimid parade decribed by a highly enthusiastic visitor to Egypt in the late eleventh or very early twelfth century included naval troops or marines armed with crossbows plus a special corps of foot soldiers called *sabarbariya*, named after their distinctive staff weapon which had an exceptionally long blade.[851] The question of infantry staff weapons or pole-arms is difficult in Europe and even more so in the medieval Islamic world. Several weapons with special names are mentioned, but only occasionally described, and as yet it has been almost impossible to link these named weapons with those shown in pictorial sources. Fakhr al-Din Mubarakshah lists several infantry pole-arms in his early thirteenth-century Persian text, describing them as being suitable for foot soldiers fighting in disciplined and ordered ranks.[852] Beyond that he adds virtually nothing.

The mid-thirteenth-century Crusader, De Joinville, recorded how Islamic infantrymen armed with maces attacked German cavalry in Syria, pulling the *couvertures*, caparisons or horse-armour from their horses.[853] Just over half a century earlier, in a battle outside Jaffa during the Third Crusade, an anonymous Crusader source stated that the Muslims carried several javelins at a time.[854] This has sometimes been incorrectly interpreted to mean that they threw several at once, though this is not the case in the original text. In reality foot soldiers armed with such javelins almost always carried several, as is shown in Islamic art from these centuries.

Fortunately, the post-Fatimid military scholar al-Tarsusi, writing for Saladin, goes into some detail about the skills and techniques required by an infantry archer. These are again drawn from the previous 'Abbasid period and include how to hold the bow flat when shooting over a wall or perhaps fortified parapet, how infantry archers caught in the open should stand back-to-back to defend themselves, or if they were alone should find something to put their back against.[855] The death of one of Saladin's most highly regarded *mamluks*, Aibak al-Akhrish, during the fighting outside Acre showed such techniques in action. It was also described in heroic detail by Baha al-Din. Aibak's horse having been killed under him, he put his back against a rock and fought until his quiver was empty, then fought with sword until overwhelmed by the enemy's numbers.[856]

A further technique was that of shooting 'under a shield' which was done by passing the left or bow-arm through the two straps then pulling the *guige* tight around the neck to stop the shield from slipping around the arm. This was probably only possible when using the thumb-draw because in this technique the arrow went to the right of the bow.[857] Interestingly enough, exactly this technique is shown on a little-known mid-eighth-century wall-painting from the Umayyad Caliphal Palace at Khirbat al-Mafjar near Jericho in Palestine.

Rather later, the epic Turkish poem known as the *Danishmandname* describes the hero dismounting from his horse, 'undoing his archery equipment' which probably referred to the belt carrying the quiver and bowcase, then hanging them over the pommel of his saddle before advancing to fight on foot.[858] The pictorial evidence confirms that a bulky quiver and bowcase, of the form designed for use on horseback, was rarely used on foot, and where it is shown the artist may have left it there to indicate the high military status of the dismounted figure in question.

Arrowguides to shoot short arrows were used on foot, just as they were on horseback. In Fatimid armies from the period of the early Crusades, such archers reportedly used tiny arrows or darts one span or no more than 20 cm long, known as *jarad*.[859] Far to the west at Sabta (Ceuta), the highly esteemed local infantry archers used the Arab bow and light, long distance arrows to harass their foes.[860] The Arab bow was, incidentally, substantially longer in dimension that the Persian or Turkish bow and was designed for use on foot. The archers of Sabta were almost certainly working within the traditional but highly developed 'school' of archery described in Ibn Maymun's archery text. Written in Morocco during the thirteenth century, it is believed to have been a plea in favour of continued use of the Arab style of infantry archery and against a current move towards crossbows which, already popular in al-Andalus, the author regarded as weak, unreliable and clumsy.[861]

In addition to training to work as a member of a team and to use his weapons effectively, a cavalryman also had to be able to ride properly. There were two basic styles of horse riding in the medieval Islamic world. The first and earliest style was based upon that of the bedouin Arabs of the desert. Though originally used in warfare it was later largely reserved for long distance riding, racing and courier communications. The second was the 'high school' style of riding which developed later and reached its peak in twelfth- and thirteenth-century Egypt and al-Andalus.[862] While the former was probably associated with the padded, unframed form of saddle, the latter was associated with the fully developed saddle with a wooden tree or frame, and a suspended leather seat under which there was a tunnel or hollow to keep weight and chafing away from the horse's spine.

A number of pictorial sources rather unexpectedly also show men riding side-saddle in the immediate pre-Islamic and early Islamic periods. In all cases the riders can tentatively be identified as representing Arabs, so it is possible that riding side-saddle in such a manner was a 'third style', though only used when travelling slowly over long distances and as an alternative to avoid fatigue. The *furusiya* treatises that deal specifically with horse-riding emphasize a firm seat or *thabat*, to be achieved through practising bareback. The resulting style of military horsemanship did not involve rising in the saddle, as would be the case in the later medieval and early modern *a la jinete* riding technique seen in North Africa and Spain.[863] Instead it would seem to have been the original that lay behind the *a la brida*, Spanish and indeed American 'cowboy' method of riding. In the early days the most suitable saddle for this 'high school' style seems to have been known as the Khwaraymian pattern. It was characterized by a raised pommel and cantle, single or doubled girth, breast strap, pads beneath each side of the saddle, and horse cloth or saddle cloth.[864] The remains of three such saddles, probably dating from the late thirteenth century and one of them practically complete though in several pieces, have recently been excavated in the Citadel of Damascus.

Most sources agreed that the horsemanship of the professional Islamic soldier was better than that of the bedouin, and the constant practice as well as initial training that such skill required was probably one of the reasons why citizen armies declined in favour of professional ones from the late eighth to tenth centuries.[865] Whether there really was a revival in cavalry skills during the Great Seljuk Sultanate remains a matter of debate. However, it has been claimed that continuing training involved horsemanship, archery and swordplay, and that cavalrymen were expected to play polo at least once a week.[866]

Nizam al-Mulk, in the *Siyasat Nama* he wrote for the Great Seljuk Sultan in 1091, recommended a training programme for *ghulams* that would take several years. It began with 'One year on foot at the stirrup of a horseman' although the trainee himself was not allowed to ride. Next he was 'given a small Turkish horse … Thus served for a year with horse and whip. In the third year to be given a belt, in the fourth a quiver and bowcase to be fastened to the belt while mounted, in the fifth year to be given a better saddle and decorated bridle plus a handsome cloak and a *dabbus* mace'. Further changes in his status concerned duties rather than appearance, except in the eighth year when he got a black felt hat decorated with silver wire and another fine cloak.[867] *Chub* maces were clearly important as marks of the status of guards at court, these being gilded or silvered according to rank.[868]

Training for the military élite of the Fatimid army was based upon the *hujra* already used by the previous 'Abbasid and Ikhshidid governors of Egypt. These seem to have been like military academies where young recruits learned a variety of skills including horsemanship as well as military techniques and, for the select few, also literacy.[869] After a period of decline this *hujra* system was revived by the *wazir* al-Afdal when it seemed that the training became more specifically military in response to a threat posed by the Latin Crusader. The fact that the *hujra* remained in operation for the rest of the Fatimid period surely indicates that it was seen as a success.[870]

Almost all these training structures made considerable use of eunuchs as instructors or teachers. Sometimes known as *tawashi*, they remained important under Saladin and the Ayyubids but thereafter declined.[871] Another source by al-Wahrani, claiming to quote Saladin, indicated that the Sultan himself believed that the education of a scholar should also include archery and the use of arms.[872] Polo had reached Syria and Egypt by the time of Saladin, if not substantially earlier, and became very popular in both Ayyubid and Mamluk court circles. Saladin's sons were said to have played polo, ridden and practised archery outside the Citadel of Damascus every evening. This may well have been the normal education for the ruling class.[873] On the other hand military leadership and command skills were obtained on the battlefield and by experience of war while in the company of one's own family members, at least until the rise of the Mamluk Sultanate in the mid-thirteenth century.[874]

Where *mamluks* and *ghulams* themselves were concerned, they remained technically slaves while *kuttubi* students in school and under training. Once this was complete the trained man received his *'itaqa* certificate and was freed as a fully trained soldier. At this moment he was usually also given his first full set of military clothing, arms, armour, horses and other necessities.[875] The *Sirat al-Malik al-Zahir* or 'Life of Baybars' by 'Abd al-Zahir stated that in every Mamluk household there was an instructor for lance-fighting while a great many of Sultan Baybars' own *mamluks* also learned the 'fire game' on horseback. This was, however, describing a time of particular emergency.[876] Nevertheless there can be little doubt that Mamluk soldiers received much better and more intensive training than did their largely tribal Mongol opponents, both in riding skills and the use of weapons.[877]

To the west and a little earlier, the training of the élite *huffaz* of the Muwahhid ruler is said to have been done as rapidly as possible and to have included the usual skills of riding and archery, plus the less common ones of swimming and rowing. Whether the latter was really in 'small boats' as has been suggested, or was to prepare the men for service in the formidable Muwahhidun fleet is unclear.[878] Nowhere else in the medieval Islamic world, it would seem, were high status soldiers trained as oarsmen for the galleys, this being a very low status occupation. On the other hand Muwahhid Morocco was different, and the story of Moorish operations, commercial, exploratory and warlike, in the Atlantic has rarely been told.[879]

The *maydans* or training grounds deserve more study than they have received. In tenth- and eleventh-century Damascus, under Fatimid rule, there was a large *maydan* for cavalry training close to the walled city, although it was also used by merchants, markets and craftsmen, presumably on days when it was not needed by the soldiers. Nur al-Din maintained *maydans* at both Aleppo and Damascus in the second half of the twelfth century. There were two outside Damascus known as the 'Green' or grassy *maydan* which was close to the river Barada west of the walled city, and the self-explanatory 'Stony' *maydan* which was south of the city. Outside Aleppo the 'Black' *maydan* was east of the city near the new Yaruqi Turcoman quarter, while the 'Green' *maydan* was inside the citadel.[880] The *maydan* of early twelfth century Mardin was directly beneath the walls of the citadel,[881] while there was also a *maydan* just outside the city walls of Mosul in northern Iraq.[882] Here there was also a market for soldiers called the Mahallat Suq al-Turkman near the *maydan*.[883] The major efforts put into the building and maintaining of such *maydan* training areas during the later Ayyubid and early Mamluk Sultanate shows not only how important they were, but also the military commitment of these dynasties. Similarly the decay into which many were subsequently allowed to fall was regarded as showing the opposite.[884]

In these *maydans*, military training often became virtually a spectator sport. It clearly attracted many people from the neighbouring cities. It might also be fair to assume that the men taking part often regarded exercises in the *maydan* almost as sports. If so, they would merely have been mirroring the pleasure that the knightly class and aristocracies of Western Europe took in the *tournament*. There were several types of exercise, some involving individual skills, some rooted in teamwork, some seemingly just to make a fine display.

Amongst the most dramatic must have been those involving use of the cavalry spear or lance. Surviving *furusiya* manuscripts from the Mamluk Sultanate strongly suggest that there was almost an outbreak of 'lance fever' in the later thirteenth century, so keen were cavalry to use this most prized of weapons, just as the public were keen to watch them doing so.[885]

The exercises or games involved striking at a target called a *birjas* which consisted of seven blocks of wood on top of each other, the topmost also having a wooden ring. A cavalryman was supposed to charge past, using the point of his spear to lift the block with a ring without knocking over the rest.[886] Another exercise involved striking a small target on the ground while charging past at speed;[887] this being identical to much later British Army tent-pegging as learned in India. A third exercise involved a revolving wooden horseman mounted on a pole and armed with a mace and shield which spun around when the figure was struck.[888] This exercise or game eventually reached Western Europe in a simplified form and became part of the entertainment at tournaments.

The only exercises with the sword or sabre which were done in public view in the *maydan* were probably those on horseback. According to 'Abd Allah Muhibb al-Din al-Tabari, writing about Mamluk training before 1295, fencing on horseback involved practice against a green reed thrust into the ground or against a row of such reeds. The aim was to reduce the height of these fresh reeds, little by little with a cut on each pass. There were also fencing exercises between pairs of horsemen, hopefully with blunted weapons.[889] Other exercises involving use of the sword appear less dramatic and may normally have been done in the privacy of the home, courtyard or barracks. They involved fencing against an opponent and striking at various targets to strengthen the arm and improve accuracy.[890]

According to 'Abd Allah Muhibb al-Din al-Tabari, such individual sword practice normally involved a mound of clay on a table, striking this from different positions and angles, sometimes with from five to one hundred layers of felt over the clay which then had to be cut. Men also practised striking from a sitting or kneeling position to strengthen their upper body and arms.[891] When fully trained in all these skills, a *mamluk* was supposedly able to choose whether to kill or merely incapacitate a foe; honing his skill with further practice against sheets of paper and cotton filled pillows.

The wrestling exercises which *mamluks* undertook were unlikely to have been done in public, given the social and religious attitudes of the time.[892] The *Danishmandname* written by 'Arif 'Ali of Toqat in the fourteenth century often describes Turkish champions wrestling and seizing each other by the belt.[893] Otherwise very little is known about the skills involved, though they may have been similar to the famous wrestling bouts still performed, very much in public, on the island of Sarayiçi outside the Turkish city of Edirne.

Archery training appears to have involved different types of *maydan* according to the exercise in question. The best archers, presumably on foot, were not only able to loose three arrows in one and a half seconds, but could hit a target about 1 m wide at a range of approximately 70 m, though speed and accuracy are unlikely to have featured in a single exercise. The target was rather larger if the archer was mounted.[894]

Different skills were demanded in the *qighaj* or *qiqaj* and *qabaq* archery exercises. The *qighaj* or *qiqaj* involved shooting at a low target on the ground and the *qabaq* at a high target above the archer's head, both to be shot at while the man rode past at the *sawq*; that is urging or driving his horse. Both exercises were then completed by the *jawaldan* or wheeling aside. Writing in the mid-fourteenth century, Taybugha al-Baklamishi al-Yunani maintained that such exercises were based upon nomadic Turkish and *fursan* or classical Islamic cavalry traditions.[895] In this context it is interesting to recall that al-Jahiz, in his work on the varying military skills of rival peoples or formations in the early ninth century 'Abbasid army, reported the Khurasanis' claim to military superiority was partly on the basis that they knew how to 'wheel aside'.[896]

According to 'Abd Allah Muhibb al-Din al-Tabari, writing about training in the Mamluk Sultanate during the final decade of the thirteenth century, the horse-archer not only had to learn how to hold his reins, stand in his stirrups and lean forward while shooting, but should loose at the *qabaq* from a range of just over 6.5 m.[897] Shooting at the *qabaq* was clearly very popular amongst the Bahri Mamluks, particularly in the period from 1260 to 1295. Its purpose as a military exercise was probably to improve dexterity and the target was normally shot at before being passed; in other words from the front or side. Shooting backwards at the target, in what is now called the Parthian Shot, was regarded as a sort of trick without much military relevance.[898]

In contrast, shooting at the *qiqaj* or ground target had a very direct military application. A horse-archer needed to be able to do this over both his left and right thigh or in any other downwards direction.[899] Shooting horizontally was, of course, also a necessary skill, if less impressive for onlookers.[900] It was against a target called a *buttiya* padded with cotton, probably covered with leather and which was mounted on four legs. It was usually at the same height as the archer's chest.[901]

A new and different sort of *maydan* was established by Sultan Baybars I outside the Citadel of Cairo. Known as the Maydan al-Sabaq, it was probably for long range flight-shooting rather than horse racing as was sometimes thought.[902] Unfortunately it is not known whether any of the archery ranges near Sabta (Ceuta) in northern Morocco were of the long-range variety, but it is clear that they were used not only for shooting with the ordinary bows but also with the 'aqqara crossbow.[903]

Another unusual variation on archery training was recorded in Syria in the year 968. It was known as an 'ajala and consisted of a stuffed animal mounted on a four-wheeled cart or trolley pulled behind a horseman with long ropes. It represented a hunted animal and sometimes had a smaller stuffed animal close behind to represent the huntsman's own dog. How common this device was at other times or in other regions is unknown.[904] With the probable exception of this remarkable moving target, the similarity between infantry archery training methods and skills in the medieval Islamic world and those recorded amongst the élite Tatar guards of late Manchu China is remarkable.[905] Both probably developed in response to the overriding threat posed by horse-archery, initially from the Turco-Mongol peoples of the Central Asian steppes. Whereas the Chinese tradition has survived as a sport, that of the Islamic Middle East has sadly disappeared.

MILITARY EQUIPMENT

Until recently the archaeological evidence for medieval Islamic arms, armour and other forms of military equipment has been very sparse. That which does exist includes religious relics whose true origins and dating have been seriously questioned by non-Muslim scholars and equally vehemently defended by Muslim scholars. While an abundance of magnificent and often beautifully decorated armour and weaponry dating from the sixteenth century onwards can be found in many museums, most of it Ottoman Turkish, Iranian or Moghul Indian, the majority of items from earlier centuries seem to be in private collections or highly specialized museums that are not always open to the public. More recently a substantial quantity of new and largely organic material has come to light in Syria, but most of it awaits complete study and publication.

Thus students of this highy specialized and little-known field have tended to be forced to rely upon written and pictorial evidence, with all the problems and limitations that implies. Where Islamic written sources are concerned, almost entirely being in Arabic, Persian and Turkish, there are still unanswered questions about the precise meaning of many terms as used in a particular region or culture at a specific time. To a lesser extent the study of Western European military equipment has suffered from the same problems of terminology; words sometimes remaining constant for centuries while the objects they describe changed.

Within the Islamic world words could have subtly different meanings in different regions, and could slightly change such meanings when being transferred from one Islamic language to another. Thus a piece of military equipment might first appear in Turkish pre- or very early Islamic Central Asia, be adopted and slightly modified in Farsi (Persian) before being adopted and again slightly modified in Arabic. Several terms then jumped across the religious divide and appeared in more or less distorted forms within various Western European languages – with or without having first passed through Byzantine Greek.

Even the occasional specialist and highly detailed source such as al-Tarsusi's *Tabsira Arbab al-Lubab*, written for Saladin early in his reign, can present the military historian with new problems because so many of the complicated weapons described are clearly experimental and probably impractical. On the other hand, once this is understood, there can be a great deal of more realistic information below the surface, since al-Tarsusi's strange devices were based upon a foundation of real and even everyday military technology. Having overcome that problem, there can be further pitfalls in the translation of the terminology of medieval Islamic raw materials, metallic alloys, even weights and measures. For example the Iraqi *ratl* is understood to have weighed something over 405 g while the Syrian *ratl* was over four and a half times times as heavy at 1,850 g.[906] Meanwhile the Egyptian *ratl* is sometimes interpreted at 330 g.

As if problems with the interpretation of terminology were not bad enough, there is the question of how to interpret the illustration of military equipment, horse-harness and so on in the very varied styles and forms of Islamic art. Some historians have seemingly given up, dismissing Islamic art as no help whatsoever. Then there is the question of quite what 'Islamic art' was. The Coptic Christian art of Egypt, the Jacobite Christian art of Syria and the Nestorian Christian art of Iraq often have more in common with the art produced by Muslims in these same countries than with the more obviously Christian art of the Byzantine world and Latin or Catholic Western Europe.

Within the Iberian Peninsula there is very little representational art of a strictly Islamic origin, but the art of the indigenous Mozarab Christians which originated in Islamic al-Andalus is very diferent from that of the Christians of northern Iberia, and has, therefore, often been taken as illustrating, at least to some degree, the military equipment and costume of al-Andalus itself. In some other frontier or peripheral regions there are different problems of stylistic attribution and content. Taking twelfth century Norman Sicily as an example, the carved lintel over the north door of the Church of La Martorana in Palermo has been described as being in a very Egyptian style.[907] It also included one of the finest representations of warriors, one of whom is a mailed archer who might well reflect the military equipment of North Africa or late Fatimid Egypt.

Then there are the more famous painted panels in the ceiling of the Capella Palatina in Palermo which are clearly Islamic in style and largely so in content. They illustrate numerous military figures with a variety of equipment. Some art historians regard them as the finest surviving examples of Fatimid art, while others believe that they are a truer reflection of Islamic North Africa,[908] or they could simply be seen as demonstrating the high degree of Islamic influence within the armies of Norman Sicily itself.

Despite the free flow of ideas, technology and the highly developed trade networks of the medieval Islamic world, each of the main regions retained some distinctive characteristics in its arms and armour. Those of eastern Iran and the settled regions of Transoxania are well described in Firdawsi's epic poem, the *Shahname* written around 1000. Armour for men and horses mainly consisted of mail and lamellar, plus quilted soft armour such as the *gubr* for a man and the *bargustuwan* for a horse. A normal array of weapons was employed, along with the lasso and various siege machines or devices.[909] Essentially the same were similarly used in the Middle East and the frontier regions facing the Byzantine Empire. Here quilted soft armour may have been popular amongst the Kurds; one force of Kurdish cavalry facing the Byzantines in 998 being equipped with a quilted 'combat tunic', a helmet and two javelins per man.[910] These sound like light cavalry.

Following the Turkish conquest of Anatolia, mail and lamellar were also used in the Seljuk Sultanate of Rum but after that state fragmented at the end of the thirteenth century, standards of equipment seem to have fallen, at least amongst the Turcoman forces of the small successor states or *beyliks*. One Western European observer claimed that the Turks of early fourteenth-century Anatolia had no armour except a 'leather hauberk'.[911] The latter probably meant a lamellar cuirass of hardened leather or rawhide, though it might also have meant a style of leather cuirass made of laminated leather hoops which has only recently been discovered (see below). A generation or two later the epic *Danishmandname* written by 'Arif 'Ali of Toqat described the élite of Turkish warriors being armed with spear, sword, *hançar* or large dagger, mace and archery equipment. After prolonged combat, the poet often describes horse harness and *cevşen* lamellar armour as being 'in tatters'.[912]

There has been a tendency to assume that the light equipment and minimal armour supposedly preferred by Arab tribesmen meant that they were virtually unarmoured. This had clearly not been the case in earlier centuries and even in the mid-twelfth century, the port-city of Aden and probably its hinterland reportedly had 'arms in immeasurable quantities'.[913] In the absence of further information it might be safer to assume that, within a general tradition of light cavalry and infantry warfare, the military equipment of the tribes and peoples of the Arabian Peninsula varied according to their wealth.

Wealth, proximity to sources of manufacture, supply, and major trade routes clearly had a major impact on arms and armour in Egypt and the Fertile Crescent during the period of the Crusades. In technological terms the Fatimid army may actually have been slightly in advance of the early Crusaders.[914] In other respects it relied upon largely the same array of arms and armour as was seen elsewhere around the Mediterranean and may therefore have had as much in common with Christian Italy as with Islamic Iran. Nor is there real evidence that its troops were particularly lightly equipped; certainly not where the élite cavalry were concerned. In the late eleventh and early twelfth centuries the latter used *tijfaf* horse armour, *kazaghand* mail-lined and padded armour, the *jawshan* lamellar cuirass and the normal *dir'* mail hauberk.[915]

A detailed description of a big Fatimid military procession to mark the First Day of the Year listed not only the troops involved, but in many cases their equipment. It was written by a Shi'a sympathizer, Ibn al-Tu'wair in the late eleventh or early twelfth century. In addition to more usual equipment, the weapons included maces of the *amud, dabbus, latt* and *gurz* types, plus various kinds of infantry staff weapon or polearm. One such was the *sabarbara* which was a broad-bladed spear more than 5 cubits (*c.* 229 cm) long of which more than 3 cubits (*c.* 137 cm) consisted of the blade. The author also mentioned the short *furanjiya* spear, various other obscure infantry staff weapons and versions of javelin but without describing them, the large *lamt* leather shield of Saharan origin, and hand-held crossbows carried by marines.[916]

The widespread use of leather armour that had characterized the eastern parts of the medieval Islamic world was also seen in Egypt, though it was not mentioned by Ibn al-Tu'wair, perhaps because it was recognized as being rather cheap, not very 'splendid' and perhaps unsuitable for parades. It was, however, noted by the Muslims' Crusader foes. A late twelfth-century French *chanson de geste* called *Les Chétifs*, which formed part of what is now known as the *Crusade Cycle*, has a leading Saracen warrior wearing just such leather armour in addition to more normal protection. It included *cauces ploieïces* or pliable chausses, and a *fort clavain* strong neck or shoulder piece, as well as a helmet of *quir boli* hardened leather.[917]

In overall terms the evidence strongly suggests that various forms of leather armour became even more important in the Mamluk Sultanate from the mid-thirteenth century onwards. In his *Life of Baybars*, 'Abd al-Zahir reported that in a time of great danger from the Mongols, Sultan Baybars ordered all troops to maintain or perhaps upgrade their military equipment.

> They had no occupation but to obtain their equipment and to increase this and *jawshans* of *kimukht* [rawhide] gilded and silvered and *jawshan*-style [lamellar] horse-armour and Frankish [Western European] helmets.[918]

The Italian military theorist Fidenzio of Padua writing around 1291, claimed that the Mamluks only had leather armour, that their arms were unprotected so that it was easier for them to use the bow, that their legs were similarly unarmoured and that they had no horse armour.[919] Either Fidenzio was exaggerating or, more probably, he was describing the poorly equipped bulk of the army while 'Abd al-Zahir had been writing about the élite. In that case both were, in their ways, correct. Almost two generations later, in 1335, another Italian writer named Giacomo di Verona described the Mamluk garrison of Cairo and this time based his account upon his own observation. The cavalry, he said, were mounted on small horses when compared to what he was used to seeing in Italian armies, had iron helmets but only leather armour, and were mainly armed with bows; '*quod in capete portant unum capellum parvum de ferro et aliqui habebant carrocias aliqui vero non, sed armaturas de coreis*'.[920]

Although some of the numerically small military élites of North Africa appear to have been reasonably well armoured, the bulk of the largely Berber tribal warriors went virtually unarmoured. For example, only a few of the Lamtuna Berbers slain in a battle between Murabitun and Gudala Berbers in 1056 were found to have been wearing mail armour. The great majority relied solely on their *lamt* leather shields.[921] Similarly the cavalry of the early Muwahhidun state in mid-twelfth-century Morocco relied on small *daraqah* leather shields. Otherwise their weapons mainly consisted of *rumh* spear or lance and *sayf* straight sword, with occasional references to a large *khanjar* dagger which had been introduced from the east.[922]

The situation was very different in al-Andalus where it appears that military equipment was abundant and armour was not restricted to the élite. A particularly detailed account of the army of the Umayyad Caliphate of Cordova in the late tenth century listed their armour as abundant *dir'* mail hauberks as well as *jawshan* lamellar cuirasses plus *tijfaf* soft armour which could also refer to horse-armour. The weapons included *'amud* mace and *tabarzin* axe as well as the more common spear and sword.[923] There is every reason to believe that essentially the same arms and armour was used by Andalusian troops throughout the eleventh and twelfth centuries. Describing such local Andalusian Islamic cavalry in the thirteenth century, Ibn Sa'id al-Maghribi still used the term *jawshan* to emphasize the 'armoured whole' of the heavy cavalryman, though his main armour remained the *dir'* mail hauberk.[924]

Whether the originally lamellar *jawshan* cuirass was still really being used in al-Andalus at a time when Andalusian troops were considered to be under such strong Western European technological and stylistic influence is less clear. On the other hand, some of the earliest evidence for the Western European coat-of-plates also comes from late twelfth- and thirteenth-century Spain, so perhaps this is further evidence for the *jawshan* being one of the most important precursors of the coat-of-plates.[925] Ibn Sa'id also noted that the Andalusian cavalryman normally used a large wooden *turs* shield while his North African Berber counterpart used a lighter leather *daraqa*.[926] Thereafter, European technological and stylistic influence declined in the last Islamic Andalusian state of Granada while that of North Africa increased. Even so, Granadan cavalry if not infantry were often regarded as being more heavily armoured than the Berber volunteers who came from North Africa, while being regarded as lightly armoured when compared to the bulk of Spanish Christian men-at-arms.

When looking at Islamic weapons by type, it is natural to start with the sword since this had such high status in Islamic civilization. Some of the most revered objects in the Islamic Reliquary now in the Topkapi Museum in Istanbul are, in fact, swords traditionally associated with the Prophet Muhammad, his closest Companions, and the earliest Caliphs. Religiously less significant but still highly respected relics from several later caliphs and rulers again include swords which they are supposed to have possessed or used.

By the eleventh century it was traditional in the Islamic world to designate sword-blades according to their geographical origins, though this may already have been developing into a typology of designs which in turn were believed to have had their origins in one part of the world or another. The most famous of all Arabic texts on swords was, of course, that of Ya'qub Ibn Ishaq al-Kindi who wrote for the 'Abbasid Caliph al-Mu'tasim in the first half of the ninth century.[927] It was such a thorough and monumental work that nothing else seems to have been considered necessary for several centuries.[928] Yet this remarkable piece of medieval scholarship is sometimes difficult to interpret, often because the meanings of certain words have changed over the centuries. Indeed the whole subject of early medieval and 'Abbasid-period Islamic swords became cluttered with myths and misunderstanding that are only now being untangled.[929]

Several of these myths took root at an early date and so even the work of the great Islamic scientist Muhammad Ibn Ahmad al-Biruni, writing in the first half of the eleventh century, has to be approached with caution. In his *Kitab al-Jamahir* he stated that the swords of Rum (the Byzantine Empire and perhaps parts of southern Europe), of the Rus (Kievan Russia and perhaps the Scandinavian merchants who came to the Islamic world via Russia) and the Saqalibah (the Slav peoples of eastern Europe) were made from *shabraqan* 'male iron' which is commonly though perhaps misleadingly translated as an early or primitive form of steel.[930] The same was also the case with *Qala'* swords which are generally believed to have come from beyond the eastern frontiers of Islam, though references to *Qala' Rumi* or 'Byzantine *Qala*'' swords rather suggests that the term now denoted a form rather than an origin. This interpretation is strengthened by the fact that al-Biruni also noted that *Qala'* swords could have either a spine or a fuller groove down their blades, so perhaps these features were what distinguished a *Qala'* sword. The swords of the Rus and the Saqalibah were both also pattern welded.[931]

According to al-Biruni, *fuladh* or true steel was made from *narm ahan* 'female' or soft iron, reportedly in the province of Harat in what is now western Afghanistan from where it was sent in the form of 'eggs' or small ingots to make *Hindi* swords.[932] Though their name, *Hindi*, denoted an Indian origin it now seems likely that the term indicated a style or form rather than necessarily a place of manufacture. In fact al-Biruni himself points out that *Hindi* and *Sarandi* (Ceylonese or Sri Lankan) swords were both sometimes called *Hindi*.[933] Swords of *fuladh* steel were also more brittle than those of the Rus which had *shaburqan* 'hard iron' edges and *narm ahan* 'soft iron' cores.[934] Al-Biruni then used the term *Firind* for the surface patterning now called watering, the nature of which, he pointed out, could indicate high quality.[935]

Historians of Islamic arms and armour still tend to disagree about the true nature or characteristics of the swords called *Qarajuli*, *Qarachuri* and other variations on this name. However, the bulk of the evidence tilts heavily in favour of them being single-edged and perhaps slightly though not necessarily curved. If single-edged and straight, they could be what is now sometimes called a *palash* and thus have been comparable to, or indeed the same as, the similarly dated Byzantine *rhomphaion*. Long, slender-bladed and clearly curved swords that could be described as true sabres had been known in Turkish Central Asia for several centuries, probably entering the eastern provinces of the Islamic world by the late ninth century and then moving westward by or during the eleventh century. Nevertheless, it is clear that the true sabre did not become widely popular within the central Islamic heartlands of the Middle East until after the Mongol invasions of the thirteenth century.

Writing in Turkish-ruled Islamic northern India in the early thirteenth century, Fakhr al-Din Mubarakshah stated that the *qalachuri* sword was curved.[936] Unfortunately, an equally prolonged argument has concerned the origins of the Turkish word *Kilij*. This normally referred to a sabre and its similarity with variations of the word *Qalachuri* seem obvious, though another derivation may yet be found. Daggers are frequently mentioned but rarely described. Some could be small, like that kept in his boot by a hero of the Turkish epic poem, *The Book of Dede Korkut*.[937] In contrast the *khanjar* fighting knife was almost a short sword.

Maces were considerably more varied and, as battlefield weapons, were more important than daggers. The winged or flanged form was once thought to be a medieval development, probably of Middle Eastern Iranian or even Indian origin. The geographical attribution may well be correct but the discovery of a fully formed spiked copper-alloy mace in the ruins of the third century Syro-Roman frontier fortress of Dura-Europos in eastern Syria pushes back the weapon's origins many centuries. The apparent lack of any comparable weapon elsewhere in the Roman World supports the identification of this particular mace as having belonged to either a Parthian refugee in the defending garrison, or a member of the Sassanian army which took Dura-Europos. In either case, the weapon's origins were east of Rome's eastern frontier.[938]

Maces, particularly those with zoomorphic heads, featured prominently in pre-Islamic and early Islamic Turkish culture in Central Asia,[939] and their symbolic function as ceremonial or particularly high-status weapons would continue among Muslim Turks beyond the medieval period. A more recent study of close combat weapons from the eighth-century 'Abbasid period to the fourteenth-century Mamluk Sultanate shows that maces remained important weapons amongst the heavily armoured cavalry, some being so heavy that only the strongest of men could use them properly. Within the medieval Islamic context these were again regarded as élite weapons and were specifically designed for use against an armoured foe. Their shapes, sizes and designs were also remarkably varied.[940]

Al-Tarsusi, writing for Saladin, explained that some were 'all of iron' while others had wooden hafts or handles. Their heads came in forms known as the *latt* which was long and fluted, the *'amud* which was the heaviest, and the *dabbus* which may have been simpler and smaller. Al-Tarsusi also mentions a fourth form which he called the *khurz* which he said was particularly effective but was, tantalizingly, of 'secret' construction.[941] This latter weapon was the Turkish *gurz* which may well have still been a novelty in ex-Fatimid Egypt. It would seem that the Turkish *gurz* could include those with zoomorphic and even anthropomorphic heads, but may more generally have been of the flanged variety. The latter shape would have been more difficult to cast in metal than some of the others, and might well have been seen as a bit of a technological secret.

Cast bronze maces are known to have been used in Iran in the eleventh and twelfth centuries, continuing throughout Seljuk domination into the Khwarazmshah period. Several still exist, mostly with elements of inlaid silver decoration. The medieval Turkish *Book of Dede Korkut* several times mentions maces with six ridges,[942] which seems to have been normal. Meanwhile the *macon* mace and more specialized *martel* 'war hammer' or *mals de fer* 'iron hammer' were often placed in the hands of Saracen foes in French *chansons de geste* such as the late twelfth-century *Les Chétifs*,[943] and Graindor de Douai's *Le Chanson d'Antioche* of c. 1190.[944]

Until recently there has been considerable misunderstanding about the medieval Islamic *tabarzin* or war-axe. The word was usually translated as 'saddle axe' from *tabar* axe and *zin* saddle, therefore being assumed to refer to a relatively small, single-handed axe as seen in later Islamic centuries.[945] However, such weapons rarely appeared in medieval Islamic art. Instead it has now been convincingly argued that the *tabarzin* was not a light 'saddle axe' for use by cavalry. In fact the term seems to have been just another variation of the Persian word *tabr* axe, as used from the pre-Islamic Sassanian Empire to the late tenth century, plus the early Persian suffix *zin* indicating that the object in question was a weapon. In other words *tabarzin* merely meant military axe or war-axe.

Furthermore, there was then a significant decline in the use of axes as weapons of war from the tenth century onwards. One reason for this decline may have been that the large axe was a very expensive and difficult weapon to manufacture, having often incorporated an iron or partially iron haft. For this reason the war-axe was to some extent replaced by the simple *dabbus* mace. It is worth noting that the very large and similarly expensive iron *'amud* form of mace also declined during this period of economic and political fragmentation.[946] These centuries were, incidentally, those which seem to have seen a significant increase in the use of various styles of hardened leather armour. The war-axe was probably regarded as obsolete during the twelfth century when the original meaning of *tabarzin* may have altered. Meanwhile, from the late eleventh or early twelfth century onwards the simple word *tabr* was used for all forms of axe, including work tools. The *tabarzin* war-axe may then have been revived at a considerably later date, as a lighter weapon and with slightly different meaning.[947]

Other forms of war-axe were also used; amongst the most notable being the Persian *nachakh* which was called a *najikh* in most Arabic sources. According to al-Tarsusi writing in twelfth-century Egypt, this weapon had a blade shaped like a half-moon and was particularly effective as a cavalry weapon against men on foot.[948] A late twelfth-century Persian source described the *nachakh* as similar to the *tabarzin* but with a larger blade.[949] A third war-axe of possible Iranian origin was the *durbash*. This, however, remains very obscure and, by the fourteenth century, sometimes seems to have been similar to the *nachakh*.[950]

The spear was such a common weapon that it was rarely described in detail unless it was of an unusual form. Generally called a *rumh* in Arabic, a *nizah* in Persian and a *sungu* or *sünü* in Turkish, there were variants that are now not always easy to distinguish. For example the Arabic *quntariya* clearly stemmed from the Byzantine Greek *kontarion* and may have had a relatively broad blade. According to the twelfth-century Syrian warrior and scholar, Usama Ibn Munqidh, this *quntariya* could be used in a sideways cutting motion as well as a straightforward thrust, and when used laterally in this manner by a cavalryman could cause very severe injuries to an opponent's horse.[951]

Usama also described a seemingly unsuccessful composite lance consisting of two *rumh* spears spliced together. This *rumah mu'allifah* was 18–20 cubits (9–10 m) long and was carried by a man on a horse, but was so long and heavy that it trailed along the ground.[952] Developed by the people of Hims in central Syria it may, in reality, have been intended primarily as a long infantry pike. On the other hand, when the mid-thirteenth to early fourteenth century Turkish *Book of Dede Korkut* epic mentioned the length of a cavalryman's spear, it was usually 60 spans long[953] (approximately 12 m), which must surely have been a poetic or heroic exaggeration. The *Book of Dede Korkut* does confirm the existence of spears with bamboo shafts as mentioned in Byzantine sources and illustrated in Arab manuscripts. For the Turks, however, such a weapon was used by low-status warriors.

The identification and description of infantry staff weapons is difficult in virtually all medieval cultures except that of China where detailed information is abundant. This may also indicate the higher prestige of foot soldiers in China than elsewhere. Al-Tarsusi, writing in twelfth-century Egypt, is clearer than most where staff weapons or pole-arms are concerned. He draws particular attention to the *furayjiya*, which may have been a mistranscription or variation of *faranjiya*, which, he maintained, was 'like' a *mizraq* javelin. This probably meant that its blade and socket formed a larger portion of the whole weapon than was the case with, for example, an ordinary spear. Whether the *faranjiya* and *furayjiya* really did have some association with the Franj, Franks or Western Europeans is unclear, but it is interesting to note that one of the pole-arms used in al-Andalus had a broad blade 'like the swords of the Franks'. This might, however, refer to spears with wings or flanges between the blade and the socket,[954] as seen in so much medieval European and rather less medieval Islamic art.

Other forms of infantry supposed pole-arms included the *dariya*. Al-Tarsusi specifically stated that the blade formed one-third of this weapon's total length. Another was the *sabarbara* which was 5 cubits (*c.* 2.29 m) in length with a blade one *fitr* (*c.* 17 cm) wide and 1 cubit (*c.* 46 cm) long,[955] thus leaving 4 cubits (*c.* 1.8 m) for the haft. Slightly earlier a unit of Fatimid infantry called *sariya* carried what must surely have been a form of pike, 7 cubits (*c.* 3.2 m) long and having a lance-blade on a long iron 'neck' plus a socket.[956]

It has been suggested that the medieval Western European *guisarme*, or *guasarma* as it was known in the Christian regions of the Iberian peninsula, developed from the long hafted war-axe seen in late eleventh-century Mozarab and other pictorial sources. This early medieval Iberian axe was clearly different from those of the rest of Western and specifically Northern or Scandinavian Europe during this period, and is very likely to have been of Arab-Islamic origin.[957]

Differentiating between the shorter forms of infantry pole-arm to be wielded and javelins to be thrown is not always easy in medieval Islamic terminology. For example, the term *harba* has often been translated as a heavy javelin. It had been used since the earliest years of Islamic history but, by the tenth century, almost certainly meant a staff weapon. Furthermore, the *harba* often also seems to have had a symbolic function, more like a standard than a fighting weapon. In late tenth-century al-Andalus it was described as having a large blade 'like a Frankish sword', half of which could apparently be coloured and decorated for ceremonial occasions.[958] It was mentioned in most parts of the Islamic world, Arab, Iranian, Turkish and northern Indian, throughout most of the medieval period.

The most common term for a real javelin was *mizraq*. Used by cavalry and infantry, usually with a slender blade to pierce armour or shields, it was again found in almost all Islamic languages from at least the tenth century onwards but was originally Arabic. The *khisht* seems to have been a small or lighter javelin, again used by both horsemen and foot soldiers in Arabic and Persian-speaking regions, though probably being of Persian origin.

Like the sword, the bow attracted a great deal of scholarly attention from both medieval and modern scholars, being one of the highest status weapons in Islamic history. The oldest form of bow, which retained prestige because of its association with the Prophet Muhammad and his Companions, was the *qaws hijazi*, 'bow of western Arabia' otherwise known as the Arab bow. It was believed to have been made of simple wood, but with a varied cross-section. Yet there is evidence that the pre-Islamic and first Islamic Arabs also knew of the composite bow and it was been suggested that the continued use of a simple bow was because the long-horned cattle or long-horned goats which provided the traditional materials for composite bows were not available in Arabia. Given the clear trade in other items of military equipment over long distances, this explanation should be treated with caution. Even the *qaws hijazi* was best made from *nab'* wood, in Latin *grewia tenax*, which was imported into Arabia from various directions, though *cornus mas* and *chadara velutina* could also be used.[959]

Many Muslims soon adopted the superior composite bow, but in the early centuries this almost certainly included quite long weapons more suited for archery on foot than on horseback and still incorporating long, inflexible and often angled 'ears' at the outer ends. The latter bows are likely to have been the same as those in the Byzantine Empire and Iran, and they reached all parts of the Islamic world including al-Andalus in the far west. Here, during the tenth century, large war-bows were divided into the Arab or *qaws hijazi*, and *qaws 'ajamiyya* or foreign bows.[960]

Surviving specialized texts dealing with archery contain a remarkable amount of detailed information and it is interesting to note that the terminology of the composite bow in al-Tarsusi's book, written in the twelfth century for Saladin, is largely of Persian origin.[961] The relative lack of Turkish archery terminology in the early thirteenth-century Persian text by Fakhr al-Din Mubarakshah also points to it being based on earlier, pre-Seljuk traditions of Islamic archery. Both these sources might therefore suggest that earlier forms of essentially Persian angled composite bows remained in widespread use.

This was clearly the case in North Africa and al-Andalus where the Turkish-style recurved composite never made much impact, though it was known by the later medieval period. Ibn Maymun, writing in thirteenth-century Morocco, added some other pieces of information about earlier forms of bow. He stated that the traditional *qaws hijazi* could be of a single piece of wood or of two joined lengthways, or could be 'backed' by an additional piece of wood to make it stronger, the entire process being finished by carving the wood to shape. A third form of bow, known as *wasiti* or 'between' was essentially of wood though reinforced with goat horn on the belly or front and sinew at the back. This was between the Arab or Hijazi and the Persian bows. All were, nevertheless, the height of a man when unstrung, thus being equivalent in overall size to what later became known as the English longbow. Clearly these were not the short Turkish recurved and fully composite bow.[962]

Most of the bending in a composite bow was near the grip. In the earlier angled form with stiff ears the latter acted as levers and made the draw easier, but they also absorbed much of the energy of the release, this making the overall bow less efficient than the fully recurved Turkish type.[963] It was also weaker in construction[964] and, in certain variants, may have posed the danger of the bowstring whipping around the angle of the ears. The angled form was similarly more difficult to use on horseback because the long, stiff ears could strike the horse when released. In fact it seems possible that, when using the angled form in this manner the mounted archer held his bow in a similar manner to that of Japanese horse archers. Their weapons were again large, but whereas the Japanese continued to use a very long bow on horseback the great majority of Islamic horse-archers abandoned the eared form in favour of the smoothly recurved Turkish form during the twelfth and thirteenth centuries.[965]

The short but thick and very powerful recurved composite bow, generally known as the Turkish bow, has been described as the ultimate cavalry weapon before the development of hand-held guns. It may have reached the eastern and even the central regions of the medieval Islamic world before the Seljuk invasions of the eleventh century, yet it was the latter series of conquests which really led to the Turkish recurved composite bow becoming the archetypal weapon of later medieval Islamic soldiers. This remarkable weapon could have the same length draw as a simple longbow though being much shorter. Weight for weight it could also achieve about twice the range of the simple bow.[966]

Such bows were usually described by their draw weight and each bow was, among the tribal Turks, probably made to suit the size and strength of a particular individual. This was not the case in the later medieval Islamic centuries when bows were mass-produced in a limited number of draw-weights. Only a very strong man could repeatedly use a bow with over 75 kg draw weight. Consequently, those normally used against the invading Crusaders are estimated to have had a draw weight of some 50 kg.[967]

According to Taybugha, writing in the later fourteenth century, the normal Turkish-style composite war-bow was known in the Mamluk Sultanate as the Damascus bow,[968] perhaps because the Syrian capital had become a major centre of almost mass production. Such weapons naturally appeared in many Western European sources concerning the Crusades, the Saracen foe and the Middle East in general, both historical and fictional. The mid-twelfth-century *Chanson d'Antioche* and several other parts of what is called *The Crusade Cycle* refer to the Muslims' 'bows of horn', while the Crusader and chronicler De Joinville similarly mentioned the Mamluks' *ars de cor*.[969]

Several accounts of bows or bowstrings being slackened by damp have been taken as evidence that they were made of rawhide or sinew rather than a vegetable fibre.[970] Ibn Maymun's archery text, written in thirteenth-century Morocco, specifically states that a variety of bowstrings were used in the medieval Islamic world. Each had advantages and disadvantages: those of hide tending to stretch in the cold or damp while those of silk or sinew were better, but not good in great heat. They were, he claimed, used by 'Slavs'. Those of gut were, in contrast, only good in hot climates. Meanwhile arrowstrings of bamboo, by which he might mean long grass, were used by Nubians and Persians.[971]

Archaeological research has shown that flint was still being used for arrowheads in Arabia shortly before the rise of Islam while there is evidence of flint also being used for Arabian spearheads even in the 'Abbasid period.[972] Nevertheless, in both cases these might have been for hunting rather than warfare. Most medieval sources, especially those from what could be regarded as the receiving end, agreed on the great penetrating power of Turkish arrows shot from composite bows.[973] However, it is also clear that the lightness of such arrows often limited their ability to penetrate reasonably strong forms of armour.

There has been some difficulty in differentiating between different sorts of arrows, assuming that the names given to arrows within one language had a clear-cut and specific meaning. It was, for example, suggested that the Arabic term *sahm* originally meant an arrow with a reed shaft, but that the word was later applied to a greater variety of arrows. Experimentation shows that arrows made wholly or partially of reed have the advantage of very quickly absorbing the vibration caused by going round the bow and thus soon straighten out. In this respect they were more effective than simple wooden arrows, but were also more difficult to make straight in the first place.[974] Some historians have interpreted the *nabl* as the original form of quite heavy Arab arrow to be shot from the large *qaws hijazi* bow, whereas others have assumed the Arab *nabl* to have been of reed and to have been lighter than the Persian *nushaba* arrow. The latter has similarly been assumed to have been a straightforward wooden arrow. Here it is perhaps significant that the medieval Turkish *Book of Dede Korkut* mentioned arrows being made of beech or hornbeam.[975] The same text also referred to quivers containing 80 or 90 arrows, though this may again have been a poetic exaggeration.[976]

Documentary information which provides specific weights for arrows and their constituent parts including arrowheads has been particularly difficult to interpret. One of the most ambitious such efforts focused on the *Nihayat al-Su'l* Mamluk *furusiya* treatise. The lightest possible arrow weighed 332 g and was considered suitable for the gentlest bow but needed a skilled archer to use it. The next arrow weighed 360 g and was suitable for a bow somewhat stiffer than the gentle (*layyin*) type but not as stiff as a medium stiffness bow. The arrow of 456 g was suitable for the true medium bow, the arrow of 498 g being suitable for a bow somewhat stiffer than the medium but not as stiff as the stiffest. The 600 g arrow was suitable for the stiffest bow and was the heaviest available arrow for use with a hand-held bow.[977] These were all war or target arrows rather than the flight competition arrows in which the iron head was sometimes replaced by a piece of bone, ivory or horn and in which the centre of gravity consequently shifted towards the tail.[978] They were also considerably heavier than the admittedly desiccated and fragmented late medieval arrows recently excavated in the Citadel of Damascus.[979]

A number of texts described the arrowguide, including two from opposite ends of the thirteenth-century Islamic world. Fakhr al-Din Mubarakshah, writing in northern India about what was called the *navak* in Persian, described it as a device for shooting short arrows or darts which, in its simplest version, consisted of a groove of split bamboo kept in place by a cord which was itself held by the drawing hand. Both groove and dart were pulled back together but only the dart was released.[980]

Ibn Maymun, writing in Morocco about that was called a *majra* in Arabic, agreed that it was a hollow guide or trough down which a short arrow or *husban* was shot. Basing his text upon earlier works from the 'Abbasid period he maintained that it had been invented by the Persians for use against the Turks who were unable to pick up the short *husban* and shoot it back because they lacked this device. It was notably accurate and very powerful against armour because of its very long draw or pull. The *majra* could also shoot stone pellets, small iron missiles called *himmas al-amir* or 'the prince's beans'. The *majra* itself was four fingers (7–8 cm) longer than an ordinary arrow and when the string was released the missile was propelled by a cord or small bead which ran along the trough.[981]

The pellet-bow or *qaws al-bunduq* was a hunting weapon and would not normally have been used in warfare. It had been recorded in the Middle East since the tenth century but has sometimes been wrongly translated as a form of crossbow. The blowpipe had similarly been used as a hunting weapon since at least Roman times though the earliest illustration in Islamic art is of an example of finely inlaid metalwork dating from 1223. Its Persian name of *tufak* was eventually adopted for the earliest forms of small but long-barrelled gun, which has led to further confusion, while its Arabic name of *zabtana* entered various European languages and in some similarly came to mean an early form of hand-held gun.[982]

The simple *bunduq* unbaked clay pellets that could be shot from both these sorts of weapon would not be expected to have survived. However, a substantial number have been found in the Citadel of Damascus, mostly believed to date from the late Mamluk and early Ottoman periods. Their sizes are remarkably consistent, falling in groups which range from 19–25 mm diameter, though the great majority are from 22–23 mm, plus a few which are considerably smaller.[983]

The crossbow was used much more widely in the medieval Islamic world than is generally realized. It was adopted at a remarkably early date and appeared in the same forms as would be used in Western Europe. Nevertheless this usage tended to be restricted to specific military circumstances. The earliest supposed reference, a *hadith* or Saying of the Prophet which supposedly concerned the pre-Islamic Sassanian Empire in Iran, actually concerned the *qaws nawakiyah* or bow with an arrow-guide (see above).[984] In the mid- to late ninth century the Armenian Thomas Arsruni stated that the soldiers of the Caliph commonly used the *virgahan* which might have been a crossbow but which could have been an arrow guide.[985] However, only a few years later the chronicler Muhammad Ibn Jarir al-Tabari specifically mentioned the *qaws al-rijl* or 'foot bow' being used by rebels.[986] During the tenth to twelfth centuries the crossbow was largely restricted to siege and naval warfare in the Islamic Middle East, Maghrib and al-Andalus. There then seems to have been an increase in its use in the wake of the Mongol invasions of the thirteenth century,[987] though again primarily in defence of fortified places.

The terminology also becomes slightly clearer. For example, it has been assumed that the terms *jawza* 'nut' and *qufl* 'lock' were both used for the small revolving element holding the bowstring and released by the trigger. However, it also seems possible that the *qufl* could sometimes be a peg thrust upwards by the trigger to push the string from the slot or notch used in some simpler and some larger crossbows. Fortunately, the later medieval Islamic Middle East produced archers or scholars who described fourteenth-century crossbows in great detail. The best was Taybugha al-Baklamishi who, writing in the Mamluk Sultanate, claimed that of the various types of non-standard bow in current use, the 'Franks' or Western Europeans used the *jarkh*, the Maghribis or North Africans and Andalusians the *laqsha*, the Persian and Turks the *zanburak* which was actually a blowpipe, and 'Muslims', by which he meant the Mamluk themselves, the *bunduq* or pellet bow. Taybugha also noted that, for naval operations, the most useful crossbows were made of yew rather than being of composite construction which was vulnerable to wet.[988]

Each of the real crossbows used in the Islamic world had its own history. The Arabic *jarkh*, for example, came from the Persian *charkh* while the Turkish term *ğarkh* came from Persian via eastern dialect of Arabic.[989] The original Persian word meant a circle or ring which almost certainly referred to the winch or windlass with which it was spanned. The *charkh* and its linguistic variants was, therefore, originally a large weapon, sometimes perhaps mounted on a pedestal, and used in static positions rather than being carried by infantry in open battle. Various sources make clear that it could shoot notably large bolts, arrows or other missiles.[990] One of the earliest clear references to such a weapon is found in the *Shahmanah* by Firdawsi, dating from around 1000. In this eastern Iranian epic poem the *kaman charkh* 'ring bow' or 'winch bow' was, however, used by foot soldiers from the Baghdad suburb of Karkh lined up in battle array:[991]

The warriors from Baghdad who were with Zanga,
The son of Shawaran, picked men of Karkh.

He ordered that their arbalists (*kamanhai charkh*) to take,
Their place afoot before the elephants.
And had two miles of mountains fronted them,
They would have pierced the rocks' hearts with their arrows.
No one was able to withstand their shots.[992]

It is just possible that here the name indicated a hand-held crossbow with a
stirrup, the word *charkh* or ring indicating the spanning stirrup at the end of
the stock.[993] Elsewhere in the *Shahnamah* such weapons were operated by Rumi,
Byzantine troops commanded by a bishop in defence of a fortified wall:

He bade magicians bring up mighty stones
Upon the walls, he summoned many experts
From Rum, and stationed troops upon the ramparts
A prelate shrewd of heart set up thereupon
Ballistas [*manjaniq*, mangonels], catapults ['*aradha*] and arbalists [*kamanhai charkh*]
And shields of wolf-hide.[994]

It is interesting to note that both these quotations from the *Shahnamah* concern
troops from west of al-Firdawsi's own homeland, and there are in general fewer
references to the *charkh* or *jarkh* in eastern Iranian sources than there are in the
Middle East. Even the Seljuk Turks' use of these weapons in 1150 was in Iraq,
against fortified Baghdad.[995]

The *qaws al-lawlab* was presumably a variation on the same concept or was
simply the preferred term in eleventh- and twelfth-century Fatimid Egypt. The
Arabic word *lawlab* could be translated in several ways, but during this period
was most likely to mean a straightforward winch. As the *qaws al-lawlab* could
shoot a bolt which either weighed, or had an arrowhead which weighed, 5 *ratl*[996]
(over 1.5 kg) it was clearly not a portable infantry weapon.

Just over a century and a half later al-Tarsusi, writing in Egypt for Saladin,
regarded the *jarkh* and the '*aqqar* forms of crossbow to be too well known to
require explanation. Both were again spanned with a *lawlab*. Sadly the *lawlab* in
question was also too well-known to need further explanation. Al-Tarsusi did
comment that the *jarkh* and '*aqqar* were less powerful than the mechanical *qaws
al-ziyar*. This might imply that they were grouped amongst the heavier forms
of crossbow, sometimes mounted on frames or pedestals, which were used from
fixed positions or ships rather than being carried by a single man like the *qaws
al-rijl*. It also seems that they usually incorporated a simple bow of yew wood
without horn or sinew, though olive wood from North Africa or Yemen could
also be used.[997]

On the other hand al-Tarsusi did consider the *qaws al-rijl* 'foot bow' and
qaws al-rikab 'stirrup bow' worth commenting upon. Both had been used by

the Fatimid army of Egypt during the later eleventh and first half of the twelfth century,[998] being lighter and smaller forms of crossbow which could be spanned, shot and presumably also carried by one man. As such they were the same as the most common forms of crossbow in medieval Europe, though having been adopted at a slightly earlier date. For al-Tarsusi the main or only difference between them was that the *qaws al-rijl* lacked the spanning stirrup, the string being pulled back with a spanning strap and hooks. This might imply that, at this time in Egypt and the Islamic Middle East, the *qaws al-rikab* did not require a strap and hooks, perhaps being a smaller and weaker but considerably faster weapon to span, load and shoot. Al-Tarsusi also noted that the bow was not of composite construction.[999]

The final form of crossbow was called the *'aqqara*, 'terrifier' or 'stunner'. Normally spanned with two feet rather than a stirrup and best made from yew and boxwood, it seems to have been considered particularly suitable for naval warfare.[1000] That may well have been why the *'aqqara* was so often associated with North Africa, the most highly regarded marines and sailors of the later medieval Islamic world coming from this region. Writing in 1373 but drawing upon both current and earlier sources, the Mamluk specialist in siege weaponry, Ibn Aranbugha al-Zardkash, added two technical illustrations to his traditional account of the *qaws 'aqqar*. In both cases the crossbows appear to have the usual revolving release nut and are spanned with a winch or windlass. In one case the spanning device is separate and in the other it has been placed directly on or over the rear of the stock.[1001]

Before leaving crossbows, something can be said about the missiles they shot. Such information obviously sheds useful light on the power and size of the weapons themselves. For example, Taybugha put the weight of the bolt shot by an *'aqqar* at 10.5 *dirhams* (about 32.5 g) whereas that of the ordinary *qaws al-rikab* weighed a little less at 9 *dirhams* (about 28 g).[1002] Two complete but entirely desiccated late medieval crossbow bolts recently excavated in the Citadel of Damascus were between 36 and 37 cm long and had considerably heavier iron heads than were recorded on the numerous broken arrows also found.[1003]

Back in the 1920s two massive crossbow staves were similarly found in the Citadel of Damascus, one being of almost entirely composite construction and 1.9 m long. A number of comparable but slightly smaller crossbow staves from Syria, one with an optimum radio-carbon dating of 1215, are currently in a private collection awaiting further study. The second crossbow stave found in Damascus in the 1920s was 2 m long and had a core of palm wood reinforced with sinew and horn. Two supposed all-iron 'crossbow bolts' were discovered at the same time, having rings to attach incendiary substances and large wooden plugs at their butt-ends. These latter were, however, almost certainly missiles to be fired from the very earliest forms of medieval cannon (see below).[1004]

As in so many other aspects of military technology, the medieval Islamic world used a greater variety of shields than were seen in Western Europe during the same period. This mainly applied to methods of construction, but was also seen in shapes and sizes. The twelfth-century Egyptian military writer and theoretician al-Tarsusi listed a significant number and also stated that iron shields were used by 'some people'. Unfortunately he provided no further details, although archaeologists found the remains of a circular shield consisting of iron segments at Bistam-Kala in north-eastern Iran. Originally this probably had a wooden foundation and has been dated by its context to the twelfth or thirteenth century. At 62 cm diameter, this was a full shield rather than a smaller buckler. Most supposedly 'iron shields', however, were more likely to have had metallic reinforcements rather than being entirely covered with metal. Such shields certainly existed in non-Islamic Central Asia while also appearing in both Islamic and medieval European art. Archaeological evidence has recently been found on the fringes of the medieval Islamic world in the northern Caucasus.[1005]

The other shields listed by al-Tarsusi were more straightforward, consisting of the leather *lamt*, the round *turs* which was normally of wood, the elongated *tariqa* with a pointed base and the *januwiya* which was elongated like the *tariqa* but had a flattened base. The *tariqa* was used by the 'Franks' and Byzantines and was very suitable for cavalry whereas the *januwiya* was normally used by infantry as a protection against archers.[1006] The Islamic foot soldiers' habit of using long shields to form a shield-wall was also noted by their Crusader foes. A southern French *troubadour* described just such a Saracen shield-wall in his late twelfth-century *chanson de geste* entitled *La Siège de Barbastre* when he called the type of shield in question a *talevaz*.[1007]

The *lamt* was amongst the most famous and valuable of medieval Islamic shields, but also became the stuff of legend. It could offer great protection which, amongst Berbers such as the Lamtuna tribe, was capable of protecting a man and a good part of his horse.[1008] It was probably made of several layers of leather glued together.[1009] Modern experiments have also shown that rawhide shields, which the *lamt* is presumed to have been, are much more effective against arrows than even the best of tanned leather, including *cuir bouilli*.[1010]

The most common form of leather shield was the *daraqa* which was smaller and usually round. On the other hand an almost heart-shaped version appeared in Morocco and al-Andalus in the thirteenth century, if not earlier, and may have represented a coming together of the *daraqa* and *lamt* traditions. This very distinctive leather shield was almost invariably associated with light cavalry, especially in Granada. In the later medieval Christian Iberian states it was known as the *adarga* and as such would be taken to the Americas by the Conquistadores. The *gawsipar* or 'leather shield' of Persian-speaking regions is believed to have been the same as the *daraqa* of the Arab countries.[1011]

The most distinctive shields used by Turkish, Mongol and some other peoples from Central Asia was the *qalqan* made of a spiral of cane bound together with cotton thread. This term was already being commonly used for the shield in thirteenth-century Turkish sources,[1012] and had appeared in pictorial sources since at least the twelfth century. A considerable number of later Turkish spiral cane shields survive in museums and private collections, mostly of Ottoman origin and often with their cotton binding forming magnificent coloured decorations. Much more recently fragments of such a shield have also been found in the Citadel of Damascus, and are believed to date from the early part of the Mamluk Sultanate, probably from the second half of the thirteenth century. This sort of shield must always have incorporated a substantial metallic boss to protect the hand-grip and to fill the 'hole' where the cane spiral begins. This in turn lent itself to further metallic elements being added as a method of strengthening the spiral, limiting the danger of blows making it unwind and also as a form of decoration. Several examples of such metallic reinforcement have been found by archaeologists within an Islamic context, usually Turkish.[1013]

The main forms of armour used in the Islamic world from at least the eighth century onwards were the mail hauberk and the lamellar cuirasses, either of metal or of some form of leather, plus soft armour. Élite troops, when serving as heavy cavalry especially in the richer and better equipped armies of the Middle East, wore mail and lamellar together. This certainly applied to the pre-Seljuk, slave-recruited *ghulams* or *mamluks* of the tenth and eleventh centuries.[1014]

Wearing two layers of armour was still clearly common practice in the twelfth century when the Syrian warrior and author, Usama Ibn Munqidh, referred not only to mail *dir'* hauberks being worn with *jawshan* cuirasses, but also two layers of mail being worn.[1015] This was, however, still not proof against a powerful lance thrust.[1016] Nevertheless the hauberks in question are likely to have been heavy. A number of as yet unpublished mail armours from a twelfth- or thirteenth-century context in Syria are said to weigh from 15–20 kg each. A small fragment from one of these consists of iron rings made of round wire with an external diameter of from 1.1–1.3 cm. This is not very similar to European mail of around the same period, but is virtually identical to third century Roman and Sassanian mail from Dura Europos. Perhaps such tentative information can be taken as evidence of a continuing tradition of mail-making in the Middle East from late classical to medieval Islamic times.

Where the mail *dir'* itself was concerned, all the evidence shows that this was essentially the same as the Western European mail hauberk. These were often worn with mail *mighfars* or coifs which seem to have been much more common in the early Islamic and specifically Arab world than they had been in early medieval Western Europe. Armour incorporating mail coifs had been used by late Roman armies and one of the clearest illustrations is in fact from the third century Roman frontier fortress of Dura Europos in eastern Syria. Medieval pictorial sources suggest that the Arab-Islamic *mighfar* tended to cover more of the face that the normal Western European mail coif, as might be expected in a part of the world where archery featured so prominently. This was also confirmed in poetry, including that from eleventh-century al-Andalus,[1017] as well as Arabic literary sources from twelfth-century North Africa.[1018]

The *kazaghand* and variations on this word were another distinctive and sophisticated form of mail body armour. In Egypt al-Tarsusi described what he called the *kazghanda* as being made of mail covered by padded silk cloth or brocade,[1019] while in Syria a few decades later Usama Ibn Munqidh described one especially strong *kazaghand* as including two layers of mail, one a long 'Frankish' *dir'* or hauberk captured from the Crusaders, and the second a *dir'* which was not Crusader and which reached only to the middle of the body. The resulting armour was then padded with felt, rabbit hair and silk waste. In all cases the armour almost certainly had fabric across both its inner and outer surfaces.[1020] The *kazaghand* eventually reached Western Europe as the *jazerant* and other variations on this term, but one of the earliest references in Western literature was in the late twelfth-century poem, the *Siège de Barbastre*, where several Saracens were said to wear an *auberc jazerant*.[1021]

These armours, especially the lamellar *jawshans*, could be very heavy. According to the Persian chronicler Maulana Minhaj al-Din, the Salgharid or early thirteenth-century *atabeg* ruler of Fars in south-western Iran, Sa'd Ibn Zangi, wore an armour that nobody else could lift.[1022] Though an exaggeration, this must surely have been a metallic rather than hardened leather or rawhide lamellar *jawshan*, probably of the large type that included arm pieces and tassets to cover the hips, buttocks and thighs. The later Turkish *Book of Dede Korkut* also makes several references to the weight of armour upon the wearer's shoulders, and the fact this armour jangled, again showing it to have been metallic and probably lameller.[1023]

Al-Tarsusi, in his twelfth century text written for Saladin, stated that the lamellar *jawshan* could be made of iron or horn or leather and was normally laced with gut,[1024] while in the late tenth century the iron *jawshans* worn by Turkish *ghulams* seem to have been regarded as novelties by their Fatimid rivals.[1025] A few decades earlier the arsenal of armour allocated to the *ghulams* defending Tarsus included what were called Tibetan *jawshans*. Unfortunately there is no means of telling what material they were made of,[1026] but in later centuries Tibet and neighbouring regions of eastern China were famous for very extensive, long-hemmed and heavy iron lamellar cuirasses, often laced with silk.[1027]

Scale armour is much more of a problem in the medieval Islamic world, just as it is in most of its medieval neighbours. Most supposed evidence for such a form of construction comes from highly stylized and probably misleading representational art and from written sources that could often be interpreted as mail just as easily as they could be interpreted as scale.[1028] The limited archaeological evidence does, however, suggest that scale rather than mail armour might have been characteristic of some parts of pre-Islamic India, with lamellar being used in those regions under Central Asian influence.[1029] The first undoubtedly scale form of armour used in the medieval Islamic world was the *qarqal*. This was a scale-lined and fabric-covered cuirass which was widely adopted in the Mamluk Sultanate. Its name was of Persian origin and first appeared in Arabic in the fourteenth century,[1030] while the armour itself may either have been of Mongol inspiration or based upon longer-established Chinese forms introduced into the eastern regions of the Islamic world by the Mongols.[1031] The sudden appearance of scale-lined armours in Russia and Europe around the same period similarly strengthens the idea of a Mongol or Chinese origin.

Additional limb defences had been more of a feature of Islamic armour during the first centuries of Islamic history than they were during the following period.[1032] This was clearly not caused by a poverty of resources. Where rigid arm defences rather than the sleeves of a mail hauberk are concerned, their decline might have resulted from the adoption of stirrups which made it easier and more practical for a horseman to carry and use a shield. On the other hand the Arab and Persian *sa'ad* or vambrace continued to be occasionally mentioned from the seventh century onwards, eventually being replaced in Persian regions by the *bazuband* and in Turkish by the *qolcaq* or *qulluq* during the late thirteenth and fourteenth centuries.

Any abandonment of additional leg armours is less clear, though such additional pieces of armour always remained rare and probably restricted to a minority of the heavy cavalry élite. Mail leg protections appeared in Islamic and Byzantine sources in the eleventh century. In Arabic-speaking regions such a defence was known as *ranat hadid* 'iron leggings' and *kalsat zarad* or sometimes as *saq al-muza*, literally meaning 'banana leggings' or 'banana skins' for descriptive reasons.[1033] In later medieval Turkish regions, additional pieces of armour for the arms and legs called *budluq* were largely within the same tradition as Iran rather than the Arab countries. The *Book of Dede Korkut* makes the interesting point that these were laced on after the warrior had donned his main body armour.[1034]

Soft armour was clearly very widespread in the early medieval Islamic period, probably more so than anywhere else except India where, in fact, much of the textile technology probably originated. It remained popular until at least the fourteenth century, and even longer in Islamic sub-Saharan Africa and India. Such armours should not be regarded as an inferior alternative to metallic or even leather armour. In reality they were a light, effective and easily made protection suitable for the sort of light cavalry warfare which dominated so much of the medieval Islamic world. Soft armour could also be combined with other forms of protection. In particular it was worn beneath, sometimes over, and combined with mail protection. Soft armours were also, of course, suitable in the notably hot climates of some Islamic countries.

These armours included the *jubba*, an Arabic term from the Turkish *cebe*, and eventually being adopted in Western Europe as the *jupon*. Like the *kazaghand*, the *jubba* could incorporate mail, though apparently did not necessarily do so. The *garwa* or *karwa* (also mentioned above under field fortifications) has sometimes been interpreted as a form of eastern Iranian and Afghan soft armour.[1035] However, even the description by al-Juzjani is not entirely clear: 'They make a piece of armour entirely of cattle-skin [*gaw*] with on each side a good thickness of cotton and decorated cloth in the manner of a stuffed bag. This is called *garwa*. This is worn by the infantry of Ghur upon their shoulders and they are covered head to foot.'[1036] The effectiveness of such Islamic soft armour was confirmed by the Crusader, De Joinville, who took a *gamboison d'estoupes* from a dead Saracen and used it against arrows during the campaign around Mansurah in Egypt in 1250. This he did because previous wounds meant that he would not wear his own normal armour.[1037]

The history of Islamic helmets differed from that of medieval Western Europe, generally reflecting a preference for good visibility and mobility at the cost of less protection. The basic traditional form in the Arab Middle East and perhaps further afield was the iron *baida* or 'egg'. Advances in metallurgy within the Islamic world meant that these were soon being forged in substantial quantities from a single piece of iron, probably before such one-piece helmets reappeared in Western Europe or even in the Byzantine Empire. At the same time the Central Asian tradition of segmented helmets in which the elements were either riveted directly to one another or to an iron frame, spread throughout the Islamic world. Helmets were, of course, an obvious object upon which to demonstrate wealth or status, and as a result most of the techniques of inlay and surface decoration found in other forms of Islamic metalwork were also found on helmets. Furthermore, the use of gilding apparently became so widespread that it was almost used as an anti-corrosion technique.

A large number of terms were used for what are assumed to have been different shaped designs of helmet. The term *khud* and its many variants probably meant a helmet of segmented construction, as distinct from the presumed one-piece *baida*, or it could be that the *khud* was pointed whereas the *baida* was rounded. Unfortunately it has only occasionally been possible to attach one name to one form, and it may have been that in many cases such terms were unspecific. In other cases distinctive forms do not seem to have had particular names. An example of the latter might be the so-called 'turban helmet'; this name being a modern European term to identify a particular form. The earliest surviving such 'turban helmet' is inscribed with the name of the mid-fourteenth-century Ottoman Turkish ruler Orhan. It originally seems to have had a nasal, eye cusps and rim hooks to support a mail aventail.[1038]

Meanwhile lighter helmets made of organic materials were used in several, perhaps most, regions of the medieval Islamic world. These were usually referred to as versions of *khud*. Recently discovered examples from Syria include pointed and rounded and almost flat-topped helmets, with or without brims.[1039] An early reference to this remarkable sort of protection was the *khudh* helmets made of palm leaves or perhaps more correctly palm stems, used by the 'poor of Baghdad' during early 'Abbasid civil wars. In poetic versions of this event the headgear was called a *mighfar* and in another was said to have been made of *qaratis* or 'leaves of paper'.[1040] The latter cannot be entirely dismissed as fanciful, bearing in mind the highly effective lacquered papier mâché helmets used many centuries later in Japan.

Writing in the second half of the twelfth century, al-Tarsusi provided a detailed description of how to make a *khudh* helmet from *kimukht* rawhide.[1041] De Joinville's comment that the large turbans worn by Muslim warriors in mid-thirteenth-century Egypt were proof against sword-cuts should,[1042] however, be treated with caution as there is strong evidence that small or closer-fitting iron helmets were often worn beneath such turbans.

While the *mighfar* was strictly speaking a mail coif that covered the entire head, other elements were often added to various forms of basic helmet. Quite realistic face-mask visors appeared in late Seljuk art from the thirteenth century and are much more clearly shown in eastern Islamic art of the fourteenth century onwards.[1043] Physical examples of such moveable or removeable anthropo-morphic visors have not yet been found in a Middle Eastern Islamic context from this period, though they were used in Iran rather later. The only known examples come from Central Asian Turkish and Turco-Mongol locations, some but not all of which were Islamic, plus Byzantine examples (see vol. 1). Their dating is similarly controversial with some scholars insisting that none date from before the Mongol invasions.[1044]

Written references to face-covering protections can be difficult to interpret, though most of those dating from before the later fourteenth century probably concern mail aventails rather than rigid visors; moveable or otherwise. One such is in the *Danishmandname* by 'Arif 'Ali of Toqat. Here a mail aventail hanging over the face and attached to a Turkish helmet was called a *niqab* (modern *nikab*) or veil, and had to be raised to identify the person wearing the helmet.[1045] Another variation on the theme of face-protections seems to have originated in the Iberian Peninsula. Here a very distinctive form of otherwise straightforward conical helmet had a fixed partial or full visor with large eye-holes. It appeared in the art of the Christian states of northern Spain but was usually, though not invariably, associated with 'evil' figures or infidels. This, and the fact that such helmets appeared in the Iberian peninsula much earlier than they did north of the Pyrenees, might suggests that this sort of helmet originated in Islamic al-Andalus to the south. This could again reflect the greater importance of archery within the region.

It is widely assumed that horse-armour was rare or even unknown in the early medieval Islamic period because it does not apparently appear in Islamic art before the later thirteenth century. On the other hand, documentary sources make it abundantly clear that various forms of horse-armour were widespread, and that its use continued uninterruptedly in Iran following the Arab-Islamic conquest.[1046] The most popular type seems to have been of quilted or padded construction, this being reflected in the most common Arabic term for horse-armour which was *tijfaf*. This was used by Fatimid heavy cavalry from the late tenth century onwards, while the riders wore mail *dir'* hauberks.[1047] Nasir-i Khusrau, visiting Fatimid Egypt in 1047, described the Caliphal Canal Cutting ceremony during which: 'each horse is covered with *zirh* [mail] or *jawshan* [lamellar]. A helmet is placed on the pommel of the saddle'.[1048] *Tijfaf* quilted horse-armour was also used in al-Andalus in the late tenth century,[1049] and there is no reason to suppose that it did not remain in fashion for a long time after that, perhaps never falling from favour and becoming the immediate source of inspiration for the sudden appearance of comparable horse-armours in later twelfth-century Western Europe.

Prior to the thirteenth century, references to horse-armour of scale, lamellar or mail were rare, though they can be found. In early thirteenth-century Islamic northern India, the Iranian terms *bargustuwan*, *gustawan*, *baghltaq* and *pardum* used for such horse-armour show that it had been introduced from that direction.[1050] Another Indian tradition of horse-armour survived further south and may have been related to early Arab-Islamic styles.[1051] Persian terminology was also adopted in the Mamluk Sultanate in the later thirteenth and fourteenth centuries, probably indicating that the old-fashioned quilted or felt form was being abandoned in favour of hardened leather horse-armours, though *tijfaf* was mentioned in the *Nihayat al-Su'l* along with the more modern *bardhunb*. The latter almost certainly coming from the Persia *par dum*.[1052]

In most parts of the world and during most periods, horse-armour was primarily a defence against arrows, but even in these circumstances it was probably more effective against long-distance harassment than close-range shooting. This was clearly true in the Islamic world where light horse-armour of quilted, leather, lamellar, mail or, at a later date, mail-and-plate construction was relatively widespread whereas plated iron horse-armour of the later medieval Western European form was effectively unknown. Generally speaking, the construction of horse-armour reflected that used for the rider's own armour, though there tended to be a time-lag with horse-armour continuing to use old-fashioned or outdated techniques. Thus a cavalryman of the fourteenth century Mamluk Sultanate could wear the latest style of scale-lined *qarqal* cuirass while his horse's armour was still made of hardened leather.

The armour for the horse's head, usually known in later Europe as a *chamfron*, was also used in the medieval Islamic world. It was variously known as a *burqu'*, a *sari* and probably as a *tishtaniya* in al-Andalus. Most would almost certainly have been of hardened leather until plated forms became popular, along with lamellar armour for the body of the horse, during the fourteenth century. Nevertheless, there is some evidence that rigid metal *chamfrons* were known in Egypt and neighbouring Islamic territories some centuries earlier, and that these were almost certainly descended from late Roman forms of horse-armour. For example, part of a sheet metal *chamfron* was found during excavations at the southern Nubian capital of Soba. The surface was covered with a pattern of small holes while there were holes around the edges suggesting that the metal had originally been sewn to a layer of strong cloth or leather.[1053] Horses with what could be *chamfrons* appear in several Nubian wall-paintings from the cathedral at Faras and in at least one fragmentary Egyptian painted manuscript which is probably from the early Fatimid period. In late tenth-century al-Andalus a piece of horse-armour called a *tashtina* could be gilded.[1054] The term is Arabized Latin and is highly likely to have been a *chamfron*; a comparable item of horse-armour known as a *testinia* also being mentioned in mid-eleventh century Aragon.[1055]

DISTRIBUTION

One aspect of medieval Islamic military organization which not only seems to have been more highly developed than that of Western Europe, but which also reflected different social, political and military attitudes was the state arsenal. It was often called a *zardkhana* and had been a feature of Islamic states since very early days. Such arsenals largely existed because the provision and safe storage of military equipment was regarded as a state responsibility. This was almost as true in periods of acute political fragmentation as it had been under the days of the previous virtually united Caliphates and would be under the large territorial states or empires which emerged in later centuries.

Even in the mid-tenth century, when the power of the 'Abbasid Caliphs was in steep decline in Syria and Cilicia, the Caliph in Baghdad not only sent élite *ghulam* troops to the threatened frontier city of Tarsus but undertook to supply them with armour for men and horses.[1056] The new Caliphal power of the Fatimids, which arose in North Africa before conquering and moving to Egypt, continued to put great effort into maintaining military arsenals. These manufactured as well as storing and distributing military equipment to Fatimid armies. Apparently weapons were issued free of charge, but if a man lost anything without good reason, its cost would be deducted from his pay.[1057] In the face of the Crusader threat, three main arsenals existed in Fatimid Egypt, there being around 3,000 craftsmen employed in that known as the 'Treasury of Banners' in Cairo.[1058]

Other Fatimid military arsenals were probably maintained elsewhere, certainly in Alexandria. This was ransacked during a revolt in 1066 and, according to the chronicler al-Qalqashandi, had contained the full array of war material: *sayf* swords, *rumh* lances, *tabr* axes, *sikkin* daggers, *qaws* bows, *nushab* arrows, *kinana* quivers, *dabbus* and *'asa* maces or batons, *baydah* helmets, *mighfar* mail coifs, *dir'* mail hauberks and *turs* shields. In addition there were supplies for use in siege warfare: *manjaniq* stone-throwing mangonels, *siham al-khita'ih* 'chinese' or chemical fire arrows, *makahil al-barud* jars of saltpetre for use in or as incendiary weapons, *qawarir al-naft* Greek Fire grenades, and *sata'ir* screens, palisades or mantlets.[1059]

Al-Qalqashandi appears to have been quoting from some official inventory, because he also listed hunting weapons which, in addition to the usual sorts, also included the *qaws al-bunduq* pellet bow and the *zabatanah* blowpipe.[1060] He made an interesting distinction between the Arab bow 'which is made of wood and one half swells [rises] to the other half', perhaps indicating that it had a regularly curved shape rather than the recurved shape normal in composite bows, and the Persian bow 'made in parts of wood and horn and sinew and glue'.[1061] The objects which al-Qalqashandi described as 'Royal' and perhaps for use on parade or by Caliphal bodyguards, included a form of *dabbus* mace whose rounded head was covered with red and black silk damask, other seemingly normal and undecorated weapons, the *daraqa latifa* or small *daraqah* shield, a *samsam* style of sword, flags, musical instruments and a remarkable decorated parasol or sunshade for the ruler himself (see below).[1062]

Another arsenal for supposedly ordinary weapons contained a form of *zaradiyyah* mail hauberk 'disguised' in 'accurate' (perhaps accurately tailored) silk and finished in silver, a gilded *jawshan* lamellar cuirass, *khudh* helmets finished in gold and silver, normal *sayf* swords, *qaljuriyah* swords which were almost certainly single-edged or even slightly curved sabres, *rumah* spears of the *qanah* and *quntariya* types which were painted and gilded, and *asinna* blades which may perhaps not yet have been attached to their hilts or shafts. Amongst the *qaws* bows which had been 'tested and from the best workmanship', were *qaws al-rijal wa'l-rikab* crossbows of the foot and stirrup type. The *qaws al-lawlab* crossbows spanned with screws or more likely a winch were those which shot bolts reportedly weighing 5 Egyptian *ratl* (approximately 1,650 g on the assumption that the eleventh-century Egyptian *ratl* is correctly interpreted as 330 g). Finally, al-Qalqashandi mentioned *nabl* arrows for Arab bows using the *majra* or arrow-guide; these arrows presumably being of a distinctive design or especially short length.[1063]

Information concerning the *suqs* or markets where independent craftsmen made and sold military equipment is much less detailed. Nevertheless we know that the weapons market or *suq al-silah* of Aleppo was just west of the great mosque in the twelfth century,[1064] and that the Third Crusade's siege and Saladin's countersiege of Acre used up so many munitions that Saladin could not get enough replacements even from the distant provinces of his realm. Similarly after the battle of Arsuf that same year, armourers were reportedly working overtime.[1065]

Sultan Baybars' order that his troops maintain their gear in good condition similarly resulted in all being: 'completely absorbed in preparing the *barkustuwan* [horse-armour] of horses, making *jawshan* [cuirasses], polishing *zirih* [mail hauberks], inlaying helmets and making *juwh al-khayl* [frontals for the horses, or perhaps *chamfrons*]'. It also resulted in the arms bazaar being very crowded with men and horses, the price of iron going up considerably, along with the wages of blacksmiths, armourers and polishers.[1066] Essentially the same systems were used in North Africa and al-Andalus, the Muwahhid rulers being specifically responsible for equipping their own élite *huffaz* soldiers.[1067] This tradition of governments being primarily responsible for the arming and equipping of soldiers was paralleled by the lack of weapons among the ordinary public. Or at least civilians did not normally wear arms, much to the surprise of many Western European visitors. Travellers and merchants often went armed while on their journeys, but it seems to have been common for such people to be obliged to leave their weapons with guards at a city gate when they arrived, then collecting them as they left.[1068]

Whereas a great deal is known about the arsenals and distribution systems in the medieval Islamic world, considerably less is known about the costs involved, especially when compared with the sometimes remarkably detailed facts which survive in some European archives. On the other hand, this dearth of information may reflect a lack of research into this highly specialized aspect of medieval Islamic economic history. Most of what is available comes from anecdotal and admittedly unreliable sources, as when a market became flooded with captured equipment after a notable victory. One such was the aftermath of the battle of Manzikert in 1071 when the cost of armaments slumped. However, the relative value of certain items may have remained constant; in this case a helmet cost half a *dinar* while a cuirass cost one-third of a *dinar*.[1069] As the Mongol hordes swept into Syria in 1299, the cost of military equipment in Cairo shot up, 'the body of a *jawshan*' lamellar cuirass rising from the normal 10 *dirhams* to 5 *dinars* which was the equivalent of 100 *dirhams*.[1070] This source also specified that the original 10 *dirhams* price was the same as that of two sheep in autumn; that is when sheep were cheap. In other words a *jawshan* without its arm-pieces and tassets for the thighs was not usually expensive. Perhaps the style of lamellar cuirass in question was actually made of hardened leather, fragments of just such armour from around this period having recently been excavated in the Citadel of Damascus.

MANUFACTURE, TRADE AND STRATEGIC MATERIALS

One of the most striking features of the economic history of the medieval Islamic world was the remarkably limited number of sources of iron ore within the core provinces. The main such sources were all on or beyond the frontiers of the Islamic world during the period under consideration. Small wonder, therefore, that the Muslims put great effort into utilizing those sources that they did control, including the iron mines of North Africa which the Romans had tended to neglect because they had access to easier sources elsewhere.[1071] The same was true within the Iberian Peninsula, though it appears that the richest mines were still in the Christian north rather than the Islamic south of the peninsula.[1072]

Another way of dealing with the problem of a shortage of suitable iron resources was to further develop existing trade networks and to open up new ones. This led to the creation of what was almost certainly the biggest, most complex and most efficient system of long-distance trade in raw materials seen before modern times. At the time, most attention by travellers and chroniclers focused on high-value and exotic goods, but it may have been the bulk transport of metals, timber, food and other such everyday things which really underpinned the economic success of the early medieval Islamic world.

A third feature was the prominent role played by governments and state-enterprises in those aspects of the economy with military relevance. This was, however, more apparent in some states than others, most notably in those with the strongest central authorities and the most urgent shortages of military supplies. Egypt fell within this bracket, and under Fatimid rule the Caliphal government seems to have dominated arms manufacture. Weapons factories employing 3,000 workers were said to have been established by al-Zahir during the first half of the eleventh century. They were housed in a special new building next to the Eastern Palace and within the fortified Caliphal city of al-Qahira (Cairo). This facility was so important that, after being destroyed by fire in 1068/9, it was promptly rebuilt elsewhere.[1073]

The question of steel in the medieval Islamic world has been discussed for many years. It is now clear that the term *fuladh* should be translated as a form of steel and that it was widely exported in the form of small ingots often called 'eggs' or 'cakes'. A number of these have recently been found during the archaeological excavation of a late Mamluk Sultanate arms workshop in the Citadel of Damascus. Their weights range from 0.74 kg to 1.21 kg.[1074] Other research shows evidence of steel production at Merv in what is now Turkmenistan in the ninth and tenth centuries.[1075] It has also been suggested that steel was produced on the coast of East Africa while the sources make it clear that India was another major source.

Forging steel ingots into high-quality blades may have been done at some of these primary production centres, but most seems to have been focused on the major medieval Islamic cities. Here craftsmen are believed to have worked with imported ingots. Unfortunately the resulting blades were sometimes known by their place of manufacture and sometimes by the origin of their steel. The proper Islamic 'damascene' blade of the medieval period was not made in the same way as the pattern-welded blades of Europe. It was, in fact, a truly remarkable piece of medieval technology and craftsmanship, with greater flexibility than European swords. It was also almost unbreakable, though it could eventually be bent. The actual surface pattern resulted from the application of an acidic substance which highlighted the metallurgical structure and thus the quality of the blade: the more the forging the finer the pattern and the better the quality. However, these blades could easily became fragile if overheated or reheated, so very accurate temperature control was critical during their manufacture.[1076]

The similarity in metalworking techniques across the vast Islamic world was quite remarkable and indicated rapid transfers of technologies as well as a highly developed trade in both raw, partially worked and completed materials. Sometimes these similarities in craftsmanship crossed the boundaries between materials. For example, a very similar method of making sword-hilts could be seen in al-Andalus, where most hilts were of iron, and in both Palestine and Iran where they were often of bronze. Yet in both cases they were almost entirely different in structure from the sword-hilts of Western and Northern Europe.

The abundance of bronze elements in so many pieces of military equipment should probably be regarded as further evidence of the medieval Islamic world's shortage of iron, certainly when compared with Europe during the same period. The use of stone arrow and spear heads for hunting in Arabia has already been mentioned, and there were also supposed examples of bronze blades in southern Jordan,[1077] as well as Lotosan in northern Iran.[1078]

What cannot be disputed is the very widespread used of open-mould casting to make the metallic elements of horse harness, detailed evidence of this having been found in tenth-century Iran.[1079] This technique produced objects in which the 'back' consisted of a flat surface. Perhaps this lent itself to the system of making sword-quillons, daggers, scabbard suspension points and various other small military items of two pieces sandwiched together, flat surface to flat surface, which can be seen in so many objects from the medieval Islamic world.

The most dramatic example is a slender and slightly curved sabre excavated in a ninth- to eleventh-century archaeological context at Nishapur in north-eastern

Iran. Its quillons and scabbard fitting are made in precisely this manner while the decorative motifs in these bronze elements are closer to those of Altaic Turkish culture than to those of pre-Islamic Sassanian Iran. The same was also, of course, true of the weapon's curved blade. In fact the styles, if not the weapon itself, were almost certainly brought to the eastern Islamic world by Turkish recruits, whether as *ghulams* of slave origin or as free volunteers.[1080]

Some bronze matrices, used to make one-use-only moulds to cast quillons and scabbard-mounts, are also understood to come from western Iran or Iraq. They were designed for an entirely different form of sword; a straight, broad and almost certainly Arab-style *sayf* which had many features in common with the much earlier Roman *gladius*. Once thought to date from the ninth or tenth century, they are now said to be thirteenth or fourteenth century, while the clearest illustrations of the sort of sword and scabbard in question actually date from the tenth to early twelfth century.[1081] Whatever their true date, they are further evidence for the continuing importance of bronze in the manufacture of military equipment.

Large quantities of horn were similarly required for the manufacture of composite bows. Here the mid-tenth-century Andalusian agricultural handbook known as the *Calendar of Cordoba* offers another fascinating bit of information, stating that June was the month when officials went to collect the horn of deers and wild male goats to make bows.[1082] Wood was another raw material that had vital strategic importance and here many provinces of the Islamic world again found themselves at a disadvantage. Timber was, of course, needed for ship building and to make the charcoal which was the most important fuel in metalworking. In addition to being used in the manufacture of wood-framed saddles,[1083] wood was, surprisingly perhaps, used to make various forms of protection for the human body, namely armour and helmets. According to Maulana Minhaj al-Din writing about the Khalj rulers of Lakhanawati in northern India, an Islamic army attacked a Tibetan fort but were defeated in 1244. The enemy Tibetans, the chronicler wrote: 'had defences made of bamboo [the word used was for young shoots of male bamboo] made into cuirasses, body armour, shields and helmets, all slips of it crudely fastened and stitched overlapping each other'.[1084]

Writing a few years earlier, Fakhr al-Din Mubarakshah had mentioned wooden helmets being used in northern India,[1085] while supposedly wooden helmets were said to have been imported into al-Andalus all the way from India.[1086] Until recently, such references seemed inexplicable, but once again the remarkable recent finds in the Citadel of Damascus might provide an answer. Here several complete helmets were made entirely of organic material except for some suspension rings for straps or aventails. Most were lined with blocks of wood and seem more like very substantial sola topees than businesslike helmets. These are low-domed with small brims, but one extraordinary example is conical in shape and is lined with slender, vertical segments of wood. It should also be mentioned that a number of more substantial 'organic' helmets were made of several layers of hardened leather, without any visible wooden elements.

Because the biggest sources of iron lay on or beyond the frontiers of the medieval Islamic world, craftsmen in the north-eastern regions relied to a considerable degree on iron from the Farghana valley in what is now eastern Uzbekistan. Ore from here appears to have been best in terms in quality and it is likely that the Transoxanian iron-working centres at Asbijab and Khwarazm used iron from Farghana.[1087] A third region of Transoxania, Shash, lay higher in the wooded hills and was known as a major centre for the manufacture of bows, arrows[1088] and perhaps saddles.

During the early Islamic centuries the next most important iron-working centres after Farghana were Khurasan in north-eastern Iran, Kirman in the south-east and Fars in the south-west. Iron-working in the southern island of Hormuz and in north-western Iran was rarely mentioned before 1300. Other Iranian centres which rose to importance were Bafq and Sugh in the centre of the country and the Alburz and Zanjan area in the north. Meanwhile Harat in Afghanistan produced steel 'cakes' to be made into sword blades elsewhere, including Sind and Multan in what is now Pakistan.[1089] Ghur in central Afghanistan was also a major arms manufacturing centre, famed for its *jawshan* lamellar cuirasses and *zirih* mail hauberks as early as the tenth century.[1090] In western Iran, the main sources of iron were again in frontier regions such as Azarbayjan,[1091] while the Kubachi region of Caucasus remained famous for its arms production from at least the sixth to fourteenth centuries.[1092]

The Fertile Crescent consisting of greater Syria, parts of south-eastern Turkey and what is now Iraq was the very heartland of medieval Islamic civilization, yet it was also one of the poorest in metallurgical resources, especially iron. Only Egypt might have been worse off. Nevertheless, the mid-tenth-century chronicler and geographer Hasan Ibn Ahmad al-Hamdani wrote that the armourers of Babil, by which he meant what is now southern Iraq, made *dir'* mail hauberks that were heavier than those of the Rum or Byzantines. This, he said, was also true of the *dir'* made in Bahrayn, now the Gulf coast of Saudi Arabia as well as Bahrayn Island itself, and of Oman and Yemen.[1093] A generation later the Arab geographical writer Kamal al-Din Ibn al-'Adim of Aleppo noted that Mississa (Misis) in Cilicia had been a vital centre of military production close to the Byzantine frontier, famous for making wood-framed saddles, bridles, spurs, sword-scabbards, maces and *mah'zuz* 'perforated iron' used in siege warfare. The latter was probably a reference to the elements used in iron lamellar armour.[1094]

The local sources of iron in Syria had been exploited for centuries if not millennia, and by the medieval period they were beginning to run out.[1095] Yet the city of Damascus retained its reputation for very high quality iron and steel manufacture through the twelfth and thirteenth centuries.[1096] The Lebanon and Anti-Lebanon ranges still produced iron ore,[1097] as did the Ajlun hills of northern Jordan, which is why both these areas became centres of conflict during the Crusades. Such relatively small-scale sources fed the forges of Damascus, as did the iron mines of the northern Syrian coastal mountains and Anatolia.[1098]

Damascus was, of course, best known for its damascene sword-blades but there was also a specialist 'market of the spearmakers' in the city in the late thirteenth century.[1099] Half a century earlier, under Ayyubid rule, Damascus had become the largest centre for the manufacture of bows. In fact production was so intense that it became almost a production-line technique with bows now being made in three standardized strengths, each with its own associated training schedule.[1100] Other military markets in Damascus included those for saddlemakers and for armourers, both of which were said to be 'under the Citadel', meaning that they were effectively in the shadow of its towering walls. The vitally important horse-market in Damascus is likely to have been a little further away, while there were comparable horse-markets in Hama and Aleppo.[1101]

The iron mines of the Jabal Ajlun in Jordan have been located between Dayr Allah and Ajlun town, dominated by Saladin's castle of Qal'at al-Rabadh. During the Ayyubid and Mamluk periods their exploitation was probably a government enterprise. This was significant enough for Saladin to transfer his governor Izz al-Din from the mountain above Beirut to Ajlun in 1184/5. Both these regions were centres of iron mining and it has been suggested that the actual iron-producing area near Ba'abda, in the Lebanese mountains overlooking Beirut, was probably held by the Muslims before they took Beirut itself in 1187. There might even have been a transfer of skilled workers to the Ajlun area. If these men included captives this could have resulted in a 'Frankish' presence which in turn accounted for local place names such as Kufrinjah and Wadi Kufrinjah, from 'village of the Franks' and 'valley of the village of the Franks'.[1102]

Swords had been made in the Balqa' region of central Jordan since at least the ninth century, but they were usually described as being of poor quality. The iron resources of Egypt similarly had a poor reputation, along with the resulting blades. Almost more important were the oases west of the Nile valley (now often called 'The New Valley') which were a major source of the alum. This chemical was used in the tanning of the leather which was itself a vital military material for horse-harness and many other objects. The oases themselves formed an 'iqta fief under the Ayyubids and were expected to produce a 1,000 *quintals*, roughly 100,000 kg, of alum per year.[1103]

Information about centres of military manufacture in the western regions of the Islamic world tends to be rather patchy. For example, in Islamic Sicily the inhabitants of the 'new quarter' established around the cathedral mosque in Palermo included armourers as well as soldiers.[1104] In Sabta (Ceuta) on the northern tip of Morocco, there were reportedly 40 bowyers' workshops from the later twelfth century onwards. In the later years these probably made crossbows rather than bows, and may always have done so.[1105] In complete contrast the famous *lamt* form of large leather shield had originally been made by the Berber tribes of the Sahara and neighbouring semi-desert regions. Later in the Middle Ages *lamt* shields were more likely being manufactured in quite large quantities in Moroccan cities such as Fez.[1106]

Across the Straits of Gibraltar in al-Andalus, armaments were made in many if not most of the major cities. Some earned a perhaps mythical or at least not entirely justified reputation for specific forms of production: Cordoba for leather, hence the English and European term *cordwain*; Toledo for sword-blades; and Saragossa for helmets. Ibn Sa'id al-Maghribi was more specific and probably reliable in stating that, during the thirteenth century, Murcia was famous for mail hauberks and *jawshan* cuirasses.

Another feature of arms manufacture in the medieval Islamic world, as it was of so many other forms of industrial production, was the high degree of craft specialization. By the tenth century, for example, metalworkers seem to have been divided into distinctive groups making specific military items.[1107] This may not have applied to those using organic materials, however. One individual or workshop was probably responsible for the entire process of making a Turkish-style composite bow. This could take one or even two years as the stages had to be spread out and were dependent upon climate, season or weather, partly because long periods of drying were involved.[1108] On the other hand the wages paid to such craftsmen could vary according to circumstances. 'Abd al-Zahir in his biography of the Mamluk Sultan Baybars I noted that during a period of emergency the 'wages of blacksmiths, armourers and polishers' went up considerably.[1109]

Finished or partially finished military equipment was traded over long distances, as were raw materials. The trade which most caught the attention of chroniclers and geographers was that of the best quality and most prestigious sword-blades. However, other items were also involved. For example, tenth-century Andalus imported 'Indian caps and helmets of wood' along with Indian spears and swords.[1110]

Al-Andalus can actually be taken as a good example of such trade because its medieval economy has been studied in detail. The country itself was on the furthest western fringe of the medieval Islamic world while also being wealthy enough to play a significant role in long-distance trade. Military imports from distant parts included armour from North Africa, bows from Yemen, almost certainly of the traditional Arab form used by infantry, saddles and tents from Iraq, armour from Khurasan, bows from the Turkish lands beyond Iran, probably of the shorter composite form, spears, javelins and helmets from north of the

Pyrenees.[1111] In return al-Andalus exported horse-harness and all forms of weapons and armour, some of the latter gilded, to North Africa, as well as swords to India and China.[1112] By the twelfth century Sabta (Ceuta) may have become the largest single destination for Genoese goods, perhaps including arms but these must surely have been for further export from Sabta to other western Islamic destinations.

In addition to a straightforward trade in military goods, such items were also used as diplomatic gifts or bribes, as when Count Joscelin II of Edessa bought peace when his castle at Tal Bashir was besieged by the Seljuks in 1149. The tribute he sent included a gift of 12 'complete armours for horsemen'.[1113] Over a century later the Mamluk Sultan Baybars I sent a shipload of handsome gifts to Khan Berek of the Mongol Golden Horde in order to cement one of the most important strategic alliances of the medieval period. This was significant enough to be described in detail by 'Abd al-Zahir in his biography of the Sultan. Unfortunately it has also been mistranslated in published versions, and actually included several examples of the *qaws halaq* or 'ring bow' which might be a stirrup crossbow (see *kaman charkh* above) or a form of pellet bow, plus some *qaws bunduq* which certainly were pellet bows.[1114]

There is also abundant and unsurprising evidence for the re-use of captured military equipment. This was most useful when taken from rival Islamic armies rather than from Christian foes, but it does seem that the first Turkish raiders into eleventh-century Byzantine Anatolia, before the battle of Manzikert, seized huge quantities of arms and armour which they then carried home, presumably for resale.[1115]

FORTIFICATION

The different regions of the medieval Islamic world faced varied forms of threat. This, and the differing traditions of each region, resulted in distinctive fortifications. In the eastern regions, plus Iran and Iraq, warfare was almost entirely internal, between competing dynasties, until the Mongol invasions of the thirteenth century. There were also relatively few urban fortifications and citadels. That indefatigable Shi'a pilgrim and traveller Nasir-i Khusrau described one such citadel that he saw in the mid-eleventh century. This was Samiran, in the mountains inland from the vital Gulf port of Sirraf. He wrote that it had a castle with a triple enceinte or circuit-wall, an underground passage which brought water from a nearby river, and a garrison of a thousand 'very loyal' soldiers plus their families.[1116]

The large city of Mosul does not appear to have had a citadel until the middle of the eleventh century; this eventually being destroyed by the Mongols two hundred years later.[1117] In the northern parts of the Fertile Crescent and the foothills of Anatolia there had been a more significant threat from the Byzantine Empire. Consequently, as Nasir-i Khusraw again wrote, the fortifications of such frontier zones were highly developed and incorporated 'raised platforms for war machines and archers'.[1118] This was clearly true of the Diyar Rabia and Diyar Bakr regions which formed enclosed, oasis-like valleys closely linked both politically and militarily to the northern Jazira. They were notably strongly fortified in the tenth and eleventh centuries, as warlike border zones with militarized Islamic populations.[1119] Most of the surviving and impressive fortifications of the city of Diyarbakir are, however, early thirteenth-century Artuqid strengthenings and updatings of what had already existed in the eleventh century.[1120] There were similarly many citadels in the fortified towns of the neighbouring Mayyafariqin area in the early eleventh century.[1121]

To the south, on the other side of the Tur 'Abin hills in the fertile region of Diyar Mudar, the ancient city of Harran had been given new fortifications around 1059, these subsequently being strengthened after the earthquakes of 1114 or 1157.[1122] Harran is particularly interesting because a Sabian community had flourished here under tolerant Islamic rule until the 1030s but were then caught up in a struggle between invading Byzantines and local Banu Numayr rulers, converting to Islam under pressure and thus bringing to an end an ancient religious community. Also known as Mandaeans, a tiny community survives in southern Iraq, with a diaspora in other parts of the world.

The main Sabian temple, which had been greatly enlarged during the early Islamic period, was then made into a fortress by the Numayrid ruler. In 1192 it was further strengthened by Saladin's brother, al-'Adil, before his more famous reconstruction of the Citadel of Damascus.[1123] Not far from Harran, al-Ruha (Edessa to the Crusaders, now Urfa in Turkey) had a much stronger citadel on a naturally defensible rock. Though fortified for a very long time, most of the existing structure is medieval Islamic. It was strengthened in the eighth century, rebuilt in the early ninth century and again by the Mamluks in the late fourteenth century.[1124]

The great Euphrates river forms the southern boundary of the Jazira, beyond which stretch the steppes and semi-desert of Syria and Arabia. However the Euphrates valley was more than a mere frontier, though it would serve the latter purpose for centuries during the later medieval period, lying between the Mamluk Sultanate to the west and the Mongols and their successors to the east. Only with the Ottoman conquests of the sixteenth century would this part of the Islamic world be politically reunited.

In earlier centuries the Euphrates and its narrow but fertile valley formed a vital strategic and commercial corridor between Iraq and Mediterranean Syria. The major states or dynasties of the Middle East always sought to control the valley, but when they were unable to do so it fell, often in sections, under the domination of Arab tribal dynasties whose power-bases lay in the steppe regions on either side of the river. The tribal dynasties also had castles, sometimes built to defend their part of the valley against attack by tribes or religious movements such as the Qarmatians raiding from bases further inside Arabia.[1125] For all these reasons, the Euphrates valley contains or is overlooked by several imposing fortresses and fortified cities. Those in that part of the valley which runs across the steppes tended to be built of brick. They include the castle of Rahba near what is now the Iraqi frontier. Its existing fortifications were probably largely built by Nur al-Din in the second half of the twelfth century.[1126] The walled city of Raqqa had been laid out and fortified by the 'Abbasid Caliphs in the late eighth century and had a substantial eleventh- to thirteenth-century citadel,[1127] while the massive fortress of Qal'at Jabar was built in the early twelfth century to face the Crusader occupiers of Edessa.

Northern Syria itself had become an exposed frontier region in the tenth century as a result of Byzantine expansion, and so its ports and mountain passes were fortified.[1128] The sophistication of these outposts was again confirmed by the observations of the Persian-speaking traveller, Nasir-i Khusraw, in the mid-eleventh century.[1129]

Many of the castles erected by the Crusaders a couple of generations later were, in fact, built upon the foundations of these earlier Arab-Islamic defences.[1130] It was from Arab military architects that the Crusaders learned how to store the water which formed a vital element in the defence of any such position in the Middle East, some of the Islamic castles using cisterns carved from the rock, while others used large ceramic containers called khawabi.[1131] Rather surprisingly the massive tel, or site of millennia of ancient habitation on the eastern side of the medieval city of Aleppo, does not appear to have been seriously fortified before the twelfth century.[1132]

Following the establishment of the Latin Crusader States in the heart of the Islamic Middle East, there were major efforts to strengthen existing fortifications and to build new ones. Then came the devastating Mongol invasions of the second half of the thirteenth century, followed by generations of frontier warfare, raiding and counter-raiding between the Mamluk Sultanate and the Mongol Il-Khans.[1133] This resulted in a perhaps even greater focus on fortification in the later thirteenth century, especially as the initial Mongol onslaughts had damaged so many existing military structures.[1134] Once the Mamluks felt confident of their re-established defences, not much further work was done until a new threat arose in the form of Timur-i Lenk (Tamerlane) at the end of the fourteenth century.[1135]

Central Syria and Lebanon had faced a threat from the Byzantines by sea as well as by land, after which came the Crusader and then the Mongol menace.

The Fatimid Caliphate's ambitions in these regions resulted in the building of fortifications, especially as the Fatimids were rarely strong enough to be able to control the countryside, despite holding the main cities.[1136] For example, Ba'albek in the inland Baqa'a valley of Lebanon became a major military centre in the Fatimid period, with its huge Roman temple complex eventually becoming one of the most extraordinary medieval fortresses in the Middle East.[1137]

A perhaps more unexpected aspect of the eleventh century in Syria was the appearance of relatively small castles set on hilltops but not associated with towns or significant trade routes. These served as military centres for local aristocratic families and were clearly intended to dominate and protect agricultural regions. As such they had a great deal in common with the archetypal medieval European castle.[1138] Many, in fact, also looked like European castles but had no connection with the Crusaders.

It was in central Syria that major changes in the design of Islamic fortifications were first seen or recorded. Though there may have been experiments somewhat earlier at places like Harran (see above), the earliest and one of the most dramatic was al-'Adil's complete rebuilding of the Citadel of Damascus in the first years of the thirteenth century. These changes focused upon bigger towers placed closer together, more strongly constructed and projecting further from the curtain wall. As before, the towers served as artillery bastions but now mounted much more powerful and heavier counterweight *trebuchets*.[1139]

Saladin's reign in the later twelfth century had seen the construction of a number of new castles. However, a programme of strengthening and repairing captured Crusader castles prior to further campaigns against shrinking Crusader territory was more characteristic of his Ayyubid successors and the subsequent Mamluk Sultanate.[1140] Not all the castles built in what is normally regarded as the Crusader or anti-Crusader period were built with the Crusader threat in mind. A number of smaller fortifications looked east in strategic terms. These included those of Shumaimis and Tadmur (Palmyra) which, like distant Rahba, were ruled from Hims in the early thirteenth century, all being strengthened during this period. In fact al-Malik al-Mujahid Shirkuh II, the Ayyubid ruler of Hims, governed a huge area of steppe and semi-desert extending from the cultivated Orontes valley to that of the Euphrates. Here it is worth noting that the dramatic hilltop fortress of Qal'at Ibn Ma'an overlooking the oasis of Palmyra and normally attributed to the seventeenth century Lebanese *Amir* Fakhr al-Din al-Ma'ani II, was first built in the late twelfth or first half of the thirteenth century.[1141]

South of Syria, the powerful Arab tribes in what is now Jordan also built small fortresses in high places during the century or so prior to the arrival of the Crusaders. This was part of a process of sedentarization. Many were, in fact, located close to the traditional *hilla* or camping grounds of these originally bedouin tribes.[1142] In Palestine, however, there were few external threats and even the coast lay at the limits of the range of Byzantine naval raiding. The main danger seems to have come from bedouin raiders who often took advantage of any decline in government authority. Ramla, which had been established on the coastal plain as a new centre of provincial government during the early Islamic period, now declined while Jerusalem increased in importance, becoming not merely a religious centre but also an administrative one. This probably reflected its more defensible location when compared with unfortified Ramla. The Fatimid Caliphate rebuilt its walls following an earthquake in 1033, often using masonry from collapsed churches.

The area of the city was also reduced by about a third, leaving the old Jewish quarter south of the Temple Mount outside the new walls. The Jews were therefore allocated a new quarter in the north-eastern corner of Jerusalem. In response to a request by the inhabitants of Jerusalem in 1063, the Fatimid government ordered each religiously distinct quarter to strengthen the fortifications in its part of the city.[1143] Meanwhile the highest and strongest point remained the so-called Citadel of David which would feature prominently during the First Crusade.

After Saladin liberated Jerusalem from the Latin Kingdom of Jerusalem in 1187 little new work was done on its defences. In 1219 they were breached once again and this time they were not repaired. During the Mamluk period Jerusalem lay south of the main Mongol threat, so only the Citadel was reconstructed in 1310 to house a local garrison, while the city of Jerusalem remained effectively open until it was absorbed into the Ottoman Turkish Empire. The existing walls largely consist of Ottoman repairs on top of the work of previous rulers.[1144]

During the late twelfth and thirteenth centuries Saladin and his Ayyubid successors seem to have put more effort into defences east of the river Jordan, in what are now the Kingdom of Jordan and the southernmost provinces of Syria. Here the massive Roman theatre in Busra was converted into one of the most extraordinary fortresses in the Middle East while a brand new castle was built above Ajlun, watching the Crusader castle of Belvoir on the other side of the Jordan valley. The Ayyubids also added a new and larger tower to the largely abandoned early Islamic fortification of Qal'at Amman overlooking the town below.[1145] A small fortified outpost at Qal'at al-Salt appears to have been a new foundation, but that in the eastern oasis of Azraq was based upon a long-abandoned Roman frontier fortress.

The small tribal forts in southern Jordan have already been mentioned. Some of these were then taken over and expanded by the Crusaders,[1146] before falling to Saladin and in a few cases being considerably enlarged by the Mamluk Sultans. For Islamic rulers, the primary purpose of such Jordanian castles was to protect communications between Egypt and Syria, Cairo and Damascus. The same was probably true of Saladin's island castle of Jazirat Fara'un at the northern end of the Gulf of Aqaba, especially in the light of Reynaud de Châtillon's daring naval excursions into the Red Sea.[1147]

In the mid-eleventh century Nasir-i Khusrau had travelled across much of the Arabian Peninsula; his account mentioning the strong and in some areas numerous fortresses in this too-often forgotten corner of the medieval Middle East.[1148] According to Nasir-i Khusrau the fortress of al-Ahsa, close to the Gulf Coast of what is now Saudi Arabia, had four strong earth walls,[1149] almost certainly made of unfired mud-brick in much the same way that central Arabian fortresses were built from pre-Islamic times to the early twentieth century century.

Relatively little study has been made of Islamic fortifications in Egypt other than the superb Fatimid gates of what had been the closed Caliphal city of al-Qahira (Cairo), Saladin's fortress of Qal'at al-Jindi in western Sinai and the Citadel, again begun by Saladin, which still dominates the skyline of Cairo. Little survives elsewhere, especially from the period before Saladin, though a number of urban defences, citadels and more isolated castles were mentioned in written sources. The majority appear to have been made of brick, fired or unfired, before Saladin introduced a new style of fortification from Syria in the late twelfth century. Apart from a largely undated and crumbling tribal citadel on a hill dominating the oasis of Siwa close to the Libyan frontier, the only other largely complete Islamic mud-brick castle seems to be that of 'Ayn Umm Dabiki on the northern edge of the western oasis of Kharga. This is believed to date from the twelfth century and to reflect a pre-Ayyubid and perhaps Fatimid tradition of military architecture.[1150]

The oasis citadel or fortified village of Siwa should perhaps be regarded as representing medieval North African rather than Egyptian fortifications. A number of *ribats* or small fortifications had been built along the vulnerable North African coast as garrison centres to resist Christian piracy from the other side of the Mediterranean. These are usually of stone, but there was also a local Maghribi or North African tradition of quickly built fortifications made of rammed earth. The Middle Eastern tradition of fired brick was added to this to create a distinctive synthesis of eastern and western ideas. While towers became fewer, gates became bigger and stronger than had been seen in the pre-Islamic Roman and Byzantine military architecture of North Africa. Building standards seemed to decline once again during the early Fatimid period and the Berber Sanhaja tribal dynasties which succeeded them. On the other hand, new ideas of fortification began to arrive under Fatimid rule.[1151]

The situation was different once again in the medieval Islamic world's furthest west, in Morocco. Here, from the eleventh to thirteenth centuries, elements of Andalusian military architecture began to be adopted under Murabitun and Muwahhidun rule.[1152] The concept of the fortified coastal *ribat* also spread from North Africa and al-Andalus to Morocco's Atlantic coast, a region which had never before faced a naval threat except for a couple of extraordinary Viking raids.[1153] The oldest such *ribat* on the Atlantic coast was at Tit, initially built in the first half of the twelfth century although the existing fortifications date from the second half of that century. They consist of stone on a concrete foundation, in a style which reflected the current mixture of North African and Andalusian military ideas.[1154]

An independent tradition of military architecture had appeared in al-Andalus during the ninth century. One of its features was a particularly good use of stone, as the Muslims' Visigothic predecessors had done. These early Islamic fortifications incorporated the same small but close-spaced towers seen in the early Islamic Middle East, but as the centuries passed and siege technologies became more effective, so towers projected further and became more widely spaced.[1155] Unlike North Africa, Islamic al-Andalus faced a real and constant threat to its land-frontier. Consequently, several impressive fortresses were built. They were probably larger and more advanced than anything else in early medieval Europe, perhaps even including the Balkan provinces of the Byzantine Empire.

One of the most striking is that of Gormaz. Here recent archaeological investigations indicate that it is slightly older than once believed, being constructed soon after 940.[1156] After falling to the Christian Spaniards by 1059 there was further building, though this does not seem to have had a particularly defensive purpose. Consequently most of the fortifications of Gormaz that can still be seen are from the period of the Caliphate or Cordova,[1157] with some fourteenth-century modifications.[1158] Cities served as major base areas at some distance behind the frontier. One such was Badajoz which again received its first fortified circuit wall in the tenth century. This would be strengthened in the eleventh century when a citadel or *qasaba* (*alcazaba* in Spanish) was added, and again under the Muwahhidun in the twelfth century.[1159]

Until the late eleventh century most towers in al-Andalus were solid, at least in their lower parts.[1160] The Andalusians also continued to erect much smaller, simple and usually rectangular isolated towers as part of their frontier defences well into the Muwahhid period. Some were of stone while others were of tabby; that is a simple form of very hard concrete (see below).[1161] The increasing pressure of the Spanish and Portuguese Christian Reconquista, and the steady loss of territory, naturally led to ever greater emphasis being placed on the frontier and urban fortifications of al-Andalus.[1162] These largely continued previous Caliphal Andalusian military-architectural traditions but tended to be less regular in plan, making greater use of the lie of the land and of natural defensive features. Many towns also had a *qasaba* citadel added at their highest points.[1163]

Unfortunately the collapse of central government and the emergence of numerous small *ta'ifa* statelets, as well as changes in their recruitment policies, often seem to have meant that there were not enough men to man these strong and perhaps over-extensive fortifications. This would presumably also have been seen in the second and third *ta'ifa* periods after the collapse of Murabitun and Muwahhidun power respectively. Certainly the success of the Crusader siege of Lisbon in 1147 fitted this pattern, the city having inherited excellent defences from the Murabitun but possessing too few men to defend them adequately.[1164] Lisbon was also not helped by the fact that its strong neighbour, Ibn Wazir the ruler of Evora, had a truce with the Portuguese king and so refused to help. Instead he advised the defenders to try and buy off their attackers, but this did not work with a Crusader army which included large numbers of fanatical, religiously motivated volunteers from Northern Europe.[1165]

After the fall of Lisbon, the Muwahhidun took control of what remained of Islamic al-Andalus. They again strengthened many of its fortifications and were responsible for introducing a number of dramatic new ideas. These can, for example, be seen as Cacares. Here the old Roman and Umayyad defences were restored in the mid-twelfth century because the city, which had once been at a safe distance from the Christian frontier, now served as a vital element in a new frontier zone. It resisted, fell, was retaken and eventually fell for the last time in 1229.[1166]

The fall of Lisbon also provided the Christians with something which they had not previously used; a forward naval base on the Atlantic coast of the Iberian Peninsula. This meant that what are now the Algarve region of southern Portugal and the Atlantic coast of Spain from Portugal to the Straits of Gibraltar were exposed to serious threat from the sea. Consequently they were now strongly fortified, with particular emphasis being given to Seville which served as the centre of Muwahhidun power in what remained of al-Andalus.[1167]

A different sort of fortification is believed to have emerged on the eastern side of al-Andalus in the late twelfth and thirteenth century, or at least these defences served a function which is less well documented elsewhere. Here in the mountains of what would soon become southern Aragon, the primary role of many fortifications was to serve as refuges. They ranged from simple towers to large walled enclosures to hold people, their goods, perhaps their animals, and were usually very different in form to the castles of Western Europe during the same period.[1168]

In the last surviving Islamic state of Granada, Islamic fortifications continued to develop along sometimes distinctive lines. The Nasrid dynasty which ruled Granada from 1232 until 1492 inherited the fortifications and the military architectural styles of the Muwahhidun and Moroccan Marinids. These included the *qasaba* or urban citadel, the *hisn* or castle and the *qalahurra* or tower incorporating a luxurious residence for the ruler. Another inherited feature was the *barraniya* separate external towers standing a short distance from the curtain wall but linked to it by a bridge. The *suluqiya* was a later development, consisting of a lower defensive wall outside the main line of fortifications.[1169]

Building upon what they had inherited, both physically and in terms of architectural knowledge, the rulers of Granada constructed an impressive line of fortifications along the *thugur* or military provinces which formed their land frontier. It stretched from Vera near the Mediterranean coast to Algeciras just west of Gibraltar, and consisted of stone towers plus castles located on sometimes remarkably inaccessible hilltops. Most were concentrated along the vulnerable western part of this frontier. The forts themselves were strictly within existing traditions of Andalusian military architecture, though incorporating a few new Spanish ideas, with a major emphasis on the storage of drinking water for the garrison and its animals. The Nasrids also strengthened urban defences, especially in the *thugur*. Here there were also numerous hilltop *tali'a* towers used for observation and linked to a central fortress by various signal systems. All these varied fortifications again provided refuges for the local population and their animals in case of Christian Spanish attack.[1170]

The methods of construction varied from region to region, but always relied upon sufficient numbers of skilled craftsmen being available. Al-Harawi, in his book of military advice for Saladin and his successors, highlighted this requirement only in a general sense and in particular relation to siege warfare. Somewhat later, Sultan Baybars I is said to have given specific orders to those in command of fortresses to 'maintain carpentry and stone-cutting equipment'.[1171]

Standards of masonry had been very good during the early Islamic Umayyad and 'Abbasid periods. This continued into the Fatimid era but in many other areas seems to have fallen, almost certainly as a result of political fragmentation and economic decline. For example, those parts of the castle of Shayzar in central Syria which could date from the period when the town and fortress formed a tiny statelet ruled by the Banu Munqidh clan tend to be of cruder construction than those dating from the previous period, or indeed of the subsequent renovation by Nur al-Din.[1172]

Even Saladin's big castle on the island of Jazirat Fara'un in the Gulf of Aqaba lacked finely dressed stone, probably because it was erected in a hurry to face a threat posed by the Crusaders in Outrejordain in what is now southern Jordan.[1173] It was also built in an area lacking a supply of trained labourers, most of whom would probably have been brought from Egypt proper. In contrast the single Ayyubid tower on the Citadel of Amman is made entirely of finely embossed masonry.[1174] It was almost certainly erected quite early in Saladin's reign, before his great victory at Hattin in 1187 as such a tower would seem to have had very little purpose afterwards.

While Syria, eastern Anatolia and Armenia were the heartlands of the finest stone architecture during the early medieval period, an equally sophisticated tradition of brick architecture existed in Iraq. Such traditions were based upon the availability of suitable building material. The brick tradition of Iraq also spread far up the Euphrates valley into what is now eastern Syria, into the Jazira region between the rivers Euphrates and Tigris, and across much of the steppe-lands of the Syrian Desert. As a result medieval fortifications along the Syrian and Iraqi Euphrates itself tended to be of brick whereas those of the hills to the north were of stone. Where the Euphrates emerged from the Anatolian hills the two styles merged. The two traditions similarly existed side by side in and around Damascus which lay between the mountains and the desert. Here the main public buildings were of superbly cut stone, the domestic buildings were often of crude stone, rubble and brick, while the fortifications of the city were, in the tenth century, at least partially of mud brick.[1175]

In early medieval Egypt both mud-brick and fired-brick were used for domestic, religious and military architecture before the Ayyubid period. At the same time, however, stone was used where necessary and where available. This Egyptian brick tradition continued in the Nile Delta almost until modern times, even for important religious buildings, for the simple reason that stone did not exist on the alluvial plain.

Rammed earth, rubble and concrete were not the only materials used for building fortifications in medieval North Africa and al-Andalus, but they were surely the most distinctive. Tamped earth walls had been a feature of North Africa and the Iberian Peninsula in the pre-Islamic period. It has, in fact, been suggested that the Arabic word *tabiya* for this sort of construction came from a Basque word, via the Romance (early Spanish) *tapia*. It was then from Arabic that English took the term *tabby* which is used as an alternative word for *cob* construction. Such tamped earth certainly became widespread in Islamic al-Andalus, especially for domestic buildings.[1176]

The Romans had become masters in the use of concrete and such techniques had not been lost in the Iberian peninsula when the Romans left. In al-Andalus a quick and cheap form of concrete reappeared in the ninth century, consisting of gravel, soil and lime laid in formers.[1177] It was being used to build fortifications by at least the eleventh century,[1178] if not earlier, around Cordova, and spread to North Africa during the twelfth century.[1179] Earlier fortifications in this area had often been of freestone (essentially consisting of available pieces of stone fitted together as well as possible) and compacted rubble. In al-Andalus, meanwhile, the pressure of the Christian Reconquista led to an increasing use of both concrete and ashlar or finely cut stone, with less use of freestone.[1180]

The materials from which a fortification was made naturally had an influence upon what defensive features it could incorporate. Generally speaking it would appear that building in well-cut ashlar enabled a military architect to be bolder in his design, though this was not invariably the case. The elements seen within

Islamic fortifications during these centuries were varied and often advanced, though it would be an oversimplification merely to claim that the Muslims were in advance of the Western Europeans or indeed of the Byzantines. One feature that does, however, seem to be credited to Islamic architects or those from the Islamic world, was the *talus*. This additional sloping element along the base of a wall was designed to make the task of enemy siege-miners more difficult at a time when such mining usually aimed at the base and foundations of the wall itself rather than seeking to tunnel deep beneath it.

The *burj*, major or central tower had been the essential feature of Islamic fortification since the earliest days and was in itself evidence of the strength of Sassanian-Iranian rather than Romano-Byzantine influence.[1181] The addition of larger towers in the thirteenth century was evidence of the spread of counterweight trebuchets. The fact that these were seen in minor castles as well as major fortifications indicated just how important such new siege weapons rapidly became.[1182]

In North Africa and al-Andalus even more distinctive towers were developed. In addition to bastions with superimposed vaulted rooms, as seen in the Middle East, the *barraniya* towers were erected just outside the main curtain wall of a citadel or city.[1183] Called *albarrana* in Spanish, they were linked to the main fortress by a narrow bridge which could, presumably, be removed or blocked in an emergency. Seen first in al-Andalus in the twelfth century, they spread to North Africa in the thirteenth.[1184] The *qalahurra* or tower which included some sort of luxurious residence for a ruler or governor may have been a later development, apparently first built by the North African Marinid rulers of Gibraltar in the mid-fourteenth century but then adopted in Granada and elsewhere.[1185]

The *machicolis* or *machicolation* was an additional element in a fortified wall or tower which enabled defenders to drop missiles or shoot downwards upon enemies attacking a gate, postern door or simply the base of the wall or tower. They came in a variety of forms, though the simple box machicolation protruding out of a wall above an entrance had been known in Syria during the immediate pre-Islamic period.[1186]

Gates were always potentially a weak point in any fortification. Hence considerable thought and often considerable expense went into their design. The bent entrance was called a *bashura* in Arabic while each right-angled turn was called a *darga*. It was probably brought westward from Central Asia during the early medieval 'Abbasid period but was far from being universally adopted. Where a bent entrance system was used, it was normally an integral part of a newly built gate but could be added ahead of existing ancient gates, as seems to have been done with the Roman triple-arched 'straight-through' Bab Sharqi 'Eastern Gate' of the walled city of Damascus. Here the central and southern entrances were blocked while an additional wall was built in front of the northern entrance.

There may have been similar additions in front of the superb late eleventh-century gates of the sacred Fatimid Caliphal palace-city of al-Qahira (Cairo), though these had disappeared by the fifteenth century.[1187] The stone gates and walls replaced the earlier Fatimid brick fortifications. However, the gates themselves may have been as much symbolic statements of power and separation as they were defensive structure. Despite being built between 1087 and 1092, they were straight-through in design but set back deep within pairs of towers and threatened by arrow-slits on both sides of the entrance-way. The presumed pre-Crusader and probably Fatimid eastern gate of the fortified city of Ascalon in southern Palestine was flanked by a pair of massive but barely projecting towers while no evidence of a bent entrance system has been found.[1188] The same appears to have been the case with the decorated fortified gates of Harran which date from the tenth and eleventh centuries.[1189]

The gates of major Middle Eastern fortifications built in the twelfth and thirteenth centuries, during the course of the Crusades, normally incorporated bent entrances. Examples include Saladin's castle of Qal'at al-Jindi in Sinai, his Citadel overlooking Cairo and his gates within Cairo's city wall. One of the most elaborate was the huge gate complex of the Citadel of Aleppo with its multiple turns,[1190] built in 1211. There were plenty of simpler examples in Iraq from the early thirteenth century onwards. The idea had probably been adopted in al-Andalus by the eleventh century[1191] and in Morocco before the end of the twelfth century, apparently reaching Tunisia from al-Andalus rather than from the Middle East in the thirteenth century.[1192]

The portcullis, despite having been used in the Roman Empire, does not seem to have survived or at least not been widely used in Islamic military architecture. Al-Andalus might have been an exception, but there is disagreement even here.[1193] On the other hand it did appear in later Spanish Christian fortifications, where it was known as the *rastrillo*. The bastion or additional fortified space ahead of a gate or other such vulnerable point was, however, employed. In al-Andalus these were often added during the eleventh to thirteenth centuries, including bastions containing superimposed vaulted rooms.[1194]

Urban fortifications seem to have been more widespread and more advanced in the medieval Islamic world than in Western Europe, at least until the later twelfth and thirteenth centuries. This clearly reflected the considerably more urbanized nature of Islamic civilization as well as its generally greater wealth. Such defences included a number of standard elements which, in Arabic-speaking regions, were the city-wall or *sur*, the gates or *abwab* (plural of *bab*), the citadel or *qala'a* and the *maydan* training ground usually associated with such fortified cities.

Most, though not all, of the regions that became the medieval Islamic world had been urbanized before the coming of Islam. Several also had their own distinctive styles of urban fortification, usually reflecting the degree of threat faced by towns and cities. In this respect, one of the most fortified was Transoxania in Central Asia, whose urban centres had incorporated sometimes massive citadels for many centuries. They remained a feature throughout the medieval periods and later centuries.

Most did not, however, incorporate large, or in some cases any, wall towers other than the *burj* protecting their often elaborate gate. Instead these Central Asian urban fortifications relied upon massive, tall and sometimes multiple walls, usually of mud-bricks and sometimes with small half-round towers which only projected a short distance. Such a tradition of urban fortification seems to have remained characteristic for much of the eastern Islamic world for many centuries. Travelling in 1047, Nasir-i Khusrau noted that the important Iranian city of Isfahan had a crenellated wall but he made no mention of wall towers.[1195]

Much the same may have been true in southern Iraq and the Jazira during the 'Abbasid period, though the inner circuit wall of the D-shaped fortified city of Raqqa on the lip of the Euphrates valley did include an extraordinary number of half-round towers of fired-brick.[1196] The outer circuit wall had none. Raqqa would play only a minor role during the period of the Crusades, but the city of Mosul would be the power-centre from which the first really effective counter-Crusade or *jihad* campaigns would be launched by 'Imad al-Din Zangi in the mid-twelfth century.

Mosul had been fortified by the Umayyad Caliphs but this wall was destroyed in the late eighth century. Thereafter significant defences were not considered necessary and there were no changes until the 'Uqaylid Arab ruler Sharaf al-Dawla rebuilt the city's defences in 1081/2 during his struggle to save the city from Seljuk Turkish conquest. This seems to have been a very simple fortification, lacking a ditch or even, reportedly, ramparts. Both features were added by the local Turkish governor, Shams al-Dawla Jukrimish in 1104/5, against a possible attack by his supposed Great Seljuk overlord. 'Imad al-Din Zangi strengthened them further in 1132 and added a new gate. By 1184 the city of Mosul had two walls with many closely spaced towers and a covered chamber inside the main or inner wall. These references to a doubled wall may, in fact, indicate that the Seljuks or their *atabeg* successors had extended the defences to include a citadel to the north. Furthermore, Mosul had at least 11 gates during *atabeg* times in the twelfth and early thirteenth centuries.[1197] In addition to a *maydan* training ground, Mosul had what was called a *dar al-mamlaka* which is usually translated as 'government houses',[1198] but which might better be seen as barracks for *mamluk* or *ghulam* troops.

To the north-west, Amida, also known as the city of Diyar Bakr, was considered by Nasir-i Khusrau in 1047 to possess the greatest fortifications in the world. The city itself had four gates which 'included no wood' and behind the crenellations of the main wall was a passage in which an armoured man could move and fight with ease. On each tower was a 'platform' for the combatants while there was an open space 15 cubits (7.5 m) wide between the inner and outer walls. The outer wall was made in the same way as the inner but incorporated towers that were only 10 cubits (about 5 m) high.[1199]

The greatest city in northern Syria was, of course, Aleppo which, in the eleventh century had a circuit wall which Nasir-i Khusrau claimed was 25 cubits (about 12.5 m) high. Within this, the city itself was crowded by the standards that Nasir-i Khusrau was used to, most of the houses being of stone. Aleppo had also remained prosperous despite recent political upheavals.[1200] The massive *tel* on the eastern side of the medieval walled city served as a refuge long before it was itself properly fortified. Today it remains one of the most remarkable sites in the Middle East, not least because the steep slopes of the man-made hill are still substantially covered with smooth stone slabs, laid during the reign of the Ayyubid ruler al-Malik al-Zahir by 1203/4. Thus the slope became a vast glacis surrounded by a deep moat. A small entrance tower was added at the same time, but this is now dwarfed by the huge twin-towered entrance complex with its five *darga* right-angled turns and five iron doors added just over ten years later.[1201] Above the stone slabs of the glacis rise the circuit wall with its dramatic, closely spaced rectangular towers.

Nasir-i Khusrau was just as impressed by certain aspects of the mid-eleventh century fortifications of Tripoli in Lebanon. The city he visited was on the coast where the port-quarter of al-Mina now stands. The later medieval and modern city of Tripoli shifted slightly inland after the expulsion of the Crusaders in the late thirteenth century. In Nasir-i Khusrau's time Tripoli owed at least nominal allegiance to the Fatimid Caliphate. It had an iron gate in its eastern or land wall, while the wall itself included battlements and embrasures. He wrote that: 'along the battlements are placed 'arradah [man-powered stone-throwing mangonels] for their fear of the Greeks [Byzantines] who are wont to attack the place in their ships'.[1202] Further south Nasir-i Khusrau noted that the Fatimid-held port of Acre was also defended by a chain which could be lowered deeper into the water to allow ships to pass in and out.[1203]

In addition to its surviving Roman gates with their early Islamic modifications and reportedly mud-brick city wall, a citadel was added to the fortifications of Damascus in the late eleventh century by the Seljuk Turks. This appears to have been the first such citadel in the long history of the Syrian capital and it was subsequently surrounded by the more famous early thirteenth-century Ayyubid citadel walls. Nevertheless much of this Seljuk fortress remains and its masonry is clearly different to that of the Ayyubid wall which stands only a few metres away.[1204]

Little is known about the fortifications of Cairo before the Fatimid *wazir* Badr al-Jamali rebuilt the partly symbolic gates. Saladin then altered the entire system of defence. However, the evidence suggests that, although quite simple, these defences were also effective. The early Fatimid fortifications on the northern side of Cairo included a mud-brick wall, wide enough for two horsemen to ride abreast, two gates and a broad ditch with one bridge. This enabled the Fatimid garrison to sortie from the fortified city and defeat a determined Qarmatian attack in 971.[1205]

The new wall built by Badr al-Jamali extended the area of the palace-city a short distance north and south. According to the chronicler al-Maqrizi: 'he made before the gateway a great *zallaqa* [glacis] of blocks of granite in order that, in case an assault were made, the horses of the cavalry would fail to get a firm footing on the hard and slippery stone'.[1206] The Fatimid defence of the exposed city of Bilbays on the eastern edge of the Nile desert may have been more typical of this period, consisting of a single, relatively low wall, probably of mud brick, without a ditch and with no mention of towers.[1207]

The massive programme of fortification in Cairo,[1208] instigated by Saladin and continued by his successors, was based upon Syrian prototypes. This was clearly the case with the great Citadel of Cairo.[1209] Saladin also started an ambitious project of extending the fortifications to enclose virtually the entire city which now consisted of much more that the ex-Caliphal 'palace city' of al-Qahira. In fact Cairo had grown throughout the early Islamic period, gradually extending northwards from the Coptic Christian town clustered around the ancient Romano-Byzantine fortress known to Medieval Europeans of 'Babylon'. These extensions included the first Arab-Islamic garrison quarter of Fustat, plus other garrison areas, palace and commercial quarters, the last of which was Fatimid al-Qahira. Other quarters or villages and market-gardens extended westwards to the river Nile and the river port of Bulaq.

Work began on Saladin's city wall in 1185 but even this ambitious scheme could not enclose everything between the Muqattam hills and the river. Consequently many people had to be moved from the already damaged suburb of Fustat into the new enclosed area. In fact some of the excavated southern wall can be seen to cut through the foundations of demolished houses in what had been part of Fustat. Furthermore, the island of Ruda and the suburb of Giza on the Nile's western bank could be said to have formed part of the city by Saladin's day, and certainly did so under his successors. The military reasons for these urban fortifications were themselves also new. Egypt's rulers no longer protected themselves from the local population by living inside a fortified palace and garrison complex. What Saladin intended was to protect Egypt's capital from external attack, most obviously from the Latin Crusader States or from another European Crusade.

The Citadel, while available as a refuge from a disaffected population, primarily served as the key and strongest point of Cairo's defences.[1210] Much of what can be seen today was actually built for Saladin's successor, al-ʿAdil, who greatly strengthened Saladin's initial plan, reflecting the need for much larger towers as artillery bastions. Otherwise the main difference between al-ʿAdil's work on the Citadel of Cairo and that on the Citadel of Damascus was that in the former al-ʿAdil modified what Saladin had begun, whereas in the latter he started from scratch, merely enclosing the old Seljuk fortress.[1211]

Another feature of medieval Islamic urban fortification is especially visible in North Africa and al-Andalus, perhaps because the pressure of hugely expanding urban populations had been less in this part of the Islamic world. This was a habit of extending city walls so broadly that they enclosed large areas of intensively cultivated and often irrigated land, as well as during the main urban centre and occasional hamlets. Such a large area often enabled the defenders to grow food during a prolonged siege.[1212]

The danger of spreading a defending garrison too thinly was to a great extent counterbalanced by the normally small size of besieging forces, obliging the latter to focus their attacks upon only part of the defences. Few of the Islamic cities of al-Andalus were that big. Here huge effort was put into the storage of drinking water or protection of a source of such drinking water. Cacares is a well preserved example. Its inner wall was built on essentially the same lines as that of the Roman city wall, plus square or octagonal external *barraniya* towers beyond.[1213] A very large water cistern was constructed in the centre of the *qasr* citadel, probably dating from the mid-twelfth-century Muwahhid period.[1214]

Most of the fortified structures now described as castles in the Islamic Middle East were actually citadels, in the sense that they formed a physical part of the defences of small towns or large villages. As such their purpose, and often their design, was closer to that of the recognized citadels which served as key points in the defence of cities. This was also true of the eastern regions of the medieval Islamic world, though here there were more isolated hill or mountaintop castles. Few have been studied, but it is clear that most were characterized by a full use of naturally defensive features, often resulting in rather rambling walled enclosures strengthened by towers.

In Syria, at Shayzar, a large fortress dominated a small town. It can be regarded as a good example of a medieval Arab-Islamic castle that never fell to the Crusaders and thus never incorporated European workmanship.[1215] Once again it made full use of its position on a steep, elongated and very narrow spur of rock with the valley of the river Orontes on its eastern side and an almost as sudden slope on the west. The fortress ended at the abrupt northern end of the spur where an entrance led down to the town and to a strategically important bridge over the river. At the southern end of the site the spur was cut by a deep, broad man-made fosse which isolated the fortress from the continuing hill beyond. The walls and towers made this remarkably strong position stronger still.

Busra was entirely different. Here a substantial town lay in a flat, fertile but entirely open plain. The only substantial feature was a superbly preserved and massively built Roman theatre from the second century AD. This was converted into a remarkable D-shaped fortress from the late eleventh to mid-thirteenth centuries.[1216] The first towers were added to its entrances by a local Turkish commander whose inscription gives the date 1089, ten years before the arrival of the First Crusade in neighbouring Palestine. A slightly later tower was added to the original curved outer wall in the mid-twelfth century. However, the most dramatic changes came in the first half of the thirteenth century when the Roman theatre was entirely enclosed by a new wall with originally nine massive, closely spaced new towers of the artillery bastion form comparable to those seen at Harran and Damascus.

Five of the great towers at Busra were credited to the Ayyubid Sultan al-'Adil. In 1211 he also attempted to fortify the isolated hill known as Mount Tabor in northern Palestine, providing it with a curtain wall 1,750 m long, ten towers and a substantial garrison which was probably intended to raid the area around Crusader-held Acre. Indeed, the fortification of Mount Tabor may have contributed to the launching of the Fifth Crusade which, though it failed to retake the fortress, did convince the Muslims to demolish it. This was another clear case of the benefits of having a powerful castle being outweighed by the potential danger that same castle posed if it fell into enemy hands.[1217]

The detailed planning of these Islamic castles in Syria and its neighbours seems to have been at least as carefully thought out as that of their Crusader counterparts. In fact a detailed analysis of the castle built by Saladin overlooking Ajlun on the eastern side of the Jordan valley, and the similarly dated Crusader castle at Belvoir facing it on the western side of the Jordan valley, suggests that Ajlun was superior in terms of the positioning of its towers, the area covered by archery from arrow-slits and its lack of 'dead ground'.[1218] This interpretation might be disputed, but there can be little doubt that the tendency of Western historians to assume that the most magnificent of castles within the presumed area of the Latin Crusader States were therefore Crusader castles is often misplaced.

For example, the superb fortress of Subayba where the south-western slopes of Mount Hermon merge into the northern edge of the Golan Heights was long believed to be the Crusader 'castle of Banyas'. In reality the latter was a relatively feeble affair. Qal'at al-Subayba itself was built to protect the road to Damascus from Galilee, not the road to Galilee and Acre from Damascus. It was started for the ruler of Damascus in 1228 to face a Crusader threat which materialized a year later. Subayba was strengthened further by the Mamluk Sultan Baybars after 1260, when the Mongol threat was present and real.[1219] However, once the Crusader and Mongol menaces had disappeared, Qal'at al-Subayba lost much major strategic purpose and remained virtually untouched. As a result it now stands as one of the most important examples of an Islamic fortress rather than urban citadel architecture dating from the period of the Crusades.

The castle of Gormaz in central Spain was another example of the Islamic military architects' use of a steep hilltop location which was then fortified with a long circuit wall plus towers. However, Gormaz was too early to have the massive artillery-emplacement towers which characterized later examples. The ninth to early eleventh-century Caliphal period in al-Andalus also saw the construction of some substantial garrison fortresses in lower lying or more accessible hilltop locations. These were usually rectangular and owed much to the early Islamic Syrian-Umayyad period and to even earlier Romano-Byzantine forms. Some, like that of 'Akabat al-Baqar (El Vacar) north of Cordova, were made of concrete and look quite astonishingly twentieth century!

At the other end of the scale were simple, rectangular *qubba* towers. Some of these had an outer or enclosure wall but many did not, instead standing alone on hilltops across the southern half of the Iberian Peninsula.[1220] Small castles known as *sajra* also appeared in the tenth century. They again tended to be on hilltop locations but had an exterior wall, a cistern, and were usually associated with a nearby settlement. Many were also located in strategic passes, perhaps to seal such routes or cut the escape of raiders.[1221] The small circular towers known as *al-tal'iya* (*atalayas* in Spanish) are more likely to have served as watchtowers or as refuges, and were found throughout the Islamic territory of al-Andalus.[1222] Almost all these varied structures continued to be used in some way or another while Islamic authority survived.

Other forms of building were similarly fortified in the Islamic world, perhaps most notably the *khans* which were placed at sometimes remarkably regular intervals along the main overland trade routes, almost like medieval motels. Islam was a highly commercial and remarkably mobile civilization. So the free, safe progress of merchant caravans was much in the interests of local rulers. The early development of the fortified *khan* can be traced back to early Islamic Iran and Transoxania, though even here the system was probably based upon earlier refuges for travellers, merchants and pilgrims.[1223]

Nor were such 'highway' forts limited to the eastern provinces, even in the early medieval period. The Fatimid authorities built small towers as outposts from which to protect the main caravan routes in Syria.[1224] They may also have provided refuges, even if only as a strong point beside which travellers could erect their tents. The most famous and best preserved such *khans* are, however, those of central Anatolia. Their construction was encouraged by the Seljuk Sultans of Rum as part of an enthusiastic promotion and revival of trade. However, as Seljuk authority collapsed, these strongly fortified mercantile structures are known to have been used occasionally as forts in the late thirteenth and early fourteenth centuries.[1225]

The use of caves as refuges is as ancient as the history of mankind itself. Their use as military bases from which to attack enemies is, sadly, likely to be equally ancient. Within the medieval Islamic world this was naturally more characteristic of hilly or mountainous areas. One early example was recorded during a Druze rebellion in 1031 against Nasr Ibn Salih, the Mirdasid ruler of Aleppo. This uprising was concentrated in the Jabal Summaq hills where, according to the chronicler Yahya Ibn Sa'id al-Antaki, the rebels destroyed mosques and 'took defensive positions in lofty and inaccessible caves'.[1226] From here the Druze also raided Byzantine territory on the Syrian coast. As a result the Byzantine governor of Antioch joined forces with the army of Aleppo to besiege the caves, driving out the rebels with fire and smoke. Several generations later Usama Ibn Munqidh recalled the enemies of Shayzar doing the same in central Syria, as well as the comparable difficulty faced by troops who had to attack these hideouts.[1227]

Nor were 'cave fortresses' restricted to the Middle East. It has been suggested that the strong point known as *Hisn Tarik*, the Castle of Tarik, in medieval Arabic histories of Gibraltar was in reality a fortified cave now called St Michaels Cave.[1228] Another fascinating but difficult reference to the use of caves as strong points in this area comes from the *Heimskringla* Norse epic. The section concerning King Sigurd of Norway's Crusade in 1100 describes his passage through the Straits of Gibraltar and how, on some unidentified 'island', he and his men battled with a Moorish army holed up in a cave which had a wall across the front. The 'island' in question might well have been the peninsula of Gibraltar itself.[1229]

SIEGE WARFARE

Technical manuals concerning siege warfare were written in the Islamic Middle East at a very early date. Unfortunately, their texts have largely been lost though their titles and the names of their authors are known through passing references in other sources. In some cases fragments of text survive, again as quotes elsewhere. The earliest known was a book on war-machines by the Banu Musa Ibn Shakir brothers who are more famous for their remarkably advanced civil engineering texts. They worked in mid-ninth-century Iraq and fragments of their book entitled *Al-Hijal* survive in a later work by al-Khwaraymi called *Mafatih al-'Ulum*, though the identification of these passages is not entirely confirmed. Section 10 of the Banu Musa brothers' *Al-Hijal* was said to mention *manjaniq* and *'arrada* stone-throwing machines. Interestingly, these two were presented as being essentially the same, as would also be the case in the last Mamluk texts on the subject. The brothers also mentioned the *jarkh* crossbow, the *zanburaq* blowpipe and military 'palisades'.[1230] Unfortunately no further details are known, though fire-weapons and the *dabbaba* protective shed did appear elsewhere in their work.[1231]

Al-Khwarizmi's own book, dating from the late tenth century, was in two parts whose titles translate as '*The Science of the Invention and Manufacture of War Machines*' and '*The Science of their Use*'. He does, however, describe the key elements of the *manjaniq* in detail, showing it to have been the early, man-powered form of mangonel that had been introduced to the Islamic world from Central Asia, almost certainly via Transoxania in the late seventh or early eighth century. This was roughly the same time that the device reached the Byzantine Empire.[1232] Even in the late eleventh century not all the peoples of the Eurasian or Central Asian steppes had access to this technology. For example, the Byzantine Princess Anna Comnena pointed out that, whereas the Islamic Turks did, the largely pagan Cumans (Kipchaqs) did not.[1233] Other evidence tends to suggests that Islamic siege technology and the mechanical weapons involved were superior to those of the invading Western Europeans at the start of the Crusades, and they were undoubtedly superior by the time the Latin States finally disappeared from the Middle East.

When al-Tarsusi wrote his famous text for Saladin in the second half of the twelfth century, the basic man-powered *manjaniq* or mangonel had evolved into a number of different forms. These ranged from very simple, quick to erect and easy to operate versions of various sizes, to larger, more complicated and accurate forms, some of which incorporated a significant degree of protection for the team of men who pulled the traction ropes. Al-Tarsusi was drawing upon older and well-established military-technical knowledge (see below).

A variety of technological traditions also fed into the sophisticated siege machines available to the Turco-Islamic rulers of northern India in the thirteenth century. The basic machines, however, seem to have been the same as those long used in neighbouring Iran, Afghanistan and Transoxania, plus some features from the Indian heritage.[1234] Essentially the same military technology was again available in Islamic North Africa where, for example, even the not particularly wealthy or powerful Hafsid rulers of Tunisia used the usual array of siege weapons at the end of the thirteenth century.[1235] Further west, the Muwahhidun of Morocco and al-Andalus were renowned for their technical capabilities in both offensive and defensive siege warfare.

The availability and quality of suitable timber featured prominently in such aspects of warfare, but this is not to say that only the biggest, strongest and straightest pieces of wood had military value. During their siege of Jerusalem in 1187, Saladin's troops used olive and other local trees to make 'engines'. These trees would probably have tended to be relatively small, gnarled and far from straight, but were still clearly useful for something.[1236]

What a stone-throwing mangonel needed above all was a strong, straight and flexible beamsling. Although the Chinese often, and perhaps normally, built theirs up from many laths, the Muslims apparently relied on a single piece of wood.[1237] There does not even seem to be clear evidence of the lower part of such a beamsling being reinforced with shorter timbers, as seen in Europe. The chronicles indicate that, when it came to besieging Crusader-held fortifications in Syria, Lebanon and Palestine, the best trees for mangonels were found in the mountains of southern Lebanon. Here there were sufficient examples up to 21 cubits high (over 10 m).[1238] Although these were not the huge cedars of Lebanon which still survive in the north of the country, they were substantial trees which could provide timbers for the vital mangonel beamslings.

During preparations for the final Mamluk siege of Acre in 1291 we know that, having been felled and probably roughly trimmed, the wood was taken from southern Lebanon to Damascus for construction. The mangonels were then transported in a disassembled condition to the siege-lines where they were reassembled. Others were made elsewhere, including a particularly large example at Hisn al-Akrad (Crac de Chevaliers, by now in Mamluk hands) which may have used timber from Mount Lebanon itself. It then required 100 ox-drawn waggons and a full month to transport the elements to Acre via Damascus.[1239]

All the evidence shows that the late thirteenth century Mamluk Sultanate in Egypt and Syria was among the most advanced states in the world when it came to siege technology. Its assembled knowledge was later brought together in a remarkable book called *Al-Aniq fi'l-Manajniq* by Ibn Aranbugha al-Zardkash. He completed it in 775 AH/1374 AD and, by that date, included the newer technology of guns.[1240] Fortunately this exceptional work survives complete and with detailed though stylized technical illustrations. A recent in-depth study of the text has attempted to understand and to reconstruct, on a smaller scale, many machines described by Ibn Aranbugha al-Zardkash. The result shows how they could serve as practical weapons,[1241] though perhaps with a tendency to assume too great a usage of iron and an occasional tendency to overcomplication.[1242]

According to al-Tarsusi writing in the second half of the twelfth century, siege towers, rams and protective sheds or shelters were too well known to need further comment in his technical manual. Unfortunately, other sources seem to have felt the same and as a result less is known about them than about more complicated siege machines. In fact the only item within these categories that al-Tarsusi described as one of his 'exotics' may have been rare or even experimental. This was the *shabaka* or moveable screen which, he said, could be used to protect men who operated the mangonels and were thus exposed to enemy archery or counter-bombardment. Its frame, he wrote, was similar to that of the *ziyar*, in other words was essentially rectangular and could be 'aimed' to face in any direction. Its defensive potential came from the fact that flexible materials were stretched across the frame to absorb the shock of missiles.[1243] Quite how the moveable mechanism of this *shabaka* was itself protected is less clear. Nevertheless, the principle was similar to that of the felt screen that was erected by a unit in the Mamluk army during the final siege of Acre in 1291, to both obscure and protect the men behind it.

Siege warfare during the period of the Crusades proved that the most important of all these devices was the beamsling or traction-powered stone-throwing mangonel or *manjaniq* as it was called in Arabic. This was based upon a concept that resulted in a weapon which was much simpler and notably more effective than the old torsion-powered weapons of the Graeco-Roman military technology, including both the double and single-armed varieties. Almost certainly invented and initially developed in China, the beamsling *manjaniq* achieved greater range with a bigger missile.[1244]

Modern experiments show that, with a properly trained team of rope-pullers and a skilled 'aimer' controlling the moment of release, even the man-powered versions could be as accurate as the complicated devices used by Hellenistic Greeks, Romans and early Byzantines. Once the counterweight version had been invented and developed, even greater range, power and accuracy could be achieved, though with a notably reduced rate of shooting.[1245] The technical measurements and proportions given by al-Tarsusi were also similar to those found in Chinese sources.[1246]

Not surprisingly, the beamsling *manjaniq* rapidly spread throughout the medieval Islamic world, including the western regions.[1247] In fact it became so common that the device was itself used as a simile to explain the appearance of less well-known devices. Thus when Nasir-i Khusrau, travelling through Iraq in 1047, wanted to describe the wooden *khashab* 'lighthouse' with its beacon to guide ships upriver from Basra, he wrote that it stood on four legs 'like a *manjaniq*'.[1248] Two and a half centuries later, during their conquest of the exceptionally strongly fortified Crusader-held coastal city of Acre, the Mamluk army used not only an astonishing number of *manjaniqs*, but also a remarkable variety including the *ifranji* 'Frankish', the *shaytani* 'devilish', the *qarabugha* 'black-bull' and the small anti-personnel *lu'ab*.[1249]

The names given to individual types and sizes of *manjaniq* changed slightly over the years, and this has led to some confusion. On the other hand the basic forms remained constant. There were several even amongst those powered by a team of men. In al-Tarsusi's text these were the *'arabi*, the *turki* or *farsi*, the *ifranji* or *rumi*, and the *lu'ab* which could be swivelled to aim in any direction.[1250] The *'arabi* was the most accurate and reliable but was complicated to erect, not least because it provided protection for the men operating it. The *turki* was the easiest to erect, and the picture in al-Tarsusi's text shows it to be practically identical to the earliest illustration outside China, which came from immediately pre-Islamic Transoxania.[1251] The *ifranji* incorporated features which seemed to overcome some problems inherent in the simple Turkish form.

In all those mangonels powered by a team of men, the role of the *rami* or 'shooter' was very important. It was he who gave the order for the rope-pullers to take up the tension, then to pull hard and in unison. Furthermore it was he who initially held the sling and its missile to his chest at the correct angle, releasing it at precisely the right moment to achieve maximum accuracy as the team pulled on the ropes.[1252] These were clearly skilled as well as courageous men.

Al-Tarsusi did not mention the *shaytani* which was a small, fast shooting type which first appeared during the siege of Damietta in Egypt in 1218.[1253] During the thirteenth century it seems to have been the only one still powered by teams of men pulling ropes, with the possible exception of the debatable *'arrada* (see below). In Islamic northern India several man-powered forms were still used and had a variety of names. Here the man-powered form which could be turned to aim in any direction appears to have been called a *manjaniq al-'arus* or 'bride *manjaniq*'. This was probably a typical military sexual pun and had been known since the first Islamic century.[1254]

There has been considerable disagreement about the identity of a stone-throwing siege engine called an *'arrada*. A widely accepted view maintains that it was a single-armed torsion-powered machine, developed from the Graeco-Roman *onagros*,[1255] but other scholars maintain that the *'arrada* was a very early form of man-powered beamsling weapon. It is said to have been known since the time of the Prophet Muhammad, in which case it might have been the first form of beamsling weapon in this part of the world. A reference to *'arradas* in the mid-ninth century stated that they needed large quantities of rope, which certainly suggests a man-powered mangonel.

In the mid-eleventh century Nasir-i Khusrau said that the battlements of Tripoli in Lebanon had many such *'arradas*.[1256] Islamic armies continued to use them throughout their struggle against the invading Crusaders, and the texts seem to suggest that it was quite easy to change the aim of these light weapons. Arabic and Spanish sources similarly state that *'arradas* were used in North Africa and al-Andalus, frequently being placed in the tops of fortified towers. Indeed the Christian Spanish term *algarrada* stemmed from the Arabic *al-'arrada*.

Finally, Ibn Aranbugha al-Zardkash in his late fourteenth-century *Al-Aniq fi'l-Manajaniq* made it entirely clear that, in his day, the *manjaniq 'arrada* was an ordinary man-powered type.[1257] There seems little reason to assume it to have been fundamentally different in earlier centuries. Ibn Aranbugha's manuscript also includes several illustrations which show such a weapon mounted on a fortified tower, sometimes alone and sometimes with other weapons.[1258]

It is generally believed that the counterweight mangonel, usually known as a *trebuchet*, was invented somewhere in the Middle East during the twelfth century. Unfortunately, it did not have a specific or separate name, either in the Islamic World, the Byzantine Empire, or even in Western Europe. In the Islamic regions it was still a *manjaniq*, though of a particular type with a variety of names according to its size and various details of construction or design. Compared with the traction, man-powered versions it could, and eventually always did, incorporate a heavier frame and a longer beamsling with a larger proportion of that length on the 'shooting' rather than the 'pulling' side of the fulcrum axle.[1259] This beam was always, even from the very earliest days of the invention, pulled back by a winch or comparable mechanism.

The resulting weapon was known in China as the 'Islamic throwing machine', showing that, for the people of the Far East, it had been introduced from the west. This did not, of course, prove that the counterweight mangonel was invented in the Islamic rather than the Byzantine regions of the Middle East or Eastern Mediterranean. Nevertheless, a more recent look at the evidence reinforces the widespread belief that Muslims can take the credit, but it also seems probable that the earliest forms of counterweight mangonel appeared, perhaps not suprisingly, on the war-torn, long-established, strongly fortified and highly militarized frontier between Islamic and Byzantine civilizations. Here it can be argued that the obscure *manjaniq h-r-ri* (short vowels missing)[1260] mounted on three of the towers of Tarsus in the last decades before this strongly fortified town fell to the Byzantines, lacked pulling teams or had a counterweight consisting of a bag of rocks, just like the earliest confirmed description of a counterweight *manjaniq* by al-Tarsusi two centuries later.[1261] Furthermore, other evidence from shortly before the Crusades and during the first decades of the Latin Crusader States refers to missiles that seem too big to be shot from man-powered versions.[1262]

Al-Tarsusi's famous description and illustration of a counterweight *manjaniq* clearly indicate a very primitive form of counterweight. In fact the need to excavate a hole within its base-frame to stop this counterweight hitting the ground surely suggests that it was a modified man-powered type. Al-Tarsusi's reference to a *jarkh* crossbow forming part of the loading mechanism,[1263] or perhaps of the release mechanism,[1264] and its clear inclusion in an accompanying illustration, has caused major problems of interpretation. Perhaps, as with so many other peculiar weapons in al-Tarsusi's text, the author did not fully understand what he was describing. Perhaps the illustration should be ignored and the word *jarkh* should be looked at again. It could perhaps be interpreted simply as a winch or windlass, as used in the early forms of *jarkh* or *charkh* crossbow, and not be a crossbow at all. What al-Tarsusi did, however, make clear was that his primitive counterweight weapon could be operated by one man.

During the early thirteenth century the most common form of counterweight *manjaniq* was the *maghribi* or North African type; this version of its name first being used in an account of the Crusader siege of Damietta in 1218.[1265] Elsewhere the *manjaniq maghribi* seems to have been regarded as a variation of the *farsi* or the *turki* or was simply called a *manjaniq harbi* or 'war mangonel'. Ibn Aranbugha al-Zardkash, writing in the 1370s, indicated that the *manjaniq turki* was by then the simplest of the counterweight types,[1266] while he called the simplest of those with a winch attached to the base-frame as a *manjaniq harbi* or *manjaniq rumi*.[1267] It would probably be safest to say that such names were flexible in their application, varying not only from century to century but from region to region.

Al-Tarsusi stated that even his seemingly primitive counterweight *manjaniq* could throw a rock weighing 50 *ratl* (16.5 kg if he was using Egyptian measurements, over 90 kg if he was using Syrian measurements but only 20 kg if he was using the Iraqi *ratl*). Since he was writing for Saladin, in Egypt, the Egyptian measurement seems more likely.

The carefully carved stone mangonel balls found in the castle of Sahyun weigh between 50 and 300 kg.[1268] Having been found in several parts of the site, they are assumed to have been shot into the castle by its Islamic attackers, though a missile weighing 300 kg surely cannot date from Saladin's successful siege of 1188 when the Crusaders lost Sahyun, never to regain it. More likely they date from a subsequent inter-Islamic conflict. Similar missiles have been found in the Citadel of Damascus,[1269] and in the Citadel of Hims. According to an account of the siege of Hims in 1248, one mangonel ball weighed 140 Syrian *ratl*.[1270] These were clearly thrown by the very largest *manjaniqs*, the normal weight of missile being from 90–136 kg. It would have required counterweights ranging from 5–15 tonnes to shoot even these.[1271] The largest yet found in North Africa came from an early fourteenth-century Marinid siege of Tlemsen in western Algeria. It was about 2 m in circumference and weighed 230 kg.[1272] It would take even gunpowder firearms a century or so of development to be able to exceed these giant weapons.

The moveable direction type of *manjaniq* similarly evolved over the years. The earliest recorded version was the *lu'ab*, as described by al-Tarsusi in the twelfth century. This was a small, anti-personnel machine in which the beamsling was mounted on a single pole with a swivel mechanism on the top which meant that it could be traversed in any direction.[1273] It was still known by this name at the siege of Acre in 1291. According to Ibn Aranbugha al-Zardkash and some other sources, a more powerful version of the same principle was known as the *manjaniq sultani*. Here the beamsling was still on a single pole and could traverse in any direction, but the traction end of the arm was divided into two which curved to each side. Each end was pulled by a team, perhaps usually of four people with ropes. The two curved arms then swung down past the central supporting pole and were not obstructed by it.[1274] A version of the 'Frankish' *manjaniq* in which the beamsling was either mounted on a single bifurcated pole or was itself divided into two, was reported at the siege of Caesarea in 1265.[1275] Perhaps this was the same as the traversable *manjaniq ifranji* which Ibn Aranbugha al-Zardkash and some other sources subsequently described as being the same as the *manjaniq sultani* but with two counterweights instead of the two teams of rope-pullers.[1276]

The strangest and, on the face of it, most unlikely modifications of the beamsling *manjaniq* were those which shot, or more correctly threw, large arrows or flighted javelins. Its origins may have been in knowledge of the Hellenistic Macedonian *kestros* or *cestrosphendone* dart-throwing sling. However, this knowledge must surely have been theoretical rather than practical as there is no apparent evidence of this Hellenistic weapon being used during the intervening centuries.[1277] Perhaps the earliest known use of such a machine was during a siege of Ahlat in 1229, when a siege weapon called a *manjaniq qarabugha* was said to be a modification of the basic *maghribi manjaniq*.[1278]

They were used again during the final Mamluk siege of Acre in 1291 where their effectiveness was described by an observer on the receiving end, the anonymous Templar of Tyre:

> After this the enemy brought up their *carabohas*, small hand-operated Turkish devices with a high rate of shooting which did more damage to our men than the larger engines did, since in the places where the *carabohas* were shooting, no one dared to come out into the open. In front of the *carabohas* they had made the rampart so strong and so high that no one could strike or shoot at those shooting [the *carabohas*].[1279]

Clearly the men operating these *carabohas* were below the upper line of the rampart while the *caraboha* itself could still shoot over it, as would have been the case with the javelin-throwing *manjaniq* described by Ibn Aranbugha al-Zardkash.[1280] Unfortunately Ibn Aranbugha called his arrow-throwing counterweight weapon a *ziyar* (see below), though still a variation of the *qarabugha*. Furthermore, his basic *qarabugha* was an ordinary stone-throwing, counterweight mangonel.[1281] It could have a 'graduated' counterweight to refine the accuracy of the shot,[1282] but otherwise the only feature which these *qarabughas* had in common was their incorporation of a fixed winch system as part of the overall structure.

Torsion-powered siege weapons, which had been so popular and apparently effective in Hellenistic and Roman times, had slumped in popularity; superseded by the simpler, more reliable and in most respects more powerful beamsling mangonel. Nevertheless, some version did survive, usually being used for highly specific tasks. Even here, however, their design seems to have been simplified and to have incorporated fewer metallic elements. The most commonly mentioned was the *qaws ziyar* or 'skein bow'. The version famously described by al-Tarsusi in his text for Saladin was again an extreme or experimental form; in this case being a giant *qaws ziyar*. The basic concept was to have two skeins of fibres tightly stretched between or wrapped around a wooden frame. Two separate 'bow arms' were then threaded through the skeins and twisted to create a rotary tension. A bowstring was then attached to the longer, nocked ends of the two 'bow arms', as in the similarly torsion-powered Byzantine *alakation* and Western European *espringal*.

The resulting tension was said to be very considerable, so much so that al-Tarsusi's giant machine needed a winch incorporating four-pulleys and representing the strength of 20 men to pull it back. It was, he said, to be used against towers and other fortifications.[1283] While al-Tarsusi's oversized device might have remained in the realm of experimentation, other more practical and presumably smaller *ziyar* 'skein bows' were used in both defensive and offensive siege warfare. Al-Harawi, who was similarly writing for Saladin or his first successor, mentioned them in his list of necessary equipment. The Mamluk Sultanate used the *ziyar* in the 1250s, and they were mentioned in Morocco in 1298.[1284]

All are likely to have been mounted on some sort of frame or pedestal and could be used to shoot large arrows or bolts, in some cases perhaps with incendiary material attached, or to shoot grenades filled with an incendiary substance. Whether the torsion-powered machine was still considered a useful weapon by the second half of the fourteenth century is unclear, but it did appear in various forms in Ibn Aranbugha al-Zardkash's *Al-Aniq fi'l-Manajaniq*. By then the term *ziyar* had, confusingly, been transferred to the arrow-throwing but counterweight beamsling weapon,[1285] and the refined but still counterweight arrow-throwing *manjaniq ziyar al-akhr*, 'ultimate' *manjaniq ziyar*.[1286]

Torsion weapons in Ibn Aranbugha's treatise probably include the *ziyar yarami ka*,[1287] with just one 'rigid' arm unlike the two separate arms of al-Tarsusi's earlier *qaws ziyar*. If this interpretation is correct, then the *ziyar yarami ka* would seem to be the final known reference to a single-armed torsion weapon like the ancient Roman *onager*. It is worth noting that it appears only once in Ibn Aranbugha's illustrations.

As far as Ibn Aranbugha al-Zardkash was concerned, the normal two-armed torsion-powered siege weapon was called a *kuskanjil*. Unlike al-Tarsusi's work, that by Ibn Aranbugha, is believed to be firmly rooted in reality, though perhaps an outdated reality. His complex versions of *kuskanjil* include an example with two bows or pairs of arms called the *kuskanjil bi-qawayn*,[1288] and another with 'three strings' called the *kuskanjil bi'thalatha awtar*.[1289] The former brings to mind al-Tarsusi's supposedly experimental triple *qaws ziyar* and references to multi-shot crossbows in later medieval Italy (see vol. 1), while the latter recalls the multi-stringed crossbows of medieval China and Indo-China.[1290]

The remarkable array of weapons and defensive devices available within the medieval Islamic world were used in different ways in defensive and in offensive siege warfare. Military commanders also had varying priorities in these situations. These are sometimes mentioned in chronicles, and are listed in detail in military manuals. For example: as the city of Granada prepared to resist siege by the Murabitun in the eleventh century, its garrison and people strengthened the fortifications, constructed water cisterns and flour-mills, and stored military equipment including shields, arrows and 'arradah stone-throwing machines. Writing about a century and a half later in the Middle East, al-Harawi provided a huge list of weapons and military materiel that the commander of a fortified place should have at his immediate disposal. He then went on to advise that water supplies outside the fortress should be polluted or poisoned, along with efforts to 'spread disease' with animal carcasses and ordure, though only downwind of the defended position. The commander's garrison should attack the enemy camp as the besiegers were trying to set it up; in other words before their field fortifications were in place or too strong. For this attack the commander should select cavalry, plenty of archers, naft throwers and men with large siege crossbows. Thereafter his men should continue to make night sorties with incendiary weapons.[1291]

During the Mamluk period major urban citadels such as Damascus and Aleppo clearly had their own arsenals for the storage, maintenance and perhaps manufacture, of military equipment. There was also a mill to grind flour for bread in the citadel of Damascus.[1292] At the time of the First Crusade the Islamic castle of Harenc in north-western Syria appears to have been used as a regional arsenal, storing military equipment for other castles.[1293] A comparable distribution system seems to have operated in the eleventh-century Andalusian ta'ifa state of Granada, with some frontier castles serving as munitions and food depots for several garrisons.[1294] The ability of the Murabit-held fortified city of Saragossa to endure a nine-month siege surely shows that it had contained abundant supplies, though in the end the city surrendered after the defeat or delay of a relieving army.[1295]

Even a ruined, ungarrisoned and almost deserted fortified town could still be useful. That seems to have been the condition of Mayyarfariqin by the early twelfth century, as a result of frequent conquest and reconquest. Nevertheless, a small force of passing soldiers could erect their tents within its broken walls through fear of the 'bandits' who roamed the country outside.[1296] More normally, a significant fortified town like Mayyarfariqin could be expected to contain a garrison and perhaps also an urban militia. Such local forces were sometimes highly effective, the ahdath of Aleppo driving back several attempts to storm their walls during the Seljuk Turkish siege of 1071 before eventually accepting honourable surrender terms.[1297]

Elsewhere the chronicles show that cities and their surrounding villages could cooperate in defence. This was clearly the case in the Ghuta of southern Syria. Here the fortified city of Damascus with its formidable ahdath militia, and the villages of the irrigated Ghuta itself combined to defeat several raids and even serious invasions in the tenth and eleventh centuries.[1298]

After the Murabitun governor of Saragossa in al-Andalus died, the citizens organized their own defence and continued to resist, fighting hard although many people died of hunger, until the failure of relief forced them to surrender in 1118.[1299] Towards the western end of the Andalusian frontier across what are now Spain and Portugal, the old Roman and Umayyad fortifications of Cacares were restored in the mid-twelfth century, the city probably becoming a sort of border *ribat* garrisoned by volunteers.[1300] Garrisons of professional soldiers were, of course, also required and the defence of urban citadels was almost invariably allocated to such troops. They similarly garrisoned castles, though in times of peace these sometimes seem to have contained little more than a token force. Professional garrisons included infantry and cavalry, as well as technical troops and non-combatant support personnel where required. In eleventh-century Fatimid-ruled Syria, garrisons which included several hundred cavalry appear to have been concentrated in a small number of fortified places a few days' march apart.[1301] Perhaps there were also some smaller outposts in between, held by infantry and local auxiliaries.

In 1047, according to Nasir-i Khusrau, the important city of Tripoli in Lebanon always had a Fatimid garrison; their pay coming from the taxes demanded from ships using the port.[1302] The professionals of the garrison which defended Jerusalem so vigorously against the First Crusade in 1099 were from, or included troops from, the élite *'askar* of the Fatimid *wazir* al-Afdal.[1303] Ten years later the citadel of Seljuk-ruled Mosul in northern Iraq reportedly had a garrison of 1,500 soldiers.[1304] In 1285 that of the Mamluk-held castle and fortified hilltop town of Marqab on the Syrian coast included 1,000 cavalry under 150 *amirs* or officers, plus numerous auxiliaries.[1305] Marqab was, of course, a very important outpost close to the remaining Crusader enclaves and was responsible for the defence of a vulnerable stretch of coastline. Furthermore, it was in a somewhat isolated position, separated by mountains from the main Mamluk military centres of Damascus and Aleppo.

Other garrisons were considerably smaller. According to the *Devise des Chemins de Babiloine*, a Hospitaller intelligence report written around the time of the fall of Acre to the Mamluks, the garrison in the great Egyptian port city of Alexandria only consisted of 90 cavalry and about 100 bedouin Arab auxiliaries. If Alexandria was seriously threatened, however, the main Mamluk army was based not far away in Cairo.

A few centuries earlier in al-Andalus the great castle of Gormaz would seem, on the basis of archaeological research, to have had a quite small permanent garrison. On the other hand it contained facilities for a large army including many horses, presumably because Gormaz served as a fortified military base for offensive and defensive operations.[1306] The large number of horses which could be housed and fed in Gormaz were not all necessarily cavalry mounts. They may have included the many pack animals which were habitually used by medieval Islamic armies. In this context it is worth noting that the defenders of Damascus and the surrounding Ghuta area were recorded as using donkeys to carry loads of stones for men armed with slings in the tenth and eleventh centuries. In all probability they carried other weapons and supplies as well.[1307]

Scattered information can be pieced together to get some idea of how walls and towers were manned when a fortified place came under attack. Damascus in the tenth and eleventh centuries could be taken as typical. Here the alarm or *nafir* was sounded when an assault occurred, after which militiamen and garrison soldiers took up their positions armed with slings and bows.[1308] Here it is abundantly clear that archers were of paramount importance, being drawn from both professional soldiers and local *ahdath* militias. In particular, archers were stationed 'above the gates' of Damascus to defend their approaches.[1309] In tenth-century Tarsus, to the north in Cilicia, infantry were issued with the hand-held *qaws al-rijl* or crossbows for the defence of walls and towers.[1310] Crossbows and handbows were similarly used to defend the walls of Tyre against a Crusader assault in 1124.[1311] Less than a generation later defenders using *jarkh* crossbows shooting *nishab* arrows in defence of a castle in the region of Diyar Bakr injured so many of Imad al-Din Zanki's troops. As a result, when the castle eventually surrendered, Zanki had their thumbs cut off so that they could never again shoot crossbows.[1312] This action itself indicates that on this occasion the *jarkh* was almost certainly a portable crossbow in which the archer squeezed the trigger upwards against the stock, as with normal European crossbows of this and later centuries.

During the defeat of the Second Crusade outside Damascus, the Crusaders suffered particularly heavily from *jarkh* shooting *nabl* and *saham* types of arrows from the walls of the city.[1313] A century earlier Islamic and Christian sources confirm that the Islamic troops of Ibn Hud, the ruler of Saragossa defending Barbastro in 1046, included crossbowmen. A later account of the same event specified the presence of 600 *rumat 'aqqara* crossbowmen.[1314]

Manjaniq mangonels were similarly used in defence of fortified places. This had been standard practice since early Islamic times and was still the case in tenth- and eleventh-century Damascus.[1315] During a civil war in Aleppo in 1024 both sides used *manjaniqs* and *'arradas*, the latter serving as long-range antipersonnel weapons from the summit of the still virtually unfortified citadel against people ransacking houses in the city below.[1316] Later in the same century, when the Seljuk Great Sultan Malik Shah besieged Aleppo, his horse was killed beneath him by a *manjaniq* stone shot from the city. This happened when the Turkish ruler went forward to inspect the construction of protective screens against the defenders' arrows, and surely indicates considerable skill amongst the defenders of Aleppo.[1317]

Early twelfth-century Saragossa in northern al-Andalus was reportedly defended by 20 *manjaniqs*,[1318] and almost a century and a half later Sultan Baybars I of Egypt ensured that there were plenty of *manjaniqs* in Alexandria to defend the city and its port against a feared Crusader naval assault.[1319] Recent archaeological excavation in the citadel of Hims in Syria uncovered another cache of *manjaniq* balls, but what made this particular find unusual was that the missiles were neatly arranged, apparently just as a *manjaniq* crew would have left them ready for use.[1320]

Most other siege machines were similarly used in both defence and attack. Among the simplest devices were the grain-sacks stuffed with straw and mats woven from reeds that the Fatimid defenders of Jerusalem erected to protect their own artillery from the First Crusade's mangonels.[1321] In his early thirteenth-century *Kitab al-Mukhtar*, Zayn al-Din Jawbari al-Dimashqi claimed to include sections from a lost work by or about the pre-Islamic Sassanian Iranians. The eighth section of his work dealt with weapons and contained a discussion of the *manjaniq* and how it should be used in defensive siege warfare. There is no evidence that the Sassanians knew about the beamsling *manjaniq* until the final decades of their empire and the text itself could be interpreted as referring to any form of missile-shooting siege machine. It is nevertheless interesting because it sheds light on techniques of defensive counter-bombardment:

> If the besiegers have a *mirma* [throwing machine] or a wooden tower, the defenders construct a machine against this. It consists of two long timbers, on top of which a *saqala* [platform] is carried with a *darabzin* [balustrade, railing] surrounding it. With ropes, rollers, rings and a *lawlab* [windlass] this scaffolding can be elevated and be let down along a second other beam to the [desired] height. This can reach beyond the moat [to attack the enemy machine or tower]. Also archers, fire projectors and others can use the platform or even a moveable platform on the beam to attack the enemy.[1322]

Comparable devices were mentioned in Byzantine military texts and were repeated in later medieval Western Europe. Something rather less complicated but still requiring a sound knowledge of ropes and timber was used by the defenders of Tyre against the Crusaders in 1111–12. Not surprisingly, it was a sailor or Fatimid naval officer who was credited with inventing this machine for dropping things onto the Crusaders' wooden siege-tower:

> A long beam of unseasoned timber was set up on the wall in front of the tower. On top of it, forming a T-shaped cross, another beam 40 cubits [about 20 m] long swung on pulleys worked by a winch in the manner of a ship's mast, directed by whoever was operating the machine. At one end of the pivoting beam was an iron spar and at the other end ropes running on pulleys by means of which the operators could hoist buckets of dung and refuse and empty them over the Franks in the tower … Then the sailor had grape-panniers and baskets filled with oil, pitch, wood shavings, resin and

cane-bark, set on fire and hoisted up in the manner described to the level of the Frankish tower.[1323]

With this the defenders of Tyre burned the Crusaders' assault tower.

Previously the same naval officer had devised a method of dealing with the rams which the Crusaders had mounted inside their assault towers. It consisted of iron *kulalib* hooks, lowered over the city wall to catch and deflect the rams.[1324] Another method of combating a besieger's assault tower was to build a counter-tower inside the walls, since the primary purpose of all such towers was to achieve a height advantage over the enemy. There are many references to this practice in medieval Islamic warfare, especially in the twelfth century and perhaps most notably during a siege of Damietta in Egypt in 1169.[1325]

The success of sorties and stratagems by the defenders must often have depended upon the nature of the immediate surroundings. Those located in a high position may have had the advantage of inaccessibility, but sorties might have been correspondingly difficult or dangerous since surprise may have been difficult to achieve and the men involved still had to get back safely. In contrast a city like Damascus was low-lying and accessible, but was also largely surrounded by dense cultivation, orchards and villages. The militia defenders of tenth- and eleventh-century Damascus are, for example, known to have used the larger country houses as strongpoints from which to harass invaders.[1326] Groves of huge walnut trees were similarly used to ambush besiegers. Furthermore this dense terrain came almost up to the city walls.[1327] The garrison and probably also local militias similarly used positions in the cultivated Ghuta from which to attack Crusader foragers and stragglers during the disastrous Second Crusade.[1328] Such men would, of course, have had the advantage of knowing the countryside much better than did the Western European invaders.

An entirely unrelated stratagem was employed by the governor of Aleppo when besieged by Saladin. He sent his men out of a postern gate at night carrying lighted torches. The men then extinguished these torches, returned inside the wall in darkness then relit their torches to repeat the manoeuvre, thus giving the illusion of a larger garrison.[1329]

One of the simplest and most ancient methods of forcing a fortified town or city to surrender was the gradual destruction of its economic surroundings. Even a tribal army without a proper siege train could do this. Furthermore, such tactics resulted in minimal casualties to the attackers and left the valuable defences intact. The Kilabi bedouin Arab tribal army in northern Syria could, for example, intimidate a city into submission by threatening to pasture the tribe's flocks in surrounding fields and to chop down the orchards.[1330] On the other hand it was probably a desire to avoid casualties and to win a city intact which led Imad al-Din Zangi to try to make Amida (Diyar Bakr) surrender by cutting down its orchards.[1331] The only real drawback was the length of time such an approach took. On at least one occasion around 1119, the Artuqid ruler Il-Ghazi found he could not retain his Arab and Turcoman auxiliaries because they were satisfied with their loot and wanted to go home.

When a full-scale siege was imposed, the commander of the attacking force tended to follow a generally agreed sequence of actions. These were set out in al-Harthami's military manual written in the early ninth century, as it survives in considerably later texts from the Mamluk Sultanate. For a start, a commander should have the following materials and men available: scaling ropes, siege ladders, grappling irons or hooks, mangonels, archers, slingers, *naft* incendiary throwers, skilled craftsmen and workers to build the siege machines. The attack should begin with the smallest engines and weapons, then gradually build up to bigger weapons so as to undermine the defenders' morale. Meanwhile the commander should post cavalry about the distance of an arrow shot facing the enemy's gates, to keep watch in case of sorties. Furthermore, the besiegers should excavate trenches and erect field fortifications because they themselves were vulnerable to counter-attack.[1332]

Nur al-Din's army in mid- to later twelfth-century Syria followed essentially this procedure, starting with the erection of palisades then starting the excavation of mines, followed by the construction of siege towers and other such devices.[1333]

Even the Arab tribal armies of tenth- and eleventh-century Syria knew how to use the latest siege technology,[1334] yet it does not seem to have been usual to keep anything other than the most complicated or metal parts of larger machines in store. Consequently the need to build siege weaponry could make surprise attack difficult. This was the case when the army of the early twelfth-century Seljuk Turkish commander Bursuq built siege machines at Ma'arat for his forthcoming assault on Crusader-held Zardana. News of these preparations reached Prince Roger at Antioch who started making his own preparations which resulted in Bursuq's defeat.[1335]

The weather could be another problem, especially in a summer campaign. During Saladin's desultory siege of Mosul in 1184 his men were permitted not to wear their armour because it was so hot, but as a consequence the siege could not be pressed hard.[1336] Meanwhile there was a substantial increase in the number of mangonels used in major sieges, surely reflecting their increasing effectiveness. During the early Crusader period from three to ten such machines seem to have been normal, but by the end of the thirteenth century this had risen to 20 and eventually to 70.[1337] The moral as well as the physical impact must have been tremendous.

The psychological aspects of medieval siege warfare seem to have been better understood in the Islamic world than anywhere else outside China. Fakhr al-Din Mubarakshah, writing for an Islamic ruler in early thirteenth-century northern

India, noted the moral effect of the constant noise of mangonels and other siege machines.[1338] He also pointed to the usefulness of sowing rumours and false information within an enemy fortress.[1339]

The most costly method of taking a fortified place was by direct assault, at least in terms of blood spilled. Even this, however, was done in as organized and intimidating a manner as possible. After bombardment and mining, Il-Ghazi attacked Crusader-occupied Atharib in 1119: 'with an assault of armed men attacking in three ranks, shooting in arrows and with a huge number of javelins'.[1340] However, it seems that here the defences had already been weakened and as a result the garrison surrendered before the attacking troops came into contact. Something similar happened when Shams al-Muluk attacked Crusader-held Banyas. Here the morale of the garrison collapsed when the Islamic soldiers approached their walls with *al-daraq al-jafatiyat* 'vaulted shields' or mantlets. They were accompanied by Khurasani troops and wall breakers, as well as Turkish cavalry who dismounted in a body and discharged a hail of arrows at the defenders on the wall.[1341]

The theory behind such assault tactics was described by al-Harawi in his manual for Saladin. He pointed out that assault parties must always be commanded by the best available officers. The men themselves should be heavily armoured and have 'all necessary assault equipment' which would include *naft* incendiary grenades, the elements needed to erect palisades, tools to demolish walls, battering rams and material for *zahafat* which might be translated as protective roofs or mobile towers. As soon as the wall was breached, these heavily armoured men should move forward to occupy the breach. At that point they should offer enemy *aman* which was an opportunity to surrender on terms. *Aman* would, in fact, already have been offered at the start of the siege.[1342]

Saladin's siege of the Crusader-held castle of Burzay has been taken as an example of how he and his commanders adopted this approach.[1343] Nor was it the only example. In a much more substantial siege of the city of Diyar Bakr in 1183, Saladin's army used mangonels to clear the defenders, and in particular the archers from the walls; his infantry then stormed the outer wall with scaling ladders. Once this was taken, Saladin's mangonels and miners turned their attention to the much stronger inner wall.[1344]

Four years earlier in 1179, Saladin had captured the incomplete Templar castle at Bayt al-Ahzan (Vadum Iacob). This had to be taken as quickly as possible because the King of Jerusalem's relief army was approaching rapidly. In the event the fortifications fell to assault. This was led by the 'common people' or non-professional volunteers who stormed up a slope that was supposedly so steep that they had to cut footholds with axes. When the place fell, the 'apostates', those who had been Muslim but who had converted to Christianity, were slaughtered.

This would have included the turcopoles, while the same fate befell the garrison's crossbowmen.

The dead, including men and animals, were then reportedly thrown into a well and covered with earth and lime. Many bodies of men and animals, including individual skeletons showing appalling blade injuries, have recently been found by archaeologists, but not as yet the well mentioned by the chronicler.[1345] Here it is perhaps worth noting Fakhr al-Din Mubarakshah's advice that a final assault should be launched before or at dawn.[1346] There are plenty of examples of this being done; perhaps the most famous being the Ottoman Turkish conquest of Constantinople in 1453.

A full-scale assault was not always necessary, and even when it was, the fortification and its garrison would normally be softened up beforehand. Here archers with various forms of weapon played a major role. The quantity of matériel used could also be enormous. When the Seljuk Great Sultan Alp Arslan attacked Aleppo in 1070, he had 80,000 heavy 'hardwood' arrows distributed to his men so that they could shoot over the city walls to bombard residential areas inside.[1347] According to the *Cronica Adefonsi Imperatoris*, large or heavy arrows described as 'spears' by those on the receiving end were shot by the Murabitun besieging Coimbra in Portugal in 1117. They were probably the large form of bolts shot by perhaps pedestal or frame-mounted crossbows.[1348] Such missiles were dramatic enough to appear in French *chansons de geste* accounts of warfare against Islamic armies; several references to such Moorish *bozon* or *bouzon* appearing in Aimeri de Narbonne's late twelfth-century *Siège de Barbastre*.[1349]

The form of crossbow most commonly used in siege warfare in North Africa and al-Andalus was the *qaws 'aqqara* which, it was said, was 'used by attackers to keep defenders away from loopholes'.[1350] The range of such Islamic weapons is not known, but in eleventh century China a large crossbow, spanned by a winch and used in siege warfare, is said to have achieved a range of just over 1 km.[1351] This is well within the bounds of possibility for the larger forms of weapon and, given the accounts of castles and their known location, seems to have been seen in the Islamic world as well as China.

Nevertheless, the great bulk of archery bombardment relied upon individual archers who had to get much closer to their target. Not surprisingly they protected themselves with large shields, mantlets, palisades and armour. In fact Saladin's archers attacking Jerusalem in 1187 were, according to the anonymous author of the *Libellus*: 'Well armoured down to their heels.'[1352] Such men carried portable weapons, either handheld bows or crossbows. During the thirteenth century the bows often seem to have used *majra* arrow-guides to shoot short darts, unless a remarkable number of the men were actually issued with crossbows. A little-known account of the final siege of Acre in 1291 in the Scottish *Chronicle of Lanercost* may have been based on a verbal account by Othon de Grandson who visited Scotland after surviving the fall of Acre. This specifically mentions the huge numbers of 'locusts', short arrows or darts shot by the Mamluks.[1353]

Unlike their Crusader and Spanish foes, the Islamic armies of the twelfth and thirteenth centuries made surprisingly little use of wooden siege towers, mobile or static. This was almost certainly because of the effectiveness of incendiary weapons within the Islamic world, plus, perhaps, a shortage of timber for what was already regarded as an old-fashioned idea. None the less, wooden *burj* towers were mentioned in theoretical manuals where it was made clear that their primary purpose was to provide the attacking force's archers and light siege engines with a height advantage over the defenders. One was used in precisely this manner during the Seljuk Turkish siege of the Armenian city of Ani in 1064.[1354]

Wooden towers rarely seem to have been considered as a means of scaling a wall.[1355] A tower might also be erected simply as an observation post to assess the progress of a siege, especially in flat terrain. This practice was certainly seen in North Africa and al-Andalus where the tower was known as a *marqaba, daydaban* or *shira'*.[1356] Artificial ramps and platforms were probably more significant. One of the most dramatic examples was during the Seljuk Turkish siege of the Armenian city of Ani in 1064. Here the Turks built platforms of earth-filled sacks on which they mounted siege machines shooting *naft* incendiaries. They were furthermore manned by archers shooting short darts from *husban* arrowguides.[1357]

The real effectiveness of artillery bombardment is still difficult to assess. The written sources tend to exaggerate. The bombardment often went hand-in-hand with mining, and the damage was almost invariably repaired once the siege was over. In the eleventh and early twelfth centuries the primary purpose of the still quite small, man-powered stone-throwing mangonels was to drive defenders from exposed positions on the summits of walls and towers. These weapons might also be capable of damaging wall-head defences, machicolations and other relatively weak structures. They are unlikely to have been able to bring down any but the weakest of walls.

A particularly detailed description of such a bombardment concerned Il-Ghazi's campaign of 1119. That year his army attacked the walls of Atharib where: 'In addition three of four times every day they deprived the towers of their defences and destroyed the defenders with savage blows by way of petraries and the apparatus of various engines'.[1358] Shortly afterwards Il-Ghazi attacked Zardana with the same machines he had used against Atharib. This time they seem to have been used by night as well as by day.[1359] The *Danishmandname* Turkish epic poem by 'Arif 'Ali of Toqat clearly describes the main threat posed by the stones shot from the *manciliq* mangonels as being against people rather than structures. Even so the Christian defenders of Qarqariya launched a sortie in an attempt to burn them.[1360]

Only with the further development and large-scale adoption of counterweight *trebuchets* could such machines significantly damage the main structure of a seriously fortified wall. During the first half of the thirteenth century these new machines, especially it seems the *manjaniq al-maghribi*, could smash at the older styles of city wall. Sultan al-Kamil's sieges of Harran and Edessa in 1236 provide dramatic examples, according to Ibn al-Muqaffa':

> The Sultan returned to Harran, and took up position against its fortress, and he besieged it for some days, and it resisted, and he set up a *manjaniq al-maghribi*, and he took it by the sword ... And he went to Edessa, and he took up position against its fortress, and it was more fortified and more impregnable than the fortress of Harran, but it did not withstand the *manjaniq al-maghribi*, for it demolished its curtain wall the day it was set up against it, and it was also taken by the sword.[1361]

Al-Kamil apparently had one *manjaniq al-maghribi* on these occasions. The number brought by the Mamluk Sultanate against Crusader-held Acre in 1291 was considerably greater. They took two days to erect and may have been grouped into batteries, or perhaps the bombardment focused upon vulnerable or weak parts of the defences. The latter was clearly the case when the last Zirid ruler of the *ta'ifa* kingdom of Granada in al-Andalus besieged Christian-held Aledo in the late eleventh century. Here the Muslims built outworks opposite what they assessed as vulnerable stretches of the defences. They then erected mangonels and other siege machines, but nevertheless their attack failed.[1362]

During a successful siege of the huge Hospitaller castle of Crac des Chevaliers in 1271, the Mamluks assembled mangonels in a battery for use against ramparts while their miners undermined a tower.[1363] Given the very limited space available where mangonels could be grouped, the sources may be correct in mentioning one such battery. It also seems unlikely that miners would have been working directly underneath the section of wall that the *manjaniqs* bombarded, as the missiles as well as debris would have fallen just there.

The most effective way of seriously damaging or bringing down a wall remained mining, though of course circumstances did not always allow effective excavation, especially in some coastal locations in Palestine and Egypt where the water-table reached or almost reached the foundations. Elsewhere the wall might not only be built directly on hard rock, but that rock might be in the form of a cliff too high for miners to reach. The most vulnerable walls included those built on or above friable rock beneath a shallow depth of earth. This may have been the case at Atharib which Il-Ghazi's army attacked in 1119. Here, according to a Crusader chronicler: 'he sent men from different sides to dig out a cave made underground, and he prepared fuses by grafting together dry pieces of wood so that when they reached the towers and put in that same kindling they would collapse, being supported by posts'.[1364]

The sources, both Islamic and Christian, strongly suggest that mining was more often directed against towers than against section of curtain wall, though the reasons for this are unclear. Perhaps angles were more prone to fall away when cracked than were sections of wall which might continue to be supported by the undamaged wall on either side. Here it is important to restate the fact that medieval siege mines were normally excavated just beneath the foundations rather than attacking the stone foundations themselves or plunging deeper below them. The whole point of the exercise was to cause such foundations to collapse and thus crack the wall above.

When seeking to damage a wall directly, a ram was intended to do much the same as large mangonel stones; namely to fracture the masonry or brick by repeated horizontal blows on the same point. The ram or *kabsh* was not only known in theory but was used, albeit not very often, in practice.[1365] The tactical weakness of this technique was that the ram and the men operating it had to be protected. This involved the erection of various forms of sturdy shed or angled roof. But such structures would be largely of wood, and thus vulnerable to the very advanced incendiary weaponry available in the Islamic world. They could themselves be protected with layers of earth or sacks of earth or wet animal hides against both fire and heavy objects dropped from above. Once large counterweight *manjaniqs* became available, vulnerable rams in their hardly less vulnerable 'sheds' fell from favour.

Even so, the associated technology remained available for use where circumstances were suitable. Amongst the most common protective roof was the *dabbaba* or 'rat'.[1366] Another was the *sannura* or 'cat' which may have incorporated a *kabsh* ram within its basic structure.[1367] Another perhaps more advanced form was the *zahhafa* which, being described as similar to a *dabbaba*, was used by the Mamluk army under Sultan Baybars I against Crusader-held Caesarea. This was, however, one of the last occasions when such a device was recorded.[1368]

A more original method of shielding sappers and men moving up into their assault positions was employed during the final Mamluk siege of Acre in 1291. It was also described, with evident pride, by the man responsible in his account of the fall of this last Crusader outpost. Baybars al-Mansuri was a *mamluk* who commanded a small but seemingly specialist contingent from Karak in what is now southern Jordan.

The outer wall of the King's Tower, a key element in the fortifications of Acre, had already been brought down but the collapsed masonry was too jumbled for the Muslims to make an assault. So, the night after it had fallen, Baybars al-Mansuri had his men make a long felt screen and then:

Between two posts opposite the dilapidated tower I placed a pulley rigged with ropes similar to a ship's. There I hoisted the felt into place like a dam. This was done under the wing of night, unknown to the people of Acre who, when they rose in the morning and saw the screen, shot *manjaniqs* and arrows against it. These had no effect and behind the screen Baybars' men made a path along which the Sultan's army subsequently stormed the damaged tower.[1369]

The reference to a ship's rigging recalls the role of a Fatimid naval officer in defence of Tyre over a century and a half earlier.

The Templar of Tyre saw the Mamluks' final preparations for their assault on Acre from the other side:

> The Saracens made small sacks of hemp cloth and filled them with sand. Every man carried one of these sacks on the neck of his horse and tossed it to the Saracens who were there behind the *buches* [screens] at that point. Then when night fell, they took the sacks and spread them across the tops of the stones and smoothed them out like a road.[1370]

A more dramatic method of undermining the walls of an enemy-held city was to direct a river against its foundations. This was only possible in specific circumstances and at suitable times of year, but the Muwahhidun managed to do it on one occasion in the twelfth century; first damming a river to build up a head of water, then releasing it all at once.[1371]

Organizing the besiegers' camp was not only a matter of providing it with field fortifications against sorties or a relief army. It had to be efficient, healthy and help maintain the army's morale. If a siege was prolonged, the tents might have to be replaced by more permanent structures. This happened when Aleppo was besieged by Manju Takin late in the tenth century; resulting in the building of houses, baths and markets to maintain a siege that lasted 13 months, the winter being the most difficult time.[1372]

Something similar happened in Saladin's huge camp while he besieged the besiegers of Acre; the latter town being held by Saladin's garrison. This camp was located a few kilometres inland from the actual siege-lines and was visited by 'Abd al-Latif Baghdadi who later wrote an account of what he saw. There were about 7,000 assorted shops or workshops, including 140 farriers' shops, all under the supervision of their own *shurta* (police) chiefs. When the soldiers moved to clean ground after the first site got dirty and unhealthy, the merchants paid the soldiers to move their goods. There was also a large market for cloth and weapons, old and new.

A European visitor would probably have been astonished by the more than 1,000 public *hamams* or baths, most of which were managed by Maghribis (North Africans). Apparently two or three Maghribis would join together to dig a pit 2 cubits (about 1 m) deep which they then filled with water. Then with the resulting mud they made a basin and a surrounding wall which they covered with planks and matting. Local wood was cut as fuel to heat the water where tired men could wash and bathe for a *dirham* or so.[1373]

Away in Islamic northern India, the early thirteenth century military writer Fakhr al-Din Mubarakshah went into great detail about the need for many different sorts of support personnel in such military camps. They included those who provided pleasant cooling drinks for the working men and the fighters, and those who washed the dead and prepared them for proper burial. Fakhr al-Din also noted the importance of providing the troops with good, interesting, spiced food.[1374]

Even before a siege began, the attacking army had to get itself and its cumbersome equipment to the target. This could sometimes be extremely difficult, especially in mountainous regions, and made huge demands upon the support personnel as well as the fighting troops. Small wonder that the act of establishing an effective siege was sometimes seen as being as much of a triumph as the siege itself. Clearly Sultan Baybars I felt this way when writing to Prince Bohemond VI about his capture of the Crusader-held castle of Akkar in northern Lebanon, as quoted by Ibn al-Furat: 'How we transported the mangonels there through mountains where the birds think it too difficult to nest; how patiently we hauled them, troubled by mud and struggling against rain.'[1375]

A besieging army would need specialized troops in its ranks, some of whom formed a technological élite. They might be quite numerous, especially if a commander knew that his campaign would result in a major siege. Otherwise they would have to be summoned when needed, which seems to have been the case after Saladin retook the town of Tartus but failed to take its citadel. He therefore had a large force of siege specialists sent from Aleppo, which had long been famous for miners and others with useful skills.[1376] A generation earlier, the infantry in Nur al-Din's Syrian army not only included archers, crossbowmen and spearmen but also *hajjarun* 'stone men' who took stones from enemy fortifications and may also have served the siege weapons, *naqqabun* sappers and miners. These various specialists were drawn from Aleppo in Syria, Armenia in Anatolia and Khurasan in eastern Iran.[1377] Ayyubid and Mamluk sources continue to refer to *naqqabun, hajjarun* and *najjarun* carpenters; the latter also being employed in mining operations where they strengthened the tunnels and erected pit-props. The skilled act of setting up and lighting fires at the end of such mining tunnels was known as *'allaqa*.[1378]

PYROTECHNICS AND CHEMICAL WARFARE

In the seventh century, during the first phase of the confrontation between the Byzantine Empire and the rising power of the Islamic Caliphate, it is generally accepted that the Byzantines enjoyed a clear advantage in terms of incendiary weapons. The most obvious example was, of course, Greek Fire. However, the basic knowledge behind this terrifying substance seems to have come from cities which were conqured by Arab-Islamic forces during the first or second waves of Islamic expansion, so it would seem highly likely that the chemical skills which underpinned Greek Fire and other comparable weapons was almost immediately available to the Caliphate.

Close study of the following centuries shows that Islamic forces, both on land and at sea, were employing the same chemical-based weapons as their Byzantine foes within at least two centuries. Furthermore, it seems that by the tenth century the Fatimids, and probably some other Islamic states as well, were in advance of Byzantium in this field.[1379] This would certainly not have been surprising, given the extraordinary flourishing of science and techology within the Islamic world around this time.

Perhaps even more significant was the fact that the Islamic world had easy access to the mineral oil which was needed for the large-scale utilization of the latest forms of incendiary weapons. These were not only in places like northern Iraq, where oil actually oozed on to the surface of the earth, but close to the shores of the Dead Sea. Bitumen extracted here was, in fact, a valuable export during the tenth and eleventh centuries.[1380] Small wonder that the armies of dynasties which ruled Egypt and dominated Palestine were often known for their skill with incendiary weapons. Even in the second half of the thirteenth century, when the whole nature of such warfare was changing with the development of what became gunpowder, many of Sultan Baybars I's own most élite *mamluk* soldiers are said to have learned 'the fire game'.[1381] Although this obscure game or training exercise was often on horseback, it was almost certainly done as a means of developing the men's skills and perhaps getting their horses used to such substances.

All save the most specialized of medieval texts tended to be somewhat cavalier with their use of terminology, and this is just as true of words relating to different forms or aspects of fire-weapons. In the Arabic texts, for example, *nar* and *naft* were sometimes not distinguished. Strictly speaking *nar* simply meant fire whereas *naft* originally meant oil or chemical based incendiary substances or a variety of such substances. Later, during the transition from what might loosely be regarded as petroleum-oil based incendiaries to primitive forms of gunpowder, the term *naft* continued to be used for a while, adding further confusion to the issue.

Incendiary weapons could be quite simple; certainly simpler than the Greek Fire syphons used by both the Byzantine Empire and some of its Islamic foes which have so caught the imagination of historians and film-makers. In fact, simpler weapons were almost certainly more reliable if marginally less terrifying.

For example, Daylami infantry from northern Iran threw javelins with incendiary materials attached against wooden field fortifications in the tenth century. Fire troops were also sent against the fortified town of 'Azaz in north Syria (now just over the border in Turkey) by the Seljuk Turkish commander Taj al-Dawla Tutush in 1079.[1382] The heads of large crossbow bolts were described as having been heated before being shot at Crusader mangonels in order to set them on fire during the Third Crusade's siege of Acre. Quite how this was done without setting fire either to the crossbow bolts or the weapon which shot them is unexplained.[1383]

It was clearly common to put *naft* into containers which could be thrown or dropped.[1384] These ranged from small grenades called *karaz* made of glass or clay, to the larger *qidr* to be thrown from a siege machine.[1385] The grenades would seem to have been very common. A large number of thick-walled and often slightly decorated medieval earthenware containers have been found in many parts of the Islamic world, and in a small number of cases beyond its borders. These are of a suitable size to be thrown by hand, but for several generations historians have been unable to agree about their function.[1386] The idea that they were incendiary grenades was strenuously disputed by those who argued in favour of containers for mercury or other valuable substances. More recently, however, chemical analysis of residual material inside some of these containers shows that many had been used as incendiary weapons.

Some of the earliest were found in pre-Islamic sites in Transoxania, including Afrasiab-Samarkand. Others date from the entire Islamic period down to the fifteenth century, but not later. By then, of course, gunpowder fire-arms had been introduced. The containers were often found at the base of fortified walls and some were decorated with the words *Fatch-Fatch*, 'War-War'.[1387] On balance the evidence now points to the greater number, if not all, having been made as grenades, being the *qarura* or 'pots of *naft*' often mentioned in Islamic siege warfare.[1388] Furthermore, the very thick walls of many could have caused an almost explosive fire effect once other chemicals had been added to simple Greek Fire *naft* in the later medieval period.

There appears to have been a notable increase in the use of such *naft* during the early Crusader period, perhaps because the Western European invaders used so much timber on their siege technology and perhaps, at first, in their fortifications. The evidence also shows that in siege warfare *naft* was more effective against towns than against castles, presumably because the domestic buildings of the former contained more timber and were thus more vulnerable to fire.[1389] Furthermore, *naft* was usually used in containers to be thrown, either by hand, by *manjaniq* mangonels or other such missile weapons.

Here al-Tarsusi mentioned that it was necessary to pad the containers of *naft* if they were to be thrown from a *manjaniq*,[1390] otherwise they might break and thus endanger the machine and its crew. *Naft* could similarly be used as an anti-personnel or at least a demoralizing weapon in siege warfare. Usama Ibn Munqidh recalled how a Turkish soldier attacked the tower of a castle with a bottle of *naft*, terrifying the defenders, after which the Turk's comrades followed him into the attack.[1391] The Crusader and chronicler De Joinville noted that the Muslims shot what he called Greek Fire from an *arbalestre à tour* or large form of crossbow during the struggle for Damietta in 1250.[1392] Arabic sources confirm this, stating that the *jarkh* large crossbow spanned by a windlass was used in late thirteenth-century Yemen to shoot arrows or *naft*.[1393] In the twelfth century al-Tarsusi even described a special container which enabled 'eggs' filled with the *naft* to be shot from an ordinary *qaws al-rijl* portable crossbow.[1394]

Al-Tarsusi's contribution may once again have remained in the realm of experimentation, but there was no denying the significance of *naft* itself. During the Crusader siege of Acre from 1189 to 1191 it was so important that swimmers took it into the city, around the flanks of the besieging Crusader army.[1395] The 'Abbasid Caliph in Baghdad, though politically hostile to Saladin, nevertheless sent him 'a body of experts, skilled in throwing *naft*, as well as two loads of that inflammable substance' during the prolonged siege of Acre.[1396] During the early Mamluk period, in the second half of the thirteenth century and into the fourteenth, *naft* was so precious, and potentially so dangerous in the wrong hands, that *naft* equipment was only stored in 'royal arsenals'.[1397] By then, however, the use of traditional petroleum-based *naft* had declined, presumably because the Crusaders had learned what Middle Eastern people long knew; namely to keep exposed wood to a minimum both in fortifications and in siege weaponry.

Efforts to use *naft* in open battle went back many centuries in Islamic history, though rarely with much success. The idea was noted by the Crusaders and found its way back to France where it was included in at least one late twelfth-century *chanson de geste*, *Les Chétifs*, where the Saracens supposedly throw Greek Fire in open battle.[1398] The only time that the Mamluk army really used *naft* in this manner on a large scale was another failure. It was against invading Mongols in 1299, at the battle of Wadi al-Khazindar, where 500 *naft* throwers led the Mamluk force. However, Mongols refused to come into range and either the *naft* or its fuses burned out before it could be used.[1399]

While *naft* virtually disappeared on land, it remained a vital weapon in naval warfare where ships proved to be suitable targets.[1400] The same was the case in river warfare. Sometimes the two came together, as they did during the initial fighting around Mansoura in the Nile Delta in 1249. As a result *naft* was, most unusually by this date, used in open battle against wooden bridges over irrigation canals, between boats fighting in the river and canals, and against field fortifications. Amongst the most dramatic weapons on this occasion were *qidr 'iraqi*, 'Iraqi pots' thrown by *manjaniqs*. These exploded when they struck and may have had very early forms of incendiary rather than exposive gunpowder inside them.[1401] Or perhaps the containers simply burst on impact.

The idea of projecting Greek Fire or *naft* through a large syringe, to create a medieval form of flame-thrower, was certainly not limited to the Byzantine Empire. Such a copper tube and syringe was called a *naffata*, *zarraqa* or *mukhula* in Arabic,[1402] though there is some doubt about the latter term.[1403] The best description of a *zarraqat al-naft* appears in an Arabic poem quoted by al-Tanukhi in the later tenth century:[1404]

> It is a yellow tube, in the mouth of which is a dribble of the same colour.
> When it comes to throw, it competes with the wind and flies as quickly.
> It envelopes one, when it blows,
> In a cloak of darkness which grows like a protecting fortress.
> It has a handle like a pigtail from the back of a man's head.
> When one pulls this towards oneself,
> It releases its wind which striked like a lance.

A more prosaic description of the *zarraqa* or *naffata* noted that it had a small box of *naft* attached to the pump by pipes in order to form a compact unit. The ignition element was called a *warda* or 'rose' fixed to the tip of the nozzle which was lit when ready to be used. The resulting *shihab* or jet of fire was as long as one spear; perhaps 3 or 4 m but surely no more. The engineer and scientist al-Jazari, working in twelfth-century Amida (Diyar Bakr), added further details when he wrote that the copper-sheathed pistons used for raising water in one of his advanced machines were similar to those used in the syphons which discharged *naft*. According to al-Jazari, each piston had a suction pipe and a delivery pipe, each with a non-return clack valve,[1405] without which the weapon would, of course, have exploded.

During the siege of Acre by the Third Crusade, the son of a Damascus coppersmith offered to help destroy the Crusaders' siege machines. He was not one of the professional *naft* soldiers, and his presumption offended the latter. Perhaps he was a mere 'volunteer'. This unnamed but clearly brilliant craftsman was eventually allowed to try, and the containers of *naft* which he made, and which were apparently thrown by one of the garrison's existing mangonels, were a success.[1406] This technology was known right across the medieval Islamic world and a hand-pump to project *naft* was mentioned in late tenth- or early eleventh-century al-Andalus, though on this occasion it was used in naval warfare.[1407] Such Islamic weapons were again mentioned in the French epic poem, *Les Chétifs*, where the Saracens use '*cofinaius d'arrain fu griois alumer*'.[1408]

Gunpowder, as is well known, was first developed in China. The key element which distinguished it from previous incendiary mixtures was saltpetre, potassium nitrate. Nevertheless, in a military context gunpowder was initially used as an incendiary rather than an explosive. This technology reached the Islamic Middle East remarkably soon after it had appeared in China. In fact some of the ceramic grenades used to burn down the barracks-suburb of Fustat in Cairo in 1168 have been found to contain traces of saltpetre. This does not mean that these grenades were explosive; merely that there is strong evidence that the most powerful incendiary mixtures already included saltpetre.[1409]

The close technological link between Egypt, the Persian Gulf and China had already been shown by an adoption of the hinged stern rudder on some ships, this being another Chinese invention, as well as other aspects of technology. Written sources similarly confirm that saltpetre was used in Iran before 1230, prior to the Mongol invasion, but most names or terms associated with its technology again indicate a Chinese origin or a strong Chinese influence.[1410] The first indisputable Arabic mention of saltpetre was in a text by al-Baytar dating from the first half of the thirteenth century. He was from al-Andalus but had spent many years in Egypt, and he again referred to saltpetre, potassium nitrate, as 'Snow of China'.[1411]

The history of gunpowder within the Islamic world remains a matter of quite heated debate,[1412] but there can be little doubt that the term *naft* had come to mean or include gunpowder by the second half of the fourteenth century. The problem is what happened during the second half of the thirteenth and the first half of the fourteenth centuries. Some answers can be found in the writings of Hasan al-Rammah who died in his thirties in 1294/5. He had, for example, a clearer and more effective recipe for refining potassium nitrate than anything found in contemporary Western European sources. While the famous text by Roger Bacon does not mention fuses at all, and those in the *Liber Igneum* are unclear,[1413] Hasan al-Rammah goes into fuses in detail.[1414] Furthermore, Hasan's recipe would make an effective blackpowder, or early form of gunpowder, while that in the *Liber Igneum* would be reasonable and that of Roger Bacon simply did not work in modern tests.[1415] Like al-Tarsusi, Hasan al-Rammah seems to have extended his writings into the realm of experimental weapons that were probably ineffective and almost certainly never used; at least not in any number. These remarkable ideas included military rockets and rocket-powered torpedoes for use against ships.[1416]

Amongst the most interesting but also most frustrating sections of Hasan al-Rammah's text is his reference to a *dawa'* or 'remedy' for the earliest type of gunpowder to be used in a *midfa'*. The latter term would be used for a form of gun or 'handmortar' in the fourteenth century.[1417] It nevertheless seems unlikely, though not impossible, that experiments with gunpowder as a means of discharging a missile from a container or tube were being undertaken in the late thirteenth-century Mamluk Sultanate.[1418]

While doubt has been cast on apparent references to saltpetre in the mid-thirteenth-century Iberian Peninsula,[1419] it has been suggested that a lack of known sources of petroleum or bitumen in the Islamic West may have encouraged an early use of explosive gunpowder.[1420] This is said to date from as early as 1204, slightly more clearly at Seville in 1248,[1421] and in southern Morocco in 1274. The latter case is particularly interesting because it appears to report iron fragments being shot from some sort of container, or perhaps mine, during the siege of the oasis town of Sijilmasa by the Marinid Sultan Abu Yusuf.[1422]

An all too often neglected aspect of this incendiary and explosive medieval warfare was the attempt to protect men and structures from such weapons. Al-Tarsusi describes a form of fire-resistant cloth and head-covering which could also be used for a horse's caparison if *naft* was being thrown from horseback.[1423] It consisted of two layers of felt impregnated with a fire-resistant substance. The latter, he suggests, could be made of 'muddy' or 'alluvial' asbestos, gum arabic, red ochre, gypsum, white flour and egg-white made into a paste with wine vinegar. This was then smeared on all the surfaces of the felt. Otherwise he suggested that the best way to protect a larger structure from fire weapons was to cover it with vinegar-soaked felt. Around the same time or slightly earlier, the *naffatun* or fire-troops in Nur al-Din's army in northern Iraq and Syria wore protective clothing impregnated with *talq*, consisting of silicate of magnesium and powdered mica.[1424] One of the strongest pieces of evidence for *naft* evolving from a purely incendiary to a primarily explosive substance in the later thirteenth century was the disappearance of such protective clothing from the written sources.[1425]

COMMUNICATION, TRANSPORT AND SUPPORT SERVICES

The nature of habitation and the very uneven spread of population in the medieval Islamic world put huge demands on communications and transport. Vast distances were often involved, not only on land but at sea. Indeed coastal navigation played a major role within and between certain regions. For example, strategic considerations meant that the rulers of Egypt often sought to dominate Syria. However, overland links between Egypt and Syria, across the deserts of the Sinai Peninsula and southern Palestine were so slow and difficult that maritime links between the Delta region of northern Egypt and the coastal towns of Palestine, Lebanon, Syria and sometimes Cilicia were more important. Hence, in Fatimid times as in many others, the fleet carried military supplies to coastal regions while camel caravans did the same for Fatimid possessions inland.[1426]

Similarly, the disruption caused by the Banu Hilal's and Banu Sulaym's migration westward from Egypt into Libya and Tunisia in the mid-eleventh century meant that the sea routes between the Islamic Middle East and North Africa became even more important.[1427] This was also the time when the rising power of the Italian maritime republics was challenging what had been Islamic naval domination of much of the Mediterranean.

The major Islamic states of the Middle East did, however, benefit from a well-established tradition of government-run, long-distance communications systems. This was the *barid* which was comparable to a postal service reserved for official government use. It was not, however, a permanent institution and as each Caliphate or major state rose and fell it almost certainly had to re-establish a *barid*. Yet the principle remained well-known and understood. For example, the Fatimid Caliphate in Egypt, parts of Syria and North Africa operated a *barid* under the authority of a *sahib al-barid*.[1428] There was also reference to a *diwan al-barid* or government postal department in 1024.[1429] Around 1100 the Fatimids still employed a team of professional overland messengers known as *faij* to carry urgent messages between Cairo and Tunisia.[1430] On the other hand it has been suggested that the Zangid rulers of northern Iraq and the Jazira were the first to use camels for the *barid*.[1431]

Meanwhile a short series of warning beacons was erected from the frontier with the Latin Crusader Kingdom of Jerusalem to Damascus in the mid-twelfth century. This was because the forces on the border were weak, with most troops being stationed in Damascus itself. They were expected to react quickly, even if only to ward off the Crusader rustlers who often raided the flocks grazing on the Golan plateau.[1432] Some elements of the Fatimid and Zangid systems were probably still in existence when Saladin took control of Egypt and Syria. His Ayyubid successors clearly had their own *barid* postal systems which made use of a pigeon-post and *najjabun* human couriers, just as the Fatimids had done.[1433] These were supplemented by a much faster but also more limited emergency signal chain of fire-beacons.[1434]

The use of carrier pigeons in the Jazira region was confirmed during Imad al-Din Zangi's campaigns early in the twelfth century, one such bird being intercepted then released with a false message to confuse the foe. The 'Abbasid Caliph al-Nasir in late twelfth- and early thirteenth-century Baghdad forbade anyone to have carrier pigeons except with his authority,[1435] and in 1225, the year al-Nasir died, a carrier-pigeon service was in operation between Baghdad and Irbil.[1436] Not much is known about how precisely such pigeon-posts were operated but, in his memoirs, Abu'l-Fida the Ayyubid ruler of Hama mentioned that there was a pigeon house for messages on the wall of the al-Naqfi gate of Hama in the early fourteenth century.[1437]

Some historians have suggested that the exceptionally efficient *barid* in the subsequent Mamluk Sultanate of Egypt and Syria had been copied from that of the Mongols,[1438] but this might be an exaggeration. The *barid* set up by the Mamluk Sultan Baybars I nevertheless differed from that of the Ayyubids in being more permanent. In the 1280s Sultan Qalawun even provided the couriers with special insignia, so that no one would have any excuse for hindering their progress or failing to help them when asked.[1439]

This fully developed Mamluk *barid* of the late thirteenth and fourteenth centuries was separate from the equally efficient system of *khans* or caravansaries that the Mamluk Sultans erected for merchants' caravans, pilgrims and other such travellers. It included a chain of beacons, visible by day as smoke and by night as fire, whose northern terminals were at al-Bira and al-Rahba overlooking the river Euphrates. These were on the Sultanate's tense and often wartorn frontier with the Mongol Il-Khans of Iraq and Iran. Both outposts were also fortresses with substantial arsenals. From here the chains of beacons ran via Palmyra, Damascus, Baysan and Nablus to Gaza in southern Palestine. From there couriers or pigeons carried urgent messages to Cairo. Additional pigeon-posts within Syria and Egypt each had their own government-run *burj* pigeon towers.[1440]

In general terms, the command and control systems available to Islamic military leaders were equivalent to those seen in the Byzantine Empire and were superior to those of almost all Christian Western Europe. This was almost certainly the case when it came to the use of musical instruments as a means of issuing commands (see above for music as a means of maintaining morale). However, Islamic armies, like those of all medieval states, lacked a really effective system of staff officers. This greatly inhibited the manoeuvring of large formations once a battle had started. Even with drums, flags and messengers, reaction times were slow and results uncertain.[1441] These problems were, on the other hand, well understood and military treatises such as the *Nihayat al-Su'l* attempted to provide answers. What is less clear is whether the solutions contained in these medieval Islamic texts were original or were drawn from ancient, pre-Islamic sources. It is similarly uncertain if they reflected current practice or were seen as some sort of unattainable ideal. The *Nihayat al-Su'l* similarly linked problems of command and control with the threat posed by spies and deserters.[1442]

Flags and banners were, perhaps, the most ubiquitous method of issuing simple instructions as well as enabling units and armies to identify one another. We know that in the Fatimid army flags were displayed each day, before the day's march began, but it is not clear whether this was simply to identify units or to indicate that the march was indeed about to start.[1443]

Banners had certainly been used as rallying points by the *ahdath* part-time militia of Damascus in 1020,[1444] and a few years later in al-Andalus the fleeing Zirid army of Granada was rallied when its commander personally seized the banners and made the retreating drummer stand. As the man beat his drum and the banner waved, the troops reportedly turned and defeated the rival army of Malaga. Both sides seem, incidentally, to have consisted of cavalry.[1445] Those Crusader chroniclers who witnessed Saladin's army attacking at the battle of Arsuf in 1191, recalled how they did so 'with ensigns fixed to their lances' and when the Islamic cavalry charged they were preceded by men with 'clarions and trumpets and tambours'.[1446]

The importance of drummers and standard-bearers was highlighted in many an epic account of heroism or prowess. In his account of the life of the Mamluk Sultan Baybars I, 'Abd al-Zahir described a battle between opposing Islamic forces when Baybars reportedly won the day when: 'He charged on until he reached the banners and broke through them, shattered the spear [shafts], shot down the drummer and scattered the army'.[1447] A similar episode featured in the epic thirteenth–fourteenth-century Turkish poem, the *Danishmandname*, when archers tipped the balance by bringing down the enemy's standard bearer.[1448] Comparable feats had been recorded much earlier, during the early days of Arab-Islamic expansion.

Musical instruments were not the only audible method of passing orders, keeping units together or distinguishing friend from foe. In the Fatimid army, and probably most other Islamic forces as well, a battlecry was decided before combat; this usually being one of the many Names of God.[1449] During the late Fatimid period the Syrian Arab *amir*, Usama Ibn Munqidh, recalled how a *buq* trumpet or bugle was used to keep order on the march, to announce stopping and starting, when a small force of cavalry was passing through dangerous nominally Crusader territory in southern Palestine.[1450] It also seems that Ayyubid armies had their own forms of battlefield code, especially when using *kussat* cymbals and *buq* trumpets, in order to stop the enemy understanding the messages. Men with loud, trained voices were similarly employed as battlefield criers, but whether any form of code-words was used is unknown. All these systems were continued by the army of the Mamluk Sultanate.[1451]

The medieval Islamic world was linked and criss-crossed by the most astonishing network of trade or caravan routes. These were not usually metalled 'roads' of the sort associated with the Roman Empire. Baggage animals had largely replaced wheeled transport and so paved roads were unnecessary and often inconvenient. Instead the states' involvement in maintaining such routes focused on building or repairing bridges, providing secure resting places or shelter, putting down banditry and keeping routes clear through mountain passes and forests. As a result Islamic armies were capable of covering remarkable distances very quickly.

On the other hand, adverse weather could endanger a military force, just as it could a merchant caravan. This happened when Shirkuh's army was caught in a sandstorm while crossing the Sinai Peninsula on its way from Syria to Egypt.[1452] It is also important to realize that state boundaries, even those between the Islamic States and the Latin Crusader States, did not necessarily stop an army on the march. It really depended upon how strong the force was, what threat if any it was deemed to pose, and whether the rulers of the territory thus violated thought it worth challenging the trespassers. Hence Islamic armies were still able to travel between Syria and Egypt even when the Latin Kingdom of Jerusalem occupied southern Palestine as far as the Gulf of Aqaba plus Oultrejourdain in what is now southern Jordan. Smaller caravans or groups were more vulnerable to attack and often had to pay a 'toll' to ensure safe passage.

Maritime and river transport was similarly well developed but was divided into clearly distinct zones. On one side there was the Mediterranean with its northern and western extensions, the Black Sea and what is sometimes called the 'Mediterranean Atlantic'. The latter was an area of ocean between the Straits of Gibraltar, the western Atlantic coast of the Iberian Peninsula, the coasts of north-west Africa as far south as Mauretania and perhaps Senegal, the Canary Islands and perhaps as far as Madeira. The eastern seas of the Islamic world consisted of the Persian (Arabian) Gulf and the Red Sea, both feeding into the Indian Ocean. Medieval Islamic mariners knew and sailed all of the Indian Ocean north of the equator, with extension further south to Madagascar and along the African coast virtually to the border of modern South Africa. They knew of all, and visited most of, the islands of the Indian Ocean other than those far to the south. They similarly traded with or knew of the islands of the Indonesian archipelago at least as far as Timor and probably Papua, so close to the continental mass of Australia that it seem incredible that they would not at least have heard about it from local sailors. Beyond the myriad islands of south-east Asia, Islamic merchants and at times Islamic shipping traded with southern China.[1453]

These vast economic and cultural hinterlands lay within what might be regarded as the world-view or mindset of the educated commercial, cultural and political élites of the medieval Islamic world. It was very different, both in scope and in understanding, to what currently existed within the confines of medieval Western Europe. On the other hand, all was not always plain sailing in these oceans and Middle Eastern Islamic trade often suffered as a result of political events far outside the Islamic or even Christian worlds. For example, the decline of the Indianized Buddhist and largely maritime kingdom of Srivijaya in what are now western Indonesia and peninsular Malaysia severely interrupted Arab long distance trade with south-east Asia in the late twelfth century.[1454] This seems to have had a direct impact upon the trading wealth, and thus military potential, of places like Yemen, Egypt and perhaps Iraq. At a much more local level, low water in the Nile could and did interrupt vital river navigation in Egypt.

These could be regarded as passing difficulties. The Islamic Middle East's acute and worsening shortage of timber for shipbuilding was more fundamental. Egypt was particularly poor in wood and iron, to the extent that some Nile boats had superstructures made partly of clay. Egyptian governments did what they could to maintain groves of acacia trees for shipbuilding, but these never formed real forests and were never sufficient.[1455]

Crete had served as an important source of timber while under Islamic rule, but after the Byzantine Empire reconquered the island, Egypt had to import timber from wherever it could,[1456] including southern Anatolia and India via Aden and the Hijaz during the Fatimid period.[1457] The Fatimids even turned to Venice which was prepared to defy a Papal ban and smuggle shipbuilding timber.[1458] Even after the First Crusade, Italian merchants from Amalfi and Genoa were similarly selling timber in Egypt during the reign of the Fatimid Caliph al-Amir (1101–30).[1459]

Saladin and his Ayyubid successors faced the same problems and were particularly keen to promote trade with Italy. In 1173 it was the maritime republic of Pisa which defied a Papal ban and signed a commercial treaty with Saladin, agreeing to sell iron, timber and pitch to Egypt, all of which were essential for shipbuilding. This treaty was confirmed again in 1215.[1460] Egypt's last 'forests' disappeared or were used up during the Mamluk Sultanate. Meanwhile the forests of Syria and Lebanon, which were also under Mamluk rule, remained small and so the Mamluks continued to import timber from southern Anatolia.[1461]

Paradoxically, the increasing size but reduced numbers of Islamic shipping in the Mediterranean may have reflected this shortage of timber as well as the growing need for ships to be able to defend themselves against Christian pirates. This trend was noted in the tenth and eleventh centuries, though it may have started earlier, and it had the added benefit of enabling such vessels to carry more drinking water and thus travel greater distances between stops.[1462] Despite the perils and the growth of Christian, especially Italian, competition, the evidence strongly suggests that most goods and people travelling between Egypt and Tunisia around the time of the First Crusade went by sea rather than overland.[1463]

The western region of the medieval Islamic world, from Tunisia to Morocco and including al-Andalus in what are now Spain and Portugal, was much more richly endowed with forests, including timber suitable for ships. Several major centres of shipbuilding were, in fact, located on the Atlantic coast at Qasr Banu Wardas (Alcacer do Sal) and Shalab (Silves) in southern Portugal, as well as Seville and Algeciras in Spain.[1464] Medieval Islamic navigation in the Atlantic has been a neglected subject but was clearly important.[1465] It was significant that the mid-tenth century, largely agricultural, Calendar of Cordova noted that ships could go to sea from 13 April onwards; earlier than that the seas were closed because of winter weather.[1466] In addition to being a major *dar al-sina* or arsenal for shipbuilding, Qasr Banu Wardas was the centre of a major fishing industry, sending fleets far out into the Atlantic.[1467] There are even said to have been whalers from al-Andalus off the coast of Ireland in the eleventh century.[1468]

Ports were as important as ships for naval communications and warfare. However, fully protected harbours, especially those with man-made quays, remained rare and it was still common practice either to beach a ship for loading and unloading, or to anchor offshore, transferring people and goods between ship and land by smaller boats. In such circumstances the twin steering oars, still used in many places instead of hinged rudders, could be used as legs to keep a vessel upright when beached.[1469]

There were plenty of sheltered roadsteads, ports and man-made or man-improved harbours around the Mediterranean and along the medieval Islamic world's eastern coasts. Those along the Atlantic coast of al-Andalus have also been mentioned. Less well-known are the ports that were developed along the Atlantic coast of Morocco during the Middle Ages. These included Tanja (Tangier), Azila, Sala, Anfa (now a suburb of Casablanca) and Azammur. Tangier had a fortified wall because of the threat from Christian Iberian and even Viking Scandinavian attack, but the other Maghribi Atlantic ports were unwalled before the eleventh century. Some were actually located a few kilometres inland and most ships either beached or moored off-shore, though Azila had a stone mole or jetty to protect its harbour.[1470] Still further south were other coastal towns, though it is unclear whether they also served as ports.

The degree to which medieval Islamic governments not only controlled but were directly involved in trade, especially in strategic materials, made them much more similar to the Byzantine Empire or China than to most of Latin Christian Western Europe. In Fatimid Egypt, for example, all imports of iron, timber and pitch had to be delivered to government agents.[1471] Furthermore, the remarkable documents from the Cairo Geniza include detailed accounts of how Egyptian Jewish merchants were involved in these and related trades. They show that six distinct types of iron and steel were imported into Egypt from the east, largely from India. This became the chief commodity for Jewish merchants in Cairo during the Fatimid period.[1472] Meanwhile nothing concerned with arms or the manufacture of arms came from Europe. In fact there was remarkably little trade with Europe when compared with Egypt's huge trade with the east.[1473]

Given the terrain and distances across which Islamic armies campaigned during this period it is hardly surprising that Islamic governments developed sophisticated systems of supply and support. Drinking water was perhaps the single most important item, after the provision of weapons. Here even the anonymous author of the *Gesta Francorum* noted that each man in the Fatimid army defeated by the First Crusade outside Ascalon on 12 August 1099 had a water-bottle around his neck.[1474] That the Crusaders could fight on that high summer day without such a basic piece of equipment seems incredible.

The mid-twelfth-century army of Nur al-Din, campaigning in the Jazira and Syria, was supported by an array of what might today be called non-combatants, though such a distinction did not exist at the time of the Crusades. They included imams to lead the prayers and offer spiritual support, Koran readers, *qadis* or men qualified to make legal decisions, scribes, interpreters, doctors, surgeons and many others.[1475] The *atlab al-mira* or supply train was under the command of an *amir*, but otherwise the troops seem to have looked after themselves, relying of the *sabila* or merchants who followed the army and set up a *suq al-ʿaskar* or soldiers' market at each camping place.[1476] This was what all previous Islamic armies had done, including that of the Seljuq Turks, and would form the basis of what came later.

A great deal is known about how Saladin's army and those of his Ayyubid successors was maintained on campaign. Their technical services and supply mechanisms were based upon previous Fatimid and Zangid systems, forming part of what was known as the *thuql*. It was responsible for all sorts of weaponry, including any siege train, as well as medical support.[1477] The specialized *naqqabun* miners and engineers, *naffatun* fire troops, *zarraqun* fire throwers and other siege technicians or specialists in castle and citadel garrisons were similarly considered to be part of this *thuql*.[1478] So were the *sassa* squires or horse-handlers and those handling mules or donkeys and camels, each being assigned to a specific group.[1479] Among the most active and hazardous roles assigned to the *thuql* was that of resupplying castles under enemy siege. It also seems to have been responsible for sending ships into besieged coastal towns, as happened at Acre during the Third Crusade.[1480]

The quality of medical care, both public and private, in the main cities of the medieval Islamic world is well known. It included hospitals for psychological as well as physical disorders. To what extent the same trained medical personnel were involved in looking after sick and injured soldiers is unknown. There was, nevertheless, a military medical service in many Islamic armies. That of the Ayyubid Sultanates formed part of the *thuql* and could establish what were, in effect, mobile or field hospitals. On particularly long campaigns these seem to have been set up near the armies' encampments though not necessarily within them.[1481]

The Ayyubid *suq al-ʿaskar* or soldiers' market was not part of the government run *thuql*, but was reputed to be very well organized and also supplied some military needs as a back-up to the official *thuql*.[1482] This *suq al-ʿaskar* could similarly purchase prisoners from their captors after a victory, such unfortunates being destined for ransom or slavery according to circumstances.[1483] At the same time the *thuql* and the *suq al-ʿaskar* themselves were often the targets of enemy attack. After Saladin conquered the Crusader castle of La Fève, following his victory at the battle of Hattin, the structure was dismantled and all useful or portable equipment that had been left behind by the Templars was loaded on to animals and perhaps waggons, to be taken across the river Jordan. However, this caravan of booty was intercepted by a Hospitaller garrison from the still unconquered castle of Belvoir in January 1188.[1484]

The numbers of animals required by armies and their support services could be extraordinary. The military stables of the Fatimid Caliphate, for example, were said to have maintained 30,000 transport camels in the late tenth century. The great majority were dromedaries, single-humped Arabian camels, but the Fatimids also used a small number of *bukht* two-humped Bactrian camels which were reportedly capable of carrying twice the load of a dromedary.[1485] In the Mamluk Sultanate, each élite *mamluk* soldier was allocated at least one or two baggage camels on campaign, while troops of the lower prestige *halqa* forces were allowed three baggage camels for every two men.[1486]

The number of horses maintained by the tenth century Fatimid government stables was considerably less than the number of camels, though 12,000 is no small number.[1487] However, it is clear that there were very substantial differences in quality and price between ordinary, good and thoroughbred horses, as was the case in Western Europe during this period.[1488] The Arabian breed had the highest prestige, and rulers such as the early Mamluk Sultans sometimes distributed extra money to their soldiers so that they could purchase horses directly from Arab bedouin tribes.[1489] The animals in question were described as light but with great endurance, physically much larger than the Mongol ponies ridden by the Mamluks' main opponents, but also needing to be stall fed.[1490] The intelligence of the Arabian horse was then, as now, proverbial. Senior Mamluk *amirs* or officers were given horses by the ruling Sultan twice a year. Otherwise a *mamluk* got his first horse on qualifying and being freed as a fully trained cavalryman. Thereafter he only received a replacement if he could prove that the animal had died.[1491]

While there were wide price differentials between qualities of animal, prices from country to country across the Islamic Middle East differed less. For reasons which are likely to have been connected to the ongoing warfare with the Crusader States, the overall cost of horses increased during the later Fatimid, Ayyubid and early Mamluk centuries, but then dipped after the Crusaders had been expelled at the end of the thirteenth century.[1492] Even so, the preparations for a military campaign saw prices rise temporarily, but sometimes dramatically. In Egypt, in the year 1300 as the army readied itself for a campaign against Mongol invaders in northern Syria, the cost of an ordinary warhorse jumped from 300 to 1,000 *dirhams*.[1493] Lacking any real pastures of its own, medieval Egypt could never be a breeder of really large numbers of horses. Instead the animals were imported from many places, some quite distant. The best came from the Bahrayn and Hijaz areas of Arabia while good horses also came from Barqa in what is now Libya and from elsewhere in North Africa. In the late thirteenth century Marco Polo reported that Aden was rich in horses which were then sold to Egypt as cavalry mounts, although he was probably referring to a wider area of Yemen than merely the city and vicinity of Aden.[1494] He also noted that the Hadramawt region north-east of Aden also exported horses to India.[1495]

NAVAL AND RIVERINE WARFARE

Even though the sea played such a major part in the trade and communications networks of the medieval Islamic world, naval warfare was relatively rare. This was largely because the Islamic states were already on the strategic defensive in the Mediterranean, with the notable exception of Anatolia, which would become a special case; while in the eastern seas including the Indian Ocean traffic continued to be overwhelmingly peaceful as it had been for centuries.

There are a number of paradoxes in the naval history of medieval Islamic civilization. In the Mediterranean, for example, the Muslim Arabs had largely learned their skills of naval warfare from the Byzantine Empire while there is virtually no evidence of the Byzantines learning from their Islamic foes. Nevertheless, by the thirteenth century the Islamic fleets seem to have had access to, and made use of, superior theoretical naval knowledge than the Byzantines.[1496] This was despite the fact that the power of the Islamic fleets was itself in decline relative to that of the Italians and other Christian powers of the western Mediterranean. Theoretical knowledge was one thing; practical application and the means to make use of such knowledge was quite another. Similarly, the Byzantine fleets were in such steep decline that a direct comparison with those of the Islamic states did not necessarily mean much.

The Fatimid Caliphate in North Africa, Egypt and Syria was the major Islamic naval power in the eastern Mediterranean from the tenth to early twelfth century. In practical terms the major role of the Fatimid fleet was to protect its naval supply lines. Very little was done in terms of offensive operations and once the Fatimid capital had been transferred from Tunisia to Cairo, the main effort of the Fatimid navy was to ensure the security of convoys between Egyptian ports and Tripoli in Lebanon.[1497] The latter remained the Fatimids' most important naval base on the Syro-Palestinian coast,[1498] and was still a major naval centre when the First Crusade arrived.

Thereafter Egyptian naval power saw a gradual decline until Saladin attempted to revive the fleet before the Third Crusade. Saladin had, of course, inherited the now much reduced Fatimid navy and its administrative structures.[1499] However, his own efforts to rebuild a lost naval power largely failed.[1500] This was not for want of trying, or of a commitment of resources. Yet the basic problems remained; namely lack of timber, a lack of qualified sailors and the very poor strategic location of Egypt as a significant naval powerbase. Saladin's efforts were, on the other hand, more successful in the Red Sea, not only defeating Reynald de Châtillon's naval and coastal operations in that region but also sending successful military expeditions to Yemen.[1501]

The Mamluk Sultanate which took over from the Ayyubids, initially in Egypt and shortly afterwards in most of Syria, inherited what remained of the Ayyubid fleet but itself maintained no permanent navy. Instead the Mamluks relied on organizing, building and recruiting as and when needed.[1502] The result was not particularly successful, despite occasionally massive efforts and a few fleeting victories. On the other hand there seems to have been an attempt to maintain the theoretical, technological or knowledge base. As a result Ibn Mangli's manual on naval warfare, dating from the mid-fourteenth century is not only unique in medieval Arabic military literature but contains remarkably detailed and advanced information (see below).[1503] Putting such knowledge into practice was again a different matter.

Although the Seljuk Sultan Sulayman Shah operated a fleet out of Tarsus against the Armenian-Byzantine governor Philaretus of Antioch in 1085, perhaps in cooperation with Ibn Ammar of Tripoli,[1504] Turkish naval history in the Mediterranean really began in the thirteenth century. It was then that the Seljuk Sultanate of Rum emerged as a new naval power, at least in terms of Islamic naval history. In other respects it was almost like a Byzantine fleet reborn in a new guise. This is clear in the very pronounced Byzantine Greek and even Italian influence in this first real Turkish navy.[1505] When the Seljuk Sultanate of Rum fragmented, a number of new and soon more formidable fleets emerged under the flags of Turkish coastal *beyliks* or *amirates*. Their naval history really belongs to the fourteenth century and one of them, the Ottoman Turks, would eventually compete for naval domination throughout the entire Mediterranean and beyond.

The decline of Islamic maritime power was much less apparent in the western than in the eastern Mediterranean. Nevertheless there was a decline which started in the late tenth and early eleventh centuries. Again it was essentially a result of increasing Italian maritime power.[1506] On the other hand Sicilian Islamic fleets remained active,[1507] and there may have been a limited revival in thirteenth-century Tunisia where the early Hafsid fleet was used in several combined operations against rivals and rebellious coastal cities.[1508] Further west the maritime decline of al-Andalus appears to have halted altogether, at least for a few centuries. The navy of the Nasrid *amirate* of Granada, the last remaining Andalusian Islamic state, was clearly very effective. Its main arsenal was at Almeria and it not only launched retaliatory raids against Aragon and Majorca,[1509] but annexed Sabta (Ceuta) in northern Morocco in 1306.

With such a flourishing maritime tradition it is hardly surprising that the shipping of the medieval Islamic world was technologically advanced.[1510] The change from skin-first to frame-first hull construction also demanded less highly skilled labourers and was much faster, as well as requiring fewer baulks of really large or particularly straight timbers.[1511] On the other hand there were clearly significant differences between the naval and technological traditions of the main 'nautical regions' of the medieval Islamic world. The main such regions were the Mediterranean and linked seas including the Black Sea in the west, and the Indian Ocean and its linked seas including the Persian Gulf and Red Sea in the east. Between the two there was what almost amounted to a separate maritime tradition; that of the great river Nile.

The Nile was, in fact, often referred to as a 'sea' rather than a mere river in medieval Arabic texts. Like the lower reaches of the Euphrates, Tigris and Karun rivers in southern Iraq and south-western Iran, the Nile had its own traditions of ship design, construction and navigation. In some respects these bridged the eastern and western seas. There was an occasionally cleared but often clogged 'Canal of the Commander of the Faithful' linking the Gulf of Suez with the Nile just north of Cairo; thus by extension linking the Indian Ocean, Red Sea and Mediterranean. There was, nevertheless, a remarkable degree of continuity in the design and decoration of Nile ships from the immediately pre-Islamic Byzantine, through the medieval to the early modern period. Rigging does not seem to have changed at all, while the main changes were to hull construction which was more susceptible to outside technological influences.[1512]

Islamic shipping in the Mediterranean inherited Romano-Byzantine naval technology, to which eastern influences had been added during the early Islamic centuries. These may also have been seen during the brief period of Sassanian Iranian occupation of Syria, Egypt and parts of Anatolia shortly before the coming of Islam. The triangular lateen sail, rather than the almost trapezoid lug sail, was, for example, adopted almost universally across the Mediterranean by the tenth and eleventh centuries.

Another interesting but more contentious question concerns the introduction of the hinged stern rudder: it is possible that the single sweep over the sternpost of small boats, as often mentioned in written sources and occasionally seen in eleventh century Islamic illustrations, might have contributed to the adoption of this stern rudder.[1513] On the other hand there is also strong evidence that the Indian Ocean style of real hinged stern rudder, as clearly known in the Persian Gulf, Euphrates, Tigris and Red Sea, was similarly adopted on the river Nile and from there the eastern Mediterranean.

Perhaps the most dramatic and, from a military point of view, most significant new development in early medieval Mediterranean shipping was the development of much bigger, three-masted and perhaps multi-decked vessels. This clearly happened earlier in the Islamic than in the Christian countries around the Mediterranean.[1514] The chronicler Ibn al-Athir quoted an earlier source when describing a particularly large vessel from al-Andalus that had been captured and reused by the Fatimids in 955. Its dimensions were said to be 84 m long, 33.5 m broad;[1515] somewhat longer than HMS *Victory* and about twice as wide.

Another source, apparently concerning the year 1137, described a particularly large ship which seems to have been built in Almeria in al-Andalus. It belonged to the government and was regarded as being safer against pirates than were smaller ships.[1516] A further reference to a large ship concerned the one vessel to escape from the Crusader blockade of Tyre in 1187. This was not only bigger than the others involved but had a notably experienced crew.[1517] The written sources indicate that the largest Islamic merchant ships of this period had a capacity of 1,000 tonnes and, when used as troop transports, could carry 1,500 men. On the other hand, it is not known how far such voyages went bearing in mind how much drinking water would be required by such a large number of passengers, not to mention the crew.[1518]

These were essentially transports rather than fighting ships, but they also needed to be able to defend themselves. From at least the ninth century onwards some of the bigger ships had fighting castles at their sterns, though the 'castellated' wooden forecastle may not have appeared until the late eleventh century. The first examples were probably seen in the Murabitun fleet operating from Morocco and al-Andalus.[1519] By this time it seems that Islamic ships were already noted for tall superstructures which were added for defensive purposes.[1520] Once again this was noted by their Christian foes, as when Aimeri de Narbonne described a Moorish fleet in his late twelfth century *Siège de Barbastre*. Each *nef* or transport ship had an *engin* or unidentified siege machine and four *chastiaus* 'castles', in each of which were 20 crossbowmen. Though probably a poetic exaggeration, it nevertheless demonstrated how impressive such ships could appear to their opponents.[1521]

In addition to a small number of very large ships, there were a larger number like the *qunbar* which, being related to the Byzantine *kombarion*, was the most common Islamic seagoing merchant ship in the Mediterranean. The *qarib* was a large coastal barge capable of very long journeys, while the *ghurab* was a relatively light transport galley. One *ghurab* was described in 1190 as being powered by 140 oars.[1522]

It seems that essentially the same sorts of Mediterranean ship were used beyond Gibraltar in the 'Mediterranean Atlantic', though it also seems likely that more strongly built versions were developed in this region to deal with Atlantic weather. One such was probably the *jabeque*, or *xebec* used in both Granada and Morocco, though the earliest known reference to such a vessel was not until 1344.[1523] It is similarly interesting that later forms of galley with fewer and larger oars appeared at a particularly early date in Granada. These were evenly spaced rather than grouped, with each oar being pulled by several men rather than one man per oar.[1524] Might such a development have again reflected the rougher conditions of the Atlantic? Finally there is evidence that Islamic Andalusian ships had adopted some aspects of the northern European ocean-going *cog* by the mid-thirteenth century, though this comes from the Mediterranean rather than the Atlantic shores of al-Andalus.[1525]

It is clear that the Muslims developed some form of advanced maritime horse-transportation capability earlier than either the Byzantine Empire or Western Europe.[1526] This may have been another case of technological influence from the eastern seas where the exportation of horses from Arabia to India became significant during the medieval period. Although such early Islamic capabilities in the Mediterranean initially involved small numbers of animals, by the late tenth century a specialized Arab-Islamic vessel known as the *tarida* could carry 40 horses.[1527] The fully developed *tarida* of the late twelfth century is understood to have had a twin stern with a ramp between which could be dropped directly on to a beach to allow men and animals to disembark.[1528]

The main fighting ship remained the galley. There were several sizes in the Islamic fleets, as there were in the Byzantine navy, but the standard Islamic galley in the Mediterranean was the *shini*. It had from 140–180 oarsmen, while the oars themselves were arranged in one or two banks; the two-bank system becoming more popular in the later medieval period. The *shini* could carry up to 150 fighting men or marines, most of whom were stationed in the forecastle.[1529]

The unique naval treatise written by Muhammad Ibn Mangli al-Qahiri in the mid-fourteenth-century Mamluk Sultanate was based upon the Byzantine Emperor Leo IV's *Naumachica*, but had been updated to take account of recent developments. Ibn Mangli was himself a *muqaddam* and 'commander of forty' in the lower prestige *halqa*. As an old man he became *naqib al-jaysh* in Alexandria where he wrote his remarkable treatise entitled *Al-akham al-mulukiya wa'l-dawabat al-namusiya*. It described naval tactics, types of warship, naval equipment and weaponry, including guns. Ibn Mangli also noted changes to the prow of a warship since Roman times, the abandonment of the shipbreaking ram and the way the forecastle had become a base for powerful weapons, while also including remarkably practical advice for those fighting at sea.[1530]

Traditionally there had been a significantly lesser role for warships in the Indian Ocean, Persian Gulf and Red Sea than in the Mediterranean. As a result little is known about them, though they were probably much like the merchant ships seen in these seas. There were almost certainly no permanent war fleets until much later, in fact not until after the arrival of the Portuguese at the end of the fifteenth century. Nevertheless it does seem that 'armed ships' rather than dedicated warships sometimes accompanied precious cargoes, and that ships were converted for military purposes when required. The clearest information for the later medieval period is found in Ibn Battuta's accounts of his travels in the fourteenth century. Here he mentioned *tarida* transports carrying horses and armed cavalry, the use of *manjaniqs* mounted on board ships for use against shore targets, and the employment of permanent 'African' marines aboard some Islamic warships.[1531]

Perhaps the most striking feature of Islamic ships in the Indian Ocean and linked seas was the fact that so many of them had hulls which were stitched rather than nailed together. This seemingly primitive system was in reality very effective, cheap and flexible. It also permitted the construction of remarkably large hulls.[1532] Another feature was the hinged stern rudder, reputedly invented in China, which was probably known in the Persian Gulf and Red Sea by the tenth and certainly by the early twelfth century. Enclosed deck cabins are similarly believed to have been more typical of these eastern seas, including the Indian Ocean.[1533] This was presumably for climatic reasons. Similarly there was much less use of galleys requiring large numbers of oarsmen, primarily because of the problem of providing sufficient on-board drinking water.[1534] Another feature which appeared earlier in Islamic Indian Ocean vessels was the masthead observation position or crow's nest, this being more important for ships that sailed long distances out of sight of land than those which hugged the coastlines. It was then apparently adopted by Islamic vessels in the Mediterranean before being taken up by Byzantine and Western European shipwrights.[1535]

The Islamic states which bordered the Mediterranean sometimes faced significant problems when it came to raising sufficient naval crews. Al-Andalus and North Africa seemed to escape this difficulty and the peoples of the Maghrib earned a reputation as the finest mariners in the Islamic world. Egypt, despite its flourishing maritime trade, did not itself have a strong naval tradition with only the ports of the Nile Delta being able to supply trained crews. Furthermore, much of the population involved still seem to have been Coptic Christians. On the other hand there is evidence that the first Arab-Islamic fleets operating from Egypt in the seventh and eighth centuries were manned by Yemeni Arab settlers, or at least these newcomers served as marines.

The Syrian, Lebanese and to a lesser extent Palestinian coast had a strong naval orientation but again many local seafarers were Christians rather than Muslims. The same would clearly be the case when the new Turkish states of Anatolia turned to naval warfare, but here the Islamic *sultans*, *amirs* and *beys* managed to get their ex-Byzantine, Christian coastal populations 'on board' in a very literal sense. This may have been largely because their most immediate foes were Latin rather than fellow Orthodox Christians.

The difficulty of recruiting sufficient and adequately trained naval personnel would remain for the rulers of Egypt throughout this period. The Fatimids, for example, had good relations with the neighbouring Libyan province of Barqa (Cyrenaica) over which they had at least nominal suzerainty. Although Barqa had only a small population, its Arab bedouin inhabitants rapidly earned a fine if unexpected reputation as sailors, but also as pirates. These communities probably took over many of the later Fatimid Caliphate's naval duties in the eleventh and twelfth centuries.[1536] Furthermore, there were many Italian so-called 'renegades' in the North African Islamic fleets sent against Genoa in the eleventh century, and these are likely to have included relatively highly skilled individuals rather than ordinary sailors or oarsmen.[1537] The skills of Islamic naval crews as well as the size and power of their ships were often emphasized in twelfth-century French *chansons de geste* and comparable epic poetry from other parts of the Christian western Mediterranean.[1538] In most cases, however, this seems to have reflected the impact made by Maghribi, North African and Andalusian fleets rather than those of the Middle East.

Ayyubid Egypt continued to wrestle with the same shortage of trained crews that had plagued the Fatimid fleet.[1539] The Maghribis retained their reputation as the best mariners in the Islamic world,[1540] and it has been suggested that Saladin's conquest of a substantial part of the Libyan coast was partly to make as many as possible of its maritime population available as sailors. Meanwhile he also recruited naval crews from further west, from what are now Tunisia, Algeria and Morocco.[1541]

The next dynasty to rule Egypt and Syria, the Mamluk Sultanate, is believed to have had a negative attitude towards the sea, and Sultan Baybars I was himself quoted as saying that the sea was the realm of 'peasants and rabble'.[1542] However, this might have been overstated, since the Mamluk ruling and military élites tended to regard anyone who was not a *mamluk* as peasants and rabble. Another interesting snippet of information from 'Abd al-Zahir's *Life of Baybars* also suggests that previous Mamluk and perhaps even late Ayyubid rulers had taken crews from the fighting galleys to serve aboard sailing transports and *haraqa* fireships.[1543] This might suggest some unclear change in naval emphasis.

Information about Mamluk fleets from the early fourteenth century, which would almost certainly have applied to later thirteenth-century vessels as well, indicated that there were distinct and separate ranks on board ship. Ten officers seem to have been normal in a warship with a *qa'id* or *muqaddam* in charge of the fighting marines while a *ra'is al-milaha* was in charge of the ship and its crew.[1544] From the earliest years of Islamic naval history, it was clear that marines, naval crews and galley oarsmen were expected to fight. The latter were neither excused nor regarded as untrustworthy.

The majority of professional marines were at first archers and even in the Fatimid fleet crossbowmen formed a minority.[1545] About 500 such 'infantry from the fleet' took part in a massive Caliphal military parade and procession in the late eleventh or early twelfth century, being armed with ordinary Arab bows and *qisi al-rijl wa'l-rikab*, 'foot' and 'stirrup' crossbows.[1546] Two and a half centuries later the main fighting strength of the Granadan fleet in southern Andalusia similarly consisted of archers and crossbowmen.[1547]

The other weaponry found aboard medieval Islamic ships was similar to that recorded on the Christian side of the Mediterranean. We are also fortunate in having the very late tenth- or early eleventh-century Serçe Liman shipwreck from the south-western tip of Anatolia. It was not an Islamic warship, but was a merchant vessel containing a remarkable array of weapons. Amongst them are at least ten distinct forms of pole arm including two not seen in medieval Western Europe, plus spears and javelins, an axe which seems to have been more of a weapon than a working tool, and two or three swords.

There was also a spike with rings attached which may have formed the central suspension point for a ceremonial parasol, perhaps originally with some sort of decoration thrust on to the spike.[1548] Another strange object could be described as a blunt spearhead. It was found still in its sheath. If the ringed spike was from a ceremonial parade parasol, then perhaps this seemingly ceremonial rather than practical blunt blade may have been a ceremonial *harba* or other such decorative parade weapon. Perhaps the Serçe Liman ship was carrying a gift of ceremonial weapons from a senior to a junior ruler. Finally, it has been suggested that the fragmentary remains of one of the scabbards could indicate that one of the swords had been slightly curved. The best preserved of the swords was, however, of a double-edged, straight-bladed form.[1549]

The Muslims used incendiary weapons at sea just as effectively as they did on land. This capability went back at least to the ninth century and would be seen again during the course of the Crusades. One of the most successful uses of fire-ships was in defence of the Nile port of Damietta in Egypt against Crusader attack in 1169.[1550] By the thirteenth century, however, there is some debate about the precise meaning of the term *harraqa* (pl. *harariq*) and it has been suggested that it no longer meant a fireship but a small form of galley.[1551] However, the *harraqa* had been a galley of ordinary size but armed with a fire-projector or other form of incendiary weapon since at least the tenth century.[1552] Perhaps the new form was a smaller oared craft, suitable for the enclosed water of the Nile Delta, but still armed with fire-weapons.

The *harraqa* type of ship used by the last Ayyubid Sultan of Egypt, al-Salih, against Crusader invaders in 1250 and again at Damietta, was almost certainly a small ship with a *naft* flame projector or thrower mounted on board. This weapon could also be removed. The ship itself was almost certainly oared rather than powered by sails, being small, fast and very manoeuvrable. Furthermore it has been described as smaller than the incendiary-armed *cheland* used by the Byzantine fleet in the mid-tenth century. The flame thrower on such a *harraqa* was operated by *naffatun* specialist incendiary troops.[1553]

Occasional references in European sources to 'serpents' being carried aboard Saracen ships probably referred to a form of pyrotechnic weapons and almost certainly not to real reptiles.[1554] Certainly the new sections of the naval treatise written by Ibn Mangli al-Qahiri in the mid-fourteenth century, rather than those parts translated from the Byzantine Emperor Leo VI's *Naumachica*, included instructions on how fire projection tubes or other incendiary weapons could be hidden by a false floor.[1555] The lower deck, or at least an enclosed or roofed area, could similarly serve as an area where a ship's surgeon treated casualties.[1556] Even more remarkable, perhaps, was Ibn Mangli's reference to the use of guns at sea.[1557]

Another area of disagreement between scholars concerns this question of the carriage of drinking water in medieval Islamic ships. It has been suggested that in at least some Islamic regions, a Chinese system of water barrels was adopted,[1558] but other scholars have disputed this and claim that Islamic ships continued to carry drinking water in ceramic amphorae or waterskins. There is strong evidence that the Fatimid fleet of 1126 used these old-fashioned jars, resulting in greater weight for the amount of water carried and thus a reduced operational range.[1559]

The limited range of galleys, both as individual ships but more especially as fleets, dominated a great deal of naval strategy and intelligence gathering. Eastern Mediterranean naval campaigns of this period and earlier were similarly constrained by the fact that almost no ships ventured from harbour or at least from the immediate coasts when the seas were 'closed' from late autumn to early spring. Even when the seas were 'open' in summer, ships in the Mediterranean tended to follow the coastlines and rarely headed into the open sea out of sight of land. This limited the strategic range of all ships because they often followed what would today look like circuitous routes. The biggest constraint on the operational range of galleys, with their large crews of oarsmen labouring under often intense sun, was the amount of drinking water that a galley could carry. The availability of accessible sources of fresh water along their route was of paramount importance. Naturally enough, those who ruled a coast would try to stop enemy shipping coming ashore to replenish their water supplies at the limited number of freshwater streams or springs.[1560]

Even the Fatimid-held outpost of Ascalon in early twelfth-century southern Palestine could be virtually cut off from Egypt, at least by sea, during winter. Consequently winter was a good time for the neighbouring Crusader outposts to raid or attack.[1561] Thereafter the fall of Ascalon in 1153 meant that Islamic fleets operating from Egypt lost a hugely significant forward base, the coast further north already being in Crusader, Armenian or Byzantine hands until Saladin's conquests after the battle of Hattin in 1187.

Until the Third Crusade the primary function of Saladin's own fleet was to raid Christian shipping in the Eastern Mediterranean, the success or otherwise of each operation being judged in the number of prisoners taken. This could be substantial if a pilgrim ship was intercepted.[1562] Occasional raids attacked Crusader ports, or at least the vessels moored offshore. During the siege of Acre by the Third Crusade, Saladin's fleet also did what it could to support the garrison, but was clearly outnumbered if not necessarily as outclassed as

Western sources tended to suggest. In fact the fall of Acre, and the capture of the substantial number of both fighting galleys and transport vessels bottled up in its harbour, meant that for some years Saladin's navy almost ceased to exist.[1563]

Saladin's fleet was notably more successful in the Red Sea. Here it not only enjoyed a numerical advantage but was much more experienced in these highly specialized waters. Furthermore, it can be assumed that Saladin's naval crews had a better knowledge of the very few sources of drinking water around the coasts of the Red Sea. Yet even here Saladin and his successors continued the policy of the preceding Fatimids who like all other rulers of the Red Sea littoral and the Gulf of Aden beyond, assembled warfleets from available shipping as and when a threat emerged.[1564]

It often seemed that governments put greater effort into creating and maintaining coastal bases than in the building and maintaining of naval fleets. From 1160 onwards the Muwahhidun in North Africa and al-Andalus, for example, built what seems to have been an entirely new town and port on the western flank of the peninsula of Gibraltar. This became what is now the town of Gibraltar but was, at the time, intended as a secure base from which to conduct major campaigns within al-Andalus.[1565]

The sources make it clear that a great deal of effort traditionally went into naval security and intelligence in the medieval Islamic world. This particularly concerned the security of ports and harbours.[1566] On the other hand the very strict legal code which governed all aspects of Islamic life, both private and public, meant that every foreign vessel entering or approaching an Islamic port had to be treated with respect until it had been proved to be 'false' or was otherwise breaking the rules. Its crew would then, at least theoretically, be arrested and sent to be judged by the local Islamic legal authorities.[1567] Nevertheless, this system was not entirely successful since equally determined efforts by the Latin Lusignan or originally Crusader rulers of Cyprus resulted in many spies penetrating Egypt at least as far as Cairo.[1568]

Islamic warships and their commanders have been credited with fundamentally changing the tactics of small-scale naval warfare in the Mediterranean during the early medieval period. By the tenth century this had shifted from raiding coasts to attacking ships at sea. Larger fleets were still primarily concerned with assaulting coastal positions, but for small squadrons and individual galleys the primary target became anything vulnerable that was caught out in the open. This in turn resulted in a much greater need for ships, including transport or sailing vessels, to be able to defend themselves.[1569]

Such a shift in tactics was primarily responsible for the development of a convoy system in which groups of ships could not only support each other if attacked at sea, but were better able to protect themselves if moored or beached for the night. Like so much Arabic naval terminology, the word *ustul* or convoy came from a Greek term, *stolos*.[1570] One such convoy was recorded in a document found in the Cairo Geniza. It concerned a merchant convoy of four or more ships that had anchored or beached in an unnamed harbour between Alexandria and Sicily. They were attacked at night by ten galleys, each reportedly containing 100 warriors. Some of the enemy disembarked and tried to seize or burn the merchant ships but only succeeded in taking one which then got stuck on rocks and was abandoned. The firebrands hurled at the other Islamic vessels were extinguished by crews and passengers working together.[1571]

The same sources also show that, in times of tension, marines were placed aboard some merchant ships, perhaps those carrying valuable cargos or which were big enough to support lesser vessels. Large ships clearly used their height advantage when challenged by low-freeboard galleys, as when King Richard of England attacked a notably tall Islamic ship between Cyprus and Syria. The latter's crew were at first able to defend themselves with 'arrows and darts', the javelins thrown downwards proving particularly effective.[1572] A century or so earlier, the ships of an Islamic relief fleet sent from North Africa to help the city of Palermo during the Norman invasion of Sicily protected themselves from stones and arrows by erecting felt coverings.[1573]

The enemy might also be tricked, as when an Islamic ship slipped out of Acre and through the surrounding Christian blockade during the Third Crusade's siege of the city. It was able to do so because the crew shaved off their beards to look like Christian sailors.[1574] Eighty years later Sultan Baybars I of Egypt is said to have ordered the ships of the Mamluk fleet he sent against Cyprus in 1271 to be painted black 'like Christian ships' and fly banners with crosses. This time, however, the Islamic fleet was defeated.[1575]

Some major Islamic fleets were supported, organized and financed through a government department, as was the army. Saladin himself was credited with establishing a *diwan* or special ministry for the navy in 1181.[1576] Among the sources of revenue set aside for this ministry and its fleet were the proceeds or taxes from the sale of natron (hydrated sodium carbonate, a mineral found in dried-up lake beds most notably the Wadi Natrun west of the Nile Delta) which initially produced 8,000 *dinars* annually but rose to 15,500 *dinars* in 1190.[1577]

Information from the early fourteenth-century Mamluk period shows that these organization structures remained in place largely unchanged, with an *amir al-ma'* or *amir al-bahr* as the most senior officer in command of the Egyptian fleet.[1578] The Muwahhidun fleet was perhaps the most powerful created in North Africa during the period under consideration. In the mid-twelfth century it was able to send 70 ships including *shini* fighting-galleys, *tarida* horse transports and smaller *shilindi* as part of a campaign to conquer Tunisia.[1579] The Nasrid fleet of Granada was naturally smaller, but was carefully structured into squadrons. The term *ustul* was used for such a unit as well as for a convoy, and they were commanded by a *qa'id al-bahr* 'commander of the sea' or *qa'id al-ustul* 'squadon commander'.[1580]

The defence of coasts was another important consideration. Around the Mediterranean this was a reaction to what each side called piracy, either Christian or Islamic. The resulting small fortified watchtowers were not the same as the earlier *ribats*, many of which were more like small castles. This new form of tower was first seen in North Africa and the Messina region of eastern Sicily from the eleventh century onwards. The first to appear in the Italian mainland dated from the twelfth century and seem to have been based on Islamic models.[1581] Indeed they came to be known as Saraceno towers, though this probably reflected their role against Saracen raids rather than the origins of their design. Along the coast of the amirate of Granada such towers and the larger *ribats* were manned by religiously motivated volunteers,[1582] which may well have been the case elsewhere as well.

Meanwhile coastal towns and harbours similarly had to be protected. Travelling around the Islamic Middle East in 1047, the Persian pilgrim Nasir-i Khusrau believed that no fewer than 1,000 boats were always in the area of Tinnis in Egypt. He was, of course, referring to the shallow-draught fishing vessels of Lake Manzala, but Nasir-i Khusrau also noted that Tinnis itself had a strong garrison for fear of attack by Franks or Greeks, European or Byzantine pirates.[1583] Saladin had the fortifications of several ports strengthened and at Damietta these included two towers with a chain slung between them to stop enemy ships sailing up the Nile from the sea.[1584] The defences of Palermo in Sicily similarly included a harbour chain under Islamic rule.[1585]

More detailed accounts of what could happen when a harbour was attacked come from North Africa. One such occasion was around the year 1100 when Mahdia in Tunisia was blockaded by Siculo-Norman or Italian pirates. Some individual ships managed to break through the blockade including a notably large Andalusian vessel which fought its way out, though another from Morocco was driven ashore and captured.[1586] Writing later in the fourteenth century, the Mamluk military theoretician al-Ansari mentioned a blockade of Sabta (Ceuta) by Christian ships during the previous century. Here the enemy were forced to withdraw under pressure from Moroccan ships, but one Christian vessel had trouble manoeuvring and was attacked by archers whose arrows so fouled the halyards that the crew were unable to hoist their sails. As a result the ship was overtaken and captured.[1587]

Difficulties of command and communication meant that large naval battles or fleet action were highly unpredictable and were therefore generally avoided, as was also the case on the Christian side of the Mediterranean.[1588] On the other hand the Byzantine Emperor Leo VI in his *Naumachica* noted that the Muslims of Cicilia in southern Anatolia were well trained in naval warfare and generally employed much the same tactics that they used on land. This included the use of large shields or mantlets which protected the crews and marines until they got close enough to an enemy ship to board her.[1589]

Boarding tactics remained the only certain way of defeating and capturing an enemy ship. However, Ibn Mangli's mid-fourteenth-century Mamluk manual on naval warfare also contained ideas about how a small fleet could be arrayed for a major confrontation at sea. These were almost certainly the same as those used earlier, including by Byzantine fleets. The most common was a loose crescent-shaped formation. A more compact one could be adopted but was less popular. Such fleets could also use feigned retreat and other such stratagems.[1590] One of the very rare references we have to ships' crews training as squadrons rather than as individual ships was in 'Abd al-Zahir's biography of Sultan Baybars I, who is said to have arranged mock naval battle in the Nile at Cairo as a form of squadron training.[1591]

Galleys could, of course, operate and manoeuvre on the broad Nile, and certainly did so in the period of the Crusades.[1592] However, we more often hear of old ships being sunk in the river which, though broad, was shallow where it flowed into the sea at places like Damietta.[1593] Once again 'Abd al-Zahir's biography of Sultan Baybars I goes one better by recording how his hero, the Mamluk Sultan, had the Nile mouth at Damietta narrowed with specially cut stones so only small or narrow ships could enter.[1594]

WESTERN SUDAN

The central and western regions of the Sahara, together with the central and western regions of the Sahel farther south, were drawn into the Islamic world during the medieval period. In some ways they became comparable to the eastern Sahara, eastern Sudan and Ethiopia which survived as albeit a shrinking extension of the medieval Christian world. The Murabitun, who were an Islamic reformist and subsequently conquering movement, have been discussed above as part of the main medieval Islamic world because their activities were largely directed northwards. Thus their military history and military systems have been seen as part of those of Morocco, some other parts of North Africa and of al-Andalus. In reality the Murabitun also directed some of their energies southwards and eastwards, into what are now Senegal, the Gambia, Mali and parts of eastern Guinea.

Here the Murabitun, like other Islamic merchants, soldiers and missionaries, met flourishing but, for Muslims, very alien cultures that existed in varied forms throughout the sub-Saharan Sahel or steppe regions. These stretched from the Atlantic in the west to the Christian Nubian states and upper Nile regions of what is now the Republic of Sudan. In simplistic terms, civilizations like that of pre-Islamic Mali were characterized by social hierarchies in which the lowest levels were virtually enslaved by the upper levels. On the other hand this very wide, indeed stark social differentiation often resulted in the enslaved captives of defeated armies being enlisted in the victor's army where they could hope to rise to high rank.[1595] Another feature was the tendency of pre-Islamic kingship in such states to often have a strongly religious element, sometimes resulting in rulers with semi-divine status.[1596]

The spread of Islam into most of this vast region of Africa between the tenth and fourteenth centuries resulted in one of the most profound cultural changes of the Middle Ages. At the same time there was a massive increase in iron-working which, although it had been known earlier, now became much more common and spread right down to village level.[1597]

The military traditions of these societies of course varied, but it would be true to say that infantry archery played a dominant role in most. The bows involved were large and of simple, one-piece wooden construction. Several medieval Arabic geographical and travellers' accounts make this clear, and also refer to the use of poisoned arrows in a few regions.[1598] These same sources refer to large leather or rawhide shields, sometimes described as being comparable to the *lamt* shields of Saharan Berber tribes, being used by *Sudani*, 'black' in Arabic, peoples of the sub-Saharan belt; similarly their use of *mizraq* javelins and hardwood maces or clubs.[1599]

The horse had clearly been introduced to the western parts of the sub-Saharan region before the coming of Islam, but perhaps not very much before. The first clear evidence of horses in the western Sahel is, for example, some terracotta models from the Niger river region. These have been dated to the period between 500 AD and 1000 AD.[1600] Thereafter the widespread adoption and breeding of horses as military mounts could be regarded as being as important in military and political terms, as the coming of Islam was in broader cultural terms. Whereas infantry had entirely dominated warfare in earlier times, cavalry became the supreme arm during the thirteenth century.[1601] In many cases this actually occurred before a state or people converted to Islam. In other places the two processes happened almost at the same time.

2

The Mongols in the West

THE MILITARY TECHNOLOGICAL BACKGROUND

After the initial wave of Arab-Islamic expansion and conquest in the seventh and eighth centuries brought Islam to Transoxania, its further penetration of Central Asia was almost entirely by peaceful means. Merchants travelling the so-called Silk Roads between the Islamic Middle East and China played a major role in this process. One of the most significant Central Asian populations to convert to Islam during the early centuries was, however, that of the settled, agricultural peasant communities in the Qarluk Turkish tribal state. Like so many such Inner Asian Turkish and indeed Mongol tribal states, that of the Qarluks was dominated by a tribal aristocracy that was either nomadic, semi-nomadic or at least of recent nomadic origin. Nevertheless, as in so many of the often ephemeral states in this part of the world, a substantial proportion of its people actually consisted of agricultural peasant villagers and somewhat smaller mercantile urban communities. The Qarluk state did not itself become officially Islamic. The first recognizable Inner Asian and supposedly 'nomadic' Turkish states to do so was that of the Qarakhanids which was recognized as Islamic around the mid-tenth century.[1]

In broader strategic and political terms it is important to recognize that some of the subsequent Mongol thrusts westward were not necessarily or overtly intended as campaigns of conquest. The assault upon the Khwarazmshahs of Transoxania was a result of Mongol competition with another major power which was perceived as a rival for domination within Inner Asia. Clearly the Khwarazmshahs had their own ambitions in this area. Once the invasion of Khwarazmian territory in Transoxania had started, however, the Mongols were almost inevitably drawn into the crushing and conquest of the entire Khwarazmian state. This had, by then, also expanded westward to such an extent that it was rivalling the revived 'Abbasid Caliphal state in western Iran and Iraq. Having gone that far, and having then crushed the 'Abbasid Caliphate in Iraq, the western Mongol armies almost seem to have been drawn willy-nilly deeper into the Islamic heartlands of the Middle East. Similarly, the Mongol rivalry with the vast Kipchaq Turkish khanate or khanates of the western steppes drew them into conflict with Russia and eventually with Hungary, Poland and ever deeper into Central Europe.[2]

Several generations of armchair strategists have expressed surprise that the Latin Crusader States of the Middle East, who were by now in clear retreat, did not seize upon an alliance with the Mongols as a means of not only saving themselves but somehow crushing the Islamic forces of the Middle East in a two-fronted attack. Yet for the people of the Crusader States themselves the first waves of Mongol campaigns were seen as a threat, just as they were by the Latins' Islamic neighbours. Indeed some Crusader chronicles seemed to reflect a comparable fear and horror of the Mongols with their strange and seemingly alien culture.[3] The Papacy in Rome eventually toyed with the idea of some huge, almost worldwide, strategic alliance between Latin Christendom and the Mongol Great Khan, as did several senior Western European rulers. Nevertheless, most though not all of the political, military and cultural élites of the Crusader States continued to fear these strange newcomers.[4]

Mongol warfare and military organization reflected the nature of Mongol society. This was also the case with other societies. Yet in the harsh environment of Inner Asia, peoples and tribes probably competed for limited resources in an even fiercer and more desperate manner than in most other parts of the world. This was as true in the true steppes as it was in the forested steppes and the forests. The Mongols were themselves, of course, not simply a steppe people. Several of their constituent tribes were forest-dwellers, and even the steppe tribes were competing for more than just good grasslands. They competed, for example, for rivers that could supply plentiful fish as an alternative source of food.[5]

Nor were the Mongols' western neighbours, rivals and future victims, the Turks, static in terms of cultural and political developments. The essentially tribal states of the Turco-Mongol steppe regions had risen and fallen for millennia, some of them establishing empires that almost stood comparison with that of the Mongol 'World Conqueror' Genghis Khan himself. Within such states, amongst both the nomads and the settled peoples whom they so often dominated, there were economic, cultural and indeed religious changes as well as political ones. Nevertheless, these may have been most dramatic and deep rooted along the margins of the steppes where the largely Turkish dominant peoples interacted most closely with settled populations who were themselves often neither Turkish nor Mongol.

One interesting example was at the furthest western end of the vast Eurasian steppes, in what became Moldavia, where the steppe grasslands met the foothills of the densely forested Carpathian Mountains. Here archaeological investigations suggest that local societies became increasingly militarized during the tenth to twelfth centuries.[6] Being at the western end of the huge steppe 'corridor' which stretched eastwards to China, Moldavia was one of those areas where once-nomadic peoples, pushed by stronger rivals, were often shoved westward out of the steppes altogether and into the foothills where they settled. Meanwhile the existing local populations were in turn pushed further into the mountains.[7] Comparable processes are likely to have been taking place in many other areas, especially where the steppes were bordered by mountains or uplands which could serve as refuges for weaker populations.

Another fate of defeated tribes or those that had been expelled from the steppes was to be absorbed by a neighbouring and powerful settled state. This had often happened along the frontiers of China. It happened to a rather lesser extent along the steppe frontiers of the Islamic world and most certainly occurred in the Byzantine-ruled Balkans. The Pechenegs and Kipchaqs of this area have already been mentioned in the chapter dealing with Byzantine military matters (see vol. 1). Here the Kipchaqs played a role in the creation of the second Bulgarian state during the late twelfth and early thirteenth centuries,[8] while there is archaeological evidence to show that Kipchaqs were settling amongst, and being assimilated into, the local Vlach (Romanian) populations of the Carpathian foothills during this same period.[9] Thereafter the Kipchaqs, though supposedly crushed by the Mongols, would be of particular importance in the military history of the Byzantines, the Mamluk Sultanate and the western regions of the Mongol 'World Empire'.

The astonishing military successes and empire-building of Genghis Khan in the early thirteenth century have tended to overshadow the previous history of the Mongols. Peoples and leaders had emerged from Mongol-speaking culture long before the rise of Genghis Khan himself, though not, perhaps, to the extent that the Turks had been a seedbed of empires. Nevertheless, some scholars have gone as far as to suggest that early Mongol culture served as a model for Oghuz and Seljuk Turkish state and military organization.[10] One thing that can be said with reasonable certainty is that the Mongols were under stronger and more direct Chinese cultural influence than were the Turks. Furthermore, they also had close cultural links with semi-nomadic, forest-dwelling and settled peoples further east in what are now Manchuria in north-eastern China, and Korea.

Once the astonishing wave of Mongol conquest and expansion began in the thirteenth century, certain military features became clear. Those Mongol armies which invaded eastern Iran were very big when compared with local Islamic forces.[11] What is more, Mongol society and its military systems enabled Mongol military leaders to use such large numbers more effectively than had been seen before.[12] This continued to be the case as the Mongols pressed deeper into the Islamic world, Hülegü invading 'Abbasid Iraq with some 70,000 men.[13]

What seems almost more remarkable is that the Mongols continued to be able to field remarkably large armies even after they themselves had ceased to be a truly nomadic society. This cultural and economic transformation was well under way during the second half of the thirteenth century, but the degree to which it caused, or was reflected in, various more detailed aspects of military organization remains a matter of debate amongst military historians. One seemingly small example is the question of whether the Mongol invaders of the Islamic Middle East were instrumental in the readoption of heavily armoured cavalry in this region, or whether they themselves adopted heavy cavalry tactics as a result of their military experiences in this region.

RECRUITMENT, ORGANIZATION AND MOTIVATION

The ethnic, cultural, military and political makeup of Central and Inner Asia was much more complex than is generally realized. Although Turks dominated most of the steppe lowlands and Mongols dominated the regions to the north-east, many upland and mountainous areas of what are now the newly independent post-Soviet states in Central Asia had been dominated by an Iranian-speaking, castle-dwelling aristocracy of *dihqans*. It was only during the Qarakhanid period from the late tenth to early thirteenth centuries that Turkish domination became almost universal, while the local authority and military role of the *dihqans* rapidly declined.[14]

It was also during this period that the military prestige of the Turks spread across the entire Islamic world, even into regions where Turkish soldiers were virtually unknown. This is shown in the work of an early twelfth-century writer in al-Andalus, at the furthest western end of the medieval Islamic world. Here Sa'id al-Andalusi was, in fact, expressing a generally accepted view when he maintained in his *'Book of the Categories of Nations'* that the Chinese were the most advanced in science, technology and the graphic arts, whereas the Turks: 'distinguish themselves by their ability to wage war and by the construction of arms, and by being the best horsemen and tacticians. They have the sharpest eyes when it comes to throwing spears, striking with swords, or shooting arrows'.[15] At this stage, of course, most Muslims outside the frontier regions of Central Asia had hardly heard of the Mongols.

In terms of military recruitment, the Mongols, though more ruthless than their Turkish predecessors, did continue age-old steppe practices when dealing with defeated rivals. This had previously resulted in the defeated ruling élites either leaving to seek their military fortunes elsewhere or declining in status to merge with the mass of the ordinary population. The latter then recognized their conquerors as rulers. The only real difference with the Mongols was that when they were the conquerors they tended to be much more drastic in their removal of defeated élites. Yet even here there were numerous and increasing cases where the losers were absorbed into Mongol armies.

The strictly 'Mongol' army, if such a thing ever existed, was regarded by many of its Islamic rivals, victims and subsequently subjects as more of a militia than a professional army such as those which by then dominated warfare throughout most of the Islamic world.[16] This militia or 'people in arms' method of raising very large forces had been characteristic of much or indeed most of Inner Asia long before the rise of Genghis Khan. States dominated by nomadic tribes could and often did raise substantial numbers of warriors from subordinate, settled and even urban populations. This had been particularly apparent in the Semirecyë region south of Lake Balkash.[17] Further west, the Romanian-speaking semi-nomadic Vlachs of the upland regions of the Balkans also often gave military support to supposedly nomadic Turkish 'steppe states', most notably to the Kipchaqs in the twelfth and early thirteenth centuries.[18] In turn the army of Johaniya of Wallachia and northern Bulgaria, when fighting against the Crusader conquerors of Constantinople in 1205, included many lightly armoured pagan Kipchaq horse-archers.[19]

The military relationship between steppe and immediately neighbouring peoples was, once again, more complex than is often recognized. Such a relationship would rapidly re-emerge in the wake of the first waves of Mongol conquests. Nor did it only involve peoples to the south and west. The Oirats, for example, had been a separate Mongol tribe living in the Siberian forests rather than the steppes. During the maelstrom of Mongol 'world conquests', a group separated and re-emerged as the Kalmuks. Although their new name was Turkish, the Kalmuks did not follow the Turks into the Islamic fold. Instead they remained pagan and migrated westward during the period of Hülegü's campaigns. While most of those other Mongols who came west and settled in or north of the Islamic world soon themselves became Muslim, the Kalmuks remained fiercely anti-Islamic, largely adopting Buddhism during the fifteenth to seventeenth centuries. Today they remain the only Buddhist 'nation' within the geographical boundaries of Europe, with their own Russian province of Kalmykiya north of the Caucasus Mountains.[20]

The Turkification of some Mongol tribes or groups went hand-in-hand with the rapid absorption of 'defeated' existing Turkish peoples within the western reaches of the Mongol Great Khan's empire. By 1256 it has been estimated that most of the Mongol armies campaigning in the Middle East actually consisted of a Mongol élite with a larger mass of Turkish soldiers, all commanded by a Mongol officer corps. These armies similarly included a small number of Chinese artillerymen and siege specialists, among the best known of whom was a Chinese general named Kuo K'an who served under Hülegü.[21]

The organization of Mongol armies inevitably changed or developed during and after the period of sudden expansion. They also adopted much from their predecessors. One such were the Qara Khitai whose defeat of the Seljuk Great Sultanate in Transoxania in 1141 probably gave rise to, or additional strength to, the European legend of Prester John as a powerful 'enemy of the Saracens' somewhere in the eastern parts of the world. Briefly ruling a huge territory on both sides of the Tien-Shan Mountains, these Qara Khitai were very Chinese in culture, which made them different to most of the other more Turkish empires of Inner Asia.[22] Furthermore, the administration of their state and the organization of their army were so similar to that of the subsequent early Mongol 'World Empire' that some degree of influence seems indisputable.

What the Qara or 'Black' Khitai, the eastern Khitai, the Kitans and the Mongols shared, and which distinguished them from the Turks, both Islamic and not-yet Islamic, was this strong degree of Chinese influence upon so many aspects of their culture, not least upon its military aspects. It is also important not to read too much into the word 'tribe' when looking at Mongol social, political and military organization. To some extent the term 'clan' might be more appropriate, and to think in terms of one or more ruling or dominant tribe-clans with the rest of society consisting of ordinary tribe-clans or conquered peoples. Membership of such social units was fluid, especially for those who were outside the very top or élite groups. Yet even the dominant tribe or clan could be joined or left according to circumstances.[23]

In strictly military terms the basic Mongol district or *qirat* was also in some ways a military unit, being theoretically expected to maintain 1,000 men each.[24] The Mongol term *tümen* is less straightforward. It was used to refer to a large military unit theoretically of 10,000 men,[25] but may also have referred to an area of land that was expected to provide provisions for the *tümen* military unit.[26] This terminology largely remained in use even after the Mongol army in Iran and Iraq changed from being a force of nomadic occupiers into a settled and largely assimilated military aristocracy.[27] Nevertheless it is clear that the traditional Mongol military and payment structure was already breaking down by the time of the Il-Khanid ruler Ghazan I in the final years of the thirteenth and the first of the fourteenth centuries. This resulted in the Il-Khans' adoption of the well-established Islamic *'iqta* system of military fiefs.[28] More surprisingly, perhaps, was the fact that the already large Mongol army in Il-Khanid Iran and Iraq is understood to have increased yet further in size. Meanwhile its nature was changing.[29]

Little study has been undertaken into the motivation of the Mongol armies; there almost being a tendency to dismiss Genghis Khan's followers as bloodcrazed barbarians who followed and almost worshipped a leader who brought them booty and glory. In reality the Mongol warriors' motivation is likely to have been just as varied and complex as that of any other fighting force. Because the true

Mongol population was so small, estimated at between one and two million in the time of Genghis Khan himself, the lives and welfare of their soldiers were very precious to Mongol commanders or rulers. Furthermore, because the original Mongol army was more like a militia, the adult male Mongol population was, in effect, the army. Great care was therefore taken to keep the troops content and they were rarely driven too hard. Wherever possible, the Mongols' own wounded were never left on the battlefield even in cases of a defeat, and it was considered criminal for a leader to lose men through carelessness. This resulted in Mongol armies generally avoiding close combat or indeed any combat that was expensive in the lives of their own troops.[30]

On the other hand religion is unlikely to have played so important, and certainly not so unifying, a role as it did in, for example, medieval Islamic and Christian armies. There were in fact many Nestorian Christians in Central and Inner Asia in the twelfth and thirteenth centuries, especially amongst settled populations and in the Semirecyë region. There were also Nestorian Christians amongst the nomads. At the same time there were large numbers of Buddhists, Manichaeans and, more suprisingly perhaps, Muslims. The Turkish Qarakhanid Great Qaghan of Balasaghun in Semirecyë is believed to have been the first Islamic ruler to have submitted to the Qarakhitai. The latter was described in Islamic sources as a 'pagan', but may in reality have been a Manichaean or Christian.[31] This humiliation of Islam would be remembered for several decades and actually resulted in the first wave of Mongol conquerors being welcomed as liberators from the Qarakhitai.[32]

Nevertheless, the greatest number of people in Genghis Khan's armies is likely to have adhered to traditional or indigenous shamanistic beliefs.[33] These involved some interesting ideas which had a direct impact upon military campaigns. The most obvious was the use of 'rain-stones', pebbles that were believed to possess what might in modern terms be called magical powers to influence the weather. This use of rain-stones seems originally to have been a Turkish shamanistic belief but was adopted by the Mongols in the early thirteenth century,[34] and remained in use in some areas even when the Turks and western Mongols converted to Islam. The ritual sacrifice of horses was never on a sufficient scale to have an impact upon military capabilities, yet it was common amongst the pre-Islamic Kipchaq and Oghuz Turks, as well as the Mongols of the westernmost Khanate of the Golden Horde. Here it was only abandoned with the latter's conversion to Islam in the later thirteenth century.

Medieval Mongol society sometimes seems to have been more dour and disciplined than that of the medieval Turks, perhaps reflecting Buddhist Chinese influence, whereas the Turks largely converted to Islam and adopted the more individualistic values characteristic of Islamic civilization.[35] It has similarly been suggested that the pre-Islamic Turkish wood and stone *balbals* or simple carvings of human figures which dot the Eurasian steppes and some neighbouring territory were a replacement for an earlier practice of human sacrifice, but this again remains unproven.[36] Certainly the taking of the heads of slain foes and hanging them on the harness of the hero's horse appears in some Central Asian epic poems, including those of the Mongols.[37] Another idea that reflected the priorities of ancient Mongol society was the belief that the thumb was the seat of an individual's soul. The thumb was, of course, vital in the Turco-Mongol style of archery and to destroy the thumbs of defeated warriors was a terrible punishment.[38] One feature is clear above all others: that the Mongol rulers and occupiers of Iran and Iraq began to lose their distinct identity after converting to Islam at the end of the thirteenth century.[39] This did not occur to the same extent amongst those Mongol Khanates of the western steppes, Transoxania and western Siberia which eventually adopted Islam as their state religion. Apart from such religious changes, their nomadic or semi-nomadic culture and forms of military organization remained largely unchanged. What happened, however, was that these western Mongol Khanates ceased to be Mongol in much more than name; instead being to a greater or lesser extent Turcified by those Turkish-Islamic peoples whom they had so recently conquered.

STRATEGY, TACTICS AND TRAINING

The Mongols' belief that they had a preordained mission to conquer the world does not seem to have existed in the early days of expansion, probably developing as a result of the Mongols' astonishing early successes.[40] Perhaps it was copied from the Turks who certainly had such a concept in both previous and later centuries. Once the idea had taken hold, however, it left little room for real cooperation with other civilizations. In the Middle East, for example, the Mongols seemed as unready and unwilling to cooperate with the Latin Crusader States against their mutual Islamic foes as the Latins were to cooperate with them.[41] Even Hülegü's idea of an alliance only came after his quarrel with Berke, the Khan of the similarly Mongol Golden Horde.[42] On the other hand, the Mongols' more local alliance with the Armenians started earlier and became deeply entrenched.[43] This did not stop the Mamluk Sultanate of Egypt and Syria greatly fearing the emergence of some strategic alliance between Latins and Mongols.[44]

The degree of devastation and slaughter which marked the Mongol conquests continues to astonish many historians. It seems, in fact, to have been a conscious strategic policy based upon, or growing out of, earlier traditions of smaller-scale warfare between competing tribes. Here, in an almost complete reversal of what was considered normal in medieval Islamic and Byzantine warfare, the object had been to utterly crush an enemy and to remove them as potential competitors for very scarce natural resources.[45] Such a different attitude towards warfare came as a monumental shock to the Mongols' Islamic and Christian opponents during the first waves of conquest. The resulting strategy of terror, as it would be seen by such opponents, clearly undermined enemy morale and it would be many years before rivals such as the Mamluk Sultanate learned to be similarly determined, though rarely if ever as ruthless.

When conducting an offensive, the Mongols usually relied upon having, and usually achieving, an overwhelming numerical advantage. Indeed their rulers attempted to muster considerably more troops than they expected to need. This was feasible because the warriors in question were expected to be supported by their families.[46] As a result the army with which Hülegü invaded Iran in the 1250s is said to have included two out of every ten available Mongol fighting men, and this was, of course, only for one campaign on one front while the Mongols were similarly invading China.[47]

The disadvantages of fielding such huge armies soon became apparent when, in 1260, Hülegü withdrew most of his forces from Syria because the already limited available fodder and grazing had been used up. The Mamluks also learned to take advantage of the Mongols' numbers by burning dry grasslands to reduce the fodder for the invading Mongols' ponies still further. According to the Christian Syrian chronicler Bar Hebraeus, an earlier Mongol campaign stalled in the summer of 1244 because the hard, dry ground damaged their ponies' legs and unshod hooves.[48]

When it came to tactics, the Mongols had their own established traditions as well as those of their numerous defeated enemies upon which to draw. Genghis Khan himself dictated an *Art of War* which was recorded and written down for his followers. It was based upon the five key elements of speed, suddenness, ferocity, variety of tactics and iron discipline.[49] The traditional view of Mongol open battlefield tactics maintains that they employed a mixture of light, medium and heavy cavalry until the mid-thirteenth century; that is during their greatest period of conquest.[50] The Il-Khanid state established by the Mongols in Iran and Iraq is then said to have tried to overcome the difficulties which their first invasions faced in Syria by imitating its Mamluk foes. This is believed to have resulting in Il-Khanid armies adopting various Islamic military traditions, including shower-shooting rather than harassment horse-archery tactics, the wearing of heavier armour and the mass production of hardened leather armour.[51]

A recent alternative interpretation suggested that Mongol warfare had, from the start, relied upon a mixture of horse archery and heavy armoured close-combat cavalry. This, it was suggested, represented an improved version of traditional steppe tactics which resulted in the Mongols having larger numbers of heavy cavalry than their steppe foes.[52] It has even been suggested that such Mongol heavy cavalry riding armoured horses were more heavily armoured than the average mid-thirteenth-century Western European knight,[53] at least by the time that the Mongols invaded Europe. This Mongol heavy cavalry may have been concentrated into the Great Khan's own guard regiments and, according to this interpretation, is likely to have existed in greater numbers than the similar heavily armoured cavalry élite of the Mamluk Sultanate.[54] Such a thesis remains unproven, but it is interesting to note that, on the basis of recent archaeological discoveries in Syria, there was a dramatic increase in the use of substantial pieces of heavy, hardened or layered leather armour in the Mamluk garrisons at the time of the greatest Mongol threat.

Genghis Khan's own *Art of War* paid close attention to battlefield stratagems and tricks. No less than 15 were listed, including one called the 'Throw into Disorder Tactics' consisting of stampeding oxen or wild horses into the enemy's lines in order to disrupt them. Centuries earlier a virtually identical stratagem had been used by the pre-Islamic Turks against the first Arab-Islamic invaders of Central Asia. Then there were the 'Confuse and Intimidate' tactics which involved lighting multiple fires, mounting straw dummies on spare horses, or tying branches to the tails of horses to raise additional dust, all of which were designed to give the impression of larger numbers. Most of the other tactics in the list were more straightforward,[55] and it is clear that such ideas really were used in warfare. For example, the Mongols are reported to have tied dummy figures on to spare horses at the battle of Perwan in Afghanistan in 1221 and during their invasion of Hungary a generation later.[56]

Mongol battle arrays were varied and sometimes complex; certainly more so than the interesting but simplistic interpretation found in plans of assorted eastern people published in Berlin in 1940.[57] Many of them were, of course, shared with other Central and Inner Asian peoples of the same and earlier periods. One of the most interesting such arrays was described, with a plan, by the early thirteenth-century Islamic northern Indian military writer Fakhr al-Din Mubarakshah. His 'Battle Array of the Turks when the Khaqan is present' may be based on what was traditionally known of Qarakhitai military practice.[58] It consisted of nine circular units, three-by-three, which is practically identical to the Chinese *jing* formation. The Chinese name actually means a waterwell, but it was the Chinese written character *jing*, which was important. The formation is said to have been developed or perfected by Chinese armies of the T'ang period and again consisted of nine units forming a three-by-three square. Here any external three could form a front to face a Central Asian, usually Turkish, enemy while the remaining six provided support, rear and flank protection. They could also be used to extend the front and outflank the enemy as required.

Fakhr al-Din Mubarakshah's 'Battle Array of the Turks' placed the non-combatant artificers, harem and herds in the central unit, this being the only one which could not form a front. The Chinese *jing* version of the same concept was discussed in great depth in a military text known as the *'Questions and Replies Between T'ang Taizong and Li Weigong'*, Li Weigong being the official title of general Li Qing who commanded the T'ang conquest of the Yangtze valley and also campaigned successfully against the Turks.[59] Another favourite battlefield tactic used by the Mongols once they had surrounded a foe was to leave one small gap open, which the Mongols could control, letting only as many as their commander wished to escape.

Whatever the role and importance of armoured cavalry, horse-archery remained central to Central Asian steppe tactics. This was as true of the Mongols as it had been of their predecessors. It is clear that long range harassment tactics on their own often failed to break a discplined foe, though it could cause considerable losses in horses. That must clearly have been why even the most traditional Turco-Mongol armies of the Eurasian steppes had to be able to close with the enemy to achieve a final or decisive victory.

The resulting combination of tactics, as employed by the Mongols themselves, was well described in the *Historia Tartarorum*, written in Poland in 1247 but based upon earlier accounts including that of Carpini. According to this source:

> A number of them [Mongol cavalrymen], each supplied with several quivers complete with arrows, begin to shoot before their opponents' arrows can reach them, sometimes even ahead of time when they are not in range. As soon as their arrows can reach the mark unhindered they are said owing to the density of their fire to rain arrows rather than to shoot them. If they find their enemies unprepared, they surround them suddenly in a ring leaving only a single way of escape, and attack them fiercely with a hail of javelins.[60]

The *Historia Tartarorum* goes on to recommend how best to combat these Mongols: 'If, however, there are no crossbowmen [*ballistarii*] to spare, the cavalry with armoured horses [*faleratis equis*] must be placed in the van, and these must take cover behind a wall of strong shields on the horses' heads and immediately baffle the Tartars' arrows.' A better translation might be 'strong shields before the horses' heads' or perhaps it was a misunderstanding of *chamfron* pieces of horse-armour for the animal's head.[61]

Assuming the capabilities of Mongol ponies to be comparable with those of slightly larger polo ponies, and riders of comparable endurance in the saddle, it has been estimated that this harassment horse-archery tactic could result in a Mongol horse-archer loosing 20 potentially armour-piercing arrows every ten seconds. This would be during a four minute assault by a unit of 80 horsemen in four waves of 20 men each. Such a scheme could also assume the presence of 20 more heavily armoured men in each unit, making it up to the approved total of 100. The heavy cavalrymen presumably did not attack at this stage of the battle. A further calculation suggests that a Mongol soldier with 60 arrows and five ponies could sustain active combat for 45 minutes, the ponies being changed after eight to ten minutes of fast action. Consequently an average-sized Mongol army could keep up this sort of pressure for one and a half hours.[62] Such calculations make many unproven assumptions, but there seem to be no intrinsic reasons why they should be incorrect.

Similar tactics had been used by the Kipchaq Turks in the Balkans a few decades before the arrival of the Mongols. Here they were described in some detail by Byzantine chroniclers and by Robert de Clari, a French participant in the Fourth Crusade. According to Byzantine sources the Kipchaq warriors attacked first with bows and then with javelins, tried to lure their enemies into an ambush with feigned retreat and then turned to attack them with sabres.[63] Robert de Clari further noted that each Kipchaq warrior had ten to twelve horses, which was probably an exaggeration.[64]

The shock-charge to close combat which concluded such tactics, whether by Kipchaq Turks or by Genghis Khan's Mongols, initially fell to the armoured heavy cavalry and was often done to protect the withdrawal of their own lightly armoured or unarmoured horse-archers.[65] The final battle-winning charge would also have been initially carried out by heavy cavalry, though the others might later have joined in to complete the rout. In this respect Turco-Mongol tactics were essentially the same as those of the Islamic world and most of Europe as well. Whether or not large numbers of fully armoured cavalry were an established or a new feature of twelfth-century Mongol armies, the way in which they were used was reasonably consistent. It was recorded by the Il-Khanid army in battle near Herat in 1269,[66] at the battle of Elbistan against the Mamluks in 1277,[67] and again against the Mamluks at the first and second battle of Hims in 1281 and 1299 respectively.[68] The outcomes of these battles also show that it did not always ensure victory.

In more than one of these confrontations the Mongols had been checked and forced to fight defensively; even to dismount and fight on foot. It is therefore significant that Genghis Khan's book on the *Art of War* already included in its 'Fifteen Military Tactics', one called the 'Archer's Tactics' in which the men dismounted and fought as infantry archers, sometimes using their horses as ramparts.[69] Once again this was more than a mere theory, having been recorded in use against the Mamluks in Syria, though only at times of desperation. The idea of Mongol infantry almost seems like a misnomer, but the Mongols were certainly adaptable, even if those who fought on foot in their armies were not themselves usually Mongols. An interesting variation was the 'camel riding troops of the Tartars' who were particularly feared in Damascus during the Mongol invasion of 1299–1301.[70] Pre-Islamic Turkish mounted infantry riding two-humped Bactrian camels had, of course, been recorded by the Chinese centuries earlier.

Not much seems to be known about Mongol field fortifications, though they certainly used them. On the other hand those of their Turkish predecessors in the western steppes were described by a number of outside observers. According to the Byzantine chronicler Michael Attaleites, the mid-eleventh century Pechenegs 'covered by their waggons like a wall, awaited the attack of the Byzantines', then drove back the Byzantine cavalry with arrows before pursuing them in a counter-attack.[71] A more unexpected account is found in the Scandinavian *Heimskringla*. Dating from around 1177, this history of the kings of Norway described a battle with the Kipchaq Turks in which the 'pagan king' ordered his men to dig a ditch behind which he drew up his waggons.[72] This was based upon an actual battle of 1122 or 1123 in which Scandinavian Varangian troops led by Torir Helsingr took part in Byzantine service alongside Flemings and Frenchmen.

The individual skill which most attracted the attention of those who fought against the Mongols was, naturally enough, their styles of horse-archery. One of the most detailed accounts was written by Vincent de Beauvais who based his account upon the authority of Simon de St Quentin. He stated that: 'When the archers let fly their arrows, they withdraw entirely their right arm from out their armour, and put it back when the shaft has left the bow. But only the barons and the military chiefs, the standard bearers and the constables wear this armour, so it is believed not a tenth part of them have it or wear it.'[73] The latter point clearly has a direct bearing upon the question of how many men in the Mongol armies could be described as heavy cavalry. According to Marco Polo each Mongol cavalryman carried 30 armour-piercing or long range arrows and 30 broadheaded arrows for use at close range.[74] Islamic sources further add that the *angushtvana* 'thumb ring' was used by the Mongols, though apparently with the *kaman-i guruha* pellet bow outside Isfahan in 1238.[75]

MILITARY EQUIPMENT: MANUFACTURE, TRADE AND STRATEGIC MATERIALS

The Mongols made use of whatever military equipment they could lay their hands on, their own culture having traditionally been relatively poor in arms and armour when compared with neighbours such as the Chinese, Turks and Koreans; nor does there seem to have been a specific style that could be associated with the Mongols.[76] This predatory eclecticism continued throughout the great Mongol conquests. The almost inevitable result was that Mongol armies settling in, rather than merely campaigning in, widely separated regions of Asia soon looked rather different from each other. The arms and armour used in Mongol-ruled China, judging by the limited archaeological as well as the written and pictorial evidence, soon differed from that of Il-Khanid armies in Mongol-ruled Iran and Iraq. In contrast the differences between the armies of what became the Mongol Il-Khanate and those of the Mongol Golden Horde and its smaller successor Khanates in the western steppes and neighbouring regions were relatively small.

Despite these differences, the Mongol 'World Empire' and its constituent Khanates were characterized by a quite extraordinary degree of cultural exchange between east and west, north and south. This is well known where the arts, science and technology are concerned. It can also be seen in arms, armour and the decoration of such military items. Indeed the fruitful flow of knowledge and fashions went far beyond the Mongol world itself, resulting in Chinese military technologies and styles penetrating both the later medieval Islamic world and later medieval Europe. Not so much seems to have flowed in the opposite direction, though the more advanced forms of Islamic siege technology were taken to China by the Mongols, along with a number of willing or unwilling siege technicians or engineers.

Soon after the Mongols conquered Iran they established their own system of arsenals for the manufacture and supply of military equipment.[77] The idea that the Mongol Il-Khanid army also began fielding significantly larger numbers of heavily armoured cavalry, often riding fully armoured horses, lies behind the belief that the strains this change imposed upon the finances of the Il-Khanid state led to significant administrative reforms.[78] Nevertheless, the Il-Khanate state in Iran and Iraq collapsed before its dominant Mongol political and military élites could make a full transition from their own somewhat primitive traditions of arms, armour and military manufacture to the comparable and highly sophisticated traditions of the eastern Islamic regions.[79] On the other hand, the traditions of arms and armour which developed in fourteenth-century Iran, after the fall of the Il-Khans, proved to be a fruitful amalgam of previous Islamic, Turkish and Mongol concepts.

While there is evidence of Mongol warriors using straight swords, especially in or near China, it is the curved sabre which was most commonly associated with them. It was by no means, however, a Mongol invention. Many of the people of the Eurasian steppes had carried such weapons. The earliest datable example within what might be regarded as the western half of the steppes was found near Kharkov, north of the Black Sea, in an area and period dominated by the Turco-Judaic Khazars. This particular weapon was found in association with an Umayyad Islamic *dirham* coin of 740 AD and an 'Abbasid coin of 799 AD, while the curved blade itself probably dated from the late eighth or early ninth century.[80]

Paradoxically, the Mongols themselves gave high status in their poetic epics to Nepalese sword-smiths from northern India.[81] The reasons for this are unknown, though probably associated with the spread of Buddhist culture to Inner Asia long before the rise of Genghis Khan. However, within Nepal the tradition of sword making and design seems to have been fully within the pre-Islamic

Indian tradition where there is no evidence for curved sabres before the late medieval Turco-Islamic conquests; the only curved swords being rather peculiar reverse-curved weapons which had no connection with the development of the true sabre.

There is abundant archaeological as well as documentary and, to a lesser extent, pictorial evidence that the peoples of the steppes, both Turks and Mongols, used a variety of other close-combat weapons including axes.[82] Mongol bows were of the composite type and were essentially the same as those used by the Turks. A variety of different quivers were similarly used to hold arrows, and these are normally assumed to reflect different archery techniques though they might also have been influenced by the characteristic weather of a particular region and the availability of suitable materials from which quivers could be made.

The most convincing argument yet put forward suggests that the small and open-ended quiver was not suitable for 'quick-draw' shower-shooting archery as it held too few arrows and was normally slung with the open end pointing in the wrong direction for such archery. Shower-shooting was done with a bunch of arrows being held in the hand, with their points directed downwards and actually being below the archer's elbow. Hence the quiver needed to present the arrows ready for the hand, with their points upwards and forwards. In other words the deep quiver holding numerous arrows and with its opening angled forwards was suitable, perhaps even the only style suitable, for such a shower-shooting technique.[83] This was precisely the sort of quiver most commonly associated with the Mongols in archaeological, pictorial and documentary sources.

Like the Turks, the Mongols made considerable use of shields formed of spirals of cane bound together with often highly coloured thread. The Mongol name for such a shield, *khalkha*,[84] was also clearly related to the Turkish name for the same thing, *qalqan*. A number of such shields preserved in Tibetan monasteries are said to date from the Mongol period, having been pious donations by Mongol leaders or rulers. The little study which has so far been made of these and other military relics which were brought out of Tibet during the time of the Chinese Cultural Revolution in the later twentieth century has come to the perhaps rather surprising conclusion that many of them really could date from the fourteenth century.[85] Furthermore, their structure is almost identical to a far more fragmentary late thirteenth- or early fourteenth-century Turco-Mamluk spiral cane shield found by archaeologists in the Citadel of Damascus.[86] Judging from the evidence of Arabic chronicles and geographical texts, the traditional shields used by early medieval Tibetan warriors may have been made of hardened leather rather than spiral cane, and have been of the domed form known as a *daraqa* in Arabic.[87]

Archaeological as well as other forms of evidence point to the use of hardened leather armour in many parts of Inner Asia, certainly including Tibet and probably including Mongolia, before the rise of Genghis Khan. Much of it was probably of the laced lamellar kind known in Arabic and Persian as a *jawshan*.[88] There is, indeed, strong evidence that the Mongols were poorer in iron resources than were their Turkish neighbours, but this clearly changed when the Mongols conquered so much of the known world in the thirteenth century. By the time Mongol armies swept across most of the eastern half of the Islamic world, their military élites were relatively well equipped. When they swept even further west to defeat the Kipchaqs they had the military wealth of Islamic Central Asia, much of Iran and a substantial part of China to draw upon. So much so that it has recently been suggested that most or even all of the supposed Kipchaq arms, armour and horse-armour found by archaeologists in what are now eastern Ukraine and south-western Russia are really Mongol, dating from after the destruction of the Kipchaq state. Well-known items such as a solid iron vambrace for a man's lower arm and a heavy three-piece chamfron for a horse's head may therefore be Golden Horde Mongol rather than Kipchaq Turkish.[89]

The Western European ambassador and missionary William of Rubruck described, in his account of his travels, how he saw Mongol soldiers being given better equipment by their ruler: 'I saw them being presented with iron plates and helmets from Persia.'[90] Although William of Rubruck insisted that the great majority of Mongol warriors still only possessed cheap and clumsy armour of hardened leather (see below), it could seem that the military élites or aristocracies possessed quite superb armour. Two examples were found in a cave in the Tuva region of Russia, on the border with Mongolia. They date from the late thirteenth or fourteenth century and, though not yet fully understood, are believed to have formed a set. One consisted of a sort of coat-of-plates, Chinese in inspiration and perhaps also in origin, where the scales were originally attached to a leather or fabric base. Clearly not of lamellar construction, it may possibly have served as a more limited but luxurious outer garment which did not cover the whole body. It could, in fact, have been worn with the second armour which consisted of a smaller number of larger, thicker plates, though again the complete garment would have been relatively short and was sleeveless.[91]

Further to his description of a small number of Mongol troops being given iron armour, William of Rubruck also referred to a form of leather armour which clearly struck him as strange: 'I also saw two men who appeared before Mangu armed with tunics made of curved pieces of stiff leather, which were very clumsy and cumbersome.'[92] These were almost certainly examples of a form of laminated leather armour formed into hinged hoops which went around the wearer's body, each horizontal hoop being attached by laces or straps to those above and below.

Until recently the reality behind descriptions such as that by William of Rubruck remained in the realm of historical speculation. However, within the last decade or so a substantial number of such laminated and hooped leather cuirasses have come to light in Syria and perhaps neighbouring regions to the east and north. Though found in Mamluk contexts, they are unlike anything else from the pre-Mamluk Islamic periods and are in some cases decorated in an unexpectedly Central Asian or almost Chinese style. Consequently, they may provisionally be regarded as Mongolian in inspiration if not necessarily Mongolian in origin. Furthermore, the dating tests which have so far been carried out confirm that they, like abundant other military matériel found in the same locations, almost certainly date from the early Mamluk period or even from the time of the first Mongol invasions of Islamic territory.[93]

Linking the archaeological evidence and that from contemporary outside observers with the terminology used by the Mongols themselves is not straight-forward. Nevertheless, it seems that the Mongol *khuyagh* was usually a lamellar cuirass, probably of both the metallic and hardened leather forms. This term may also have included the layered leather 'hooped' cuirasses. The term *khatangku dehel*, literally meaning 'coat as hard as steel', may originally have been a form of soft or quilted armour worn beneath a *khuyagh*. Later forms of the *khatangku dehel* may have included those lined with metallic scales, and it is likely to have been from the latter that the Middle Eastern Islamic *qarqal* and various forms of scale-lined European armours such as the *brigandine* developed.[94]

The whole question of the use of leather armour amongst nomadic peoples of the steppes needs further study. It is, for example, possible that the Crusader Robert de Clari's comment that the Kipchaqs in early thirteenth-century Byzantine service wore no armour except sheepskins did not mean 'sheepskin coats' as a form of soft armour, as is generally assumed, but might mean that they used a form of hardened, tanned, rawhide or layered leather armour.[95] Such protections have been shown to be highly effective against arrows. Meanwhile various thirteenth-century Western European sources noted the lightness and effectiveness of the Mongols' leather armour, especially against archery.[96]

The European missionary and traveller Carpini clearly stated that the Mongols used horse-armour of both leather and of iron.[97] Such protections suddenly became much more frequent in Middle Eastern and specifically Islamic armour after the Mongol invasions, and slightly more frequent in the written sources. This surely indicates that horse-armour, though known and used before the Mongols, became more widespread under their rule or military influence. Furthermore, the terminology of horse-armour also changed in the Middle East. Here the Old Persian term *bargustuwan* dropped out of use in Iran itself in favour of the new terms *kajin* or *kajim*.[98] Perhaps this reflected a shift from the old felt, quilted, occasionally scale-lined or scale-covered and very rarely mail horse-armours to a new lamellar style, usually of leather lamellae but occasionally of iron lamellae.

Finally there is the question of the manufacture of military equipment and horse-harness. In the early days of their conquests the Mongols are believed to have relied on a tradition they shared with the early Turks; namely that each man or his family made most of his own equipment.[99] This would not have applied to more advanced items such as swords or iron armour, though the latter might have been made by itinerant smiths. It almost certainly did apply to leather items, soft armour and perhaps even wood-framed saddles.

A major change occurred when the Mongols conquered substantial settled and urbanized states like China and Iran. In the latter, according to the Persian chronicler Rashid al-Din writing in the early fourteenth century, local Iranian armourers were initially unable to make the sort of arms and armour that their new Mongol rulers required. By the early fourteenth century, however, Rashid al-Din maintained that the Iranians had learned the new styles and techniques. As a result they were making Mongol-style military equipment better than the Mongols themselves.[100]

FORTIFICATION AND SIEGE WARFARE

Those regions of Central Asia which were drawn into the Islamic world during the early medieval period had their own advanced traditions of fortification (see above). The regions further east and north-east, on both sides of the Tien Shan Mountains, were similarly dotted with fortifications large and small. Here, in what is sometimes called Inner Asia, the strongest external influence upon military architecture came, not surprisingly, from China. However, there was also technological contact with Iran.[101] At the western end of the Eurasian steppes the strongest influence upon the fortifications built by so-called 'nomad empires' came from the Byzantine Empire. Here the indigenous Vlach peoples of the hills were apparently obliged to build forts for dominant Kipchaq Turks. The word galati, meaning fortress, appears in many Romanian place-names,[102] and is understood to indicate a Kipchaq presence though the word itself is ultimately of Arabic origin, stemming from qala'at, meaning a fortress or castle.[103]

Very little is known about the siege skills of Mongol armies before the rise of Genghis Khan or even during the early years of the Mongol conquests. What is clear is that they soon enlisted the technological skills of defeated opponents and subjected peoples. Consequently there were Chinese artillerymen with those Mongol armies which campaigned in the Middle East, the western steppes and Europe, even in the first such expeditions. Their numbers and effectiveness subsequently grew so that in 1253 the army of Möngke Khan had mangonels which could be dismantled into five or six pieces and brought from China to Turkestan in waggons.[104]

Amongst the most dramatic siege weapons used by the Mongols, and which certainly caught the attention of contemporary chroniclers, were what are understood to have been very large crossbows. Hülegü, for example, is said to have had 3,000 *charkh* crossbows in the army which invaded Iran, besieged the Isma'ili 'Assassin' castles in the north of that country and conquered the Iraqi capital of Baghdad. On the other hand it is far from clear whether these were large or small, of Middle Eastern or Chinese type. Some at least are likely to have been substantial frame-mounted weapons.

During the well documented Mongol siege of Baghdad, Hülegü's artillerymen used *charkh andazan* and *charkh kaman*, some of which are believed to have been multi-shot weapons. When no suitable stone was available their mangonels also shot large wooden blocks soaked in water to make them heavy.[105] It was also part of Hülegü's army which overcame the defences of the central Iranian city of Isfahan in 1237 by diverting a river in flood.[106] The fact that they were able to do this is surely further evidence of the very large numbers of men available in such Mongol forces.

COMMUNICATION, TRANSPORT AND SUPPORT SERVICES

Once again little is known about the communications systems used by Mongol armies before they began to adopt those of the peoples they conquered. Carpini did, however, mention their use of whistling arrows as a method of signalling.[107] Arrowheads with just such whistles, sometimes made of bone and sometimes of metal, have been found by archaeologists in many parts of the steppes, indicating that they were found amongst other Turco-Mongol peoples, not just the Mongols themselves. The Mongol *barid* system, which supposedly inspired the Mamluk Sultanate, is itself likely to have been built upon what the Mongols found when they conquered Transoxania and Iran rather than being a wholly new Mongol concept.

The Mongols' supposed lack of interest in the sea was really only seen in the western parts of their 'World Empire'. In the Far East they not only attempted to invade Japan but sent military expeditions to some of the islands of what is now Indonesia. In the Islamic Middle East, however, the Il-Khans seem to have had almost no ambition to control any part of the Mediterranean coast.[108] Yet they were interested in expanding their influence into the Persian Gulf. From the later fourteenth century onwards the Mongol Golden Horde and its successor Khanates controlled a large part of the coast of the Black Sea, but again showed no interest in taking to the sea. Instead the Golden Horde developed a close commercial and to some extent political relationship with Genoa, and through the Genoese with the Byzantine Empire and the Mamluk Sultanate. In this way they ensured that the Italian and other naval powers which dominated the Black Sea were friendly.

The Mongols' systems of logistical support and military supplies were efficient but also sometimes cumbersome. For example the Golden Horde army which invaded Transoxania in the late thirteenth century during one of the inter-Mongol wars which erupted soon after the fragmentation of Genghis Khan's 'World Empire' is said to have consisted of not only fighting men, but supposedly five horses, two slaves, a cart and 30 sheep or goats for every warrior.[109] Even if the figure of 250,000 troops is an exaggeration, the support allocated to each soldier must have resulted in an unwieldy army. Figures quoted in other sources for the number of spare horses and food animals such as sheep and goats required by Mongol armies were similarly huge.[110]

Even if they were partially true, they would highlight the logistical and feeding problems for men and even more so for animals that led to repeated Mongol failures after the first waves of conquest reached their highwater mark. In 1256 each 'military family' in those Mongol armies campaigning in the Middle East was said to have about 100 sheep upon which to live.[111] These forces were like 'peoples on the march' rather than armies in the normal sense, and the devastation they left in their wake was often huge. Not surprisingly the Mongol military leadership also needed to know the state or anticipated state of pasture along the routes they planned to take, usually before a campaign began, since it was essential that the animals, riding horses and food-sheep had enough to eat.[112] Unlike the Mamluks' war-horses, the Mongols' war-ponies had to live off the land, and when this proved impossible their campaign failed.

The ponies ridden by the great majority of Mongol cavalrymen were smaller than those of professional Islamic soldiers such as the *mamluks*. Some of the Mongol military élite probably rode higher quality horses, either of Turkestani, Iranian or Arabian breeds, but they would have been a small minority. This had a significant impact upon several battles in Syria where Mongol cavalry could not withstand the better mounted Mamluk cavalry unless they enjoyed overwhelming numbers. It has, in fact, been estimated that the average Mamluk horse weighed about 410 kg compared with the Mongol pony of around 275 kg, and was thus comfortably able to carry about 70 kg whereas the Mongol pony could only carry about 45 kg.[113] Because the riders weighed essentially the same, a Mongol warrior needed more ponies on campaign than a Mamluk soldier needed horses. Furthermore, the Mongol pony was really not a suitable mount for a fully armoured man,[114] still less if the animal was expected to carry horse-armour.

In 1256, in addition to the herds or flocks of animals required for food mentioned above, the typical Mongol 'military family' on campaign in the Islamic Middle East was expected to have five geldings as military mounts plus five breeding mares.[115] Under such circumstances it is hardly surprising that the relative lack of natural pasture in Syria during the summer campaigning season caused Mongol armies considerable problems. So much so that for an invasion of Mamluk territory in 1300 spare fodder for the ponies was carried on camels, but even then so many animals died that a substantial part of the Mongol invasion force ended up on foot.[116] Indeed, ecological factors would eventually play a major part in the stalling and eventual defeat of the Mongol attempts to conquer Syria.

3

The military heritage and impact of Crusading warfare on the Islamic and Mongol worlds

The cultural and political impact of the Crusades on those peoples involved, and in a broader sense upon the cultures that were drawn into these conflicts, has been widely discussed for many years. The more specific military impact has received less attention. Nevertheless it was profound. The Islamic world had already learned just about all there was to learn from the Byzantine Empire and there was as yet little to learn from medieval Western Europe. In fact, even the supposedly backward Mongols had little to learn from the Europeans, though they learned a great deal from their other foes, most notably the Chinese and the Muslims.

The most obvious flow of new or more advanced military ideas was from the Medieval Islamic world to medieval Western, Latin or Catholic Europe. This could be seen in new forms of armour though less so in weapons with the possible exception of incendiaries and gunpowder. A possible Mongol role in the transmission of the latter technology cannot be ignored. There was similarly a flow, or more correctly perhaps, a mutual exchange of ideas in the design of fortification,[1] and of increasingly powerful siege weapons.

This exchange of ideas was not the only stimulus to change. There was also the pressure of warfare itself. The period of the Crusades and the Counter-Crusades or *Jihad* witnessed some remarkable advances in, for example, the design, power and size of stone-throwing *trebuchets*. Their larger and more accurate missiles had a profound impact upon the design of fortifications and in defensive planning. On the other hand, it should never be forgotten that, at least in the initial period, the major impact of the counterweight *trebuchet* was in defence rather than in attack.[2] The role of warfare, and of the injuries as well as the disease it caused, in the spread of Islamic medical knowledge to Western Europe is less obvious. However, it is interesting to note that the influence of this much more advanced knowledge was at first upon the practical rather than the theoretical side of medieval European medicine.[3] This was especially apparent during the second half of the twelfth century which was, in many respects, the most dramatic period of such transmission.

The effect of the Crusades upon the indigenous Christian peoples of the Middle East, upon those whom the Crusades were in part launched to 'save' from supposed Islamic oppression, was entirely negative. Indeed in many areas it was catastrophic.[4] Even so, this catastrophe was not solely a result of the Crusades. The way in which several local Christian communities either rallied to, or were thought to be sympathetic to, the Mongol invaders may have been more important. Nevertheless, the *modus vivendi* which had characterized relations between Christians, Muslims and others had been gravely undermined by the Crusades well before the Mongols appeared on the scene.

The breaking of the old *convivencia* in the Iberian Peninsula similarly resulted from Christian aggression, though this was at first localized. The sudden collapse of al-Andalus in the mid- to late thirteenth century, leaving Granada as the only surviving bastion of Iberian Islam, had a much more profound impact in the rest of the Islamic world. Here there was a notable increase in anti-Christian feelings, not least in the Mamluk Sultanate of Egypt and Syria where the position of indigenous Christian *dhimmis* or Christians under Islamic rule was gravely undermined.[5] Coptic Egyptian conversion to Islam, which had previously been a trickle, became a flood in the fourteenth century, even in Upper Egypt where Christians had remained a majority and had been supported by strong links with the Christian kingdoms of Nubia. Jews, meanwhile, were not seen as a threat and therefore avoided the most fanatical elements of the persecution which scarred this period of Mamluk history.[6]

The Crusades similarly had a negative impact upon the Islamic peoples of the Middle East, causing their culture to become less outward-looking, confident and tolerant than it had been in earlier centuries. Nevertheless, the impact of the Crusades was as nothing compared with that of the Mongol invasions. In addition to huge numbers of casualties the latter resulted in massive material damage, some areas being so devastated that the results are still apparent today. On the other hand, the cultural impact was mixed. While the eastern Islamic world was, for a while, opened up to the civilization, culture and arts of China, the humiliation suffered by Islam at the hands of those perceived as pagans led to a backlash once the western Mongols and their successors converted to Islam. This in turn prompted a missionary zeal which sometimes expressed itself in military aggression and decreasing toleration of non-Islamic communities; characteristics which, rarely seen before the Mongol onslaught, are still sometimes apparent today, not least in Afghanistan.

Far more positive was the effect both the Crusades and the Mongol conquests had upon long-distance trade and patterns of trade, though even here there were losers as well as winners. From the thirteenth to the end of the fifteenth century the Black Sea became a more important hub of north–south and east–west trade than it had been. This was largely because of the stability established by the Mongol Golden Horde and maintained, more or less, by its successor Khanates. Meanwhile east–west trade seems largely to have consisted of luxury or exotic goods; north–south trade largely consisting of bulk goods such as grain and leather. It was also characterized by an extraordinary and almost unique form of slave trade. Here adolescent males and young men, supposedly captured further north or in the foothills of the Caucasus mountains, were shipped across the Black Sea, Aegean and eastern Mediterranean to become the *mamluk* military élite and, for the lucky few, the rulers of the Mamluk Sultanate of Egypt and Syria.[7]

Terminology

Ara = Arabic; Arm = Armenian; Ber = Berber; Cat = Catalan; Far = Farsi; Fle – Flemish; Geo = Georgian; Gr = Greek; Lat = Latin, including medieval Latin; ME – medieval English; MF = medieval French; MG = medieval German; MI = medieval Italian; Mon = Mongol; MS = medieval Spanish; Occ = Occitan; Por = Portuguese; Sl = Slavic (various); Tur = Turkish.

'abd [pl. 'abid] (Ara)	slave
'abid al-makhzan (Ara)	black African slaves
abtal [sing. batal] (Ara)	champions
aghzaz (Ara)	plural of Ghuzz, Turkish tribesmen
ahdath (Ara)	urban militia
'ajala (Ara)	target in form of stuffed animal on a cart
ajnad al-halqa (Ara)	troops of the Halqa units
'alam (Ara)	standard
'aliq (Ara)	allocation of feed for horses
aljamia (MS)	Latin-based dialect spoken in al-Andalus
'allaqa (Ara)	lighting incendiaries or fires
aman (Ara)	offer of an opportunity to surrender on terms
aminan (Far)	trusted confidants
amir (Ara)	officer rank or ruler of middle status
amir 'ashara (Ara)	officer rank, literally '*amir* of ten'
amir akhur (Ara)	master of horse
amir al-bahr (Ara)	naval commander, literally '*amir* of the sea'
amir al-isfahsalar (Ara)	a senior officer rank
amir al-juyush (Ara)	army commander, literally '*amir* of the soldiers'
amir al-ma' (Ara)	naval commander, literally '*amir* of the water'
amir al-umara (Ara)	army commander, literally '*amir* of the amirs'
amir arba'in (Ara)	officer rank, literally '*amir* of forty'
amir hajib (Ara)	senior officer rank
amir jandar (Ara)	officer rank
amir kabir (Ara)	officer rank
amir mi'a (Ara)	officer rank, literally '*amir* of one hundred'
amir tablkhana (Ara)	officer rank
amirate (Ara)	small state ruled by an *amir*
'amud (Ara)	form of mace
angushtvana (Far)	archer's thumb ring
ansar (Ara)	Companions of the Prophet Muhammad
'aqqara (Ara)	large crossbow
arayish (Far)	non-combatants
arbab al-qundub (Ara)	senior officer rank, literally 'lords of maces'
'ard (Ara)	military muster
'arif [pl. 'arifan] (Ara)	junior officer

'arrada (Ara)	stone-throwing siege machine, probably traction type
'asa (Ara)	mace or baton
asabiya (Ara)	sense of family or tribal loyalty
'asaqila (Ara)	former garrison troops of Ascalon
asinnat (Ara)	blades
askar (Ara)	household corps
atabeg (Tur)	originally an adviser to a young ruler, subsequently a local ruler or governor, literally 'father to the prince'
atbaru [sing. tabr] (Ara)	axes
atlab al-mira (Ara)	supply train
baghltaq (Far)	piece of horse-armour
bahriya (Ara)	élite Mamluk regiment
baida (Ara)	round form of helmet probably made of one piece, literally 'egg'
baqt (Ara)	peace agreement, from 'pact'
bar band (Far)	horse collar or neckpiece of horse-armour
barak (Ara)	annual salary
bardhunb (Ara)	crupper strap or crupper armour
bargustuwan (Far)	horse armour
barkil (Ara)	probably *turcopole*
barraniya (Ara)	freestanding external tower attached to main wall by a bridge
bashura (Ara)	bent entrance in a gate
battal (Ara)	soldier without an *'iqta* fief
bazm (Ara)	thumb-draw style of archery draw
bazuband (Far)	*vambrace*, armour for lower arm
beylik (Tur)	small state ruled by a *bey* or *beg*
birjas (Ara)	target used in cavalry training with a lance
boru (Tur)	trumpet
budluq (Tur)	thigh defences
bukht (Ara)	two-humped Bactrian camel
bunduq (Ara)	pellet or ball
buq (Ara)	trumpet
burj (Ara)	tower
burqu' (Ara)	head-armour for a horse
buttiya (Ara)	archery target
çarh (Tur)	crossbows
çauş (Tur)	official or officer
cebe (Tur)	mail-lined armour or *hauberk*
çevgen (Tur)	set of bells mounted on a staff
çevkâni (Tur)	singers
cevşen (Tur)	lamellar cuirass (see *jawshan*)
chakiran (Far)	grooms, attendants
charkh andazan (Far)	large crossbow
charkh kaman (Far)	crossbow
cherkes (Tur)	Circassians from Caucasus
chub (Far)	mace
chubha-i ahan basta (Far)	all-iron mace
cirit (Tur)	mounted combat game using blunted javelins
cura (Tur)	clarinet
da'i (Ara)	religious leader

da'wa (Ara)	religious community
dababis al-muharrafa [sing. dabbus al-muharrafa] (Ara)	spiked mace
dababis al-muharraqa [sing. dabbus al-muharraqa] (Ara)	flanged mace
dabbaba (Ara)	protective roof or shed, literally 'rat'
dabbus (Ara)	form of mace
daniyyat (Ara)	three finger-draw method of archery draw
dar al-mamlaka (Ara)	government offices or perhaps barracks for *mamluk* soldiers
dar al-sina (Ara)	arsenal for shipbuilding
darabzin (Ara)	balustrade, railing
daraq al-jafatiyat (Ara)	large shield or mantlet
daraqa (Ara)	leather shield
daraqa kamil (Ara)	large or elongated leather shield
daraqa latifa (Ara)	small leather shield
darga (Ara)	right-angled turn within a bent entrance gate
dariya (Ara)	form of infantry pole-arm
darraja (Ara)	mounted guard unit
davul (Tur)	ordinary two-sided drums
dawa' (Ara)	recipe, method or list of ingredients
daydaban (Ara)	observation tower
devsirme (Tur)	forcible recruitment of children
dhimmis (Ara)	non-Muslims who had accepted Islamic protection
dihqan (Far)	lower aristocracy
dirafsh (Far)	cobbler's awl
diwan (Ara)	government department or office
diwan al-barid (Ara)	government department in charge of postal service
diwan al-jaysh (Ara)	government department in charge of the army
duhul (Far)	kettledrum
durbash (Far)	war axe
duwal-i 'inan (Far)	straps of bridle
duwal-i rikab (Far)	straps of stirrups
ettebel (Ber, Tuareg)	drum-group
faij (Ara)	messenger
faqi (Ara)	Islamic religious scholar
farahiya, farajiya, faranjiya (Ara)	form of infantry pole-arm
farantira (Ara)	frontier or frontier zone, from medieval Spanish
fasl (Ara)	vassal
fay' (Ara)	collective booty
fida'i [pl. fidayin] (Ara)	dedicated warrior or guerrilla
firind (Ara)	surface patterning or watering on a blade
fityan (Ara & Tur)	urban militia
fuladh (Ara)	steel
furayjiya (Ara)	form of infantry pole-arm
furusiya (Ara)	skills expected of a mounted soldier
furusiya al-harbiya (Ara)	military *furusiya* skills
furusiya al-nabila (Ara)	code of noble or courtly behaviour
futuwwa (Ara)	religious brotherhood
ǧarkh (Tur)	crossbow
gawsipar (Far)	leather shield

ghazw (Ara)	raiding warfare
ghulam (Ara)	slave recruited to be trained as a soldier
ghulman al-asaghir (Ara)	lesser or perhaps younger *ghulams*
ghurab (Ara)	light transport galley
ghuzat (Ara)	volunteers
ghuzzat (Ara)	archers
gubr (Far)	quilted soft armour
gürz (Tur)	type of mace
gustawan (Far)	piece of horse-armour
hadith (Ara)	Saying attributed to the Prophet Muhammad
hadith (Far)	new part of the army of Seljuk Rum
haj (Ara)	Islamic pilgrimage to Mecca
hajib (Ara)	first or senior government minister, or army commander
hajjarun (Ara)	stone removers, masons
halqa (Ara)	part of the Ayyubid and Mamluk armies
hamalat al-silja (Ara)	arms bearers
hamam (Ara)	public bath
hançar (Tur)	large dagger
harafisha (Ara)	irregular troops, rabble
haramiya (Ara)	literally 'robbers', guerrilla troops specializing in cutting supply routes
harasbanan (Far)	sentries, pickets
harba (Ara)	javelin or symbolic weapon, standard
harim (Ara & Far)	womenfolk of a family, area reserved for women in a house
harraqa (Ara)	fire-ship
hasakdaran (Far)	calthrops
hasham (Ara)	distinct or separate military unit
hashishin (Ara)	users of hashish (cannabis)
havashi (Far & Tur)	military retainer or servant
hayasa (Far)	surcingle strap
hilal (Ara)	crescent
hilatgaran (Far)	mechanical weapons
hilla (Ara)	semi-permanent bedouin camp
himmas al-amir (Ara)	small iron arrow or dart
huffaz (Ara)	élite military units, guards
hujariya (Ara)	troops trained from youth in barracks
hujra (Ara)	barracks
humaydiya (Ara)	Kurdish tribe
husban (Ara)	short arrow or dart
hushud (Ara)	conscripts
ifranji (Ara)	Western Europeans, 'Franks'
igdish (Tur)	unclear unit in army of Seljuk Rum; see also *ikdish*
igdishbaşi (Tur)	commander of *igdish* troops
ikdish (Tur)	unclear unit in army of Seljuk Rum; see also *igdish*
ikhvan (Tur)	brotherhood
imam (Ara)	prayer leader
'imara al-wutawwaqun (Ara)	literally '*Amirs* of the necklace', senior officer rank
iqlim (Ara)	military district
'iqta (Ara)	sources of revenue, usually in form of land allocation
'iqta i'tidad (Ara)	larger '*iqta* for an officer to support specified number of soldiers

'iqta jayshi (Ara)	'iqta specifically for a soldier
'iqta tamlik (Ara)	'iqta allocated as private property
'irafa (Ara)	small military unit
isfahsalah (Ara & Far)	army commander
ispahbadh (Far)	senior officer
isti'rad (Ara)	military muster
istina (Ara)	loyalty to a patron
'itaqa (Ara)	certificate indicating completion of training and freedom from previous slave-status
jalish (Ara)	probably unit defending standardbearers
jama'a (Ara)	military formation of middle size
jamah (Ara)	wing or flank officer
jamakiya (Ara)	monthly pay
jandar [pl. jandariyya] (Ara)	members of guard unit
janib (Ara)	unclear military unit
januwiya (Ara)	mantlet
jarida (Ara)	small unit
jarkh (Ara & Far)	crossbow
javans (Tur)	military brotherhood or association
jawshan (Ara)	lamellar cuirass
jawza (Ara)	revolving release-nut of a crossbow
jigar-andazan (Far)	champions, literally 'those who hazard their lives'
jihadi (Ara)	volunteers for military *jihad*
jira khvar (Tur)	locally recruited mercenaries
jirid (Ara)	light javelin
jubba (Ara)	quilted and sometimes mail-lined armour
julban (Ara)	*mamluks* of the ruling Sultan
jund (Ara)	regional forces
jundi mutadawwan (Ara)	territorial militias
juwalduz (Far)	pack-needle, also short arrow or dart
juwh al-khayl (Ara)	frontals for the horses, or *chamfrons*
juyushi (Ara)	regular military formation, regiment
kaba zurna (Tur)	clarinet
kabsh (Ara)	ram
kafil (Ara)	senior governor
kafil al-mamlaka (Ara)	senior military rank, literally 'Defender of the State'
kajim, kajin (Far)	horse armour
kalsat zarad (Ara)	mail leg armour
kaman charkh (Far)	crossbow
kamand andazan (Far)	men with lassoes or throwers of scaling ropes
kamand halqa andazan (Far)	men with scaling ladders and ropes
kaman-i guruha (Far)	pellet bow
karadis (Ara)	squadron
karariya (Ara)	shock troops
karaz (Ara)	hand-thrown incendiary grenade
kardha-i buzurg (Far)	large dagger
kardus (Ara)	formation or squadron
karib (Ara)	sailing ship
karr wa farr (Ara)	cavalry tactic of repeated attack and withdrawal
karwah (Far)	mantlet or form of quilted soft-armour
katiba (Ara)	small cavalry formation

kazaghand, kazghanda (Far & Ara)	mail-lined and padded body armour
khadiman (Far)	servants, eunuchs
khalkha (Mon)	shield of spiral cane construction
khamis (Ara)	division or element of army
khan (Ara)	refuge for merchant caravans, sometimes fortified
khan (Tur & Mon)	ruler
khanate (Tur & Mon)	state ruled by a *khan*
khanjar (Ara & Far)	large dagger
khariji (Ara)	member of an early Islamic reformist movement
khashab (Ara)	wooden structure, 'lighthouse'
khassagan (Far)	royal guards
khassakiya (Ara)	ruler's bodyguards
khatangku dehel (Mon)	'coat as hard as steel', quilted or scale-lined armour
khawabi (Ara)	water stage containers
khawass al-khilafa (Ara)	caliphal élite regiment
khazindar (Ara)	governor of a major citadel
khisht (Far)	light javelin
khud (Ara)	helmet, probably segmented construction
khurz (Ara)	mace
khuyagh (Mon)	lamellar cuirass
kimukht (Ara)	rawhide
kinana (Ara)	quiver
kiswa (Ara)	annual or half yearly allowance for clothing expenses
kizil-elma (Tur)	ultimate goal of Turkish conquests, literally 'Red Apple'
kös (Tur)	bass drum
kulalib (Ara)	hooks
kundestabl (Tur)	master of horse
kurenay (Tur)	trumpet
kus (Tur)	drum
kuskanjil (Ara)	torsion-powered siege weapon
kuskanjil bi'thalathah awtar (Ara)	torsion-powered siege machine with 'three strings'
kuskanjil bi-qawayn (Ara)	torsion-powered siege weapon with two arms
kussat (Ara) cymbals	
kustuban (Far)	archer's partial gauntlet
kuttubi (Ara)	students, including those under military training
lahm (Ara)	daily meat ration
laqab (Ara)	personal title or indication of origin
laqsha (Ara)	type of crossbow
lasiqs (Ara)	beginners
latinia (MS)	Latin-based dialect
latt (Ara)	type of mace
layyin (Ara)	weak or practice bow
lisus (Ara)	cavalry raiders
liwa (Ara)	flag
lu'ab (Ara)	small form of traversible mangonel
lutut [sing. latt] (Ara)	maces
mafsula (Ara)	vassal
maghariba (Ara)	'westerners', usually referring to North Africans and Andalusians

mah'zuz (Ara)	probably iron lamellae, literally 'perforated'
mahmal (Ara)	symbolic howdah carried by a camel during Haj, Islamic pilgrimage to Mecca
majbudu (Ara)	field fortification
majra (Ara)	arrow-guide
makahil al-barud (Ara)	large incendiary missiles to be thrown by a *manjaniq*, literally 'jars of saltpetre'
malik (Ara)	king
mamlaka sultaniya (Ara)	*mamluks* of the ruling Sultan
mamluk (Ara)	soldier of slave-recruited origin
manciliq (Tur)	*mangonel*
manjaniq (Ara)	beamsling stone-throwing siege weapon, also used for stone-throwing siege weapons in general
manjaniq 'arrada (Ara)	small form of traction-powered beamsling stone-throwing siege weapon
manjaniq al-'arus (Ara)	traction-powered beamsling stone-throwing siege weapon
manjaniq h-r-ri (Ara)	beamsling stone-throwing siege weapon, possibly of early counterweight type (note short vowels unknown in second word)
manjaniq ziyar al-akhr (Ara)	'ultimate' version of counterweight arrow-throwing beamsling siege weapon
marqaba (Ara)	battlefield observation tower or platform
mashariqa (Ara)	'easterners', usually referring to inhabitants of the Islamic Middle East and regions further east
masri (Ara)	Egyptian
maydan al-sabaq (Ara)	archery training area
maymana (Ara)	left flank
maysara (Ara)	right flank
mehter (Tur)	military band
mehter düdüğü (Tur)	whistles or fifes
mehterhane (Tur)	military band
meteris (Tur)	mantlet
midfa' (Ara)	gun
mighfar (Ara)	coif
mihraniya (Ara)	Kurdish tribe
mirma (Ara)	throwing machine
mitrad (Ara)	small spear or javelin
mizraq (Ara)	javelin
mubariz (Ara)	champions
muhannak (Ara)	expert
muharraqa (Ara)	flanged mace
mukhula (Ara)	perhaps a projection system for *naft*, Greek Fire
muqaddam (Ara)	officer
muqaddam alf (Ara)	senior military rank, literally 'commander of a thousand'
muqaddama (Ara)	cavalry vanguard
muqaddamu al-halqa (Ara)	middle ranking officer
muqta' (Ara)	holder of an *'iqta* fief
murabit (Ara)	military volunteer, including those for service in a *ribat*
murtat (Tur)	renegade
murtaziqa (Ara)	freely enlisted soldier
murtidd (Ara)	renegade

musalla (Ara)	prayer hall
mushtarawat ajlab (Ara)	*mamluks* of the ruling Sultan
mustakhdamun (Ara)	*mamluks* not purchased by the current Sultan
mutatawwiya (Ara)	religiously motivated *jihad* volunteers
mutawwi'a (Ara)	religiously motivated *jihad* volunteers
muwallad (Ara)	early non-Arab converts to Islam attached to an existing Arab tribe, literally 'clients'
nabl [pl. nabala] (Ara)	arrow
nachakh (Far)	large-bladed war-axe
nafaqa (Ara)	additional payment on the eve of a campaign
nafatin (Ara)	incendiary troops
naffad (Tur)	*naft*, Greek Fire
naffata (Ara)	projection system for *naft*, flame-thrower
nafir (Ara)	alarm
naft (Ara)	petroleum-based incendiary mixture, Greek Fire
naft andazan (Far)	incendiary troops, literally 'fire throwers'
naft oq (Tur)	fire-arrows
najakh, najikh (Ara)	large-bladed war-axe
najjabun (Ara)	couriers
najjarun (Ara)	carpenters
naqar (Ara)	drum
naqib (Ara)	officer
naqib al-jaysh (Ara)	military commander
naqqabun (Ara)	sappers and miners
nar (Ara)	fire
narm ahan (Far)	soft or 'female' iron
nasab, nisba (Ara)	family line, as part of an individual's name
nasara (Ara)	Christians, recruited as mercenaries
navak (Far)	arrow-guide to shoot short arrows or darts
nawakiyya (Ara)	Turkish tribe
nayib (Ara)	senior governor
nayib al-sultana (Ara)	Sultan's Deputy
nazir (Ara)	keeper or inspector
nefir (Tur)	trumpet
negus (Lat)	Abyssinian ruler
nekkare (Tur)	pair of small kettle-drums
niqab (Ara)	veil
nizah (Far)	spear
nushaba (Far)	arrow
nuzul (Ara)	assembling at the end of a day's march
par dum (Far)	collar or neck armour for a horse
payk (Tur)	court page
pushtak (Far)	unknown strap or straps over the horse's back or over the saddle
qa'id (Ara)	officer rank
qa'id al-bahr (Ara)	naval commander, 'commander of the sea'
qa'id al-ustul (Ara)	naval rank, 'squadon commander'
qabaq (Ara)	horse-archery target
qadi (Ara)	man qualified to make Islamic legal decisions
qaghan (Tur)	senior ruler
qaim (Ara)	handle

qala' (Ara)	type of sword
qalahurra (Ara)	tower incorporating a luxurious residence
qalqan (Tur)	shield of a spiral of cane
qarabugha (Ara)	large form of counterweight stone-throwing siege machine
qaraghulamiya (Ara)	lower-rated *mamluk* soldiers
qarajuli, qarachuri (Far & Ara)	curved sword, sabre
qaranis (Ara)	*mamluks* recruited by a previous ruler
qaratis (Ara)	leaves of paper
qarnus (Ara)	raised pommel at the front of a saddle
qarqal (Ara & Far)	scale-lined and cloth-covered body armour
qarura (Ara)	incendiary grenade
qasaba, qasba (Ara)	citadel
qasim (Tur)	Ancient or older part of Seljuk Rum army
qawarir al-naft (Ara)	incendiary grenades
qaws 'aqqar (Ara)	type of crossbow
qaws al-lawlab (Ara)	large form of crossbow spanned with a windlass or winch
qaws al-qutn (Ara)	bow having a cotton bowstring
qaws al-rijl (Ara)	large crossbow spanned by placing feet on the bow
qaws al-rikiab (Ara)	small crossbow spanned with a spanning stirrup
qaws al-ziyar (Ara)	torsion-powered siege weapon
qaws hijazi (Ara)	bow of simple construction, not incorporating sinew or horn
qaws nawakiya (Ara)	bow used with a *nawak* arrow-guide
qidr (Ara)	pot, also a grenade
qidr 'iraqi (Ara)	incendiary grenade
qighaj, qiqaj (Ara)	horse-archery target
qirat (Mon)	district and associated military unit
qolcaq, qolluq, qulluq (Tur)	lower arm defences
qubba (Ara)	rectangular tower
qufl (Ara)	lock and release mechanism in a crossbow
quft Ara)	fortress or strongpoint
qunbar (Ara)	sailing ship
quntariya (Ara)	large cavalry lance
ra'is (Ara)	headman
ra'is al-milaha (Ara)	ship's captain
rafiq (Ara)	comrade
rami (Ara)	shooter
ranat hadid (Ara)	mail leg armour, 'iron leggings'
raqqusa (Ara)	courier
ratl (Ara)	measurement of weight
raya (Ara)	flag
raia (Ara)	raiding warfare
ribat (Ara)	small fort or garrison of such a fort
rikabiya (Ara)	Caliphal bodyguard
risman (Far)	thread
rumat 'aqqara (Ara)	crossbowmen
rumh (Ara)	spear
sa'ad (Ara)	armour for lower arm, *vambrace*
sabarbara (Ara)	broad-bladed spear
sabarbariya (Ara)	infantry armed with the *sabarbara*
saham, sahm (Ara)	arrow
sahib al-barid (Ara)	official in charge of government postal service

sajar (Ara)	humiliation
sajra (Ara)	small castle
samsam (Ara)	broad type of sword
sancaq (Tur)	banner
sanjaq (Ara)	Turkish-style banner
sannura (Ara)	protective roof or shed, literally 'cat'
saq al-muza (Ara)	mail *chausses* to protect legs
saqah (Ara)	separate unit as vanguard or rearguard
saqala (Ara)	battlefield observation platform
saqaliba (Ara)	individuals of supposed Slav origin
sarhang (Far)	military officer
sari (Ara)	piece of horse-armour, probably for the head
sariya (Ara)	small military unit
sassa (Ara)	squires or horse-handler
sata'ir (Ara)	screens, palisades or mantlets
sayfiya (Ara)	mamluk soldiers of a deceased or dismissed commander
serhenk (Tur)	senior officer, from Persian *sarhang*
shabaka (Ara)	moveable protective screen
shahrazuriya (Ara)	Kurdish tribe
shaja'a (Ara)	courage
shamshir (Far)	sword
shamsiyya al-arman (Ara)	Armenian followers of a heretical sect, supposedly 'sun-worshippers'
shari'a (Ara)	Islamic law
shatrang (Far)	chessboard, chequerboard pattern
shaykh (Ara)	respected elder figure, leader
shaykh al-ghuzat (Ara)	commander or leader of religiously motivated volunteers
shaytani (Ara)	devilish
shihab (Ara)	shooting star, flame
shihnat al-shurta (Ara)	chief of police
shilindi (Ara)	small galley
shini (Ara)	galley
shira' (Ara)	battlefield observation platform
shuj'an (Ara)	offensive cavalry
sibyan al-rikab al-khass (Ara)	Caliphal bodyguard
sibyan al-zarad (Ara)	armoured élite military unit, literally 'young men with mail armour'
siham al-khita'ih (Ara)	chemical fire-arrows, literally 'Chinese arrows'
sikkin (Ara)	dagger
silah (Ara)	military equipment in general
sinf (Ara)	sense of group identity
sipahsalar (Far)	senior military commander
sipar (Far)	shield
siparha-i farkh (Far)	broad infantry shield
siper (Tur)	arrow-guide
sudani (Ara)	individuals of sub-Saharan African origin, literally 'blacks'
sufi (Ara)	Islamic mystic, literally 'woolly'
suluqiyya (Ara)	lower defensive wall outside the main fortifications
sungu, sünü (Tur)	spear
suq (Ara)	market
suq al-'askar (Ara)	soldiers' market

suq al-silah (Ara)	arms market
sur (Ara)	city-wall
suzan (Far)	needle
ta'ifa (Ara)	faction or party, also name given to fragmented states of al-Andalus
tabarzin (Ara & Far)	axe
tabbala (Ara)	drummers
tabira (Far)	type of kettledrum
tabiya (Ara)	tamped earth method of construction
tablakhana (Ara)	middle officer rank
tabl-i ali-i osman (Tur & Far)	military band of the Ottoman Sultan
tablkhana (Ara)	arsenal of drums and musical instruments
tabr (Ara)	axe
tal'iya (Ara)	watchtower
tala'i al-'askar (Ara)	unit of reconnaissance troops
talaya (Ara)	scouts
tali'a (Ara)	scouting party or watchtower
talq (Ara)	fireproof mixture of silicate of magnesium and powdered mica
tarida (Ara)	specialized galley as horse-transport or landing-craft
tariqa [pl. tawariqah] (Ara)	shield with a pointed base
tarkash (Far)	quiver
tawa'if al-ajnad (Ara)	ordinary regiments
tawashi [pl. tawashiya] (Ara)	élite force of free cavalry, later highly rated *mamluks*
tawqi (Ara)	document allocating an *'iqta*
thabat (Ara)	firm riding seat
thagri (Ara)	frontiersmen
thughur (Ara)	frontier zone
thuql (Ara)	military supply train
tijfaf (Ara)	soft armour for man or horse, usually of felt or quilted
tir andazan (Far)	archers
tiraz (Ara)	bands of fabric around upper sleeves with dedicatory inscription
tishtaniya (Ara)	armour for horse's head, *chamfron*
tufak (Far)	blowpipe
tüfenk (Tur)	early form of handgun
tulb (Ara)	platoon
tümen (Mon)	large military unit and territory associated with its maintainance
tuq (Tur)	horse or yak tail
turs (Ara)	shield, usually of wood
uj, uji (Tur)	frontiersman
umma (Ara)	Islamic community as a whole
ustadh (Ara)	instructor
ustadh al-dar (Ara)	senior officer rank
ustul (Ara)	convoy or naval squadron
wali (Ara)	governor
waqf (Ara)	Islamic charitable trust
warda (Ara)	ignition element in a *naft*, Greek Fire, projector, literally 'rose'
wasiti (Ara)	bow of partially composite construction, literally 'middling'
wazir (Ara)	senior government minister, vizier

wusfana (Ara)	slave-recruited troops of African origin
yaruqiya (Ara)	Turkish tribe
yazaq (Ara)	advance guard
yazaq al-da'im (Ara)	élite advance guard
za'im (Ara)	leader
zabtana (Far)	blowpipe
zagaya, zaghaya (Ber)	javelin or short spear
zahafa, zahhafa (Ara)	protective roof, shed or siege tower
zanburak (Far)	blowpipe
zangiyana (Far)	frames of bell, 'jingling johnny'
zanj (Ara)	troops from the Horn of Africa
zaqaziq (Ara)	calthrops
zarad (Ara)	mail
zardkhana (Ara)	military arsenal
zarraqa (Ara)	device for projecting *naft*, flame-thrower
zarraqun (Ara)	troops equipped with fire projectors or throwers
zarzariya (Ara)	Kurdish tribe
zhupin (Far)	javelins
zil (Tur)	cymbals
ziman (Ara)	officer
ziyar yaramika (Ara)	torsion-powered siege weapons with only one arm
zurna (Tur)	large form of clarinet

Notes

Notes to Introduction

1   Russell, J. C., p. 53.
2   For the Papacy's enthusiasm for a
    'great battle' between Castile and the
    Muwahhidun (Almohades) in Spain,
    see García Fitz (1996) p. 274 n. 22.

*Notes to Chapter 1: The medieval
Islamic world*

1   Beeston, A.F.L., pp. 7–9.
2   Nicolle, D.C. (1997) *passim.*
3   Bacharach, J. L., p. 472.
4   Ayalon, D. (1976) pp. 203–4.
5   Zajaczkowski, A., *passim.*
6   Van Tongerloo, A., *passim.*
7   Bulliet, R. W., p. 99.
8   Bulliet, R. W., p. 107; Ryckmans, J.,
    passim.
9   For the origins, early history and
    development of the composite bow,
    see Credland, A. G. (1994) *passim.*
10 Allan, J. W. (1988) pp. 3–5.
11 Baker, P. *passim.*
12 Ayalon, D. (1977b) p. 287.
13 Daftary, F. (1998) pp. 123–4.
14 Usamah Ibn Munqidh (1929) p. 153.
15 Tibi, A. T., p. 100.
16 Matveev, A. (1998a) p. 15.
17 Bianquis, T. (1983) p. 547.
18 Christie, N. (1999) *passim.*; Christie,
    N. (2000) *passim.*
19 Lyons, M. C., pp. 44–5.
20 Christie, N. (2000) p. 2.
21 Lyons, M. C., pp. 45–51.

22 Lyons, M. C., p. 48.
23 Ayyuqi, *passim.*
24 Menéndez Pidal, R., p. 43.
25 Wasserstein, D., p. 295.
26 Wasserstein, D., pp. 292–3.
27 Wasserstein, D., p. 292.
28 Glick, T. F. (1979) p. 60.
29 Lacarra, J. M. (1947) pp. 68–70
    and 72.
30 Lomax, D. W., pp. 90–1 and 112–13.
31 Marsden, J. D., p. 29.
32 Bazzana, A. (1983b) p. 35.
33 Slousch, N., p. 398.
34 Wasserstein, D., pp. 86 and 284.
35 Wasserstein, D., pp. 283–4.
36 Latham, J. D. (1971) pp. 191–5.
37 Abun-Nasr, J. M., pp. 134–8.
38 Granara, W. E., pp. 70–1.
39 *Ibid.*
40 Johns, J. (1987) p. 89.
41 Johns, J. (1987) p. 96.
42 Johns, J. (1987) p. 90.
43 Bellafiore, G., pp. 217–22.
44 Lev, Y. (1980) p. 181.
45 Bianquis, T. (1983) p. 663.
46 Hamblin, W. J. (1984) p. 13.
47 Cahen, C. (1972) p. 182.
48 Hamblin, W. J. (1984) p. 157.
49 Brett, M. (1997) *passim.*
50 *Ibid.*
51 Humphreys, R. S. (1977a) p. 173.
52 Bulliet, R. W., p. 93.
53 Bulliet, R.W., p. 96.
54 Smith, G.R., pp. 71–3.
55 Lyon, B. D., p. 159.
56 Bianquis, T. (1984) p. 14.
57 Bianquis, T. (1984) p. 11.

58 Bianquis, T. (1984) p. 12.
59 Bianquis, T. (1984) pp. 13–14.
60 Zakkar, S., pp. 67–8.
61 Zakkar, S., pp. 77–9.
62 Zakkar, S., pp. 84 and 93–4.
63 Bianquis, T. (1983) pp. 479–80.
64 Prawer, J. (1980) p. 473.
65 Forey, A. (1985) pp. 178–9.
66 Bianquis, T. (1983) p. 663.
67 Hillenbrand, C. (1985) pp. 9–10.
68 Buckler, G., p. 421.
69 For an in-depth study of the way in which the Orthodox Christian and largely Greek-speaking population of Anatolia became largely Muslim and Turkish-speaking Turkey, see Vryonis, S. (1971) passim.
70 Bombaci, A., p. 344.
71 Bombaci, A., pp. 362–3.
72 'Arif 'Ali of Toqat, vol. I, pp. 54–7.
73 Weinberger, J. W., pp. 34 and 37–8.
74 Alptekin, C., p. 62.
75 Amououx-Mourad, M., p. 50.
76 Nielsen, J. S. (1991) pp. 339–40.
77 Bianquis, T. (1983) pp. 432, 436–7 and 446.
78 Lokkegaard, F., p. 269.
79 Vryonis argues strongly for significant Byzantine influence upon Seljuk Rum armies, their organization and even their costume, etc.; see Vryonis, S. (1971) pp. 467–8.
80 Dadoyan, S. B., pp. 81–106.
81 Lev, Y. (1988a) p. 77.
82 Holt, P. M. (1977) p. 56.
83 Douglas, D. C., p. 75.
84 Tanukhi, Muhassin Ibn 'Ali al-, pp. 96–6.
85 Ayalon, D. (1976) pp. 199–202.
86 Ayalon, D. (1976) pp. 202–3.
87 Zakkar, S., pp. 134–42.
88 Weinberger, J. W., pp. 42–4 and 58–61.
89 Weinberger, J. W., pp. 66–9.
90 Lambton, A. K. S. (1965) pp. 253–4.
91 Nizam al-Mulk (1960) pp. 96–7.
92 Nizam al-Mulk (1960) pp. 103–4.
93 Smith, J. M. (J. Masson Smith) (1984b) p. 313.

94 Taeschner, Fr., p. 739; on the question of who were first Turks to penetrate Anatolia during the eleventh century, see Cahen, C. (1948) passim.
95 Vryonis, S. (1971) p. 230.
96 Toumanoff, C., p. 620.
97 Vryonis, S. (1975) pp. 146 and 150–1.
98 Vryonis, S. (1971) pp. 230–1.
99 Bombaci, A., pp. 345–7.
100 Bombaci, A., p. 354.
101 Bombaci, A., p. 345.
102 Bombaci, A., pp. 345–7.
103 Cahen, C. (1968) pp. 230–4; Bombaci, A., pp. 348–9.
104 Bombaci, A., pp. 348–9.
105 Cahen, C. (1968) pp. 230–4.
106 Bombaci, A., p. 368.
107 Bombaci, A., p. 353.
108 Ibid.
109 Bombaci, A., pp. 353–4.
110 Cahen, C. (1983) p. 174.
111 Bombaci, A., pp. 358–60; Matuz, J., pp. 190–6.
112 Bombaci, A., pp. 355–6.
113 Bombaci, A., pp. 357–8 and 363–7.
114 Bombaci, A., pp. 368–9.
115 Alptekin, C., p. 62.
116 Hartman, A., pp. 76–7.
117 Rashad Mohamad, A. M., pp. 45–6 and 93.
118 Rashad Mohamad, A. M., p. 96.
119 Zanki, J. H. M. A. al-, pp. 271–2.
120 Bianquis, T. (1983) pp. 434 and 459.
121 Amououx-Mourad, M., p. 50.
122 Bianquis, T. (1983) p. 673.
123 Zakkar, S., p. 47.
124 Zakkar, S., pp. 252–4.
125 Dadoyan, S. B., pp. 72–5.
126 Dadoyan, S. B., p. 67.
127 Bianquis, T. (1983) p. 314.
128 Nicolle, D. C. (1994b) passim.; Usamah Ibn Munqidh (1930) passim.; Usamah Ibn Munqidh (1929) passim.
129 Zakkar, S., pp. 176–7.
130 Zanki, J. H. M. A. al-, p. 268.
131 Salibi, K. S. (1977) p. 156.
132 Amououx-Mourad, M., p. 51.
133 Zanki, J. H. M. A. al-, pp. 272–3.

134 Zanki, J. H. M. A. al-, pp. 254–7.
135 Zanki, J. H. M. A. al-, pp. 261–2.
136 Zanki, J. H. M. A. al-, p. 264.
137 Zanki, J. H. M. A. al-, pp. 253–4.
138 Zanki, J. H. M. A. al-, p. 265.
139 Zanki, J. H. M. A. al-, pp. 271–2.
140 Zanki, J. H. M. A. al-, pp. 273–4.
141 Zanki, J. H. M. A. al-, pp. 275–7.
142 Canard, M. (1967) p. 107.
143 Dédéyan, G., *passim.*
144 Hillenbrand, C. (1981) pp. 271–2.
145 *Ibid.*
146 Nicholson, R. L. (1973) p. 10.
147 Rose, R. B., p. 245.
148 Elisseeff, N. (1967) p. 730.
149 Elisseeff, N. (1967) p. 729.
150 Lyons, M. C., pp. 5–6.
151 Daftary, F. (1990) pp. 433–4.
152 Atiya, A. S., p. 64.
153 Richard, J. (1979c) p. 29.
154 Lev, Y. (1996) p. 145.
155 Beshir, B. J., p. 42.
156 Beshir, B. J., p. 44.
157 Beshir, B. J., p. 41; Hamblin, W. J. (1984) p. 55.
158 Hamblin, W. J. (1984) pp. 17–18.
159 Hamblin, W. J. (1984) pp. 14–15.
160 Bianquis, T. (1983) p. 229.
161 Beshir, B.J., pp. 40–1.
162 Canard, M. (1954) pp. 94–7.
163 Beshir, B. J., p. 43.
164 Hamblin, W. J. (1984) pp. 19–27.
165 Dadoyan, S. B., pp. 10–11.
166 Hamblin, W. J. (1984) p. 19.
167 Beshir, B. J., p. 42.
168 Hamblin, W. J. (1984) pp. 33–4.
169 Hamblin, W. J. (1984) pp. 61–2.
170 Lev, Y. (1996) pp. 143–4.
171 Hamblin, W. J. (1984) pp. 42–8.
172 Hamblin, W. J. (1984) pp. 19–27.
173 Hamblin, W. J. (1984) p. 55.
174 Hamblin, W. J. (1984) pp. 35 and 57–61.
175 Beshir, B. J., pp. 38–9.
176 Saleh (Salih), A. H. (1980) p. 51.
177 Beshir, B. J., p. 44; for Fatimid government relations with the bedouin, see Cahen, C. (1972)
p. 180; for a study of the bedouin in medieval Egypt, see Saleh, A. H. (1979) pp. 351–2.
178 Hamblin, W. J. (1984) pp. 57–61.
179 Beshir, B. J., pp. 38–9.
180 For a detailed study of the ethnic composition of Saladin's army, see Lev, Y. (1988b) pp. 150–8.
181 Ayalon, D. (1977a) pp. 1–3.
182 Ayalon, D. (1977a) p. 8.
183 Humphreys, R. S. (1977a) pp. 90–1.
184 Ayalon, D. (1977a) p. 23.
185 Lyon, B. D., p. 97.
186 Humphreys, R. S. (1977a) pp. 94–6.
187 Humphreys, R. S. (1977a) p. 97.
188 Bacharach, J. L., pp. 481–9.
189 Saleh, A. H. (1979) p. 350.
190 Saleh (Salih), A. H. (1980) p. 65; for a detailed study of the Egyptian bedouin under Ayyubid rule see Saleh, A. H. (1979) *passim.*
191 Saleh (Salih), A. H. (1980) p. 51.
192 Saleh, A. H. (1979) *passim.*
193 Richard, J. (1979c) p. 260.
194 De Joinville (1921) p. 233.
195 Eddé, A.-M., p. 226.
196 Eddé, A.-M., pp. 227–9.
197 Humphreys, R. S. (1977a) p. 152.
198 Eddé, A.-M., pp. 229–31.
199 Eddé, A.-M., p. 231.
200 Eddé, A.-M., pp. 232–3.
201 Humphreys, R. S. (1977a) p. 73.
202 Richard, J. (1979c) p. 222.
203 Richard, J. (1979c) p. 235.
204 Sarraf, S. al- (1996) pp. 128–9.
205 Bosworth, C. E. (1972) p. 63 n. 2.
206 Ayalon, D. (1949) p. 136.
207 Ayalon, D. (1949) pp. 136–8.
208 Amitai-Preiss, R. (1996) p. 287.
209 Humphreys, R. S. (1977a) pp. 158–9.
210 Gorelik, M. V. (1979) p. 41.
211 Humphreys, R. S. (1977a) p. 149.
212 *Ibid.*
213 Ayalon, D. (1965b) p. 11.
214 Saleh, A. H. (1978) p. 61.
215 Ziadeh, N. A., p. 24.
216 Ayalon, D. (1965b) p. 5.
217 Humphreys, R. S. (1977a) pp. 149–50.

218 Ziadeh, N. A., p. 26.
219 Hopkins, J. F. P., p. 73.
220 Brett, M. (1975) p. 82.
221 Frend, W. H. C., p. 78 n. 3.
222 Lewis, A. R. (1985) p. 143.
223 Abun-Nasr, J. M., pp. 134–8.
224 Ahmad, Aziz (1975) p. 22.
225 Bresc, H., pp. 52–3.
226 Bresc, H., p. 58.
227 Abulafia, D. (1990) p. 108.
228 Kantorowixz, E., pp. 128–30.
229 Hopkins, J. F. P., pp. 75–6.
230 Hopkins, J. F. P., pp. 74–5.
231 Hopkins, J. F. P., pp. 73–4.
232 Hopkins, J. F. P., p. 78.
233 Norris, H. T. (1982) p. 176.
234 Hopkins, J. F. P., pp. 82–3.
235 Hopkins, J. F. P., pp. 78–9.
236 Hopkins, J. F. P., pp. 79–80.
237 Hopkins, J. F. P., p. 80.
238 *Ibid.*
239 Dufourcq, pp. 90–2.
240 Hopkins, J. F. P., pp. 76–8.
241 Burns, R. I. (1976) pp. 118–20.
242 Abun-Nasr, J. M., pp. 115–16.
243 Torres Delgado, C. (1988) pp. 199–200.
244 Wasserstein, D., pp. 58–61.
245 Wasserstein, D., pp. 146–8.
246 Terrasse, H. (1965) pp. 81–3.
247 Tibi, A.T., pp. 226 and 226 n.14.
248 Wasserstein, D., pp. 146–8.
249 Menéndez Pidal, R., p. 47.
250 Schneidman, J. L., pp. 112–13.
251 Dawood, A. H. H. O. M., pp. 191–4;
     Turtushi, Muhammad Ibn Walid al-,
     passim.
252 Torres Delgado, C. (1988) pp. 201–2.
253 Arié, R., pp. 238–40.
254 Torres Delgado, C. (1988) p. 202.
255 Marsden, J. D., p. 45.
256 *Ibid.*
257 Marsden, J. D., p. 29.
258 Marsden, J. D., pp. 29–30.
259 Arié, R., pp. 241–4.
260 Bosworth, C. E. (1978b) pp. 265–9.
261 Bosworth, C. E. (1975) pp. 70–7.
262 Rice, T. T., p. 81.
263 Ashtor, E. (1976) p. 212.

264 Mirza, N. A., pp. 166–7.
265 Mirza, N. A., pp. 168–70.
266 Cahen, C. (1968) pp. 230–4.
267 Rice, T. T., p. 81.
268 Bombaci, A., p. 345.
269 Vryonis, S. (1971) p. 242.
270 Bombaci, A., p. 349.
271 Bombaci, A., pp. 348–9.
272 Bombaci, A., p. 368.
273 Bombaci, A., pp. 357–60.
274 Bianquis, T. (1983) p. 459.
275 Bianquis, T. (1983) pp. 546–7.
276 Cahen, C. (1940) p. 195.
277 Zakkar, S., p. 44.
278 Zakkar, S., pp. 273–4.
279 Zakkar, S., p. 226.
280 Cahen, C. (1965) *passim.*
281 Azhari, T.K. El-, p. 280.
282 Azhari, T. K. El-, pp. 288 and 296–7.
283 Azhari, T. K. El-, pp. 298–9.
284 Azhari, T. K. El-, pp. 302–3.
285 Azhari, T. K. El-, pp. 303–7; for the five
     categories of officials see Azhari, T. K.
     El-, pp. 309–11.
286 Cahen, C. (1940) p. 195.
287 Hillenbrand, C. (1979) pp. 275–6.
288 Zanki, J. H. M. A. al-, p. 253.
289 Zanki, J. H. M. A. al-, pp. 279–82.
290 Elisseeff, N. (1967) pp. 721–2.
291 Elisseeff, N. (1967) p. 723.
292 Mirza, N. A., p. 171.
293 Mirza, N. A., p. 172.
294 Beshir, B. J., pp. 50–1.
295 *Ibid.*
296 Bianquis, T. (1983) pp. 413 and 432.
297 Bianquis, T. (1983) p. 661.
298 Staffa, S. J., p. 84.
299 Lev, Y. (1996) p. 121.
300 Bianquis, T. (1983) p. 207.
301 Ehrenkreutz, A. S. (1972) pp. 73–4.
302 Hamblin, W. J. (1984) pp. 65–81;
     Ashtor, E. (1976) p. 192.
303 Hamblin, W. J. (1984) pp. 84–91.
304 Hamblin, W. J. (1984) pp. 92–4.
305 Canard, M. (1951) p. 373.
306 Hamblin, W. J. (1984) p. 36.
307 Hamblin, W. J. (1984) pp. 42–8.
308 Hamblin, W. J. (1984) pp. 36–41.

309   Hamblin, W. J. (1984) pp. 47–8.
310   Sanders, P., p. 239.
311   Hamblin, W. J. (1984) pp. 48–9.
312   Hamblin, W. J. (1984) pp. 52–4.
313   Lyon, B. D., p. 26.
314   Lyon, B. D., p. 34.
315   Hamblin, W. J. (1984) pp. 94–5.
316   Hamblin, W. J. (1984) pp. 63–4.
317   Saleh, A. H. (1978) pp. 46–9.
318   Adams, W. Y., pp. 524–5.
319   For a recent detailed study of the
        Ayyubid army, see Lev, Y. (1988b)
        pp. 141–60.
320   Ehrenkreutz, A. S. (1972) pp. 73–4;
        Gibb, H. A. R., pp. 304–20; Elisseeff, N.
        (1967) p. 724.
321   Lyon, B. D., p. 41.
322   Humphreys, R. S. (1977a) pp. 74–6;
        Lev, Y. (1988b) pp. 141–50.
323   Lyon, B. D., pp. 252–3.
324   Humphreys, R. S. (1977a) pp. 83–5.
325   Humphreys, R. S. (1977a) pp. 86–8.
326   For a recent and sober study of the
        administration of these forces, see Lev,
        Y. (1988b) pp. 158–69, and for a more
        traditional and detailed analysis see
        Elbeheiry, S., pp. 88–161.
327   Elbeheiry, S., pp. 46–65 and 69–76.
328   Elbeheiry, S., pp. 79–82.
329   Humphreys, R. S. (1977a) pp. 82–3.
330   Elbeheiry, S., pp. 17–21.
331   Elbeheiry, S., pp. 22–5.
332   Elbeheiry, S., pp. 26–42.
333   Humphreys, R. S. (1977a) pp. 70–1.
334   Humphreys, R. S. (1977a) pp. 77–81.
335   Cahen, C. (1972) p. 170.
336   Humphreys, R. S. (1977a) p. 94.
337   Humphreys, R. S. (1977a) pp. 94–7.
338   Humphreys, R. S. (1977a) p. 99.
339   Eddé, A.-M., p. 226.
340   Humphreys, R. S. (1977a) pp. 159–60.
341   Irwin, R. G. (1994) pp. 57, 59 and
        61–3.
342   Irwin, R. G. (1994) pp. 58–9.
343   Ayalon, D. (1953a) p. 223.
344   Ayalon, D. (1953a) p. 283.
345   Humphreys, R. S. (1977a) p. 150.
346   Ayalon, D. (1949) p. 146.

347   Humphreys, R. S. (1977a) p. 147;
        Ayalon, D. (1953a) passim.
348   Irwin, R. (1986) pp. 232–3.
349   Ziadeh, N. A., p. 24.
350   Humphreys, R. S. (1977a) pp. 81–2.
351   Amitai, R. (Amitai-Preiss) (1990)
        p. 147.
352   Humphreys, R. S. (1977a) pp. 148–9
        and 172–6.
353   Humphreys, R. S. (1977a) pp. 172–6.
354   Ayalon, D. (1954) passim.
355   Humphreys, R. S. (1977a) p. 163.
356   Humphreys, R. S. (1977a) pp. 153–6.
357   Ayalon, D. (1953b) pp. 448–52.
358   Humphreys, R. S. (1977a) p. 148.
359   Humphreys, R. S. (1977a) pp. 161–2.
360   Ayalon, D. (1972) p. 39.
361   Ayalon, D. (1960) pp. 945–7.
362   Adams, W. Y., pp. 524–5.
363   Brett, M. (1986) pp. 82–3.
364   Brett, M. (1986) p. 87.
365   Brett, M. (1986) p. 94.
366   Brunschwig, R., pp. 75–8.
367   Brunschwig, R., pp. 78–9.
368   Abun-Nasr, J. M., pp. 134–8.
369   Granara, W. E., pp. 95–6.
370   Ahmad, Aziz (1975) p. 38.
371   Lévi-Provençal, E. (1954) p. 286.
372   Le Tourneau, R., pp. 1043–4.
373   Brett, M. (1975) p. 84.
374   Norris, H. T. (1972) p. 95.
375   Norris, H. T. (1972) p. 103.
376   Norris, H. T. (1972) p. 116 n. A.
377   Norris, H. T. (1982) p. 134.
378   Norris, H. T. (1982) pp. 181–2.
379   Dufourcq, pp. 90–2.
380   Lévi Provençal, E. (1932) p. 134.
381   Torres Delgado, C. (1988) p. 198.
382   Wasserstein, D., p. 100.
383   Lourie, L., pp. 68–9.
384   Arié, R., pp. 51–2.
385   Terrasse, H. (1965) pp. 81–3.
386   De Oliveiro-Marques, A. H., pp. 70–3.
387   De Oliveiro-Marques, A. H., p. 71.
388   Burns, R. I. (1976) pp. 109–10.
389   Burns, R. I. (1976) pp. 114–15.
390   Burns, R. I. (1976) pp. 105–6.
391   Arié, R., pp. 238–40.

392   Marsden, J. D., pp. 44–5.
393   Nizam al-Mulk (1960) pp. 102–3.
394   Bombaci, A., pp. 345–7.
395   Bombaci, A., pp. 351–2.
396   Amououx-Mourad, M., p. 51.
397   Cahen, C. (1940) p. 195.
398   Elisseeff, N. (1967) pp. 728.
399   Zanki, J. H. M. A. al-, pp. 277–8.
400   Elisseeff, N. (1967) p. 729.
401   Zakkar, S., p. 276.
402   Cahen, C. (1972) pp. 168–9.
403   Cahen, C. (1972) p. 170 n. 1.
404   Bianquis, T. (1983) pp. 661–2.
405   Cahen, C. (1972) pp. 164–6.
406   Nasir-i Khusrau (1881) p. 162.
407   Beshir, B. J., pp. 45–6.
408   Lev, Y. (1980) p. 184.
409   Cahen, C. (1972) pp. 171–3.
410   Elbeheiry, S., p. 312.
411   Ehrenkreutz, A. S. (1972) pp. 74–5.
412   Humphreys, R. S. (1977a) pp. 92–3.
413   Rabie, H. M. (1972) pp. 73–4.
414   Ashtor, E. (1969) p. 265.
415   Rabie, H. M. (1972) pp. 68–9.
416   Rabie, H. M. (1972) p. 122.
417   Gibb, H. A. R., *passim.*
418   Ashtor, E. (1969) p. 229.
419   Ayalon, D. (1958) p. 48.
420   Ayalon, D. (1958) p. 261.
421   Humphreys, R. S. (1977a) pp. 165–7.
422   Smith, J. M. (J. Masson Smith) (1984b)
      p. 321.
423   Ahmad, Aziz (1975) p. 23.
424   Hopkins, J. F. P., pp. 83–4.
425   Torres Delgado, C. (1988) pp. 199–200.
426   Lévi Provençal, E. (1950–67) vol. III,
      pp. 67, 204 and 207.
427   Terrasse, H. (1965) pp. 81–3.
428   Hinds, M., *passim.*
429   Ackermann, P., *passim.*
430   Calmard, J., p. 789.
431   'Arif 'Ali of Toqat, vol. I, p. 195 and
      vol. II, p. 19.
432   Lévi Provençal, E. (1950–67) vol. III,
      p. 90.
433   Sanders, P., p. 152.
434   David-Weill, J., p. 349.
435   Elisseeff, N. (1967) p. 730.

436   Ackermann, P., p. 2773 n. 2.
437   Ettinghausen, R., pp. 381–5.
438   Leaf, W. and S. Purcell, pp. 15–16 and
      passim.
439   Leaf, W., p. 61.
440   Rice, D.S., pp. 52 and 63–5.
441   Perhaps the most visible are carved
      on fortifications in Cairo and Crac
      des Chevaliers, but also on a medieval
      bridge over what was once the Abu
      al-Munajja canal near Shubra in the
      Nile Delta.
442   The latter collection is one of the most
      significant finds of medieval arms
      and armour for many years, and is
      currently being prepared for study.
443   This supposed 'coat-of-arms' of
      the rulers of Granada can be seen,
      for example, on some stucco wall
      decorations in the Alhambra Palace in
      Granada.
444   Ahsan, M. M., p. 33.
445   Ahsan, M. M., pp. 68–9.
446   Ackermann, P., p. 2773.
447   Arié, R., pp. 245–6.
448   *Ibid.*
449   Bianquis, T. (1983) p. 673.
450   'Arif 'Ali of Toqat, *passim.*
451   Harawi, 'Ali Ibn Abu Bakr al- (1961–2)
      p. 233.
452   Verbruggen, J. F. (1977b) pp. 264–5.
453   S. Doras and R. E. Koçu, *passim.*
454   De Moraes Farias, P. F., p. 817.
455   Anon., *La Chanson de Roland*, II.
      pp. 852 and 3137.
456   Norris, H. T. (1982) p. 178.
457   Peters, R., pp. 4–5.
458   Granara, W. E., pp. 126–7.
459   Esin, E. (1994) pp. 201–4.
460   Turan, O., pp. 83–4.
461   Turan, O., p. 89.
462   Boratav, P. N., pp. 245–6.
463   Weinberger, J. W., p. 24.
464   Weinberger, J. W., p. 22.
465   Lewis, G., *passim.*
466   Laurent, J. (1971) p. 123.
467   Glaesener, H., pp. 140–2.
468   Dajani-Shakeel, H. (1991) *passim.*

469 Hillenbrand, C. (1981) p. 272.
470 Hillenbrand, C. (1985) p. 13.
471 Hillenbrand, C. (1985) pp. 13–14.
472 Rist, R., pp. 99–100.
473 Dajani-Shakeel, H. (1986) *passim*.
474 Ellenblum, R. (2003) p. 97; for the significance of Bayt al-Ahzan see Le Strange, G., p. 412, and Harawi, 'Ali Ibn Abu Bakr al- (1957) p. 51.
475 Zanki, J. H. M. A. al-, pp. 275–7.
476 Eddé, A.-M., p. 234.
477 Hillenbrand, C. (1985) p. 15.
478 Lambton, A. K. S. (1971) pp. 425–7.
479 Lambton, A. K. S. (1971) pp. 428–90.
480 Tabbaa, Y., *passim*.
481 Toueir, K. (1983) *passim*; Toueir, K. (2004) *passim*.
482 Kedar, B. Z. (1992), pp. 206–7
483 Kedar B. Z. (1982), p. 202
484 Ben-Ami, A., p. 184.
485 Hillenbrand, C. (1985) pp. 13–14.
486 Morgan, D. O. (1968) p. 153.
487 Morgan, D. O. (1968) p. 156.
488 Sivan, E., pp. 180–2.
489 Zahir, Al-Qadi Muhi al-Din Ibn 'Abd al-, pp. 115–16.
490 Frenkel, Y., p. 246.
491 Ziadeh, N. A., p. 167.
492 Ayalon, D. (1965b) pp. 47–8.
493 Cahen, C. (1951) pp. 105–6.
494 'Arif 'Ali of Toqat, vol. I, p. 351, vol. II, pp. 165–6.
495 Wittek, P., p. 300.
496 Le Tourneau, R., pp. 1043–4.
497 Wasserstein, D., p. 154.
498 Wasserstein, D., p. 141.
499 Messier, R. A., pp. 241–2.
500 Burns, R. I. (1976) pp. 118–20.
501 Mottahedeh, R. P., pp. 100–1.
502 Mottahedeh, R. P., pp. 107–10.
503 Mottahedeh, R. P., p. 94.
504 Mottahedeh, R. P., pp. 54–9 and 61.
505 Hamblin, W. J. (1984) p. 8.
506 Mottahedeh, R. P., pp. 82–5.
507 Mottahedeh, R. P., p. 89.
508 Mottahedeh, R. P., pp. 85–6.
509 Mottahedeh, R. P., p. 87.
510 *Ibid.*

511 Mottahedeh, R. P., p. 88.
512 Irwin, R. (1986) pp. 237–8.
513 Ayalon, D. (1953b) p. 475.
514 Bianquis, T. (1983) pp. 661–2.
515 Mottahedeh, R. P., pp. 110–14.
516 Humphreys, R. S. (1977b) pp. 374–5.
517 Amitai-Preiss, R. (1996) pp. 271–2.
518 Pellat, C., and W. T. Najim, pp. 74–5.
519 *Ibid.*
520 Savvides, A. G. C. (2000b) p. 368.
521 Bianquis, T. (1983) p. 62.
522 Zakkar, S., p. 40.
523 Saleh, A. H. (1978) p. 59.
524 Weinberger, J. W., pp. 30–1.
525 Bianquis, T. (1983) p. 76.
526 Zakkar, S., p. 175.
527 Zanki, J. H. M. A. al-, pp. 268–70.
528 Kedar, B. Z. (1990) pp. 154–5.
529 Usamah Ibn Munqidh (1930) p. 41; Usamah Ibn Munqidh (1929) p. 63.
530 Ibn al-Athir, *passim*.
531 Little, D. P., p. 177.
532 Zahir, Al-Qadi Muhi al-Din Ibn 'Abd al-, p. 93.
533 Abu'l-Fida, p. 17.
534 Lomax, D. W., p. 105.
535 Peters, R., pp. 3–4.
536 Jurji, E. J., p. 332.
537 Weigert, G., *passim*.
538 Ibn Anas, Iman Malik, pp. 174–5.
539 Jurji, E. J., p. 335.
540 Peters, R., pp. 5–25.
541 Ansari, 'Umar Ibn Ibrahim al-Awsi al-, pp. 113–14.
542 Frenkel, Y., pp. 241–2.
543 Frenkel, Y., p. 243.
544 Bianquis, T. (1983) p. 661.
545 Lev, Y. (2001) *passim*.
546 Anon., *La Continuation de Guillaume de Tyr (1184–1197)* p. 56.
547 De Mas Latrie, M. L., pp. 231–2.
548 Ligato, G., *passim*.
549 Claverie, P-V., pp. 508–9.
550 Forey, A. (1991) p. 279.
551 Ayalon, D. (1976) pp. 198–9.
552 Bombaci, A., p. 358.
553 Forey, A. (1991) pp. 259–60 and 265–6.
554 Claverie, P-V., pp. 510–11.

555   Goitein, S. D. (1952) pp. 163–4.

556   Goitein, S. D. (1952) pp. 164–6.

557   Goitein, S. D. (1952) p. 167 n. 1.

558   Bianquis, T. (1983) p. 229.

559   Tantum, G., pp. 199–200.

560   Friedman, Y. (2002) p. 102.

561   Forey, A. (1991) p. 275.

562   Kantorowixz, E., pp. 128–30.

563   Bosworth, C. E. (1991) pp. 984–6.

564   Sarraf, S. al- (1996) p. 118.

565   Leo VI, *passim.*

566   More focused modern research in this field is nevertheless still occasionally rediscovering or identifying such early texts, either embedded in later works or as unrecognized manuscripts in sometimes obscure libraries.

567   Ansari, 'Umar Ibn Ibrahim al-Awsi al-, pp. 113–14.

568   Harthami, Abu Sa'id al-Sha'rani al-, p. 26.

569   Harthami, Abu Sa'id al-Sha'rani al-, pp. 36–7.

570   Harthami, Abu Sa'id al-Sha'rani al-, p. 41.

571   Harthami, Abu Sa'id al-Sha'rani al-, pp. 51–2.

572   Harthami, Abu Sa'id al-Sha'rani al-, pp. 56–9 and pp. 61–2.

573   Sarraf, S. al- (1996) p. 122.

574   See Sarraf, S. al- (1996) p. 119; for a condensed and perhaps more accessible version of Sarraf's study of 'Abbasid and Mamluk furusiya see Sarraf, S. al- (2002b) *passim.*

575   Ayalon, D. (1965a) pp. 954–5.

576   Lambton, A. K. S. (1971) p. 423.

577   Lambton, A. K. S. (1971) pp. 423–4.

578   Bosworth, C. E. (1965) pp. 284–5.

579   Fakhr al-Din Mubarakshah, Muhammad Ibn Mansur; no chapter of this work has yet been translated in full, except for the section on military archery, see Fakhr-i Mudabbir (1974) *passim.*

580   Fakhr-i Mudabbir (1974) p. 78.

581   Beshir, B. J., pp. 51–2.

582   Bosworth, C. E. (1991) pp. 987–8.

583   Hamblin, W. J. (1992) *passim.*

584   Sarraf, S. al- (1996) p. 131.

585   Tarsusi, Murda Ibn 'Ali Murda al- (1947–8) p. 103.

586   Harawi, 'Ali Ibn Abu Bakr al- (1961–2) *passim.*; Hamblin, W.J. (1992) pp. 229–30.

587   Hamblin, W. J. (1992) pp. 231–3.

588   Sarraf, S. al- (1996) p. 119.

589   Sarraf, S. al- (1996) p. 125.

590   Aqsara'i, al-, *passim.*

591   Sarraf, S. al- (1996) p. 130.

592   Tantum, G., pp. 194–5.

593   Sarraf, S. al- (1996) p. 120.

594   *Ibid.*; translated in Taybugha al-Baklamishi al-Yunani.

595   Dozy, R., p. 234.

596   Sarraf, S. al- (1996) p. 120; this text was translated in N. A. Faris and R. P. Elmer, at a time when the author was still unidentified.

597   Ibn Hudayl al-Andalusi, 'Ali Ibn 'Abd al-Rahman (1924) pp. 249–62; Ibn Hudayl al-Andalusi, 'Ali Ibn 'Abd al-Rahman (1977) pp. 197–210.

598   Obolensky, D. (1974) p. 306.

599   Morgan, D. O. (1985) p. 234.

600   Ayalon, D. (1984) p. 37.

601   Bianquis, T. (1983) pp. 420–1.

602   Lyon, B. D., p. 218.

603   Ghaith, Z. M., pp. 125–6.

604   Bianquis, T. (1983) p. 324.

605   Maulana Minhaj al-Din, p. 262.

606   Lyon, B. D., p. 11.

607   Nicholson, R. L. (1973) p. 146.

608   Verbruggen, J. F. (1977b) p. 257.

609   Verbruggen, J. F. (1977b) pp. 264–5.

610   Brunschwig, R., pp. 88–94.

611   Brett, M. (1995) pp. 17–18.

612   Nicolle, D.C. (1975) p. 29.

613   Brett, M. (1995) p. 19.

614   Richard, J. (1979c) p. 23.

615   Hillenbrand, C. (1981) pp. 276–7.

616   Smail, R. C. (1982) p. 166.

617   Smail, R. C. (1982) pp. 172–4.

618   Prawer, J. (1980) p. 480.

619   Nicholson, R.L. (1973) p. 86.

620   Smail, R. C. (1982) p. 159.

621 Hamblin, W. J. (1992) pp. 234–6.
622 *Ibid.*
623 Ehrenkreutz, A. S. (1972) pp. 109–12.
624 Khowaiter, A. A., p. 39.
625 Rashad Mohamad, A. M., pp. 77–8.
626 Prawer, J. (1980) p. 481.
627 Ayalon, D. (1960) pp. 945–7.
628 *Ibid.*
629 *Ibid.*
630 Amitai-Preiss, R. (1995) pp. 202–7;
     Amitai-Preiss, R. (1999) *passim.*
631 Zozaya, J. (1992) pp. 63–4.
632 Lacarra, J. M. (1963) pp. 207–8.
633 Lacarra, J. M. (1947) p. 67.
634 Ricard, R., and L. Torres Balbás, p. 463.
635 Burns, R. I. (1986) *passim.*
636 Powell, J. M. (1999) pp. 21–2.
637 A simplistic but interesting attempt to
     differentiate the traditional battlefield
     tactics of various medieval Middle
     eastern peoples was published in
     Berlin in 1940 by Von Pawlikowski-
     Cholewa, A., including those of the
     'Abbasid Caliphate (p. 228), Ayyubid
     Egypt (p. 234) and Muwahhidun
     [Almohades] (p. 253).
638 Fakhr al-Din Mubarakshah,
     Muhammad Ibn Mansur, p. 325.
639 Cahen, C. (1971a) pp. 181–4.
640 Ansari, 'Umar Ibn Ibrahim al-Awsi al-,
     p. 95.
641 Ibn Miskawaihi, p. 174.
642 Bianquis, T. (1983) p. 183 n. 1.
643 Ansari, 'Umar Ibn Ibrahim al-Awsi al-,
     pp. 95–6.
644 Ansari, 'Umar Ibn Ibrahim al-Awsi al-,
     pp. 100–2.
645 Ansari, 'Umar Ibn Ibrahim al-Awsi al-,
     p. 106.
646 Ansari, 'Umar Ibn Ibrahim al-Awsi al-,
     pp. 104–5.
647 Ansari, 'Umar Ibn Ibrahim al-Awsi al-,
     p. 93.
648 Ameer Ali, p. 9.
649 Ibn Miskawaihi, p. 144.
650 Smith, J. M. (J. Masson Smith) (1984b)
     p. 321.
651 Beshir, B. J., pp. 51–2.
652 *Ibid.*
653 Bianquis, T. (1983) pp. 240–1.
654 Bianquis, T. (1983) pp. 660–1.
655 Greenstone, J. H., p. 166.
656 Hamblin, W. J. (1984) pp. 160–5 and
     169–79.
657 Hamblin, W. J. (1984) pp. 26–7.
658 Smail, R. C. (1956) pp. 175–6.
659 Lev, Y. (1996) p. 147.
660 Zakkar, S., pp. 206–19.
661 France, J. (1996) p. 170.
662 Martinez, A. P., pp. 129–30.
663 'Arif 'Ali of Toqat, vol. I, p. 333, vol. II,
     p. 146.
664 Miller, I., *passim*; Nasawi, Muhammad
     Ibn Ahmad al-, p. 321.
665 Fakhr al-Din Mubarakshah,
     Muhammad Ibn Mansur, p. 340.
666 Fakhr al-Din Mubarakshah,
     Muhammad Ibn Mansur, p. 336.
667 Fakhr al-Din Mubarakshah,
     Muhammad Ibn Mansur, pp. 330–3;
     translated by C. E. Bosworth with
     modifications by D. C. Nicolle, Fakhr-i
     Mudabbir (2003) *passim.*
668 Lyon, B. D., pp. 14–16.
669 Tarsusi, Murda Ibn 'Ali Murda al-
     (1947–8) pp. 125–6 and 148–9.
670 Harawi, 'Ali Ibn Abu Bakr al- (1961–2)
     p. 233.
671 Lyon, B. D., p. 93.
672 Nicolle, D. C. (2005), pp. 55–82.
673 Ibn al-Athir, p. 684.
674 Prawer, J. (1980) p. 496.
675 Nicolle, D. C. (1993b) pp. 65–79.
676 Thordeman, B., p. 236.
677 Thordeman, B., pp. 238–9.
678 Verbruggen, J. F. (1977b) pp. 264–5.
679 Brett, M. (1975) p. 82.
680 Brunschwig, R., pp. 83–5.
681 Brett, M. (1970) pp. 17–18.
682 Brett, M. (1975) pp. 82–3.
683 Brett, M. (1975) p. 81.
684 De Moraes Farias, P. F., pp. 810–11.
685 *Ibid.*
686 El Bekri (Bakri, al-), p. 314.
687 Hopkins, J. F. P. and N. Levtzion,
     p. 165.

688   Norris, H. T. (1982) p. 179.
689   Brett, M. (1975) pp. 83–4.
690   Beeler, J., pp. 176–8.
691   Brett, M. (1975) p. 83.
692   Turtushi, Muhammad Ibn Walid al-, pp. 308–9 (Arabic), trans. pp. 332–3 (trans.); translated in Lévi Provençal, E. (1950–67) p. 100.
693   Burns, R. I. (1976) pp. 118–20.
694   Ansari, 'Umar Ibn Ibrahim al-Awsi al-, pp. 83–4.
695   Ansari, 'Umar Ibn Ibrahim al-Awsi al-, p. 90.
696   Ansari, 'Umar Ibn Ibrahim al-Awsi al-, pp. 91–2.
697   Beshir, B. J., pp. 51–2.
698   Bianquis, T. (1983) p. 92.
699   Elisseeff, N. (1967) p. 738.
700   Tantum, G., p. 198.
701   Canard, M. (1965a) pp. 486–7.
702   Ansari, 'Umar Ibn Ibrahim al-Awsi al-, pp. 80–1.
703   Elbeheiry, S., pp. 226–30.
704   Elbeheiry, S., p. 244.
705   Ansari, 'Umar Ibn Ibrahim al-Awsi al-, pp. 86–7.
706   Bianquis, T. (1983) p. 105.
707   Bianquis, T. (1983) p. 183.
708   Brett, M. (1975) pp. 86–8.
709   Elisseeff, N. (1967) p. 739.
710   Harawi, 'Ali Ibn Abu Bakr al- (1961–2) p. 229.
711   Lyon, B. D., p. 106.
712   Verbruggen, J. F. (1977b) pp. 264–5.
713   Matuz, J., 190–6
714   Ansari, 'Umar Ibn Ibrahim al-Awsi al-, p. 72.
715   Bianquis, T. (1983) p. 153.
716   Martinez, A. P., pp. 130–8.
717   Ibn Hauqal (1939) p. 113; Ibn Hauqal (1964) pp. 112–13.
718   Soler del Campo, A. (1986) p. 73.
719   Ibn Miskawaihi, p. 164.
720   Bowlus, C. R., *passim*.
721   Bowlus, C. R., pp. 160–1.
722   Bowlus, C. R., pp. 163–5.
723   Currently in a private collection and as yet unpublished.
724   Boit, B. A. (1991a) pp. 39–40.
725   Smith, J. M. (J. Masson Smith) (1996) p. 251 n. 13.
726   Smith, J. M. (J. Masson Smith) (1996) p. 252 n. 16.
727   Smith, J. M. (J. Masson Smith) (1996) p. 252.
728   Smith, J. M. (J. Masson Smith) (1984b) p. 324.
729   Smith, J. M. (J. Masson Smith) (1996) p. 259.
730   Smith, J. M. (J. Masson Smith) (1996) p. 258.
731   Psellus, M., p. 68.
732   De Moraes Farias, P. F., p. 813.
733   De Moraes Farias, P. F., pp. 811–12.
734   Bianquis, T. (1983) p. 182.
735   Bianquis, T. (1983) pp. 597–8.
736   Abu'l-Fida, p. 19.
737   Lindner, R. P. (1981) pp. 10–11.
738   Marshall, C. J. (1990) p. 224.
739   Ansari, 'Umar Ibn Ibrahim al-Awsi al-, pp. 112–13.
740   Ansari, 'Umar Ibn Ibrahim al-Awsi al-, pp. 97–8.
741   Zakkar, S., p. 202.
742   Sarraf, S. al- (1996) pp. 128–9.
743   Tantum, G., pp. 198–9.
744   Lyon, B. D., pp. 297–8.
745   Anon., *The Third Crusade, Itinerarium Peregrinorum*, pp. 131–2.
746   Baha' al-Din Ibn Shaddad (1897b) p. 161.
747   Baha' al-Din Ibn Shaddad (1897a) p. 208; Baha' al-Din Ibn Shaddad (2002) p. 206.
748   Ansari, 'Umar Ibn Ibrahim al-Awsi al-, pp. 93–4.
749   Bianquis, T. (1984) p. 76.
750   Zanki, J.H.M.A. al-, pp. 275–7.
751   Arié, R., pp. 241–4.
752   Norris, H. T. (1982) pp. 135–6.
753   Kollias, T. (1984) p. 133 n. 29.
754   Elbeheiry, S., pp. 83–7.
755   Norris, H. T. (1982) p. 134.
756   Hopkins, J. F. P., pp. 75–6.
757   Ansari, 'Umar Ibn Ibrahim al-Awsi al-, p. 72.

758 Ansari, 'Umar Ibn Ibrahim al-Awsi al-, pp. 107–8.
759 Bianquis, T. (1983) p. 94.
760 Maulana Minhaj al-Din, p. 352 n. 3.
761 Maulana Minhaj al-Din, pp. 352–3.
762 Verbruggen, J. F. (1977a) *passim.*
763 Hamblin, W. J. (1984) p. 168.
764 Hamblin, W. J. (1984) pp. 27–31.
765 Bianquis, T. (1983) p. 314.
766 Hamblin, W. J. (1984) pp. 151–2.
767 A practice remarkably similar to the trench-fires men of a certain age were taught to use while camping as youngsters. Was al-Tarsusi also aware that a fire in a trench, if correctly aligned to the wind, produced a more intense heat for cooking?
768 Anon., *The Third Crusade, Itinerarium Peregrinorum*, pp. 87–8.
769 Baha' al-Din Ibn Shaddad (1897a) p. 175; Baha' al-Din Ibn Shaddad (1897b) p. 290.
770 Anon., *The Third Crusade, Itinerarium Peregrinorum*, p. 92.
771 De Joinville (1921) p. 199; De Joinville (1952) p. 257.
772 Anon., *The Book of Dede Korkut*, p. 145.
773 Anon., *The Book of Dede Korkut*, p. 94.
774 Atiya, A. S., p. 60.
775 Sarraf, S. al- (1996) p. 133 n. 59.
776 Bianquis, T. (1983) pp. 113–14.
777 Lev, Y. (1980) pp. 188–9.
778 Zanki, J.H.M.A. al-, p. 258.
779 Ayyuqi, v. p. 331.
780 Ayyuqi, v. p. 365 and passim.
781 Ayyuqi, v. p. 522.
782 Ayyuqi, v. pp. 523–4.
783 Ayyuqi, v. pp. 540–1.
784 Ayyuqi, v. p. 1153.
785 'Arif 'Ali of Toqat, vol. I, p. 333, vol. II, p. 146.
786 Aqsara'i, al-, pp. 317–40: Nicolle, D. C. (1994a) *passim.*
787 Aqsara'i, al-, p. 336.
788 Aqsara'i, al-, pp. 336–7.
789 Aqsara'i, al-, p. 337.
790 Sarraf, S. al- (1996) pp. 128–9.

791 Hamblin, W. J. (1984) pp. 145–6.
792 Anon., *Gesta Francorum, The Deeds of the Franks and other Pilgrims to Jerusalem*, p. 49; original Latin text reads, 'Et Agulani fuerunt numero tria milia; qui neque lanceas neque sagittas neque ulla arma timebant, quia omnes erant undique cooperti ferro et equi eorum, ipsique nolebant in bellum ferre arma nisi solummodo gladios'.
793 France, J. (1996) p. 169.
794 Anon., *The Third Crusade, Itinerarium Peregrinorum*, p. 78.
795 Ayyuqi, pp. 38–9.
796 De Joinville (1921) p. 198.
797 Soler del Campo, A. (1986) pp. 67–8; Norris, H. T. (1972) p. 112.
798 Beeler, J., pp. 181–3.
799 Arié, R., p. 250.
800 Burns, R.I. (1976) p. 117.
801 Burns, R.I. (1976) p. 117 n. 36.
802 Sarraf, S. al- (1996) p. 123.
803 Aqsara'i, al-, p. 193.
804 Aqsara'i, al-, *passim.*
805 Aqsara'i, al-, p. 196.
806 Aqsara'i, al-, p. 197.
807 Usamah Ibn Munqidh (1929) pp. 68–9.
808 Usamah Ibn Munqidh (1929) *passim.*
809 Usamah Ibn Munqidh (1929) p. 92.
810 Usamah Ibn Munqidh (1929) p. 66.
811 Baha' al-Din Ibn Shaddad (1897a) p. 205; Baha' al-Din Ibn Shaddad (1897b) p. 338.
812 Fakhr al-Din Mubarakshah, Muhammad Ibn Mansur, pp. 260–1.
813 Baer, E., *passim.*
814 Norris, H. T. (1982) pp. 152–3.
815 Beshir, B. J., p. 38.
816 Von Oppenhein, M., *passim.*
817 Anon, *Sassountzy David, Haykakan Zhoghovrdakan Epos*; Anon., *David of Sassoun: The Armenian Folk Epic in Four Cycles.*
818 Tarsusi, Murda Ibn 'Ali Murda al- (1968) pp. 142–4.
819 Sarraf, S. al- (2002a) p. 175.
820 Sarraf, S. al- (1996) p. 124.
821 Sarraf, S. al- (2002a) *passim.*

822 Anon., *The Third Crusade, Itinerarium Peregrinorum*, pp. 131–2.
823 Gabrieli, F., pp. 290–1.
824 De Joinville (1921) p. 179.
825 Fakhr al-Din Mubarakshah, Muhammad Ibn Mansur, p. 263.
826 'Arif 'Ali of Toqat, vol. I, p. 214 and vol. II, p. 28.
827 'Arif 'Ali of Toqat, vol. I, p. 304, vol. II, p. 117 and *passim*.
828 Canard, M. (1965c) p. 187.
829 Aqsara'i, al-, pp. 332–4.
830 *Ibid.*
831 McEwen, E., *passim*.
832 Fakhr-i Mudabbir (1974) pp. 92–4.
833 Sarraf, S. al- (1996) p. 122.
834 Anon., *Gesta Francorum, The Deeds of the Franks and other Pilgrims to Jerusalem*, p. 19.
835 Sarraf, S. al- (1996) p. 120.
836 Boudot-Lamotte, A. and F. Viré, pp. 50–1.
837 James, S., pp. 197–9.
838 Paterson, W. F. (1963) p. 14.
839 Latham, J. D. and W. F. Paterson (1965) p. 254.
840 Latham, J. D. (1968) pp. 242–3.
841 Fakhr-i Mudabbir (1974) p. 94.
842 Nicolle (forthcoming).
843 Usamah Ibn Munqidh (1929) p. 74.
844 Fakhr-i Mudabbir (1974) pp. 81–3.
845 Tarsusi, Murda Ibn 'Ali Murda al- (1968) pp. 142–4.
846 Tarsusi, Murda Ibn 'Ali Murda al- (1968) pp. 146–8.
847 Smith, J. M. (J. Masson Smith) (1984a) pp. 10 and 13–14.
848 Smith, J. M. (J. Masson Smith) (1996) p. 257 n. 33.
849 Soler del Campo, A. (1986) pp. 72–3.
850 Latham, J. D. (1970) p. 102.
851 Canard, M. (1951) p. 397.
852 Fakhr al-Din Mubarakshah, Muhammad Ibn Mansur, p. 260.
853 De Joinville (1921) p. 280; De Joinville (1952) p. 329.
854 Anon., *The Third Crusade, Itinerarium Peregrinorum*, p. 153.
855 Tarsusi, Murda Ibn 'Ali Murda al- (1968) pp. 146–8.
856 Baha' al-Din Ibn Shaddad (1897b) p. 145.
857 Paterson, W. F. (1969) pp. 27–8.
858 'Arif 'Ali of Toqat, vol. I, p. 356, vol. II, p. 171.
859 Hamblin, W. J. (1984) pp. 142–3.
860 Latham, J. D. (1971) p. 203.
861 Faris, N. A. and R. P. Elmer, p. 12.
862 Douillet, G., p. 953.
863 *Ibid.*
864 Douillet, G., p. 954.
865 Lyon, B. D., p. 5.
866 Rice, T. T., p. 81.
867 Nizam al-Mulk (1960) pp. 106–7.
868 Nizam al-Mulk (1960) p. 135; Nizam al-Mulk (1932) p. 96.
869 Beshir, B. J., pp. 46–8.
870 *Ibid.*
871 Ayalon, D. (1977b) p. 268.
872 Lyons, M. C. and D. E. P. Jackson, p. 4.
873 *Ibid.*
874 Lyons, M. C. and D. E. P. Jackson, p. 5.
875 Ayalon, D. (1951) pp. 16–17.
876 Zahir, Al-Qadi Muhi al-Din Ibn 'Abd al-, p. 215.
877 Smith, J. M. (J. Masson Smith) (1996) p. 256.
878 Norris, H. T. (1982) pp. 181–2.
879 Nicolle, D. C. (2002b) *passim*.
880 Elisseeff, N. (1967) p. 731.
881 Hillenbrand, C. (1985) p. 311.
882 Patton, D. L., pp. 46–8.
883 Patton, D. L., p. 65.
884 Ayalon, D. (1961) pp. 37–9.
885 Sarraf, S. al- (1996) p. 128.
886 Rabie, H. M. (1975) p. 156.
887 Ibn Akhi Khazam, f.184.
888 Ibn Akhi Khazam, f.179.
889 Rabie, H. M. (1975) p. 162.
890 Ibn Akhi Khazam, *passim*.
891 Rabie, H. M. (1975) p. 161.
892 Ayalon, D. (1965b) p. 57.
893 'Arif 'Ali of Toqat, *passim*.
894 Smith, J. M. (J. Masson Smith) (1984b) p. 323; Smith, J. M. (J. Masson Smith) (1996) p. 258 n. 36.

895   Latham, J. D. (1969) pp. 257–8.
896   Jahiz, al- (1915) pp. 642–6; Jahiz,
        al- (1965) pp. 15–21.
897   Rabie, H. M. (1975) p. 160.
898   Latham, J. D. (1969) p. 260.
899   Latham, J. D. (1969) p. 261.
900   Latham, J. D. (1969) pp. 261–2.
901   Rabie, H. M. (1975) p. 159.
902   Latham, J. D. (1968) p. 241.
903   Latham, J. D. (1971) pp. 202–3.
904   Ahsan, M. M., p. 223.
905   Squiers, G., *passim.*
906   Sarraf, S. al- (2002c) *passim.*
907   Ahmad, Aziz (1975) p. 99.
908   Jones, D., pp. 44–7.
909   Wolff, F., *passim.*
910   Bianquis, T. (1983) p. 241.
911   Atiya, A. S., p. 108.
912   'Arif 'Ali of Toqat, *passim.*
913   Goitein, S. D. (1954) p. 248.
914   Hamblin, W. J. (1984) pp. 138–41.
915   Hamblin, W. J. (1984) pp. 143–4.
916   Canard, M. (1952b) pp. 366–93;
        Canard, M. (1951) p. 397.
917   Anon., *The Old French Crusade Cycle,
        vol. V: Les Chétifs,* II. pp. 804–20 and
        passim.
918   Zahir, Al-Qadi Muhi al-Din Ibn 'Abd
        al-, pp. 225–9, retranslated by D. C.
        Nicolle.
919   Verbruggen, J. F. (1977b) p. 269.
920   Atiya, A. S., p. 166.
921   Norris, H. T. (1982) p. 129.
922   Baidhaq, Abu Bakr Ibn 'Ali al-Sanhagi
        al- (tr.) p. 124 (ed.) p. 76 and *passim.*
923   García Gómez, pp. 165–7.
924   Lévi Provençal, E. (1932) pp. 144–6.
925   Nicolle, D. C. (2002a) *passim.*
926   Lévi Provençal, E. (1932) pp. 144–6.
927   Kindi, al-; Hammer-Purgstall, J.
928   Sarraf, S. al- (2002a) p. 151.
929   Sarraf, S. al- (2002a) pp. 167–74.
930   Biruni, Muhammad Ibn Ahmad al-,
        p. 248.
931   Biruni, Muhammad Ibn Ahmad al-,
        p. 250.
932   Biruni, Muhammad Ibn Ahmad al-,
        p. 252.
933   Biruni, Muhammad Ibn Ahmad al-,
        p. 253.
934   Biruni, Muhammad Ibn Ahmad al-,
        p. 254.
935   Biruni, Muhammad Ibn Ahmad al-,
        pp. 252–3.
936   Fakhr al-Din Mubarakshah,
        Muhammad Ibn Mansur, p. 260.
937   Anon., *The Book of Dede Korkut,*
        p. 146.
938   James, S., pp. 189–90, where the
        weapon is described as a Roman
        cavalry mace.
939   Esin, E. (1974) *passim.*
940   Sarraf, S. al- (2002a) pp. 152–61.
941   Tarsusi, Murda Ibn 'Ali Murda al-
        (1947–8) pp. 117–18 and 139–40.
942   Anon., *The Book of Dede Korkut,
        passim.*
943   Anon., *The Old French Crusade Cycle,
        vol. V: Les Chétifs, passim.*
944   Graindor de Douai, I. p. 3202.
945   Melikian-Chirvani, A. S., p. 311.
946   Sarraf, S. al- (2002a) p. 166.
947   Sarraf, S. al- (2002a) pp. 162–5.
948   Tarsusi, Murda Ibn 'Ali Murda al-
        (1947–8) pp. 118 and 140.
949   Melikian-Chirvani, A. S., pp. 311–12.
950   *Ibid.*
951   Usamah Ibn Munqidh (1929) p. 75.
952   Usamah Ibn Munqidh (1930) p. 101;
        Usamah Ibn Munqidh (1929) p. 131.
953   Anon., *The Book of Dede Korkut,
        passim.*
954   Soler del Campo, A. (1986) pp. 64–5.
955   Tarsusi, Murda Ibn 'Ali Murda al-
        (1947–8) pp. 112–14 and 134–6.
956   Hamblin, W. J. (1984) pp. 152–3.
957   De Hoffmeyer, A. B. (1972) p. 170.
958   García Gómez, p. 165.
959   Boudot-Lamotte, A., p. 797.
960   García Gómez, p. 165.
961   Boudot-Lamotte, A. and F. Viré,
        pp. 49–50.
962   Faris, N. A. and R. P. Elmer, pp. 10–12.
963   Boit, B. A. (1991a) pp. 26–8.
964   Boit, B. A. (1991a) p. 2.
965   Boit, B. A. (1991a) p. 7.

966   McEwen, E.
967   Boit, B. A. (1991b) pp. 83–4.
968   Sarraf, S. al- (1996) p. 121.
969   Flutre, L. F., pp. 312–13.
970   Credland, A. G. (1994) p. 27.
971   Faris, N. A. and R. P. Elmer, p. 94.
972   Ahsan, M. M., p. 221.
973   Buckler, G., p. 428.
974   Miller, R. (1985a), *passim*.
975   Anon., *The Book of Dede Korkut*,
      passim.
976   *Ibid*.
977   Latham, J. D. and W. F. Paterson (1965)
      pp. 256–7.
978   Latham, J. D. and W. F. Paterson (1965)
      p. 261.
979   Other more complete and earlier
      Mamluk-period arrows from Syria,
      currently in a private collection, have
      yet to be studied.
980   Fakhr-i Mudabbir (1974) pp. 90–2.
981   Faris, N. A. and R. P. Elmer, pp. 124–6.
982   Credland, A. G. (1981) pp. 119–20.
983   Nicolle, D. C. (forthcoming).
984   Huuri, K., p. 113.
985   Huuri, K., p. 114.
986   *Ibid*.
987   Huuri, K., p. 111.
988   Paterson, W. F. (1990) *passim*.
989   Huuri, K., pp. 94–5.
990   Boudot-Lamotte, A., p. 798.
991   Wolff, F., *passim*.
992   Firdawsi (1877–80) p. 1280; Firdawsi
      (1905) p. 147.
993   Paterson, W. F. (1990) *passim*.
994   Firdawsi (1877–80) pp. 1327–8;
      Firdawsi (1905) p. 197.
995   Huuri, K., pp. 117–18.
996   Hamblin, W. J. (1984) p. 142.
997   Tarsusi, Murda Ibn 'Ali Murda al-
      (1947–8) pp. 110 and 132; Paterson, W.
      F. (1990) *passim*.
998   Hamblin, W. J. (1984) p. 142.
999   Tarsusi, Murda Ibn 'Ali Murda al-
      (1947–8) pp. 110–32.
1000 Latham, J. D. (1971) pp. 202–3.
1001 Zardkash, Ibn Urunbugha al-,
      pp. 129–31.

1002 Paterson, W. F. (1990) *passim*.
1003 Nicolle, D. C. (forthcoming).
1004 Finó, J.-F., pp. 26–7; the staves and
      'missiles' found in the Citadel of
      Damascus during the period of the
      French mandate are now in the Musèe
      de l'Armèe in Paris (both as inv. L2).
1005 Gorelik, M. V. (2004) *passim*.
1006 Tarsusi, Murda Ibn 'Ali Murda al-
      (1947–8) pp. 114–15 and 136–8.
1007 Anon., *La Siège de Barbastre*, I. p. 1222.
1008 Norris, H. T. (1982) p. 120.
1009 Buttin, F. (1960) p. 412.
1010 Mitchell, R., *passim*.
1011 Melikian-Chirvani, A. S., p. 314.
1012 'Arif 'Ali of Toqat, vol. I, pp. 229 and
      387, vol. II, pp. 42 and 203.
1013 Gorelik, M. V. (2004) *passim*.
1014 Bianquis, T. (1983) p. 153.
1015 Usamah Ibn Munqidh (1929)
      pp. 69–70 and *passim*.
1016 Usamah Ibn Munqidh (1929) *passim*.
1017 Pérès, H., pp. 350–9.
1018 Amari, M. (1880–1) vol. II, p. 399 and
      passim.
1019 Tarsusi, Murda Ibn 'Ali Murda al-
      (1947–8) pp. 116 and 138–9.
1020 Usamah Ibn Munqidh (1929)
      pp. 129–30.
1021 Anon., *La Siège de Barbastre*, *passim*.
1022 Maulana Minhaj al-Din, pp. 176–7.
1023 Anon., *The Book of Dede Korkut*,
      passim.
1024 Tarsusi, Murda Ibn 'Ali Murda al-
      (1947–8) pp. 116 and 138–9.
1025 Bianquis, T. (1983) p. 152.
1026 Canard, M. (1957) p. 49.
1027 Clarke, J., *passim*; 'Lamellar Armor and
      Helmets', in D. J. LaRocca, pp. 51–67.
1028 Nicolle, D. C. (1983) *passim*, the
      author now believes that most of
      the pictorial sources which had been
      interpreted as scale armour were in
      reality representations of mail armour.
1029 Allchin, F. R., pp. 113–18.
1030 Tazi, 'Abd al-Hadi al-, *passim*.
1031 Nicolle, D. C. (forthcoming).
1032 Nicolle, D. C. (2004a) p. 738.

1033 Bosworth, C. E. (1998) *passim*.

1034 Anon., *The Book of Dede Korkut*, p. 165.

1035 Maulana Minhaj al-Din, p. 352 n. 3.

1036 Melikian-Chirvani, A. S., pp. 313–14.

1037 De Joinville (1952) pp. 253–4.

1038 Alexander, D. G. (1984) pp. 97–8 and 104.

1039 Currently being conserved prior to study.

1040 Mas'udi, al-, vol. 6, 452, 462 and 470.

1041 Tarsusi, Murda Ibn 'Ali Murda al- (1947–8) pp. 116 and 138–9.

1042 De Joinville (1921) p. 273.

1043 Alexander, D. G. and H. Ricketts, p. 298.

1044 Gorelik, M. V. (1997) *passim*.

1045 'Arif 'Ali of Toqat, vol. I, pp. 367–8, vol. II, p. 185.

1046 Melikian-Chirvani, A. S., p. 314.

1047 Beshir, B. J., pp. 48–9.

1048 Nasir-i Khusrau (1881) pp. 46 and 137.

1049 García Gómez, p. 166.

1050 Cahen, C. (1947–8) pp. 58–60; Fakhr al-Din Mubarakshah, Muhammad Ibn Mansur, *passim*.

1051 Deloche, J., p. 35.

1052 Aqsara'i, al-, pp. 13, 143 and 319.

1053 Allason-Jones, L., p. 33.

1054 García Gómez, pp. 166–7.

1055 *Ibid*.

1056 Canard, M. (1957) p. 49.

1057 Cahen, C. (1972) p. 168.

1058 Hamblin, W. J. (1984) pp. 138–41.

1059 Qalqashandi, Ahmad Ibn 'Abd Allah al-, pp. 132–8.

1060 Qalqashandi, Ahmad Ibn 'Abd Allah al-, pp. 8–18.

1061 Qalqashandi, Ahmad Ibn 'Abd Allah al-, p. 134.

1062 Qalqashandi, Ahmad Ibn 'Abd Allah al-, pp. 473–5.

1063 Qalqashandi, Ahmad Ibn 'Abd Allah al-, p. 477.

1064 Elisseeff, N. (1967) p. 848.

1065 Lyon, B. D., pp. 322 and 341.

1066 Zahir, Al-Qadi Muhi al-Din Ibn 'Abd al-, p. 215.

1067 Norris, H. T. (1982) pp. 181–2.

1068 Canard, M. (1952a) p. 300.

1069 Cahen, C. (1934) p. 636.

1070 Ashtor, E. (1969) p. 355.

1071 Marcais, G., p. 79.

1072 Glick, T. F. (1979) *passim*.

1073 Lev, Y. (1996) p. 140.

1074 Nicolle, D. C. (forthcoming).

1075 Feuerbach, *passim*.

1076 Allan, J. W. (1979) pp. 76–8.

1077 A bronze spearhead said to date from the Ayyubid period, now in the Islamic Museum at Mazar.

1078 Willey, P., p. 150.

1079 Allan, J. W. (1979) p. 59.

1080 Allan, J. W. (1982) pp. 57–8.

1081 Alexander, D. G. and H. Nickel, p. 27.

1082 Dozy, R. (ed.) and C. Pellat (tr.), pp. 104–5.

1083 Fragments from two or three wood-framed saddles, one virtually complete, have been found in the Citadel of Damascus and are believed to date from the early Mamluk period. They are undergoing conservation prior to being studied in detail.

1084 Maulana Minhaj al-Din, p. 566.

1085 Fakhr al-Din Mubarakshah, Muhammad Ibn Mansur, p. 263.

1086 Imamuddin, S. M., p. 131.

1087 Allan, J. W. (1979) pp. 66–7.

1088 *Ibid*.

1089 *Ibid*.

1090 Anon., *Hudud al'-Alam*, p. 110.

1091 Allan, J. W. (1979) pp. 66–7.

1092 Arendt, W. (1932–4) p. 188.

1093 Hamdani, Hasan Ibn Ahmad al-, pp. 255–7.

1094 Canard, M. (1957) p. 46.

1095 Lombard, M., pp. 165–6.

1096 Hassan, A. Y. al-, pp. 38–9.

1097 Hassan, A. Y. al-, pp. 41–2.

1098 Bahnassi, A., p. 289.

1099 Somogyi, J., p. 371.

1100 Sarraf, S. al- (1996) p. 122.

1101 Ziadeh, N. A., p. 89.

1102 Miller, R. (1985b) *passim*.

1103 Huart, Cl., p. 1084.

1104 Ahmad, Aziz (1975) pp. 39–40.
1105 Latham, J. D. (1971) p. 201.
1106 Buttin, F. (1960) p. 412.
1107 Allan, J. W. (1979) p. 68.
1108 Boit, B. A. (1991a) pp. 8–18.
1109 Zahir, Al-Qadi Muhi al-Din Ibn ʿAbd al-, p. 215.
1110 Zahir, Al-Qadi Muhi al-Din Ibn ʿAbd al-,131.
1111 Imamuddin, S. M., pp. 129–31.
1112 Imamuddin, S. M., pp. 127–9.
1113 Elisseeff, N. (1967) p. 451.
1114 Zahir, Al-Qadi Muhi al-Din Ibn ʿAbd al-, pp. 189–90.
1115 Bianquis, T. (1983) p. 559.
1116 Nasir-i Khusrau (1881) p. 15.
1117 Patton, D.L., p. 46.
1118 Bianquis, T. (1983) p. 533.
1119 Bianquis, T. (1983) p. 613.
1120 Sinclair, T., p. 306.
1121 Bianquis, T. (1983) p. 320.
1122 Sinclair, T., p. 321.
1123 Hanisch, H-P., passim.
1124 Sinclair, T., pp. 305–7 and 310.
1125 Bianquis, T. (1983) p. 41.
1126 Bylinski, J., passim.
1127 Heidemann, S., pp. 49–55.
1128 Bianquis, T. (1983) pp. 5–6.
1129 Bianquis, T. (1983) p. 533.
1130 Bianquis, T. (1983) pp. 479–80.
1131 Bianquis, T. (1983) p. 482.
1132 Salibi, K. S. (1977) p. 68.
1133 Michaudel, B., passim.
1134 Zahir, Al-Qadi Muhi al-Din Ibn ʿAbd al-, pp. 117–18.
1135 Ziadeh, N. A., p. 85.
1136 Bianquis, T. (1983) p. 662.
1137 Bianquis, T. (1983) p. 426.
1138 Bianquis, T. (1983) p. 479.
1139 Chevedden, P. E. (1985) pp. 4–5.
1140 Michaudel, B., passim.
1141 Bylinski, J., passim.
1142 Bianquis, T. (1983) p. 577 n. 2.
1143 Goitein, S. D. (1982) pp. 187–8.
1144 Drory, J., pp. 191–3.
1145 Northedge, A., p. 457.
1146 Brooker, C. H. and E. A. Knauf, p. 187.
1147 Ibid.

1148 Nasir-i Khusrau (1881) pp. 215–16.
1149 Nasir-i Khusrau (1881) p. 225.
1150 Voisin, J-C., pp. 329 and 330 n. 42.
1151 Terrasse, H. (1960) p. 1319.
1152 Terrasse, H. (1960) p. 1320.
1153 Nicolle, D. C. (2000) pp. 23–32.
1154 Basset, H., pp. 118–19 and 142–3.
1155 Terrasse, H. (1960) pp. 1319–20.
1156 Banks, P. J. and J. Zozaya, pp. 680–1.
1157 Banks, P. J. and J. Zozaya, pp. 682–3.
1158 Zozaya, J. (1988) pp. 173–8.
1159 Valdés Fernández, p. 151.
1160 Zozaya, J. (1992) p. 71.
1161 Zozaya, J. (1992) pp. 65–6.
1162 For a recent study of the frontier defence system and fortresses of eleventh- to thirteenth-century al-Andalus, see García Fitz, F. (1998b) passim.
1163 Terrasse, H. (1960) p. 1320.
1164 Bennett, M. (2001) p. 78.
1165 Bennett, M. (2001) p. 80.
1166 Ricard, R. and L. Torres Balbás, pp. 448 and 457.
1167 García Fitz, F. (1990) p. 56.
1168 Bazzana, A. (1983a) passim.
1169 Fernández-Puertas, A., p. 1028.
1170 Arié, R., pp. 230–8.
1171 Zahir, Al-Qadi Muhi al-Din Ibn ʿAbd al-, pp. 225–9.
1172 Tonghini, C. and N. Montevecchi, passim.
1173 Brooker, C. H. and E. A. Knauf, p. 187.
1174 Allen, T. (1996–2003) Fig. 24.
1175 Salibi, K. S. (1977) p. 89.
1176 Glick, T. F. (1976) pp. 146 and p. 151.
1177 Terrasse, H. (1960) pp. 1319–20.
1178 Basset, H., p. 155.
1179 Terrasse, H. (1971) p. 500.
1180 Terrasse, H. (1960) p. 1320.
1181 Sourdel-Thomine, J., p. 1315.
1182 Chevedden, P. E. (1999) pp. 39–40.
1183 Terrasse, H. (1960) p. 1320.
1184 Terrasse, H. (1971) p. 500.
1185 Fernández-Puertas, A., p. 1028.
1186 Creswell, K.A.C. (1952) p. 90.
1187 Creswell, K.A.C. (1960) p. 831.
1188 Pringle, R. D. (1994) pp. 90–1.

1189 Rice, D. S., pp. 48, 52–3 and 63–6.
1190 Creswell, K. A. C. (1960) p. 831.
1191 Terrasse, H. (1960) p. 1320.
1192 Terrasse, H. (1971) p. 500.
1193 Terrasse, H. (1960) p. 1320; Zozaya, J. (1992) p. 71.
1194 Terrasse, H. (1960) p. 1320.
1195 Nasir-i Khusrau (1881) p. 252.
1196 Becker, A., pp. 3–4; Hagen, N., M. al-Khalaf, M. Meinecke and H. Mismahl, pp. 5–10.
1197 Patton, D. L., pp. 43–5.
1198 Patton, D. L., p. 4
1199 Nasir-i Khusrau (1881) p. 27.
1200 Zakkar, S., pp. 276–7.
1201 Creswell, K. A. C. (1952) pp. 123–5.
1202 Nasir-i Khusrau (1888) pp. 7–8.
1203 Nasir-i Khusrau (1888) p. 13.
1204 Hartmann-Virnich, A., *passim*; for the Ayyubid citadel see Creswell, K. A. C. (1952) p. 123, Chevedden, P. E. (1985) *passim* and Chevedden, P. E. (1999) *passim*.
1205 Bianquis, T. (1983) pp. 61–6.
1206 Creswell, K. A. C. (1952) p. 112; for the great Bab al-Nasr, Bab al-Futuh and Bab Zuwayla gates built by Badr al-Jamali see Creswell, K. A. C. (1952) pp. 113–14.
1207 Lyon, B. D., p. 8.
1208 Creswell, K. A. C. (1952) pp. 119–23.
1209 Staffa, S. J., pp. 86–8.
1210 *Ibid*.
1211 Chevedden, P. E. (1999) p. 39.
1212 Colin, G. S. (1971b) p. 470.
1213 Ricard, R. and L. Torres Balbás, pp. 464–5.
1214 Ricard, R. and L. Torres Balbás, pp. 470–1.
1215 Tonghini, C. and N. Montevecchi, *passim*.
1216 Creswell, K. A. C. (1952) p. 123; Yovitchich, C., *passim*.
1217 Molin, B. K., p. 60; Creswell, K. A. C. (1952) p. 123.
1218 Minnis, D. and Y. Bader, *passim*.
1219 Ellenblum, R. (1989) pp. 106–12.
1220 Zozaya, J. (1992) p. 65.

1221 *Ibid*.
1222 Zozaya, J. (1992) pp. 65–6.
1223 Buryakov, Y. F. *et al.*, *passim*.
1224 Bianquis, T. (1983) p. 126.
1225 Vryonis, S. (1971) p. 247.
1226 Zakkar, S., pp. 264–5; Antaki, Yahya Ibn Sa'id al-, p. 265.
1227 Usamah Ibn Munqidh (1929) *passim*; Usamah Ibn Munqidh (1930) *passim*.
1228 Norris, H. T. (1984) p. 41.
1229 Norris, H. T. (1984) p. 40.
1230 Wiedemann, E., pp. 193–200.
1231 Wiedemann, E., pp. 140 and 177–8.
1232 Hill, D. R. (1973) pp. 100–1.
1233 Comnena, Anna, p. lxx.
1234 Cahen, C. (1947–8) pp. 58–60.
1235 Brunschwig, R., p. 85.
1236 Anon., *De Expugnatione Terrae Sanctae per Saladinum, Libellus*, p. 242.
1237 Hill, D. R. (1993) p. 118.
1238 Little, D. P., p. 167.
1239 Little, D. P., p. 169.
1240 Sezgin, F. and E. Neubauer, pp. 5 and 97.
1241 Sezgin, F. and E. Neubauer, pp. 5 and 93–138.
1242 Sezgin, F. and E. Neubauer, pp. 5 and pp. 106–19.
1243 Tarsusi, Murda Ibn 'Ali Murda al- (1947–8) pp. 120 and 142.
1244 De Vries, K., pp. 133–4.
1245 De Vries, K., p. 137.
1246 Hill, D. R. (1993) p. 118.
1247 Amari, M. (1933) vol. III, pp. 706–7.
1248 Nasir-i Khusrau (1881) pp. 246–7.
1249 Little, D. P., p. 171.
1250 Tarsusi, Murda Ibn 'Ali Murda al- (1947–8) pp. 140–2 and 118–19.
1251 Nicolle, D. C. (2002c) p. 14.
1252 Hill, D. R. (1993) p. 118.
1253 Chevedden, P. E. (1985) p. 8.
1254 Nicolle, D. C. (2002c) p. 15.
1255 Cahen, C. (1960) *passim*.
1256 Nasir-i Khusrau (1881) p. 7.
1257 Zardkash, Ibn Urunbugha al-, pp. 109–10.
1258 Zardkash, Ibn Urunbugha al-, pp. 117–19.

1259 Hill, D. R. and A. Y. Hassan, pp. 101–2.
1260 Bosworth, C. E. (1993) p. 188.
1261 Nicolle, D. C. (2004b) p. 270.
1262 Lewis, B., pp. 64–5; Lévi Provençal, E. (1932) pp. 144–6; Walter the Chancellor, p. 95; Nicolle, D. C. (2004b) pp. 269–78.
1263 Chevedden, P. E. (1985) pp. 35–7 n. 9.
1264 Nicolle, D. C. (2004b) pp. 274 and 277.
1265 Chevedden, P. E. (1985) pp. 6–7.
1266 Zardkash, Ibn Urunbugha al-, pp. 109–10.
1267 Zardkash, Ibn Urunbugha al-, pp. 66–7.
1268 Finó, J.-F., p. 36.
1269 Not yet weighed and published.
1270 Approximately 304 kg according to Dr Hill, approximately 259 kg according to Dr Sarraf.
1271 Hill, D. R. (1993) p. 120.
1272 De Vries, K., pp. 137–8.
1273 Tarsusi, Murda Ibn 'Ali Murda al- (1947–8) pp. 143 and 120.
1274 Sezgin, F. and E. Neubauer, p. 106.
1275 Chevedden, P. E. (1985) pp. 7–8.
1276 Sezgin, F. and E. Neubauer, p. 107.
1277 Hollenback, G. M., passim.
1278 Chevedden, P. E. (1985) p. 7.
1279 Anon., The 'Templar of Tyre': part III of the 'Deeds of the Cypriots', p. 106.
1280 Sezgin, F. and E. Neubauer, pp. 110–1.
1281 Sezgin, F. and E. Neubauer, pp. 108–9.
1282 Sezgin, F. and E. Neubauer, p. 97.
1283 Tarsusi, Murda Ibn 'Ali Murda al- (1947–8) pp. 108–10 and 129–32.
1284 Huuri, K., p. 125.
1285 Sezgin, F. and E. Neubauer, pp. 110–11; Zardkash, Ibn Urunbugha al-, pp. 92–4.
1286 Zardkash, Ibn Urunbugha al-, pp. 95–6.
1287 Zardkash, Ibn Urunbugha al-, pp. 109–10.
1288 Zardkash, Ibn Urunbugha al-, pp. 103–4 and 107–8.
1289 Zardkash, Ibn Urunbugha al-, pp. 105–6.
1290 Turnbull, S. (2001) pp. 12–15.
1291 Harawi, 'Ali Ibn Abu Bakr al- (1961–2) pp. 237–9.
1292 Ziadeh, N. A., p. 86.
1293 Nicholson, R. L. (1940) pp. 70–1.
1294 Terrasse, H. (1965) pp. 81–3.
1295 Lacarra, J.M. (1947) p. 86.
1296 Hillenbrand, C. (1979) p. 274.
1297 Zakkar, S., pp. 185–7.
1298 Bianquis, T. (1983) p. 77.
1299 Lacarra, J. M. (1947) pp. 85–6.
1300 Ricard, R. and L. Torres Balbás, pp. 448 and 457.
1301 Bianquis, T. (1983) p. 662.
1302 Nasir-i Khusrau (1888) pp. 7–8.
1303 Ibn al-Qalanisi (1932) p. 45.
1304 Patton, D. L., p. 46.
1305 Irwin, R. (1985) p. 247.
1306 Banks, P. J. and J. Zozaya, pp. 680–1.
1307 Bianquis, T. (1983) p. 79.
1308 Bianquis, T. (1983) pp. 76–7.
1309 Bianquis, T. (1983) pp. 44, 74 and passim.
1310 Canard, M. (1957) pp. 47–51.
1311 Rogers, R., p. 78.
1312 Usamah Ibn Munqidh (1929) pp. 185–6.
1313 Ibn al-Qalanisi (1908) p. 299.
1314 Lévi Provençal, E. (1950–67) pp. 71–6.
1315 Bianquis, T. (1983) p. 138.
1316 Bianquis, T. (1983) p. 453.
1317 Bianquis, T. (1983) p. xix.
1318 Lacarra, J. M. (1947) p. 84.
1319 Ayalon, D. (1971a) p. 143.
1320 King, G., p. 4.
1321 Rogers, R., p. 58.
1322 Wiedemann, E., p. 679.
1323 Ibn al-Qalanisi (1908) pp. 179–80.
1324 Ibid.
1325 Rogers, R., p. 85.
1326 Bianquis, T. (1983) p. 77.
1327 Bianquis, T. (1983) p. 74.
1328 Nicholson, R. L. (1973) p. 112.
1329 Lyon, B. D., p. 180.
1330 Zakkar, S., p. 43.
1331 Alptekin, C., p. 132.
1332 Ansari, 'Umar Ibn Ibrahim al-Awsi al-, pp. 116–19.

1333 Elisseeff, N. (1967) pp. 747–50.
1334 Bianquis, T. (1983) p. 281.
1335 Walter the Chancellor, p. 96.
1336 Lyon, B. D., p. 229.
1337 Ayalon, D. (1956) p. 14 n. 29.
1338 Fakhr al-Din Mubarakshah,
       Muhammad Ibn Mansur, p. 422.
1339 Fakhr al-Din Mubarakshah,
       Muhammad Ibn Mansur, p. 421.
1340 Walter the Chancellor, pp. 145–6.
1341 Ibn al-Qalanisi (1932) p. 216.
1342 Harawi, 'Ali Ibn Abu Bakr al- (1961–2)
       pp. 234–6.
1343 Hamblin, W. J. (1992) pp. 231–4.
1344 Lyons, M. C. and D. E. P. Jackson,
       p. 191.
1345 Lyon, B. D., pp. 142–3.
1346 Fakhr al-Din Mubarakshah,
       Muhammad Ibn Mansur, p. 422.
1347 Bianquis, T. (1983) p. 595.
1348 Powers, J. F. (1994) p. 20.
1349 Anon., La Siège de Barbastre, passim.
1350 Colin, G. S. (1971b) p. 470.
1351 Needham, J. (1994) p. 122.
1352 Lyon, B. D., p. 273.
1353 Clifford, E. R., p. 120.
1354 Bosworth, C. E. (1971) p. 471.
1355 Ayalon, D. (1956) p. 11.
1356 Colin, G. S. (1971b) p. 470.
1357 Canard, M. (1965b) pp. 247–8;
       Bosworth, C. E. (1971) p. 471.
1358 Walter the Chancellor, pp. 145–6.
1359 Walter the Chancellor, pp. 149–50.
1360 'Arif 'Ali of Toqat, vol. I, pp. 308–9 and
       vol. II, p. 123.
1361 Chevedden, P. E. (1999) p. 38.
1362 Tibi, A. T., pp. 164–5.
1363 Cathcart King, D. J. (1949) pp. 88–92.
1364 Walter the Chancellor, pp. 145–6.
1365 Ayalon, D. (1956) p. 11.
1366 Ibid.
1367 Prawer, J. (1972) p. 349; Cahen, C.
       (1971b) pp. 469–70.
1368 Ayalon, D. (1956) pp. 11–12.
1369 Little, D. P., pp. 172–3.
1370 Anon., The 'Templar of Tyre': part III of
       the 'Deeds of the Cypriots', p. 109.
1371 Colin, G. S. (1971b) p. 470.

1372 Bianquis, T. (1983) p. 198.
1373 Maqrizi, al-, pp. 82–3.
1374 Fakhr al-Din Mubarakshah,
       Muhammad Ibn Mansur, pp. 423–4.
1375 Molin, B. K., p. 76; Ibn al-Furat, vol. 2,
       p. 148.
1376 Hackett, J. W., pp. 36–7.
1377 Elisseeff, N. (1967) p. 733.
1378 Ayalon, D. (1971a) p. 474.
1379 Christides, V. (1990b) p. 6.
1380 Bianquis, T. (1983) p. 538.
1381 Zahir, Al-Qadi Muhi al-Din Ibn 'Abd
       al-, p. 215.
1382 Bianquis, T. (1983) p. 607.
1383 Baha' al-Din Ibn Shaddad (1897b)
       p. 206; Baha' al-Din Ibn Shaddad
       (1897a) p. 120.
1384 Hill, D. R. and A. Y. Hassan, p. 108.
1385 Hill, D. R. and A. Y. Hassan, p. 109.
1386 De Saulcy, M. F., passim.
1387 Arendt, W. (1931) pp. 206–10.
1388 Colin, G. S. (1971a) p. 1055.
1389 Ayalon, D. (1956) p. 11.
1390 Tarsusi, Murda Ibn 'Ali Murda al-
       (1947–8) pp. 124–5 and pp. 147–8.
1391 Usamah Ibn Munqidh (1929)
       pp. 103–4.
1392 De Joinville (1952) p. 245.
1393 Smith, G. R., p. 120.
1394 Tarsusi, Murda Ibn 'Ali Murda al-
       (1947–8) pp. 111 and 133.
1395 Rogers, R., p. 218.
1396 Baha' al-Din Ibn Shaddad (1897a)
       p. 102; Baha' al-Din Ibn Shaddad
       (1897b) p. 176.
1397 Gabrieli, F., pp. 334–8.
1398 Anon., The Old French Crusade Cycle,
       vol. V: Les Chétifs, II. pp. 732–42.
1399 Ayalon, D. (1956) p. 14.
1400 Ayalon, D. (1956) p. 12.
1401 Hill, D. R. and A. Y. Hassan,
       pp. 111–2.
1402 Colin, G. S. (1971a) p. 1055.
1403 Ayalon, D. (1956) p. 25.
1404 Canard, M. (1946) pp. 6–7.
1405 Hill, D. R. and A. Y. Hassan, pp. 48–9.
1406 Lyon, B. D., p. 311.
1407 Partington, J. R., p. 15.

1408 Anon., *The Old French Crusade Cycle*, vol. V: *Les Chétifs*, appendix 1. p. 68; this reference comes in an additional part of the text which might be slightly later than the main verses which date from the late twelfth century.
1409 Hill, D. R. and A. Y. Hassan, p. 111.
1410 Colin, G. S. (1971a) pp. 1055–6.
1411 Partington, J. R., p. 22.
1412 Hill, D. R. and A. Y. Hassan, pp. 109–11.
1413 Foley, V. and K. Perry, pp. 203–4.
1414 Hill, D. R. and A. Y. Hassan, p. 117.
1415 Foley, V. and K. Perry, pp. 205–6.
1416 Hill, D. R. and A. Y. Hassan, pp. 117–18.
1417 Credland, A. G. (1981) p. 141 n. 17.
1418 Colin, G. S. (1971a) p. 1056; Hill, D. R. and A. Y. Hassan, pp. 113–14.
1419 Partington, J. R., p. 190.
1420 Hill, D. R. and A. Y. Hassan, p. 113.
1421 *Ibid.*
1422 Partington, J. R., p. 191; Allouche, I. S., p. 81.
1423 Tarsusi, Murda Ibn 'Ali Murda al- (1947–8) pp. 147 and 125.
1424 Elisseeff, N. (1967) p. 735.
1425 Ayalon, D. (1956) pp. 16–17.
1426 Beshir, B. J., p. 49.
1427 Goitein, S. D. (1970) p. 58.
1428 Bianquis, T. (1983) pp. 257 and 267.
1429 Bianquis, T. (1983) p. 443.
1430 Goitein, S. D. (1956) p. 394.
1431 Ziadeh, N. A., p. 36.
1432 Lyon, B. D., p. 136.
1433 Elbeheiry, S., pp. 252–4.
1434 Elbeheiry, S., p. 260.
1435 Salinger, G., p. 484.
1436 Rashad Mohamad, A. M., p. 75.
1437 Abu'l-Fida, p. 19.
1438 Ayalon, D. (1971b) p. 301.
1439 Ziadeh, N. A., p. 36.
1440 Hill, D. R. and A. Y. Hassan, p. 105.
1441 Lyon, B. D., pp. 255–6.
1442 Tantum, G., p. 196.
1443 Beshir, B. J., pp. 51–2.
1444 Bianquis, T. (1983) p. 382.
1445 Tibi, A. T., p. 140.
1446 Anon., *The Third Crusade, Itinerarium Peregrinorum*, pp. 87–8.
1447 Zahir, Al-Qadi Muhi al-Din Ibn 'Abd al-, p. 86.
1448 'Arif 'Ali of Toqat, vol. I, p. 217, vol. II, p. 31 and *passim*.
1449 Beshir, B. J., pp. 51–2.
1450 Usamah Ibn Munqidh (1930) p. 15; Usamah Ibn Munqidh (1929) p. 39.
1451 Elbeheiry, S., pp. 255–9.
1452 Lyon, B. D., p. 11.
1453 See Tibbetts, G. R., *passim*.
1454 Di Meglio, R. R., p. 114.
1455 Hill, D. R. and A. Y. Hassan, p. 127.
1456 Lombard, M., pp. 162–5.
1457 Lev, Y. (1984) p. 245.
1458 Unger, R. W., pp. 99–100.
1459 Stern, S. M., p. 533.
1460 Ashtor, E. (1976) p. 240.
1461 Ayalon, D. (1960) pp. 945–7.
1462 Unger, R. W., p. 127.
1463 Goitein, S. D. (1956) p. 394.
1464 De Oliveiro-Marques, A. H., p. 68; Lévi Provençal, E. (1950–67) vol. III, p. 110.
1465 Nicolle, D. C. (2002b) *passim*.
1466 Dozy, R. (ed.) and C. Pellat (trs) pp. 68–9.
1467 De Oliveiro-Marques, A. H., pp. 67–8.
1468 Dunlop, D. M. (1960) p. 934.
1469 Goitein, S. D. (1967) p. 318.
1470 Yarrison, J. L., pp. 227–8.
1471 Ashtor, E. (1976) p. 197.
1472 Goitein, S. D. (1955) p. 81.
1473 Goitein, S. D. (1955) pp. 82–83.
1474 Anon., *Gesta Francorum, The Deeds of the Franks and other Pilgrims to Jerusalem*, p. 95.
1475 Elisseeff, N. (1967) p. 736.
1476 Elisseeff, N. (1967) p. 737.
1477 Elbeheiry, S., pp. 169–75.
1478 Elbeheiry, S., pp. 183–91.
1479 Elbeheiry, S., pp. 194–5.
1480 Elbeheiry, S., p. 192.
1481 Elbeheiry, S., pp. 179–81.
1482 Elbeheiry, S., pp. 198–202.
1483 *Ibid.*
1484 Kedar, B. Z. and D. Pringle, p. 170.
1485 Bianquis, T. (1983) p. 207.
1486 Ayalon, D. (1958) pp. 270–1.
1487 Bianquis, T. (1983) p. 207.
1488 Ashtor, E. (1969) p. 259.

1489 Ashtor, E. (1969) p. 365.
1490 Smith, J. M. (J. Masson Smith) (1984b) p. 331, n. 75.
1491 Ayalon, D. (1958) pp. 263–9.
1492 Ashtor, E. (1969) p. 365.
1493 Ashtor, E. (1969) p. 364.
1494 Marco Polo, p. 402.
1495 Marco Polo, p. 403.
1496 Christides, V. (1984) pp. 139–43.
1497 Bianquis, T. (1983) p. 201.
1498 Bianquis, T. (1983) p. 236.
1499 Lev, Y. (1988b) pp. 161–3.
1500 Lev, Y. (1988b) pp. 175–84.
1501 Ehrenkreutz, A. S. (1955) pp. 108–10.
1502 Ayalon, D. (1960) pp. 945–7.
1503 Sarraf, S. al- (1996) p. 125.
1504 Yarnley, C. J., pp. 113–14 and 115, n. 1.
1505 Bombaci, A., p. 363.
1506 Lewis, A. R. (1951) pp. 183–4.
1507 Lewis, A. R. (1951) pp. 196–7.
1508 Brunschwig, R., pp. 94–5.
1509 Arié, R., pp. 266–71.
1510 Nicolle, D. C. (1989) passim.
1511 Kreutz, B. M. (1976) p. 104.
1512 Basch, L., pp. 23–32.
1513 Pryor, J. H. and S. Bellabarba, pp. 105–7.
1514 Pryor, J. H. and S. Bellabarba, p. 105.
1515 Kreutz, B. M. (1976) p. 106; note also the 'enormous' Islamic–Andalusian Atlantic ship described off the Île d'Yeu, near the mouth of the river Loire in the ninth century. Rouche, M., L'Aquitaine des Wisigoths aux Arabes (Paris 1979) p. 260.
1516 Goitein, S. D. (1956) p. 397.
1517 Lyon, B. D., p. 282.
1518 Hill, D. R. and A. Y. Hassan, p. 123.
1519 Pryor, J. H. and S. Bellabarba, p. 104.
1520 Christides, V. (1991) p. 17.
1521 Anon., La Siège de Barbastre, II. pp. 7131–5.
1522 Goitein, S. D. (1967) pp. 305–6.
1523 Torres Delgado, C. (1980) p. 230.
1524 Anderson, R. C., pp. 53–4.
1525 Kreutz, B. M. (1976) p. 107, n. 132.
1526 Pryor, J. H. (1982) p. 18.
1527 Bennett, M. (1993) p. 49.
1528 Bennett, M. (1993) p. 50.

1529 Christides, V. (1987) p. 76; Christides, V. (1991) p. 16; Pryor, J. H. (1988) p. 63.
1530 Sarraf, S. al- (1996) p. 125; Christides, V. (1994) p. 25.
1531 Christides, V. (1990a) pp. 87–8.
1532 Facey, W., pp. 107–65; Agius, D. A., pp. 133–78.
1533 Christides, V. (1989) p. 77.
1534 Christides, V. (1989) p. 78.
1535 Christides, V. (1989) pp. 77–8.
1536 Lev, Y. (1984) p. 252; Goitein, S. D. (1967) pp. 327–8.
1537 Bragadin, M.-A., p. 33.
1538 Walker, J. M. (1961) pp. 147–8.
1539 Ehrenkreutz, A. S. (1955) p. 111.
1540 Lyon, B. D., p. 318.
1541 Ehrenkreutz, A. S. (1955) pp. 100–5.
1542 Ayalon, D. (1965b) p. 5.
1543 Zahir, Al-Qadi Muhi al-Din Ibn 'Abd al-, p. 116.
1544 Christides, V. (1991) p. 17.
1545 Canard, M. (1952b) p. 393.
1546 Qalqashandi, Ahmad Ibn 'Abd Allah al-, p. 508.
1547 Arié, R., pp. 266–71.
1548 Schwarzer, J. K. (1991) pp. 328–30.
1549 Schwarzer, J. K. (1988) passim.
1550 Nicholson, R. L. (1973) p. 54.
1551 Pryor, J. H. (1992) p. 123.
1552 Christides, V. (1994) pp. 18–19.
1553 Haldane, D., pp. 142–3.
1554 Brooks, F. W., pp. 118–19.
1555 Christides, V. (1994) pp. 15–18.
1556 Livadas, G. K., p. 147.
1557 Sarraf, S. al- (1996) p. 125.
1558 Christides, V. (1990b) p. 7.
1559 Pryor, J. H. (1988) pp. 80–2.
1560 Lev, Y. (1995) p. 193.
1561 Bianquis, T. (1983) p. 108.
1562 Lev, Y. (1988b) pp. 168–9.
1563 Lev, Y. (1988b) pp. 172–5.
1564 Lev, Y. (1988b) pp. 170–1.
1565 Huici Miranda, A., pp. 197–8.
1566 Christides, V. (1997) pp. 269–70.
1567 Christides, V. (1997) pp. 270–1.
1568 Christides, V. (1997) p. 272.
1569 Unger, R. W., p. 101.

1570 Goitein, S. D. (1967) p. 307.
1571 Goitein, S. D. (1967) pp. 330–1.
1572 Anon., *The Third Crusade, Itinerarium Peregrinorum*, p. 57.
1573 Bennett, M. (1986) p. 53.
1574 Lyon, B.D., p. 316.
1575 Thorau, P., p. 207.
1576 Lev, Y. (1988b) pp. 166–8.
1577 Rabie, H.M. (1972) pp. 165–6.
1578 Christides, V. (1991) p. 17.
1579 Ibn Khaldun, p. 590.
1580 Arié, R., pp. 266–71.
1581 Tamari, S., pp. 32–41.
1582 Arié, R., pp. 274–5.
1583 Nasir-i Khusrau (1881) pp. 112–13.
1584 Lev, Y. (1988b) pp. 163–6.
1585 Bennett, M. (1986) p. 53.
1586 Goitein, S. D. (1956) p. 395.
1587 Latham, J. D. (1971) pp. 203–4.
1588 Lev, Y. (1995) p. 195.
1589 Kollias, T. (1984) p. 135.
1590 Christides, V. (1991) p. 17.
1591 Zahir, Al-Qadi Muhi al-Din Ibn 'Abd al-, p. 116.
1592 Pryor, J. H. (1992) p. 123.
1593 Pryor, J. H. (1992) p. 122.
1594 Zahir, Al-Qadi Muhi al-Din Ibn 'Abd al-, p. 116.
1595 Mantran, R. and C. De La Roncière, p. 379.
1596 Mantran, R. and C. De La Roncière, p. 381.
1597 Mantran, R. and C. De La Roncière, p. 376.
1598 Hopkins, J. F. P. and N. Levtzion, p. 133 and 248.
1599 Hopkins, J. F. P. and N. Levtzion, *passim.*
1600 Rivallain, J., p. 216.
1601 Mantran, R. and C. De La Roncière, p. 382.

Notes to Chapter 2: The Mongols in the West

1 Barthold, V. V. (1962a) pp. 88 and 93.
2 Rady, M., pp. 43–4.
3 Jackson, P. (1980) pp. 487–90.
4 Jackson, P. (1980) pp. 503–12.
5 Darko, E., p. 416.
6 Spinei, V. (1986) p. 77.
7 Spinei, V. (1974) pp. 414–15.
8 Anastasijevic, D. and G. Ostrogorsky, pp. 21–9.
9 Diaconu, P., p. 128.
10 Sayer, I.M., pp. 272–3.
11 Morgan, D.O. (1979) pp. 82–4.
12 Morgan, D.O. (1979) p. 88.
13 Ashtor, E. (1976) p. 249.
14 Barthold, V.V. (1962b) pp. 10–24.
15 Andalusi, Sa'il al-, p. 7.
16 Morgan, D. O. (1979) p. 81.
17 Barthold, V. V. (1962a) pp. 88–91.
18 Diaconu, P., p. 24.
19 Villehardouin (1952) p. 162; Villehardouin (1921) p. 92.
20 Boyle, J.A. (1978) p. 512.
21 Jackson, P. (1980) pp. 512–13.
22 Barthold, V. V. (1962b) p. 29.
23 Schamiloglu, U., pp. 10–13.
24 Smith, J. M. (J. Masson Smith) (1984b) p. 312.
25 Smith, J. M. (J. Masson Smith) (1984b) p. 310.
26 Morgan, D. O. (1979) pp. 89–91.
27 Martinez, A. P., pp. 202–16; also see Martinez, A. P., for a detailed study of the Il-Khanid Mongol army in the later thirteenth- and early fourteenth-century Islamic world.
28 Morgan, D. O. (1979) pp. 92–9.
29 Morgan, D. O. (1979) p. 95.
30 Onon, U., pp. 175–6.
31 Barthold, V. V. (1962a) pp. 101–3.
32 Barthold, V. V. (1962a) pp. 107–10.
33 Barthold, V. V. (1962a) p. 88.
34 Boyle, J. A. (1972) p. 190.
35 Gorelik, M.V. (1997) *passim.*
36 Boyle, J.A. (1965) pp. 145–60.
37 Heissig, W., p. 23.
38 Heissig, W., p. 22.
39 Morgan, D. O. (1979) pp. 93–6.
40 Morgan, D. O. (1989) p. 200.
41 Jackson, P. (1980) p. 483.
42 Jackson, P. (1980) p. 484.

43 Jackson, P. (1980) p. 485.
44 Jackson, P. (1980) pp. 494–9.
45 Painter, G. D., p. 34.
46 Smith, J. M. (J. Masson Smith) (1996) pp. 249–50.
47 Morgan, D. O. (1968) pp. 93–5.
48 Morgan, D. O. (1985) pp. 233–4.
49 Onon, U., pp. 176–82.
50 Martinez, A. P., pp. 138–46.
51 Smith, J. M. (J. Masson Smith) (1996) p. 260.
52 Matveev, A. (1998b) pp. 2–3.
53 Matveev, A. (1998b) p. 8; for a study of Mongol tactics at the battle of Leignitz in 1241, see Turnbull, S. (2003) *passim*.
54 Matveev, A. (1998b) p. 8.
55 Onon, U., pp. 176–82.
56 Painter, G. D., p. 69, n. 4.
57 Von Pawlikowski-Cholewa, A., p. 200.
58 Fakhr al-Din Mubarakshah, Muhammad Ibn Mansur, p. 322.
59 Ranitzsch, K. H., p. 21.
60 Painter, G. D., pp. 98–9.
61 Painter, G. D., pp. 100–1.
62 Smith, J. M. (J. Masson Smith) (1996) pp. 252–3.
63 Diaconu, P., p. 11.
64 Diaconu, P., pp. 11–12.
65 Smith, J. M. (J. Masson Smith) (1984b) p. 319.
66 Martinez, A. P., pp. 152–6.
67 Martinez, A. P., pp. 156–8.
68 Martinez, A. P., pp. 158–78.
69 Onon, U., pp. 176–82.
70 Somogyi, J., p. 375.
71 Kaegi, W. E. (1964) p. 103.
72 Diaconu, P., pp. 72–4.
73 William of Rubruck (1900) p. 261, n. 3; Gaunt, G. D., p. 21.
74 Smith, J. M. (J. Masson Smith) (1984b) p. 315.
75 Boyle, J. A. (1971) p. 6.
76 For an up-to-date book on Mongol armour from the tenth to fourteenth centuries, see Gorelik, M. V. (2002b) *passim*.

77 Smith, J. M. (J. Masson Smith) (1984b) p. 323, n. 47.
78 Martinez, A. P., pp. 178–201.
79 Smith, J. M. (J. Masson Smith) (1996) p. 263.
80 Arendt, W. (1934) p. 51.
81 Heissig, W., p. 24.
82 Comnena, Anna, p. lv; Nicolle, D. C. (1999) pp. 273–304 and Figs. pp. 698–800.
83 Smith, J. M. (J. Masson Smith) (1996) p. 260, n. 40.
84 Gorelik, M. V. (1979) p. 40.
85 'Shields', in LaRocca, D. J., pp. 92–5.
86 Currently undergoing conservation prior to closer study.
87 Dunlop, D. M. (1973) pp. 302–4.
88 Dunlop, D. M. (1973) p. 317; Nicolle, D. C. (2002a) pp. 183–6.
89 Gorelik, M. V. (1997) *passim*.
90 William of Rubruck (1955) pp. 210–11; a slightly different translation is offered in William of Rubruck (1990) pp. 259–60.
91 Matveev, A. (1998b) pp. 1–2.
92 William of Rubruck (1955) pp. 210–11; a slightly different translation is offered in William of Rubruck (1990) pp. 259–60.
93 In fact the radiocarbon dating tests done on one of these leather cuirasses resulted in an optimum date of 1220 AD (where the radiocarbon age crossed the calibration curve).
94 Gorelik, M. V. (1979) pp. 36–8.
95 Robert de Clari, p. 51.
96 Richard, J. (1979b) pp. 109–10.
97 Carpini, pp. 23–4.
98 Melikian-Chirvani, A.S., p. 314.
99 Smith, J. M. (J. Masson Smith) (1996) p. 250; Smith, J. M. (J. Masson Smith) (1984b) p. 329.
100 Gorelik, M. V. (1979) pp. 20–1.
101 See: Stein, A. (1912); Stein, A. (1933); Esin, E. (1980); Nicolle, D. C. (1990) pp. 17–9.
102 Diaconu, P., p. 24.

103 Diaconu, P., p. 29.
104 Needham, J. (1976) pp. 111 and
     n. 68.
105 Huuri, K., pp. 118 and 123; Bosworth,
     C. E. (1971) p. 472.
106 Boyle, J. A. (1971) pp. 331–6.
107 Gaunt, G. D., pp. 20–1.
108 Morgan, D. O. (1989) p. 198.
109 Morgan, D. O. (1968) p. 88.
110 Morgan, D. O. (1979) p. 86.
111 Smith, J. M. (J. Masson Smith) (1996)
     p. 249.
112 Morgan, D. O. (1979) p. 87.
113 Smith, J. M. (J. Masson Smith) (1996)
     p. 255.
114 Smith, J. M. (J. Masson Smith) (1996)
     p. 251.

115 Smith, J.M. (J. Masson Smith) (1996)
     p. 249.
116 Morgan, D.O. (1985) pp. 232–3.

*Notes to Chapter 3: The military
heritage and impact of crusading
warfare on the Islamic and Mongol
worlds*

1 Voisin, J-C., *passim.*
2 Chevedden, P. E. (1999) *passim.*
3 Paterson, L. M. (1988) pp. 118–19.
4 Hitti, P. K., *passim.*
5 Bosworth, C. E. (1972) p. 65.
6 Bosworth, C. E. (1972) pp. 65–6.
7 Balard, M. (1983) *passim.*

Bibliography

Abu'l-Fida (P. M. Holt trans.) (1983), *The Memoirs of a Syrian Prince: Abu'l-Fida, Sultan of Hamah (672–737/1273–1331)*, Wiesbaden.

Abulafia, D. (1986), 'The Anconitan Privileges in the Kingdom of Jerusalem and the Levant Trade of Ancona', in G. Airaldi and B. Z. Kedar (eds), *I Comuni Italiani nel Regno Crociato di Gerusalemme*, Genoa, pp. 523–59.

—— (1990), 'The End of Muslim Sicily', in J. M. Powell (ed.), *Muslims under Latin Rule, 1100–1300*, Princeton, pp. 103–33.

Abun-Nasr, J. M. (1987), *A History of the Maghrib in the Islamic Period*, Cambridge.

Ackermann, P. (1939), 'Standards, Banners and Badges', in A. A. Pope and P. Ackermann (eds), *A Survey of Persian Art*, vol. VI, London, pp. 2766–82.

Adams, W.Y. (1977), *Nubia, Corridor to Africa*, London.

Agius, D. A. (2002), *In the Wake of the Dhow: The Arabian Gulf and Oman*, Reading.

Ahmad, Aziz (1975), *A History of Islamic Sicily*, Edinburgh.

—— (1977), *Storia della Sicilia islamica*, Catania.

Ahsan, M. M. (1979), *Social Life under the Abbasids 176–289AH, 786–902AD*, London.

Alexander, D. G. (1984), 'Two Aspects of Islamic Arms and Armour', *Metropolitan Museum Journal*, 18, pp. 97–109.

Alexander, D. G. and H. Nickel (1980), 'Matrices for Sword Mounts', in P. De Montebello (ed.), *Notable Acquisitions 1979–80: Metropolitan Museum of Art*, New York, p. 27.

Alexander, D. G. and H. Ricketts (1985), 'Armes et armures', in S. C. Welch (ed.), *Trésors de l'Islam (Collection Rifaat Shaikh al Ard)*, Geneva.

Allan, J. W. (1979), *Persian Metal Technology, 700–1300 AD*, Oxford.

—— (1982), *Nishapur Metalwork of the Early Islamic Period*, New York.

—— (1985), "Alam wa 'Alamat: The history of Metal 'Alams', in *Encyclopedia Iranica*, vol. I, London, pp. 790–1.

—— (1988), 'Metalwork: before 1100: Bronzes: The West/Egypt', prepublication draft for *Macmillan's Encyclopedia of Art* (correspondence 3 November 1988).

—— (1996), *Ayubid Architecture* (web publication).

Allason-Jones, L. (1992), 'Catalogue of Weaponry from Soba Excavations, 8–14 cents' (unpublished).

Allchin, F. R. (1970), 'A piece of scale armour from Shaikhan-Dheri, Charsada (Shaikhan-Dheri Studies 1)', *Journal of the Royal Asiatic Society*, pp. 113–20.

Allen, T. (1996–2003), *Ayyubid Architecture*, electronic publication, Occidental, CA.

Allouche, I. S. (1945), 'Une texte relatif aux premiers canons', *Hespéris*, 32, pp. 81–4.

Alptekin, C. (1972), 'The Reign of Zangi (521–541/1127–1146)', PhD thesis, London University.

Amari, M. (1876), 'Su i fuochi da guerra usati nel Mediterraneo nell'XI e XII secolo', *Atti della Reale Academia dei Lincei*, pp. 3–16.

—— (1880–1), *Biblioteca Arabo-Sicula*, Turin and Rome.

—— (1933), *Storia dei Musulmani di Sicilia*, Catania.

Amatuccio, G. (1921), 'Saracen Archers in Southern Italy' (*De Re Militari* website, 2004).

Ameer Ali (1921), *A Short History of the Saracens*, London.

Amitai, R. (Amitai-Preiss) (1990), 'The Remaking of the Military Elite of Mamluk Egypt by Al-Nasir Muhammad b. Qalawun', *Studia Islamica*, 72, pp. 145–63.

—— (1995), *Mongols and Mamluks: The Mamluk-Ilkhanid War, 1260–1281*, Cambridge.

—— (1996), 'The Mamluk Officer Class during the reign of Sultan Baybars', in Y. Lev (ed.), *War and Society in the Eastern Mediterranean, Seventh–Fifteenth Centuries*, Leiden, pp. 267–300.

—— (1999), 'Northern Syria between the Mongols and the Mamluks: Political Boundary, Military Frontier, and Ethnic Affinities', in D. Power and N. Standen (eds), *Frontiers in Question: Eurasian Borderlands 700–1700*, London, pp. 128–52.

Amououx-Mourad, M. (1988), *Le Comté d'Edesse*, Beirut.

Anastasijevic, D. and G. Ostrogorsky (1951), 'Les Koumanes Pronoïaires', *Annuaire de l'Institut de philologie et d'histoire Orientales et Slaves*, 11, pp. 19–29.

Andalusi, Sa'id al- (S. I. Salem and A. Kumar ed. and trans.) (1991), *Science in the Medieval World: 'Book of the Categories of Nations'*, Austin, TX.

Anderson, R. C. (1976), *Oared Fighting Ships*, Kings Langley.

Anon. (1861), 'Chronica collecta a Magno presbytero – 1195' (W. Wattenbach ed.) in G. H. Pertz (ed.) *Monumenta Germaniae Historica, Scriptorum*, vol. XVII, Hanover (reprinted New York 1963).

—— (1964), *David of Sassoun: The Armenian Folk Epic in Four Cycles* (A.K. Shalian trans.), Athens, OH.

—— (1875), *De Expugnatione Terrae Sanctae per Saladinum, Libellus: Rolls Series*; vol. 66 (J. Stevenson ed.), London.

—— (1956), *Digenes Akritas* (J. Mavrogordato trans.), Oxford.

—— (1962), *Gesta Francorum, The Deeds of the Franks and other Pilgrims to Jerusalem* (R. Hill ed. and trans.), London.

—— (1937), *Hudud al-'Alam* (V. Minorsky trans.), London.

—— (1924), *La Chanson de Roland* (T.A. Jenkins ed.), London.

—— (1982), *La Continuation de Guillaume de Tyr (1184–1197)* (M. R. Morgan ed.), Paris.

—— (1926), *La Siège de Barbastre* (J.-L. Perrier ed.), Paris.

—— (1939), *Sassountzy David, Haykakan Zhoghovrdakan Epos* (anon. ed.), Erevan.

—— (1974), *The Book of Dede Korkut* (G. Lewis, trans.), London.

—— (1977), *The Old French Crusade Cycle*, vol. I: *La Naissance du Chevalier au Cygne: Elioxe* (E. J. Mickel ed.), Alabama.

—— (1977), *The Old French Crusade Cycle*, vol. I: *La Naissance du Chevalier au Cygne: Beatrix* (J. A. Nelson ed.), Alabama.

—— (1981), *The Old French Crusade Cycle*, vol. V: *Les Chétifs* (G. M. Myers ed.), Alabama.

—— (2003), *The 'Templar of Tyre': part III of the 'Deeds of the Cypriots'* (P. Crawford trans.), Aldershot.

—— (1958), *The Third Crusade, Itinerarium Peregrinorum* (K. Fenwick trans.), London.

Ansari, 'Umar Ibn Ibrahim al-Awsi al- (G.T. Scanlon trans. and ed.) (1961), *A Muslim Manual of War: being Tafrij al Kurub fi Tadbir al Hurub*, Cairo.

Antaki, Yahya Ibn Sa'id al- (L. Shikhu ed.) (1909), *Tarikh Yahya Ibn Sa'id al-Antaki*, Beirut.

Aqsara'i, al- (A.S.M. Lutful-Huq ed.) (1956), 'A Critical Edition of *Nihayat al-Su'l*', PhD thesis, London University.

Arendt, W. (1931), 'Die Spharisch-Konischen Gefässe aus Gebrannten Ton', *Zeitschrift für Historische Waffen- und Kostümkunde*, n.s. 3, pp. 206–10.

—— (1932–4), 'Sirgeron-Kubetschi', *Zeitschrift für Historische Waffen- und Kostümkunde*, n.s. 4.

—— (1934), 'Türkische Säbel aus dem VIII–IX Jahrhunderten', in A. Zakharow and W. Arendt (eds), *Studia Levedica: Archaeologischer Beitrag zur Geschichte der Altungarn im IC. Jh. Archaeologia Hungarica*, 16, pp. 48–68.

—— (1936), 'Der Nomadenhelm des Frühen Mittelalters in Osteuropa', *Zeitschrift für Historische Waffen- und Kostümkunde*, n.s. 5, pp. 26–34.

Arié, R. (1965), 'Quelques remarques sur le Costume des Musulmans d'Espagne au Temps des Nasrides', *Arabica*, 7, pp. 244–61.

'Arif 'Ali of Toqat ('Arif 'Ali de Tokat) (I. Melikoff ed. & tr.) (1960), *Danishmandname: La Geste de Melik Danişment*, Paris.

Ashgar K. G. (1969), 'The Role of the Nobility During Early Turkish Rule in India, 1210–1255', PhD thesis, Edinburgh University.

Ashtor, E. (1969), *Histoire des prix et des salaires dans l'orient médiévale*, Paris.

—— (1976), *A Social and Economic History of the Near East in the Middle Ages*, London.

—— (1983), 'L'ascendant technologique de l'Occident médiévale', *Revue Suisse d'Histoire*, 33, pp. 385–413.

Atiya, A. S. (1938), *The Crusade in the Later Middle Ages*, London.

Ayalon, D. (1949), 'The Circassians in the Mamluk Kingdom', *Journal of the American Oriental Society*, 64, pp. 135–47.

—— (1951), *L'Esclavage du Mamelouk: Oriental Notes and Studies, No. 1*, Jerusalem.

—— (1953a), 'Studies in the Structure of the Mamluk Army – I: The Army Stationed in Egypt', *Bulletin of the School of Oriental and African Studies*, 15, pp. 203–28.

—— (1953b), 'Studies in the Structure of the Mamluk Army – II: The Halqa', *Bulletin of the School of Oriental and African Studies*, 15, pp. 448–76.

—— (1954) 'Studies in the Structure of the Mamluk Army – III: Holders of Offices Connected with the Army', *Bulletin of the School of Oriental and African Studies*, 16, pp. 57–90.

—— (1956), *Gunpowder and Firearms in the Mamluk Kingdom*, London.

—— (1958), 'The System of Payment in Mamluk Military Society', *Journal of the Economic and Social History of the Orient*, 1, pp. 37–65 and 257–96.

—— (1960), 'Bahriyya: Mamluks', in *Encyclopedia of Islam*, vol. 1, 2nd edition, Leiden, pp. 945–7.

—— (1961), 'Notes on the Furusiyya Exercises and Games in the Mamluk Sultanate', *Scripta Hierosolymitana*, 9, pp. 31–62.

—— (1965a), 'Furusiyya: In the Mamluk State', in *Encyclopedia of Islam*, vol. 2, 2nd edition, Leiden, 954–5.

—— (1965b), 'The Mamluks and Naval Power: A Phase in the Struggle between Islam and Christian Europe', *Proceedings of the Israel Academy of Sciences and Humanities*, 1, pp. 1–12.

—— (1971a) 'Hisar: The Mamluk Sultanate', in *Encyclopedia of Islam*, vol. 3, 2nd edition, Leiden, pp. 472–6.

—— (1971b), 'On One of the Works of Jean Sauvaget', *Israel Oriental Studies*, 1, 298–302.

—— (1972) 'Discharges from service, banishments and imprisonments in Mamluk society', *Israel Oriental Studies*, 2, pp. 25–50.

—— (1976), 'Aspects of the Mamluk Phenomenon: The Importance of the Mamluk Institution', *Der Islam*, 53, pp. 196–225.

—— (1977a), 'Aspects of the Mamluk Phenomenon: B. Ayyubids, Kurds and Turks', *Der Islam*, 54, pp. 1–32.

—— (1977b), 'The Eunuchs in the Mamluk Sultanate', in M. Rosen-Ayalon (ed.), *Studies in Memory of Gaston Wiet*, Jerusalem, pp. 267–95.

—— (1984), 'Egypt as the Dominant Factor in Syria and Palestine during the Islamic Period', in A. Cohen and G. Baer (eds), *Egypt and Palestine – a Millennium of Association (868–1948)*, Jerusalem, pp. 17–47.

Ayyuqi (A.S. Melikian-Chirvani ed. and trans.) (1970), 'Le Roman de Varqe et Golsâh', *Arts Asiatiques*, 22 (whole volume).

Azhari, T. K. El- (1997), *The Saljuqs of Syria during the Crusades 463–549 AH/1070–1154 AD*, Berlin.

Bacharach, J. L. (1981), 'African Military Slaves in the Medieval Middle East', *International Journal of Middle East Studies*, 13, pp. 471–95.

Baer, E. (1970–1), 'The "Pila" of Jativa, a Document of Secular Urban Art in Western Islam', *Kunst des Orients*, 7, pp. 142–66.

Baha' al-Din Ibn Shaddad (Yusuf Ibn Rafi' ed.) (1897a), *Al-Nawadir al-Sultaniyah*, Cairo.

—— (C. W. Wilson trans.) (1897b), *Saladin, what befell Sultan Yusuf: Palestine Pilgrim's Text Society*, London (1997).

—— (D. C. Richards trans.) (2002), *The Rare and Excellent History of Saladin*, Aldershot.

Bahnassi, A. (1976), 'Fabrication des Épées de Damas', *Syria*, 53, pp. 281–94.

Baidhaq, Abu Bakr Ibn 'Ali al-Sanhagi (Sanhaji) al- (E. Levi-Provençal ed. and trans.) (1928), 'History of the Almohades', in *Documents Inédits d'Histoire Almohade*, Paris, 75–225 (trans.) and 50–134 (ed.).

Baker, P. (2004), Correspondence on Mamluk quilted textiles, 6 May.

Balard, M. (1983), 'Gênes et la Mer Noire (XIIIe–XVe siècle)', *Revue Historiques*, 270, pp. 31–54.

Baldwin, M. W. (1936), *Raymond III of Tripoli and the Fall of Jerusalem (1140–1187)*, Princeton.

Banks, P. J. and J. Zozaya (1984), 'Excavations of the Caliphal Fortress of Gormaz (Soria), 1979–1981: A Summary', in T. F. C. Blagg, R. F. J. Jones and S. J. Keay (eds.), *Papers in Iberian Archaeology: BAR International Series 193 (II)*, Oxford, pp. 674–703.

Barber, M. (1998), 'Frontier Warfare in the Latin Kingdom of Jerusalem: The Campaign at Jacob's Ford, 1178–79', in J. France and W. G. Zajac (eds), *The Crusades and their Sources: Essays Presented to Bernard Hamilton*, Aldershot, pp. 9–22.

Barthold, V. V. (V. and T. Minorsky trs.) (1962a), *Four Studies on the History of Central Asia*, vol. 1, *History of Semirechye*, Leiden, pp. 73–165.

—— (1962b), *Four Studies on the History of Central Asia*, vol. 1, *A Short History of Turkestan*, Leiden, pp. 1–72.

Basch, L. (1993), 'Navires et bateaux coptes: état des questions en 1991', *Graeco-Arabica*, 5, pp. 23–62.

Basset, H. (1927), 'Sanctuaires et Ferteresses Almohades', *Hesperis*, 7, pp. 117–56.

Bazzana, A. (1977), 'Problèmes d'architecture militaire au Levant espagnol: Le château d'Alcala de Chivert', *Château Gaillard* (1976) p. 8 (1977) pp. 21–46.

—— (1983a), 'Approche d'une typologie des édifices castraux de l'ancien Sharq al-Andalus', *Château Gaillard* (1982) pp. 9–10 (1983) pp. 301–28.

—— (1983b), 'Forteresses du Royaume nasride de Grenade (XIIIe–XVe siècles): la défense des frontières', *Château Gaillard*, 11, pp. 29–43.

Becker, A. (2004), 'Die 'abbasidische Stadtmauer', in V. Daiber and A. Becker (eds), *Raqqa III: Baudenkmäler und Paläste I*, Mainz, pp. 3–4.

Beech, G. T. (1993), 'A Norman-Italian Adventurer in the East: Richard of Salerno 1097–1112', *Anglo-Norman Studies*, 15 (1993) pp. 25–40.

Beeler, J. (1971), *Warfare in Feudal Europe, 730–1200*, Ithaca.

Beeston, A. F. L. (1976), *Warfare in Ancient South Arabia (2nd–3rd centuries AD)*, London.

Bellafiore, G. (1975), 'The Cathedral of Monreale', *Connoisseur*, March, pp. 216–22.

Ben-Ami, A. (1969), *Social Change in a Hostile Environment: The Crusaders' Kingdom of Jerusalem*, Princeton.

Bennett, M. (1986), 'The Status of the Squire: the Northern Evidence', in C. Harper-Bill and R. Harvey (eds), *The Ideals and Practice of Medieval Knighthood (Papers from the first and second Strawberry Hill Conferences)*, Bury St Edmunds, pp. 1–11.

—— (1993), 'Norman Naval Activity in the Mediterranean *c.* 1060–1108', *Anglo-Norman Studies*, 15, pp. 41–58 (Woodbridge).

—— (2001), 'Military aspects of the conquest of Lisbon, 1147', in J. Phillips and M. Hoch (eds) *The Second Crusade: Scope and Consequences*, Manchester, pp. 71–89.

Beshir, B. J. (1978), 'Fatimid Military Organization', *Der Islam*, 55, pp. 37–57.

Bianquis, T. (1983), *Damas et la Syrie sous la domination Fatimide (359–468/969–1076)*, Damascus.

—— (1984), 'Deux Révoltes Bédouines en Syrie Méridionale au Moyen Age', in *The Third International Conference of Bilad al-Sham: Palestine, 19–24 April 1980*, vol. 3, *History of Palestine*, Amman, pp. 11–15.

Biruni, Muhammad Ibn Ahmad al- (F. Krenkow ed.) (1936), *Kitab al-jamahir fi ma'rifat al-jawahir*, Hyderabad.

Bishko, C. J. (1963), 'The Castilian as Plainsman: The Medieval Ranching Frontier in La Mancha and Extremadura', in A. Lewis and T. McGunn (eds), *The New World Looks at its History*, Austin, pp. 46–69.

Bisson, T. N. (1986), *The Medieval Crown of Aragon*, Oxford.

Boit, B.A. (1991a), *Building a Better Bow: Technical Refinement of the Turkish Composite Bow during the Crusading Era* (unpublished paper, Ohio State University, Columbus).

—— (1991b), 'The Fruits of Adversity: Technical Refinement of the Turkish Composite Bow during the Crusading Era', MA thesis, Ohio State University.

Bombaci, A. (1978), 'The Army of the Saljuqs of Rum', *Istituto orientale di Napoli, Annali*, n.s. 38, pp. 343–69.

Boratav, P. N. (1986), 'Kizil-Elma', in *Encyclopedia of Islam*, vol. 5, 2nd edition, Leiden, pp. 245–6.

Bosworth, C.E. (1965), 'Fakhr-i Mudabbir', in *Encyclopedia of Islam*, vol. 2, 2nd edition, Leiden, pp. 284–5.

—— (1971), 'Hisar: Persia', in *Encyclopedia of Islam*, vol. 3, 2nd edition, Leiden, pp. 470–2.

Bosworth, C. E. (1972), 'Christian and Jewish Religious Dignitaries in Mamlûk Egypt and Syria: Qalqashandi's information on their Hierarchy, Titulature and Appointment (Part 1)', *International Journal of Middle East Studies*, 3 (1972) pp. 59–74.

—— (1975) 'Recruitment, Muster and Review in Medieval Islamic Armies', in V. J. Parry and M. E. Yapp (eds), *War, Technology and Society in the Middle East*, London, pp. 59–77.

—— (1978a), 'Ispahbadh', in *Encyclopedia of Islam*, vol. 4, 2nd edition, Leiden, pp. 207–8.

—— (1978b), 'Istirad ('Ard)', in *Encyclopedia of Islam*, vol. 4, 2nd edition, Leiden, pp. 265–9.

—— (1991), 'Nasihat al-Muluk', in *Encyclopedia of Islam*, vol. 7, 2nd edition, Leiden, pp. 984–8.

—— (1993), 'Abu 'Amr 'Uthman al-Tarsusi's Siyar al-Thughur and the Last Years of Arab Rule in Tarsus (Fourth/Tenth century)', *Graeco-Arabica*, 5, pp. 183–95.

——(1998), Correspondence on *saq al-muza*, January.

Boudot-Lamotte, A. (1968), *Contribution à l'Etude de l'Archerie Musulmane*, Damascus.

Boudot-Lamotte, A. and F. Viré (1970), 'Contribution á l'Etude de l'Archerie Musulmane', *Arabica*, 17, 47–68.

—— 'Kaws' (1978), in *Encyclopedia of Islam*, vol. 4, 2nd edn., Leiden, pp. 795–803.

Bowlus, C. R. (1996), 'Tactical and Strategic Weaknesses of Horse-Archers on the Eve of the First Crusade', in M. Balard (ed.), *Autour de la Première Croisade*, Paris, pp. 159–66.

Boyle, J. A. (1965), 'A Form of Horse-Sacrifice amongst the thirteenth and fourteenth century Mongols', *Central Asiatic Journal*, 10, pp. 145–50.

—— (1971), 'The Capture of Isfahan by the Mongols', in *Atti del Convegno Internazionale sul Tema: la Persia nel Medioevo*, Rome, pp. 331–6.

—— (1972), 'Turkish and Mongol shamanism in the Middle Ages', *Folklore*, 83, pp. 177–93.

—— (1978), 'Kalmuk', in *Encyclopedia of Islam*, vol. 4, 2nd edn, Leiden, p. 512.

Bragadin, M.-A. (1955), *Histoire des Republiques Maritimes Italiennes: Venise-Amalfi-Pise-Gênes*, Paris.

Brand, C. M. (1962), 'The Byzantines and Saladin, 1185–1192: Opponents of the Third Crusade', *Speculum*, 37, pp. 167–81.

Bresc, H. (1980), 'Mudejars des Pays de la Couronne d'Aragon et Sarrasins de la Sicile Normande: Le Problème d'Acculturation', in *X Congreso de Historia de la Corona de Aragon: Jaime I y su Epoca (Zaragoza, 1975), t. III*, Saragossa, pp. 51–60.

Brett, M. (1970), '*Fitnat al-Qayrawan*. A Study of Traditional Arabic Historiography', PhD thesis, University of London.

—— (1975), 'The Military Interest of the Battle of Haydran', in V. J. Parry and M. E. Yapp (eds), *War, Technology and Society in the Middle East*, London, pp. 78–88.

—— (1986), 'The City-State in Medieval Ifriqia: The Case of Tripoli', *Cahiers de Tunisie*, 34, pp. 69–94.

—— (1995), 'The Battles of Ramla (1099–1105)', in U. Vermeulen and D. De Smet (eds), *Egypt and Syria in the Fatimid, Ayyubid and Mamluk Eras: Proceedings of the 1st, 2nd and 3rd International Colloquium: Orientalia Lovaniensia Alalecta 72*, Leuven, pp. 17–37.

—— (1997), 'The Battle of Hattin, 1187', paper read at the Sixth Colloquium on Egyptian and Syrian Studies in the Fatimid, Ayyubid and Mamluk Periods, Leuven, 15 May.

Brodman, J.W. (1986), *Ransoming Captives in Crusader Spain*, Philadelphia.

Brooker, C.H. and E.A. Knauf (1988), 'Notes on Crusader Transjordan', *Zeitschrift des Deutschen Palaestina-vereins*, 104, pp. 185–8.

Brooks, F. W. (1928), 'Naval Armament in the Thirteenth Century', *Mariner's Mirror*, 14, pp. 115–31.

Brunschwig, R. (1940–7), *La Berberie Orientale sous les Hafsides des origines à la fin du XV siècle*, Paris.

Buckler, G. (1929), *Anna Comnena, a Study*, London.

Bulliet, R.W. (1975), *The Camel and the Wheel*, Cambridge MA.

Burns, R. I. (1976), 'The Muslim in the Christian Feudal Order: The Kingdom of Valencia, 1240–1280', *Studies in Medieval Culture*, 5, pp. 105–126.

—— (1986), 'The Crusade against al-Azraq: A Thirteenth Century Mudejar Revolt in International Perspective', paper read at 61st Annual meeting of the Medieval Academy of America, University of New Mexico, April.

Buryakov, Y. F., K. M. Baipakov, K. H. Tashbaeva and Y. Yakubov (eds) (1999), *The Cities and Routes of the Great Silk Road*, Tashkent.

Buttin, F. (1960), 'Les Adargues de Fès', *Hespéres Tamuda*, 1, pp. 409–455.

Bylinski, J. (2004), 'Three minor fortresses in the realm of Ayyubid rulers of Homs in Syria: Shumaimis, Tadmur (Palmyra) and al-Rahba', in N. Faucherre, J. Mesqui, N. Prouteau and J. Richard (eds.), *La Fortification au Temps des Croisades*, Rennes, pp. 151–64.

Byrne, E. H. (1920), 'Genoese Trade with Syria in the Twelfth Century', *American Historical Review*, 25, 191–219.

Cahen, C. (1934), 'La Campagne de Mantzikert, d'après les sources Musulmanes', *Byzantion*, 9, pp. 613–42.

—— (1940), *La Syrie du Nord au Temps des Croisades*, Paris.

—— (1947–8), 'Les armes chez les Ghûrides', in 'Un traité d'armurerie composé pour Saladin', *Bulletin d'Etudes Orientales*, 12, pp. 58–60.

—— (1948), 'La Première pénétration Turque en Asie-Mineure (seconde moitié du XIe. s.)', *Byzantion*, 18, pp. 5–67.

—— (1951), 'Seljukides de Rum, Byzantins et Francs d'après le Seljuknameh anonyme', *Annuaire de l'Institut de Philologie et d'Histoire Orientales et Slaves*, 11, pp. 97–106.

—— (1960), "Arrada', in *Encyclopedia of Islam*, vol. 1, 2nd edn, Leiden, pp. 658–9.

—— (1965) 'Djaysh, I: Classical', in *Encyclopedia of Islam*, vol. 2, 2nd edn, Leiden, pp. 504–9.

—— (1968), *Pre-Ottoman Turkey*, London.

—— (1970), 'Note sur l'esclavage musulman et le devshirme Ottoman: à propos des travaux récents', *Journal of the Economic and Social History of the Orient*, 13, pp. 211–18.

—— (1971a), 'Harb', in *Encyclopedia of Islam*, vol. 3, 2nd edn, Leiden, pp. 181–4.

—— (1971b), 'Hisar: General Remarks', in *Encyclopedia of Islam*, vol. 3, 2nd edn, Leiden, pp. 469–70.

—— (1972), 'L'Administration Financière de l'armée Fatimide d'après al-Makhzumi', *Journal of the Economic and Social History of the Orient*, 15, pp. 163–82.

—— (1983), *Orient et Occident au Temps des Croisades*, Paris.

Calmard, J. (1985), "Alam va 'Alamat: History', in *Encyclopedia Iranica*, vol. 1, London, pp. 785–90.

Canard, M. (1946), 'Textes relatifs à l'emploi du feu grégeois chez les Arabes', *Bulletin des Etudes Arabes (Alger)*, 24, pp. 3–7.

—— (1951), 'Le Cérémonial Fatimite et le Cérémonial Byzantin', *Byzantion*, 21, pp. 355–420.

—— (1952a), 'L'autobiographie d'un chambellan du Mahdi 'Obeidallah de Fatimide', *Hesperis*, pp. 279–329.

—— (1952b), 'La Procession du Nouvel An chez les Fatimides', *Annales de l'Institut Orientales de la Faculté des Lettres d'Alger*, 9, pp. 364–98.

—— (1954), 'Un Vizir Chrétien à l'époque fatimide: l'Arménien Bahram', *Annales de l'Institut Orientales de la Faculté des Lettres d'Alger*, 12, pp. 84–113.

—— (1957), 'Quelques Observations sur l'introduction géographique de la Bughyat at'T'aleb de Kamal ad-Din ibn al 'Adim d'Alep', *Annales de l'Institut Orientales de la Faculté des Lettres d'Alger*, 15, pp. 41–53.

—— (1965a), 'Djasus', in *Encyclopedia of Islam*, vol. 2, 2nd edn, Leiden, pp. 486–8.

—— (1965b), 'La Campagne Arménienne du Sultan Salguqide Alp Arslan et la prise d'Ani en 1064', *Revue des Etudes Arméniennes*, 2, pp. 239–59.

—— (1965c) 'Quelques aspects de la vie sociale en Syrie et Jazira au dixième siècle d'après les poètes de la Cour Hamdanide', in *Arabic and Islamic Studies in Honour of Hamilton A. R. Gibb*, Leiden, pp. 168–209.

—— (1967), 'Fatimides et Burides à l'Epoque du Calife al Hafiz l'-Din-Illah', *Revue des Eudes Islamiques*, pp. 103–17.

Carpini (W.M. Rockhill trans.) (1900), 'The Journey of Friar John of Pian de Carpine as narrated by himself', in W. W. Rockhill (ed.), *The Journey of William of Rubruck to the Eastern Parts of the World 1253–55, as narrated by himself, with two accounts of the earlier journey of John of Pian de Carpine*, London, pp. 1–32.

Cathcart King, D. J. (1949), 'The Taking of Le Krak des Chevaliers in 1271', *Antiquity*, 23, pp. 83–92.

—— (1982), 'The Trebuchet and other siege engines', *Château Gaillard*, 9–10, pp. 457–69.

Chevedden, P. E. (1985), 'Recent Archaeological Researches in the Citadel of Damascus', paper read at the meeting of the Middle East Studies Association, New Orleans, 25 November.

—— (1999), 'Fortifications and the Development of Defensive Planning in the Latin East', in D. Kagay and L. J. A. Villalon (eds), *The Circle of War in the Middle Ages*, Woodbridge, pp. 33–43.

Christides, V. (1984), 'Naval Warfare in the Eastern Mediterranean (6th–14th centuries): An Arabic Translation of Leo's "Naumachica"', *Graeco-Arabica*, 3, pp. 137–43.

—— (1987), 'Navies: Islamic', in J. R. Strayer (ed.), *Dictionary of the Middle Ages*, vol. 9, New York, pp. 73–8.

—— (1989), 'Some Remarks on the Mediterranean and Red Sea Ships in Ancient and Medieval Times: A Preliminary Report', *Tropsis*, 1, pp. 75–82 (Piraeus).

—— (1990a), 'Some Remarks on the Mediterranean and Red Sea Ships in Ancient and Medieval Times, II: Merchant-Passenger vs. Combat Ships', *Tropsis*, 2, pp. 87–99 (Piraeus).

—— (1990b), 'The Transmission of Chinese Maritime Technology by the Arabs to Europe: The Single Stern Rudder, Greek Fire, Animal Transport Ships', pre-publication draft.

—— (1991) 'Milaha: in the pre-Islamic and Medieval Arab worlds', in *Encyclopedia of Islam*, vol. 7, 2nd edn, Leiden, pp. 40–6.

—— (1994), 'New Light on Navigation and Naval Warfare in the Eastern Mediterranean, the Red Sea and the Indian Ocean (6th–14th centuries AD)', *Nubica*, 3, pp. 3–42.

—— (1997), 'Military Intelligence and Arabo-Byzantine Naval Warfare', in K. Tsiknakis (ed.), *Byzantium at War (ninth–twelfth C.)*, Athens, pp. 269–81.

Christie, N. (1999), 'Muslim Attitudes towards the Early Crusades', paper read at the Institute of Historical Research, London University, 13 December.

—— (2000), 'Hostility, Admiration and Confusion: Muslim Views of the Early Crusades', paper read at Toronto University, 4 April.

Clarke, J. (2006), 'A History of Ironworking in Tibet: Centers of Production, Styles and Techniques', in D. J. LaRocca (ed.), *Warriors of the Himalayas: Rediscovering the Arms and Armor of Tibet*, New York, pp. 21–33.

Claverie, P-V. (2000), 'Le statut des templiers capturés en Orient durant les croisades', in G. Cipollone (ed.), *La liberazione dei 'Captivi' tra Cristianità e Islam: Oltre la Crociata e il Gihad: Tolleranza e Servizio Umanitario*, Vatican, pp. 501–11.

Clavijo, Ruy Gonzales de (Guy Le Strange trans.) (1928), *Clavijo, Embassy to Tamerlane, 1403–1406*, London.

Clifford, E. R. (1961), *A Knight of Great Renown: The Life and Times of Othon de Grandson*, Chicago.

Colin, G. S. (1971a), 'Barud: General & the Maghrib', in *Encyclopedia of Islam*, vol. 1, 2nd edn, Leiden, pp. 1055–8.

—— (1971b), 'Hisar: The Muslim West', in *Encyclopedia of Islam*, vol. 3, 2nd edn, Leiden, p. 470.

Comnena, Anna (B. Leib ed. and trans.) (1967), *Annè Comnène, Alexiade*, Paris.

Credland, A. G. (1981), 'The Blowpipe in Europe and the East', *Journal of the Arms and Armour Society*, 10, pp. 119–47.

—— (1994), 'The Origins and Development of the Composite Bow', *Journal of the Society of Archer Antiquaries*, 37, pp. 19–39.

Creswell, K. A. C. (1952), 'Fortification in Islam before AD 1250', *Proceedings of the British Academy*, 308, pp. 89–125 plus plates.

—— (1960), 'Bab', in *Encyclopedia of Islam*, vol. 1, 2nd edn, Leiden, pp. 830–2.

Cuoq, J. (1986), *Islamisation de la Nubie Chretienne VIIe–XVIe Siècles*, Paris.

Curtis, E. (1912), *Roger of Sicily*, London.

Dadoyan, S. B. (1997), *The Fatimid Armenians: Culture and Political Interaction in the Middle East*, Leiden.

Daftary, F. (1990), *The Isma'ilis: their History and Doctrines*, Cambridge.

—— (1998), 'Sayyida Hurra: The Isma'ili Sulayhid Queen of Yemen', in G. R. G. Hambly (ed.), *Women in the Medieval Islamic World: Power, Patronage and Piety*, London, pp. 117–30.

Dajani-Shakeel, H. (1986), 'Al-Quds: Jerusalem in the Consciousness of the Counter-Crusade', in V. P. Goss and C. V. Bornstein (eds.), *The Meeting of Two Worlds: Cultural Exchange between East and West during the Period of the Crusades*, Kalamazoo, pp. 201–21.

—— (1991), 'A Reassessment of Some Medieval and Modern Perceptions of the Counter-Crusade', in R. A. Messier (ed.), *The Jihad in its Times: Dedicated to Andrew Stefan Ehrenkreutz*, Ann Arbor, pp. 41–70.

Darko, E. (1937), 'La Tactique Touranienne', *Byzantion*, 10, pp. 443–69; 12, 119–47.

David-Weill, J. (1960), ''Alam', in *Encyclopedia of Islam*, vol. 1, 2nd edn, Leiden, p. 349.

Dawood, A. H. H. O. M. (1965), 'A Comparative Study of Arabic and Persian Mirrors for Princes from the Second to the Sixth Century AH', PhD thesis, London.

de Clari, Robert (A. Pauphilet and E. Pognon eds.) (1952), 'La Conquête de Constantinople', in *Historiens et Chroniqueurs du Moyen Age*, Paris, pp. 1–81.

De Hoffmeyer, A. B. (1972), *Arms and Armour in Spain, a short survey*, vol. I, Madrid.

—— (1982), *Arms and Armour in Spain, a short survey*, vol. II, Madrid.

De Joinville, J. (F. Marzials trans.) (1921), *Memoirs of the Crusades by Villehardouin and de Joinville*, London, pp. 135–327.

—— (A. Pauphilet and E. Pognon eds.) (1952), 'Histoire de Saint Louis', in *Historiens et Chroniqueurs du Moyen Age*, Paris, pp. 197–366.

De Mas Latrie, M. L. (ed.) (1871), *Chronique d'Ernoul et de Bernard le Trésorier*, Paris.

De Moraes Farias, P. F. (1967), 'The Almoravids: Some Questions Concerning the Character of the Movement during its periods of Closest Contact with the Western Sudan', *Bulletin de l'Institut Fondamental d'Afrique Noir*, ser. B, 29, pp. 794–878.

De Oliveiro-Marques, A. H. (1972), *History of Portugal: vol. I, From Lusitania to Empire*, New York.

De Saulcy, M. F. (1874), 'Notes sur des Projectiles à Main, Creux et en Terre Cuite de Fabrication Arabe', *Mémoires de la Société Nationale des Antiquaires de France*, 4 ser. 5, pp. 18–34.

De Vries, K. (1992), *Medieval Military Technology*, Peterborough Ontario.

Dédéyan, G. (2001), 'Un émir arménien du Hawrân entre la principauté turque de Damas et le royaume latin de Jérusalem (1147)', in M. Balard, B. Z. Kedar and J. Riley-Smith (eds.), *Dei gesta per Francos*, Aldershot, pp. 179–85.

Deloche, J. (1989), *Military Technology in Hoysala Sculpture (Twelfth and Thirteenth Century)*, New Delhi.

Dennis, G. T. (1981), 'Flies, Mice and the Byzantine Crossbow', *Byzantine and Modern Greek Studies*, 7, pp. 1–5.

Di Meglio, R. R. (1970), 'Arab Trade with Indonesia and the Malay Peninsula', in D. S. Richards (ed.), *Islam and the Trade of Asia*, Oxford, pp. 105–35.

Diaconu, P. (1978), *Les Coumans au Bas-Danube aux XIe au XIIe siècles*, Bucharest.

Djanpoladian, R. and A. Kirpicnikov (1972), 'Mittelalterlicher Säbel mit einer Armenischen inschrift, gefunden im subpolaren Ural', *Gladius*, 10, pp. 15–23.

Doras, S. and R. E. Koçu (n.d.), *Mehterhane*, Ankara.

Douglas, D. C. (1976), *The Norman Fate 1100–1154*, London.

Douillet, G. (1965), 'Furusiyya', in *Encyclopedia of Islam*, vol. 2, 2nd edn, Leiden, pp. 953–4.

Dozy, R. (1881), *Récherches sur l'histoire et la litteratire de l'Espagne*, Leiden; reprinted Amsterdam 1965.

Dozy, R. (ed.) (C. Pellat trans.) (1961), *Le Calendrier de Cordoue*, Leiden.

Drory, J. (1981), 'Jerusalem during the Mamluk Period (1250–1517)', in L. I. Levine (ed.), *Jerusalem Cathedra: Studies in the History, Archaeology, Geography and Ethnography of the Land of Israel*, vol. 1, Jerusalem and Detroit, pp. 190–213.

Dufourcq, J. (1980), 'Rapports entre l'Afrique et l'Espagne au XIIIe siècle', *Medievalia*, 1, pp. 83–101.

Dunlop, D. M. (1960), 'Al-Bahr al-Muhit', in *Encyclopedia of Islam*, vol. 1, 2nd edn, Leiden, p. 934.

—— (1973), 'Arab Relations with Tibet in the eighth and early ninth centuries AD', *Islâm Tetkikleri Enstitüsü Dergisi*, 5, pp. 301–18.

Eddé, A.-M. (1996), 'Kurdes et Turcs dans l'Armée Ayyoubide de Syrie du Nord', in Y. Lev (ed.), *War and Society in the Eastern Mediterranean, Seventh–Fifteenth Centuries*, Leiden, pp. 225–36.

Edgington, S. (1996), 'The Doves of War: The part played by carrier pigeons in the crusades', in M. Balard (ed.), *Autour de la Première Croisade*, Paris, pp. 167–75.

Ehrenkreutz, A. S. (1955), 'The Place of Saladin in the Naval History of the Mediterranean Sea in the Middle Ages', *Journal of the American Oriental Society*, 75, pp. 100–16.

—— (1972), *Saladin*, New York.

El Bekri (Bakri, al-) (De Slane trans.) (1913), *Description de l'Afrique Septentrionale*, Paris.

Elbeheiry, S. (1972), *Les Institutions de l'Egypte au Temps des Ayyubides*, PhD thesis, University of Paris IV, 1971; published by Université de Lyon III.

Elisseeff, N. (1967), *Nur al Din: un Grand Prince Musulman de Syrie au Temps des Croisades*, Damascus.

—— (1991), 'al-Markab', in *Encyclopedia of Islam*, vol. 6, 2nd edn, Leiden, pp. 577–83.

Ellenblum, R. (1989), 'Who built Qal'at al Subayba?', *Dumbarton Oaks Papers*, 43, pp. 103–12.

—— (2001), 'Frankish and Muslim Siege Warfare and the construction of Frankish Concentric Castles', in M. Balard (ed.), *Dei Gesta per Francos*, Aldershot, pp. 187–98.

—— (2003), 'Frontier Activities: the Transformation of a Muslim Sacred Site into the Frankish Castle of Vadum Iacob', *Crusades*, 2, pp. 83–97.

Esin, E. (1974), 'L'arme zoomorphe du guerrier turc (Étude iconographique)', in G. Hazai and P. Zieme (eds), *Sprache, Geschichte und Kultur der altaischen Völker*, Berlin, pp. 193–217.

Esin, E. (1980), *A History of Pre-Islamic and Early Islamic Turkish Culture*, Istanbul.

—— (1994), 'The Oghuz Epics and Saljuq Iconography', in R. Hillenbrand (ed.), *The Arts of the Saljuqs in Iran and Anatolia*, Costa Mesa, pp. 201–9.

Ettinghausen, R. (1971), 'Hilal: In Islamic Art', in *Encyclopedia of Islam*, vol. 3, 2nd edn, Leiden, pp. 381–5.

Facey, W. (1979), *Oman, a Seafaring Nation*, Muscat.

Fakhr al-Din Mubarakshah, Muhammad Ibn Mansur (1969) (A. S. Khwansari ed.) *Adab al-Harb was al-Shuja'ah*, Tehran.

Fakhr-i Mudabbir (1974) (E. McEwen trans.), 'Adab al Harb', *The Islamic Quarterly*, 18, pp. 76–99.

—— (2003) (C. E. Bosworth trans.), 'Chapter 19 of Adab al-harb wa/l-shuja'a', unpublished text.

Faris, N.A. and R. P. Elmer (trans.) (1945), *Arab Archery*, Princeton; see also Ibn Maymun, Abu Muhammad Jamal al-Din 'Abd Allah.

Fernández-Puertas, A. (1991), 'Nasrids: art and architecture', in *Encyclopedia of Islam*, vol. 8, 2nd edn, Leiden, pp. 1028–9.

Feuerbach, A. (1998), 'Evidence for the Production of Damascus Steel, from the late ninth-early tenth century at Merv, Turkmenistan', in L. E. Nemchinova and T. M. Tallerchik (eds), *Military Archeology*, St Petersburg, pp. 309–12.

Finó, J.-F. (1970), 'Le Feu et ses usages militaires', *Gladius*, 9, pp. 15–30.

Firdawsi (1877–80) (J. A. Vullers ed.), *Shahname*, Leiden.

—— (1905) (A. G. and E. Warner trans.), *The Shahnama of Firdausi*, London.

Flutre, L.F. (1974), 'Une arbaleste fait de cor, Cléomadés 2936', *Romania*, 95, pp. 309–17.

Foley, V. and K. Perry (1979), 'In Defence of LIBER IGNEUM: Arab Alchemy, Roger Bacon and the Introduction of Gunpowder into the West', *Journal for the History of Arabic Science*, 3, pp. 200–18.

Forey, A. (1985), 'The Emergence of the Military Order in the Twelfth Century', *Journal of Ecclesiastical History*, 36, pp. 175–97.

—— (1991), 'The Military Orders and the Ransoming of Captives from Islam (twelfth to early fourteenth centuries)', *Studia Monastica*, 33, pp. 259–79.

France, J. (1996), 'Technology and the Success of the First Crusade', in Y. Lev (ed.), *War and Society in the Eastern Mediterranean, Seventh–Fifteenth centuries*, Leiden, pp. 163–76.

Frend, W. H. C. (1955) 'North Africa and Europe in the Early Middle Ages', *Transactions of the Royal Historical Society*, 5 ser. 5, pp. 61–80.

Frenkel, Y. (1996), 'The Impact of the Crusades on Rural Society and Religious Endowments: The Case of Medieval Syria (Bilad al-Sham)', in Y. Lev (ed.), *War and Society in the Eastern Mediterranean: Seventh–Fifteenth Centuries*, Leiden, pp. 237–48.

Friedman, Y. (1996), 'The Ransom of Captives in the Latin Kingdom of Jerusalem', in M. Balard (ed.), *Autour de la Première Croisade*, Paris, pp. 177–89.

—— (2002), *Encounter Between Enemies: Captivity and Ransom in the Latin Kingdom of Jerusalem*, Leiden.

Gabrieli, F. (1969), *Arab Historians of the Crusades*, London.

García Fitz, F. (1990), 'Notas Sobre la Tenencia de Fortalezas: los Castillos del Concejo de Sevilla en la Baja Edad Media', *Historia, Instituciones, Documentos*, 17, 55–81.

—— (1995), 'Las Huestes de Fernando III', in (Anon, ed.), *Fernando III y su época. IV Jornadas Nacionales de Historia Militar*, Seville, pp. 157–89.

—— (1996), 'La Batalla en su contexto estragégico; A propósito de Alarcos', in R. I. Benito and F. R. Gómez (eds), *Alarcos 1195; al-Arak 592: Actas del Congreso Internacional Conmemorativo del VIII Centenario de la Batalla de Alarcos (1995, Ciudad Real)*, Cuenca, pp. 267–82.

—— (1997), 'Tecnología militar y guerra de asedios. La experiencia castellano-leonesa, siglos XI al XIII', in G. De Boe and F. Verhaeghe (eds), *Military Studies in Medieval Europe – Papers of the 'Medieval Europe Brugge 1997' Conference*, volume 11, Zellik, pp. 33–41.

—— (1998a), 'El Cerco de Sevilla: Reflexiones sobre la guerra de Asedio en la Edad Media', in M. González Jiménez (ed.), *Sevilla 1248, Congreso Internacional Conmemorativo del 750 Aniversario de la Conquista de la Ciudad de Sevilla por Fernando III, Rey de Castilla y León*, Seville, pp. 115–54.

—— (1998b), 'Fortificaciones, fronteras y sistemas defensivos en al-Andalus, siglos XI al XIII', in (Anon, ed.), *I Congreso Internacional Fortificaciones en al-Andalus (Algeciras, Noviembre–Diciembre 1996)*, Algeciras, pp. 269–79.

—— (1999), 'La Conquista de Sevilla desde el punto de vista Militar "La Marina y la Guerra"', in (Anon, ed.), *Santander y Cantabria en la Conquista de Sevilla, 750 Aniversario (Ciclo de Conferencias Cátedra de Menéndez Pelayo, Santander 1998)*, Santander, pp. 11–28.

García Gómez, E. (1967), 'Armas, Banderas, Tièndas de Campaña, Monturas y Correos en los "Anales de Al-Hakam II" por "Isa" Razi', *Andalus*, 32, pp. 163–79.

Gaunt, G. D. (1973), 'Mongol Archers of the Thirteenth Century', *Journal of the Society of Archer Antiquaries*, 16, pp. 20–1.

Ghaith, Z. M. (1970), 'The Crusades in Arabic Poetry up to the Death of Nur al-Din', M.Litt thesis, Edinburgh University.

Gibb, H. A. R. (1951), 'The Armies of Saladin', *Cahiers d'Histoire Egyptienne*, 3, pp. 304–20.

Glaesener, H. (1946), 'L'Escalade de la Tour d'Antioche', *Revue de la Moyen Age Latin*, 2, pp. 139–48.

Glick, T. F. (1976), 'Cob Walls Revisited: The Diffusion of Tabby Construction in the Western Mediterranean World', in B. S. Hall and D. C. West (eds), *On Pre-Modern Technology and Science: Studies in Honor of Lynn White Jr.*, Malibu, pp. 147–59.

—— (1979), *Islamic and Christian Spain in the Early Middle Ages*, Princeton.

Goitein, S. D. (1952), 'Contemporary Letters on the Capture of Jerusalem by the Crusaders', *The Journal of Jewish Studies*, 3–4, pp. 162–77.

—— (1954), 'Two Eye-Witness Reports on an Expedition of the King of Kish', *Bulletin of the School of Oriental and African Studies*, 16, pp. 247–57.

—— (1955), 'The Cairo Geniza as a Source for the History of Muslim Civilization', *Studia Islamica*, 3, pp. 75–91.

—— (1956), 'Glimpses from the Cairo Geniza on Naval Warfare in the Mediterranean and on the Mongol Invasion', in (Anon, ed.), *Studi Orientalistici on Onore di Georgio Levi della Vida*, Rome, pp. 393–408.

—— (1967), *A Mediterranean Society: The Jewish Communities of the Arab World as Portrayed in the Documents of the Cairo Geniza*, Vol. 1: *Economic Foundations*, Berkeley.

—— (1970), 'Mediterranean Trade in the Eleventh Century: Some facts and problems', in M. A. Cook (ed.), *Studies in the Economic History of the Middle East*, London, pp. 51–62.

—— (1982), 'Jerusalem in the Arab Period (638–1099)', in L. I. Levine (ed.), *The Jerusalem Cathedra: Studies in the History, Archaeology, Geography and Ethnography of the Land of Israel*, vol. 2, Jerusalem and Detroit, pp. 168–96.

Gorelik, M. V. (1979), 'Oriental armour of the Near and Middle East from the eighth to the fifteenth centuries as shown in works of art', in R. Elgood (ed.), *Islamic Arms and Armour*, London, pp. 30–63.

—— (1997), Conversation on aspects of Mongol culture and military equipment, 20 November.

—— (2002a), 'Arms and Armour in South-Eastern Europe in the Second Half of the First Millenium AD', in D. C. Nicolle (ed.), *A Companion to Medieval Arms and Armour*, Woodbridge, pp. 127–47.

—— (2002b), *Armii Mongolo-Tatar, X–XIVvv*, Moscow.

—— (2004), 'Aduigi i Yuzhnom Podneprove (2-ya Polovina XIII v.-1-ya Polovina XIV v.)' (Reinforced shields and weapons of the 2nd part of the 13th – first part of the 14th cent.), in (Anon, ed.), *Materialii Issledovanya po Arkheologii Severnogo Kavkasa III*, Armavir, pp. 292–300.

Graindor de Douai (1977–87) (S. Duparc-Quic ed.), *Le Chanson d'Antioche*, Paris.

Granara, W. E. (1986), 'Political Legitimacy and Jihad in Muslim Sicily 217/827–445/1053', PhD thesis, University of Pennsylvania.

Greenstone, J. H. (1905–6), 'The Turkoman defeat at Cairo', *American Journal of Semitic Languages and Literatures*, 22, pp. 144–75.

Hackett, J. W. (1937), 'Saladin's Campaign of 1188 in Northern Syria', B Litt thesis, Oxford University.

Hagen, N., M. al-Khalaf, M. Meinecke and H. Mismahl (2004), 'Das Nordtor', in V. Daiber and A. Becker (eds), *Raqqa III: Baudenkmäler und Paläste I*, Mainz, pp. 5–10.

Haldane, D. (1999), 'The Fire-Ship of al-Salih Ayyub and Muslim Use of "Greek Fire"', in D. J. Kagay and L. J. A. Villalon (eds), *The Circle of War in the Middle Ages*, Woodbridge, pp. 137–44.

Haldon, J. F. (2001), *The Byzantine Wars: Battles and Campaigns of the Byzantine Era*, Stroud.

Haldon, J. F. and M. Byrne (1977), 'A Possible Solution to the problem of Greek Fire', *Byzantinische Zeitschrift*, 70, pp. 91–9.

Halphen, L. (1926), 'La Conquête de la Méditerranée par les Européens au XIe at aux XIIe siècles', in (Anon, ed.), *Mélanges d'histoire offerts à Henri Pirenne*, vol. 1, Bruxelles, pp. 175–80.

Hamblin, W. J. (1984), 'The Fatimid Army during the Early Crusades', PhD thesis, University of Michigan.

—— (1992), 'Saladin and Muslim Military Theory', in B. Z. Kedar (ed.), *The Horns of Hattin*, Jerusalem, pp. 228–38.

Hamdani, Hasan Ibn Ahmad al- (1931) (Al-Karmali al-Baghdadi ed.), *Al-Iklil, VIII*, Baghdad, whole volume.

Hammer-Purgstall, J. (1854), 'Sur les lames des Orientaux', *Journal Asiatique*, 8, pp. 66–79.

Hanisch, H-P. (2004), 'The Works of al-Malik al-'Adil in the citadel of Harrân', in N. Faucherre, J. Mesqui, N. Prouteau and J. Richard (eds.), *La Fortification au Temps des Croisades*, Rennes, pp. 165–78.

Harawi, 'Ali Ibn Abu Bakr al- (1957) (J. Sourdel-Thomine tr.), *Guide des Lieux de Pelerinage*, Damascus.

—— (1961–2) (J. Sourdel-Thomine trans.), 'Les Conseils du Sayh al Harawi à un Prince Ayyubide', *Bulletin d'Etudes Orientales de l'Institut Français de Damas*, 17, pp. 205–66.

Harthami, Abu Sa'id al-Sha'rani al- (1964) ('Abd al-Ra'uf ed.), *Mukhtasar Siyasat al-Hurub*, Cairo.

Hartman, A. (1975), *An-Nasir li-Din Allah (1180–1225): Politik, Region, Kultur in der späten 'Abbasidenzeit*, Berlin and New York.

Hartmann-Virnich, A. (2004), 'Les portes ayyoubides de la citadelle de Damas: le regard d'archéologie du bâti', in N. Faucherre, J. Mesqui, N. Prouteau and J. Richard, eds., *La Fortification au Temps des Croisades*, Rennes, pp. 287–311.

Hassan, A.Y. al- (1978), 'Iron and Steel Technology in Medieval Arabic Sources', *Journal for the History of Arabic Science*, 2, 31–43.

Hazai, G., 'Kipcak' (Qipchaq), in *Encyclopedia of Islam*, vol. 5, 2nd edn, Leiden, pp. 125–6.

Heidemann, S. (2004), 'Die Zitadelle von ar-Rafiqa', in V. Daiber and A. Becker (eds.), *Raqqa III: Baudenkmäler und Paläste I*, Mainz, pp. 49–55.

Heissig, W. (1989), 'Historical Realities and Elements in the Mongol Heroic Epic', in *International Association for the Study of the Cultures of Central Asia: Information Bulletin*, 16, pp. 20–26 (Moscow).

Hendrix, W. S. (1922), 'Military Tactics in the Poem of the Cid', *Modern Philology*, 20, pp. 45–8.

Hill, D. R. (1973), 'Trebuchets', *Viator*, 4, pp. 99–114.

—— (1993), *Islamic Science and Engineering*, Edinburgh.

Hill, D. R. and A. Y. Hassan (1986), *Islamic Technology: An illustrated history*, Cambridge.

Hillenbrand, C. (1979), 'The History of the Jazira 1100–1150: The Contribution of Ibn al Azraq al Fariqi', PhD thesis, Edinburgh University.

—— (1981), 'The Career of Najm al-Din Il-Ghazi', *Der Islam*, 58, pp. 250–92.

—— (1985), 'The History of the Jazira, 1100–1250: A Short Introduction', in J. Raby (ed.), *Oxford Studies in Islamic Art*, vol. 1, Oxford, pp. 9–19.

Hinds, M. (1971), 'The Banners and Battle Cries of the Arabs at Siffin', *Al Abhath*, 24, pp. 3–42.

Hitti, P. K. (1972), 'The Impact of the Crusades in Eastern Christianity', in S. A. Monroe (ed.), *Medieval and Middle Eastern Studies in Honor of Aziz Suryal Atiya*, Leiden, pp. 211–17.

Hollenback, G. M. (2005), 'A new reconstruction of the kestros or cestrosphendone', *Arms and Armour, Journal of the Royal Armouries*, 2, pp. 79–86.

Holt, P. M. (1977), 'The Structure of Government in the Mamluk Sultanate', in P. M. Holt (ed.), *The Eastern Mediterranean Lands in the Period of the Crusades*, Warminster, pp. 44–61.

—— (1985), 'Baybars' Treaty with the Lady of Beirut in 667/1269', in P. W. Edbury (ed.), *Crusade and Settlement*, Cardiff, pp. 242–5.

Hopkins, J. F. P. (1958), *Medieval Muslim Government in Barbary, until the sixth century of the Hijra*, London.

Hopkins, J. F. P. and N. Levtzion (1981), *Corpus of Early Arabic Sources for West African History*, Cambridge.

Huart, Cl. (1993), 'al-Wah', in *E.J. Brill's Encyclopedia of Islam*, vol. 7 1st edn (reprint Leiden 1993), pp. 1083–4.

Huici Miranda, A. (1956), *Historia Política del Imperio Almohade*, vol. 1, Tetuan.

Humphreys, R. S. (1977a) 'The Emergence of the Mamluk Army', *Studia Islamica*, 45, pp. 67–99 and 147–82.

—— (1977b), *From Saladin to the Mongols: The Ayyubids of Damascus 1193–1260*, Albany New York.

Huuri, K. (1941), *Zur Geschichte des mittelalterliches Geschützwens, aus Orientalischen Quellen: Studia Orientalia*, Helsinki.

Ibn Abi Zar' (1860) (A. Beaumier trans.), *Rudh al-Qartas, Histoire des Souverains du Maghreb*, Paris.

Ibn Akhi Khazam (n.d.), *Kitab al-makhzun fi jami' al-funun* (Oriental Institute, Ms. Or.C.686. St Petersburg); see A. Alikberov and E. Rezvan, 'Ibn Abi Khazzam and his Kitab al-Makhzun: The Mamluk Military Manual', *Manuscripta Orientalia*, 1/1 (July 1995) pp. 21–8.

Ibn al-Athir (1872), 'Extrait de la Chronique intitulée Kamel Altevarykh', in *Recueil des Historiens des Croisades: Historiens Orientaux*, vol. I, Paris.

Ibn al-Furat (1971) (U. Lyons trans.), *Ayyubids, Memlukes and Crusaders: Selections from the Tarikh al-duwal wa'l-Muluk of Ibn al-Furat*, Cambridge.

Ibn al-Qalanisi (1908) (H. F. Amedroz ed.), *Bi Dhayl Tarikh Dimashq: History of Damascus*, Beirut.

—— (1932) (H. A. R. Gibb trans.), *The Damascus Chronicle of the Crusades*, London.

Ibn Anas, Iman Malik (1989) (A. A. Bewley trans.), *Al-Muwatta of Iman Malik ibn Anas: The First Formulation of Islamic Law*, London.

Ibn Hauqal (Hawqal) (1939) (J. K. Kramers ed.), *Liber Imaginis Terrae, Kitab Surat al 'Ard*, Leiden.

—— (1964) (J. K. Kramers and G. Wiet trans.), *Configuration de la Terre, Kitab Surat al 'Ard*, Beirut and Paris.

Ibn Hudayl al-Andalusi, 'Ali Ibn 'Abd al-Rahman (1924) (L. Mercier trans.), *La Parure des Cavaliers et l'Insigne des Preux*, Paris.

—— (1977) (M. J. Viguera trans.), *Gala de Caballeros, Blasons de Paladines*, Madrid.

Ibn Khaldun(1934) (De Slane trans.), *Histoire des Berbers*, vol. IV, Paris.

Ibn Maymun, Abu Muhammad Jamal al-Din 'Abd Allah (1945) (N. A. Faris and R. P. Elmer trans.), *Arab Archery*, Princeton.

Ibn Miskawaihi (1921) (D. S. Margoliouth ed. and trans.), *The Eclipse of the Baghdad Khalifate*, Oxford.

Imamuddin, S. M. (1965), *Some Aspects of the Socio-Economic and Cultural History of Muslim Spain 711–1492 AD*, Leiden.

Irwin, R. (1985), 'The Mamluk Conquest of the County of Tripoli', in P. W. Edbury (ed.), *Crusade and Settlement*, Cardiff, pp. 246–50.

—— (1986), 'Factions in Medieval Egypt', *Journal of the Royal Asiatic Society*, pp. 228–46.

—— (1994), 'How Many Miles to Babylon? The Devise des Chemins de Babilone Redated', in M. Barber (ed.), *The Military Orders: Fighting for the Faith, Caring for the Sick*, Aldershot, pp. 57–63.

Jackson, P. (1980), 'The Crisis of the Holy Land in 1260', *The English Historical Review*, 176, pp. 481–513.

Jahiz, al- (1915) (C. T. Harley-Walker trans.), 'Jahiz of Basra to Al-Fath Ibn Khaqan on the Exploits of the Turks and the Army of the Khalifate in General', *Journal of the Royal Asiatic Society*, pp. 631–7.

—— (1965) ('Abd al-Salim Muhammad Harun ed.), *Rasa'il a-Jahiz*, Cairo and Baghdad.

James, S. (2004), *Excavations at Dura-Europos 1928–1937: Final Report VII: The Arms and Armour and other Military Equipment*, London.

Johns, J. (1987), 'Malik Ifriqiya: The Norman Kingdom of Africa and the Fatimids', *Libyan Studies*, 18, pp. 89–101.

Jones, A. H. M. and E. Monro (1935), *A History of Abyssinia*, Oxford.

Jones, D. (1972), 'The Cappella Palatina in Palermo: Problems of Attribution', *Art and Archaeology Research Papers*, 1, pp. 41–7.

Jurji, E. J. (1940), 'The Islamic Theory of War', *The Moslem World*, 30, 3 pp. 32–42.

Kaegi, W. E. (1964), 'The contribution of archery to the Turkish conquest of Anatolia', *Speculum*, 39, pp. 96–108.

Kanimetov, A. *et al.* eds. (1983), *Pamyatniki Kulturya i Iskusstva Kirgizii*, Leningrad.

Kantorowixz, E. (1931), *Frederick the Second 1194–1250*, London.

Kedar, B. Z. (1982), 'The Patriarch Eraclius', in B. Z. Kedar (ed.), *Outremer: Studies in the history of the Crusading kingdom of Jerusalem presented to Joshua Prawer*, Jerusalem, pp. 177–204.

—— (1990), 'The Subjected Muslims of the Frankish Levant', in J. M. Powell (ed.), *Muslims under Latin Rule, 1100–1300*, Princeton, pp. 135–74.

—— (1992), 'The Battle of Hattin Revisited', in B. Z. Kedar (ed.), *The Horns of Hattin*, Jerusalem, pp. 190–207.

Kedar, B. Z. and D. Pringle (1985), 'La Fève: A Crusader Castle in the Jezreel Valley', *Israel Exploration Journal*, 25, pp. 164–79.

Khowaiter, A. A. (1978), *Baibars the First: His Endeavours and Achievements*, London.

Kindi, Ya'qub Ibn Ishaq al- (1952) (A. R. Zaki ed.), 'Al-Suyuf wa Ajnasuha', *Bulletin of the Faculty of Letters, Fuad I University*, 14, pp. 1–36.

—— (2006) (R. G. Hoyland and B. Gilmour trans.), *Medieval Islamic Swords and Swordmaking: Kindi's Treatise 'On Swords and their kinds'*, Oxford.

King, G. (2001), 'Alumni Archaeology team make exciting discoveries in Syria', *Alumni Newsletter (SOAS)*, 23 (Autumn), pp. 3–4.

Kohlberg, E. and B. Z. Kedar (1988), 'A Melkite Physician in Frankish Jerusalem and
    Ayyubid Damascus: Muwaffaq al-Din Ya'qub b. Siqlab', *Asian and African Studies*, 22,
    pp. 113–26.
Kollias, T. (1984), 'The Taktica of Leo VI the Wise and the Arabs', *Graeco-Arabica*, 33,
    pp. 129–35.
—— (1976), 'Ships, Shipping and the Implications of Change in the Early Medieval
    Mediterranean', *Viator*, 7, pp. 79–109.
Kreutz, B.M. (1976), 'Ships, Shipping and the Implications of Change in the Early Medieval
    Mediterranean', *Viator*, 7, pp. 79–109.
Krey, A. C. (1958), *The First Crusade: The Accounts of Eye-Witnesses and Participants*,
    Gloucester, MA.
Lacarra, J. M. (1947), 'La Conquista de Zaragoza por Alfonso I', *Al Andalus*, 12, pp. 65–96.
—— (1963), 'Les villes-frontière dans l'Espagne des XIe et XIIe siècles', *Le Moyen Age*, 69,
    pp. 202–22.
Lambton, A. K. S. (1965), 'Dihkan' (Dihqan), in *Encyclopedia of Islam*, vol. 2, 2nd edn, Leiden,
    pp. 253–4.
—— (1971), 'Islamic Mirrors for Princes', in (Anon, ed.), *La Persia nel Medioevo, Atti del
    Convegno Internazionale, Roma 1970*, Rome, pp. 419–42.
LaRocca, D. J. (ed.), *Warriors of the Himalayas: Rediscovering the Arms and Armor of Tibet*,
    New York.
Latham, J. D. (1968), 'The Meaning of Maydan as-Sibaq', *Journal of Semitic Studies*, 13,
    pp. 241–8.
—— (1969), 'Notes on Mamluk Horse-archers', *Bulletin of the School of Oriental and African
    Studies*, 32, pp. 257–67.
—— (1970), 'Archers of the Middle East: the Turco-Iranian Background', *Iran*, 8, pp. 97–103.
—— (1971), 'The Strategic Position and Defence of Ceuta in the Later Muslim Period', *Islamic
    Quarterly*, 15, pp. 189–204.
Latham, J. D. and W. F. Paterson (1965), 'An Analysis of Arrow-Weights in an Islamic Military
    Manual', *Journal of Semitic Studies*, 10, pp. 253–61.
—— *Saracen Archery*, see Taybugha al-Baklamishi al-Yunani, *Ghunat al-Murami*.
Laurent, J. (1913), *Byzance et les Turcs Seldjoucides dans l'Asie Occidentale jusqu'en 1081*,
    Nancy.
—— (1928), 'Byzance et Antioche sous de Curopalate Philarète', *Revue des Etudes Arméniennes*,
    8, pp. 61–72.
—— (1971) *Etudes d'Histoire Arménienne*, Louvain.
Le Strange, G. (n.d.), *Palestine under the Moslems: A Description of Syria and the Holy Land
    from AD 650 to 1500* (reprinted Beirut 1965).
Le Tourneau, R. (1960), 'Barghawata', in *Encyclopedia of Islam*, vol. 1, 2nd edn, Leiden,
    pp. 1043–4.
Leaf, W. (1983), 'Developments in the System of Armorial Insignia during the Ayyubid and
    Mamluk Periods', *Palestine Exploration Quarterly*, 115, pp. 61–74.
Leaf, W. and S. Purcell (1986), *Heraldic Symbols: Islamic Insignia and Western Heraldry*,
    London.
Leo VI (Emperor) (1771) (M. Joly de Maizeroi trans.), *Tactica*, Paris.
Lev, Y. (1980), 'The Fatimid Army, AH 358–427/968–1036 CE: Military and Social Aspects',
    Asian and African Studies, 14, pp. 165–92.
—— (1984), 'The Fatimid Navy, Byzantium and the Mediterranean Sea 909–1036 CE/297–427
    AH', *Byzantion*, 54, pp. 220–52.

—— (1988a), 'Persecution and Conversion to Islam in Eleventh-Century Egypt', *Asian and African Studies*, 22, pp. 73–91.

—— (1988b), *Saladin in Egypt*, Leiden.

—— (1995), 'The Fatimids and Byzantium, 10th–12th Centuries', *Graeco-Arabica*, 6, pp. 190–208.

—— (1996), 'Regime, Army and Society in Medieval Egypt, 9th–12th centuries', in Y. Lev (ed.), *War and Society in the Eastern Mediterranean, 7th–15th centuries*, Leiden, pp. 115–52.

—— (2001), 'Prisoners of War during the Fatimid-Ayyubid wars with the Crusaders', in M. Gervers (ed.), *Tolerance and Intolerance*, Syracuse New York, pp. 11–28.

Lévi Provençal, E. (1932), *L'Espagne Musulmane au Xème siècle*, Paris.

—— (1950–67), *Histoire de l'Espagne Musulmane*, Paris.

—— (1954), 'Une héröine de la Résistance Musulmane en Sicile au début du XIIIe Siècle', *Oriente Moderna*, 34, pp. 283–8.

Lewis, A. R. (1951), *Naval Power and Trade in the Mediterranean AD 500–1100*, Princeton.

—— (1964), 'La féodalitè dans le Toulousain et la France mèridionale (850–1050)', *Annales du Midi*, 76, pp. 247–59.

—— (1985), 'James the Conqueror: Montpellier and Southern France', in R. I. Burns (ed.), *The Worlds of Alfonso the Learned and James the Conqueror*, Princeton, pp. 130–49.

Lewis, B. (1974), *Islam from the Prophet Muhammad to the Capture of Constantinople*, vol. 1: *Politics and War*, New York.

Lewis, G. (1998), 'Heroines and Others in the Heroic Age of the Turks', in G. R. G. Hambly (ed.), *Women in the Medieval Islamic World: Power, Patronage and Piety*, London, pp. 147–60.

Liebel, J. (1998), *Springalds and Great Crossbows*, Leeds.

Ligato, G. (2000), 'Saladino e i prigioneri di guerra', in G. Cipollone (ed.), *La liberazione dei 'captive' tra Cristianita e Islam*, Vatican, pp. 649–54.

Lindner, R. P. (1981), 'Nomadism, Horses and Huns', *Past and Present*, 92, pp. 3–19.

Little, D. P. (1986), 'The fall of 'Akka in 690/1291: The Muslim version', in M. Shalon (ed.), *Studies in Islamic History and Civilization in Honour of Professor David Ayalon*, Jerusalem, pp. 159–81.

Livadas, G. K. (1995), 'Some Questions of Medieval Nautical Technology in Kameniates' "Sack of Thessaloniki" (904 AD)', *Graeco-Arabica*, 6, pp. 145–51.

Lokkegaard, F. (1987), 'The Concepts of Peace and War in Islam', in B. P. McGuire (ed.), *War and Peace in the Middle Ages*, Copenhagen, pp. 263–81.

Lomax, D. W. (1978), *The Reconquest of Spain*, London.

Lombard, M. (1966), *Les Métaux dans l'ancient Monde du Ve au XIe siècle*, Paris.

Lourie, L. (1966), 'A Society Organized for War: Medieval Spain', *Past and Present*, 35, pp. 54–76.

Lyon, B. D. (1957), *From Fief to Indenture: The Transition from Feudal to Non-Feudal Contract in Western Europe*, Cambridge, MA.

Lyons, M. C. (2001), 'The Land of War: Europe in the Arab Hero Cycles', in A. E. Aiou and P. R. Mottadeh (eds.), *The Crusades from the Perspective of Byzantium and the Muslim World*, Washington, pp. 41–51.

Lyons, M. C. and D. E. P. Jackson (1982), *Saladin: The Politics of the Holy War*, Cambridge.

Mantran, R. and C. De La Roncière (1986), 'Africa opens up to the Old Worlds', in R. Fossier (ed.), *The Cambridge Illustrated History of the Middle Ages*, vol. III: *1250–1520*, London, pp. 356–96.

Maqrizi, al- (1980) (R. J. C. Broadhurst trans.), *A History of the Ayyubid Sultans of Egypt (Al Maqrizi)*, Boston.

Marcais, G. (1948), *La Berbérie Musulmane et l'Orient au Moyen Age*, Paris.

Marco Polo (1908) (J. Masefield trans.), *The Travels of Marco Polo*, London.

Marsden, J. D. (1967), 'The Reign of Muhammad V, Sultan of Granada', MA thesis, Manchester University.

Marshall, C.J. (1990), 'The Use of the Charge in Battle in the Latin East, 1192–1291', *Historical Research (Bulletin of the Institute of)*, 63, pp. 221–6.

Martinez, A. P. (1986–8), 'Some Notes on the Il-Xanid Army', *Archivum Eurasiae Medii Aevi*, 6, pp. 129–242.

Mas'udi, al- (1861–77) (C. Barbier de Maynard and P. De Courteille, eds. and trans.), *Muruj al-Dahab: Les Prairies d'Or*, Paris.

Matuz, J. (1973), 'Die Niedergand der anatolischen Seldschuken: Die Entscheidungsschlacht am Kösedağ', *Central Asiatic Journal*, 17, pp. 180–99.

Matveev, A. (1998a), 'A propos the causes of the success of the First Crusade: The Oriental point of view', unpublished article.

—— (1998b), 'Main Aspects of "Classic" Mongol Warfare (late twelfth – early thirteenth centuries)', in L. E. Nemchinova and T. M. Tallerchik (eds), *Military Archaeology*, St Petersburg, pp. 314–19.

Maulana Minhaj al-Din (n.d.) (H. G. Raverty trans.), *Tabakat-i Nasiri: A General History of the Muhammad Dynasties of Asia* (reprinted New Delhi 1970).

Mayer, H. E. (1978), 'Latins, Muslims and Greeks in the Latin Kingdom of Jerusalem', *History*, 63, pp. 175–92.

McEwen, E. (1977), 'Nomad Archery', paper read at Colloquy on Arts of the Eurasian Steppelands, SOAS, London, 27 June.

Melikian-Chirvani, A. S. (1981), 'Notes sur le terminologie de la metallurgie et des armes dans l'Iran Musulman', *Journal of the Economic and Social History of the Orient*, 24, pp. 310–16.

Menéndez Pidal, R. (1971), *The Cid and his Spain*, London.

Messier, R. A. (1986), 'The Christian Community of Tunis at the Time of St Louis' Crusade, AD 1270', in V. P. Goss and C. V. Bornstein (eds.), *The Meeting of Two Worlds: Cultural Exchange between East and West during the Period of the Crusades*, Kalamazoo, pp. 241–55.

Michaudel, B. (2004), 'Les refortifications ayyoubides et mameloukes en Syrie du Nord (fin XIIe-début XIVe siècles)', in N. Faucherre, J. Mesqui, N. Prouteau and J. Richard (eds.), *La Fortification au Temps des Croisades*, Rennes, pp. 179–88.

Miller, I. (1993), Correspondence on *qarajuli* swords, 2 April.

Miller, R. (1985a), 'Experimental Approaches to Ancient Near Eastern Archery', lecture at the Institute of Archaeology & Anthropology, Yarmouk University, Irbid, 5 November.

—— (1985b), 'Jabal Ajlun iron working', lecture at the Archaeological Museum, Amman.

Minnis, D. and Y. Bader (1988), 'A Comparative Analysis of Belvoir (Kawkab al-Hawa) and Qal'at al-Rabad ('Ajlun Castle)', *Annual of the Department of Antiquities of Jordan*, 32, pp. 255–64.

Mirza, N.A. (1963), 'The Syrian Isma'ilis at the Time of the Crusades', PhD thesis, Durham University.

Mitchell, P. D. (2004), *Medicine in the Crusades: Warfare, Wounds and the Medieval Surgeon*, Cambridge.

Mitchell, R. (2003), Correspondence on hardened leather armour and shields, 13 August.

Molin, B. K. (1996), 'The Role of Castles in the Political and Military History of the Crusader States and the Levant, 1187–1380', PhD thesis, Leeds University.

Morgan, D. O. (1968), *The Mongols*, Oxford.

—— (1979), 'The Mongol Armies in Persia', *Der Islam*, 56, pp. 81–96.

—— (1985), 'The Mongols in Syria, 1260–1300', in P. W. Edbury (ed.), *Crusade and Settlement:*

papers read at the first conference of the SSCLE, Cardiff, pp. 231–5.

—— (1989), 'The Mongols and the Eastern Mediterranean', in B. Arbel, B. Hamilton and D. Jacoby (eds.), *Latins and Greeks in the Eastern Mediterranean after 1204*, London, pp. 198–211.

Mottahedeh, R. P. (1980), *Loyalty and Leadership in an Early Islamic Society*, Princeton.

Mullett, M. (1996), '1098 and all that; Theophylact, Bishop of Semnea and the Alexian Reconquest of Anatolia', *Peritia*, 10, 235–53.

Nasawi, Muhammad Ibn Ahmad al (1895) (O. Houdas ed. and trans.), *Sirat-i Jalal al-Din: Histoire du Sultan Djelal ed-Din Mankobirti, Prince of Khwareym*, Paris.

Nasir-i Khusrau (1881) (G. Shefer, ed. and trans.), *Sefer Nameh: Relation du Voyage de Nassiri Khosrau*, Paris (reprinted Amsterdam 1970).

—— (1888) (G. Le Strange trans.), *Diary of a Journey through Syria and Palestine by Nâsir-i-Khusrau in 1047 AD*, London (reprinted Ann Arbor 1977).

Needham, J. (1976), 'China's Trebuchets, Manned and Counterweighted', in B. S. Hall and D. C. West (eds.), *On Pre-Modern Technology and Science: Studies in Honor of Lynn White jr.*, Malibu, pp. 107–45.

—— (1994), *Science and Civilization in China*, Vol. 5. *Chemistry and Chemical Technology, Part IV. Military Technology: Missiles and Sieges*, Cambridge.

Nicholson, R.L. (1940), *Tancred: A Study of his Career and Work*, Chicago.

—— (1973), *Joscelyn III and the Fall of the Crusader States, 1134–1199*, Leiden.

Nicolle, D. C. (1975), 'The 'Askalan Strip', *Middle East International*, 53 (November), pp. 29–31.

—— (1983), 'Arms Manufacture and the Arms Trade in South-Eastern Arabia in the Early Muslim Period', *The Journal of Oman Studies*, 6, pp. 231–8.

—— (1989), 'Shipping in Islamic Art: Seventh Through Sixteenth Century AD', *American Neptune*, 49, pp. 168–97.

—— (1990), *Attila and the Nomad Hordes*, London.

—— (1992), 'Byzantine and Islamic Arms and Armour; Evidence for Mutual Influence', *Graeco-Arabica*, 4, pp. 299–325.

—— (1993a), *Armies of the Muslim Conquests*, London.

—— (1993b), *Hattin 1187*, London.

—— (1994a), 'The Reality of Mamluk Warfare: Weapons, Armour and Tactics' (translation of Chapter Two, Lesson Seven of the Nihâyat al-Su'l), *Al-Masâq*, 7, pp. 77–111.

—— (1994b), *Saracen Faris 1050–1250 AD*, London.

—— (1994c), *Yarmuk 636 AD*, London.

—— (1995), 'No Way Overland: Evidence for Byzantine Arms and Armour on the 10th–11th Century Taurus Frontier', *Graeco-Arabica*, 6, pp. 226–45.

—— (1997), 'Arms of the Umayyad Era: Military Technology in a Time of Change', in Y. Lev (ed.), *War and Society in the Eastern Mediterranean*, Leiden and New York, pp. 9–100.

—— (1999) *Arms & Armour of the Crusading Era 1050–1350: Islam, Eastern Europe and Asia*, London.

—— (2000), 'Moors against Majus: The defence of Spain and Morocco against the Vikings 844–972 AD', *Osprey Military Journal* II/3 (May), pp. 23–32.

—— (2002a) 'Jawshan, Cuirie and Coat-of-Plates: An Alternative Line of Development for Hardened Leather Armour', in D. C. Nicolle (ed.), *A Companion to Medieval Arms and Armour*, Woodbridge, pp. 179–221 and pls. XIII–1 to XIII–45.

—— (2002b), 'Medieval Islamic Navigation in the Atlantic', *Journal of Medieval and Islamic History (Cairo)*, 2, pp. 3–14.

—— (2002c), *Medieval Siege Weapons (2): Byzantium, the Islamic World & India AD 476–1562*, Oxford.

—— (2004a), 'Silah: The Islamic Period', in *Encyclopedia of Islam, Supplement, fasc. 11–12*, 2nd edn, Leiden, pp. 736–46 plus fig.

—— (2004b), 'The Early Trebuchet: Documentary and Archaeological Evidence', in N. Faucherre, J. Mesqui, N. Prouteau and J. Richard (eds.), *La Fortification au Temps des Croisades*, Rennes, pp. 269–78.

—— (2005), *The Third Crusade 1191*, Oxford.

—— (forthcoming), *Late Mamluk & Early Ottoman Military Equipment in the Light of Finds from the Citadel of Damascus*, Damascus forthcoming, 2007.

Nielsen, J. S. (1991), 'Between Arab and Turk: Aleppo from the 11th till the 13th centuries', *Byzantinische Forschungen*, 16, pp. 323–40.

Nishimura, D. (1988), 'Crossbows, Arrow Guides, and the Solenarion', *Byzantion*, 58, pp. 422–35.

Nizam al-Mulk (1932) (S. 'Abd al-Rahman Khalkhali ed.), *Siyasat Nama*, Tehran.

—— (1960) (H. Darke trans.), *The Book of Government or Rules for Kings: The Siyasat Nama*, London.

Norris, H. T. (1972) *Saharan Myth and Saga*, Oxford.

—— (1982), *The Berbers in Arabic Literature*, London.

—— (1984), 'Caves and Strongholds from the Moorish Period around the Rock of Gibraltar', *The Maghreb Review*, 9, pp. 39–45.

Northedge, A. (1983), 'The Fortification of Qal'at 'Amman ('Amman Citadel): Preliminary Report', *Annual of the Department of Antiquities (Amman)*, 27, pp. 437–59.

Northrup, L. S. (1974), 'Muslim-Christian relations during the reign of the Mamluk Sultan al-Malik al-Mansur Qala'un (678/1279–689/1290)', MA thesis, McGill University.

Obolensky, D. (1974), 'The Byzantine Frontier Zones and Cultural Exchange', in Anon (ed.), *Actes du XIVe Congrés Internationale des Etudes byzantines (Bucarest 1971)*, vol. I, Bucharest, pp. 303–13.

—— (1978), 'The Crimea and the North before 1204', in Anon (ed.), *Byzantine Black Sea (Symposium, Birmingham University, 18–20 March 1978)*, Athens, pp. 123–33.

Onon, U. (2001), 'The Art of War under Chinggis Qahan (Genghis Khan)', in U. Onon (ed.) *The Secret History of the Mongols: The Life and Times of Chinggis Khan*, London.

Painter, G. D. (1965), 'The Tartar Relation', in R. A. Skelton, T. E. Marston and G. D. Painter (eds.), *The Vinland Map and the Tartar Relation*, New Haven, pp. 19–106.

Pálóczi Horváth, A. (1989), *Pechenegs, Cumans, Iasians: Steppes Peoples in Medieval Hungary*, Budapest.

Partington, J. R. (1960), *A History of Greek Fire and Gunpowder*, Cambridge.

Paterson, L.M. (1988), 'Military Surgery: Knights, Sergeants and Raimon of Avignon's Version of the Chirurgia of Roger of Salerno (1180–1209)', in C. Harper-Bill (ed.), *The Ideals and Practice of Medieval Knighthood: Papers from the Third Strawberry Hill Conference, II*, Woodbridge, pp. 117–46.

Paterson, W. F. (1963), 'Thumb Guards', *Journal of the Society of Archer Antiquaries*, 6, pp. 14–15.

—— (1969), 'Shooting under a Shield', *Journal of the Society of Archer Antiquaries*, 12, pp. 27–8.

—— (1983), Correspondence on Nubian, Seljuk and Italian bows, 29 January.

—— (1990), *A Guide to the Crossbow* (A.G. Credland, ed.), London.

Patton, D. L. (1982), 'A History of the Atabegs of Mosul and their Relations with the Ulama, AH 521–660/AD 1127–1262', PhD thesis, New York University.

Pellat, C. and W. T. Najim (1969), *The Life and Works of Al Jahiz*, Berkeley.

Pérès, H. (1953), *Poésie Andalouse en Arabe Classique*, Paris.

Peters, R. (1977), *Jihad in Medieval and Modern Islam*, Leiden.

Pieri, P. (1953), 'I Saraceni di Lucera nella storia militare medievale', *Archivio Storico Pugliese*, 6, pp. 94–101.

Powell, J. M. (1999), 'Frederick II and the rebellion of the Muslims of Sicily 1200–1224', in Anon (ed.), *Ulusararasi Haçlı Seferleri Sempozyumu, 23–25 Harıran 1997, Istanbul*, Ankara, pp. 13–22.

Powers, J. F. (1994), 'Life on the Cutting Edge: The Besieged Town in the Luso-Hispanic Frontier in the Twelfth Century', in I. A. Corfis (ed.), *The Medieval City under Siege*, Woodbridge, pp. 17–34.

Prawer, J. (1972), *The Crusaders' Kingdom*, New York.

—— (1980), *Crusader Institutions*, Oxford.

Pringle, R.D. (1994), 'Town Defences in the Crusader Kingdom of Jerusalem', in I. Corfis and M. Wolfe (eds), *The Medieval City under Siege*, Woodbridge, pp. 69–121.

Pryor, J. H. (1982), 'Transportation of Horses by Sea during the Era of the Crusades, Eighth Century to 1285 AD', *Mariner's Mirror*, 68, pp. 9–27 and 103–26.

—— (1988), *Geography, Technology and War: Studies in the Maritime History of the Mediterranean 649–1571*, Cambridge.

—— (1992), 'The Crusade of Emperor Frederick II: 1220–29: The Implications of the Maritime Evidence', *American Neptune*, 52, pp. 113–31.

Pryor, J. H. and S. Bellabarba (1990), 'The Medieval Muslim Ships of the Pisan Bacini', *Mariner's Mirror*, 76, pp. 99–113.

Psellus, M. (1966), *Fourteen Byzantine Rulers* (E.R.A. Sewter trans.), London.

Qalqashandi, Ahmad Ibn 'Abd Allah al- (1903–19) (Ibn al-Ghuddah ed.), *Subh al-A'sha*, Cairo.

Rabie, H. M. (1972), *The Financial System of Egypt 564–741AH/1169–1341AD*, Oxford.

—— (1975), 'The Training of the Mamluk Faris', in V. J. Parry and M. E. Yapp (eds.), *War, Technology and Society in the Middle East*, London, pp. 153–63.

Rady, M. (1991), 'The Mongol Invasion of Hungary', *Medieval World*, 3 (November–December), pp. 39–46.

Ranitzsch, K. H. (1995), *The Army of Tang China*, Stockport.

Rashad Mohamad, A. M. (1963), 'The Abbasid Caliphate (575/1179–656/1258)', PhD thesis, London University.

Rausing, E. (1967), *The Bow: Some Notes on its Origins and Development. Acta Archaeologica Lundensia, VI*, Lund.

Ricard, R. and L. Torres Balbás (1948), 'Cáceres y su cerca Almohade', *Al Andalus*, 13, pp. 446–75.

Rice, D. S. (1952), 'Medieval Harran: Studies in its Topography and Monuments, I', *Anatolian Studies*, 2, pp. 36–84.

Rice, T. T. (1961), *The Seljuks*, London.

Richard, J. (1979a), 'Les causes de victoires Mongoles d'après les historiens occidentaux du XIIIe siècle', *Central Asiatic Journal*, 23, pp. 104–17.

—— (1979b), 'Les causes de victoires Mongoles d'après les historiens occidentaux du XIIIe siècle', *Central Asiatic Journal*, 23, pp. 104–17.

—— (1979c), *The Latin Kingdom of Jerusalem*, Oxford.

—— (1986), 'Les Turcopoles: Musulmans Convertes ou Chrétiens Orientaux', *Revue des Etudes Islamiques*, 54, pp. 259–70.

—— (1998) 'Les prisoniers et leur rachat au cours des croisades', in Anon (ed.), *121e congrés nationales des Sociétés Savants. Hist. Scient. Nice 1996, Histoire médiévales – Fondations*, Paris, pp. 63–73.

Rist, R. (2003), 'Papal Policy and the Albigensian Crusades: Continuity or Change?', *Crusades*, 2, pp. 99–108.

Rivallain, J. (1996), 'The Horse, the Status Mount of Africa', in D. Alexander (ed.), *Furusiyya*, vol. 1. *The Horse in the Art of the Near East*, Riyadh, pp. 216–21.

Rogers, R. (1992), *Latin Siege Warfare in the Twelfth Century*, Oxford.

Rose, R. B. (1992), 'The Native Christians of Jerusalem, 1187–1260', in B. D. Kedar (ed.), *The Horns of Hattin*, Jerusalem and London, pp. 238–49.

Rouche, M. (1979), *L'Aquitaine des Wisigoths aux Arabes*.

Russell, J. C. (1986), 'Demographic Factors of the Crusades', in V. P. Goss and C. V. Bornstein (eds.), *The Meeting of Two Worlds: Cultural Exchange between East and West during the Period of the Crusades*, Kalamazoo, pp. 53–8.

Ryckmans, J. (1973), 'L'apparition du cheval en Arabie Ancienne', *Jaarbericht 'Ex Oriente Lux'*, 17, pp. 211–26.

Saleh (Salih), A. H. (1980), 'Le role des bedouins d'égypte à l'époque fatimide', *Rivista degli Studi Orientali*, 54, pp. 51–65.

—— (1978), 'Quelques remarques sur les bédouins d'Egypte au Moyen-Age', *Studia Islamica*, 48, pp. 45–70.

—— (1979), 'Saladins et les Bédouins d'Egypte', *Rendiconti della Reale Accademia Nazionale dei Lincei, Scienze Morali*, 34, pp. 349–54.

Salibi, K.S. (1957), 'The Maronites of Lebanon under Frankish and Mamluk Rule', *Arabica*, 4, pp. 288–303.

—— (1977), *Syria under Islam*: vol. 1; *Empire on Trial 634–1097*, New York.

Salinger, G. (1950), 'Was the Futuwa an Oriental Form of Chivalry?', *Proceedings of the American Philosophical Society*, 94, pp. 481–93.

Sanders, P. (1984), 'The Court Ceremonial of the Fatimid Caliphate in Egypt', PhD thesis, Princeton University.

Sarraf, S. al- (1996), 'Furusîyya Literature of the Mamluk Period', in D. Alexander (ed.), *Furusiyya*, volume 1. *The Horse in the Art of the Near East*, Riyadh, pp. 118–35.

—— (2002a), 'Close Combat Weapons in the Early 'Abbasid Period: Maces, Axes and Swords', in D. Nicolle (ed.), *A Companion to Medieval Arms and Armour*, Woodbridge, pp. 149–78.

—— (2002b), 'Evolution du concept du furûsiyya et de sa littérature chez les Abbassides et les Mamloukes', in E. Delpont (ed.), *Chevaux et Cavaliers Arabes dans les arts d'Orient et d'Occident*, Paris, pp. 67–71.

—— (2002c), Conversation on the conversion of medieval Arabic *ratl* weight measurements, April.

Savvides, A. G. C. (2000a), 'Can we refer to concerted action amongst Rapsomates, Caryces and the Emir Tzachas between AD 1091 and 1093?' *Byzantion*, 70, pp. 122–34.

—— (2000b), 'Kilij Arslan I of Rum, Byzantines, Crusaders and Danishmandids AD 1092–1107', *Byzantina*, 21, pp. 365–77.

Sayer, I.M. (1951), 'The Empire of the Salcuqids of Asia Minor', *Journal of Near Eastern Studies*, 10, pp. 268–80.

Schamiloglu, U. (1986), 'Tribal Politics and Social Organization in the Golden Horde', PhD thesis, Columbia University.

Schneidman, J. L. (1970), *The Rise of the Aragonese–Catalan Empire 1200–1350*, London.

Schröder, B. (1922), 'Helme und panzer aus Krokodilhaut', *Berliner Museen*, 43, pp. 11–75.

Schwarzer, J. K. (1988), 'The Eleventh Century Weapons from Serçe Limani', paper read at Third International Congress on Greek-Arabic Studies, Athens, 17–20 July.

—— (1991), 'Arms from an Eleventh Century Shipwreck', *Graeco-Arabica*, 4, pp. 327–50.

Sezgin, F. and E. Neubauer (2004) (F. Benfeghoul trans.), 'Technique militaire', in *Sciences et Technique en Islam*, vol. 5, Frankfurt, pp. 91–138.

Sinclair, T. (1983), 'Byzantine and Islamic Fortifications in the Middle East – the Photographic Exhibition', in S. Mitchell (ed.), *Armies and Frontiers in Roman and Byzantine Anatolia. British Archaeeological Reports, Int. Series 156*, Oxford, pp. 305–30.

Sivan, E. (1968), *L'Islam et la Croisade, Idéologie et propagande dans les réactions musulmanes aux croisades*, Paris.

Slousch, N. (1910), 'L'Empire des Berghouata et les origines des Blad es-Siba', *Revue du Monde Musulman*, 10, pp. 394–400.

Smail, R. C. (1956), *Crusading Warfare, 1097–1193*, Cambridge.

Smail, R. C. (1982), 'The Predicaments of Guy of Lusignan, 1183–87', in B. Z. Kedar (ed.), *Outremer, Studies in the History of the Crusading Kingdom of Jerusalem presented to Joshua Prawer*, Jerusalem, pp. 159–76.

Smbat (1980) (G. Dédéyan trans.), *La Chronique Attribué au Connétable Smbat*, Paris.

Smith, G. R. (1978), *The Ayyubids and Early Rasulids in the Yemen (567–694/1173–1295): Gibb Memorial Series, XXVI/2*, London.

Smith, J. M. (J. Masson Smith) (1984a), 'Mamluk Training and Tactics', paper read at the American Historical Association, Chicago, 30 December.

—— (1984b), '"Ayn Jalut: Mamluk Success or Mongol Failure?' *Harvard Journal of Asiatic Studies*, 44, pp. 307–45.

—— (1996) 'Mongol Society and Military in the Middle East; Antecedents and Adaptations', in Y. Lev (ed.), *War and Society in the Eastern Mediterranean, 7th–15th centuries*, Leiden, pp. 249–66.

Soler Del Campo, A. (1986), 'Sistemas de Combate en la Iconografia Mozarabe y Andalusi Altomedieval', *Boletín de la Asociación Española de Orientalistas*, 22, pp. 61–87.

—— (1993), *La evolucion del armamento medieval en el reino castellano-leonés y Al-Andalus*, Madrid.

Somogyi, J. (1948), 'Adh-Dhahabi's Record of the Destruction of Damascus by the Mongols in 699–700/1299–1300', in S. Löwinger (J. Somogyi, ed.), *Ignace Goldziher Memorial Volume, Part 1*, pp. 353–86 (Budapest).

Sourdel-Thomine, J. (1960), 'Burdj: Military Architecture in the Islamic Middle East', in *Encyclopedia of Islam*, volume 1, 2nd edn, Leiden, pp. 1315–18.

Spinei, V. (1974), 'Antichitatile nomazilor turanici din Molova în primul sfert al mileniului al II-lea', *Studii si cercetari do Istorie veche si Arheologi*, 25, pp. 389–415.

—— (1986), *Moldavia in the 11th–14th Centuries*, Bucharest.

Squiers, G. (1958), 'Tartar Training for Use of the Bow', *Journal of the Society of Archer Antiquaries*, 10, p. 10.

Staffa, S. J. (1977), *Conquest and Fusion: The Social Evolution of Cairo AD 642–1850*, Leiden.

Stein, A. (1912), *Ruins of Desert Cathay*, London.

—— (1933), *On Ancient Central Asian Tracks*, London.

Stern, S. M. (1956), 'An Original Document from the Fatimid Chancery concerning Italian merchants', in Anon (ed.), *Studi Orientalistici in Onore di Giorgio Levi della Vida*, Rome, pp. 529–38.

Tabari, al- (M.J. de Goeje) (1879–1901), *Tarikh al-Rusul wa'l-Muluk*, Leiden.

Tabbaa, Y. (1986) 'Monuments with a Message: Propagation of Jihad under Nur al-Din (1146–1174)', in V. P. Goss and C. V. Bornstein (eds.), *The Meeting of Two Worlds: Cultural Exchange between East and West during the Period of the Crusades*, Kalamazoo, pp. 223–40.

Taeschner, Fr. (1965), 'Futuwwa', in *Encyclopedia of Islam*, volume 2, 2nd edn, Leiden, pp. 961–9.

Tamari, S. (1978), 'Qal'at al Tina in Sinai, An Historical-Architectural Analysis', *Annali, Istituto Orientale di Napoli*, 38, pp. 1–78.

Tantum, G. (1979), 'Muslim warfare: a study of a medieval Muslim treatise on the art of war', in R. Elgood (ed.), *Islamic Arms and Armour*, London, pp. 187–201.

Tanukhi, Muhassin Ibn 'Ali al- (1922) (D. S. Margoliouth trans.), *The Table-Talk of a Mesopotamian Judge*, London.

Tarsusi, Murda Ibn 'Ali Murda al- (1947–8) (C. Cahen ed. and trans.), 'Une traité d'armurerie composé pour Saladin', *Bulletin d'Etudes Orientales de l'Institut Français de Damas*, 12, pp. 103–60.

—— (1968) (A. Boudot-Lamotte tr.), *Contribution à l'Etude de l'Archerie Musulmane*, Damascus.

Taybugha al-Baklamishi al-Yunani (1970), *Ghunat al-Murami* (J. D. Latham and W. F. Paterson), *Saracen Archery: An English Version and Exposition of a Mameluke Work on Archery (ca. AD 1368)*, London.

Tazi, 'Abd al-Hadi al- (2004), Correspondence on the *qarqal*, 22 June.

Terrasse, H. (1960), 'Burdj: Military architecture in the Muslim West', in *Encyclopedia of Islam*, volume 1, 2nd edn, Leiden, pp. 1318–21.

—— (1965), 'La Vie d'un Royaume Berbère du XIe siècle Espagnol: L'Emirat Ziride de Grenade', *Melanges de la Casa de Velazquez*, 1, pp. 73–85.

—— (1971), 'Hisn: The Muslim West', in *Encyclopedia of Islam*, volume 3, 2nd edn, Leiden, pp. 498–501.

Thorau, P. (1987), *The Lion of Egypt: Sultan Baybars I & the Near East in the Thirteenth Century*, London.

Thordeman, B. (1939), *Armour from the Battle of Wisby 1361*, Uppsala.

Tibbetts, G. R. (1971), *Arab Navigation in the Indian Ocean Before the Coming of the Portuguese*, London.

Tibi, A. T. (1971–2), 'The Tibyan of 'Abdullah b. Buluggin, last Zirid amir of Granada', D Phil thesis, Oxford University.

Tonghini, C. and N. Montevecchi (2004), 'The Castle of Shayzar: the results of recent archaeological investigations', in N. Faucherre, J. Mesqui, N. Prouteau and J. Richard (eds.), *La Fortification aux Temps des Croisades*, Rennes, pp. 137–50.

Torres Delgado, C. (1980), 'El Mediterráneo Nazarí. Diplomacia y Piratería, Siglos XIII–XIV', *Anuario de Estudios Medieval*, 10, pp. 227–36.

—— (1988), 'El Ejercito y las Fortificaciones del Reino Nazari di Granada', in *Gladius: Las Armas en la Historia* (special volume), Madrid, pp. 197–217.

Toueir, K. (1983), 'Heraqlah: a Unique Victory Monument of Harin ar-Rashid', *World Archaeology*, 14, pp. 296–304.

—— (2004), 'Das Hiraqla des Harun ar-Rasid', in V. Daiber and A. Becker (eds), *Raqqa III: Baudenkmäler und Paläste I*, Mainz, pp. 137–42.

Toumanoff, C. (1966), 'Armenia and Georgia', in J. M. Hussey (ed.), *The Cambridge Medieval History*, vol. IV. *The Byzantine Empire part I. Byzantium and its Neighbours*, Cambridge, pp. 593–637.

Turan, O. (1955), 'World Domination Among the Medieval Turks', *Studia Islamica*, 4, pp. 77–90.

Turnbull, S. (2001), *Siege Weapons of the Far East (1): AD 612–1300*, Oxford.

—— (2003), 'Mongol Strategy and the Battle of Leignitz 1241', *Medieval History*, 3 (November), pp. 38–45.

Turtushi, Muhammad Ibn Walid al- (1931) (M. Alarcón trans.), *Lámpara de los Príncipes*, Madrid.

—— (n.d.) (Anon, ed.), *Siraj al-Muluk*, Cairo.

Umari, Ibn Fadl Allah al- (1927) (Gaudefroy-Denombynes trans.), *Masalik el Absar fi Mamalik el Ansar*, Paris.

Unger, R. W. (1980), *The Ship in the Mediterranean Economy 600–1600*, London.

Usamah Ibn Munqidh (1929) (P. K. Hitti trans.), *The Memoirs of an Arab-Syrian Gentleman*, Princeton (reprinted Beirut, 1964).

—— (1930) (P. K. Hitti ed.), *Kitab al-I'tibar*, Princeton.

Vachon, V. (2004), 'Les Châteaux Isma'iliens du Djabal Bahra', in N. Faucherre, J. Mesqui, N. Prouteau and J. Richard (eds.), *La Fortification au Temps des Croisades*, Rennes, pp. 219–241.

Valdés Fernández (1988), 'Ciudadela y fortificación urbana: el case de Badajoz', in A. Bazzana (ed.), *Castrum III*, Madrid, pp. 143–52.

Van Tongerloo, A. (1997), 'Turcological Notes on the Mamlûk Court Literature', paper read at the Sixth Colloquium on Egyptian and Syria Studies in the Fatimid, Ayyubid and Mamluk Periods, Leuven, 16 May.

Vasiliev, A. A. (1934–50), *Byzance et les Arabes*, Brussels.

Verbruggen, J.F. (1977a), 'De Goedendag', *Militaria Belgica*, 3, pp. 65–70.

—— (1977b), *The Art of Warfare in Western Europe during the Middle Ages*, Oxford.

Villehardouin (1921) (F. Marzials tr.), *Memoirs of the Crusades by Villehardouin and de Joinville* (London 1921) pp. 1–133.

Villehardouin, G. de (1952) 'La Conquête de Constantinople' (A. Pauphilet and E. Pognon eds), in *Historiens et Chroniquers du Moyen Age*, Paris, pp. 89–194.

Voisin, J-C. (2004), 'Le Moyen-Orient des fortifications: espace d'échanges entre Byzantins, Arabo-musulmans et Occidentaux du Moyen Age', in N. Faucherre, J. Mesqui, N. Prouteau and J. Richard (eds.), *La Fortification au Temps des Croisades*, Rennes, pp. 313–29.

Von Oppenhein, M. (1926), 'Der Djerid und das Djerid-Spiel', *Islamica*, 2, pp. 590–617.

Von Pawlikowski-Cholewa, A. (1940), *Die Heere des Morgenlandes*, Berlin.

Vryonis, S. (1971), *The Decline of Medieval Hellenism in Asia Minor and the Process of Islamization from the Eleventh through the Fifteenth Century*, Berkeley.

—— (1975), 'Byzantine and Turkish Societies and their Sources of Manpower', in V. J. Parry and M. E. Yapp (eds), *War, Technology and Society in the Middle East*, London, pp. 125–52.

Walker, J. M. (1961), 'The Saracens in the Thirteenth-Century Chansons de Geste and Romances', MA thesis, London University.

Walter the Chancellor (1999) (T. S. Asbridge and S. B. Edgington, trans.), *Walter the Chancellor's The Antiochene Wars*, Aldershot.

Wasserstein, D. (1985), *The Rise and Fall of the Party Kings*, Princeton.

Weigert, G. (1996), 'A Note on Hudna: Peacemaking in Islam', in Y. Lev (ed.), *War and Society in the Eastern Mediterranean, 7th–15th Centuries*, Leiden, pp. 399–405.

Weinberger, J. W. (1984), 'The Rise of Muslim Cities in Soghdia, 700–1220', PhD thesis, University of California, Berkeley.

Whittow, M. (1996), 'How the East was Lost: The Background to the Komnenian Reconquista', in M. Mullett (ed.), *Alexios I Komnenos. Belfast Byzantine Texts and Translations 4*, Belfast, pp. 56–67.

Wiedemann, E. (1970), *Aufsätze zur Arabizchen Wissenschafts-Geschichte*, Hildesheim.

Wiet, G. (1938), 'Les relations égypto-abyssines sous les sultans Mamlouks', *Bulletin de la Société d'archéologie copte*, 4, pp. 115–40.

Willey, P. (1963), *The Castles of the Assassins*, London.

William of Rubruck (1900) (W. W. Rockhill trans.), 'The Journey of William of Rubruck', in W. W. Rockhill (ed.), *The Journey of William of Rubruck to the Eastern Parts of the World 1253–55, as narrated by himself, with two accounts of the earlier journey by John of Pian de Carpine*, London, pp. 40–283.

—— (1955) (C. Dawson trans.), 'The Journey of William of Rubruck', in C. Dawson (ed.), *The Mongol Mission*, London.

—— (1990) (P. Jackson trans.), *The Mission of Friar William of Rubruck: His journey to the court of the Great Khan Möngke 1253–1255*, London.

Wittek, P. (1936), 'Deux chapitres de l'histoire des Turcs de Roum', *Byzantion*, 6, pp. 285–319.

Wolff, F. (1965), *Glossar zu Firdosis Schahname*, Hildesheim.

Yarnley, C. J. (1972), 'Byzantine Relations with the Armenians in the Eleventh Century, with Special Reference to Cilicia', B Litt thesis, Oxford University.

Yarrison, J. L. (1982), 'Force of an Instrument of Policy: European Military Incursions and Trade in the Maghrib, 1000–1355', PhD thesis, Princeton University.

Yovitchich, C. (2004), 'La citadelle de Bosra', in N. Faucherre, J. Mesqui, N. Prouteau and J. Richard (eds), *La Fortification au Temps des Croisades*, Rennes, pp. 205–17.

Zahir, Al-Qadi Muhi al-Din Ibn 'Abd al- (1956) (S. F. Sadeque trans.), *Baybars I of Egypt: Sirat al Malik al Zahir*, Oxford.

Zajaczkowski, A. (1965; 1968–9), 'Chapitres choises du Vocabulaire arabe-kipchak 'ad-Durrat al-mudi'a fi-l-lugat at-turkiya' (three parts), *Rocznik Orientalistyczny*, 29 (1965) pp. 39–38 and 67–105; 32 (1968–9) pp. 19–61.

Zakkar, S. (1969), 'The Emirate of Aleppo 392/1002–487/1094', PhD thesis, London University.

Zanki, J. H. M. A. al- (1989), 'The Emirate of Damascus in the Early Crusading Period 488–549/1095–1153', PhD thesis, St Andrews University.

Zardkash, Ibn Urunbugha al- (1985) (M. I. Hindi ed.), *Al-aniq fi'l-manajaniq*, Aleppo.

Ziadeh, N. A. (1953), *Urban Life in Syria under the Mamluks*, Westport.

Zozaya, J. (1988), 'Evolución de un yacimiento: el castillo de Gormaz (Soria)', in A. Bazzana (ed.), *Guerre, Fortification et Habitat dans le Monde Méditerranéen au Moyen Age, Actes du colloque Guerre, habitat et fortification au Moyen Age (Madrid 1985), Castrum III*, Madrid, pp. 173–8.

—— (1992), 'The Fortifications of al-Andalus', in J. D. Dodds (ed.), *Al-Andalus: The Art of Islamic Spain*, New York, pp. 63–73.

Index